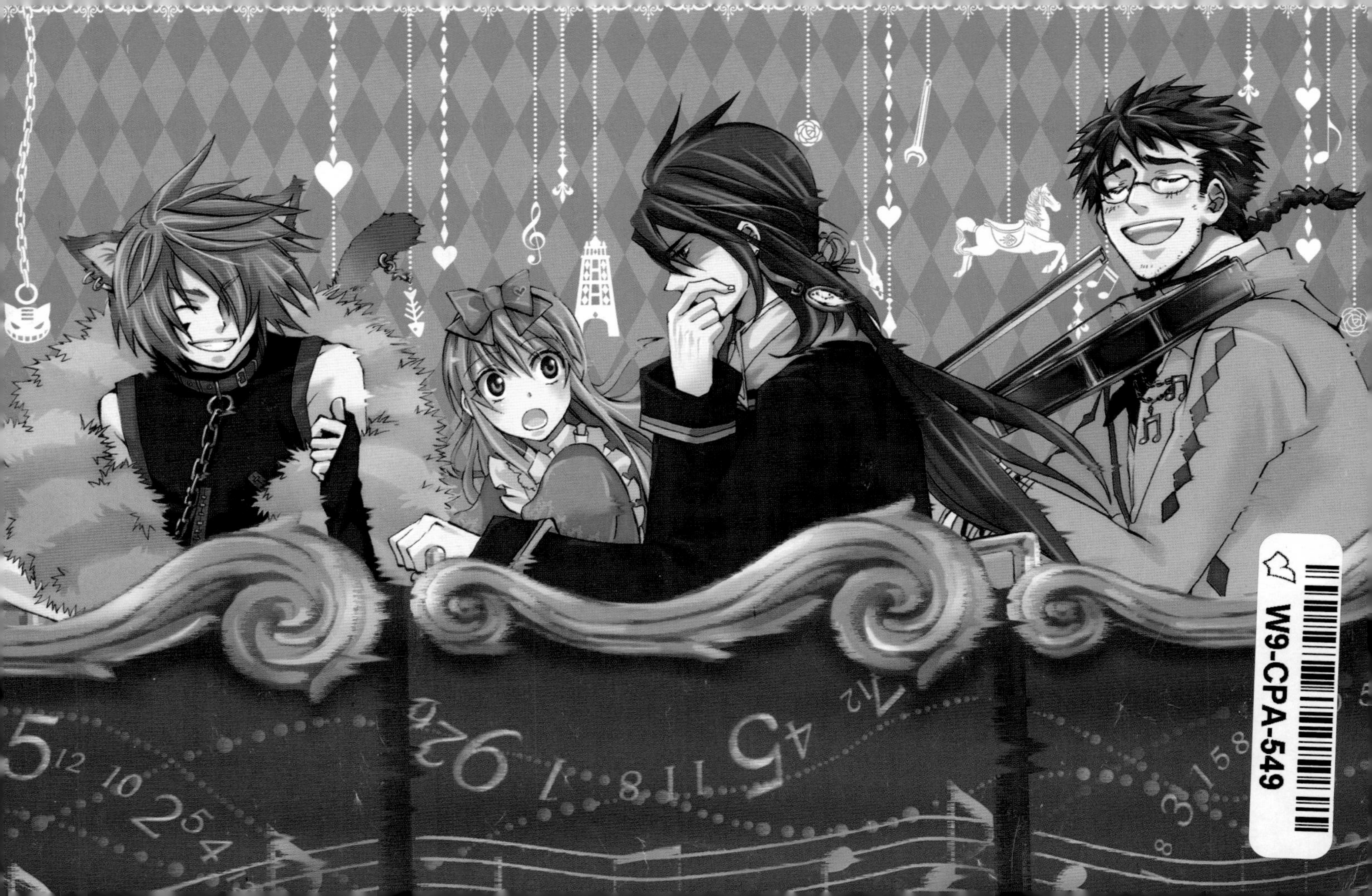

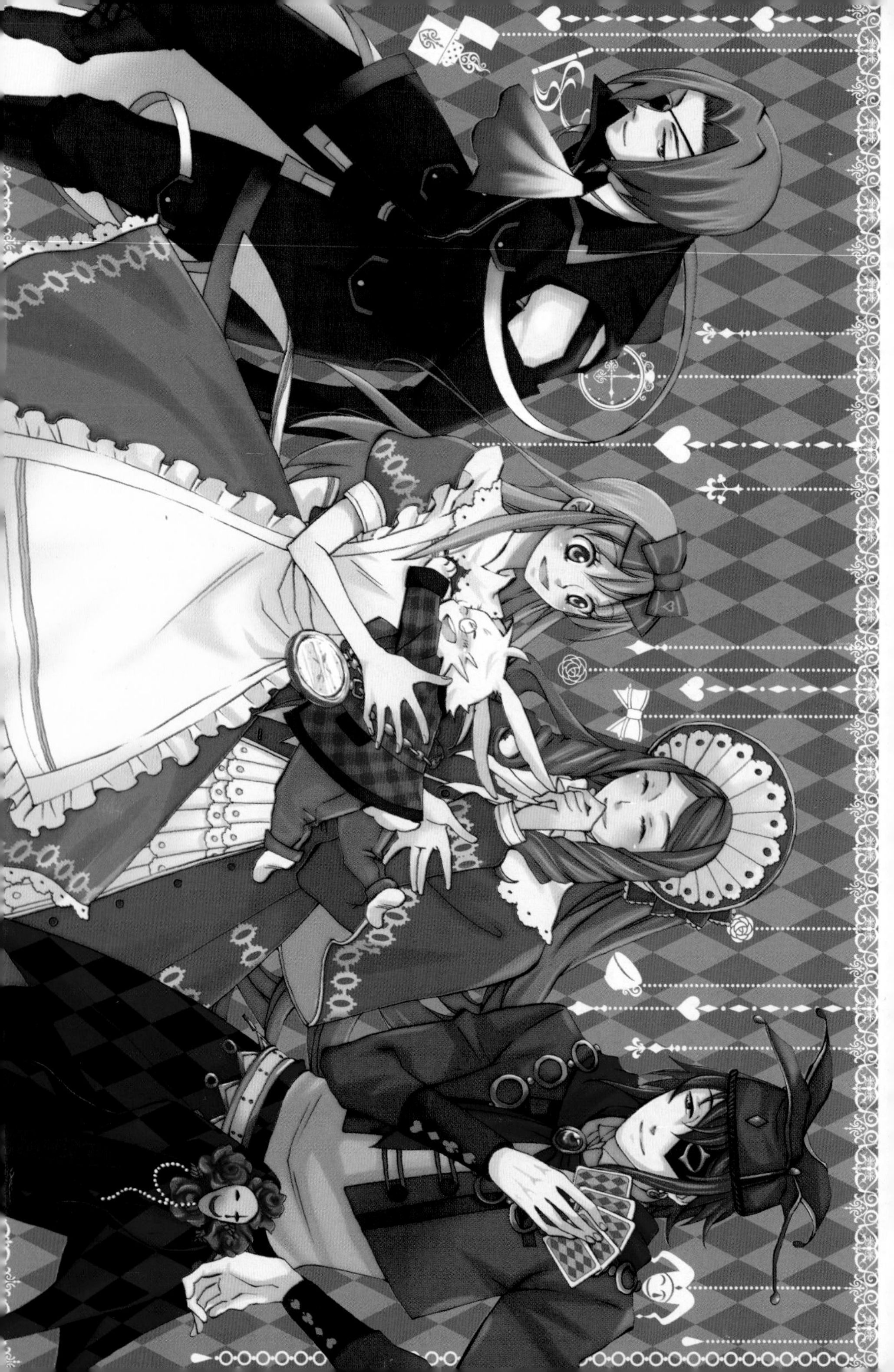

ALICE IN THE COUNTRY OF HEARTS

2

QuinRose ✕ Soumei Hoshino

ALICE IN THE COUNTRY OF HEARTS

2

CONTENTS

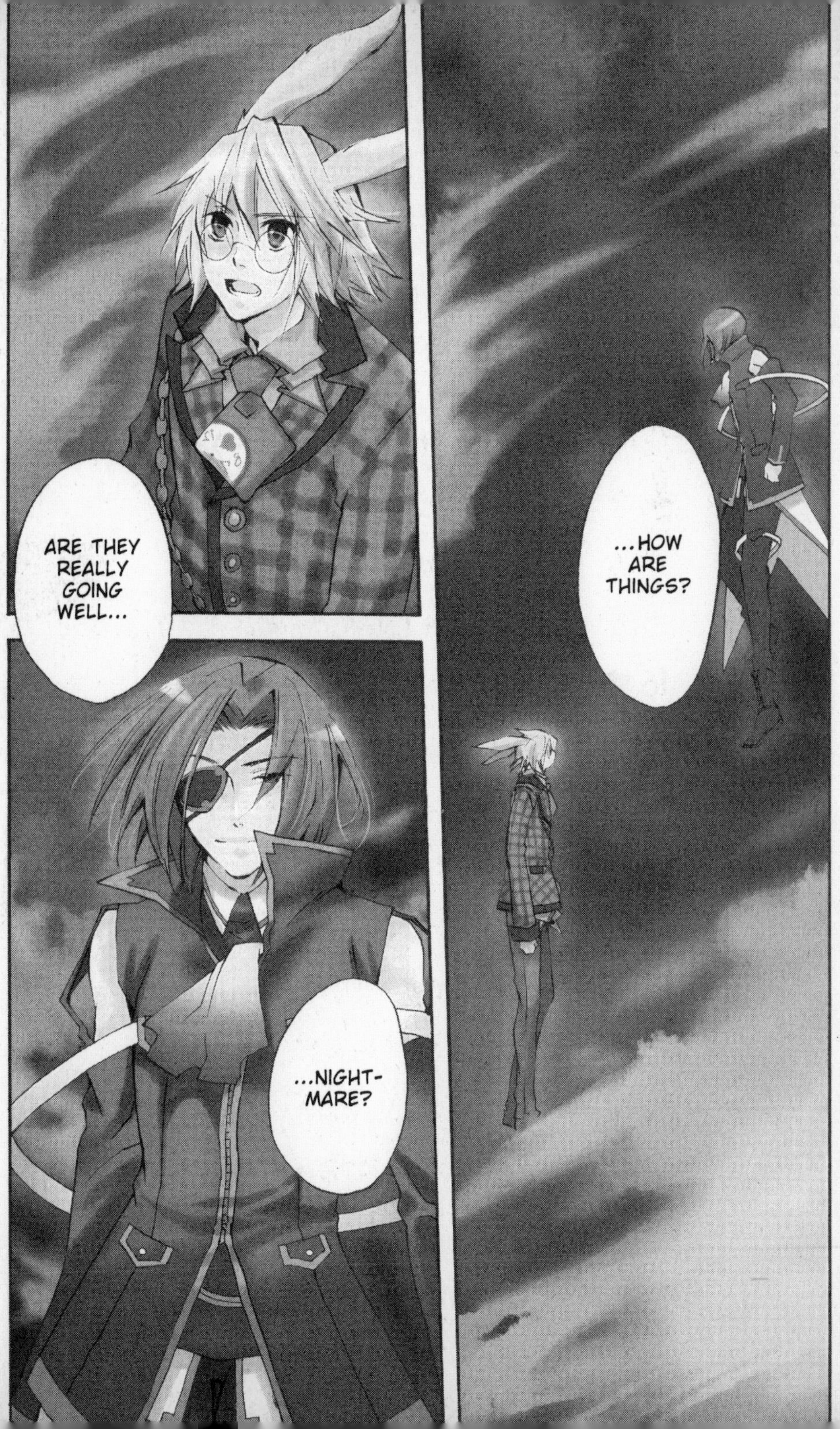
...HOW ARE THINGS?
ARE THEY REALLY GOING WELL...
...NIGHT-MARE?

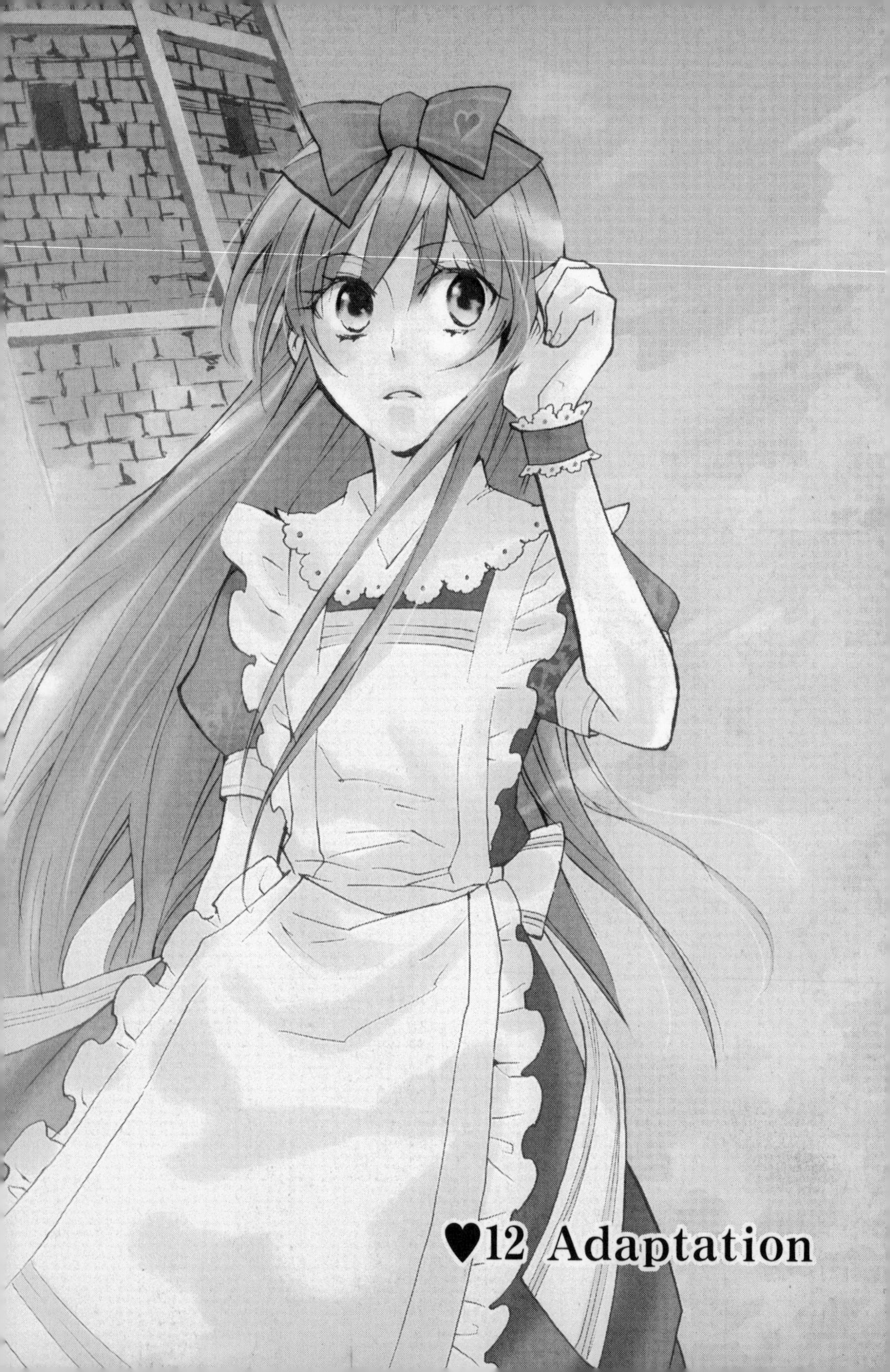
♥12 Adaptation

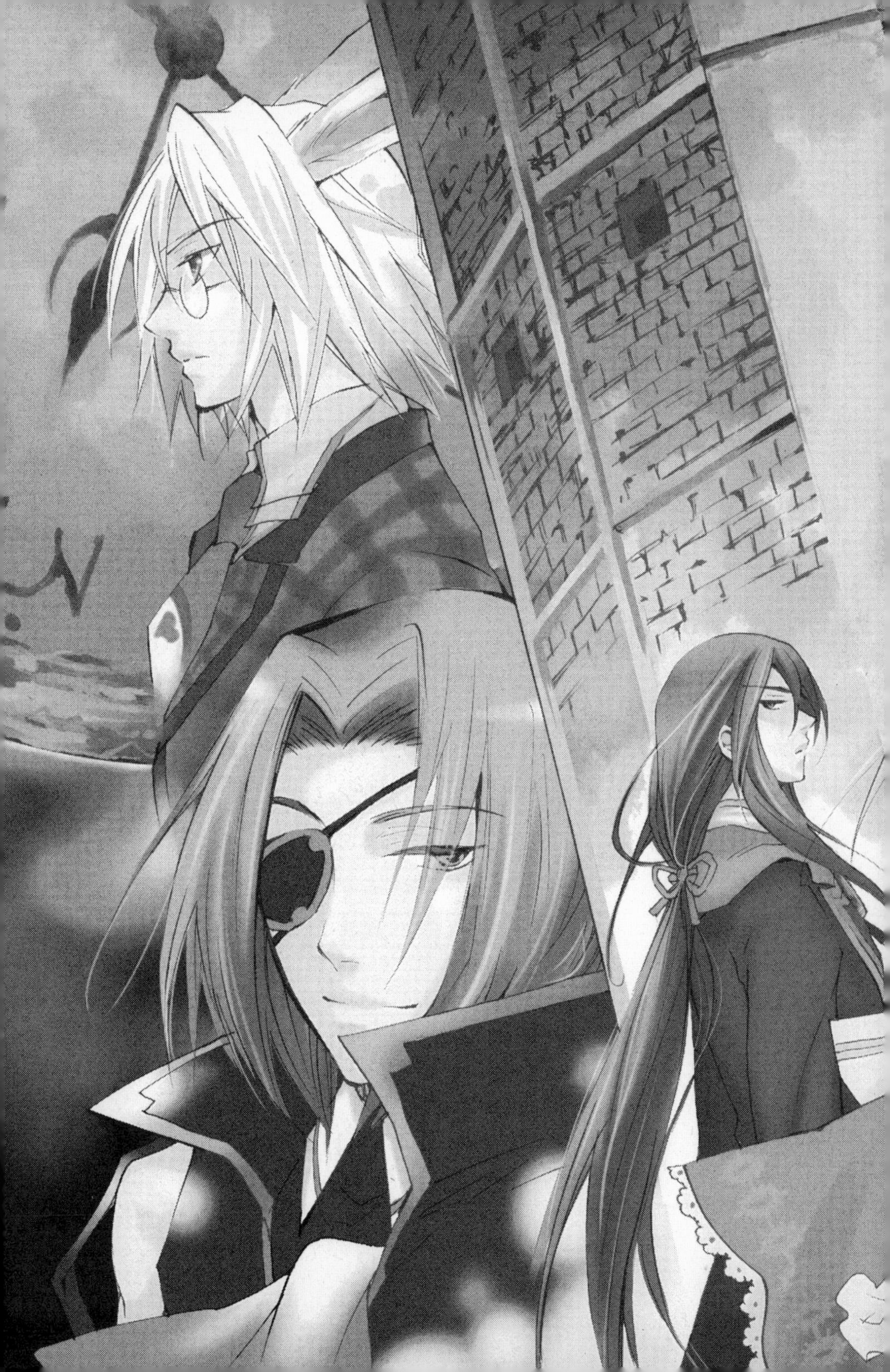

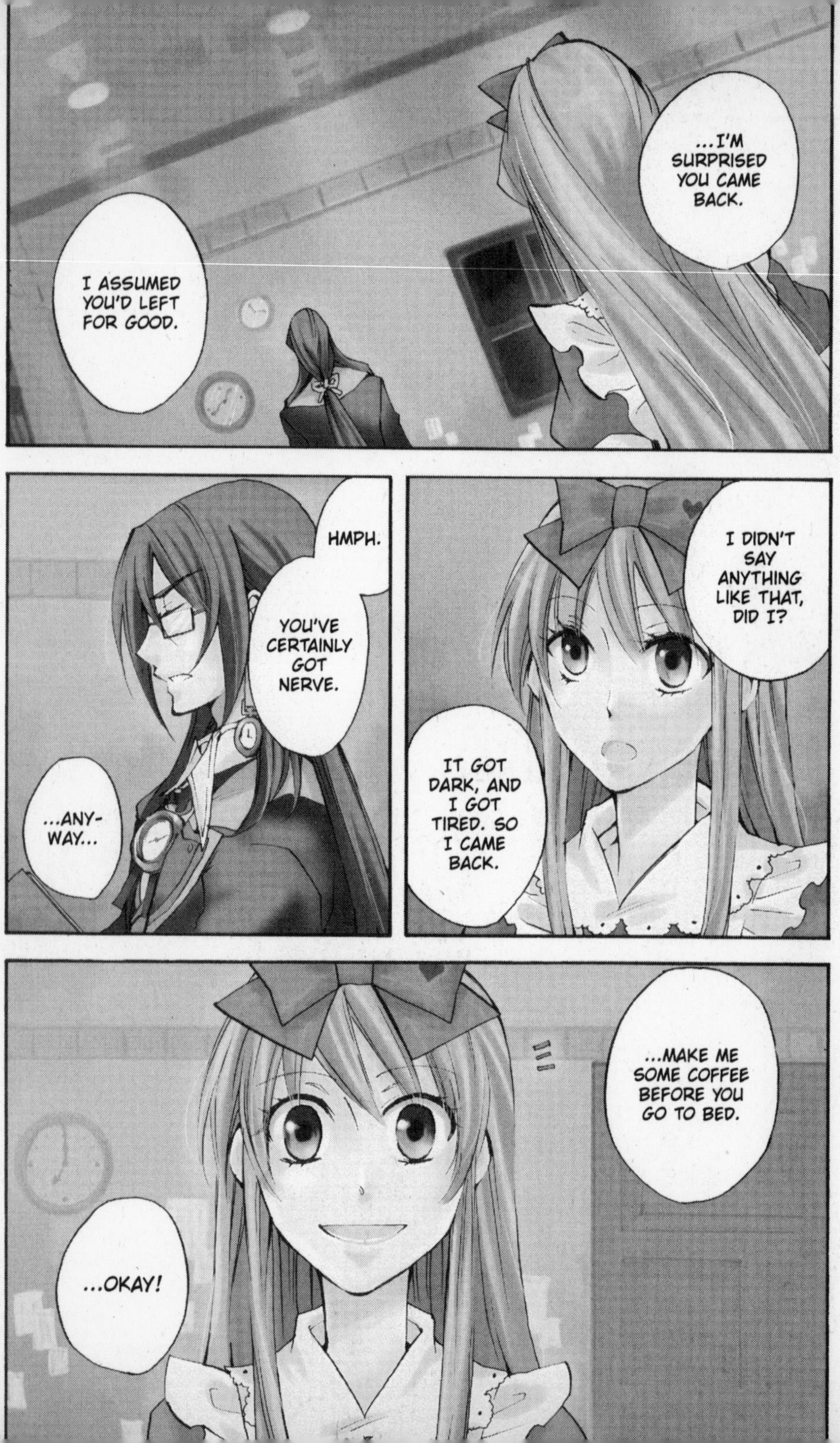
...I'M SURPRISED YOU CAME BACK.
I ASSUMED YOU'D LEFT FOR GOOD.
I DIDN'T SAY ANYTHING LIKE THAT, DID I?
IT GOT DARK, AND I GOT TIRED. SO I CAME BACK.
HMPH.
YOU'VE CERTAINLY GOT NERVE.
...ANY-WAY...
...MAKE ME SOME COFFEE BEFORE YOU GO TO BED.
...OKAY!

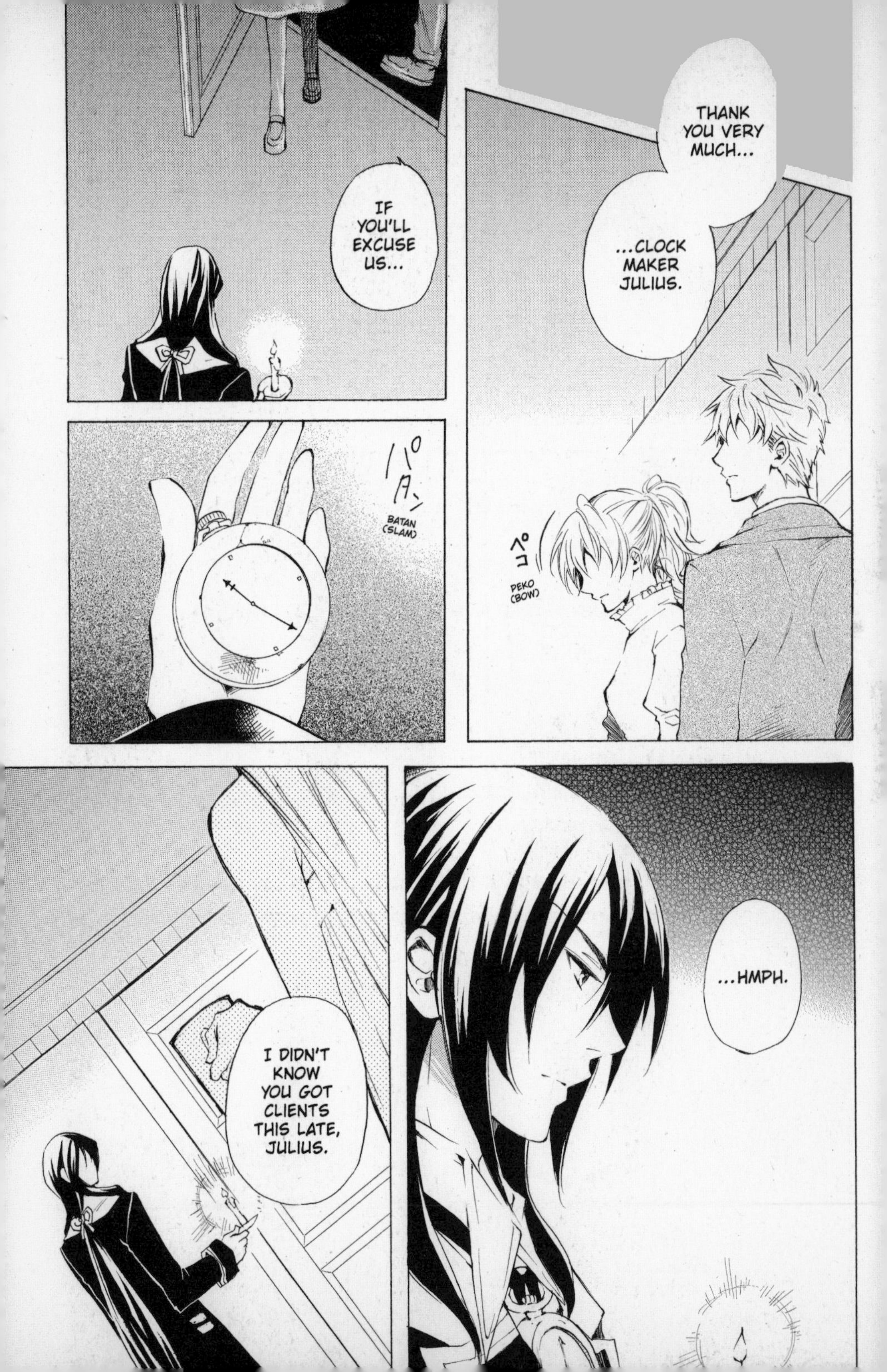

THANK YOU VERY MUCH...
...CLOCK MAKER JULIUS.
ペコ
PEKO (BOW)
IF YOU'LL EXCUSE US...
パタン
BATAN (SLAM)
...HMPH.
I DIDN'T KNOW YOU GOT CLIENTS THIS LATE, JULIUS.

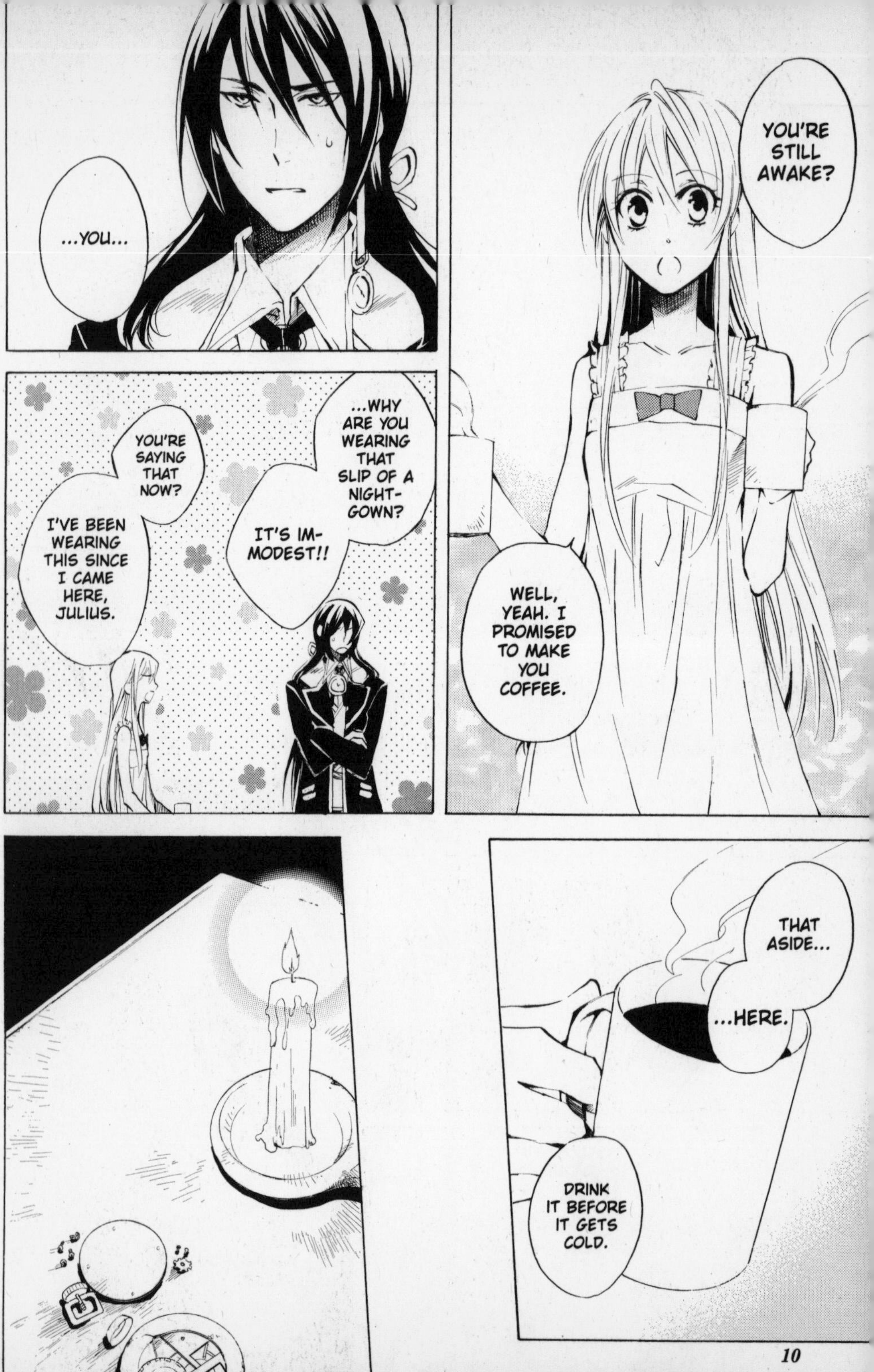
YOU'RE STILL AWAKE?
WELL, YEAH. I PROMISED TO MAKE YOU COFFEE.
...YOU...
...WHY ARE YOU WEARING THAT SLIP OF A NIGHT-GOWN?
IT'S IM-MODEST!!
YOU'RE SAYING THAT NOW?
I'VE BEEN WEARING THIS SINCE I CAME HERE, JULIUS.
THAT ASIDE...
...HERE.
DRINK IT BEFORE IT GETS COLD.

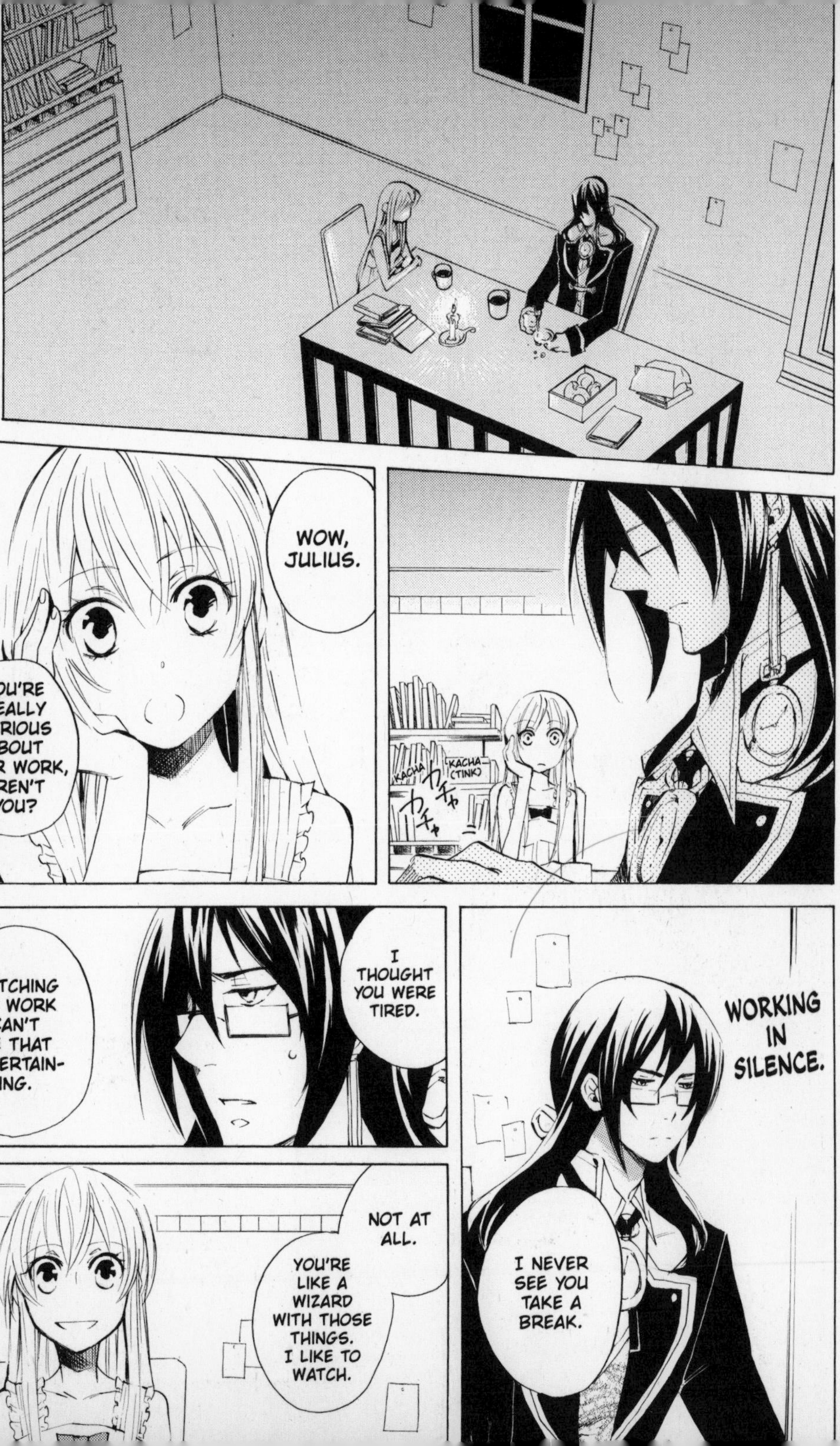
KACHA (TINK)
KACHA
カチャ カチャ
WOW, JULIUS.
YOU'RE REALLY SERIOUS ABOUT YOUR WORK, AREN'T YOU?
WORKING IN SILENCE.
I NEVER SEE YOU TAKE A BREAK.
I THOUGHT YOU WERE TIRED.
WATCHING ME WORK CAN'T BE THAT ENTERTAIN-ING.
NOT AT ALL.
YOU'RE LIKE A WIZARD WITH THOSE THINGS. I LIKE TO WATCH.

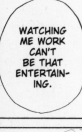

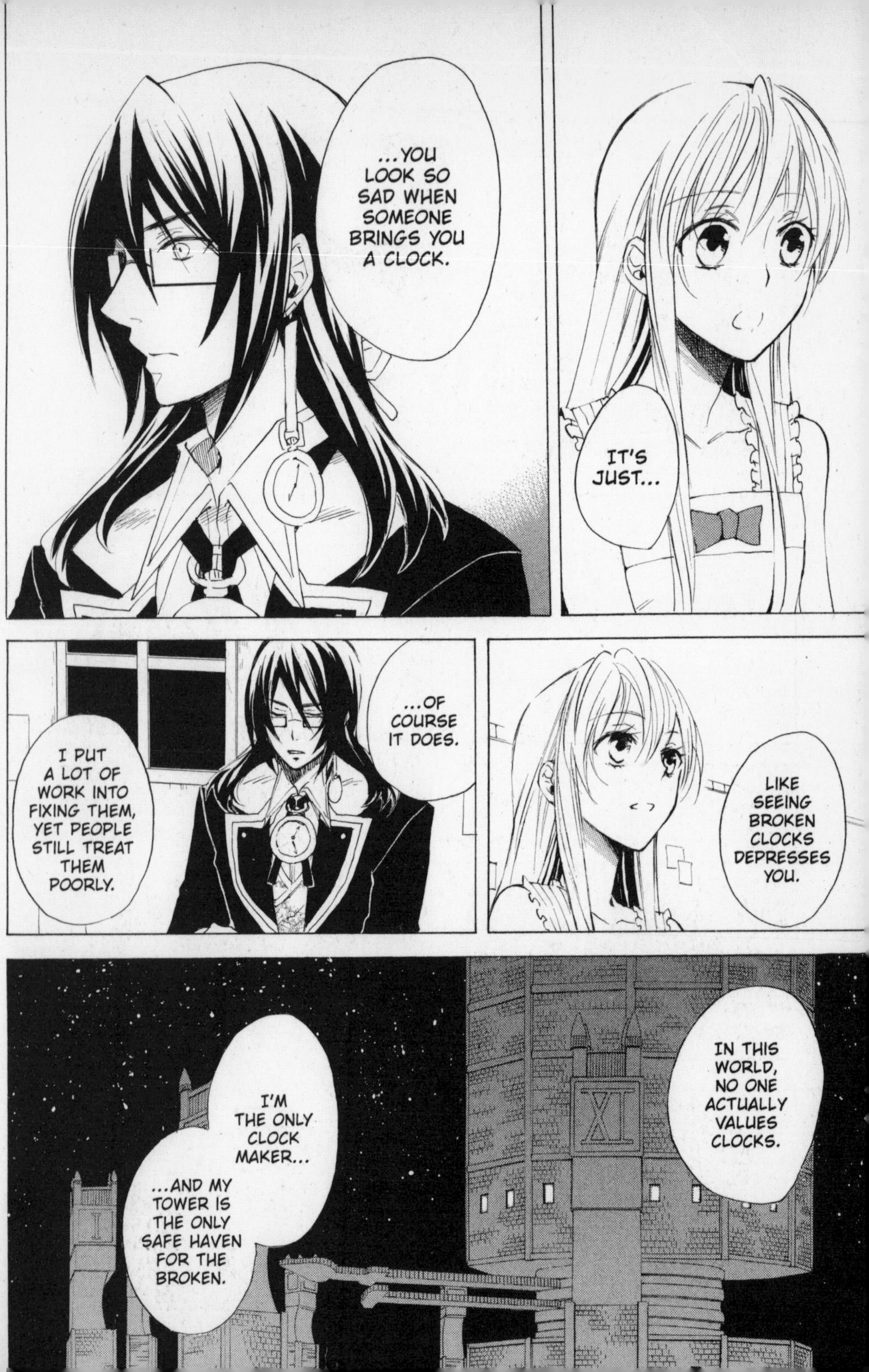
IT'S JUST...
...YOU LOOK SO SAD WHEN SOMEONE BRINGS YOU A CLOCK.
LIKE SEEING BROKEN CLOCKS DEPRESSES YOU.
...OF COURSE IT DOES.
I PUT A LOT OF WORK INTO FIXING THEM, YET PEOPLE STILL TREAT THEM POORLY.
IN THIS WORLD, NO ONE ACTUALLY VALUES CLOCKS.
I'M THE ONLY CLOCK MAKER...
...AND MY TOWER IS THE ONLY SAFE HAVEN FOR THE BROKEN.

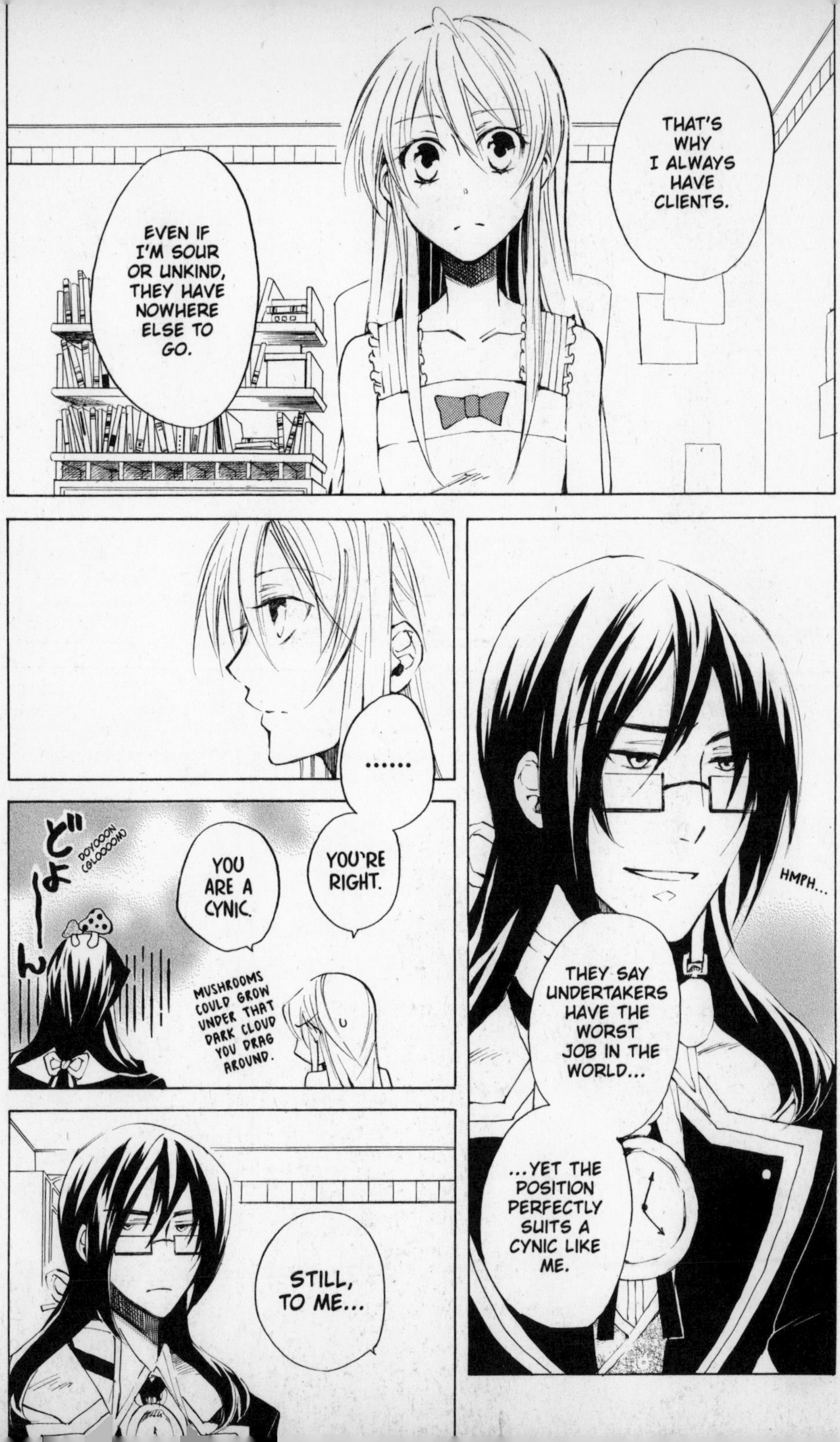

THAT'S WHY I ALWAYS HAVE CLIENTS.
EVEN IF I'M SOUR OR UNKIND, THEY HAVE NOWHERE ELSE TO GO.
HMPH...
THEY SAY UNDERTAKERS HAVE THE WORST JOB IN THE WORLD...
...YET THE POSITION PERFECTLY SUITS A CYNIC LIKE ME.
......
YOU'RE RIGHT.
YOU ARE A CYNIC.
どよーん
DOYOOON (GLOOOOM)
MUSHROOMS COULD GROW UNDER THAT DARK CLOUD YOU DRAG AROUND.
STILL, TO ME...

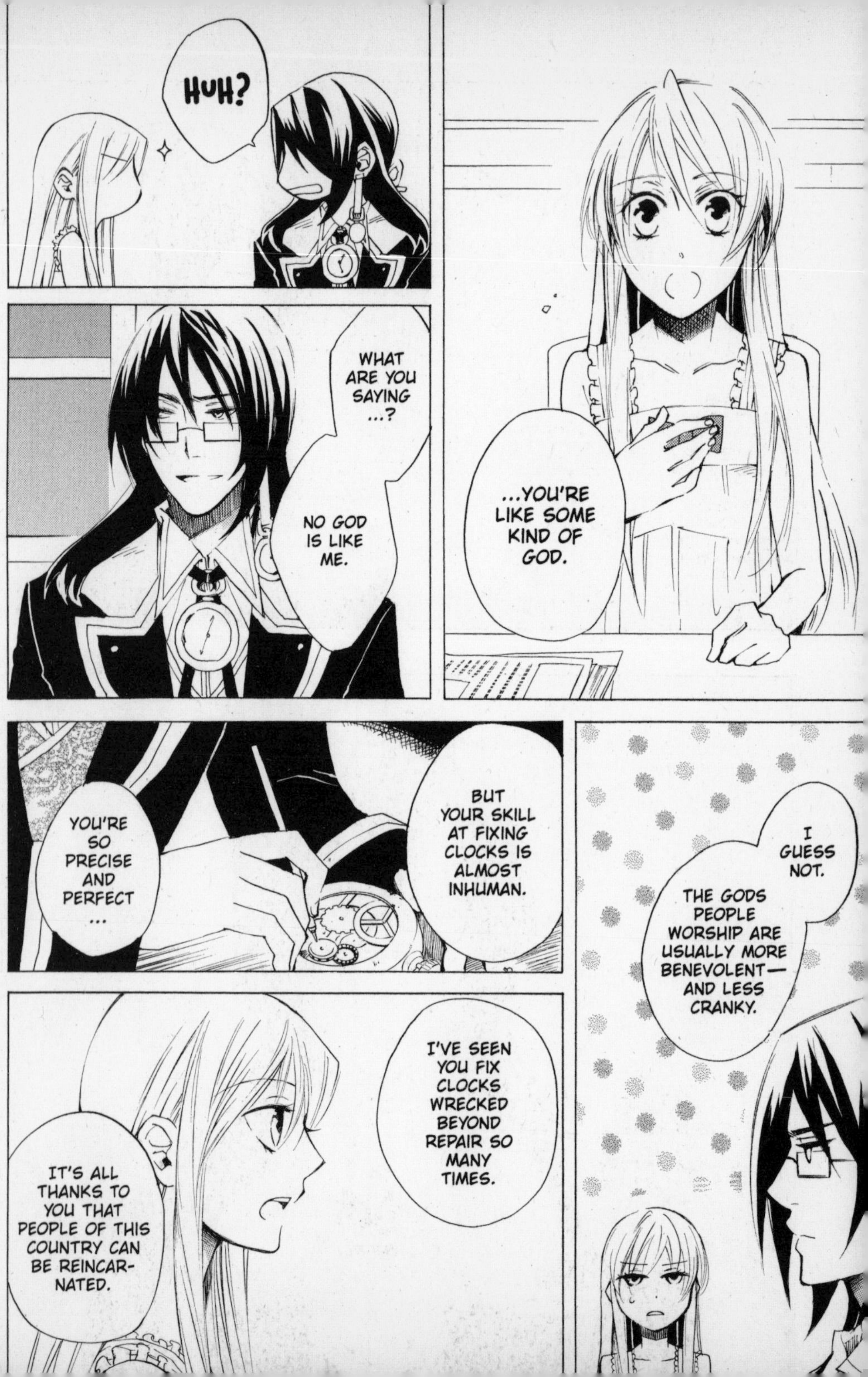
...YOU'RE LIKE SOME KIND OF GOD.
HUH?
WHAT ARE YOU SAYING ...?
NO GOD IS LIKE ME.
I GUESS NOT.
THE GODS PEOPLE WORSHIP ARE USUALLY MORE BENEVOLENT— AND LESS CRANKY.
BUT YOUR SKILL AT FIXING CLOCKS IS ALMOST INHUMAN.
YOU'RE SO PRECISE AND PERFECT ...
I'VE SEEN YOU FIX CLOCKS WRECKED BEYOND REPAIR SO MANY TIMES.
IT'S ALL THANKS TO YOU THAT PEOPLE OF THIS COUNTRY CAN BE REINCAR- NATED.

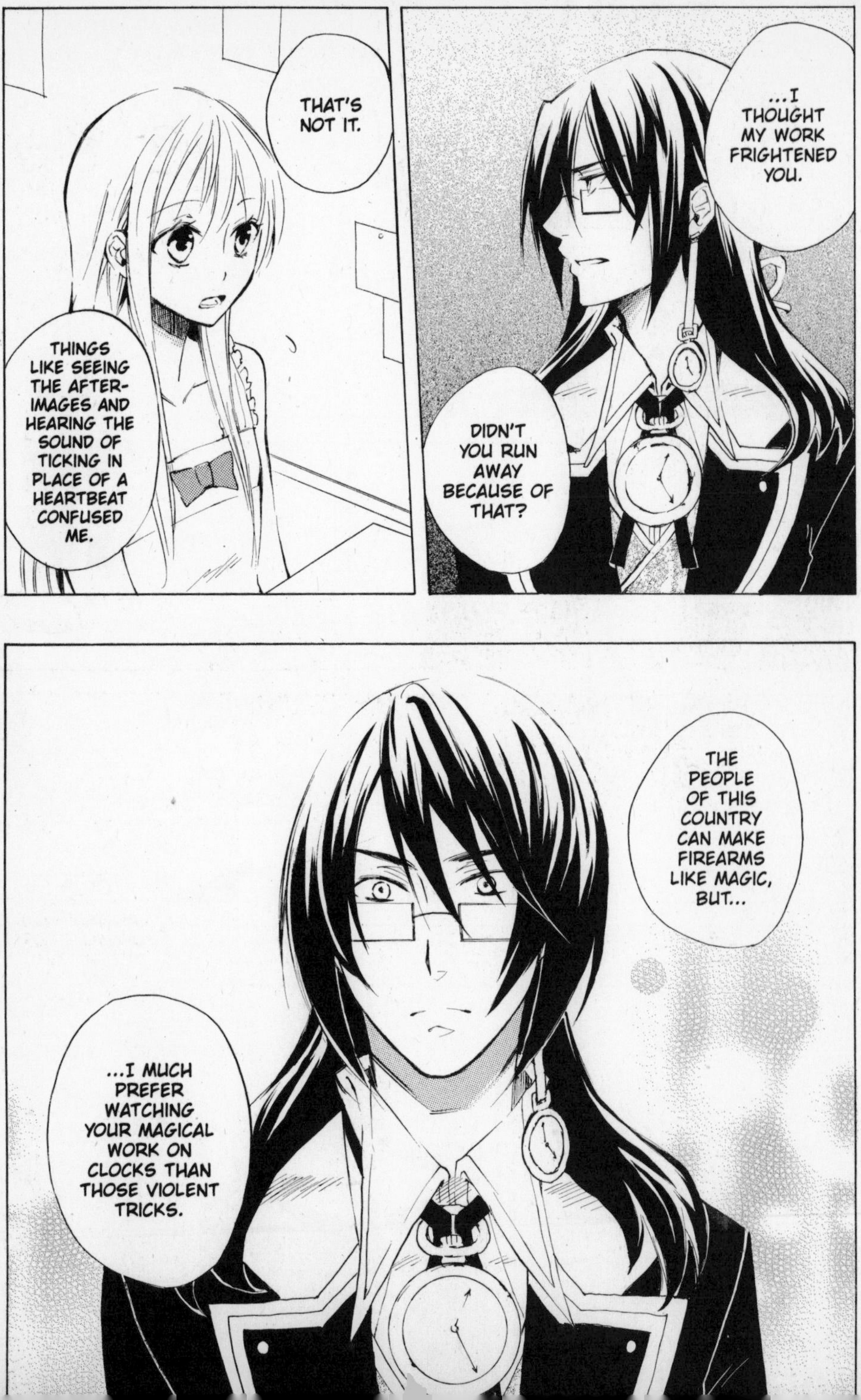
...I THOUGHT MY WORK FRIGHTENED YOU.
DIDN'T YOU RUN AWAY BECAUSE OF THAT?
THAT'S NOT IT.
THINGS LIKE SEEING THE AFTER-IMAGES AND HEARING THE SOUND OF TICKING IN PLACE OF A HEARTBEAT CONFUSED ME.
THE PEOPLE OF THIS COUNTRY CAN MAKE FIREARMS LIKE MAGIC, BUT...
...I MUCH PREFER WATCHING YOUR MAGICAL WORK ON CLOCKS THAN THOSE VIOLENT TRICKS.

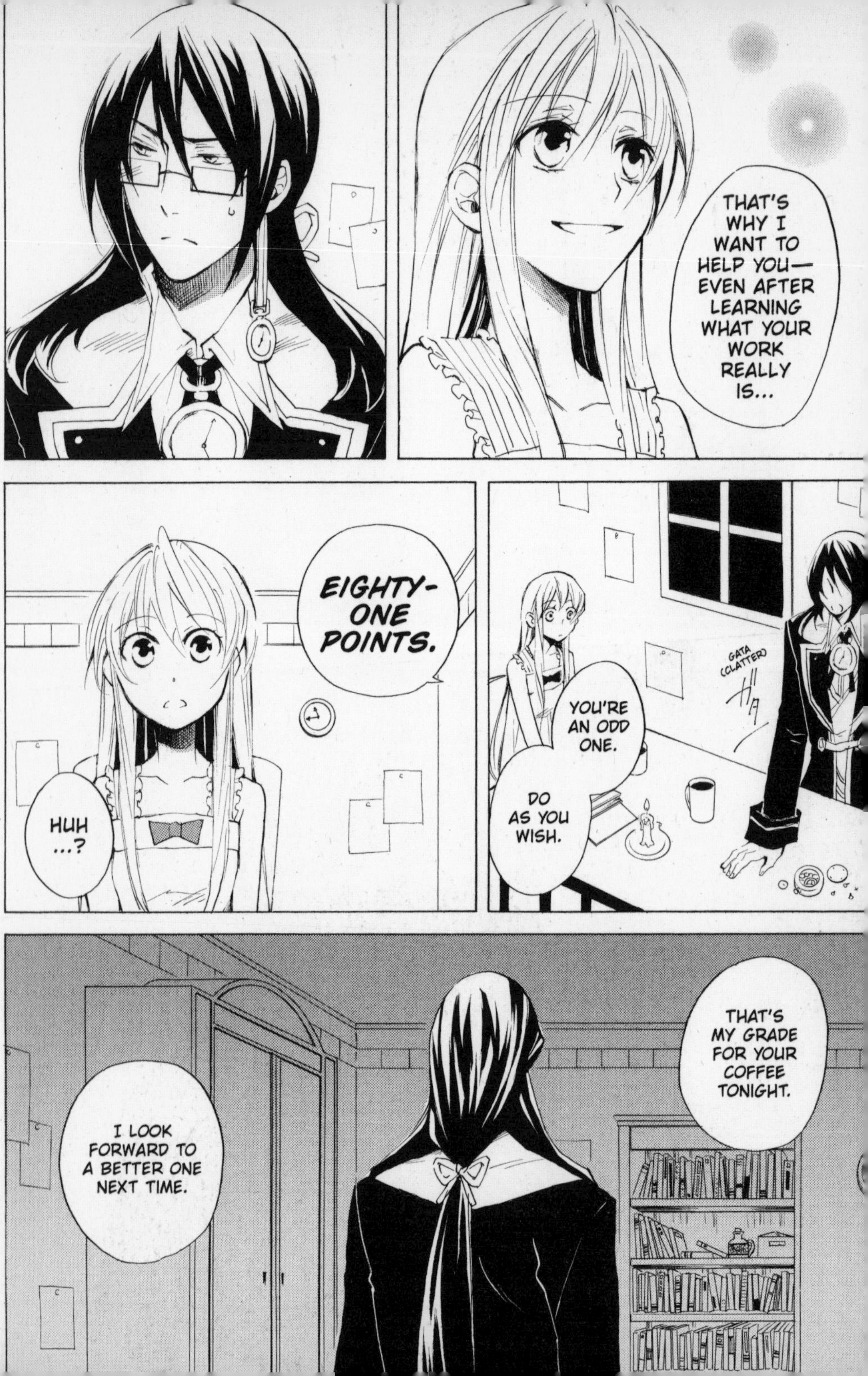
THAT'S WHY I WANT TO HELP YOU— EVEN AFTER LEARNING WHAT YOUR WORK REALLY IS...
GATA (CLATTER)
YOU'RE AN ODD ONE.
DO AS YOU WISH.
EIGHTY-ONE POINTS.
HUH ...?
THAT'S MY GRADE FOR YOUR COFFEE TONIGHT.
I LOOK FORWARD TO A BETTER ONE NEXT TIME.

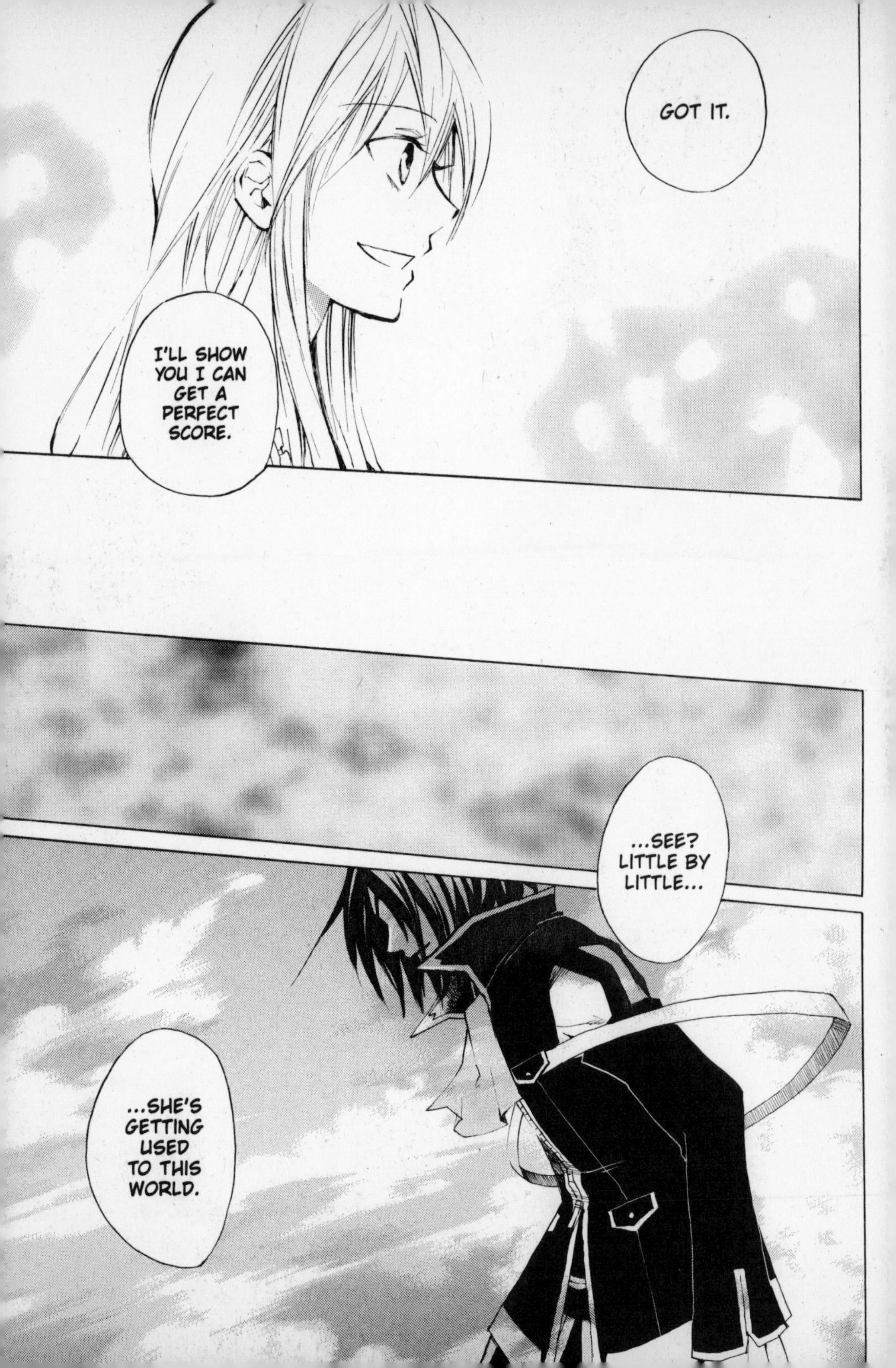
GOT IT.
I'LL SHOW YOU I CAN GET A PERFECT SCORE.
...SEE? LITTLE BY LITTLE...
...SHE'S GETTING USED TO THIS WORLD.

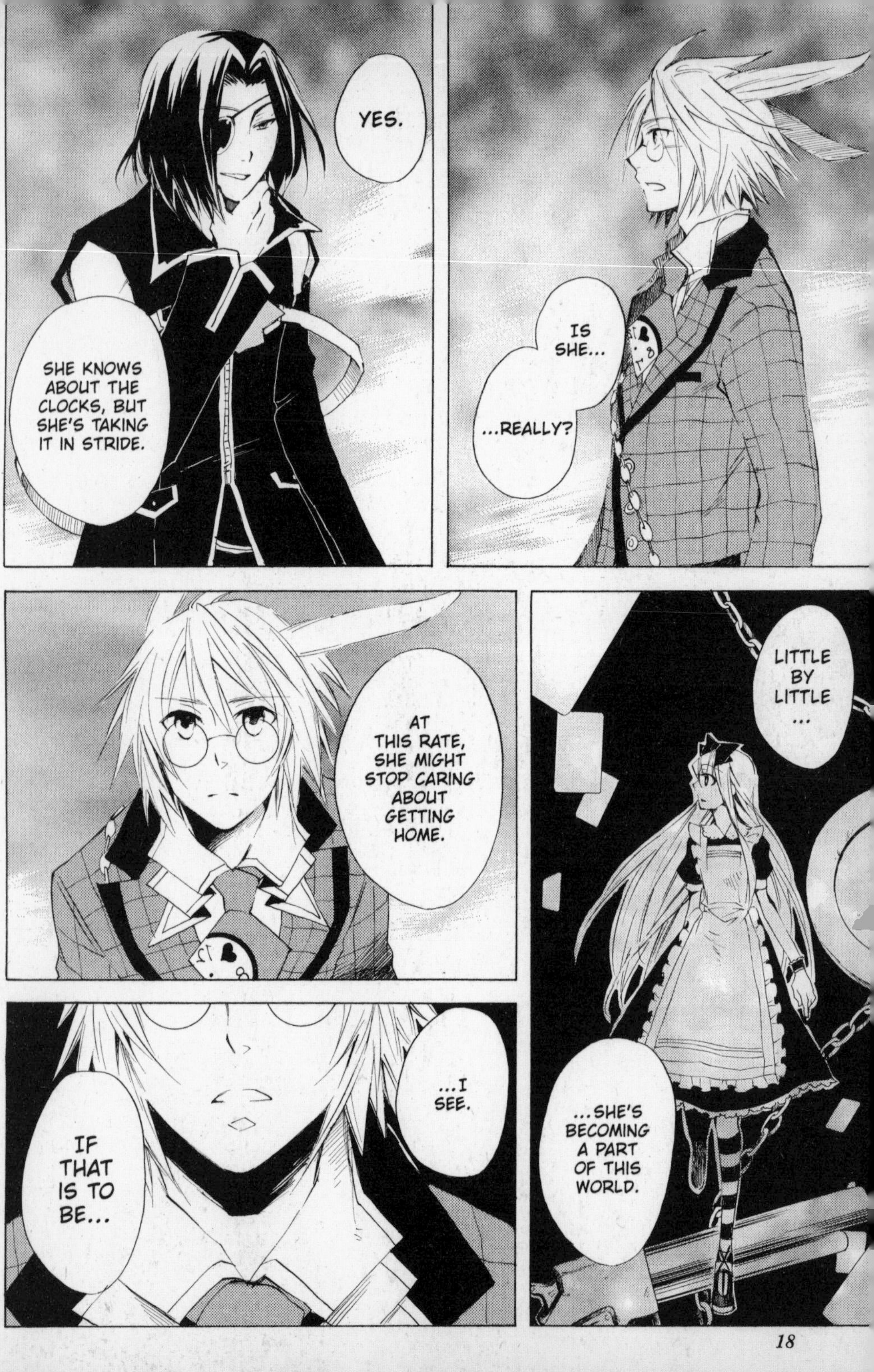
IS SHE...
...REALLY?
YES.
SHE KNOWS ABOUT THE CLOCKS, BUT SHE'S TAKING IT IN STRIDE.
LITTLE BY LITTLE...
...SHE'S BECOMING A PART OF THIS WORLD.
AT THIS RATE, SHE MIGHT STOP CARING ABOUT GETTING HOME.
...I SEE.
IF THAT IS TO BE...

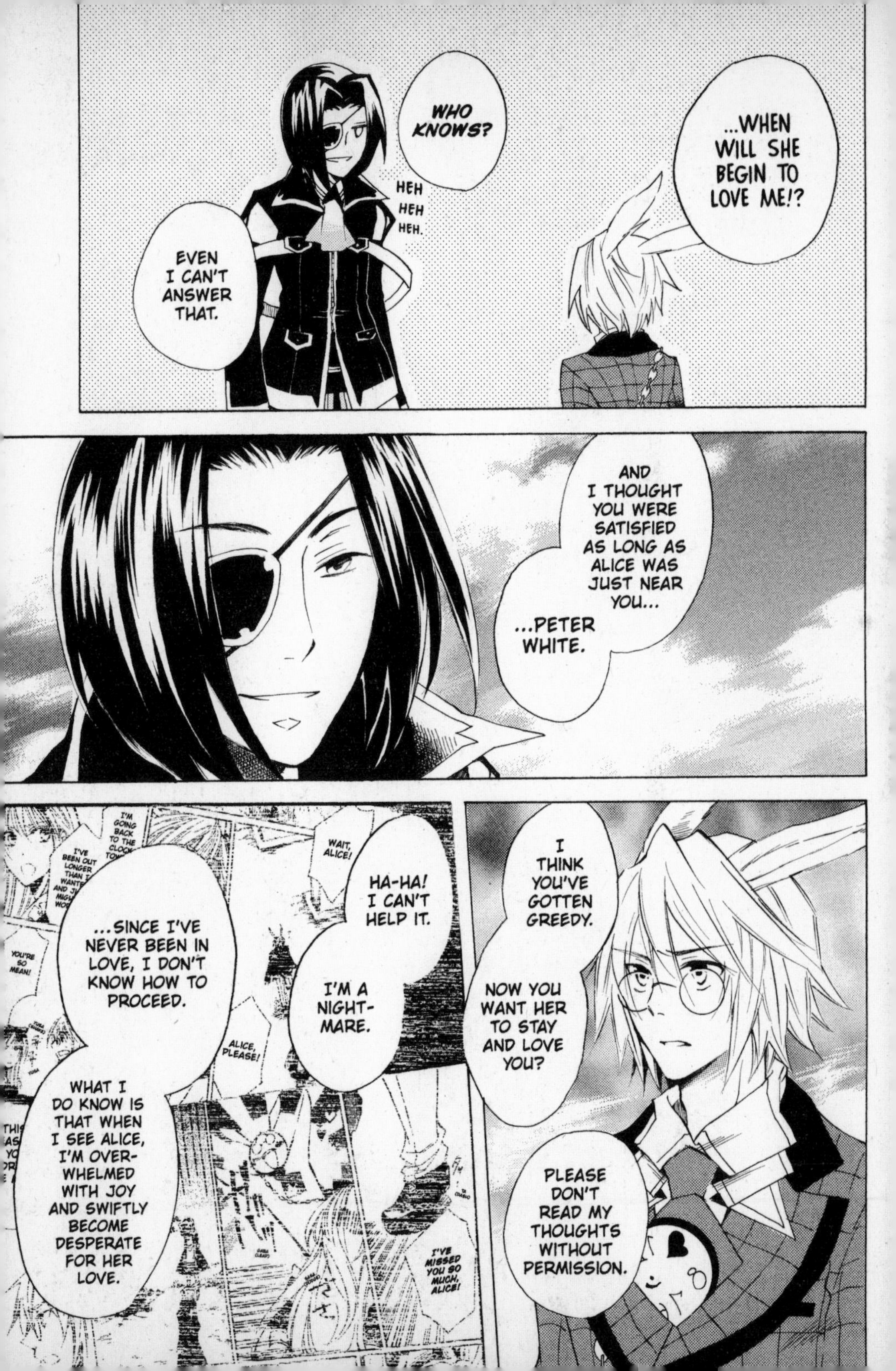
...WHEN WILL SHE BEGIN TO LOVE ME!?
WHO KNOWS?
HEH HEH HEH.
EVEN I CAN'T ANSWER THAT.
AND I THOUGHT YOU WERE SATISFIED AS LONG AS ALICE WAS JUST NEAR YOU...
...PETER WHITE.
I THINK YOU'VE GOTTEN GREEDY.
NOW YOU WANT HER TO STAY AND LOVE YOU?
PLEASE DON'T READ MY THOUGHTS WITHOUT PERMISSION.
WAIT, ALICE!
HA-HA! I CAN'T HELP IT.
I'M A NIGHT-MARE.
...SINCE I'VE NEVER BEEN IN LOVE, I DON'T KNOW HOW TO PROCEED.
YOU'RE SO MEAN!
ALICE, PLEASE!
WHAT I DO KNOW IS THAT WHEN I SEE ALICE, I'M OVER-WHELMED WITH JOY AND SWIFTLY BECOME DESPERATE FOR HER LOVE.
I'VE MISSED YOU SO MUCH, ALICE!

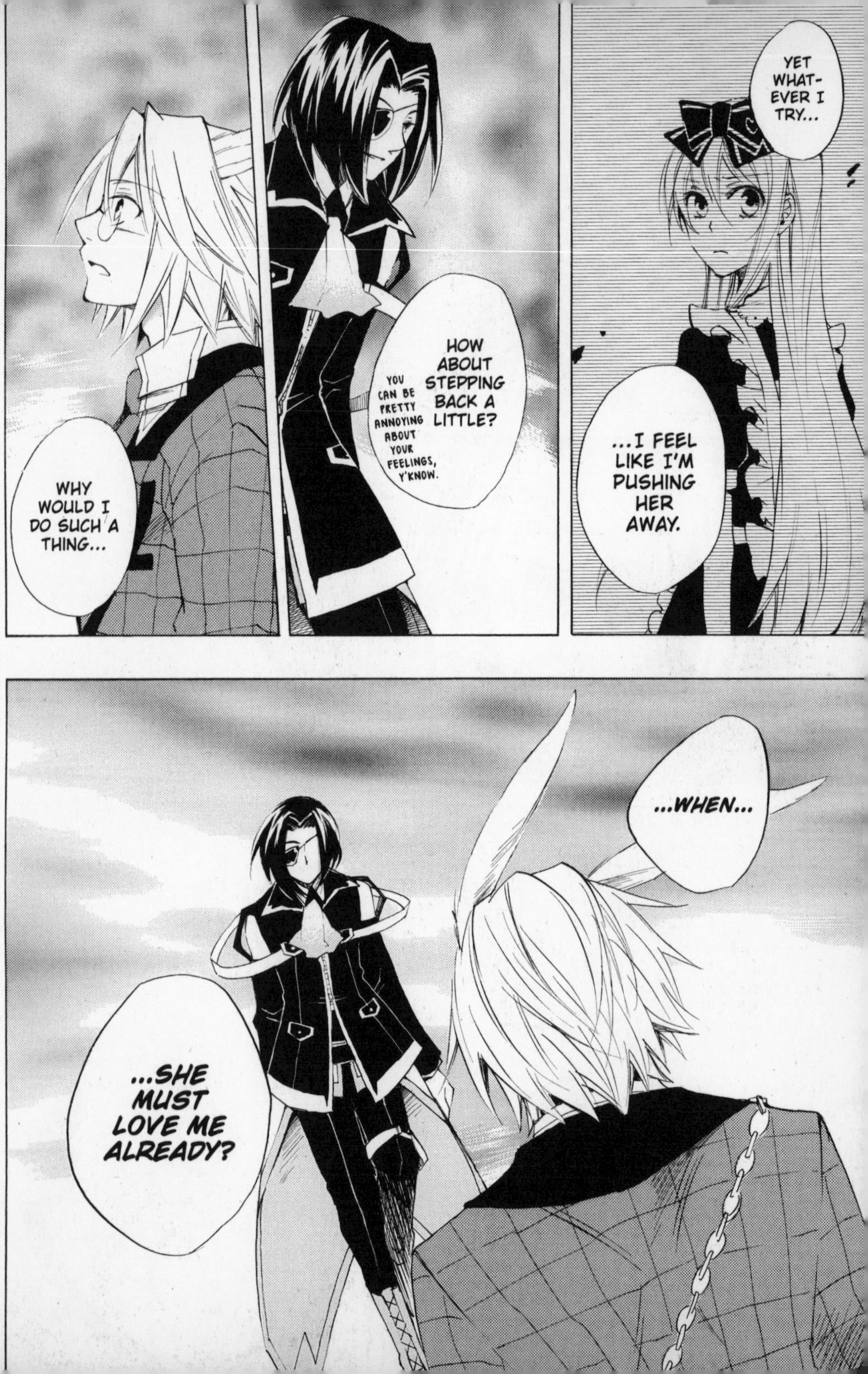
YET WHAT-EVER I TRY...
...I FEEL LIKE I'M PUSHING HER AWAY.
HOW ABOUT STEPPING BACK A LITTLE?
YOU CAN BE PRETTY ANNOYING ABOUT YOUR FEELINGS, Y'KNOW.
WHY WOULD I DO SUCH A THING...
...WHEN...
...SHE MUST LOVE ME ALREADY?

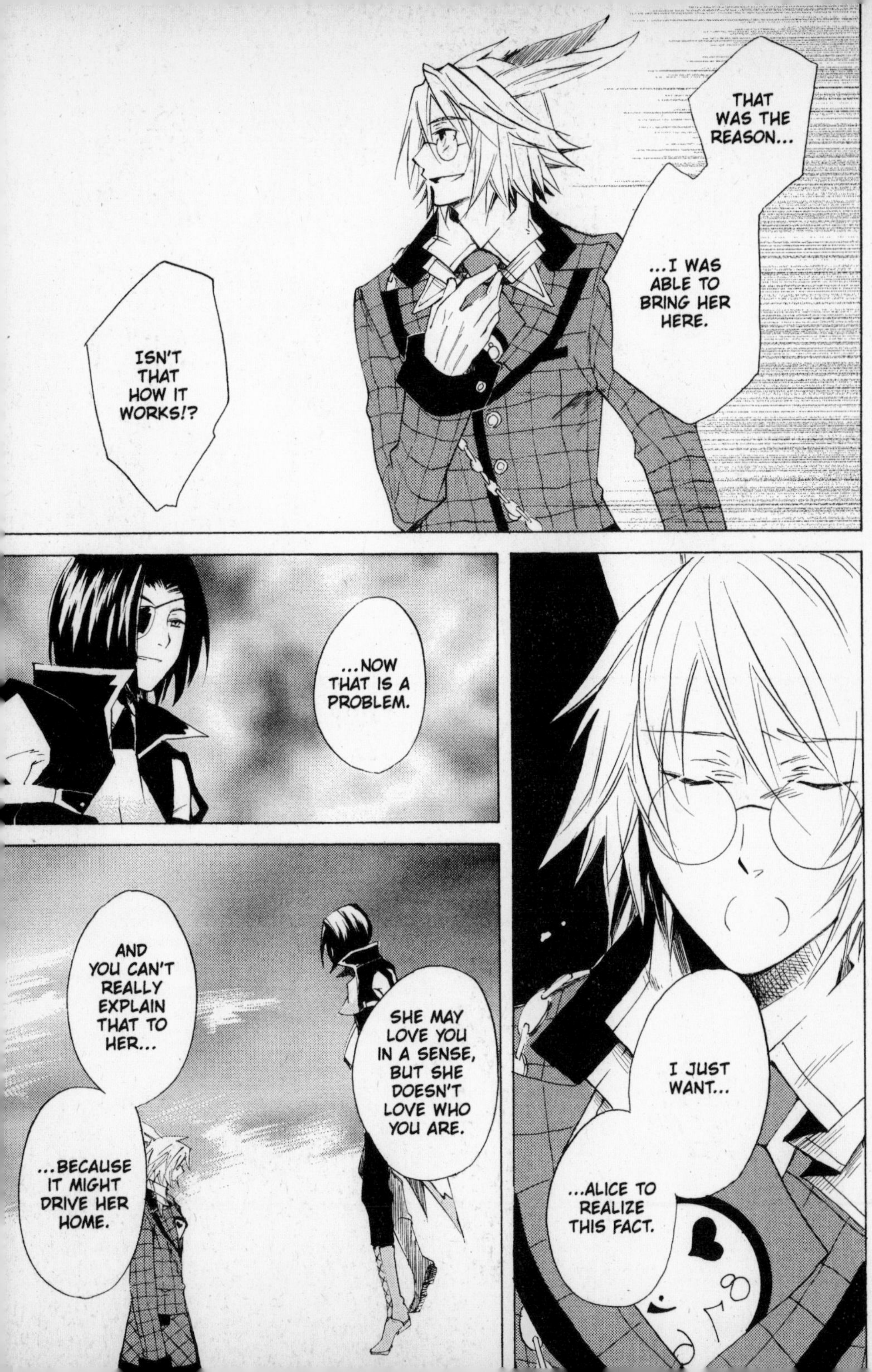
THAT WAS THE REASON...
...I WAS ABLE TO BRING HER HERE.
ISN'T THAT HOW IT WORKS!?
I JUST WANT...
...ALICE TO REALIZE THIS FACT.
...NOW THAT IS A PROBLEM.
SHE MAY LOVE YOU IN A SENSE, BUT SHE DOESN'T LOVE WHO YOU ARE.
AND YOU CAN'T REALLY EXPLAIN THAT TO HER...
...BECAUSE IT MIGHT DRIVE HER HOME.

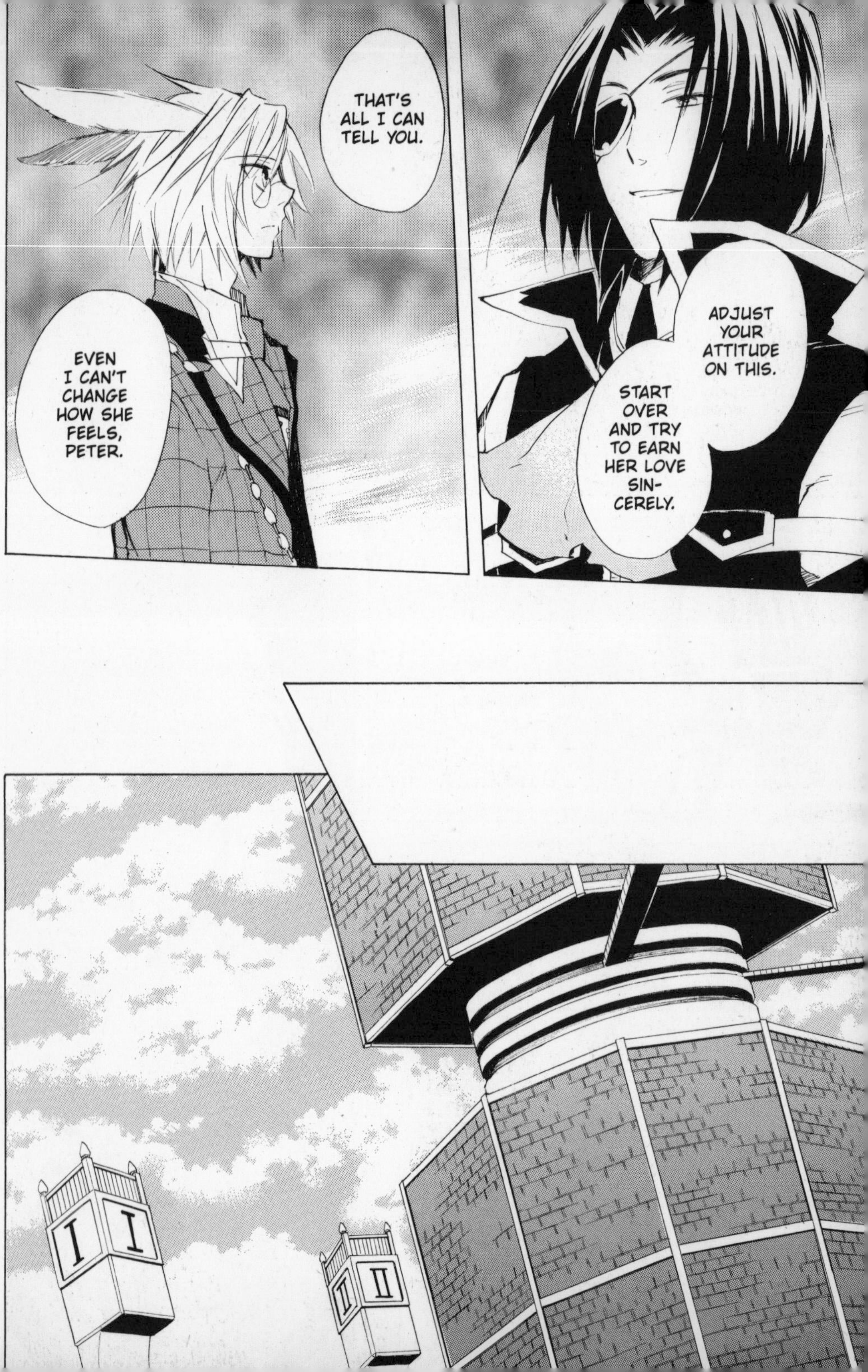
ADJUST YOUR ATTITUDE ON THIS.
START OVER AND TRY TO EARN HER LOVE SIN-CERELY.
THAT'S ALL I CAN TELL YOU.
EVEN I CAN'T CHANGE HOW SHE FEELS, PETER.

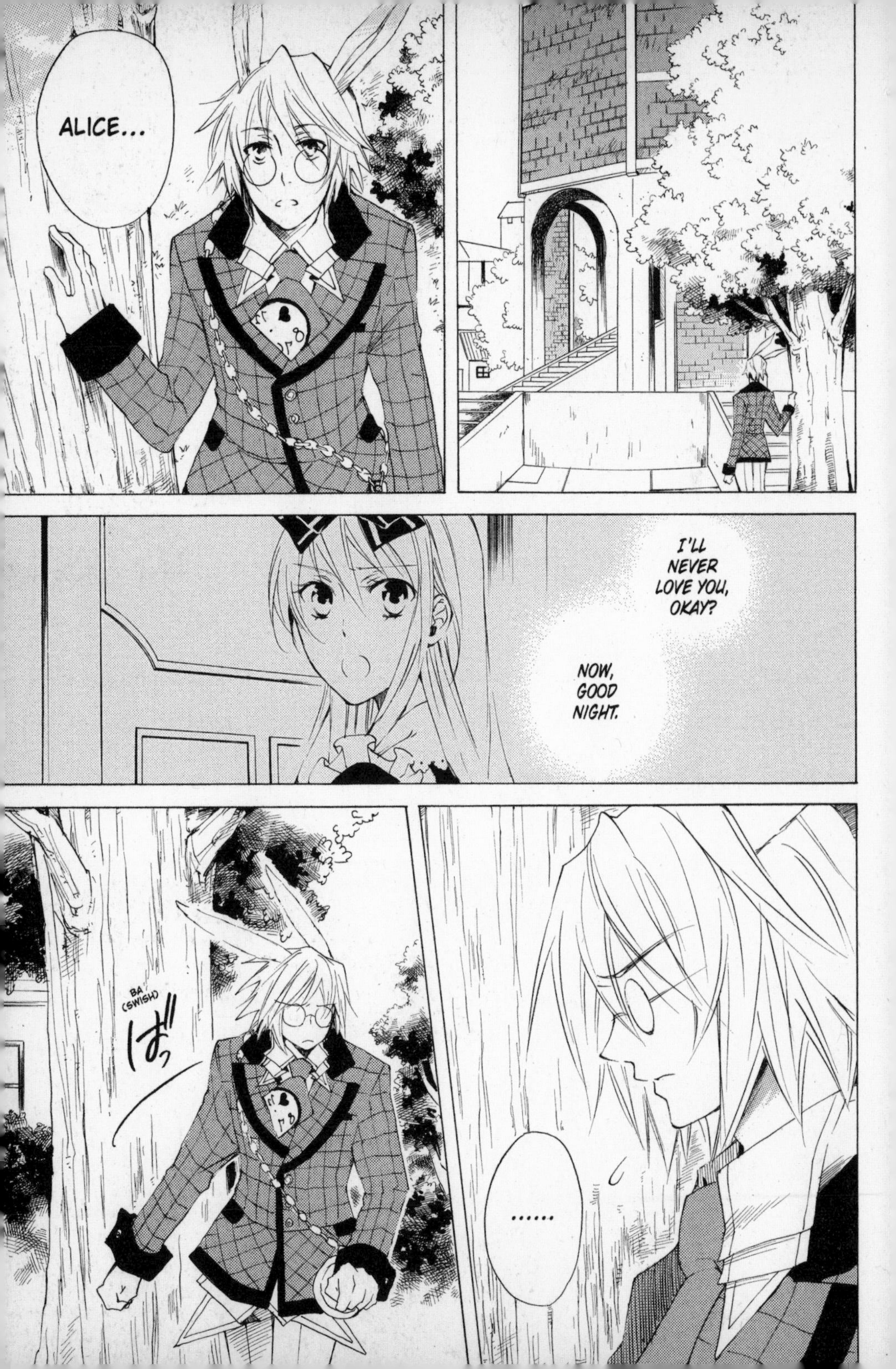
ALICE...
I'LL NEVER LOVE YOU, OKAY?
NOW, GOOD NIGHT.
......
BA (SWISH)
ばっ

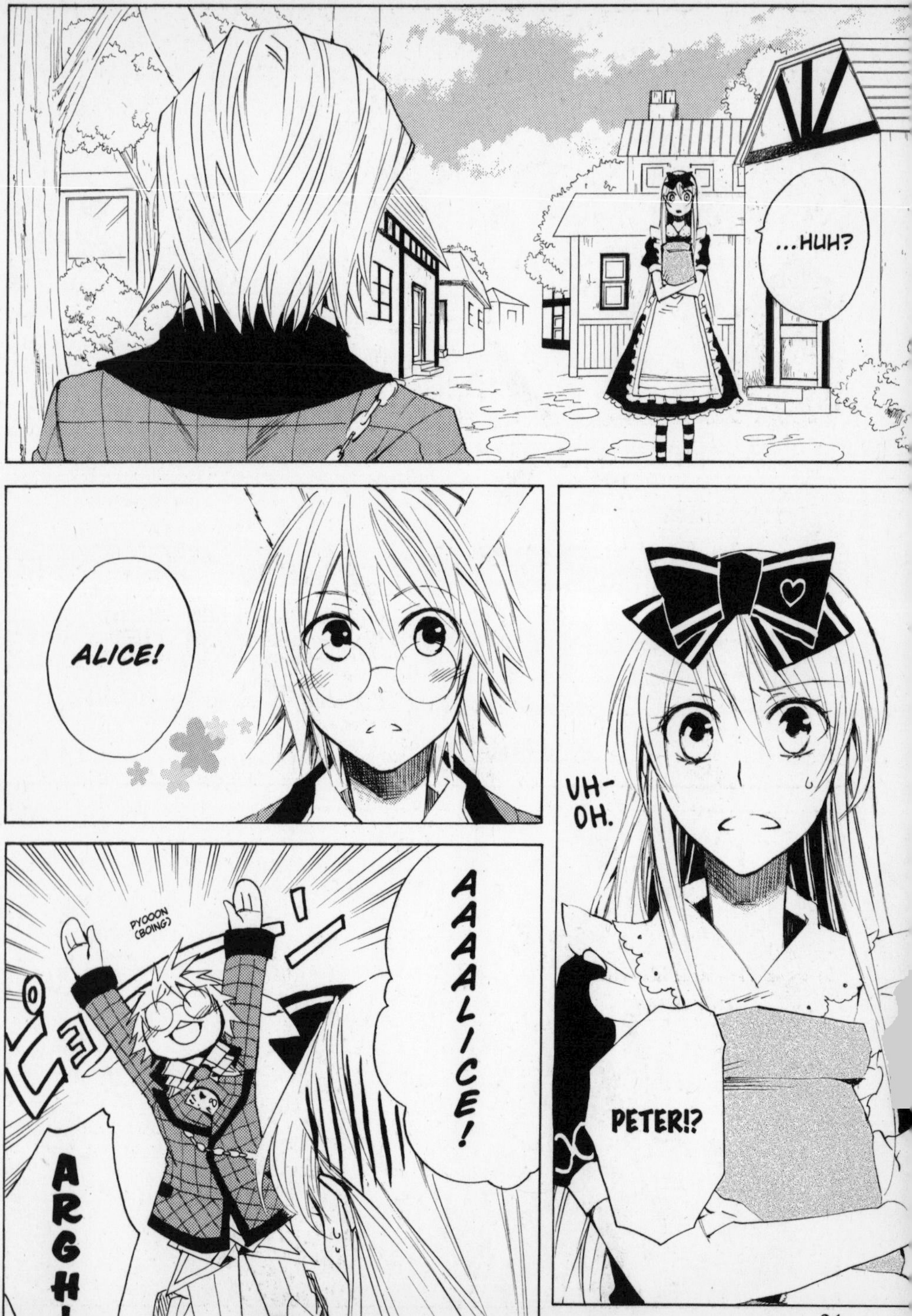
...HUH?
UH-OH.
PETER!?
ALICE!
AAAALICE!
PYOOON (BOING)
ARGH!

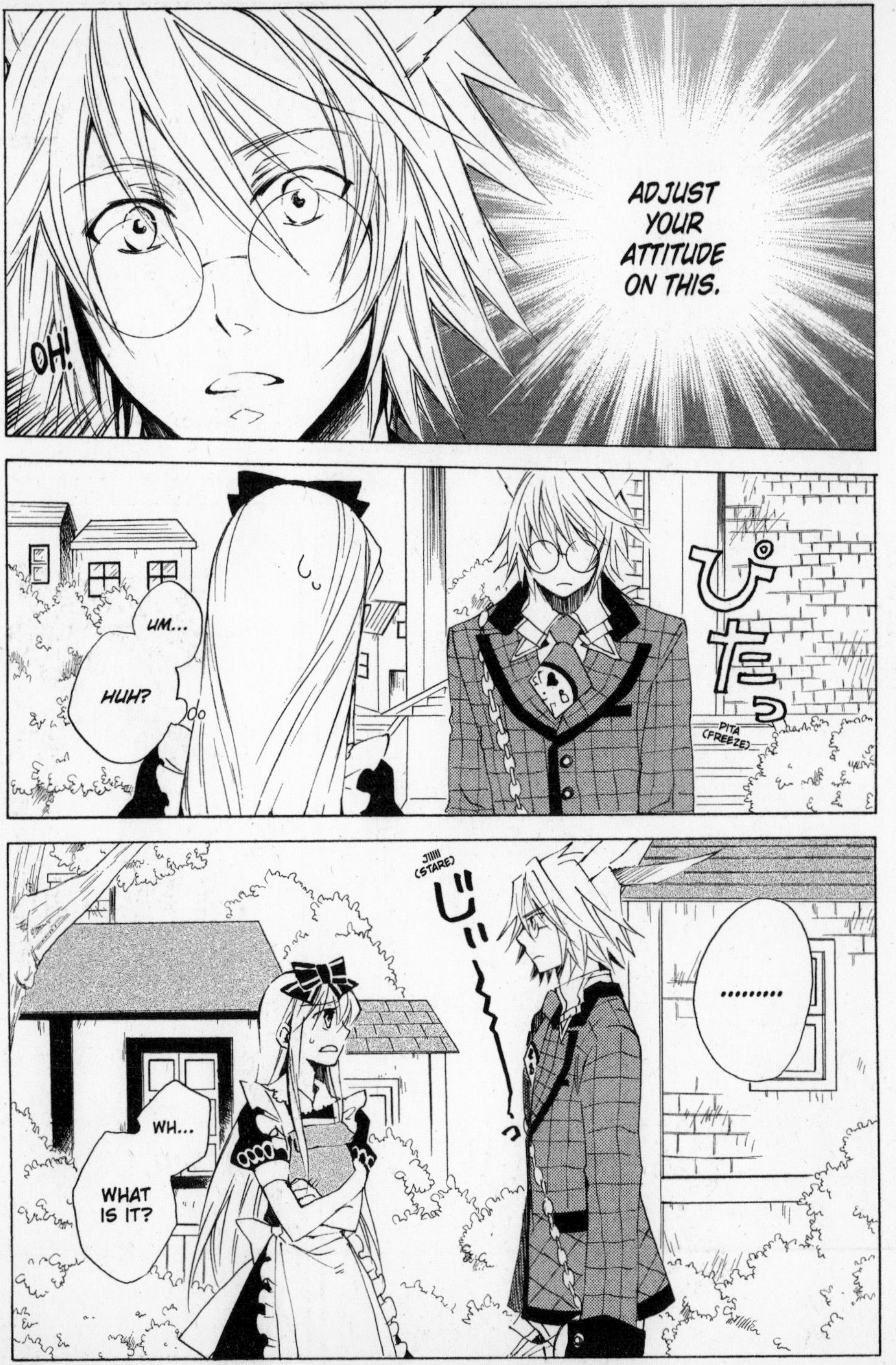
ADJUST YOUR ATTITUDE ON THIS.
OH!
ぴたっ
PITA (FREEZE)
UM...
HUH?
....
じぃ~っ
JIIIII (STARE)
WH...
WHAT IS IT?

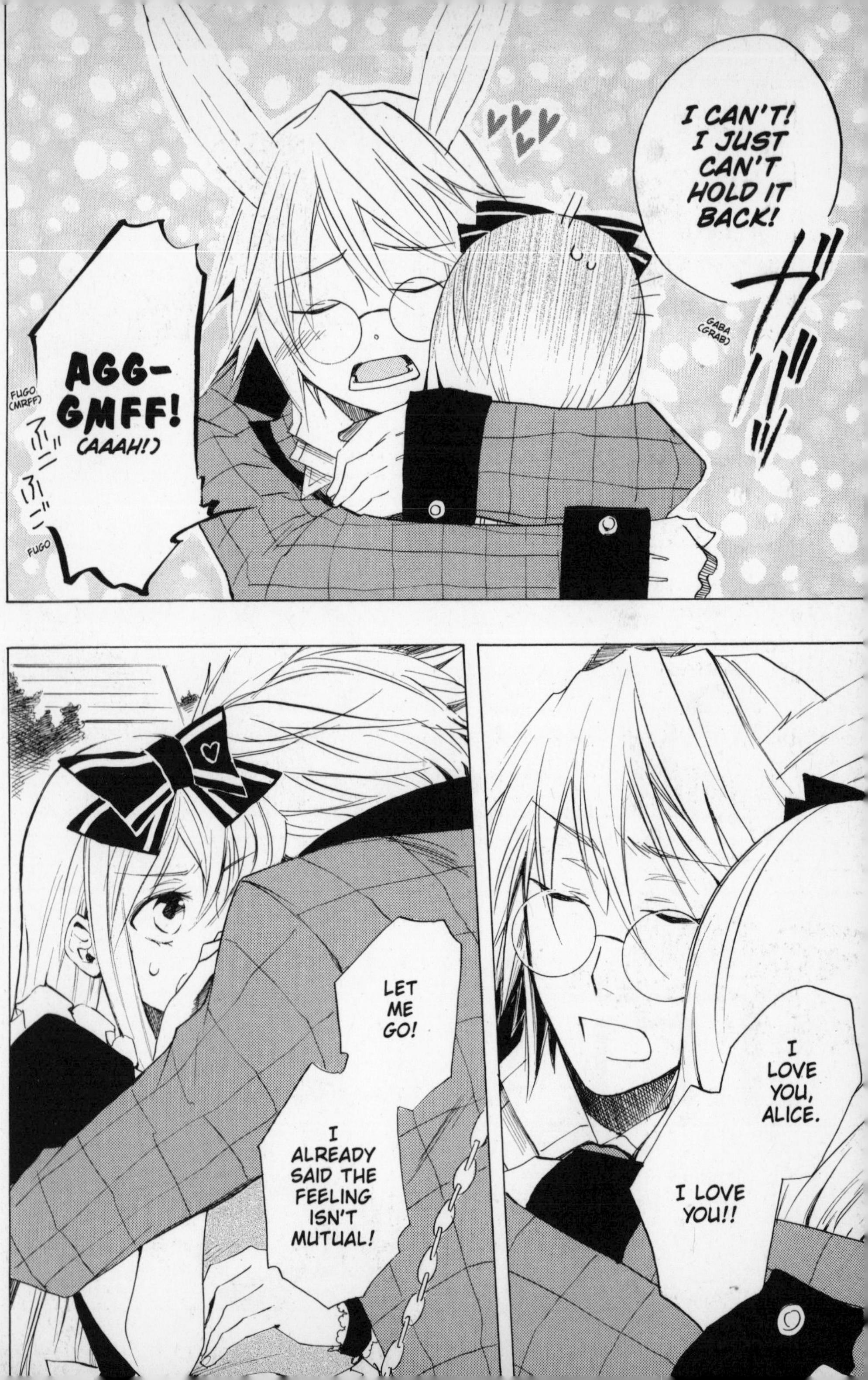
I CAN'T! I JUST CAN'T HOLD IT BACK!
GABA (GRAB)
AGG-GMFF! (AAAH!)
FUGO (MRFF)
FUGO
I LOVE YOU, ALICE.
I LOVE YOU!!
LET ME GO!
I ALREADY SAID THE FEELING ISN'T MUTUAL!

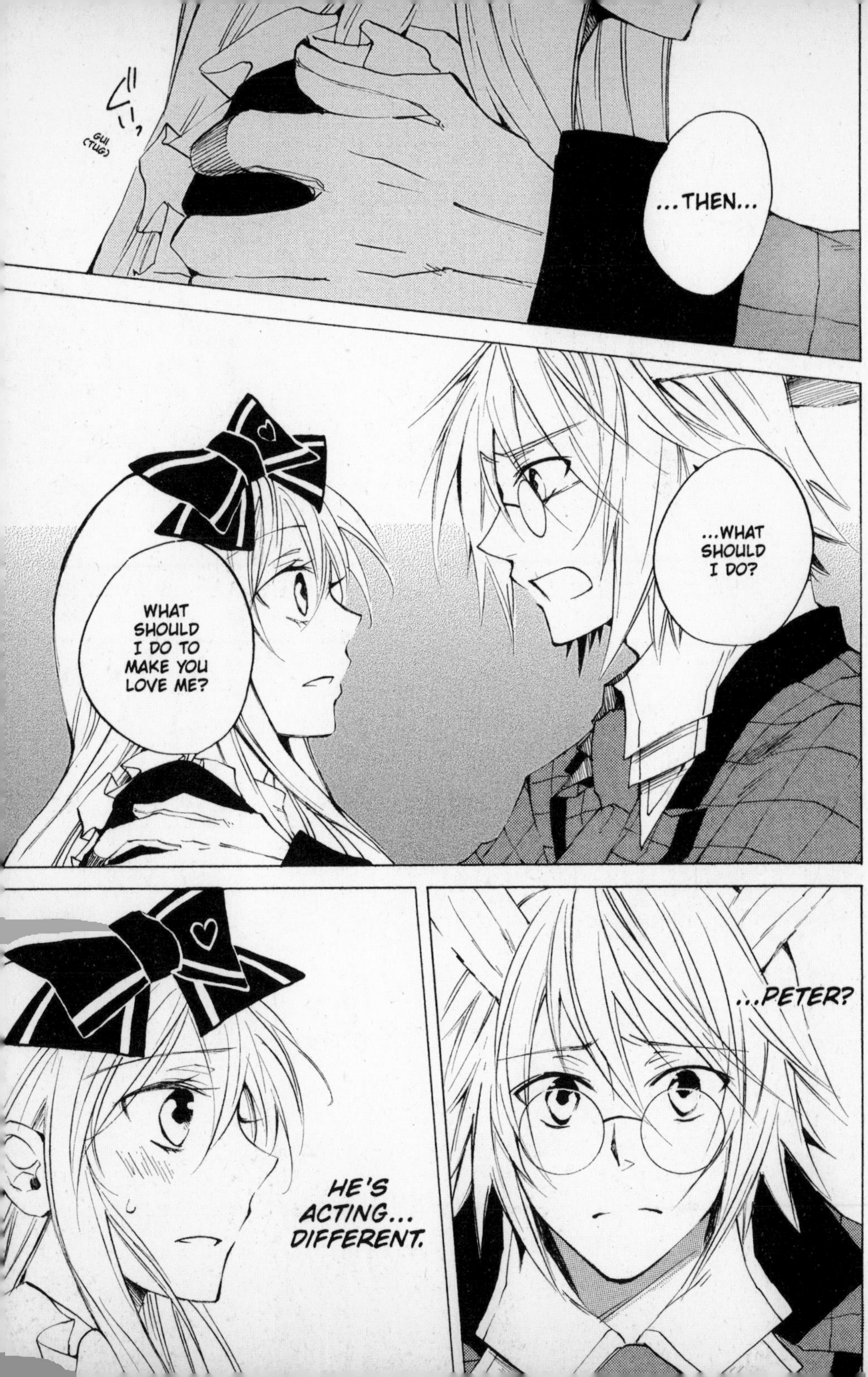
...THEN...
GUI (TUG)
...WHAT SHOULD I DO?
WHAT SHOULD I DO TO MAKE YOU LOVE ME?
...PETER?
HE'S ACTING... DIFFERENT.

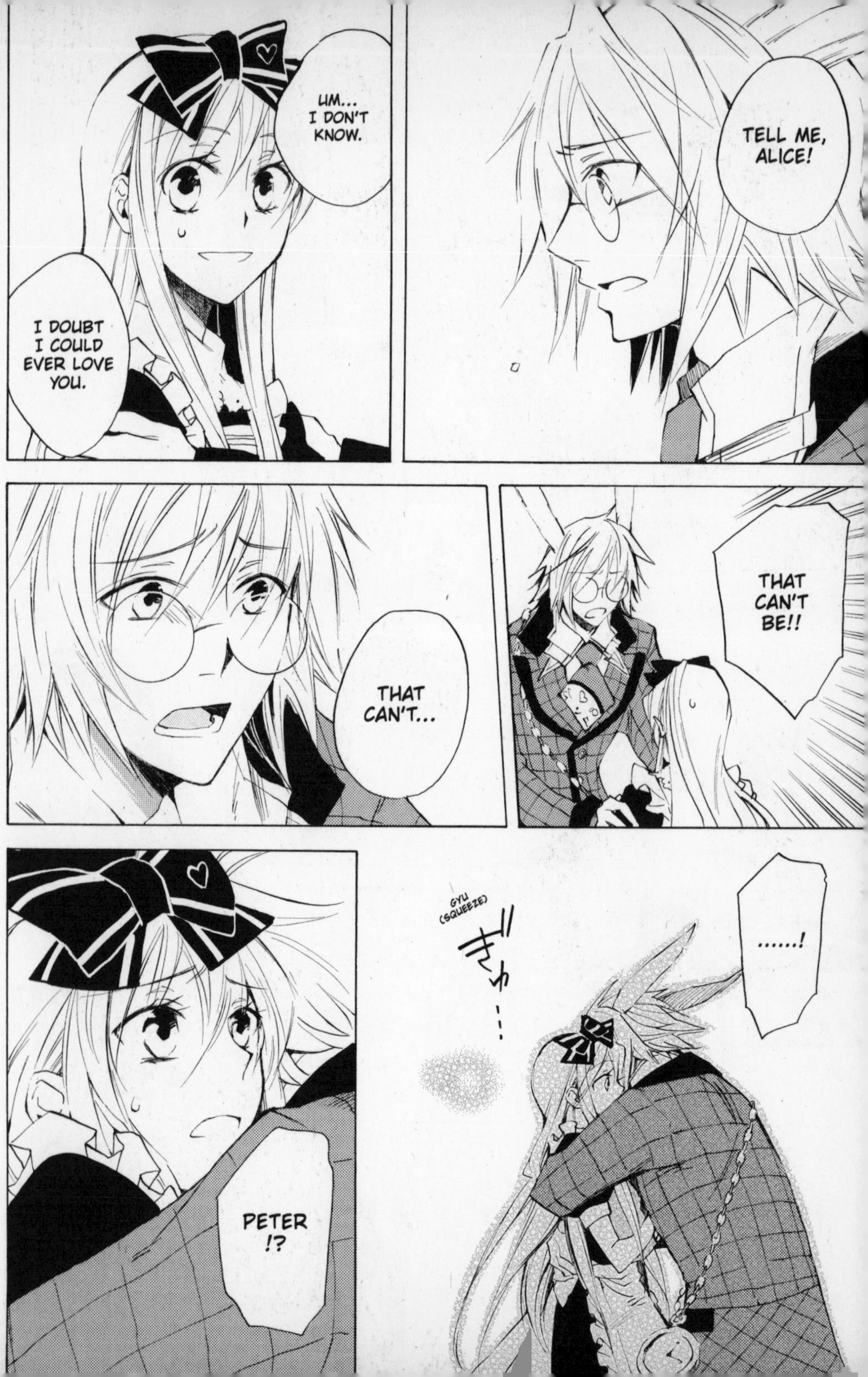
TELL ME, ALICE!
UM... I DON'T KNOW.
I DOUBT I COULD EVER LOVE YOU.
THAT CAN'T BE!!
THAT CAN'T...
......!
GYU (SQUEEZE)
PETER !?

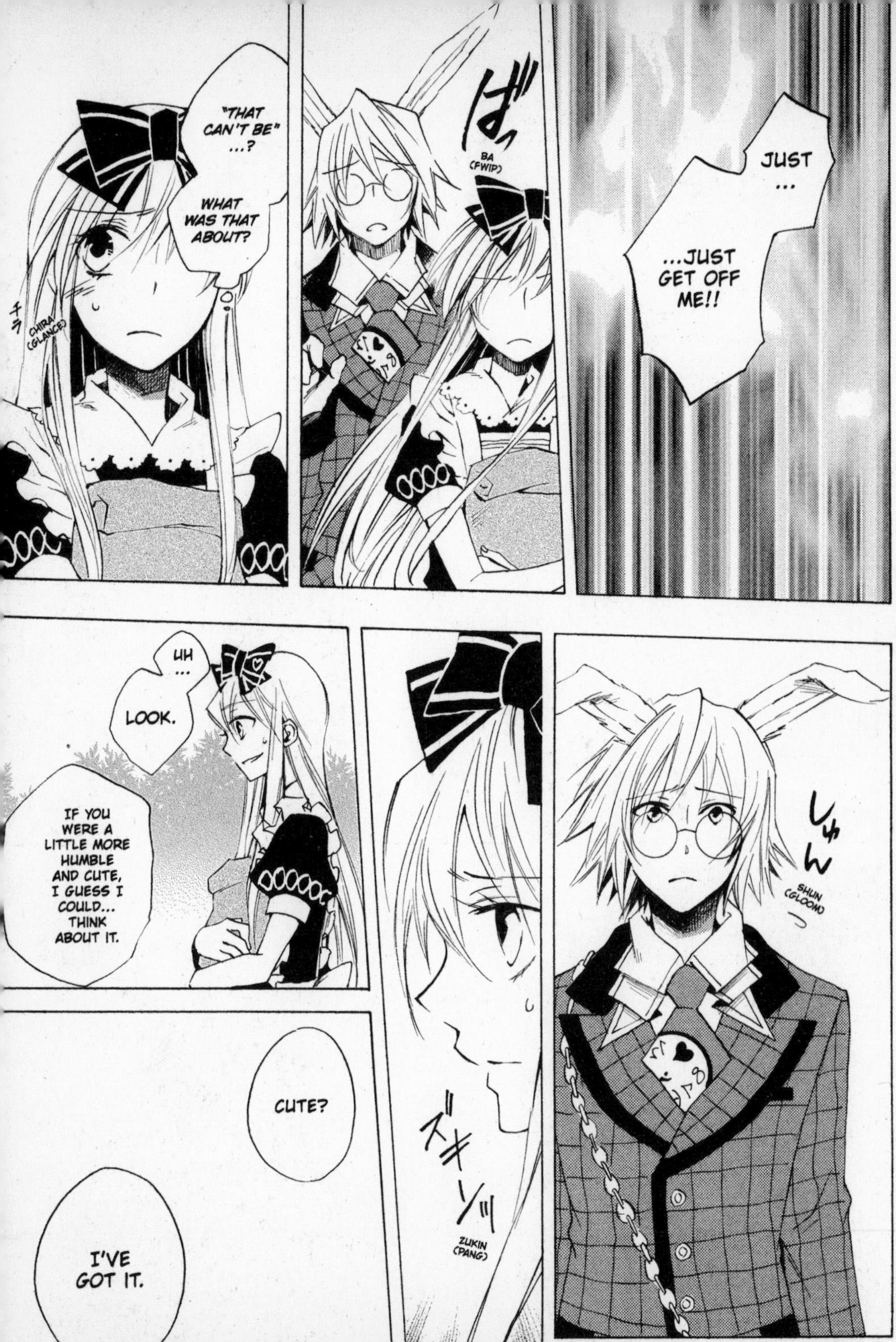
JUST ...
...JUST GET OFF ME!!
ばっ
BA (FWIP)
"THAT CAN'T BE" ...?
WHAT WAS THAT ABOUT?
チラ
CHIRA (GLANCE)
しゅん
SHUN (GLOOM)
ズキン
ZUKIN (PANG)
UH ...
LOOK.
IF YOU WERE A LITTLE MORE HUMBLE AND CUTE, I GUESS I COULD... THINK ABOUT IT.
CUTE?
I'VE GOT IT.

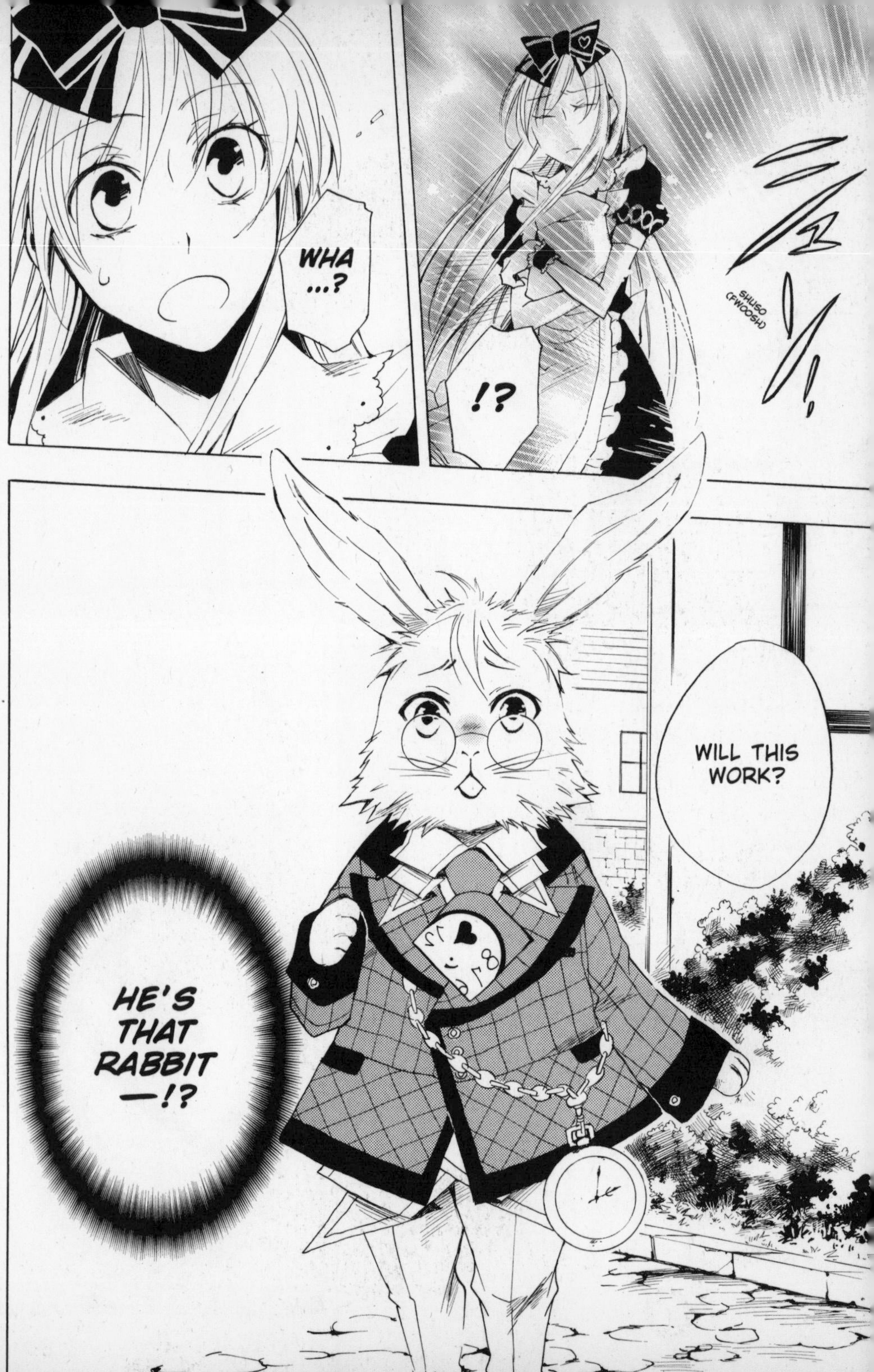
SHUSO (FWOOSH)
!?
WHA ...?
WILL THIS WORK?
HE'S THAT RABBIT —!?

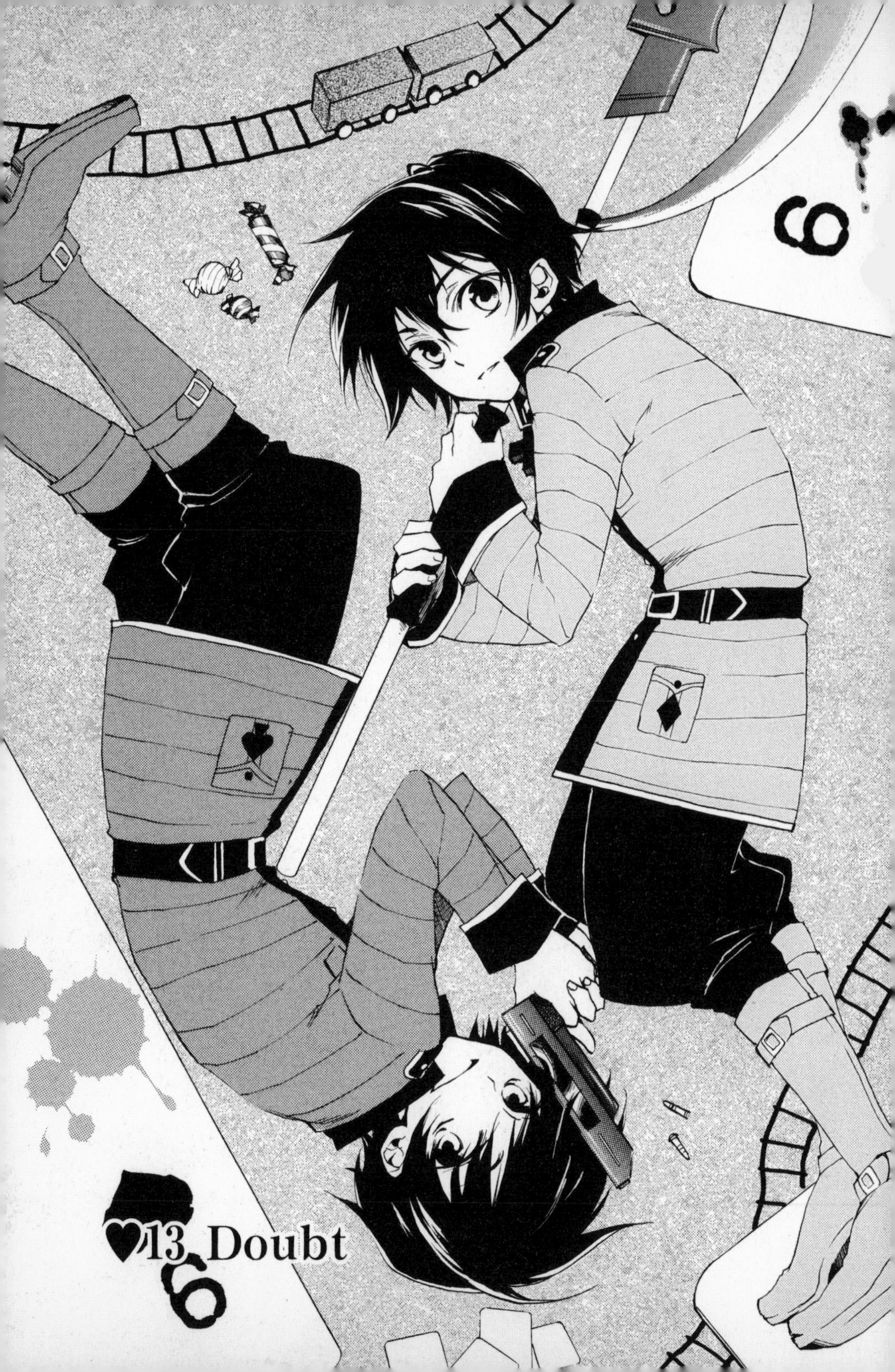

♥13 Doubt

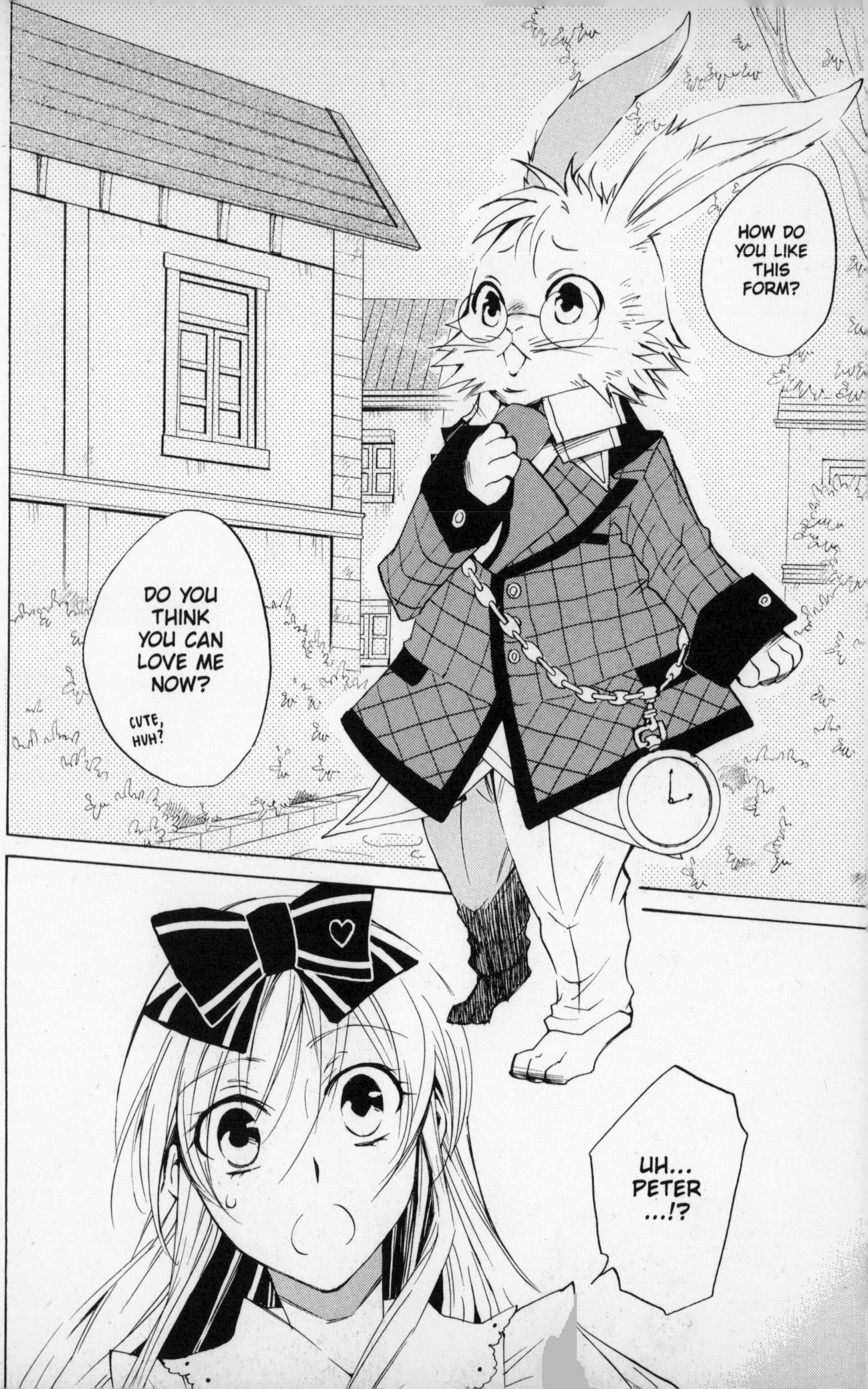
HOW DO YOU LIKE THIS FORM?
DO YOU THINK YOU CAN LOVE ME NOW?
CUTE, HUH?
UH... PETER ...!?

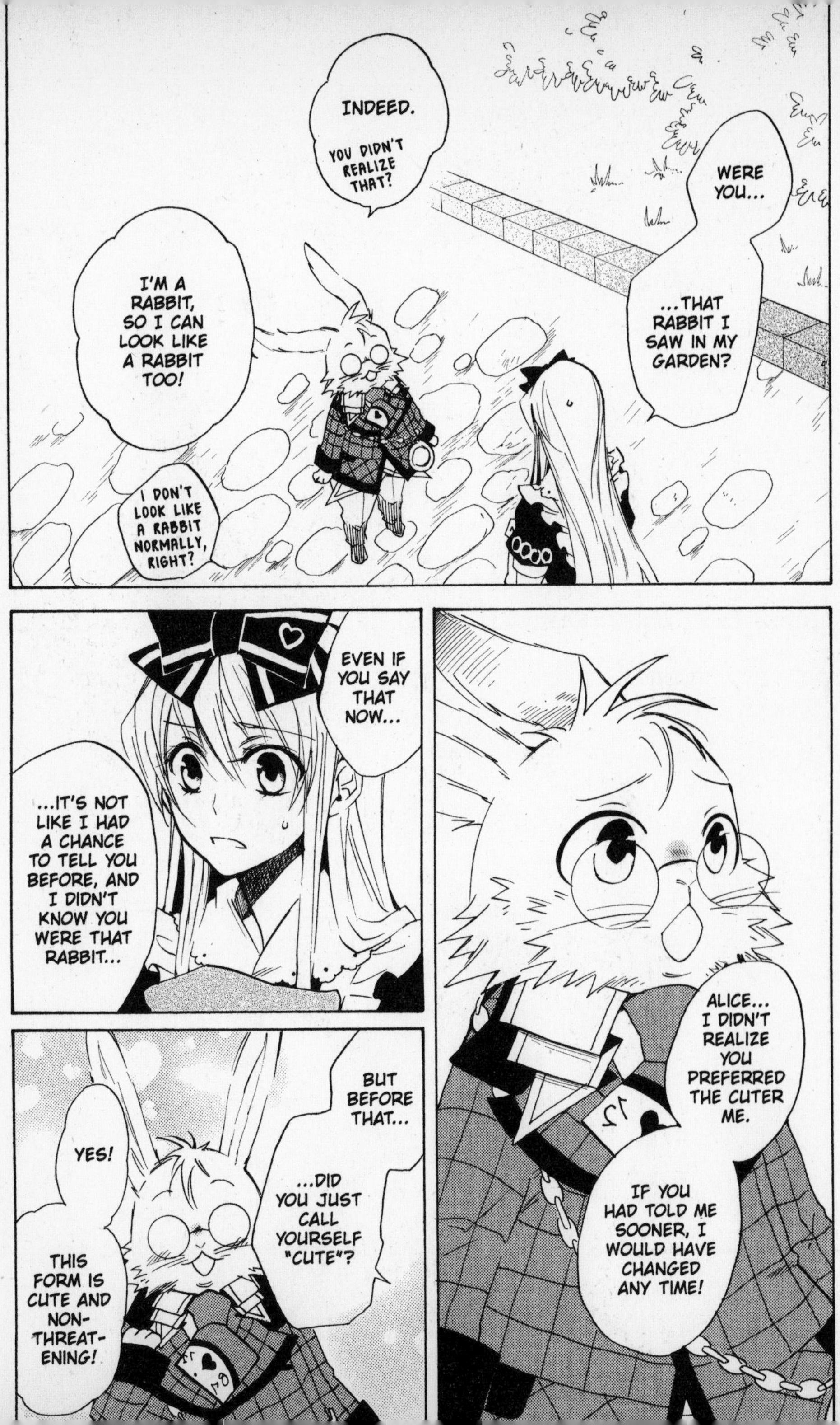
WERE YOU...
...THAT RABBIT I SAW IN MY GARDEN?
INDEED.
YOU DIDN'T REALIZE THAT?
I'M A RABBIT, SO I CAN LOOK LIKE A RABBIT TOO!
I DON'T LOOK LIKE A RABBIT NORMALLY, RIGHT?
ALICE... I DIDN'T REALIZE YOU PREFERRED THE CUTER ME.
IF YOU HAD TOLD ME SOONER, I WOULD HAVE CHANGED ANY TIME!
EVEN IF YOU SAY THAT NOW...
...IT'S NOT LIKE I HAD A CHANCE TO TELL YOU BEFORE, AND I DIDN'T KNOW YOU WERE THAT RABBIT...
BUT BEFORE THAT...
...DID YOU JUST CALL YOURSELF "CUTE"?
YES!
THIS FORM IS CUTE AND NON-THREAT-ENING!

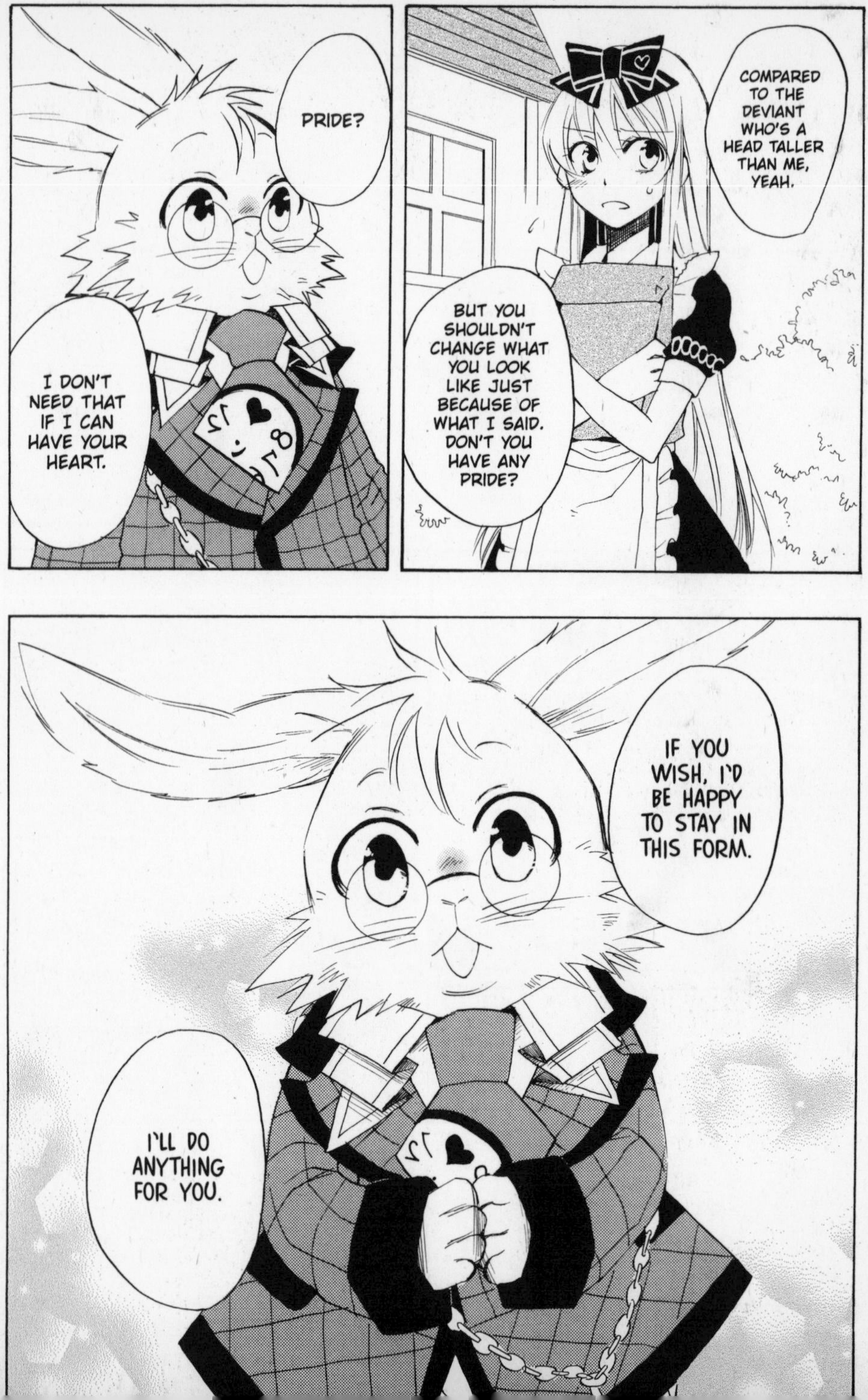
COMPARED TO THE DEVIANT WHO'S A HEAD TALLER THAN ME, YEAH.
BUT YOU SHOULDN'T CHANGE WHAT YOU LOOK LIKE JUST BECAUSE OF WHAT I SAID. DON'T YOU HAVE ANY PRIDE?
PRIDE?
I DON'T NEED THAT IF I CAN HAVE YOUR HEART.
IF YOU WISH, I'D BE HAPPY TO STAY IN THIS FORM.
I'LL DO ANYTHING FOR YOU.

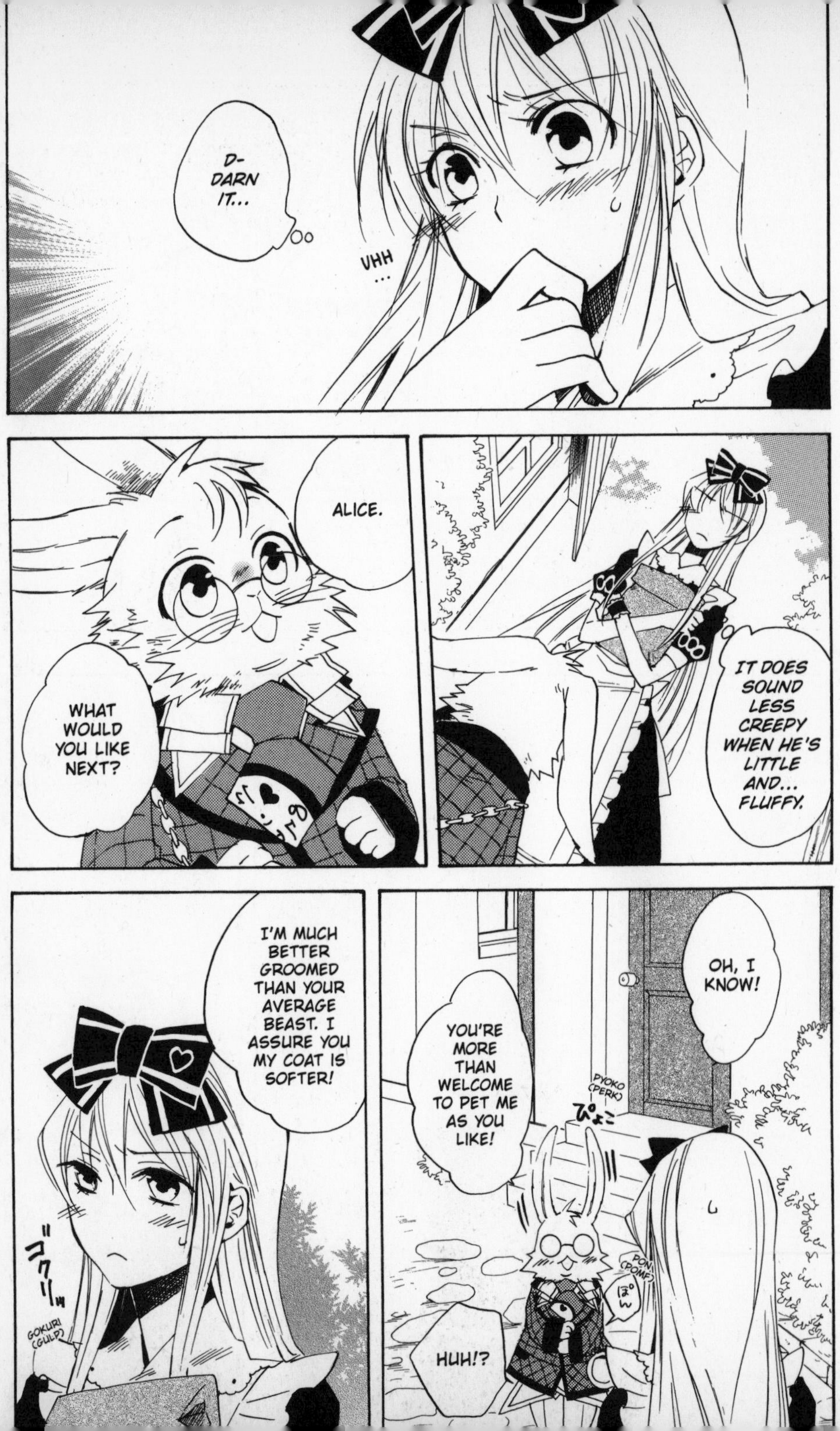
D-DARN IT...
UHH ...
IT DOES SOUND LESS CREEPY WHEN HE'S LITTLE AND... FLUFFY.
ALICE.
WHAT WOULD YOU LIKE NEXT?
OH, I KNOW!
YOU'RE MORE THAN WELCOME TO PET ME AS YOU LIKE!
PYOKO (PERK)
PON (POMF)
HUH!?
I'M MUCH BETTER GROOMED THAN YOUR AVERAGE BEAST. I ASSURE YOU MY COAT IS SOFTER!
GOKURI (GULP)

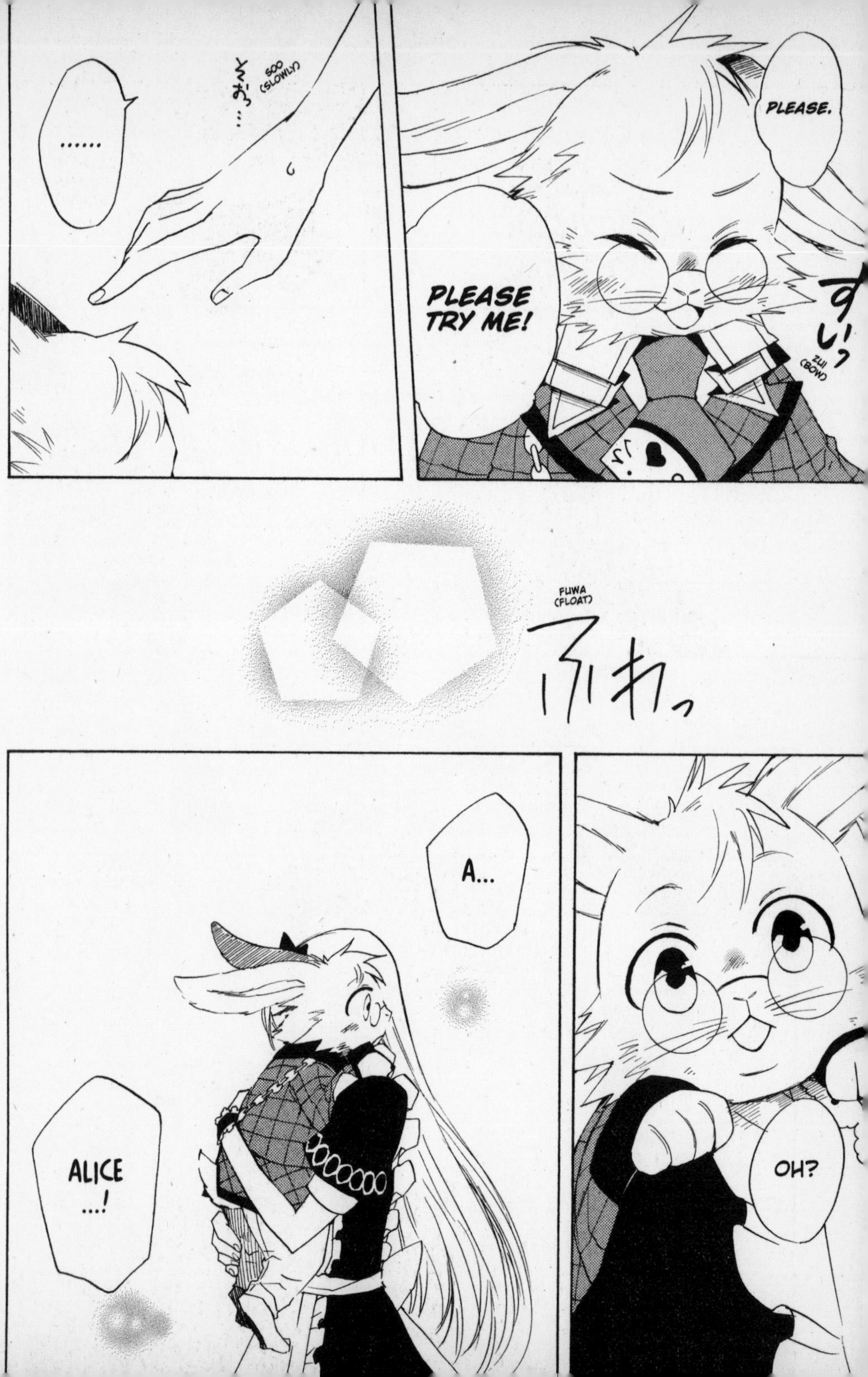
PLEASE.
PLEASE TRY ME!
すいっ
ZUI (BOW)
......
SOO (SLOWLY)
FUWA (FLOAT)
ふわっ
OH?
A...
ALICE ...!

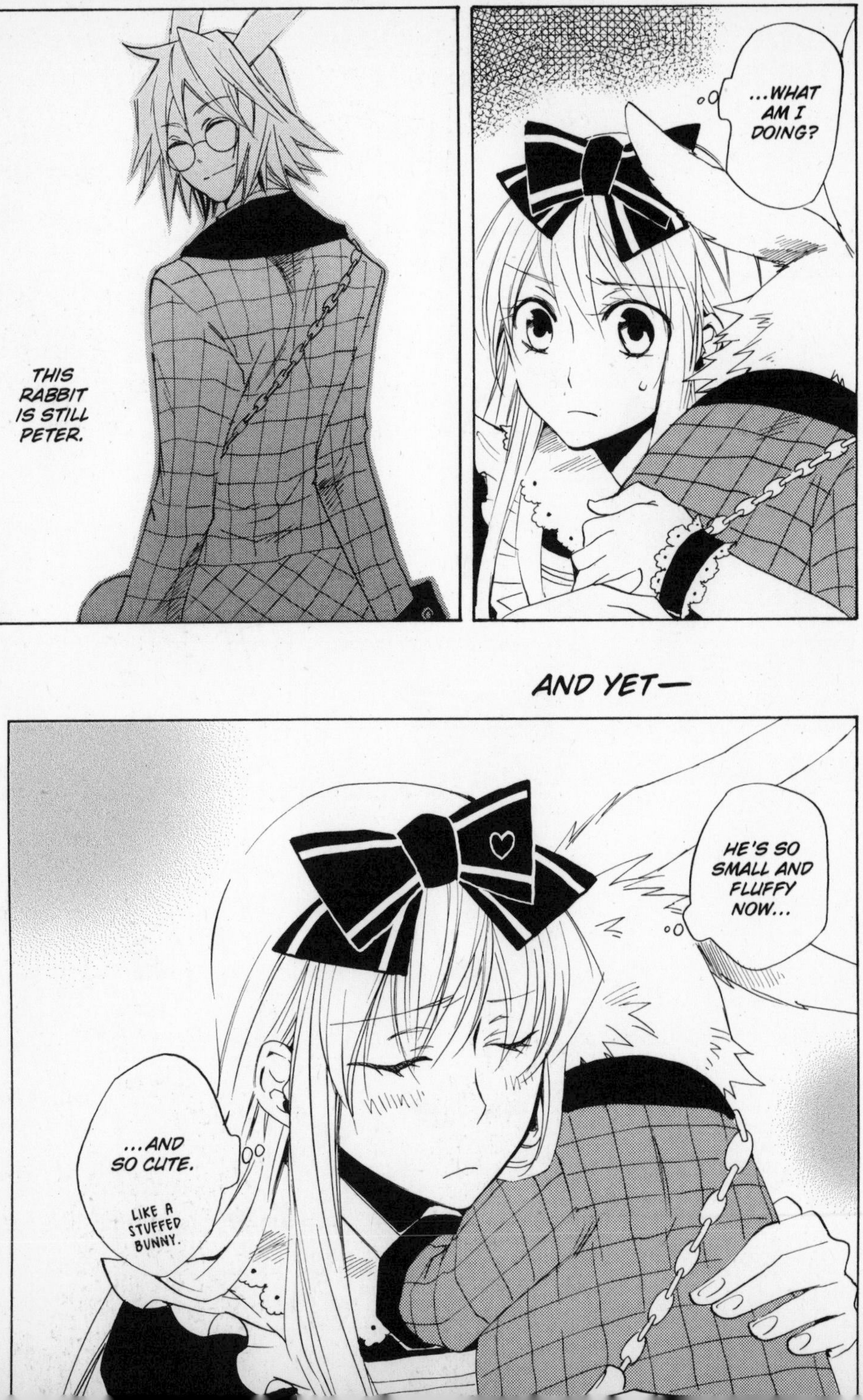
...WHAT AM I DOING?
THIS RABBIT IS STILL PETER.
AND YET—
HE'S SO SMALL AND FLUFFY NOW...
...AND SO CUTE.
LIKE A STUFFED BUNNY.

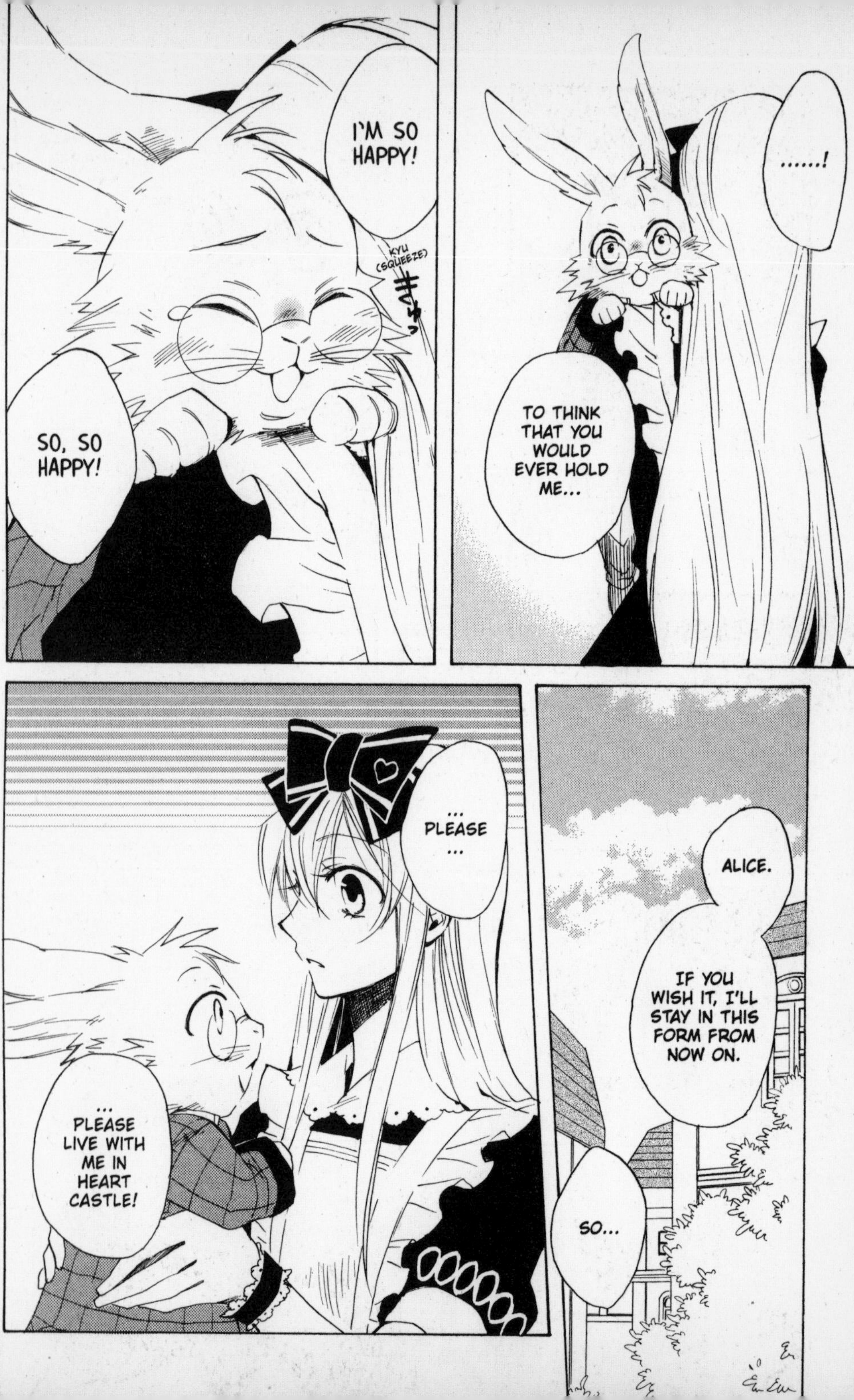

......!
TO THINK THAT YOU WOULD EVER HOLD ME...
I'M SO HAPPY!
KYU (SQUEEZE)
SO, SO HAPPY!
ALICE.
IF YOU WISH IT, I'LL STAY IN THIS FORM FROM NOW ON.
SO...
... PLEASE ...
... PLEASE LIVE WITH ME IN HEART CASTLE!

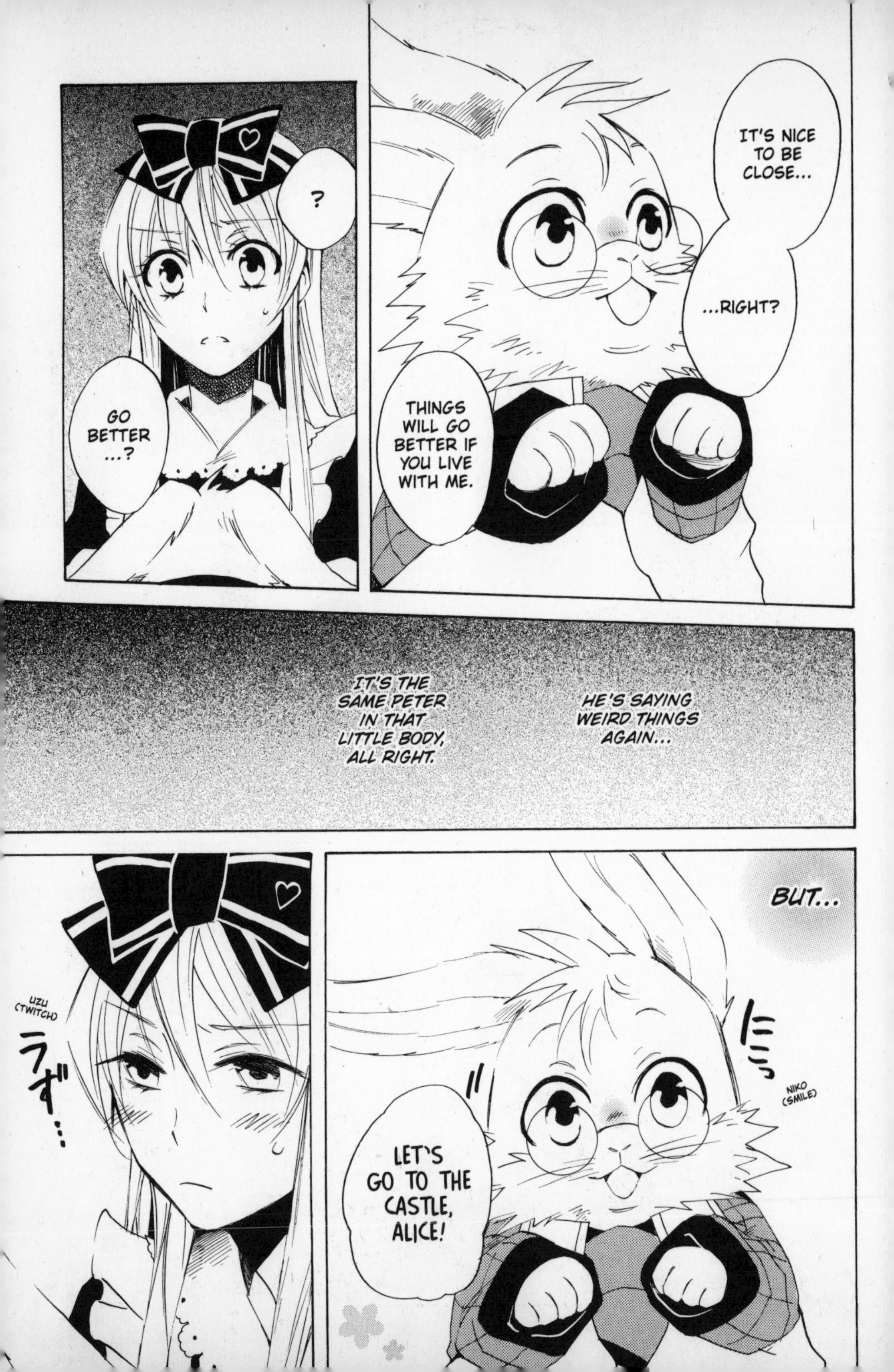
IT'S NICE TO BE CLOSE...
...RIGHT?
THINGS WILL GO BETTER IF YOU LIVE WITH ME.
?
GO BETTER ...?
HE'S SAYING WEIRD THINGS AGAIN...
IT'S THE SAME PETER IN THAT LITTLE BODY, ALL RIGHT.
BUT...
NIKO (SMILE)
LET'S GO TO THE CASTLE, ALICE!
うず…
UZU (TWITCH)

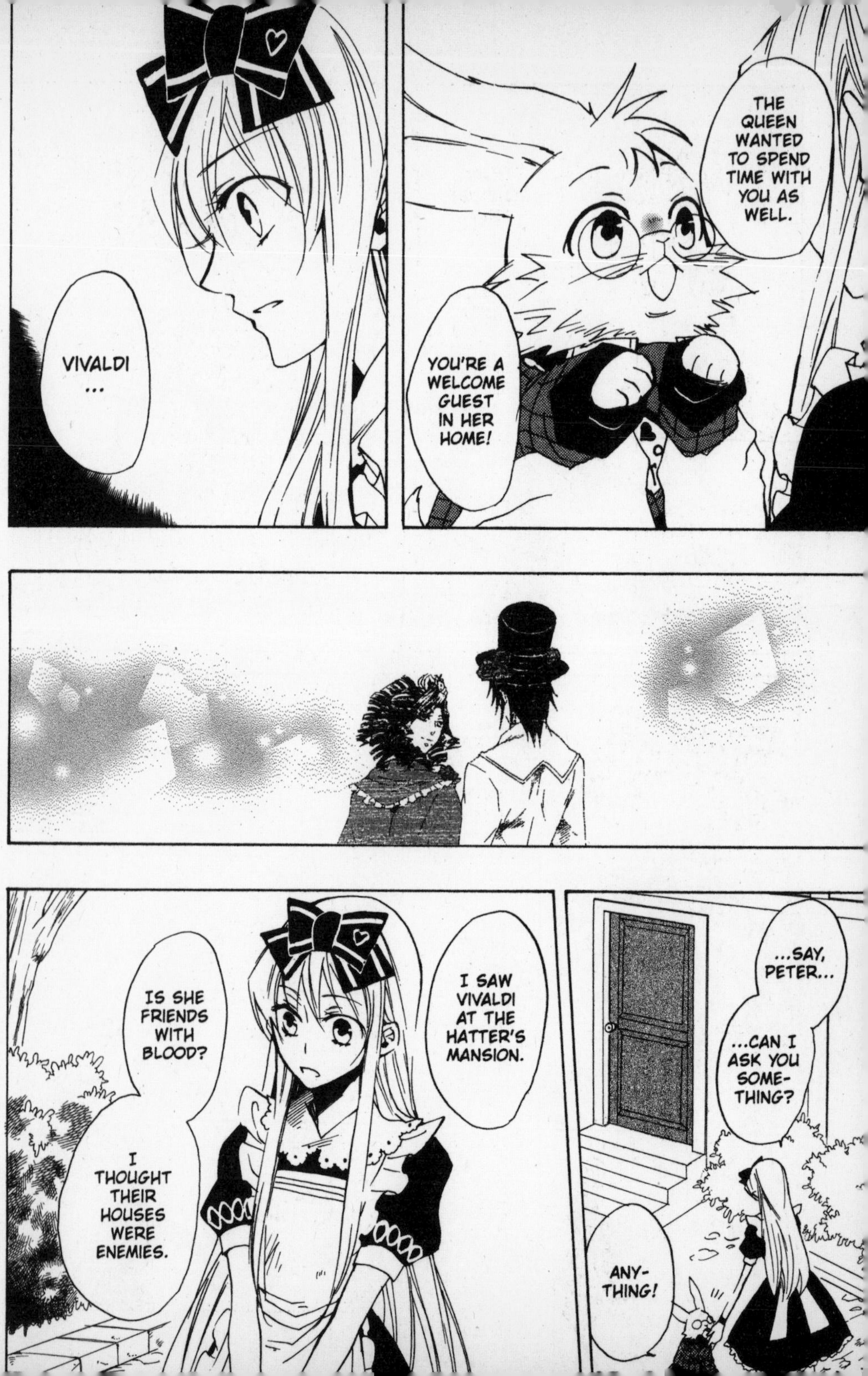
THE QUEEN WANTED TO SPEND TIME WITH YOU AS WELL.
YOU'RE A WELCOME GUEST IN HER HOME!
VIVALDI ...
...SAY, PETER...
...CAN I ASK YOU SOME-THING?
ANY-THING!
I SAW VIVALDI AT THE HATTER'S MANSION.
IS SHE FRIENDS WITH BLOOD?
I THOUGHT THEIR HOUSES WERE ENEMIES.

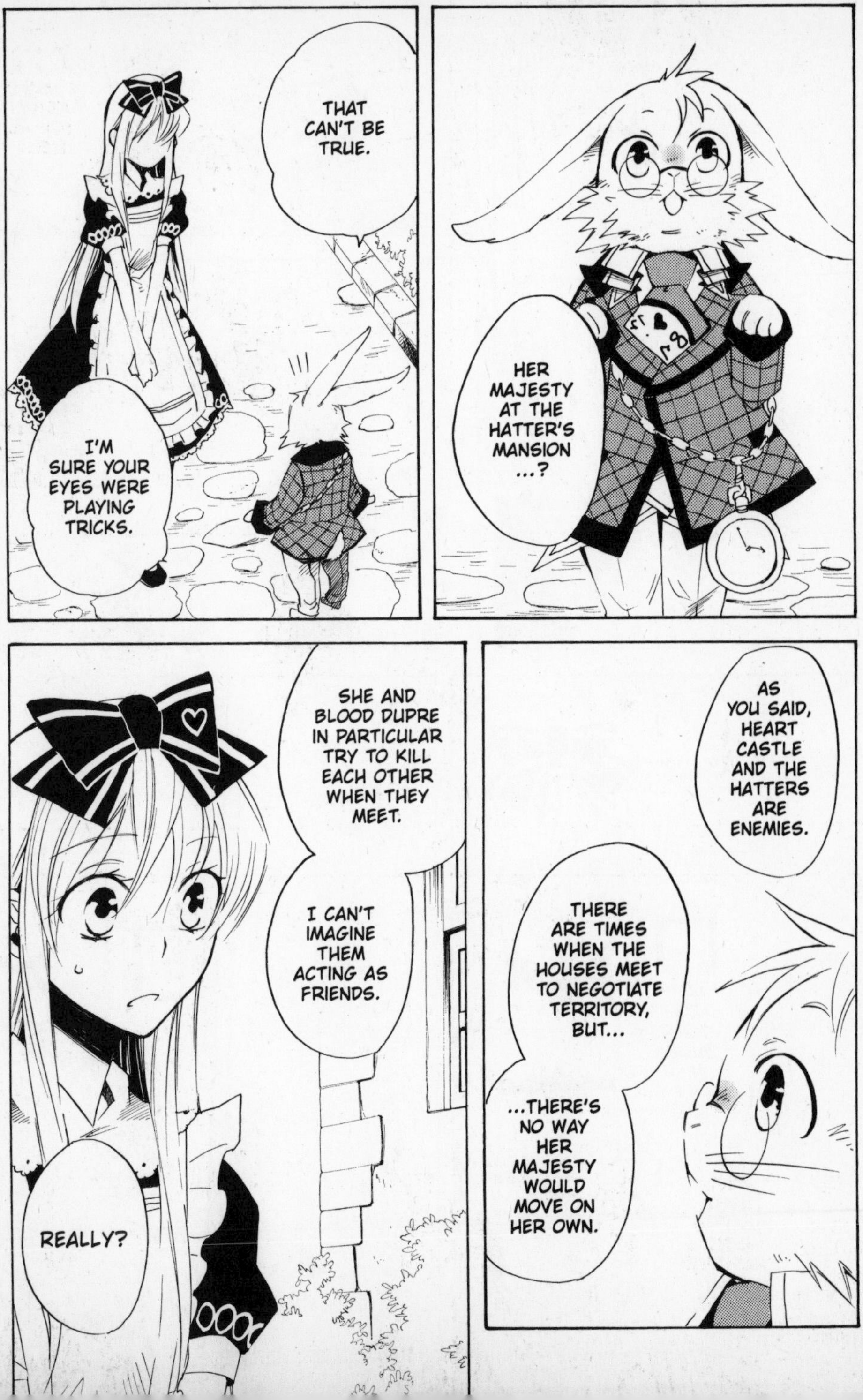
HER MAJESTY AT THE HATTER'S MANSION ...?
THAT CAN'T BE TRUE.
I'M SURE YOUR EYES WERE PLAYING TRICKS.
AS YOU SAID, HEART CASTLE AND THE HATTERS ARE ENEMIES.
THERE ARE TIMES WHEN THE HOUSES MEET TO NEGOTIATE TERRITORY, BUT...
...THERE'S NO WAY HER MAJESTY WOULD MOVE ON HER OWN.
SHE AND BLOOD DUPRE IN PARTICULAR TRY TO KILL EACH OTHER WHEN THEY MEET.
I CAN'T IMAGINE THEM ACTING AS FRIENDS.
REALLY?

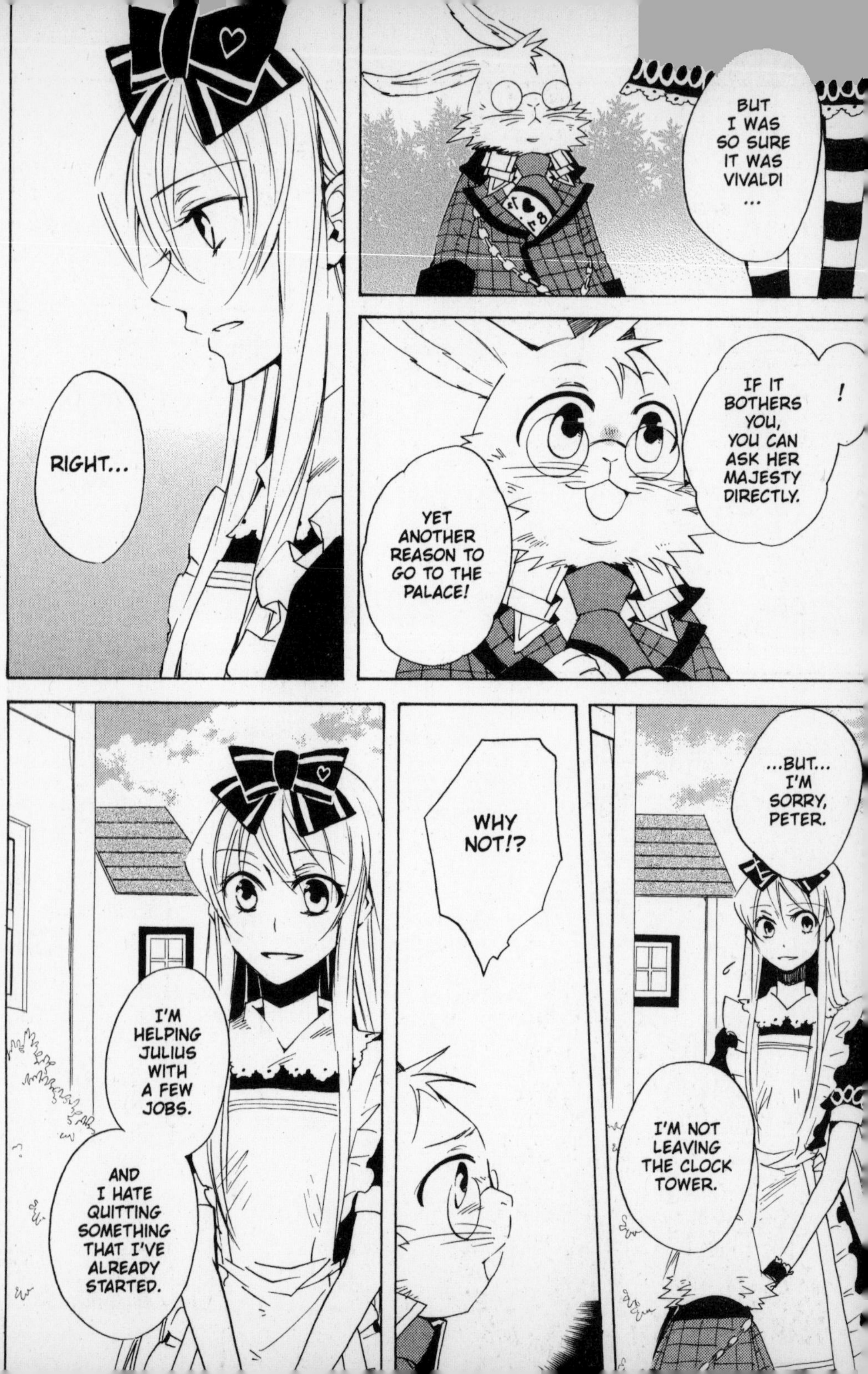
BUT I WAS SO SURE IT WAS VIVALDI ...
IF IT BOTHERS YOU, YOU CAN ASK HER MAJESTY DIRECTLY.
!
YET ANOTHER REASON TO GO TO THE PALACE!
RIGHT...
...BUT... I'M SORRY, PETER.
I'M NOT LEAVING THE CLOCK TOWER.
WHY NOT!?
I'M HELPING JULIUS WITH A FEW JOBS.
AND I HATE QUITTING SOMETHING THAT I'VE ALREADY STARTED.

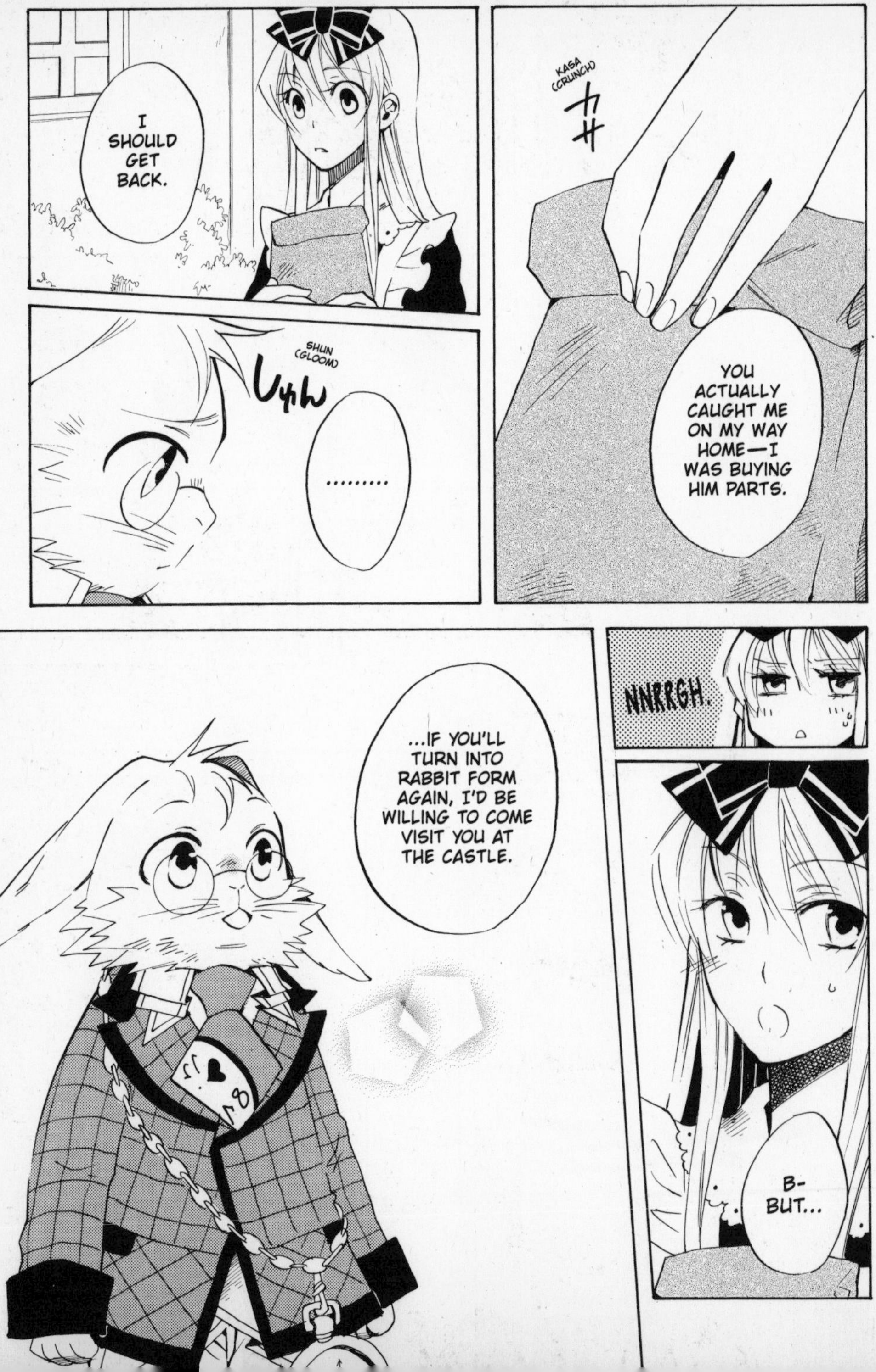
KASA (CRUNCH)
カサ
YOU ACTUALLY CAUGHT ME ON MY WAY HOME—I WAS BUYING HIM PARTS.
I SHOULD GET BACK.
SHUN (GLOOM)
しゅん
....
NNRRGH.
B-BUT...
...IF YOU'LL TURN INTO RABBIT FORM AGAIN, I'D BE WILLING TO COME VISIT YOU AT THE CASTLE.

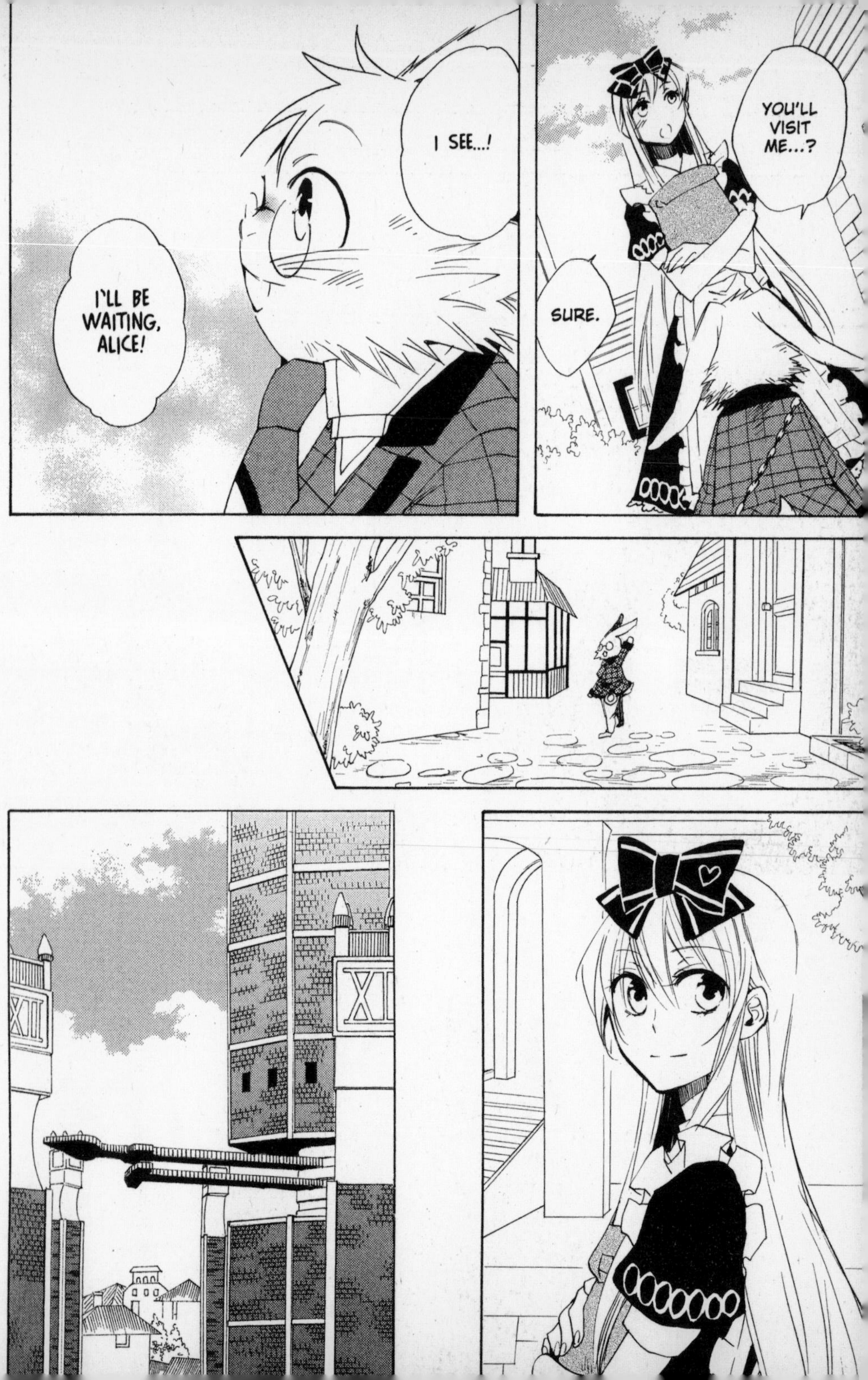
YOU'LL VISIT ME...?
SURE.
I SEE...!
I'LL BE WAITING, ALICE!

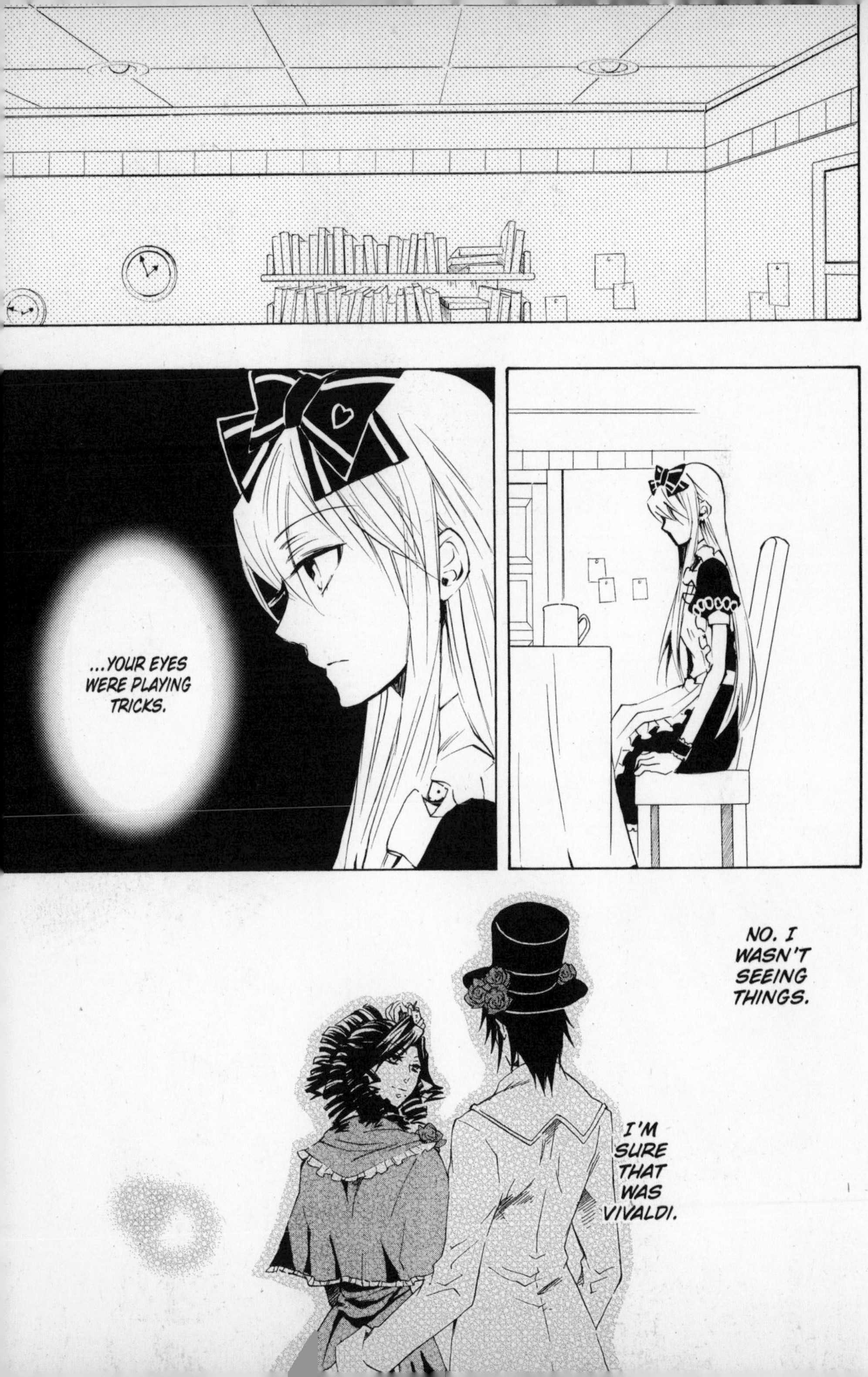
...YOUR EYES WERE PLAYING TRICKS.
NO. I WASN'T SEEING THINGS.
I'M SURE THAT WAS VIVALDI.

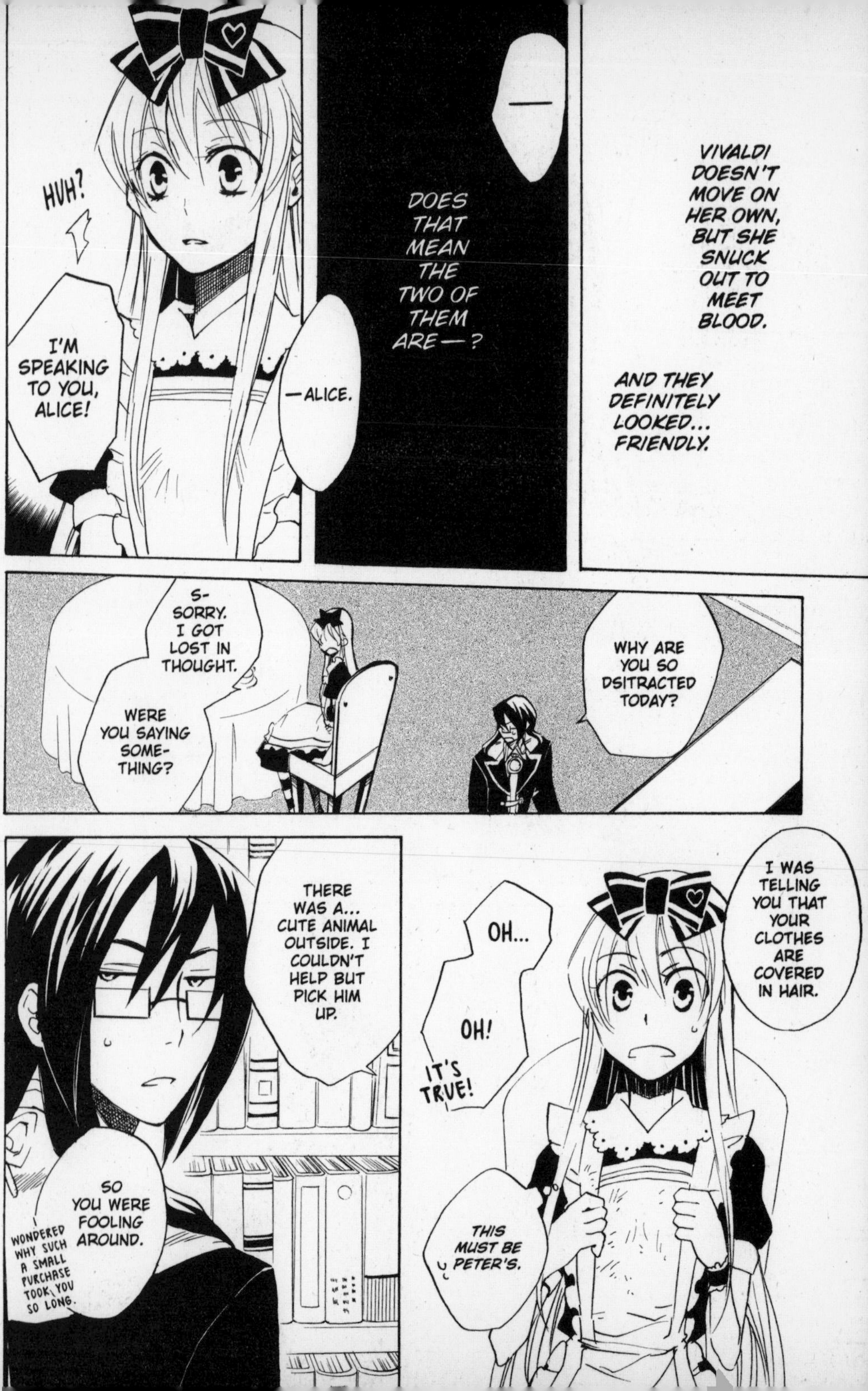
VIVALDI DOESN'T MOVE ON HER OWN, BUT SHE SNUCK OUT TO MEET BLOOD.
AND THEY DEFINITELY LOOKED... FRIENDLY.
—
DOES THAT MEAN THE TWO OF THEM ARE—?
—ALICE.
HUH?
I'M SPEAKING TO YOU, ALICE!
WHY ARE YOU SO DSITRACTED TODAY?
S-SORRY. I GOT LOST IN THOUGHT.
WERE YOU SAYING SOME-THING?
I WAS TELLING YOU THAT YOUR CLOTHES ARE COVERED IN HAIR.
OH...
OH!
IT'S TRUE!
THIS MUST BE PETER'S.
THERE WAS A... CUTE ANIMAL OUTSIDE. I COULDN'T HELP BUT PICK HIM UP.
SO YOU WERE FOOLING AROUND.
I WONDERED WHY SUCH A SMALL PURCHASE TOOK YOU SO LONG.

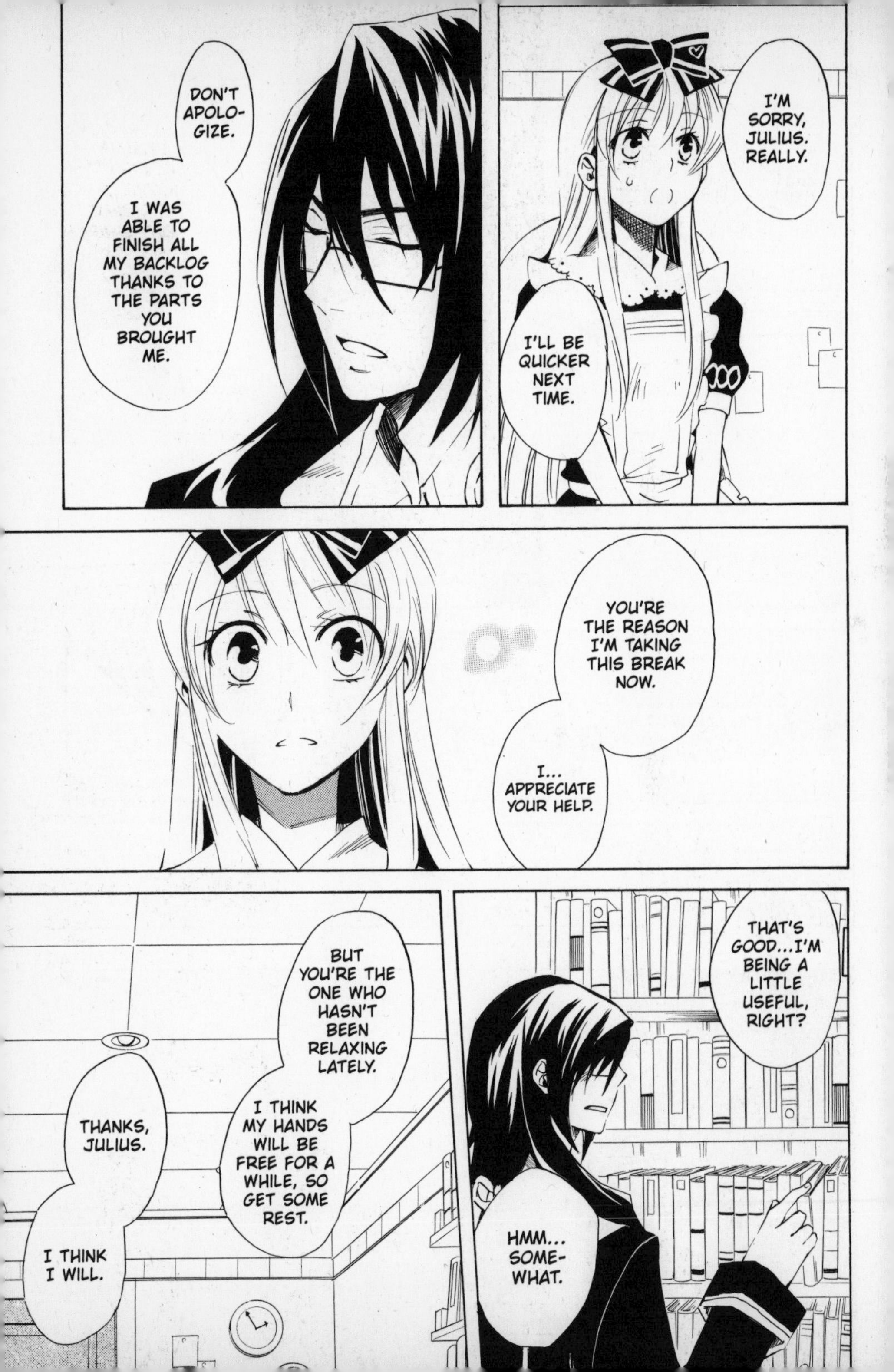
I'M SORRY, JULIUS. REALLY.
I'LL BE QUICKER NEXT TIME.
DON'T APOLOGIZE.
I WAS ABLE TO FINISH ALL MY BACKLOG THANKS TO THE PARTS YOU BROUGHT ME.
YOU'RE THE REASON I'M TAKING THIS BREAK NOW.
I... APPRECIATE YOUR HELP.
THAT'S GOOD...I'M BEING A LITTLE USEFUL, RIGHT?
HMM... SOMEWHAT.
BUT YOU'RE THE ONE WHO HASN'T BEEN RELAXING LATELY.
I THINK MY HANDS WILL BE FREE FOR A WHILE, SO GET SOME REST.
THANKS, JULIUS.
I THINK I WILL.

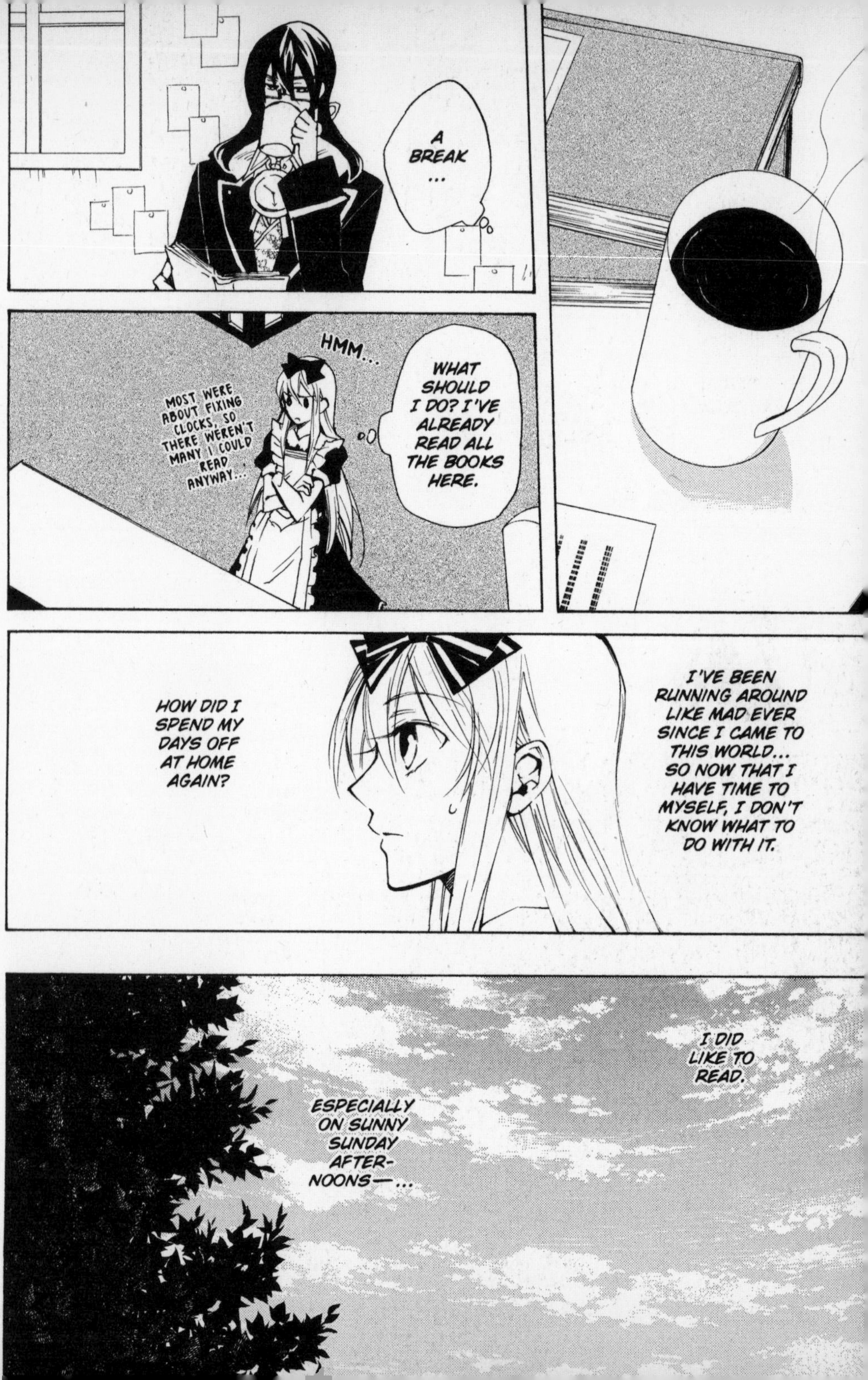
A BREAK...
HMM...
WHAT SHOULD I DO? I'VE ALREADY READ ALL THE BOOKS HERE.
MOST WERE ABOUT FIXING CLOCKS, SO THERE WEREN'T MANY I COULD READ ANYWAY...
I'VE BEEN RUNNING AROUND LIKE MAD EVER SINCE I CAME TO THIS WORLD... SO NOW THAT I HAVE TIME TO MYSELF, I DON'T KNOW WHAT TO DO WITH IT.
HOW DID I SPEND MY DAYS OFF AT HOME AGAIN?
I DID LIKE TO READ.
ESPECIALLY ON SUNNY SUNDAY AFTER-NOONS—...

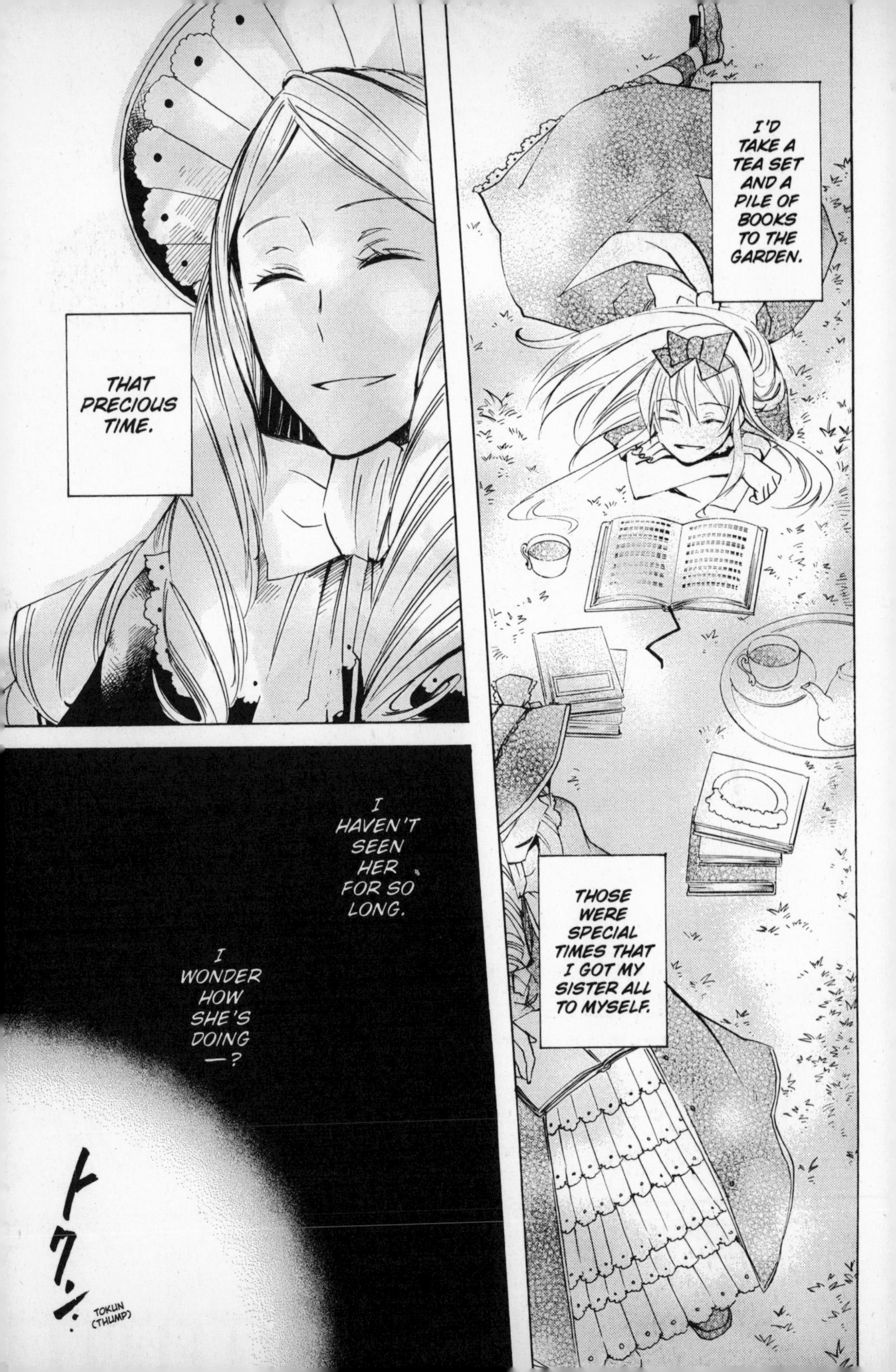
I'D TAKE A TEA SET AND A PILE OF BOOKS TO THE GARDEN.
THOSE WERE SPECIAL TIMES THAT I GOT MY SISTER ALL TO MYSELF.
THAT PRECIOUS TIME.
I HAVEN'T SEEN HER FOR SO LONG.
I WONDER HOW SHE'S DOING—?
トクン
TOKUN (THUMP)

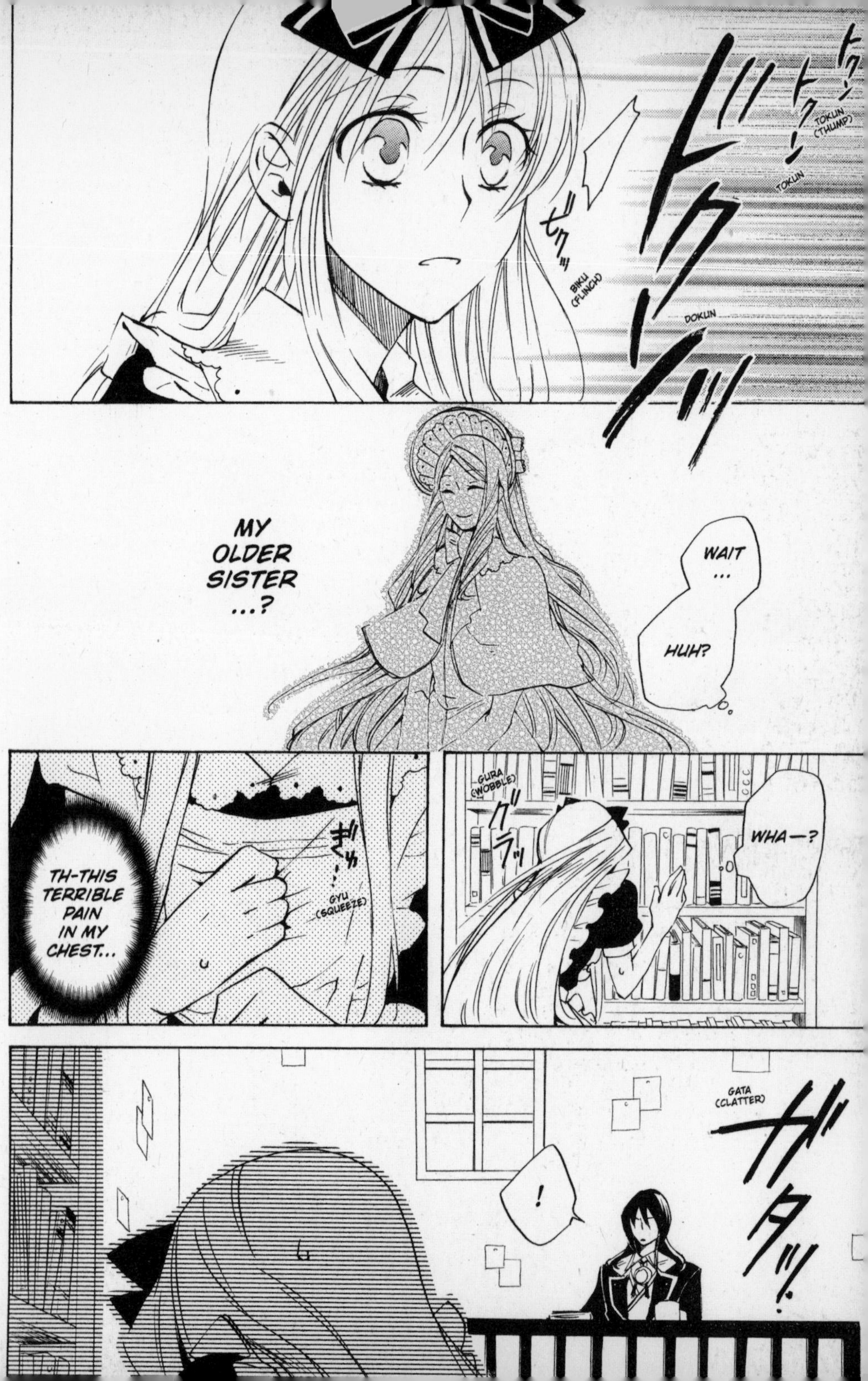
TOKUN (THUMP)
TOKUN
DOKUN
BIKU (FLINCH)
WAIT ... HUH?
MY OLDER SISTER ...?
WHA—?
GURA (WOBBLE)
GYU (SQUEEZE)
TH-THIS TERRIBLE PAIN IN MY CHEST...
GATA (CLATTER)
!

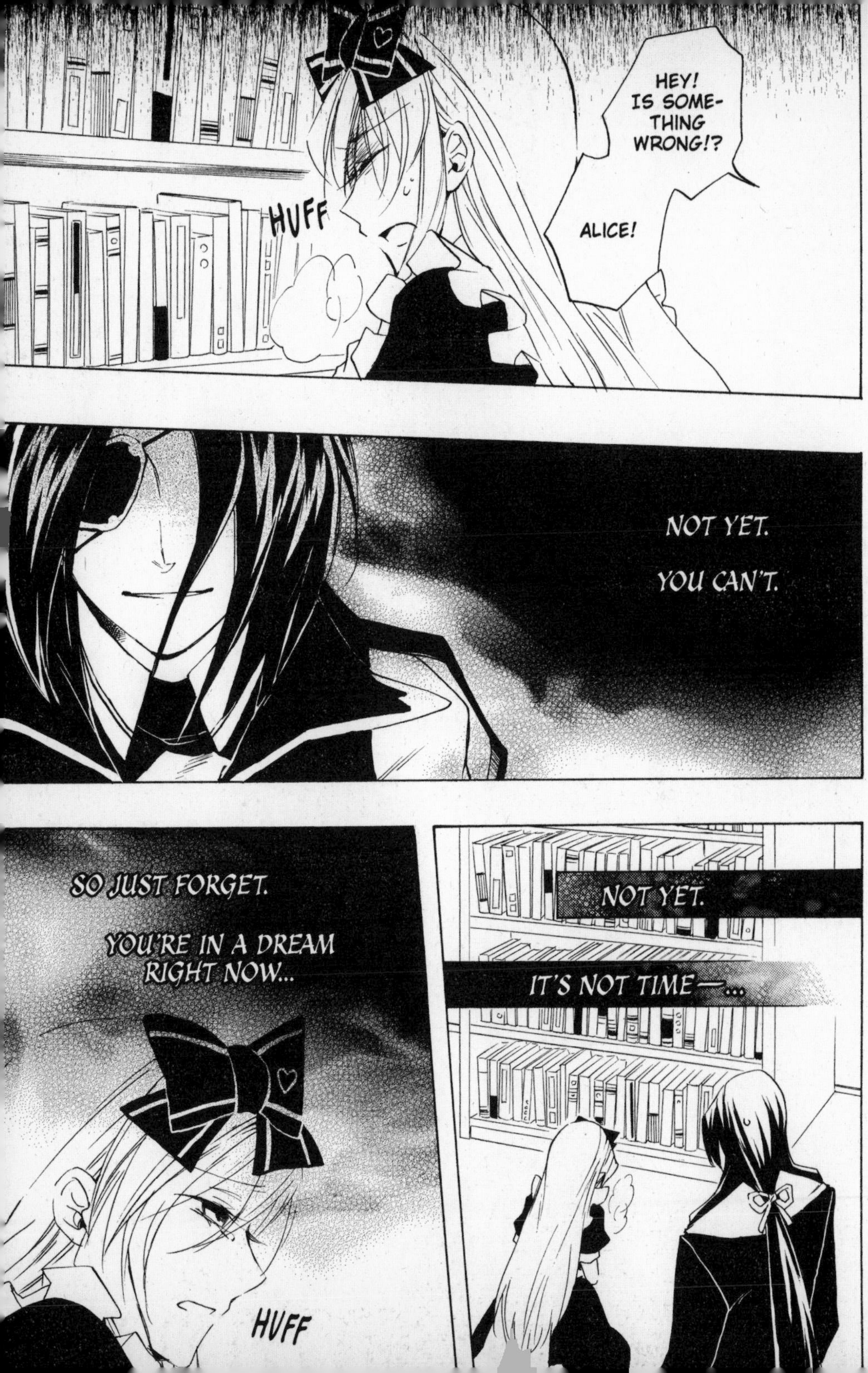
HEY! IS SOME-THING WRONG!?
ALICE!
HUFF
NOT YET.
YOU CAN'T.
NOT YET.
IT'S NOT TIME—...
SO JUST FORGET.
YOU'RE IN A DREAM RIGHT NOW...
HUFF

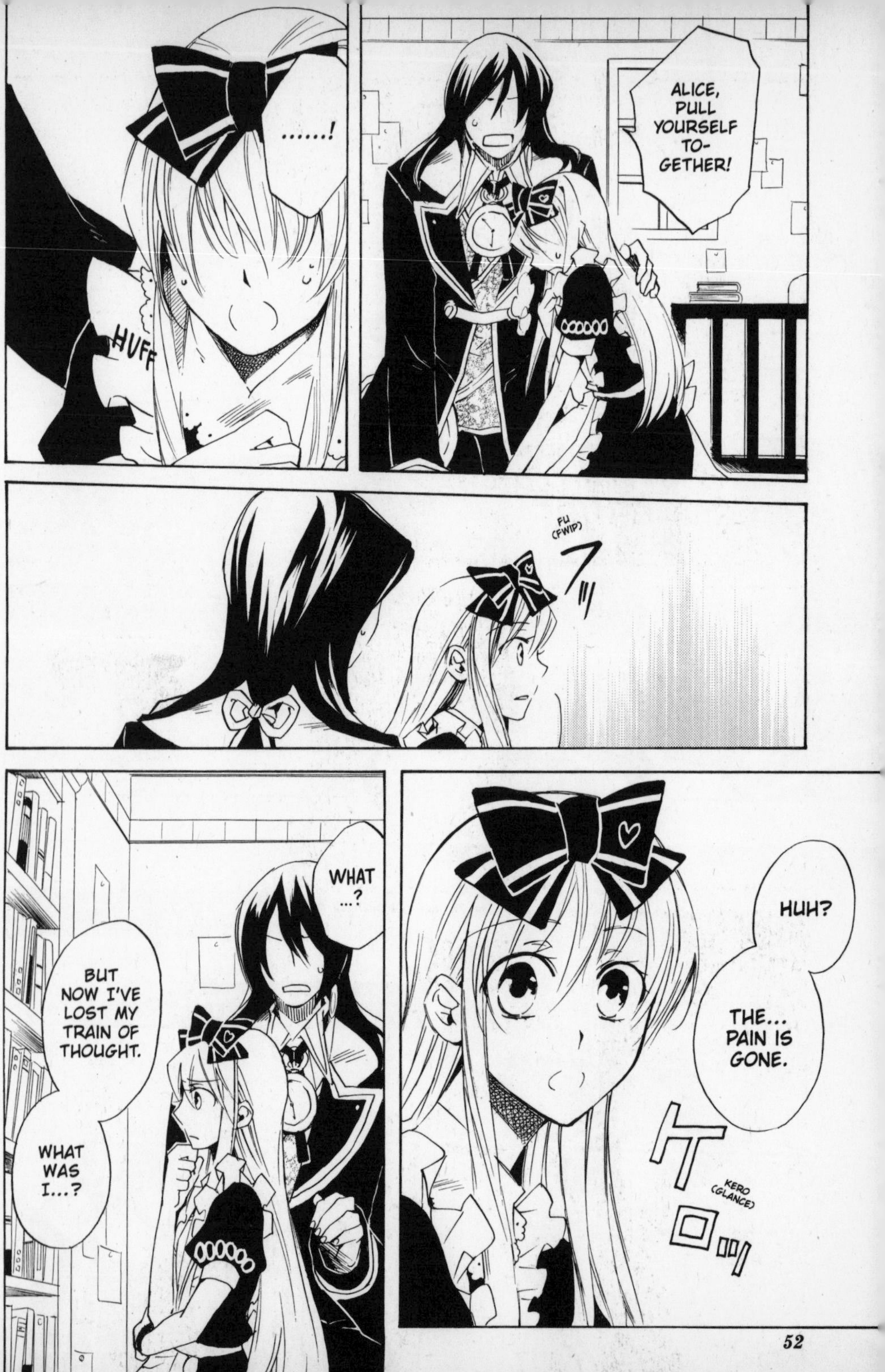
ALICE, PULL YOURSELF TO-GETHER!
......!
HUFF
FU (FWIP)
HUH?
THE... PAIN IS GONE.
KERO (GLANCE)
WHAT ...?
BUT NOW I'VE LOST MY TRAIN OF THOUGHT.
WHAT WAS I...?

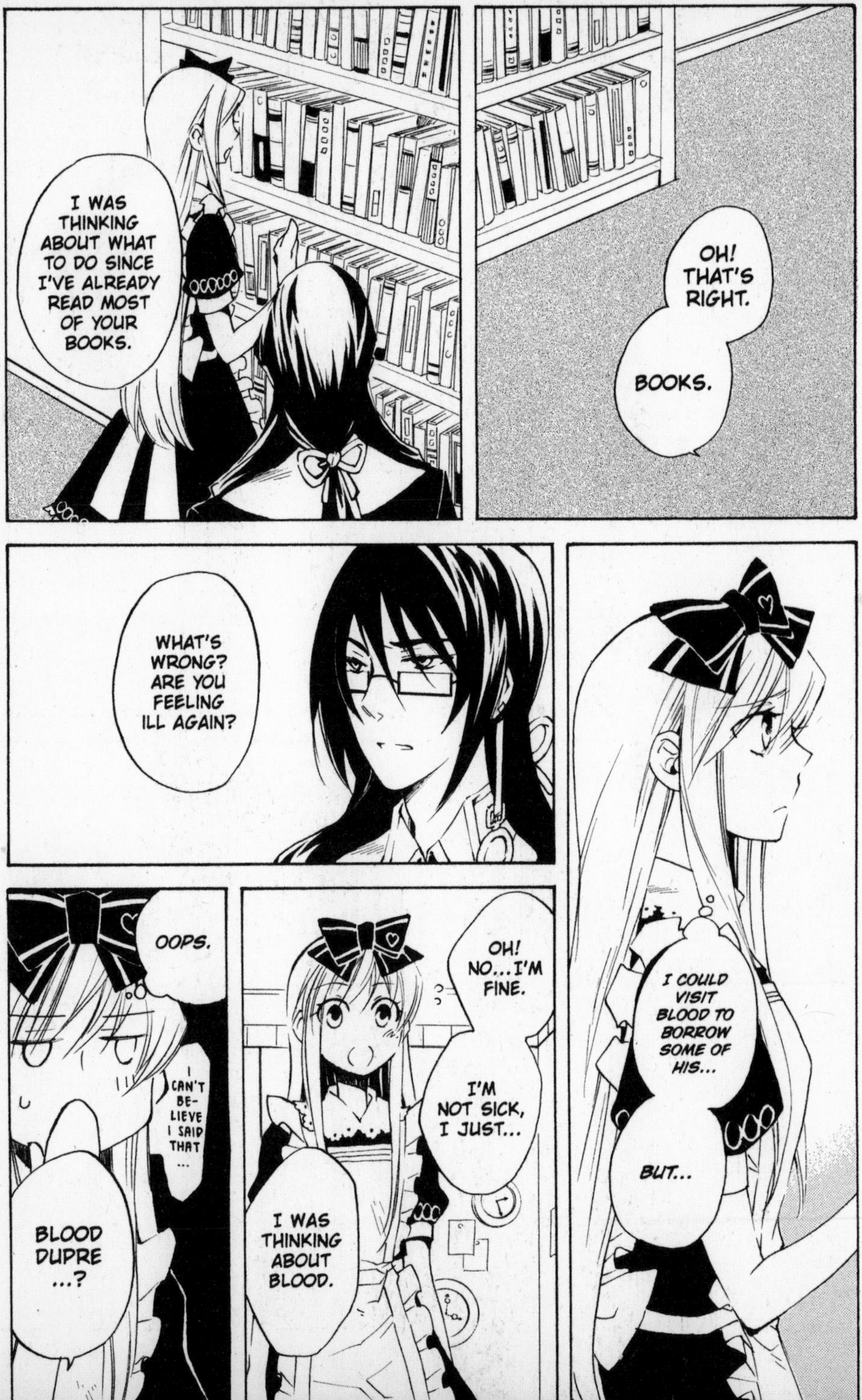
OH! THAT'S RIGHT.
BOOKS.
I WAS THINKING ABOUT WHAT TO DO SINCE I'VE ALREADY READ MOST OF YOUR BOOKS.
I COULD VISIT BLOOD TO BORROW SOME OF HIS...
BUT...
WHAT'S WRONG? ARE YOU FEELING ILL AGAIN?
OH! NO...I'M FINE.
I'M NOT SICK, I JUST...
I WAS THINKING ABOUT BLOOD.
OOPS.
I CAN'T BE-LIEVE I SAID THAT...
BLOOD DUPRE ...?

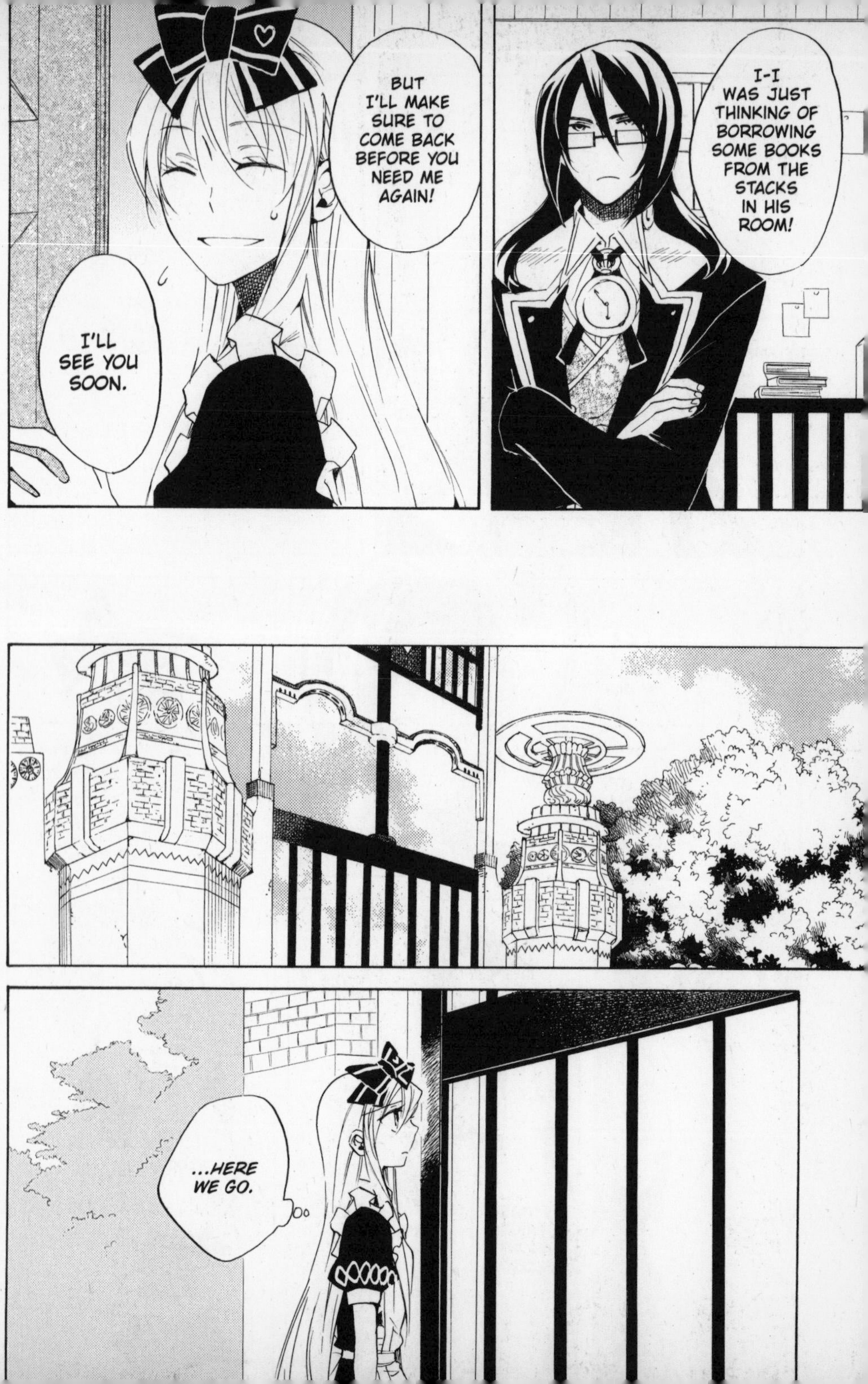
I-I WAS JUST THINKING OF BORROWING SOME BOOKS FROM THE STACKS IN HIS ROOM!
BUT I'LL MAKE SURE TO COME BACK BEFORE YOU NEED ME AGAIN!
I'LL SEE YOU SOON.
...HERE WE GO.

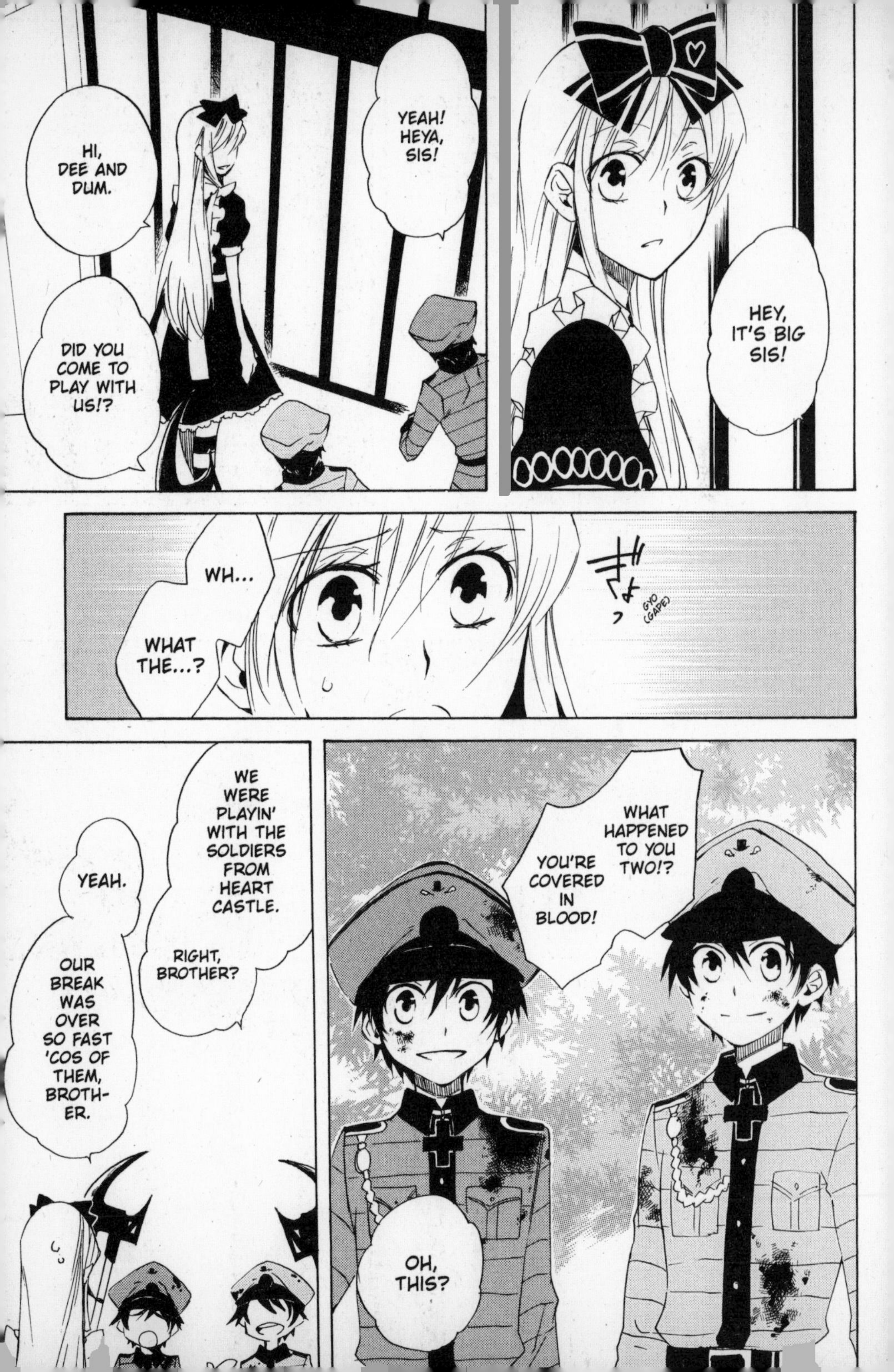
HEY, IT'S BIG SIS!
YEAH! HEYA, SIS!
HI, DEE AND DUM.
DID YOU COME TO PLAY WITH US!?
ぎょっ
GYO (GAPE)
WH...
WHAT THE...?
WHAT HAPPENED TO YOU TWO!?
YOU'RE COVERED IN BLOOD!
OH, THIS?
WE WERE PLAYIN' WITH THE SOLDIERS FROM HEART CASTLE.
RIGHT, BROTHER?
YEAH.
OUR BREAK WAS OVER SO FAST 'COS OF THEM, BROTHER.

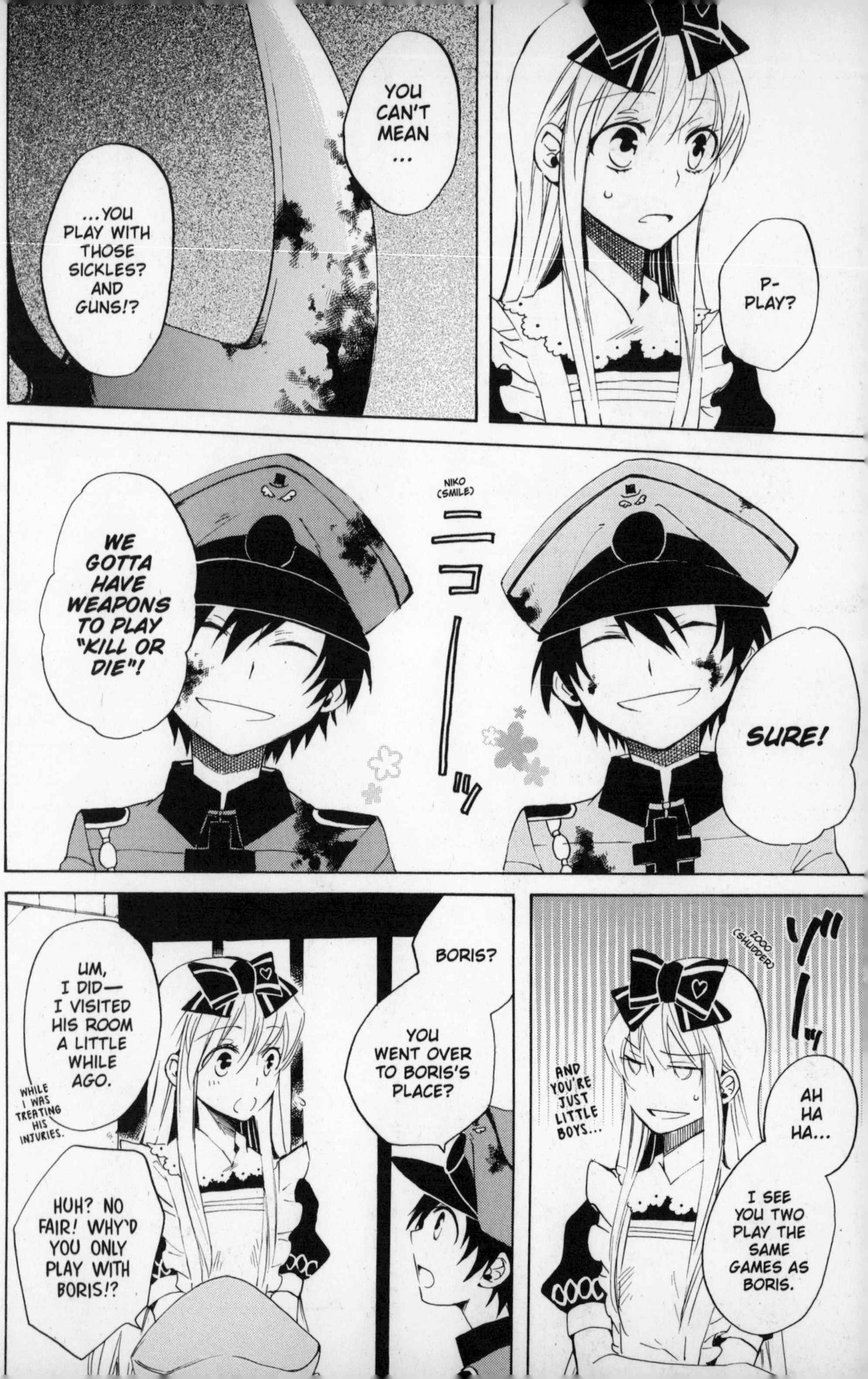
P-PLAY?
YOU CAN'T MEAN ...
...YOU PLAY WITH THOSE SICKLES? AND GUNS!?
SURE!
NIKO (SMILE)
WE GOTTA HAVE WEAPONS TO PLAY "KILL OR DIE"!
ZOOO (SHUDDER)
AH HA HA...
AND YOU'RE JUST LITTLE BOYS...
I SEE YOU TWO PLAY THE SAME GAMES AS BORIS.
BORIS?
YOU WENT OVER TO BORIS'S PLACE?
UM, I DID— I VISITED HIS ROOM A LITTLE WHILE AGO.
WHILE I WAS TREATING HIS INJURIES.
HUH? NO FAIR! WHY'D YOU ONLY PLAY WITH BORIS!?

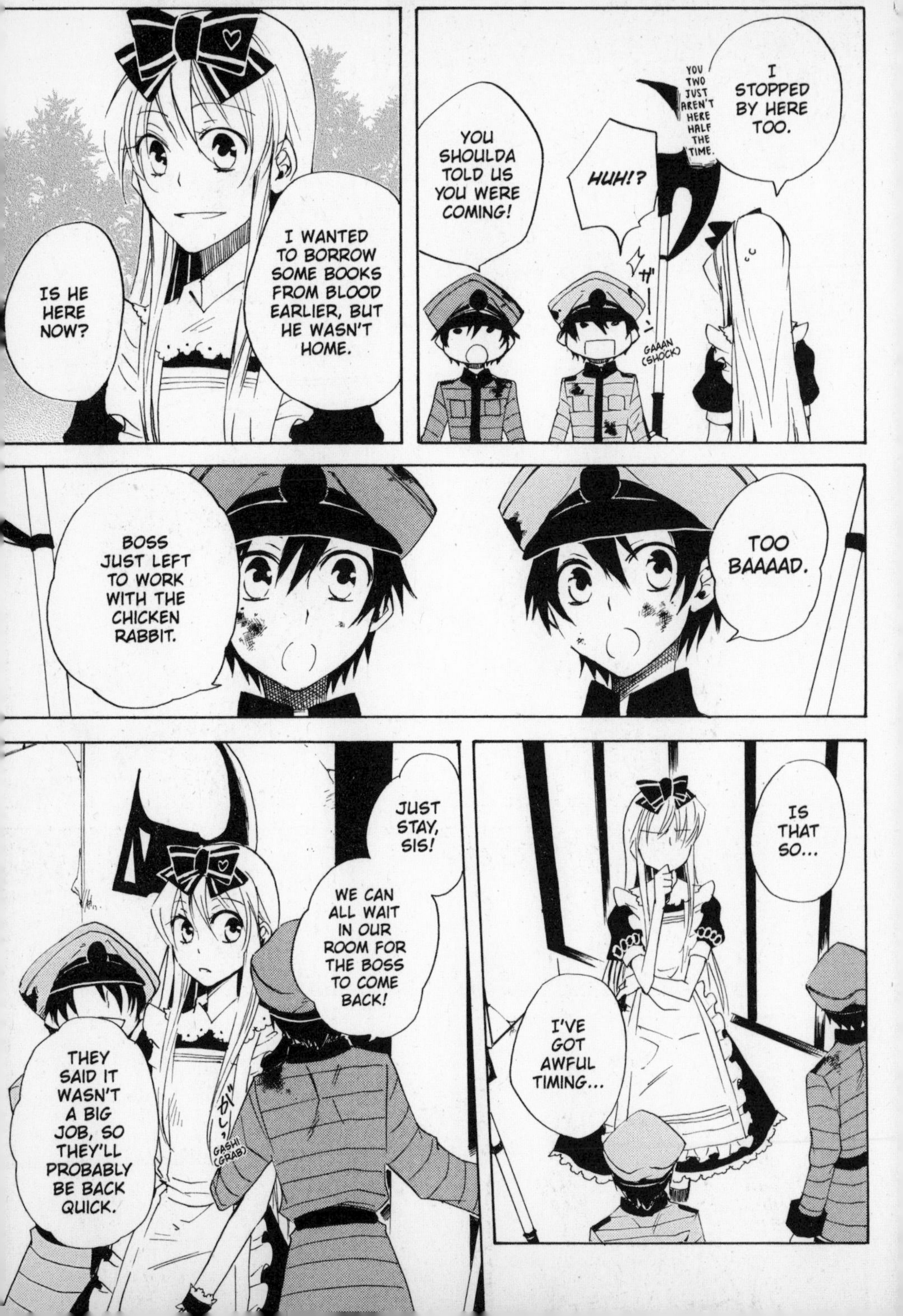
I STOPPED BY HERE TOO.
YOU TWO JUST AREN'T HERE HALF THE TIME.
HUH!?
YOU SHOULDA TOLD US YOU WERE COMING!
GAAAN (SHOCK)
I WANTED TO BORROW SOME BOOKS FROM BLOOD EARLIER, BUT HE WASN'T HOME.
IS HE HERE NOW?
TOO BAAAAD.
BOSS JUST LEFT TO WORK WITH THE CHICKEN RABBIT.
IS THAT SO...
I'VE GOT AWFUL TIMING...
JUST STAY, SIS!
WE CAN ALL WAIT IN OUR ROOM FOR THE BOSS TO COME BACK!
GASHI (GRAB)
THEY SAID IT WASN'T A BIG JOB, SO THEY'LL PROBABLY BE BACK QUICK.

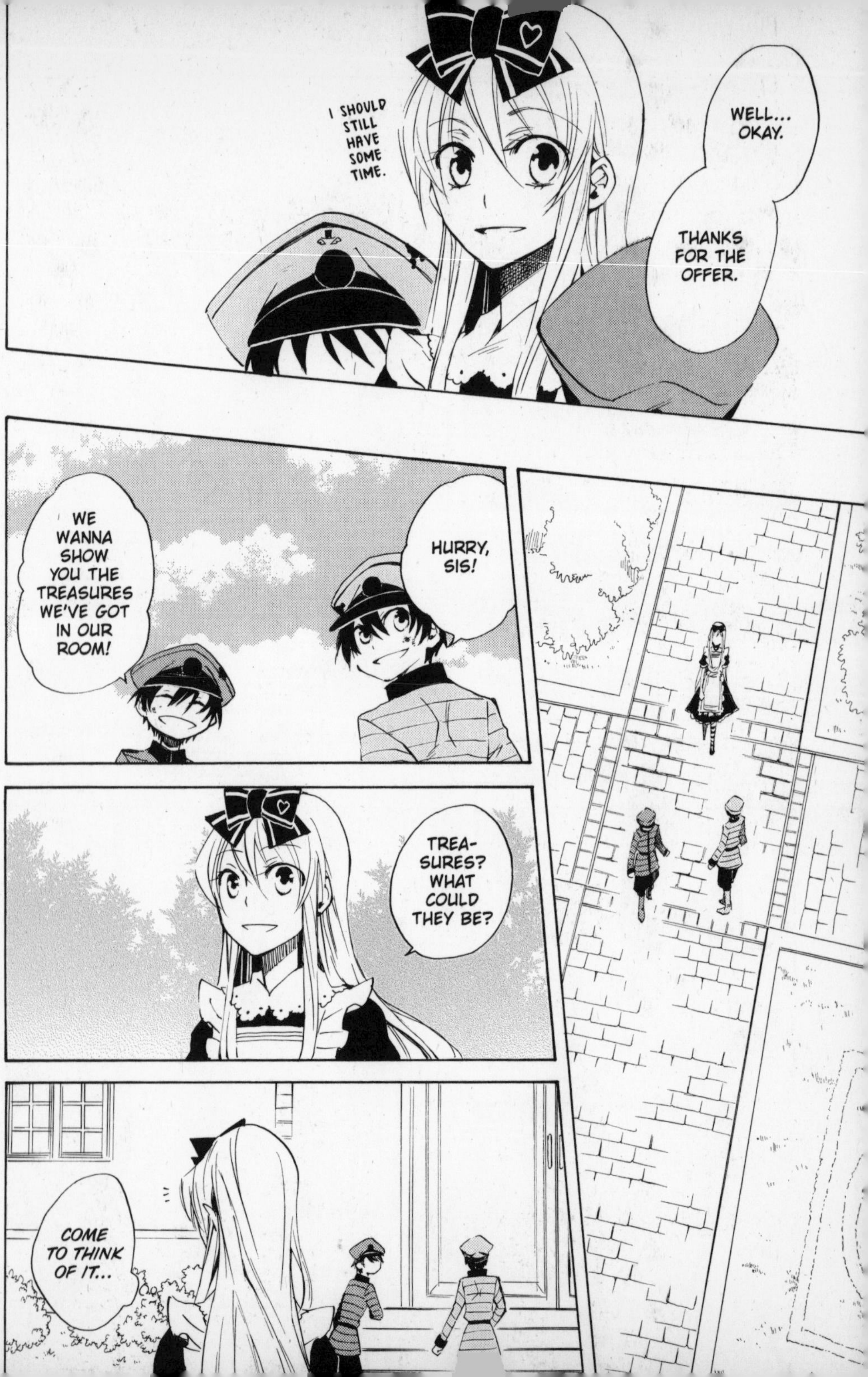
WELL... OKAY.
THANKS FOR THE OFFER.
I SHOULD STILL HAVE SOME TIME.
HURRY, SIS!
WE WANNA SHOW YOU THE TREASURES WE'VE GOT IN OUR ROOM!
TREA-SURES? WHAT COULD THEY BE?
COME TO THINK OF IT...

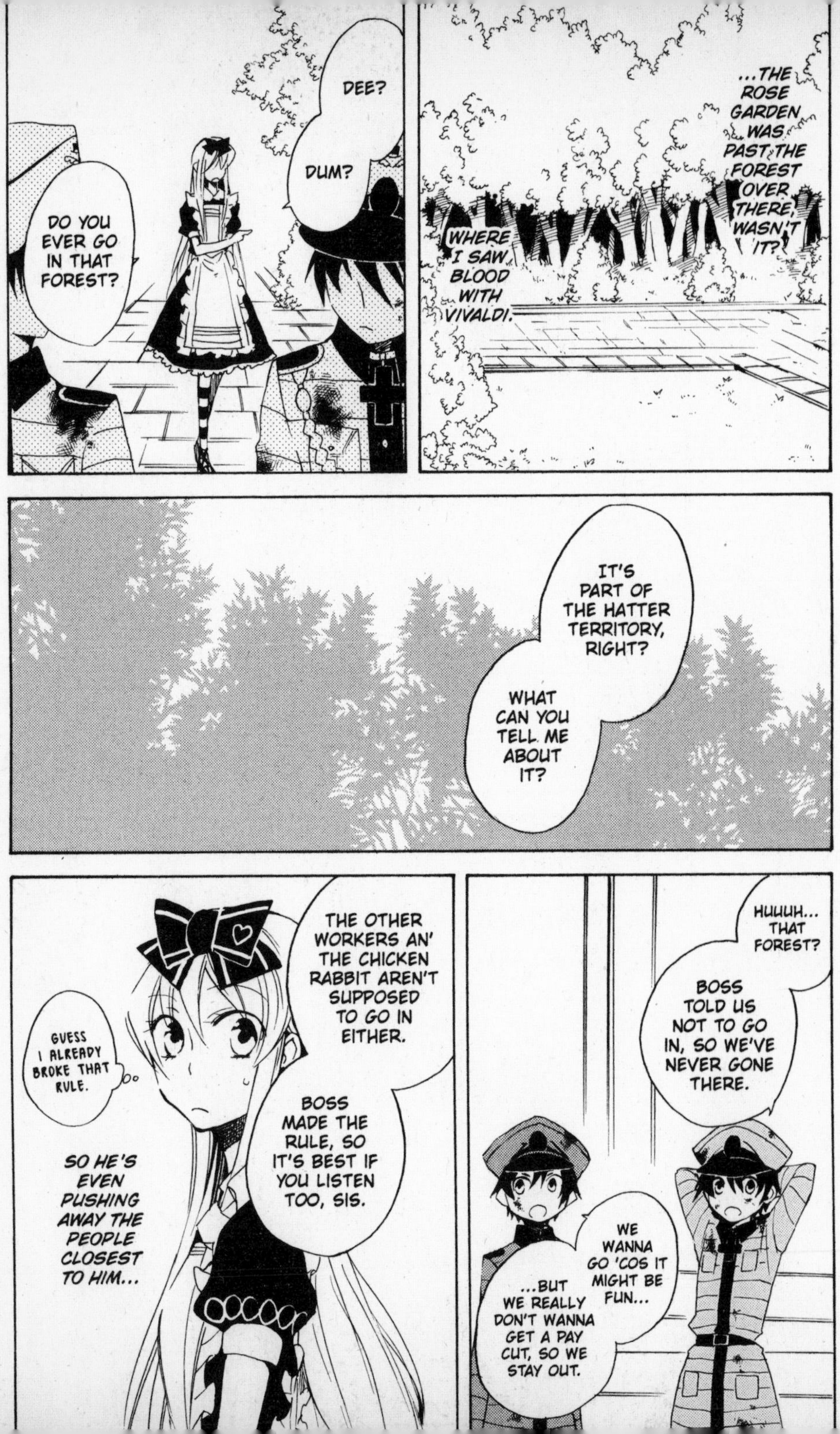
...THE ROSE GARDEN WAS PAST THE FOREST OVER THERE, WASN'T IT?
WHERE I SAW BLOOD WITH VIVALDI.
DEE?
DUM?
DO YOU EVER GO IN THAT FOREST?
IT'S PART OF THE HATTER TERRITORY, RIGHT?
WHAT CAN YOU TELL ME ABOUT IT?
HUUUH... THAT FOREST?
BOSS TOLD US NOT TO GO IN, SO WE'VE NEVER GONE THERE.
WE WANNA GO 'COS IT MIGHT BE FUN...
...BUT WE REALLY DON'T WANNA GET A PAY CUT, SO WE STAY OUT.
THE OTHER WORKERS AN' THE CHICKEN RABBIT AREN'T SUPPOSED TO GO IN EITHER.
BOSS MADE THE RULE, SO IT'S BEST IF YOU LISTEN TOO, SIS.
GUESS I ALREADY BROKE THAT RULE.
SO HE'S EVEN PUSHING AWAY THE PEOPLE CLOSEST TO HIM...

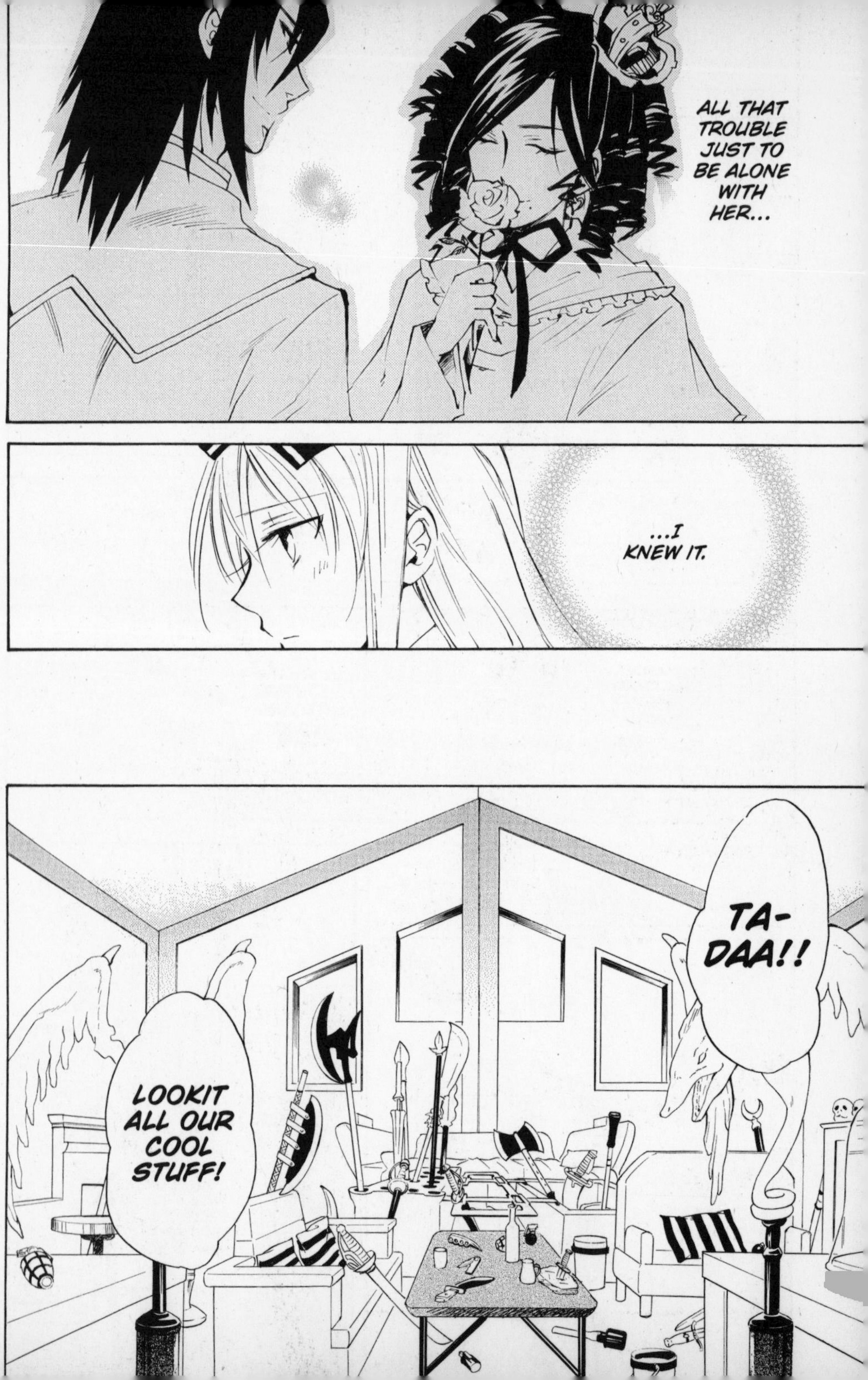
ALL THAT TROUBLE JUST TO BE ALONE WITH HER...
...I KNEW IT.
TA-DAA!!
LOOKIT ALL OUR COOL STUFF!

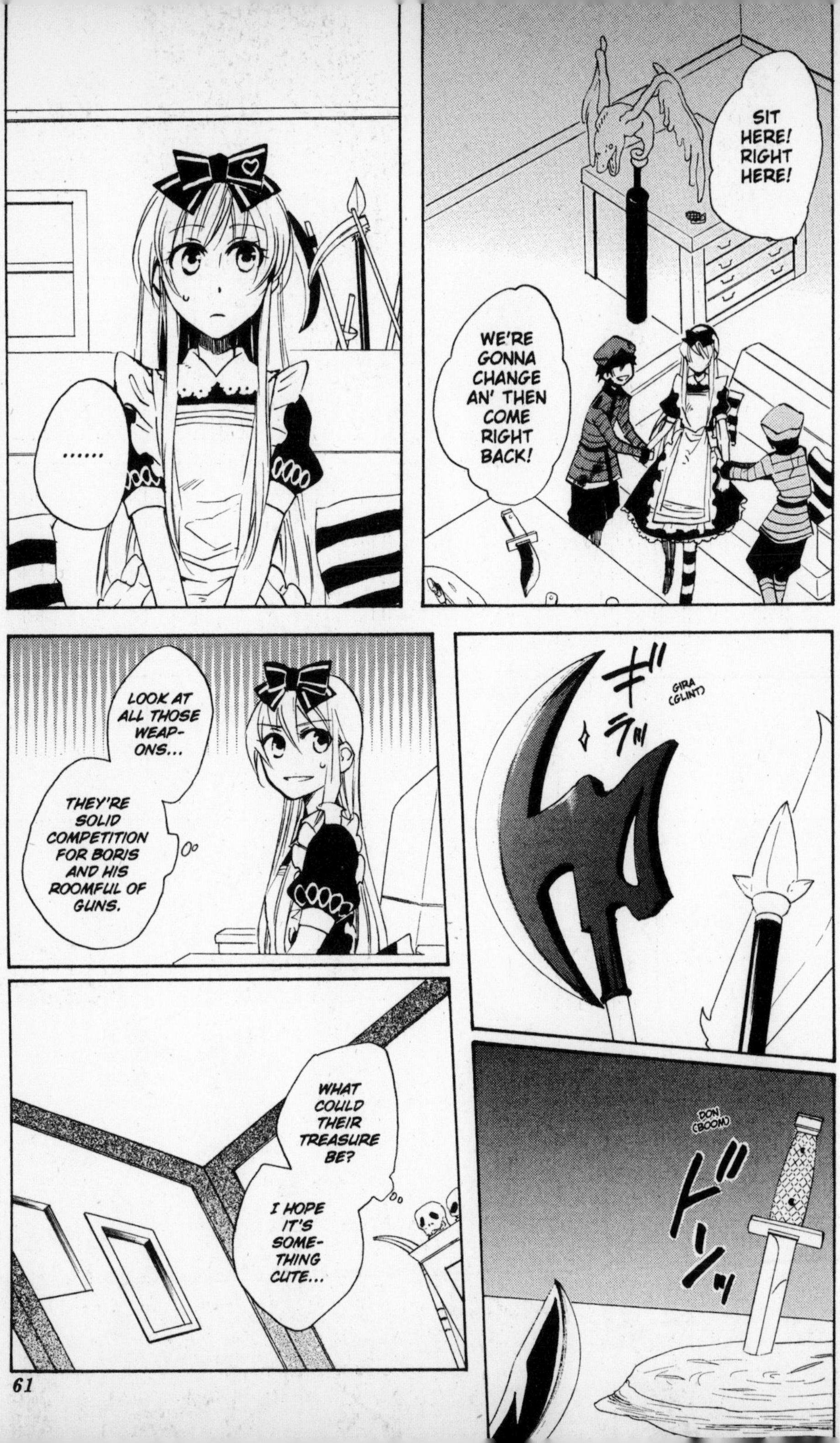

SIT HERE! RIGHT HERE!
WE'RE GONNA CHANGE AN' THEN COME RIGHT BACK!
......
ギラッ
GIRA (GLINT)
LOOK AT ALL THOSE WEAP-ONS...
THEY'RE SOLID COMPETITION FOR BORIS AND HIS ROOMFUL OF GUNS.
ドンッ
DON (BOOM)
WHAT COULD THEIR TREASURE BE?
I HOPE IT'S SOME-THING CUTE...

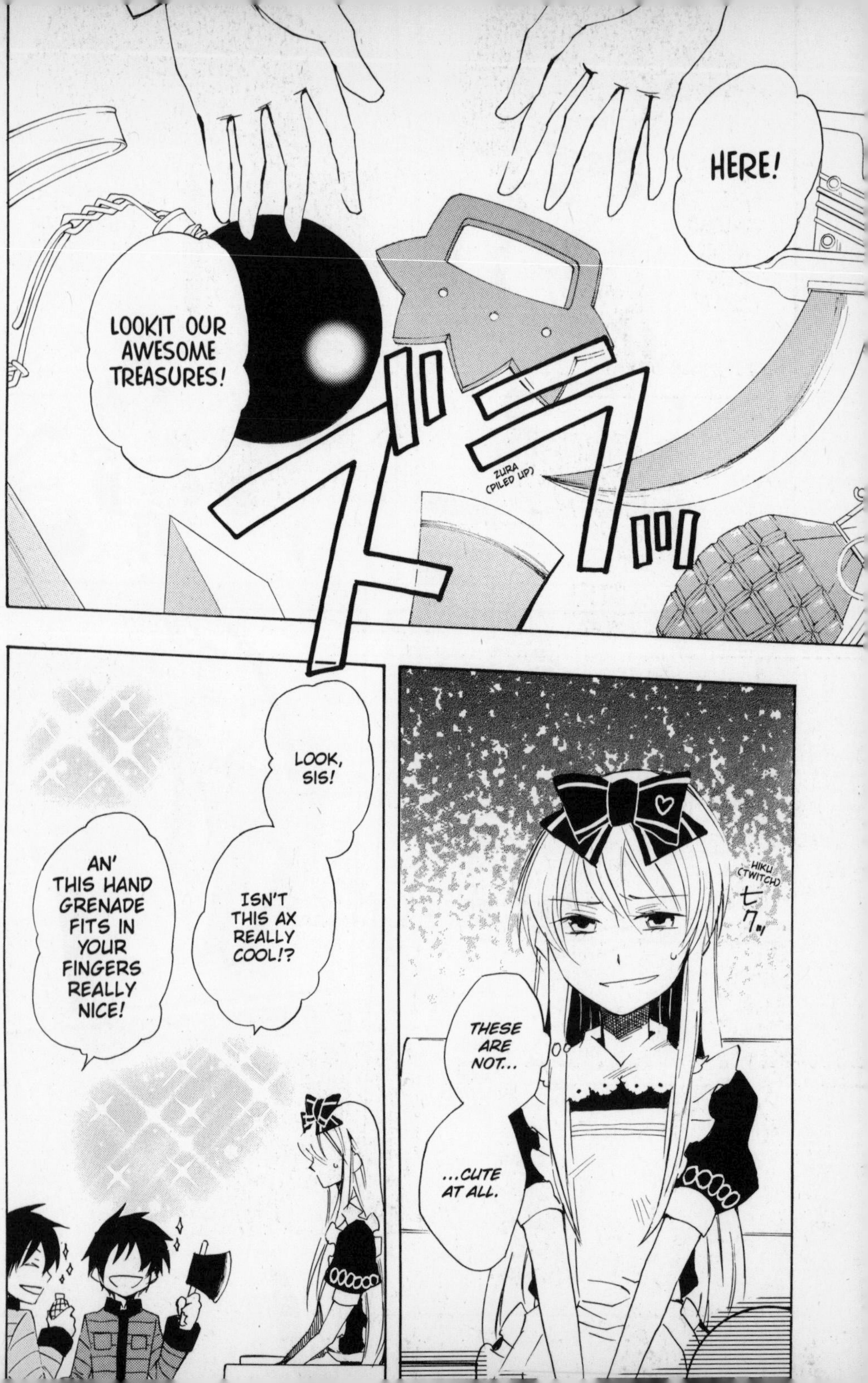
HERE!
LOOKIT OUR AWESOME TREASURES!
ZURA (PILED UP)
HIKU (TWITCH)
THESE ARE NOT...
...CUTE AT ALL.
LOOK, SIS!
ISN'T THIS AX REALLY COOL!?
AN' THIS HAND GRENADE FITS IN YOUR FINGERS REALLY NICE!

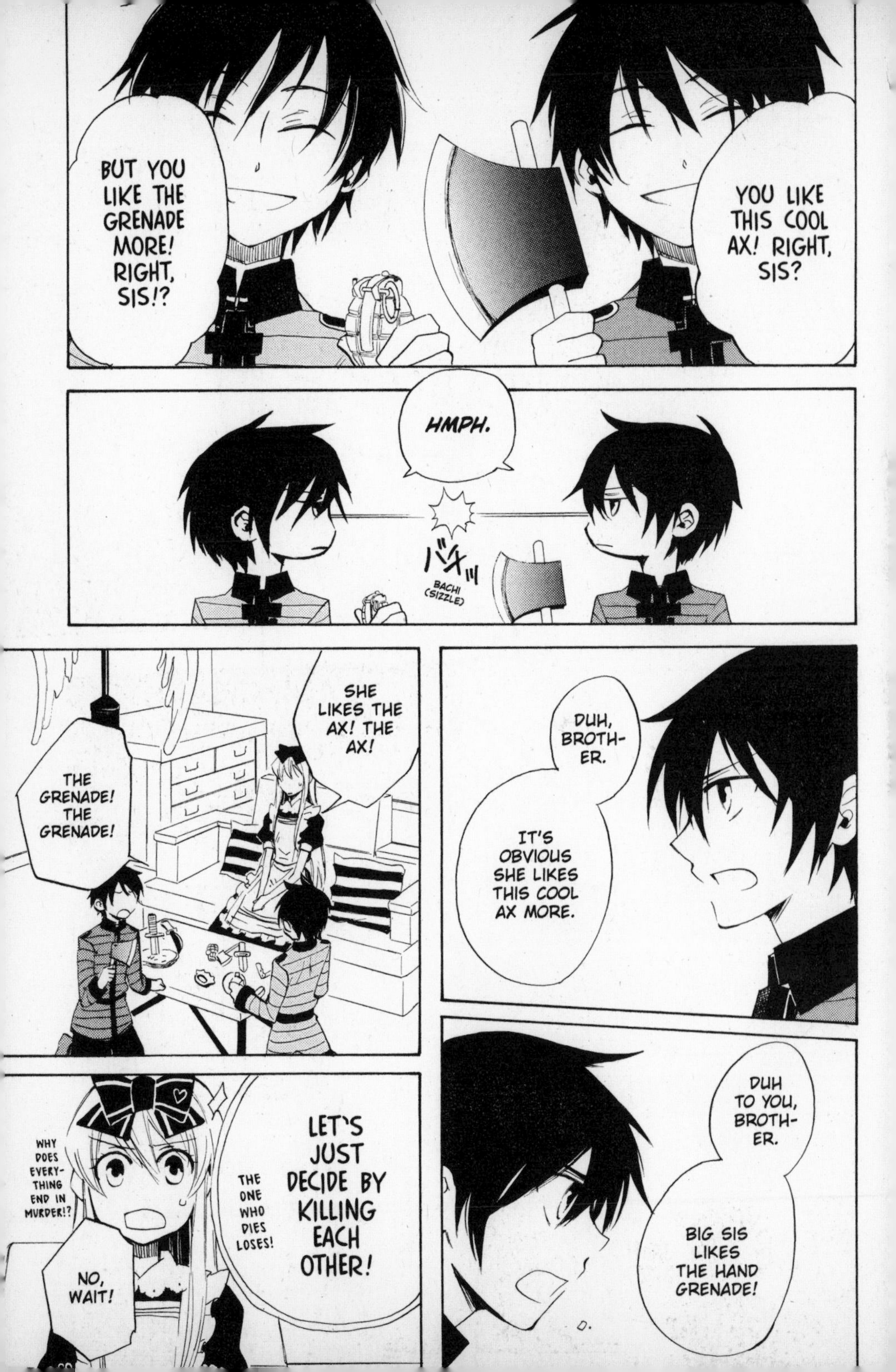
YOU LIKE THIS COOL AX! RIGHT, SIS?
BUT YOU LIKE THE GRENADE MORE! RIGHT, SIS!?
HMPH.
バチッ
BACHI (SIZZLE)
DUH, BROTHER.
IT'S OBVIOUS SHE LIKES THIS COOL AX MORE.
SHE LIKES THE AX! THE AX!
THE GRENADE! THE GRENADE!
DUH TO YOU, BROTHER.
BIG SIS LIKES THE HAND GRENADE!
LET'S JUST DECIDE BY KILLING EACH OTHER!
THE ONE WHO DIES LOSES!
WHY DOES EVERYTHING END IN MURDER!?
NO, WAIT!

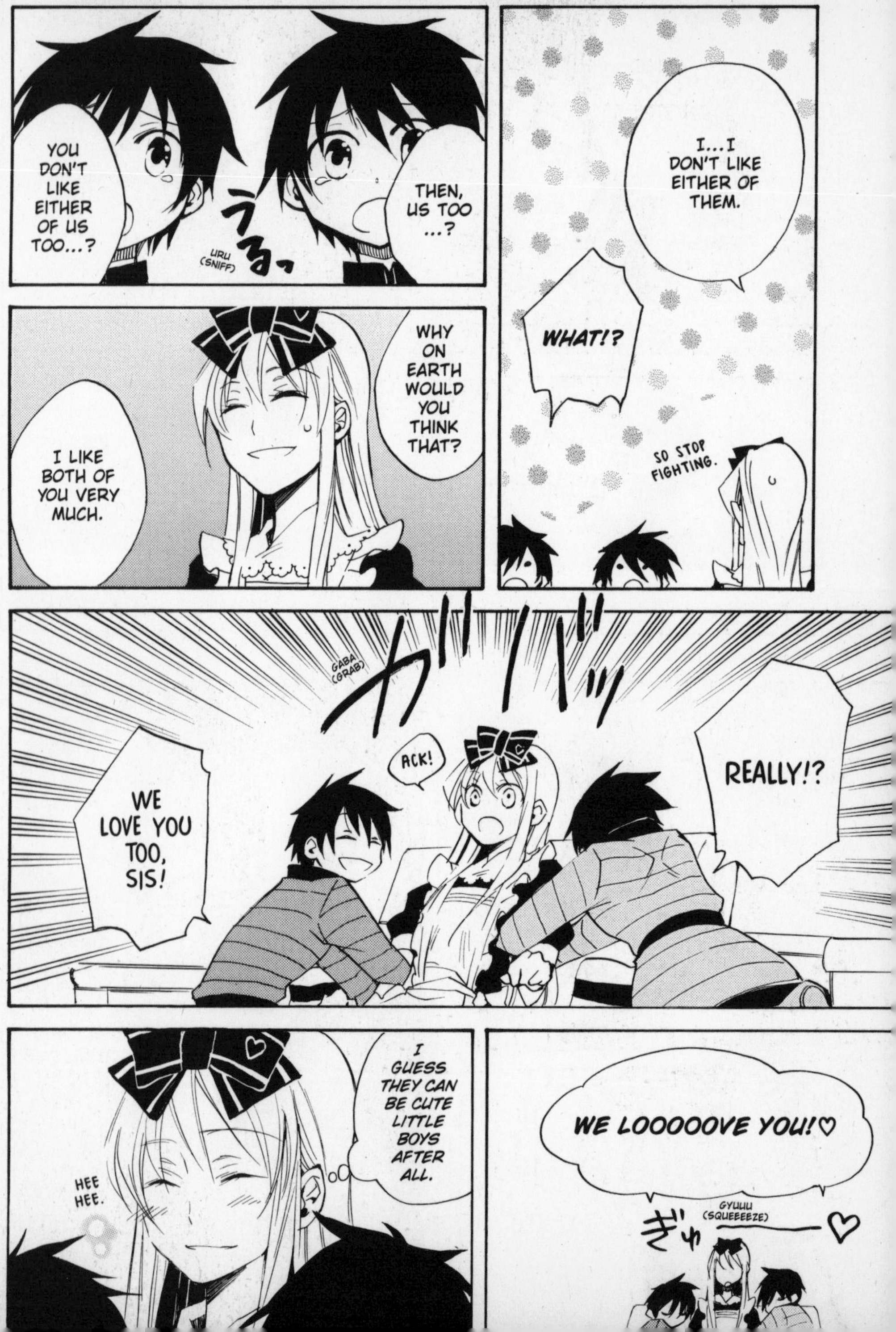
I...I DON'T LIKE EITHER OF THEM.
WHAT!?
SO STOP FIGHTING.
THEN, US TOO ...?
URU (SNIFF)
YOU DON'T LIKE EITHER OF US TOO...?
WHY ON EARTH WOULD YOU THINK THAT?
I LIKE BOTH OF YOU VERY MUCH.
GABA (GRAB)
REALLY!?
ACK!
WE LOVE YOU TOO, SIS!
WE LOOOOOVE YOU!♡
GYUUU (SQUEEEEZE)
I GUESS THEY CAN BE CUTE LITTLE BOYS AFTER ALL.
HEE HEE.

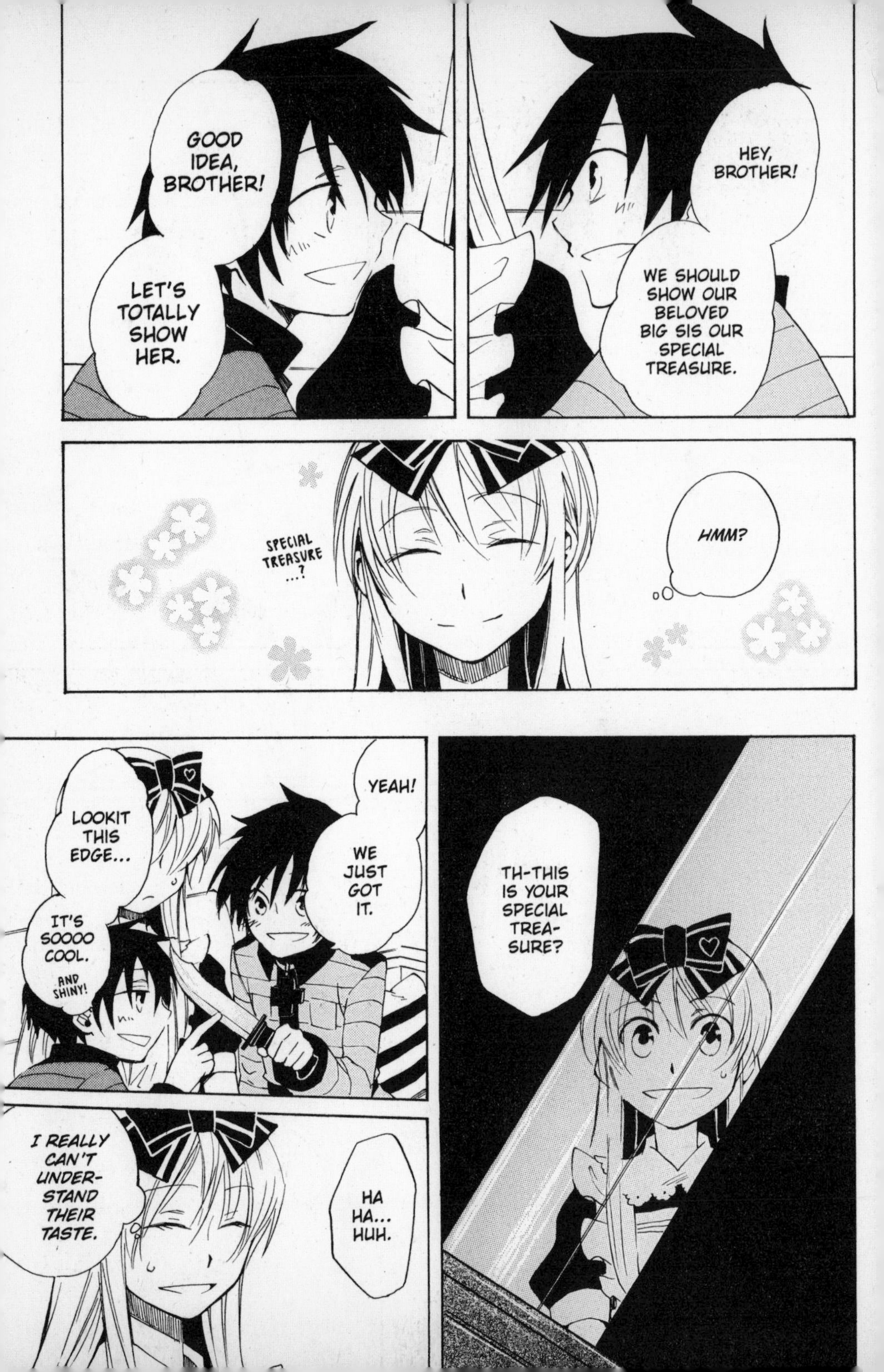
HEY, BROTHER!
WE SHOULD SHOW OUR BELOVED BIG SIS OUR SPECIAL TREASURE.
GOOD IDEA, BROTHER!
LET'S TOTALLY SHOW HER.
HMM?
SPECIAL TREASURE ...?
TH-THIS IS YOUR SPECIAL TREA-SURE?
YEAH!
WE JUST GOT IT.
LOOKIT THIS EDGE...
IT'S SOOOO COOL.
AND SHINY!
HA HA... HUH.
I REALLY CAN'T UNDER-STAND THEIR TASTE.

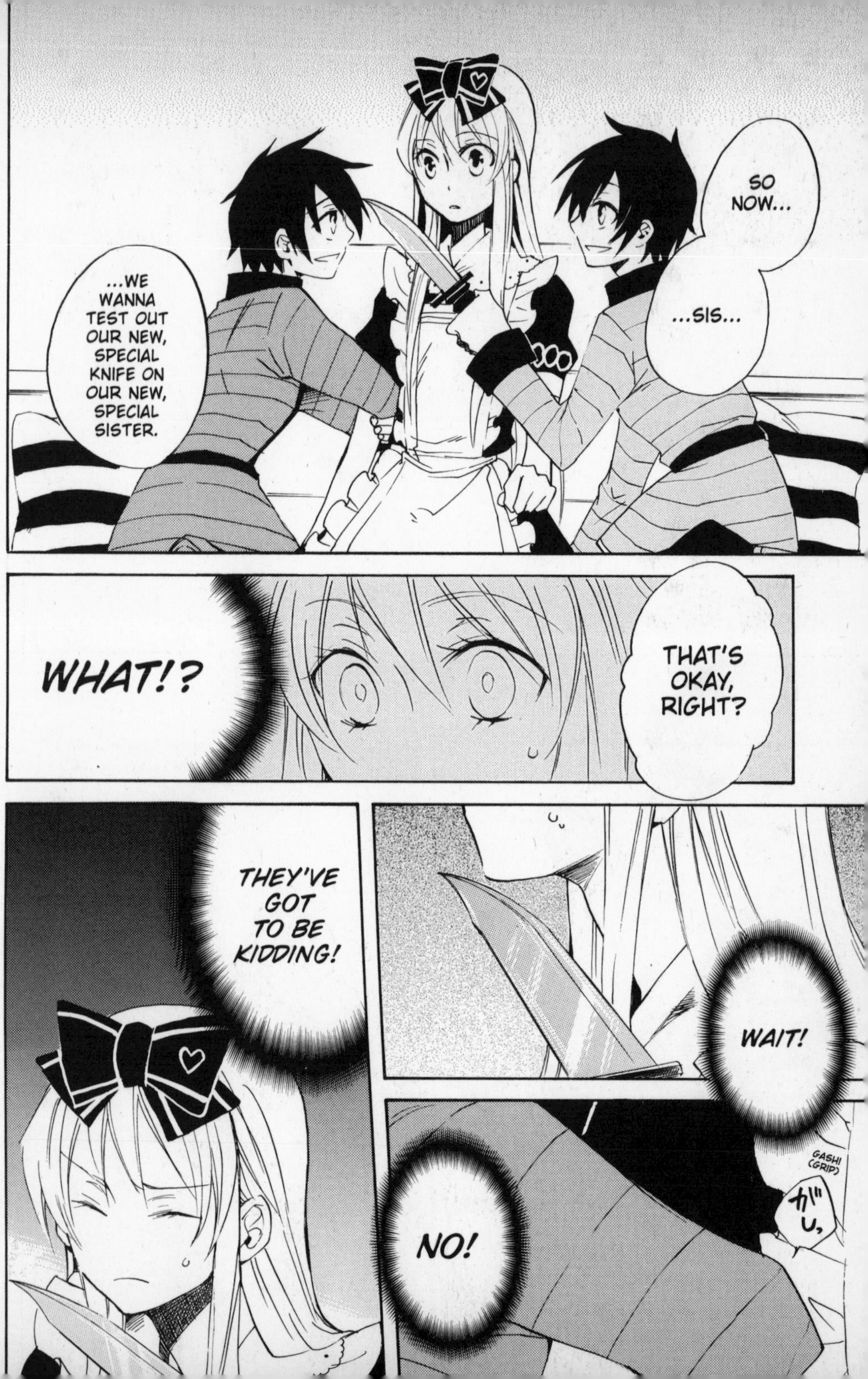
SO NOW...
...SIS...
...WE WANNA TEST OUT OUR NEW, SPECIAL KNIFE ON OUR NEW, SPECIAL SISTER.
THAT'S OKAY, RIGHT?
WHAT!?
WAIT!
GASHI (GRIP)
NO!
THEY'VE GOT TO BE KIDDING!

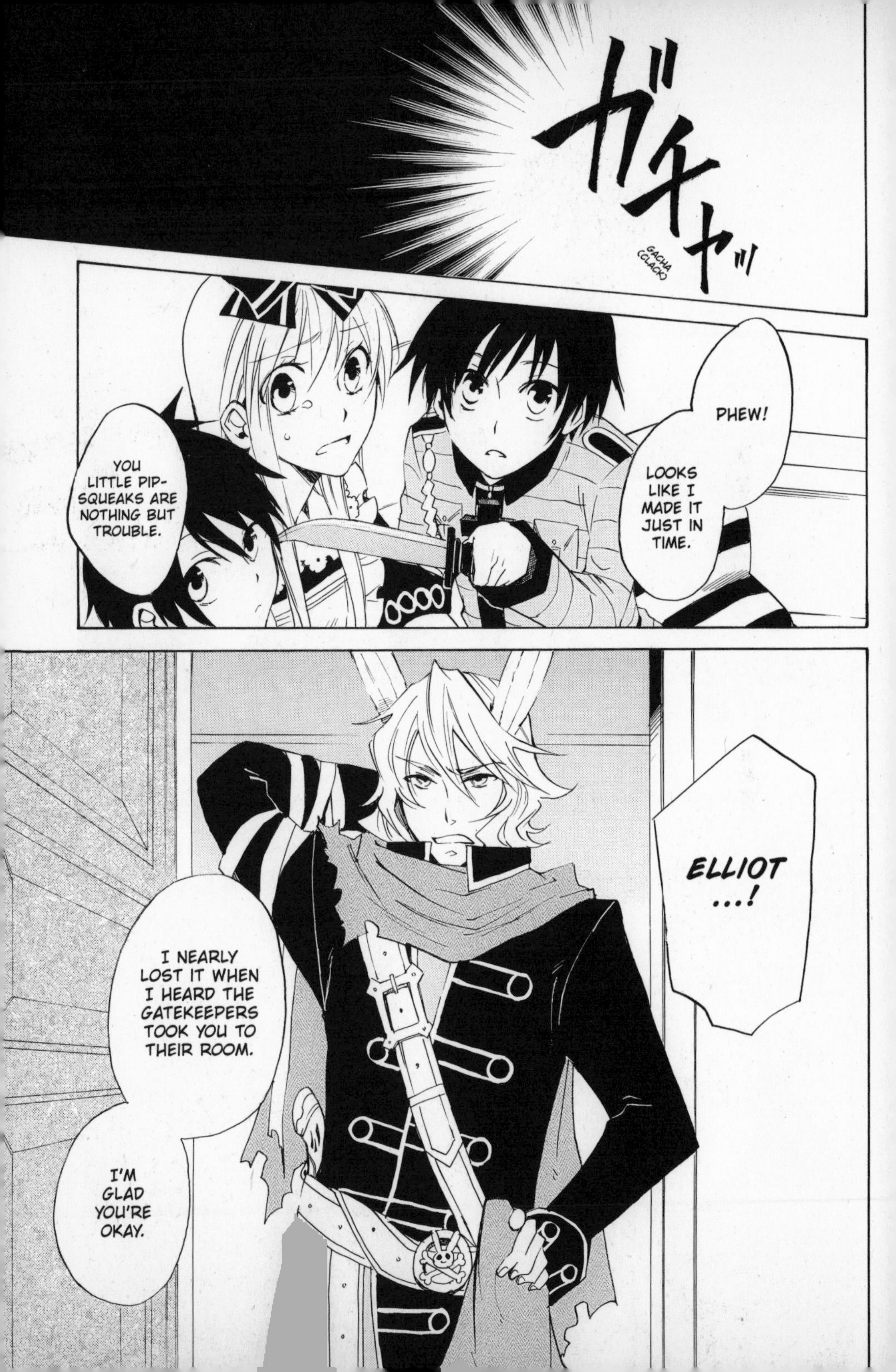
ガチャッ
GACHA (CLACK)
PHEW!
LOOKS LIKE I MADE IT JUST IN TIME.
YOU LITTLE PIP-SQUEAKS ARE NOTHING BUT TROUBLE.
ELLIOT ...!
I NEARLY LOST IT WHEN I HEARD THE GATEKEEPERS TOOK YOU TO THEIR ROOM.
I'M GLAD YOU'RE OKAY.

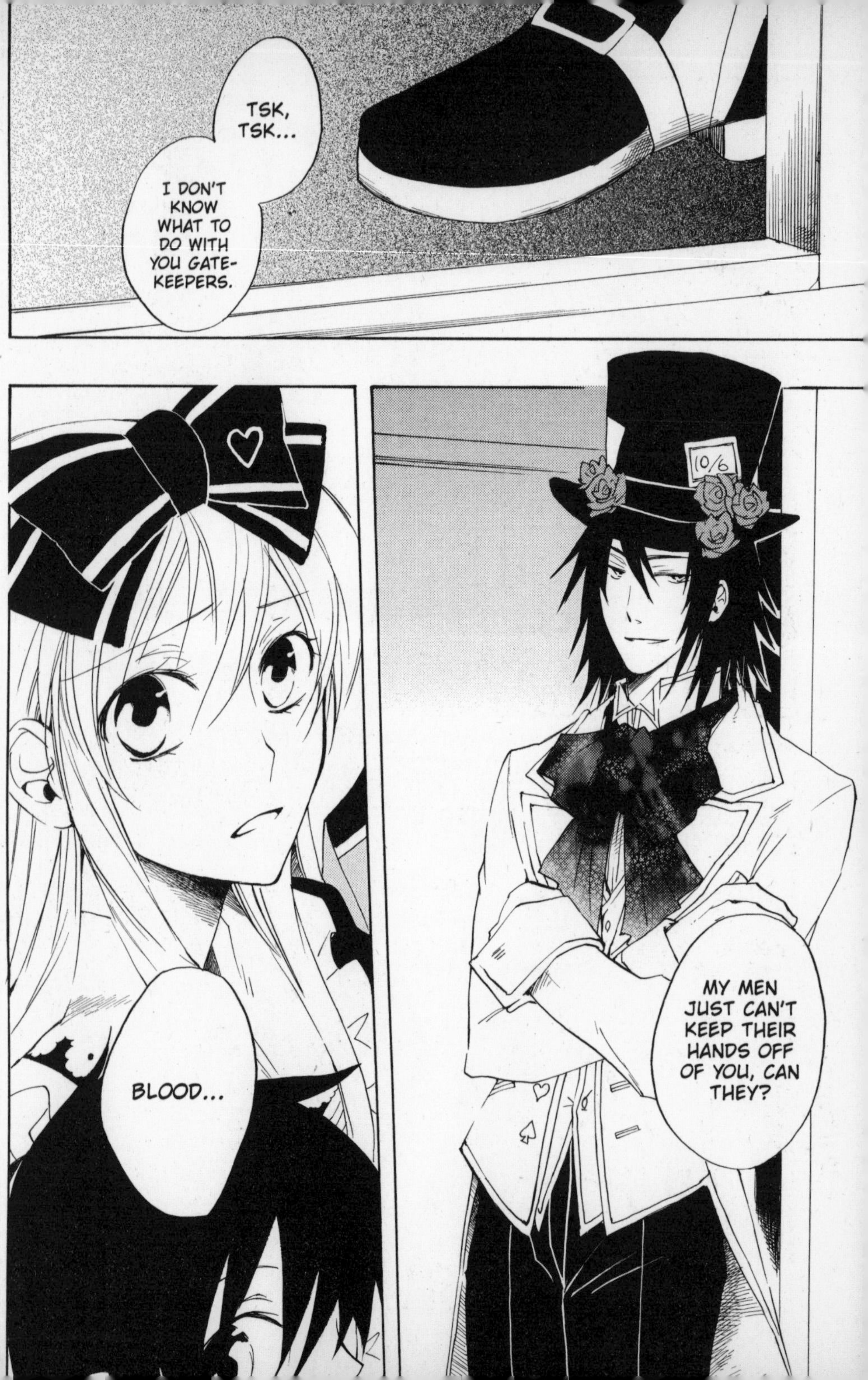
TSK, TSK...
I DON'T KNOW WHAT TO DO WITH YOU GATE-KEEPERS.
MY MEN JUST CAN'T KEEP THEIR HANDS OFF OF YOU, CAN THEY?
BLOOD...

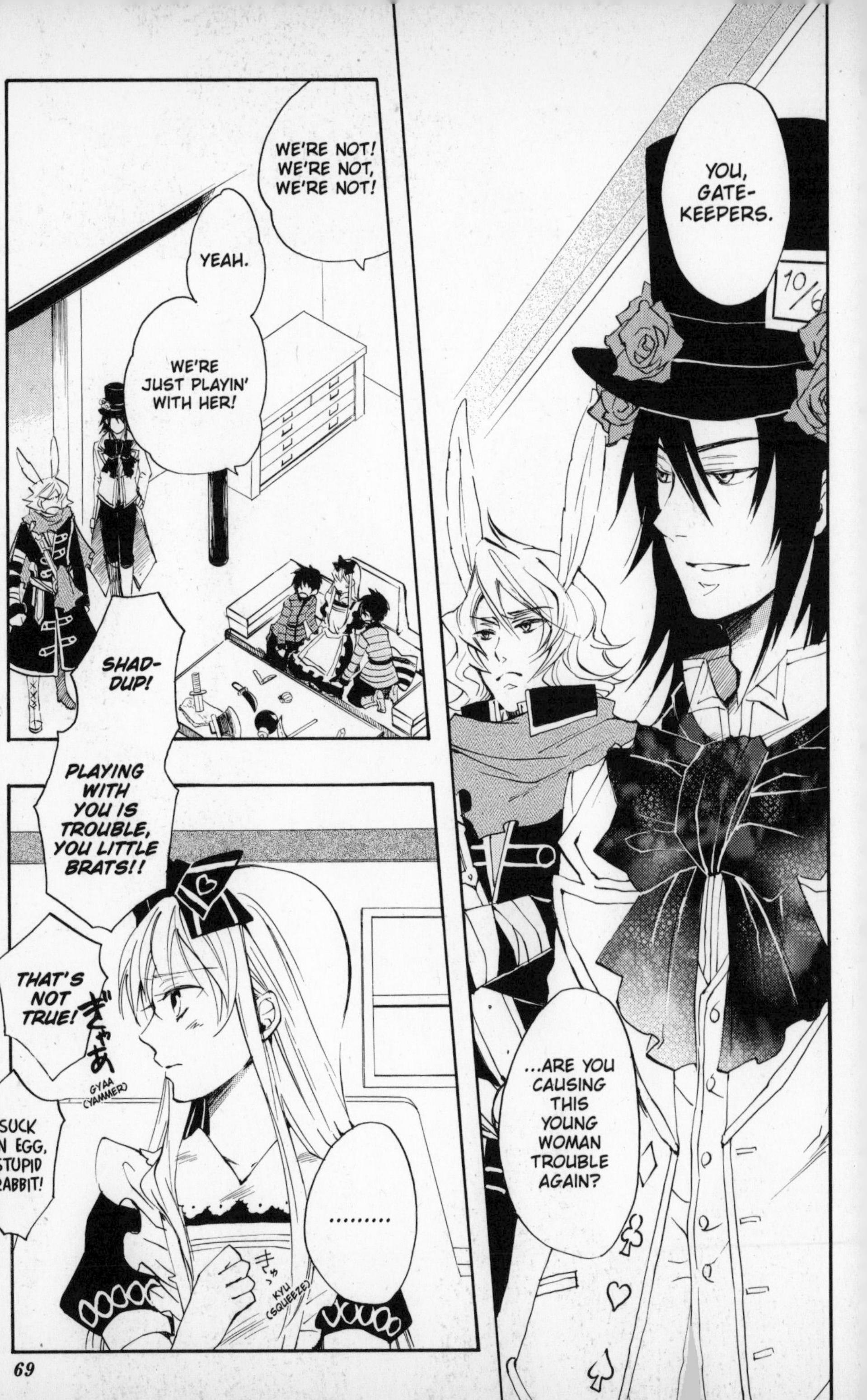
YOU, GATE-KEEPERS.
...ARE YOU CAUSING THIS YOUNG WOMAN TROUBLE AGAIN?
WE'RE NOT! WE'RE NOT, WE'RE NOT!
YEAH.
WE'RE JUST PLAYIN' WITH HER!
SHAD-DUP!
PLAYING WITH YOU IS TROUBLE, YOU LITTLE BRATS!!
THAT'S NOT TRUE!
ぎゃあ
GYAA (YAMMER)
SUCK AN EGG, STUPID RABBIT!
ぎゃあ
GYAA
....
きゅ
KYU (SQUEEZE)

♥14 Disjointing Flower

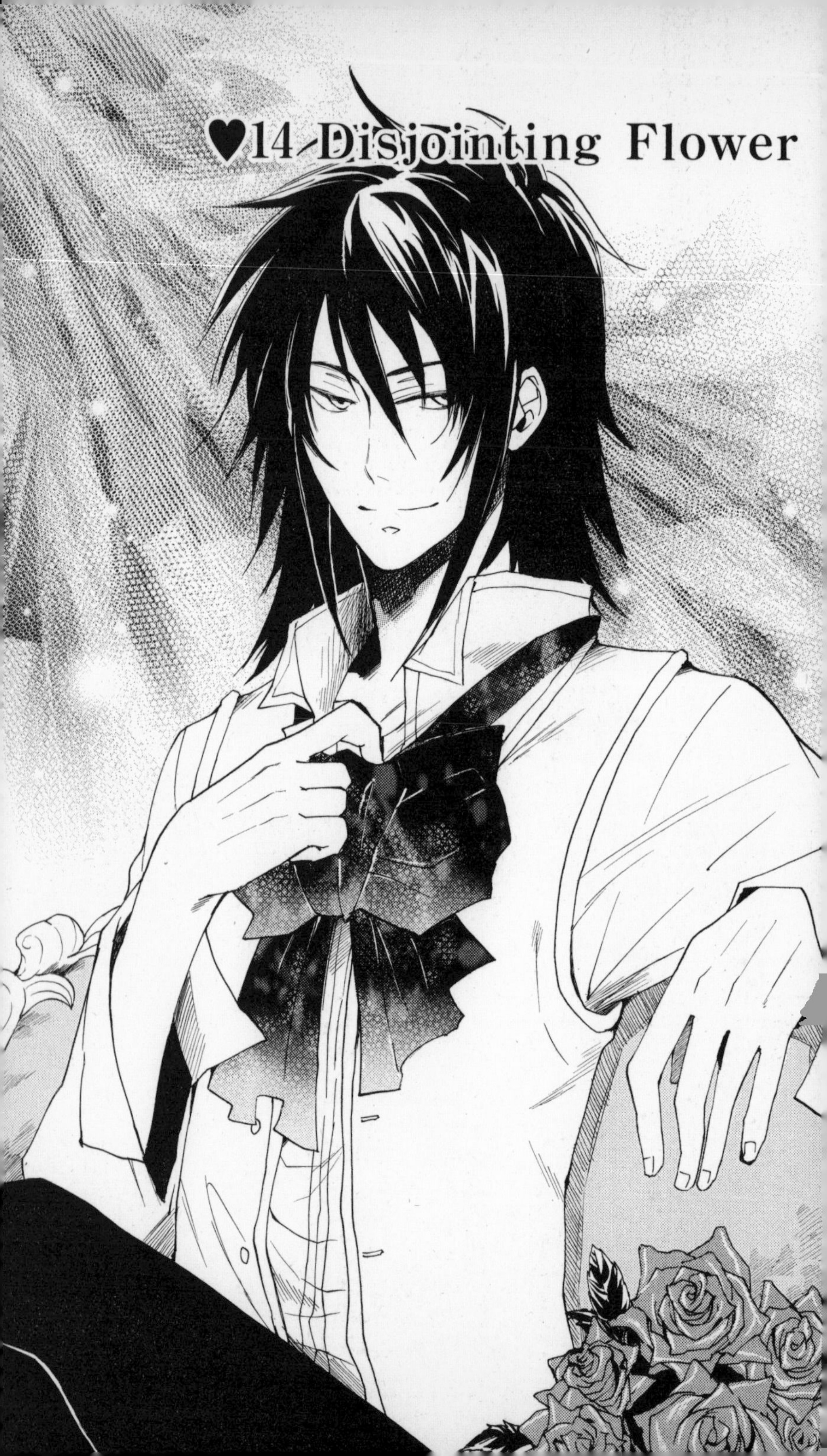

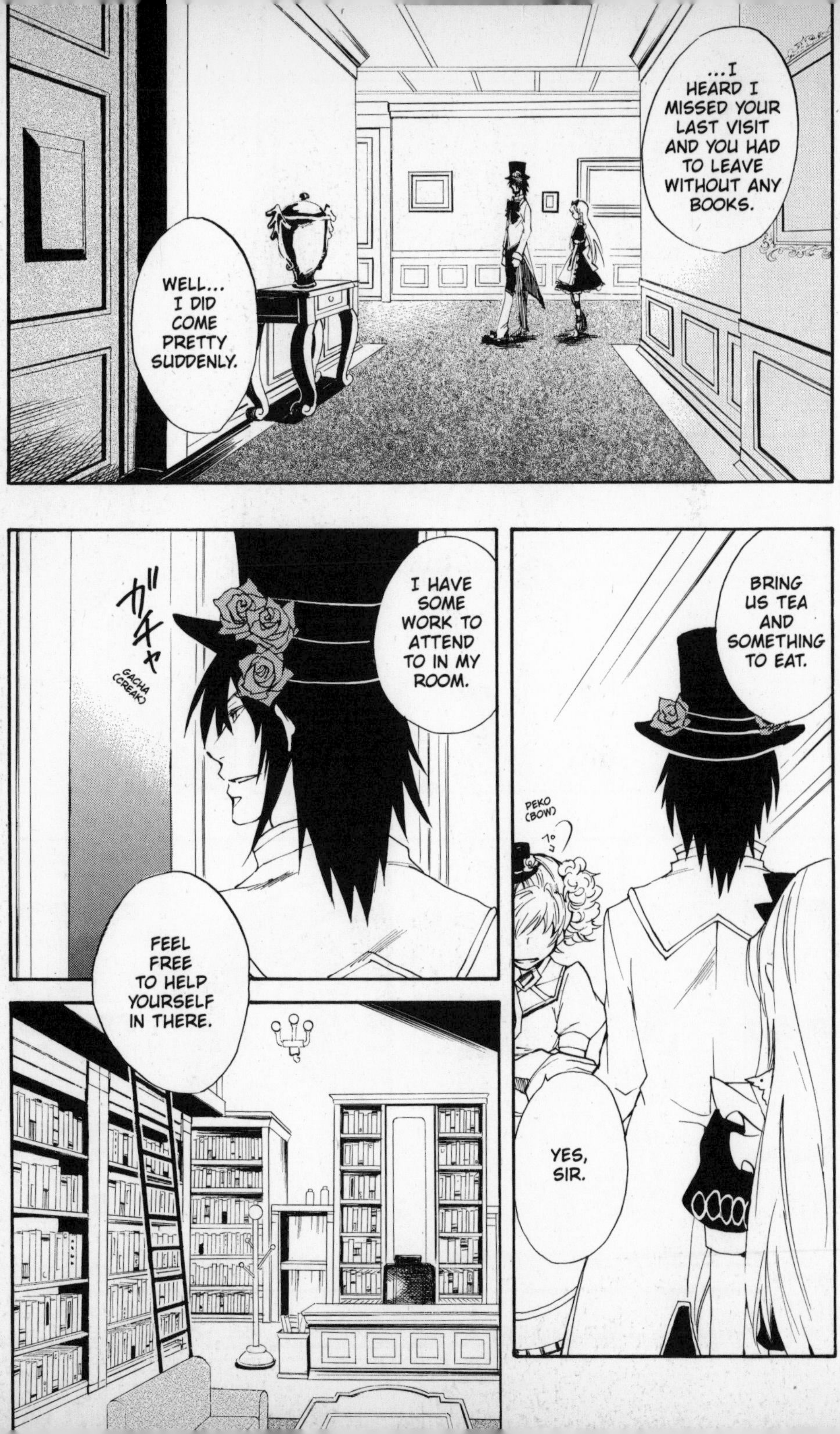
...I HEARD I MISSED YOUR LAST VISIT AND YOU HAD TO LEAVE WITHOUT ANY BOOKS.
WELL... I DID COME PRETTY SUDDENLY.
BRING US TEA AND SOMETHING TO EAT.
PEKO (BOW)
YES, SIR.
ガチャ
GACHA (CREAK)
I HAVE SOME WORK TO ATTEND TO IN MY ROOM.
FEEL FREE TO HELP YOURSELF IN THERE.

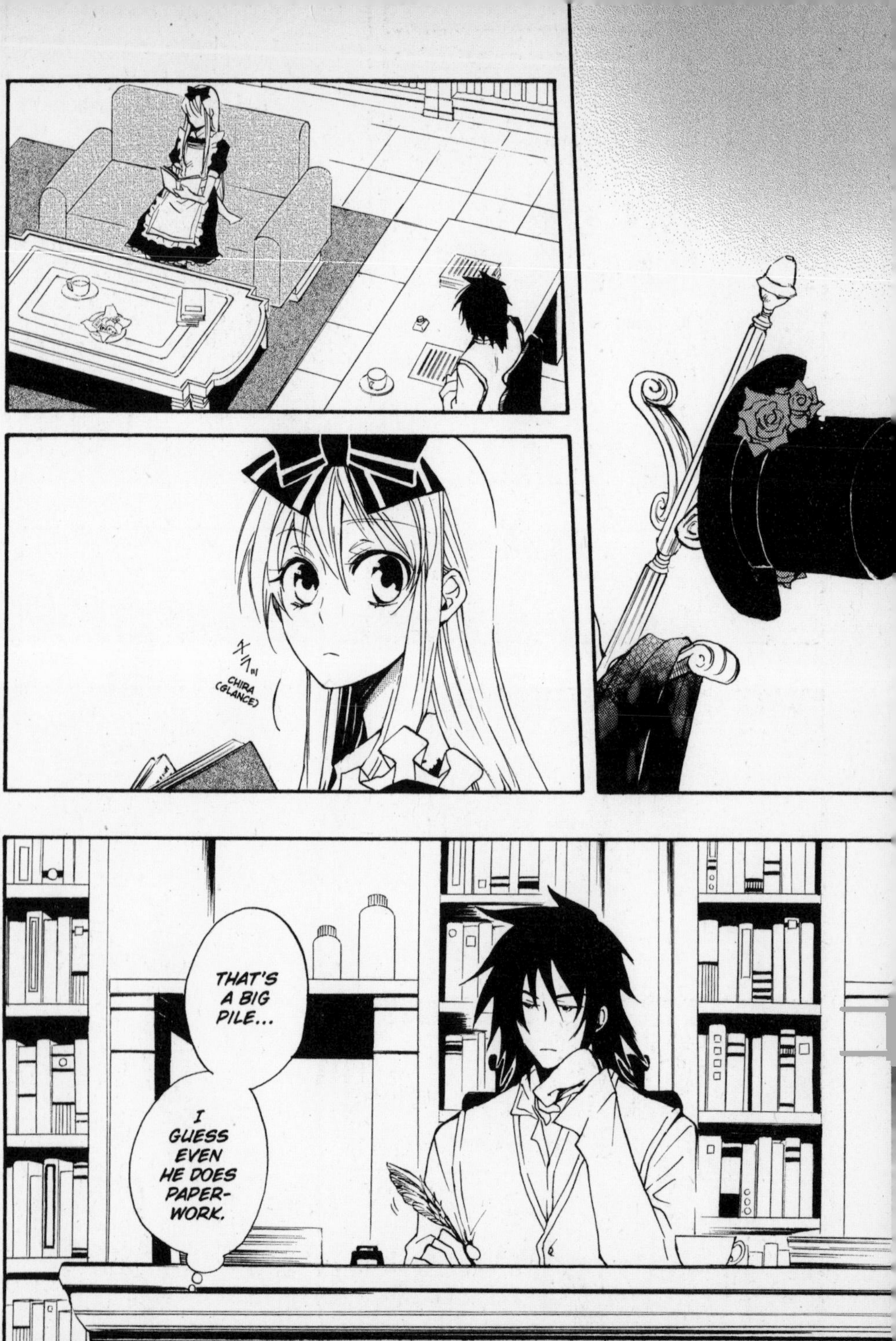
CHIRA (GLANCE)
THAT'S A BIG PILE...
I GUESS EVEN HE DOES PAPER-WORK.

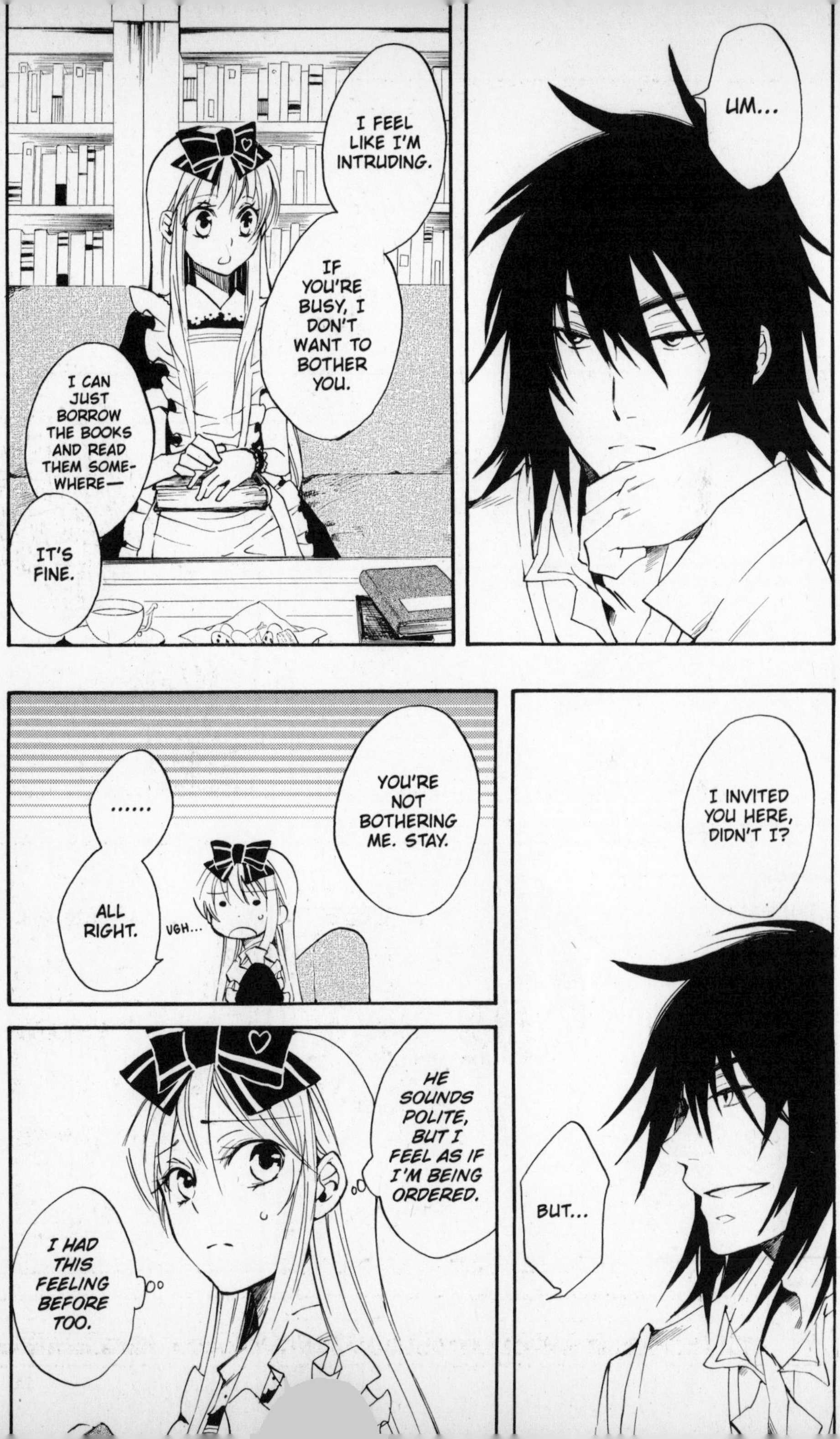
UM...
I FEEL LIKE I'M INTRUDING.
IF YOU'RE BUSY, I DON'T WANT TO BOTHER YOU.
I CAN JUST BORROW THE BOOKS AND READ THEM SOME-WHERE—
IT'S FINE.
I INVITED YOU HERE, DIDN'T I?
BUT...
YOU'RE NOT BOTHERING ME. STAY.
......
ALL RIGHT.
UGH...
HE SOUNDS POLITE, BUT I FEEL AS IF I'M BEING ORDERED.
I HAD THIS FEELING BEFORE TOO.

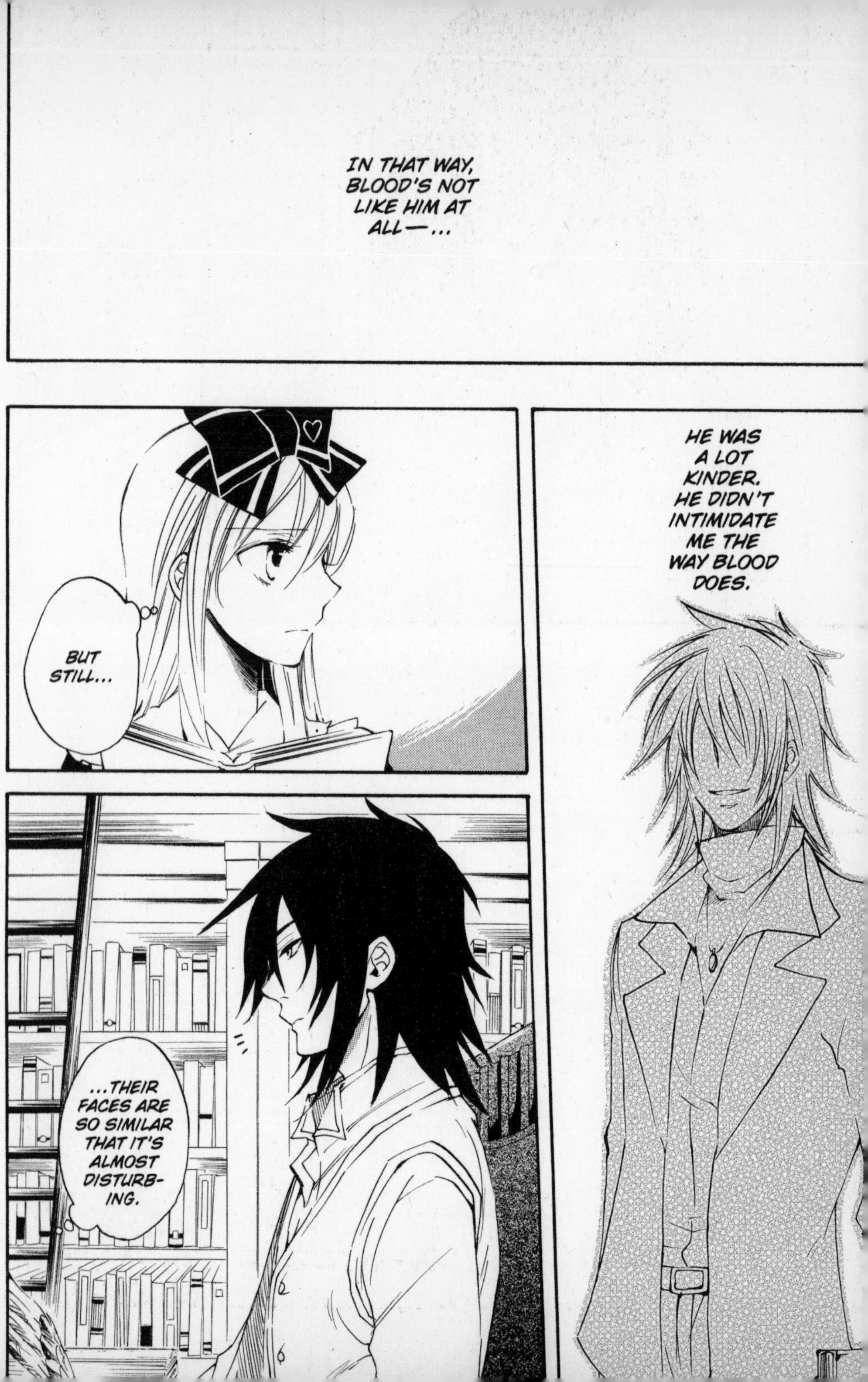
IN THAT WAY, BLOOD'S NOT LIKE HIM AT ALL—...
HE WAS A LOT KINDER. HE DIDN'T INTIMIDATE ME THE WAY BLOOD DOES.
BUT STILL...
...THEIR FACES ARE SO SIMILAR THAT IT'S ALMOST DISTURB-ING.

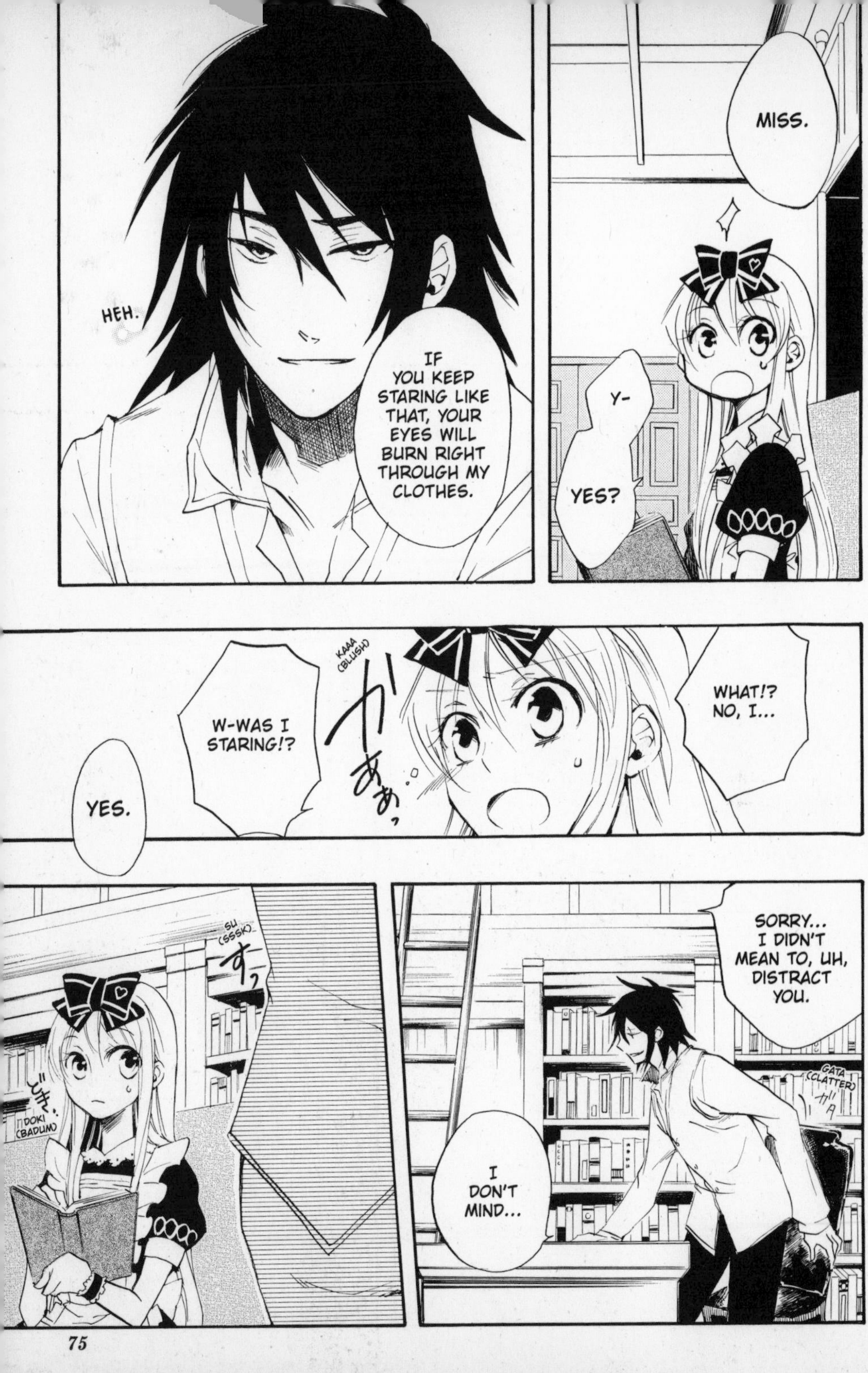

MISS.
Y-
YES?
HEH.
IF YOU KEEP STARING LIKE THAT, YOUR EYES WILL BURN RIGHT THROUGH MY CLOTHES.
WHAT!? NO, I...
KAAA (BLUSH)
かぁぁ
W-WAS I STARING!?
YES.
SORRY... I DIDN'T MEAN TO, UH, DISTRACT YOU.
GATA (CLATTER)
ガタ
I DON'T MIND...
SU (SSSK)
す
DOKI (BADUM)
どき

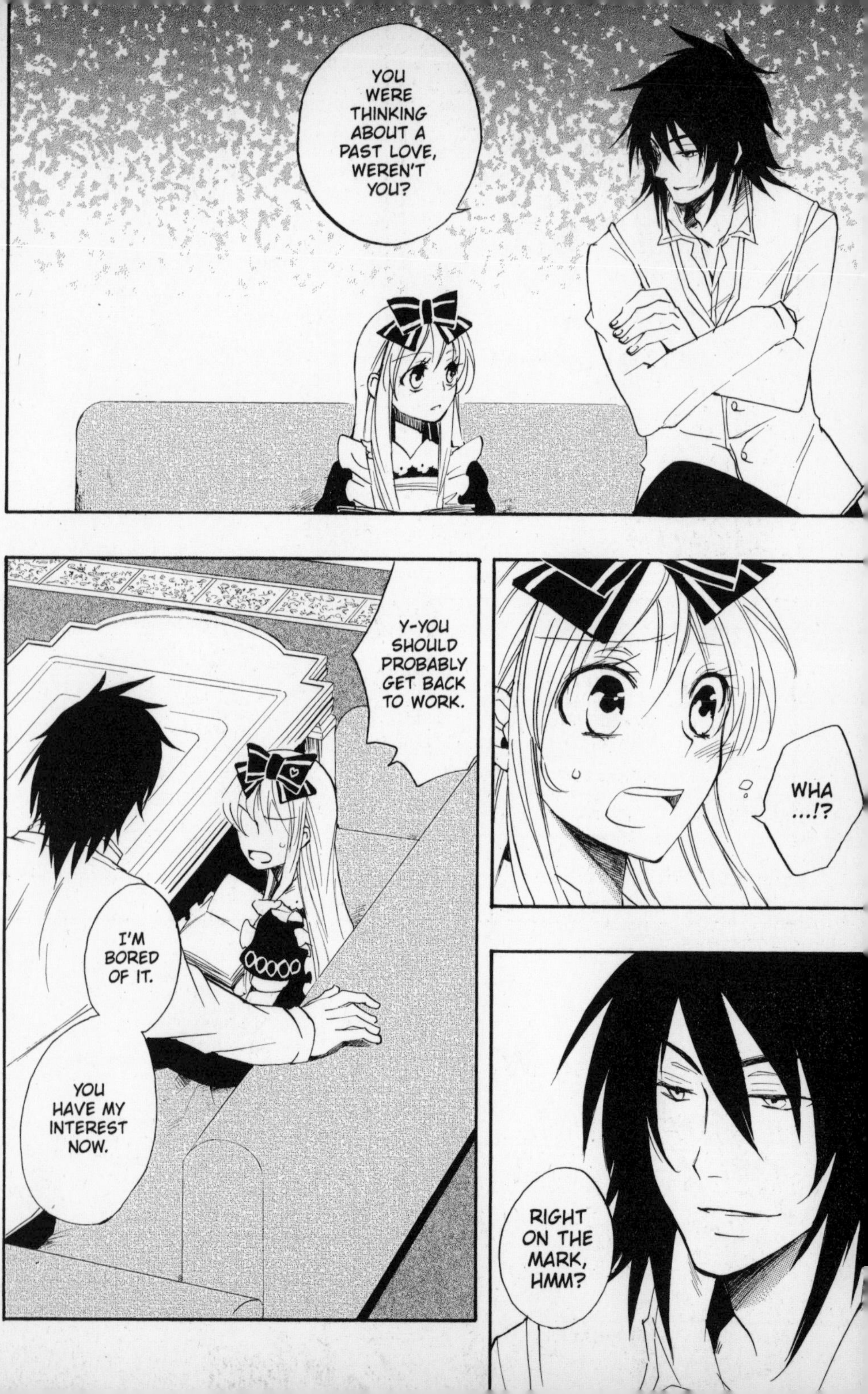
YOU WERE THINKING ABOUT A PAST LOVE, WEREN'T YOU?
WHA ...!?
RIGHT ON THE MARK, HMM?
Y-YOU SHOULD PROBABLY GET BACK TO WORK.
I'M BORED OF IT.
YOU HAVE MY INTEREST NOW.

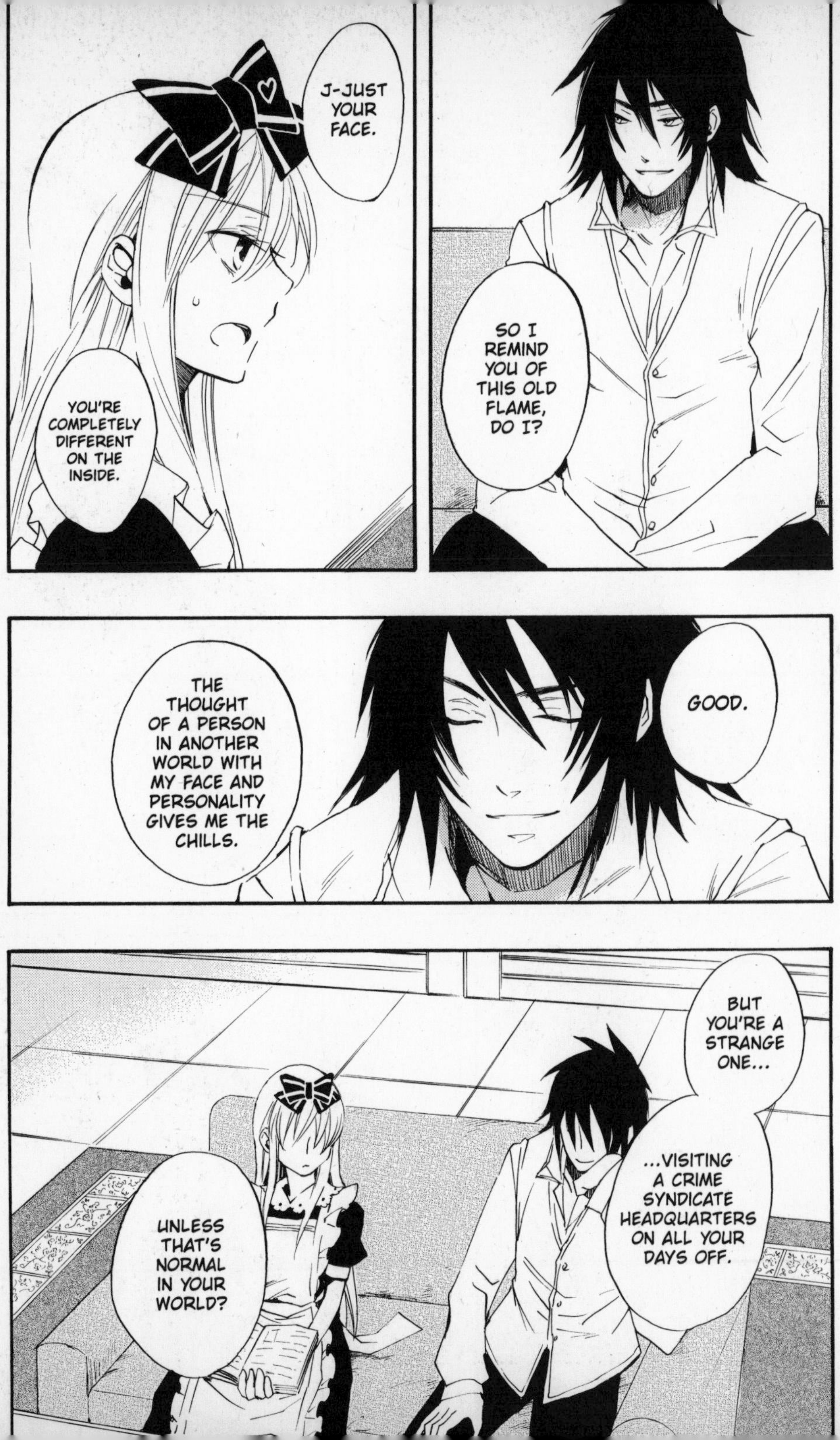
SO I REMIND YOU OF THIS OLD FLAME, DO I?
J-JUST YOUR FACE.
YOU'RE COMPLETELY DIFFERENT ON THE INSIDE.
GOOD.
THE THOUGHT OF A PERSON IN ANOTHER WORLD WITH MY FACE AND PERSONALITY GIVES ME THE CHILLS.
BUT YOU'RE A STRANGE ONE...
...VISITING A CRIME SYNDICATE HEADQUARTERS ON ALL YOUR DAYS OFF.
UNLESS THAT'S NORMAL IN YOUR WORLD?

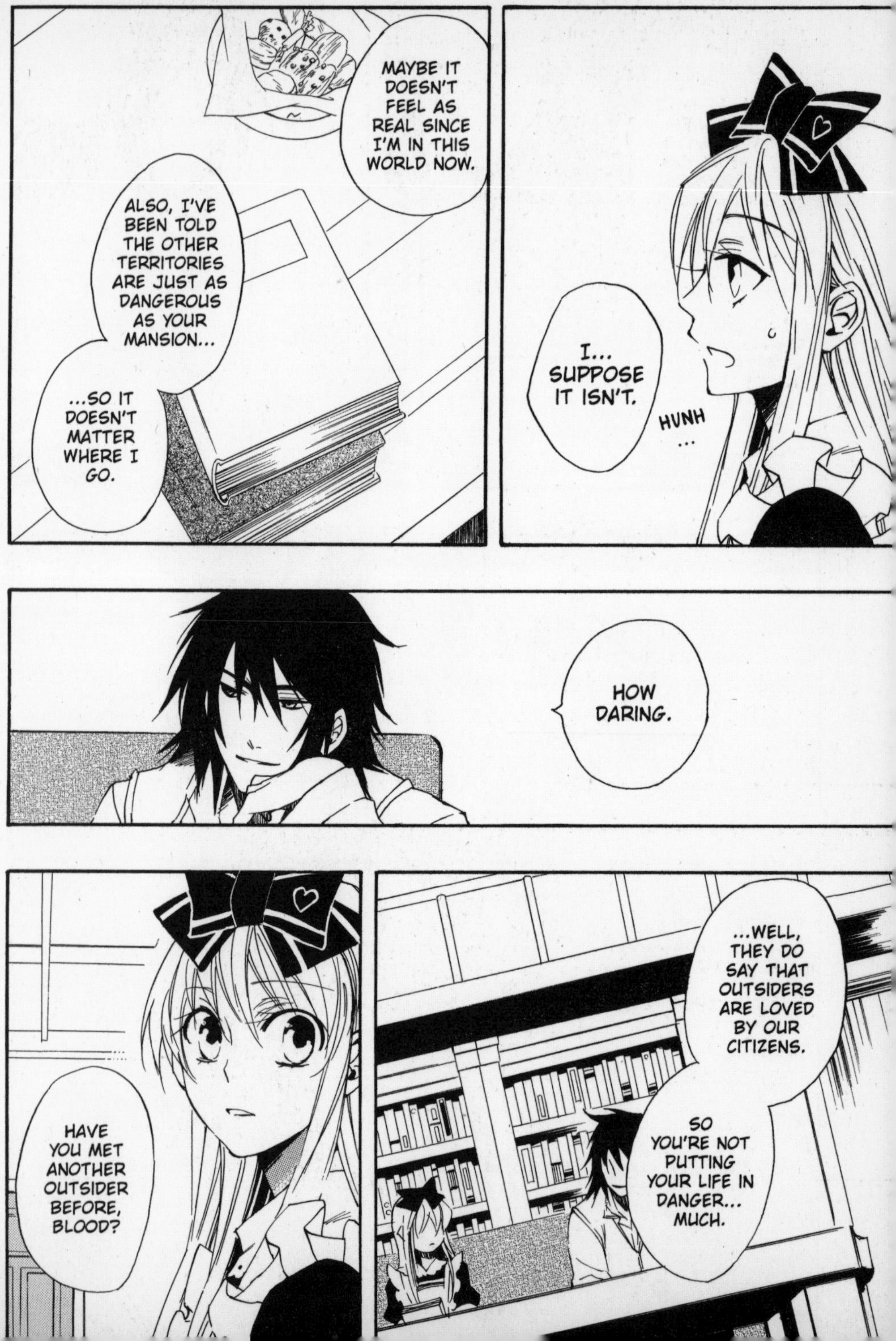
I... SUPPOSE IT ISN'T.
HUNH ...
MAYBE IT DOESN'T FEEL AS REAL SINCE I'M IN THIS WORLD NOW.
ALSO, I'VE BEEN TOLD THE OTHER TERRITORIES ARE JUST AS DANGEROUS AS YOUR MANSION...
...SO IT DOESN'T MATTER WHERE I GO.
HOW DARING.
...WELL, THEY DO SAY THAT OUTSIDERS ARE LOVED BY OUR CITIZENS.
SO YOU'RE NOT PUTTING YOUR LIFE IN DANGER... MUCH.
.....
HAVE YOU MET ANOTHER OUTSIDER BEFORE, BLOOD?

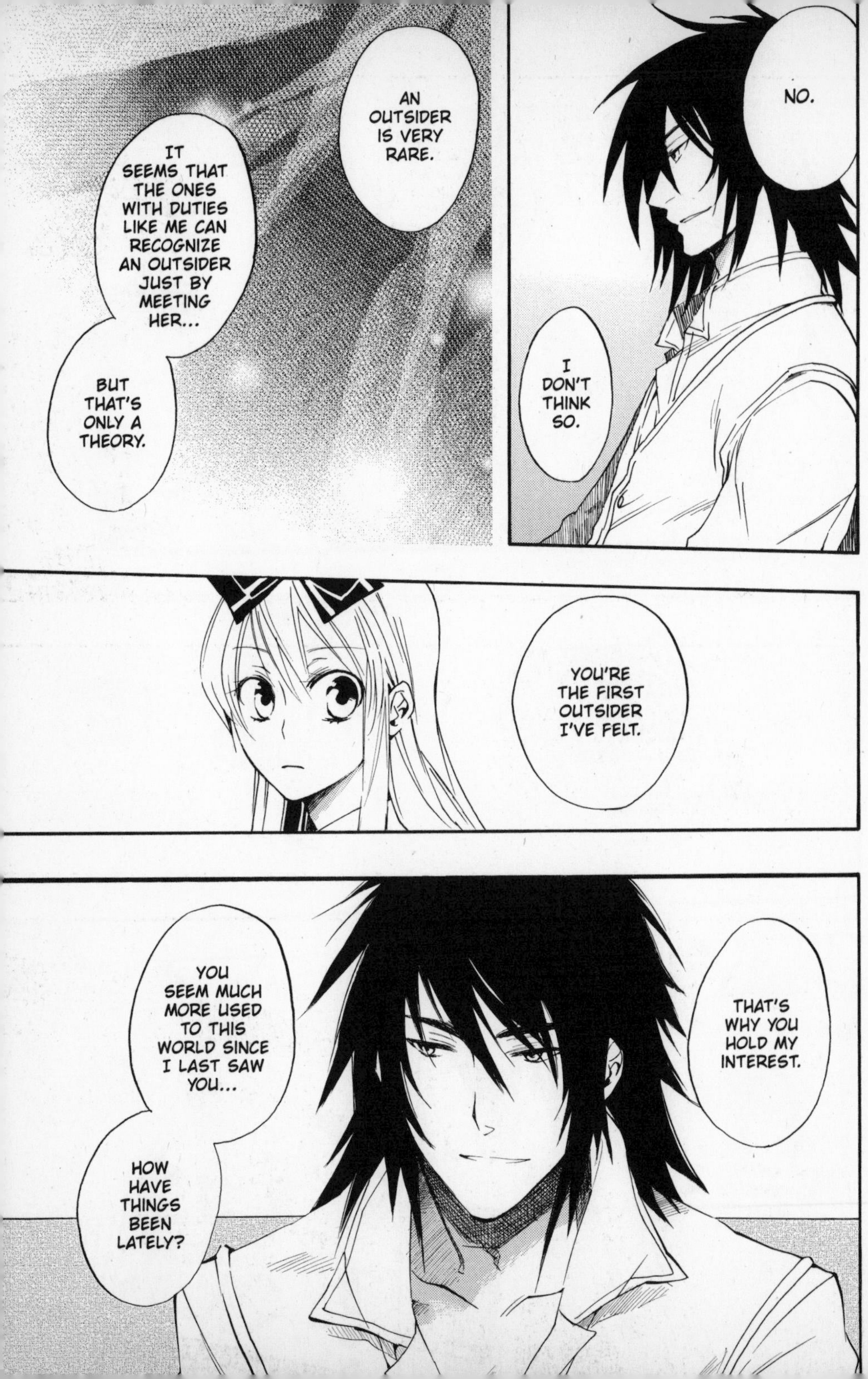
NO.
I DON'T THINK SO.
AN OUTSIDER IS VERY RARE.
IT SEEMS THAT THE ONES WITH DUTIES LIKE ME CAN RECOGNIZE AN OUTSIDER JUST BY MEETING HER...
BUT THAT'S ONLY A THEORY.
YOU'RE THE FIRST OUTSIDER I'VE FELT.
THAT'S WHY YOU HOLD MY INTEREST.
YOU SEEM MUCH MORE USED TO THIS WORLD SINCE I LAST SAW YOU...
HOW HAVE THINGS BEEN LATELY?

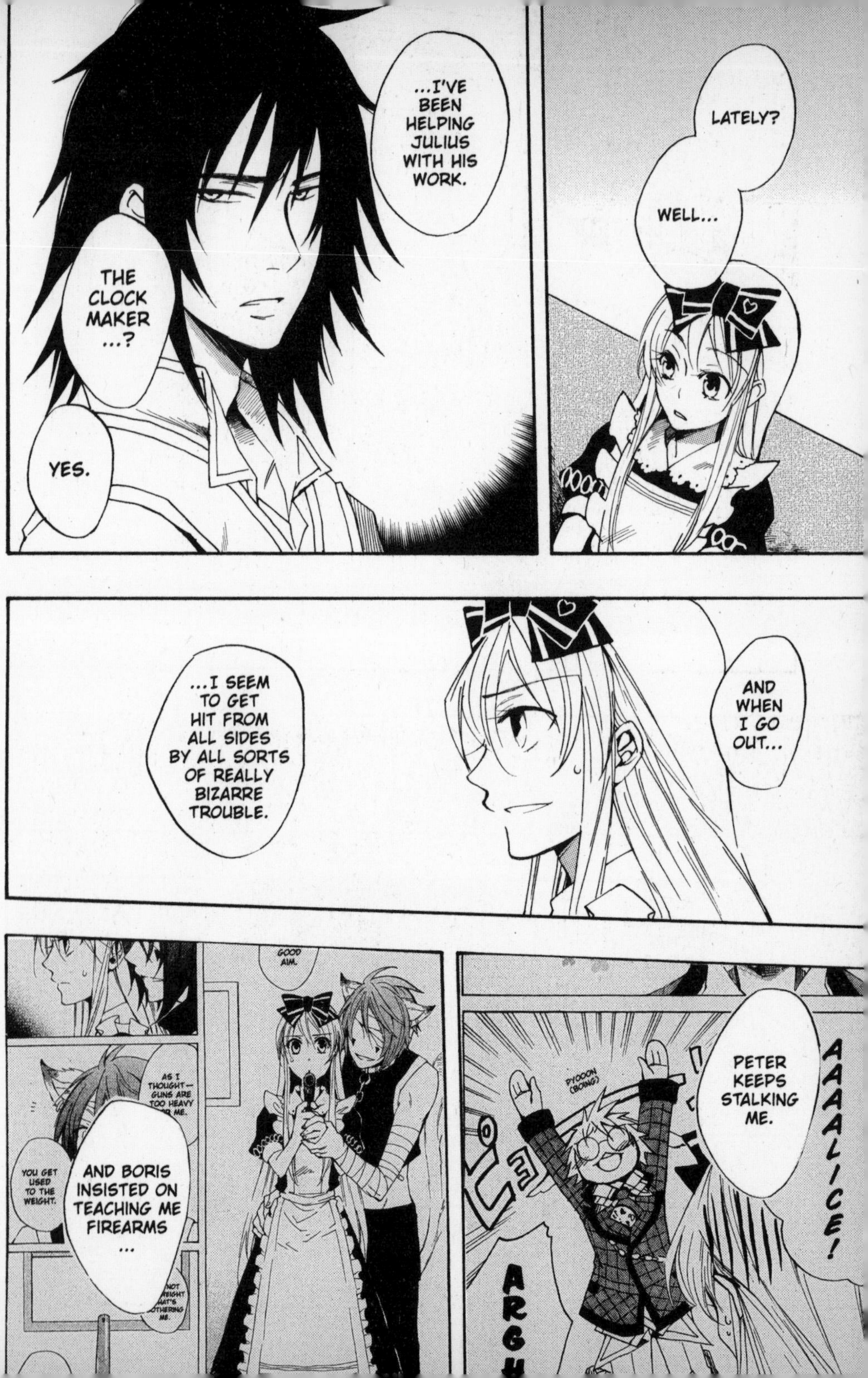
LATELY?
WELL...
...I'VE BEEN HELPING JULIUS WITH HIS WORK.
THE CLOCK MAKER ...?
YES.
AND WHEN I GO OUT...
...I SEEM TO GET HIT FROM ALL SIDES BY ALL SORTS OF REALLY BIZARRE TROUBLE.
AAAALICE!
PETER KEEPS STALKING ME.
PYOOON (BOING)
AND BORIS INSISTED ON TEACHING ME FIREARMS ...
GOOD AIM.
YOU GET USED TO THE WEIGHT.

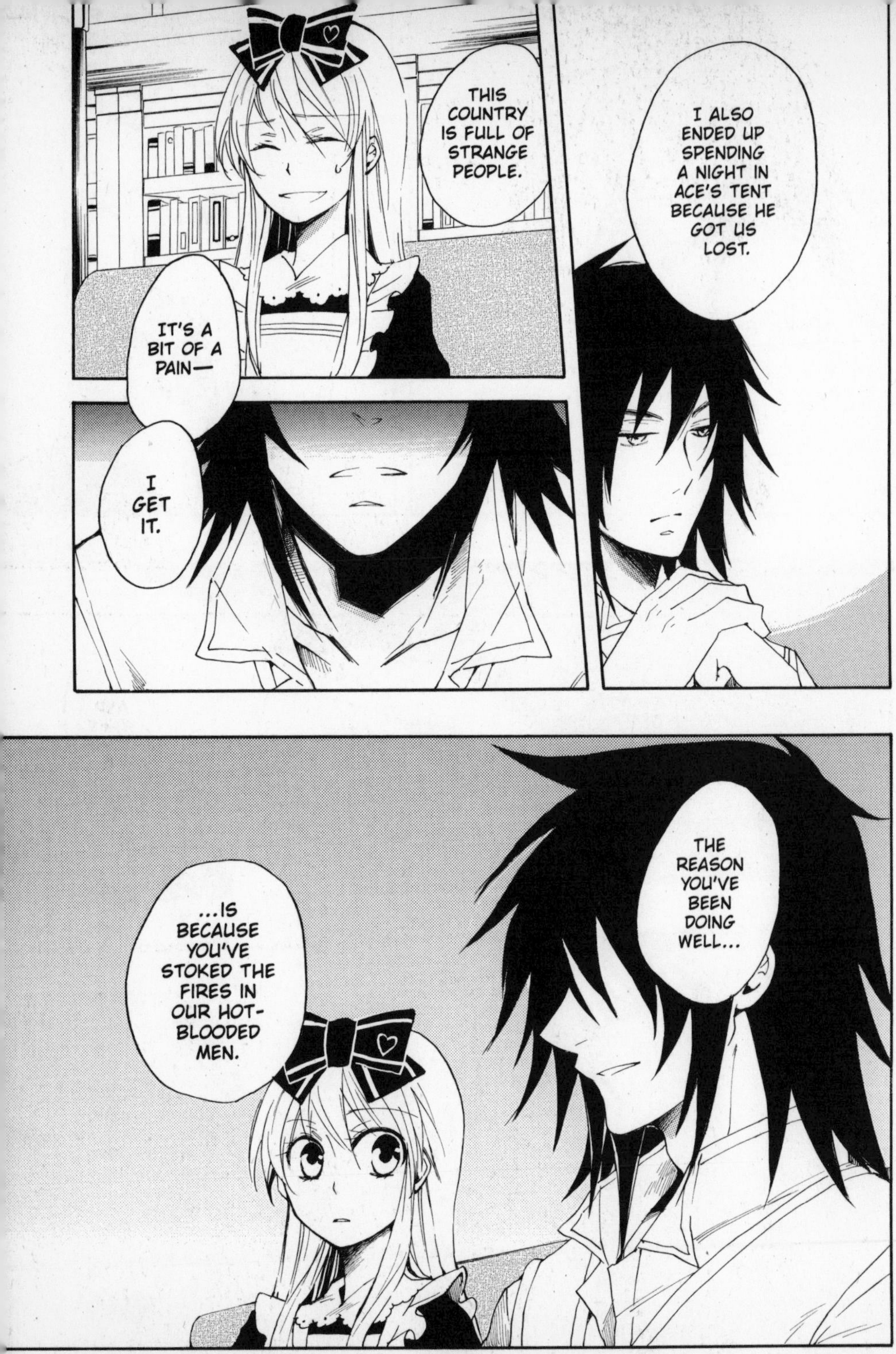
I ALSO ENDED UP SPENDING A NIGHT IN ACE'S TENT BECAUSE HE GOT US LOST.
THIS COUNTRY IS FULL OF STRANGE PEOPLE.
IT'S A BIT OF A PAIN—
I GET IT.
THE REASON YOU'VE BEEN DOING WELL...
...IS BECAUSE YOU'VE STOKED THE FIRES IN OUR HOT-BLOODED MEN.

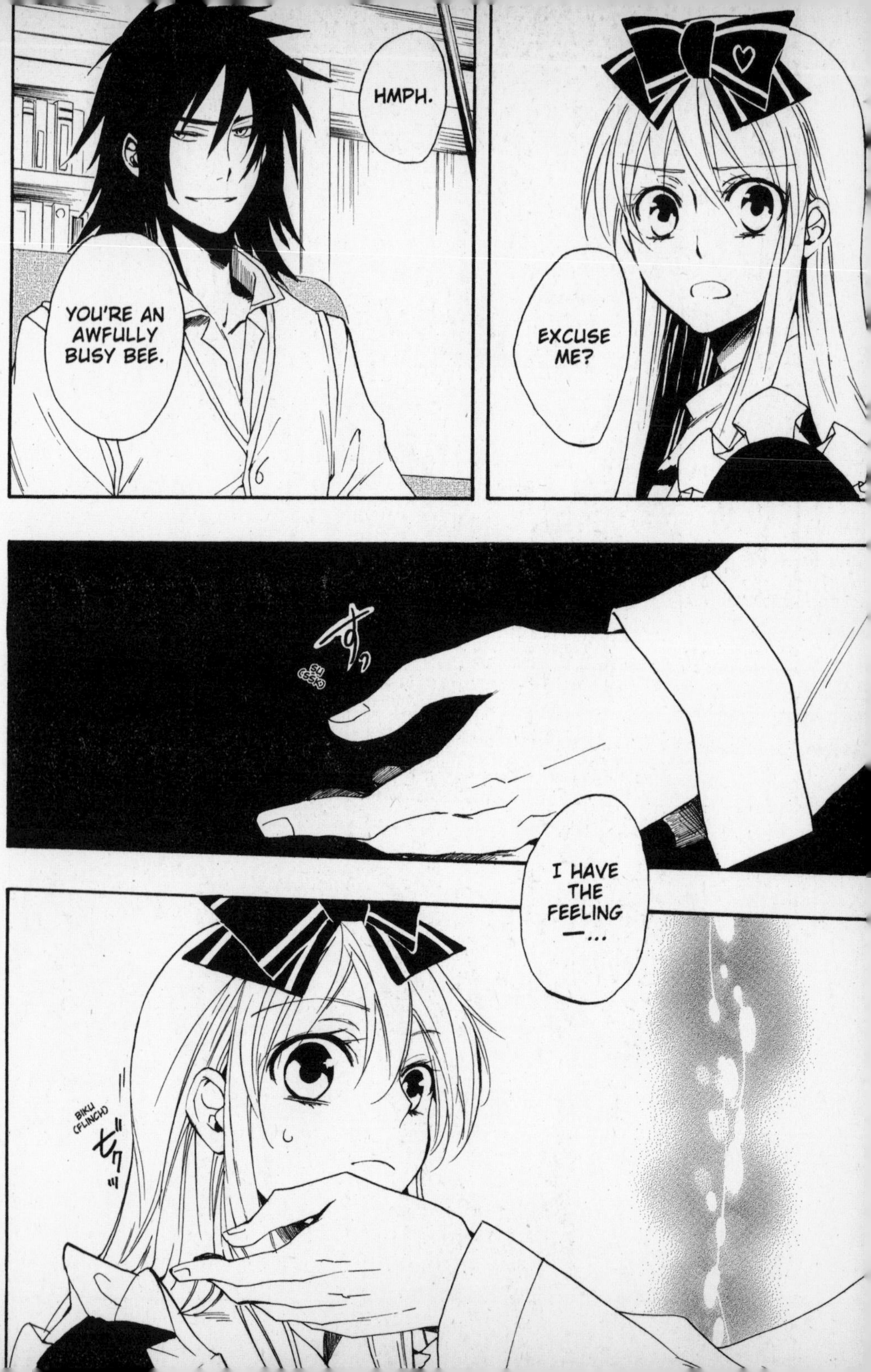
EXCUSE ME?
HMPH.
YOU'RE AN AWFULLY BUSY BEE.
SU (SSSH)
I HAVE THE FEELING —...
BIKU (FLINCH)

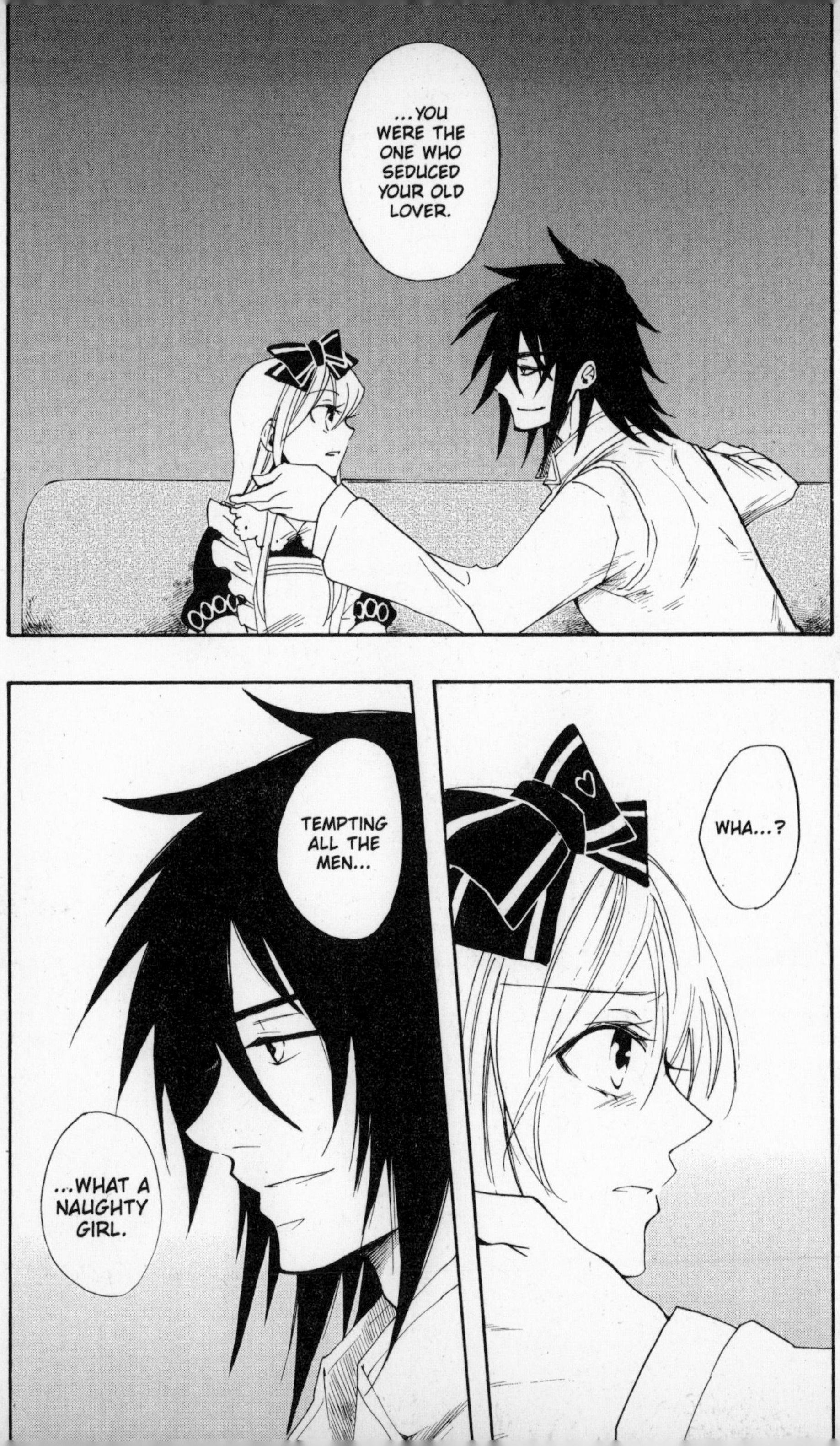
...YOU WERE THE ONE WHO SEDUCED YOUR OLD LOVER.
WHA...?
TEMPTING ALL THE MEN...
...WHAT A NAUGHTY GIRL.

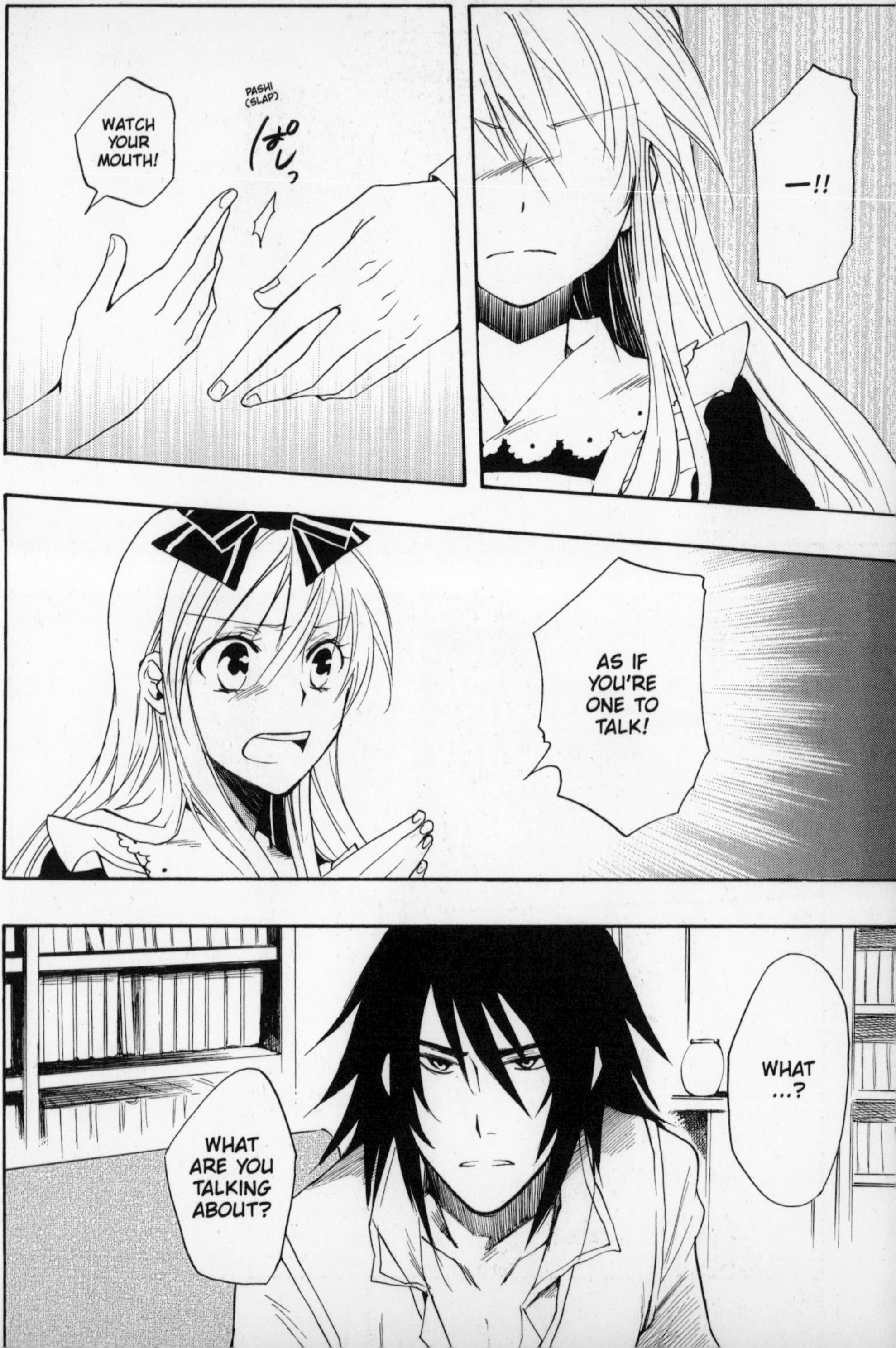
—!!
WATCH YOUR MOUTH!
PASHI (SLAP)
ぱしっ
AS IF YOU'RE ONE TO TALK!
WHAT ...?
WHAT ARE YOU TALKING ABOUT?

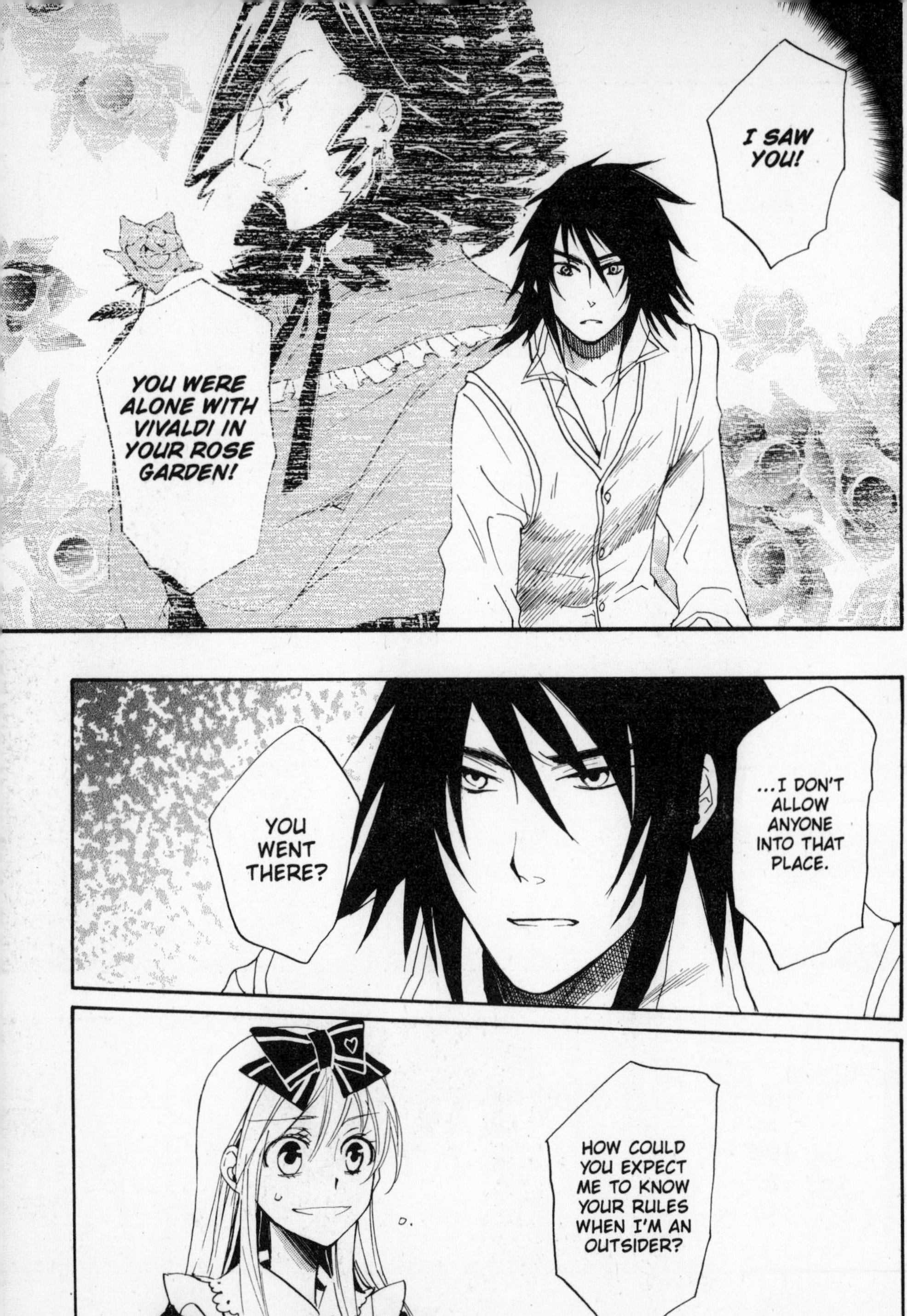
I SAW YOU!
YOU WERE ALONE WITH VIVALDI IN YOUR ROSE GARDEN!
...I DON'T ALLOW ANYONE INTO THAT PLACE.
YOU WENT THERE?
HOW COULD YOU EXPECT ME TO KNOW YOUR RULES WHEN I'M AN OUTSIDER?

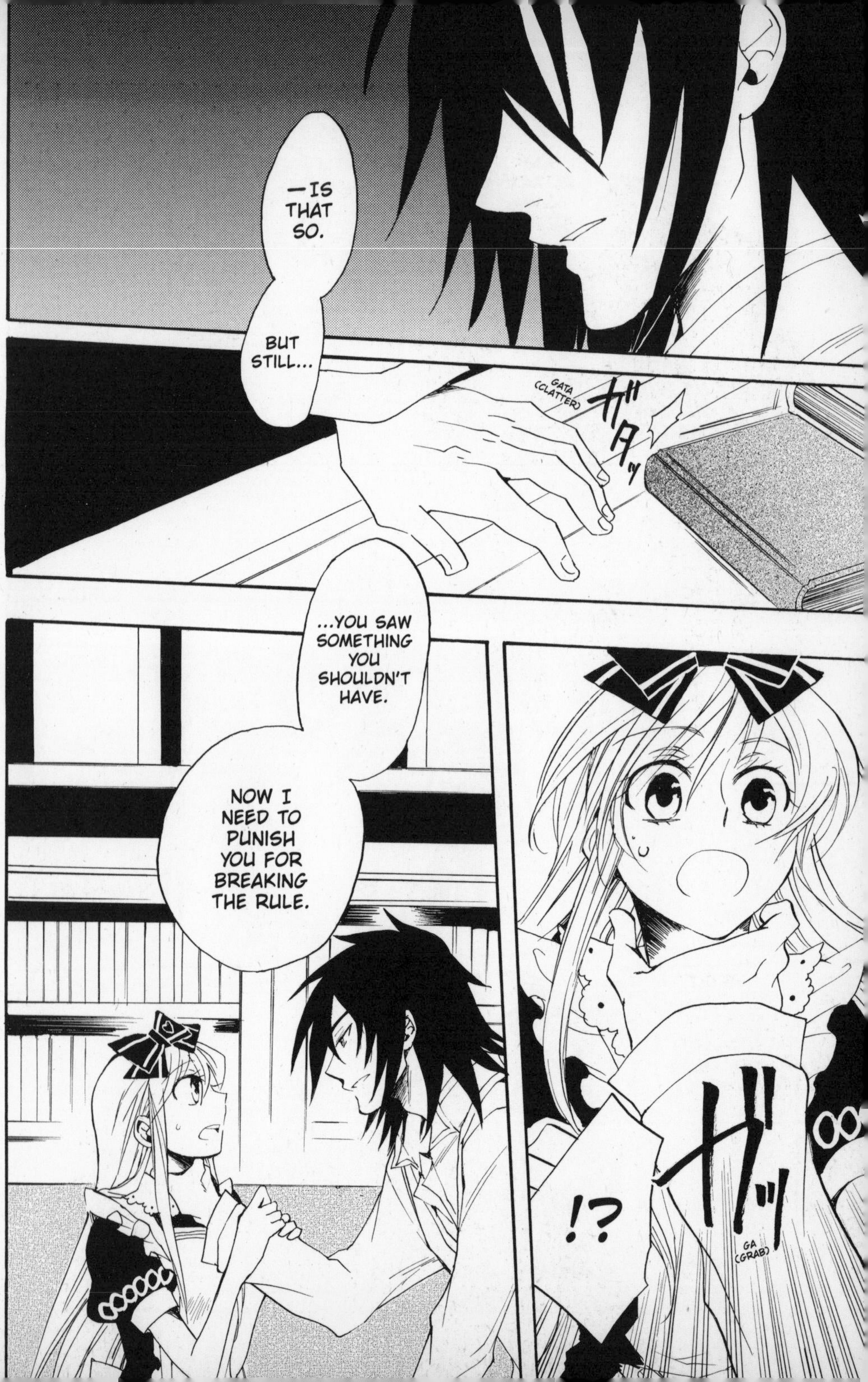
—IS THAT SO.
BUT STILL...
GATA (CLATTER)
...YOU SAW SOMETHING YOU SHOULDN'T HAVE.
NOW I NEED TO PUNISH YOU FOR BREAKING THE RULE.
GA (GRAB)
!?

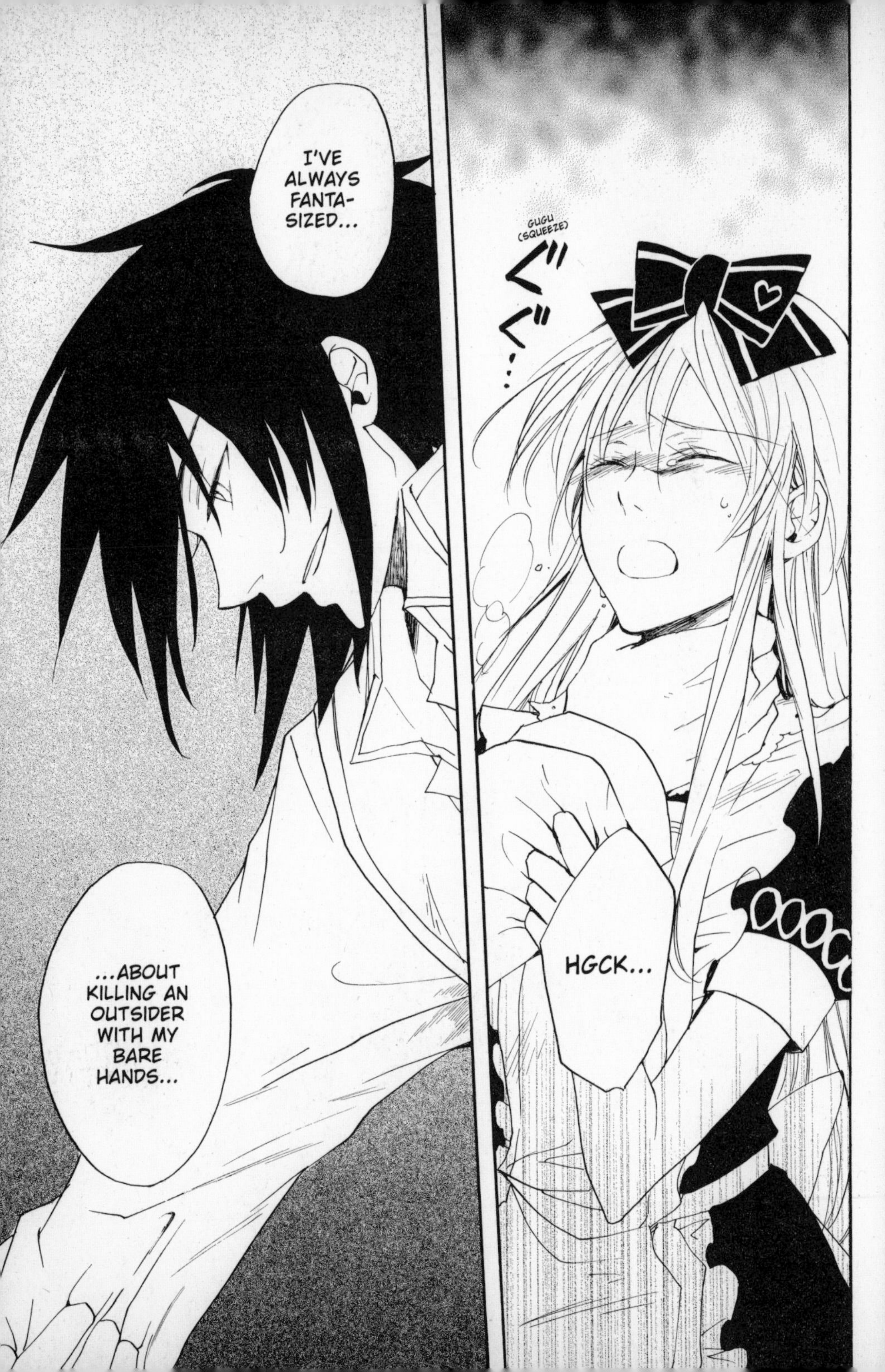
GUGU (SQUEEZE)
ぐぐ…
HGCK...
I'VE ALWAYS FANTA- SIZED...
...ABOUT KILLING AN OUTSIDER WITH MY BARE HANDS...

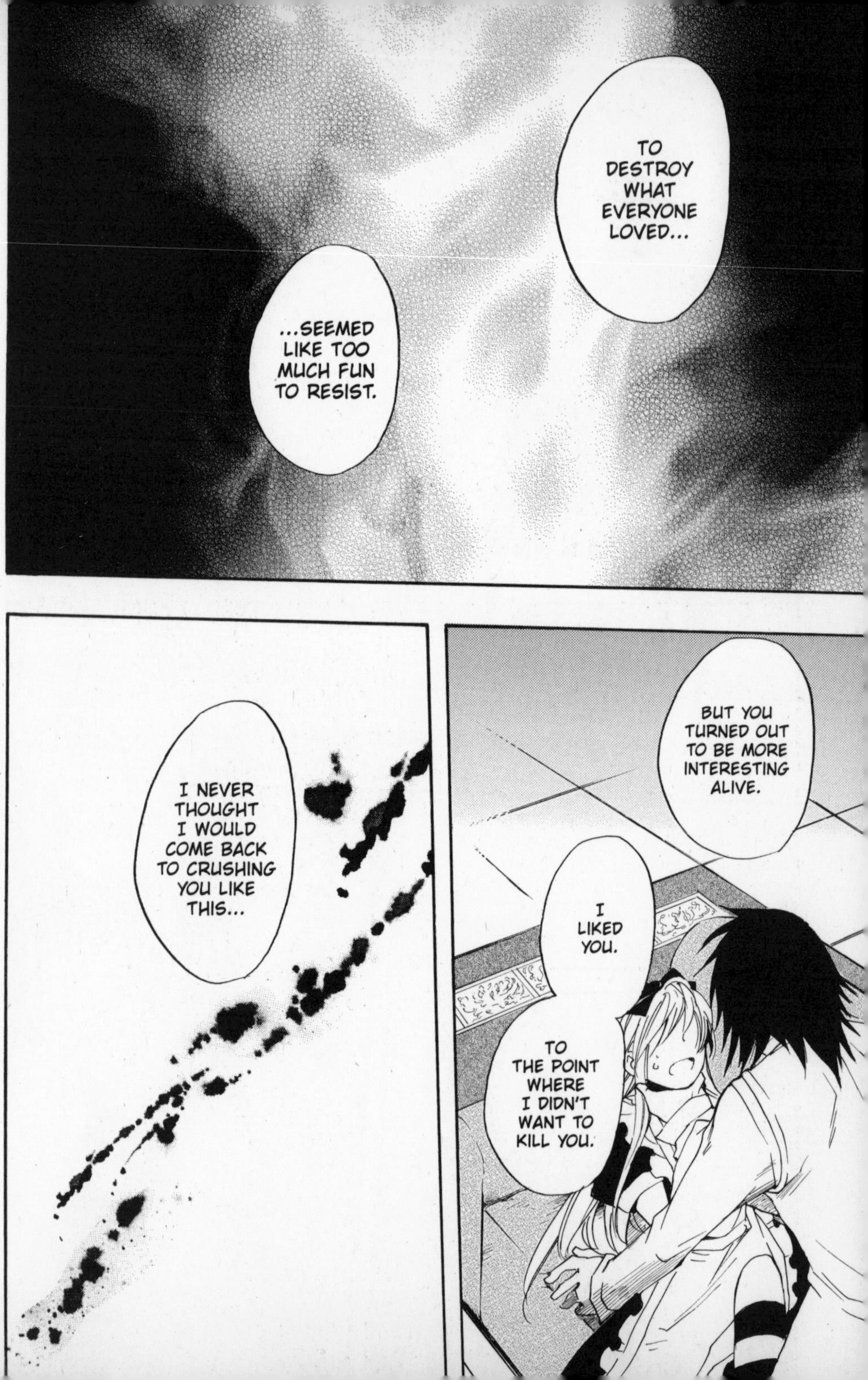
TO DESTROY WHAT EVERYONE LOVED...
...SEEMED LIKE TOO MUCH FUN TO RESIST.
BUT YOU TURNED OUT TO BE MORE INTERESTING ALIVE.
I LIKED YOU.
TO THE POINT WHERE I DIDN'T WANT TO KILL YOU.
I NEVER THOUGHT I WOULD COME BACK TO CRUSHING YOU LIKE THIS...

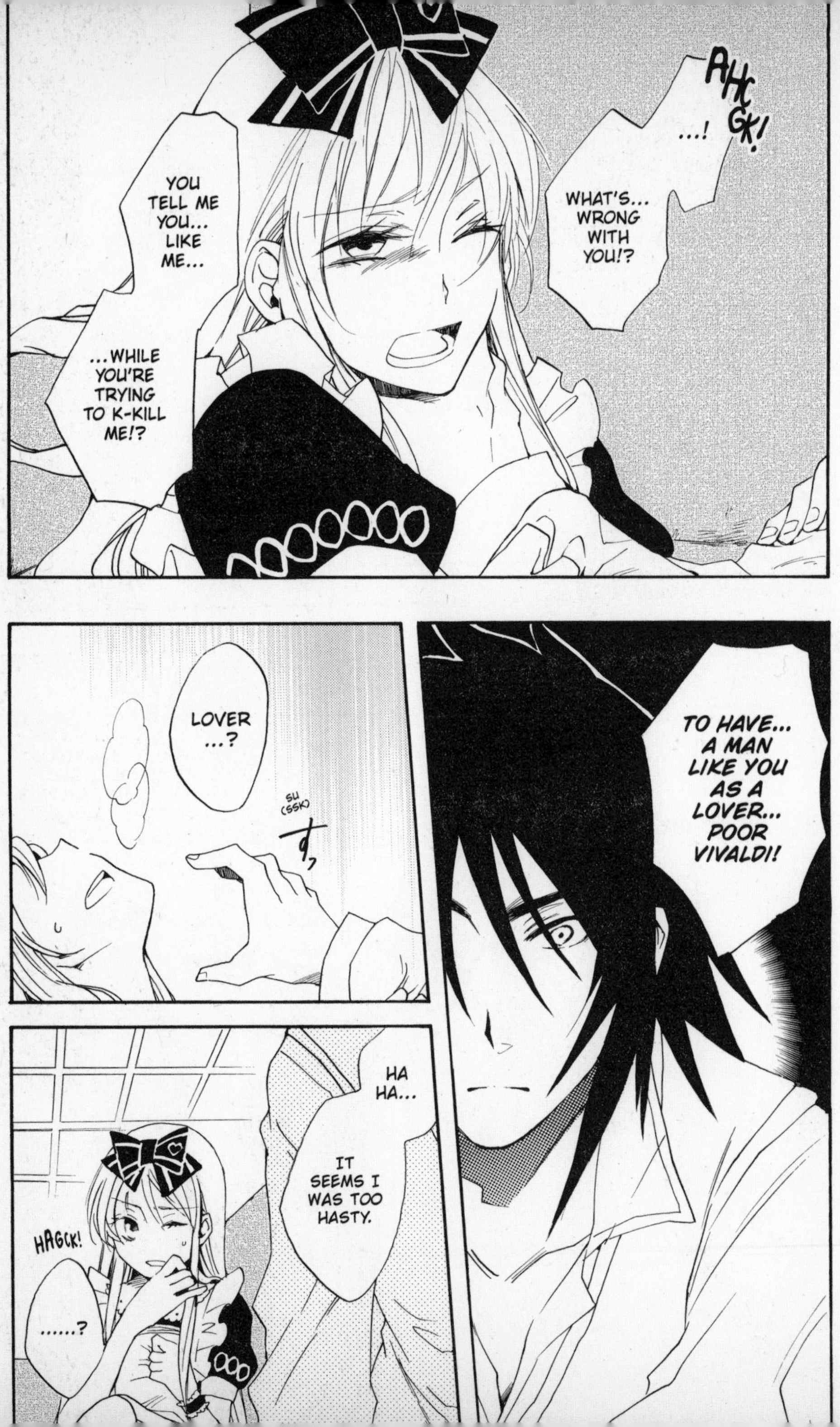
AHCGK!
...!
WHAT'S... WRONG WITH YOU!?
YOU TELL ME YOU... LIKE ME...
...WHILE YOU'RE TRYING TO K-KILL ME!?
TO HAVE... A MAN LIKE YOU AS A LOVER... POOR VIVALDI!
LOVER ...?
SU (SSK)
HA HA...
IT SEEMS I WAS TOO HASTY.
HAGCK!
......?

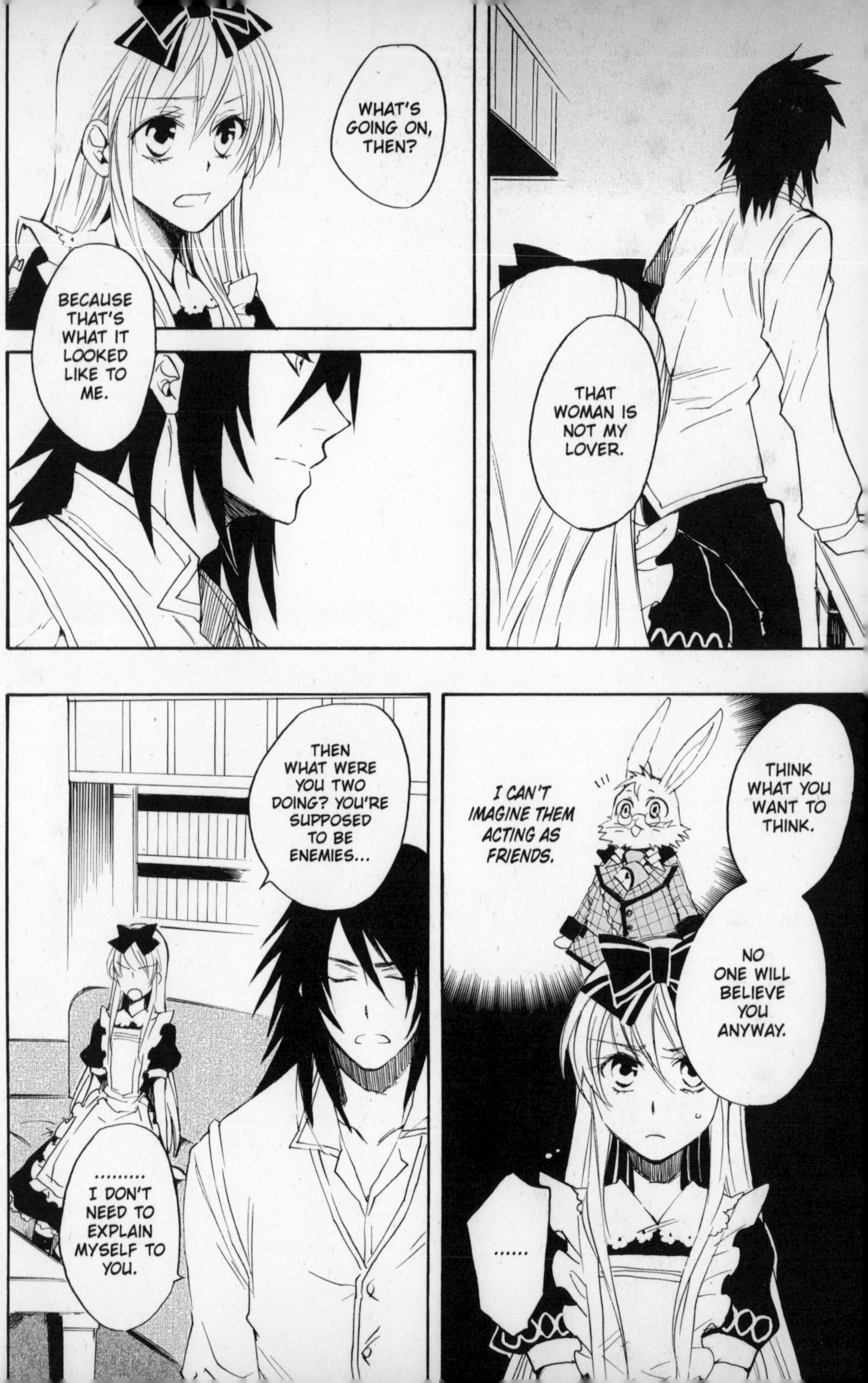
THAT WOMAN IS NOT MY LOVER.
WHAT'S GOING ON, THEN?
BECAUSE THAT'S WHAT IT LOOKED LIKE TO ME.
THINK WHAT YOU WANT TO THINK.
NO ONE WILL BELIEVE YOU ANYWAY.
I CAN'T IMAGINE THEM ACTING AS FRIENDS.
......
THEN WHAT WERE YOU TWO DOING? YOU'RE SUPPOSED TO BE ENEMIES...
.... I DON'T NEED TO EXPLAIN MYSELF TO YOU.

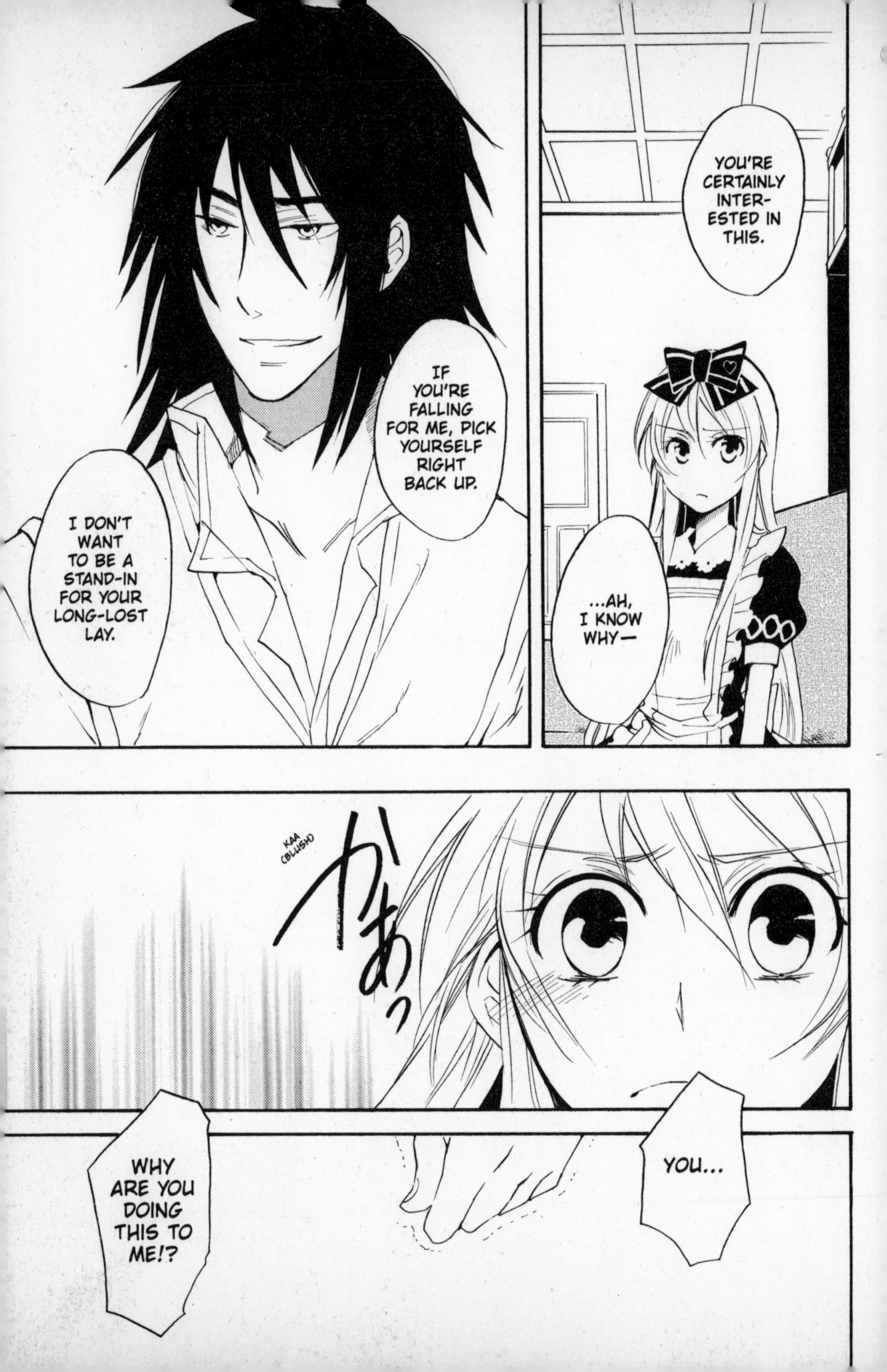
YOU'RE CERTAINLY INTER-ESTED IN THIS.
...AH, I KNOW WHY—
IF YOU'RE FALLING FOR ME, PICK YOURSELF RIGHT BACK UP.
I DON'T WANT TO BE A STAND-IN FOR YOUR LONG-LOST LAY.
かあっ
KAA (BLUSH)
YOU...
WHY ARE YOU DOING THIS TO ME!?

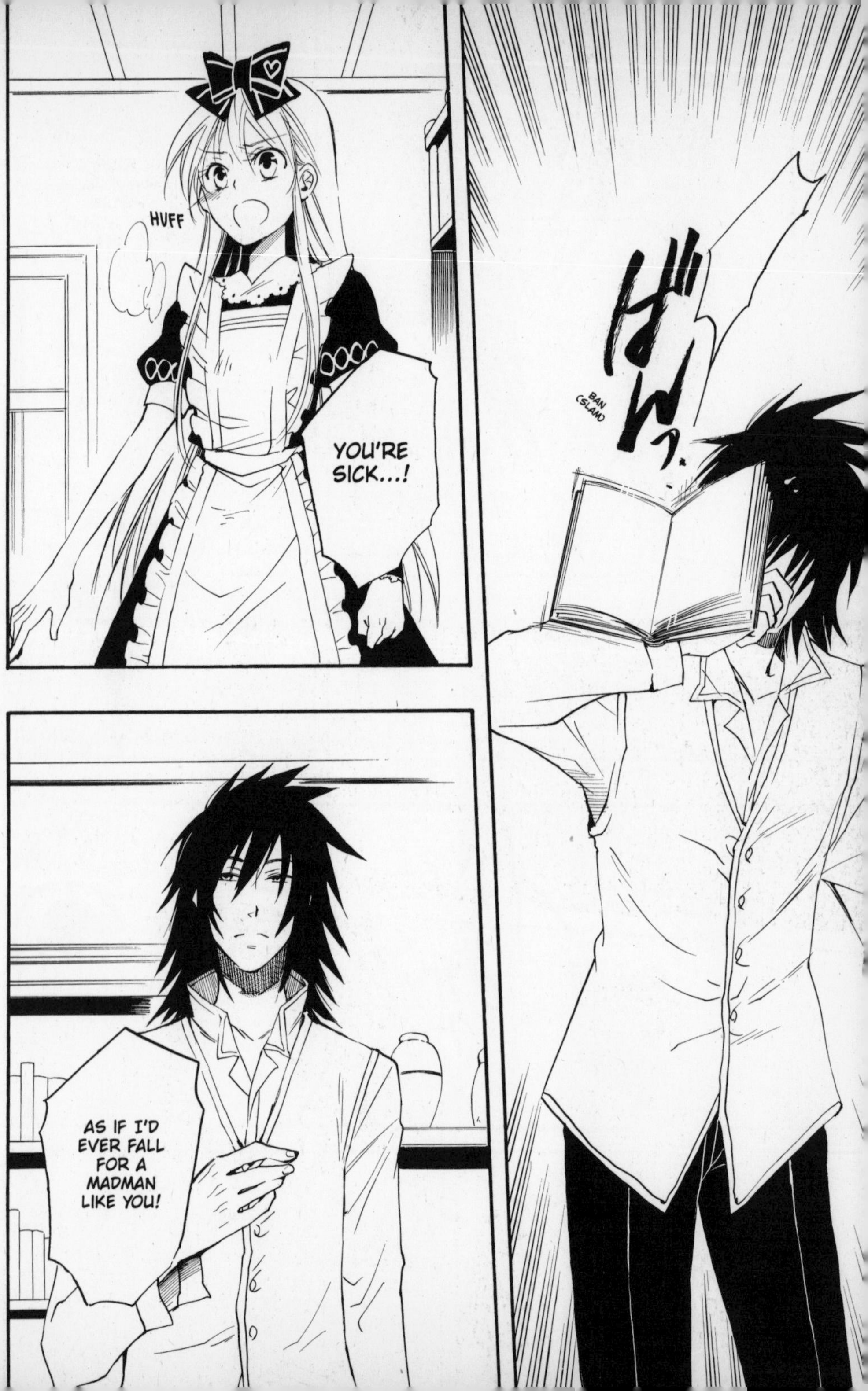
ばんっ
BAN (SLAM)
HUFF
YOU'RE SICK...!
AS IF I'D EVER FALL FOR A MADMAN LIKE YOU!

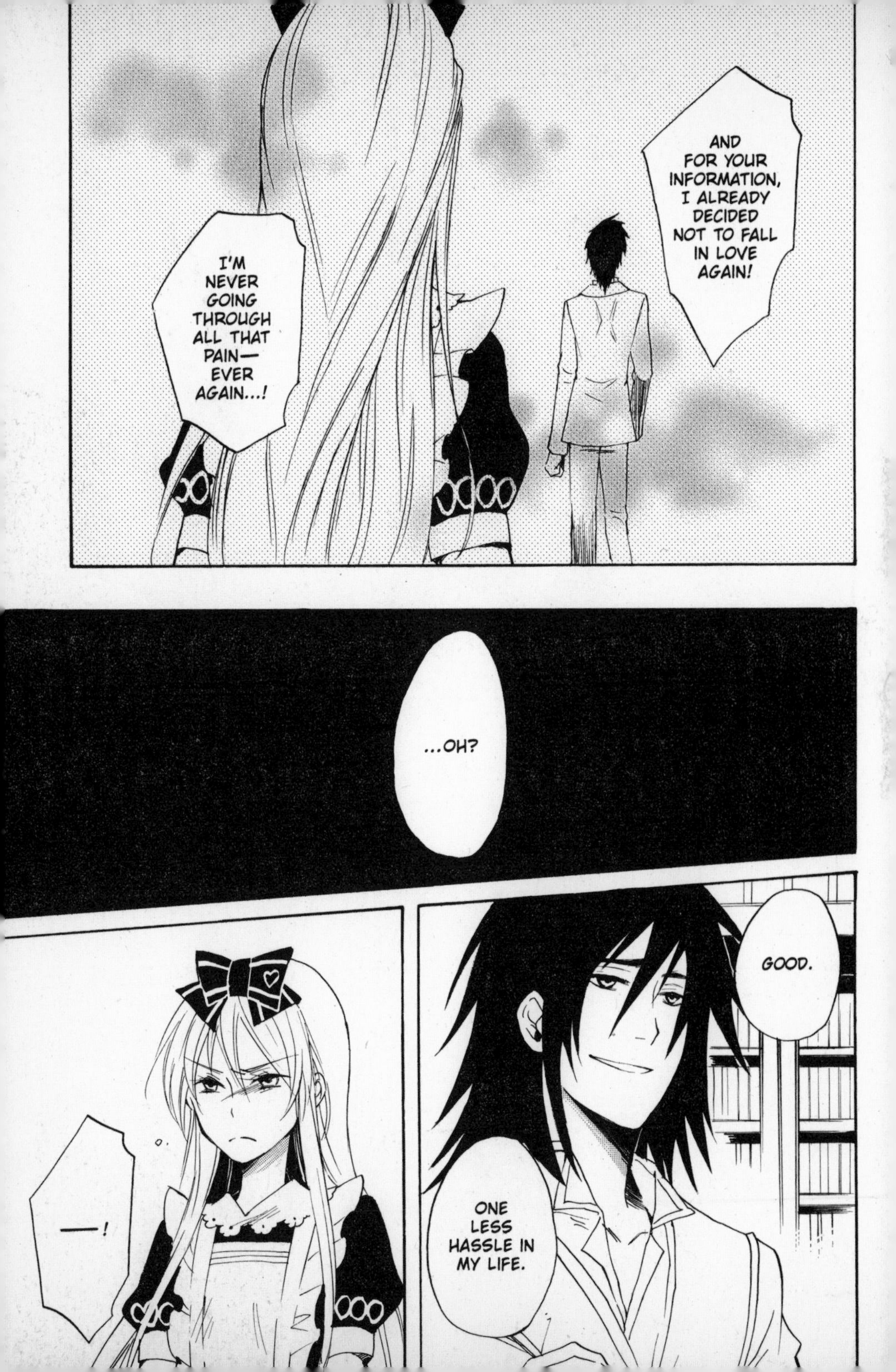
AND FOR YOUR INFORMATION, I ALREADY DECIDED NOT TO FALL IN LOVE AGAIN!
I'M NEVER GOING THROUGH ALL THAT PAIN—EVER AGAIN...!
...OH?
GOOD.
ONE LESS HASSLE IN MY LIFE.
—!

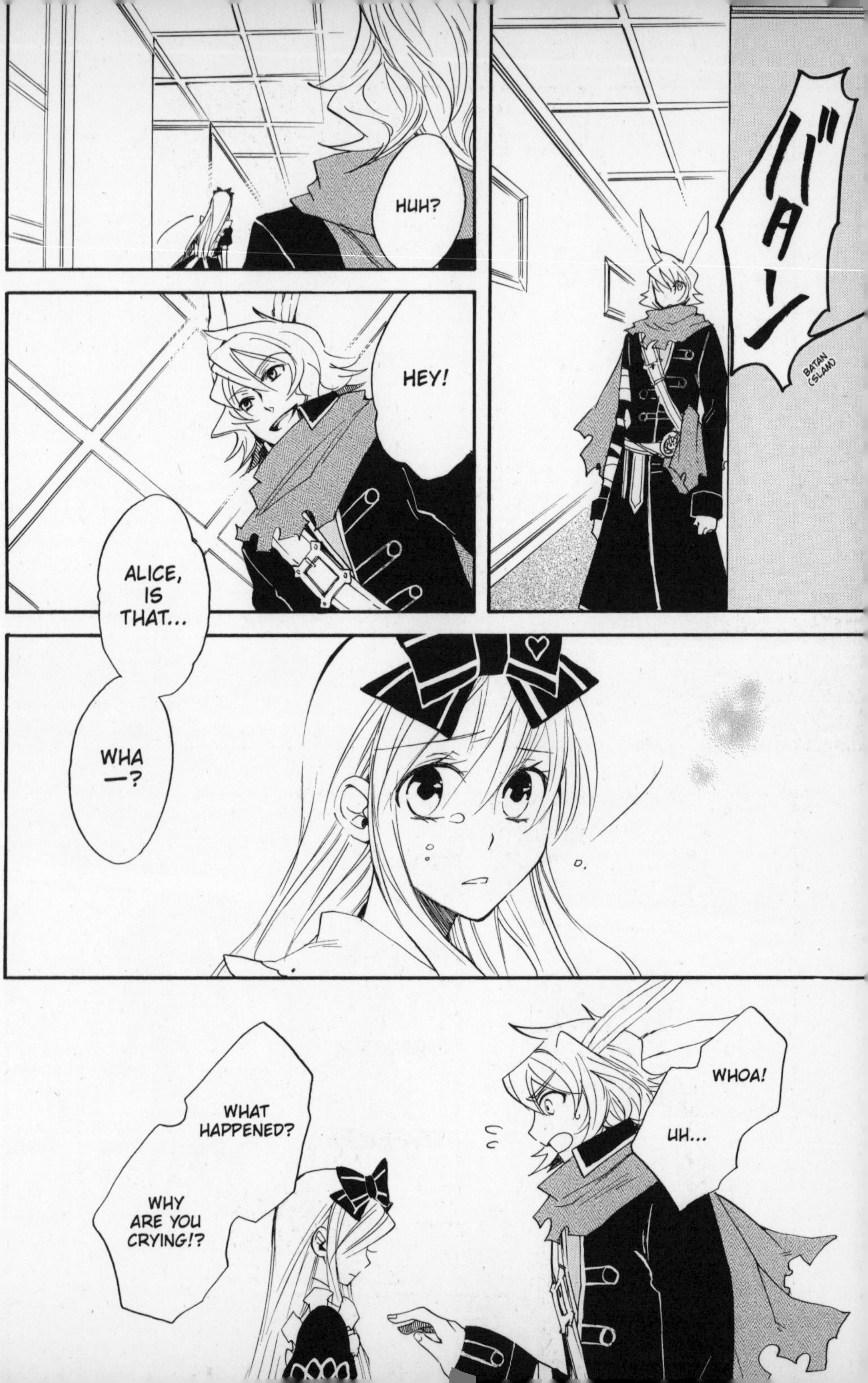
バターン
BATAN (SLAM)
HUH?
HEY!
ALICE, IS THAT...
WHA —?
WHOA!
UH...
WHAT HAPPENED?
WHY ARE YOU CRYING!?

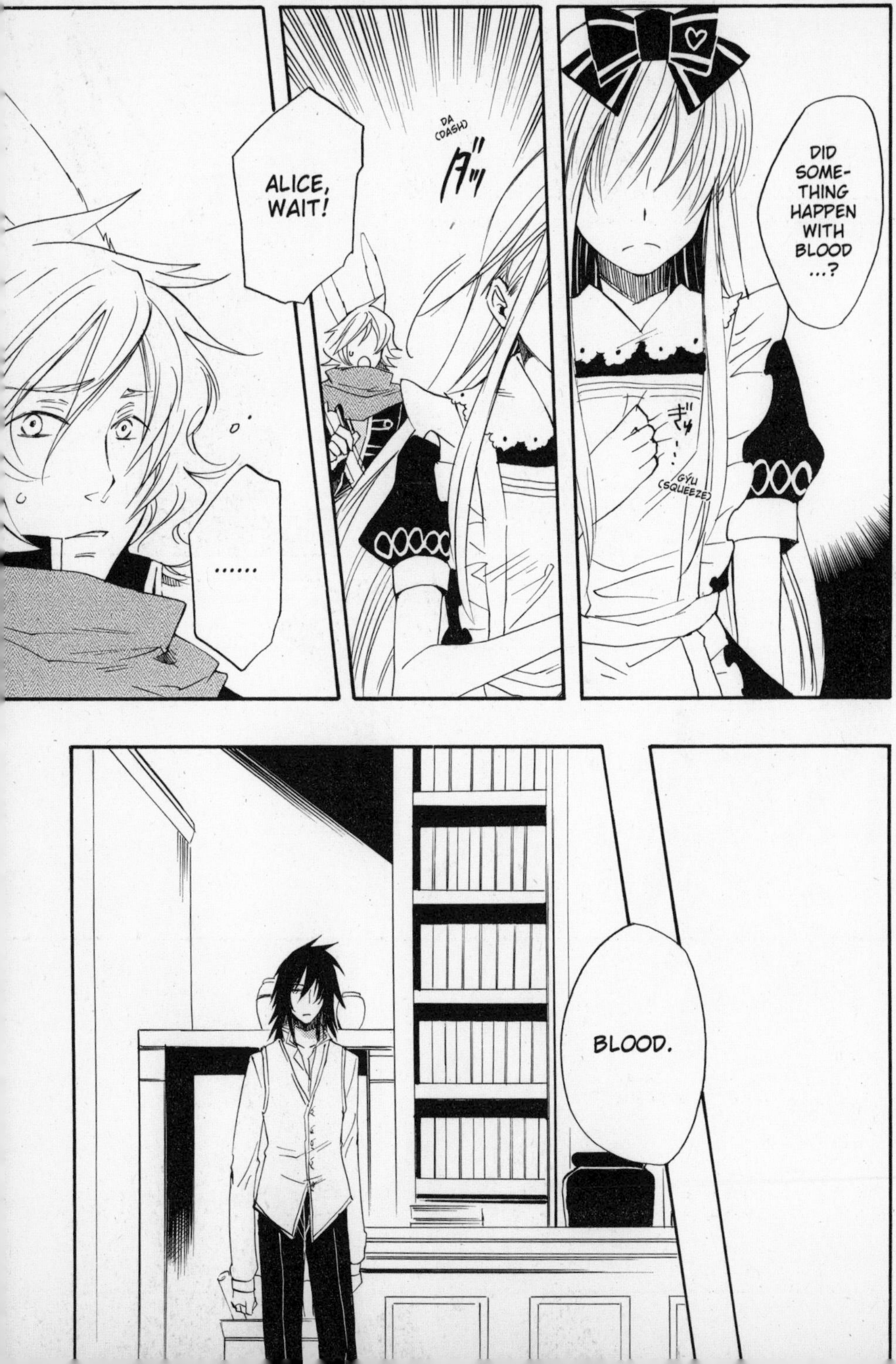
DID SOMETHING HAPPEN WITH BLOOD ...?
ぎゅ
GYU (SQUEEZE)
ダッ
DA (DASH)
ALICE, WAIT!
......
BLOOD.

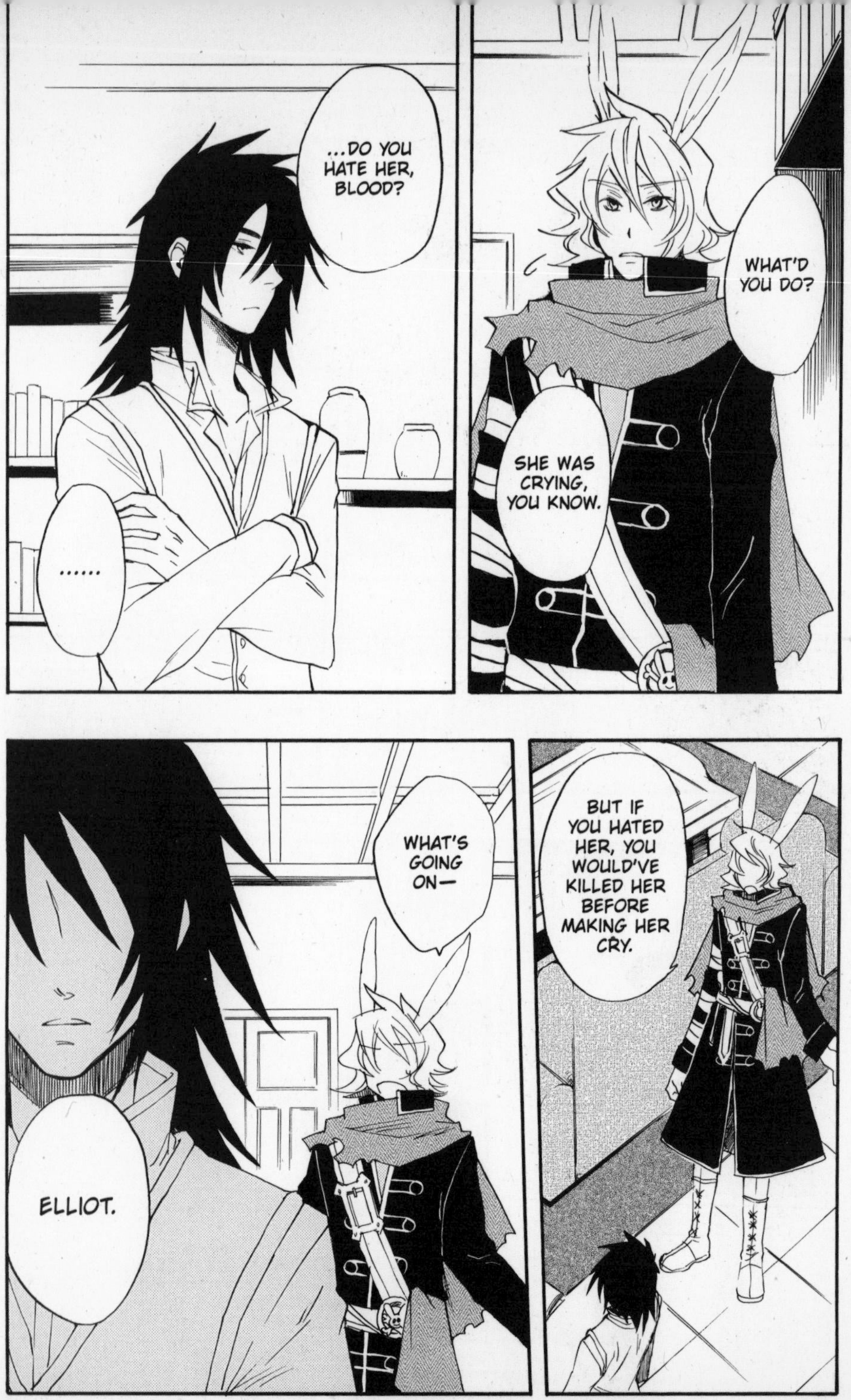
WHAT'D YOU DO?
SHE WAS CRYING, YOU KNOW.
...DO YOU HATE HER, BLOOD?
......
BUT IF YOU HATED HER, YOU WOULD'VE KILLED HER BEFORE MAKING HER CRY.
WHAT'S GOING ON—
ELLIOT.

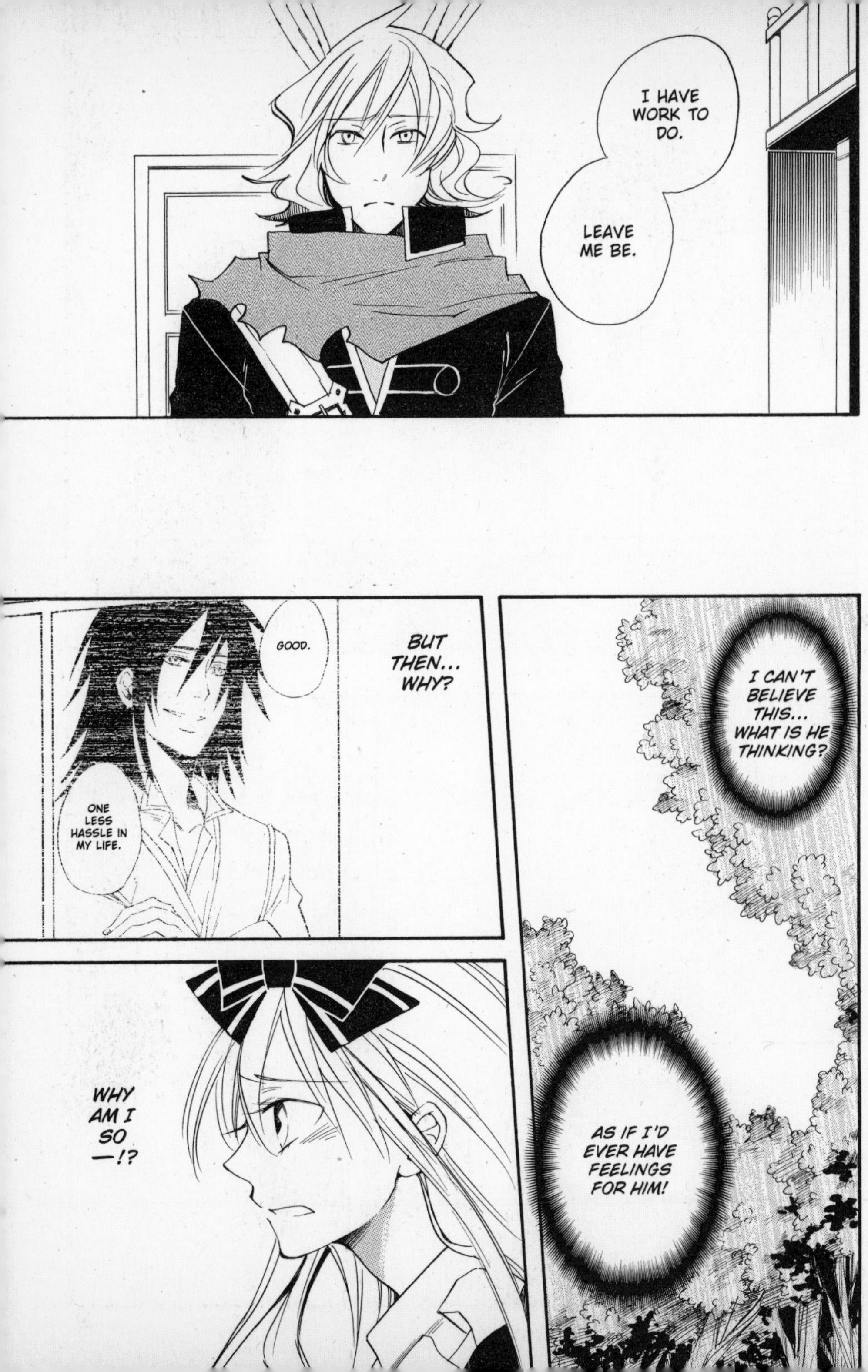
I HAVE WORK TO DO.
LEAVE ME BE.
I CAN'T BELIEVE THIS... WHAT IS HE THINKING?
AS IF I'D EVER HAVE FEELINGS FOR HIM!
BUT THEN... WHY?
GOOD.
ONE LESS HASSLE IN MY LIFE.
WHY AM I SO—!?

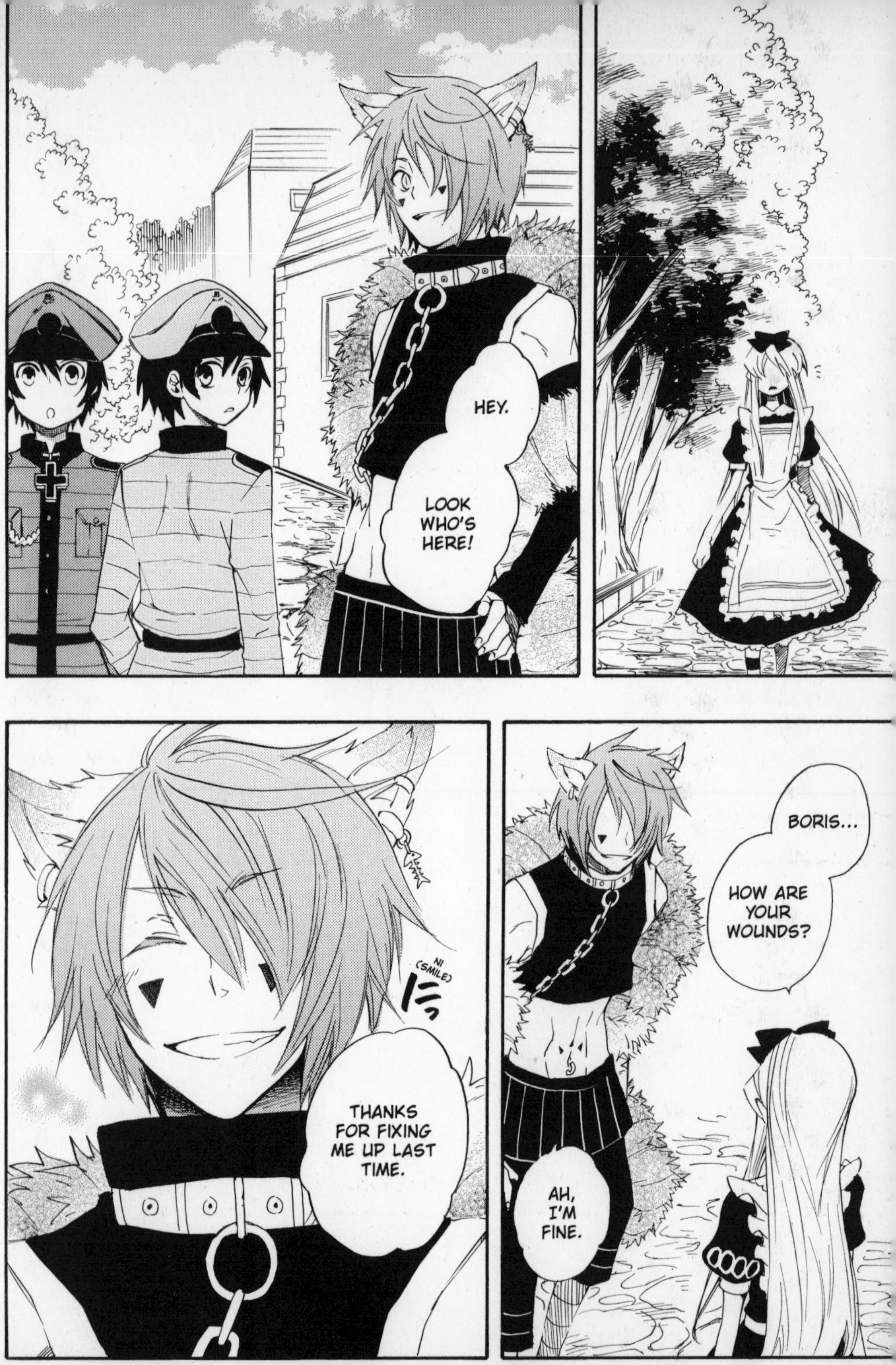
HEY.
LOOK WHO'S HERE!
BORIS...
HOW ARE YOUR WOUNDS?
AH, I'M FINE.
NI (SMILE)
THANKS FOR FIXING ME UP LAST TIME.

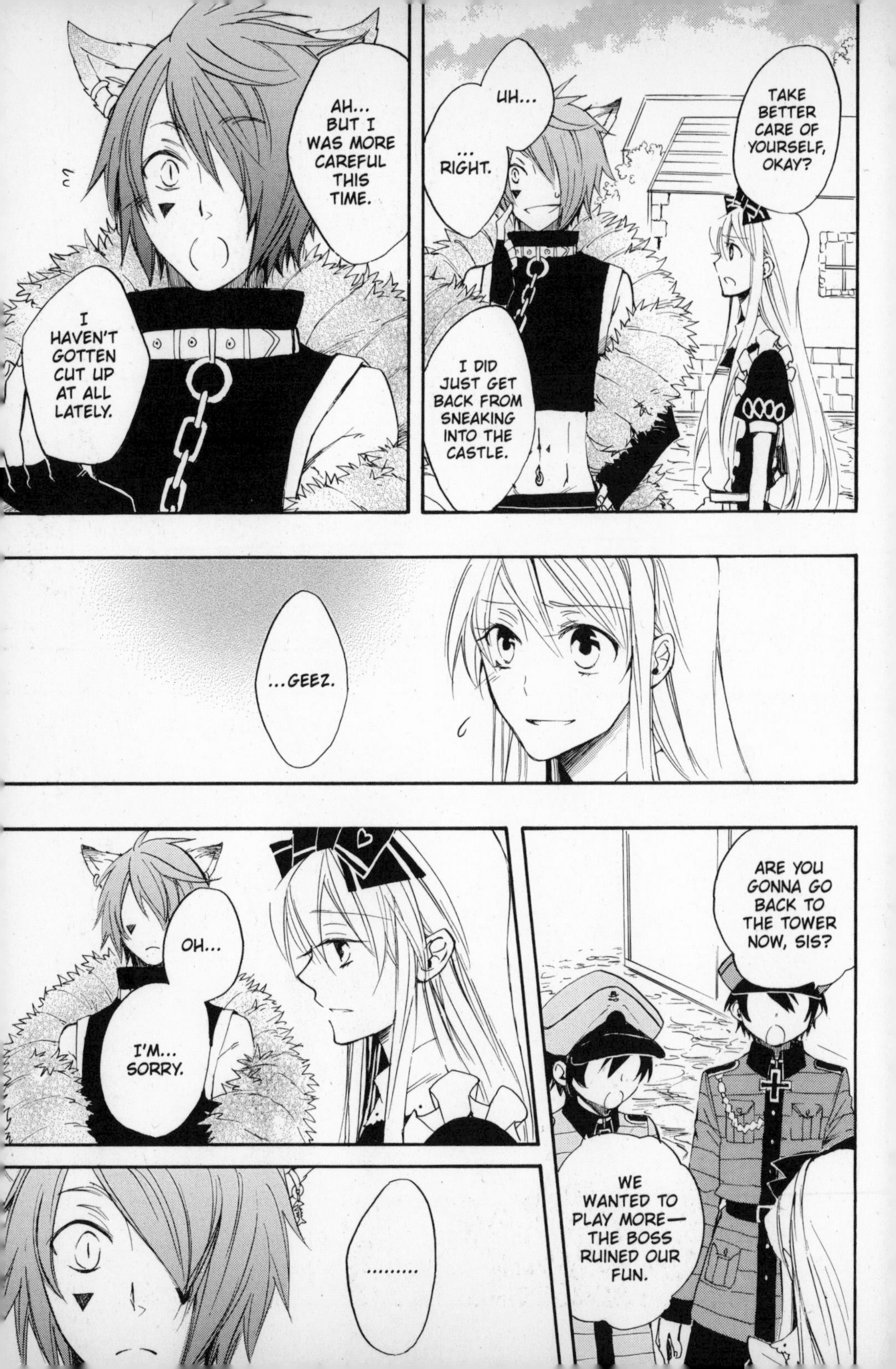
TAKE BETTER CARE OF YOURSELF, OKAY?
UH...
... RIGHT.
I DID JUST GET BACK FROM SNEAKING INTO THE CASTLE.
AH... BUT I WAS MORE CAREFUL THIS TIME.
I HAVEN'T GOTTEN CUT UP AT ALL LATELY.
...GEEZ.
ARE YOU GONNA GO BACK TO THE TOWER NOW, SIS?
WE WANTED TO PLAY MORE— THE BOSS RUINED OUR FUN.
OH...
I'M... SORRY.
....

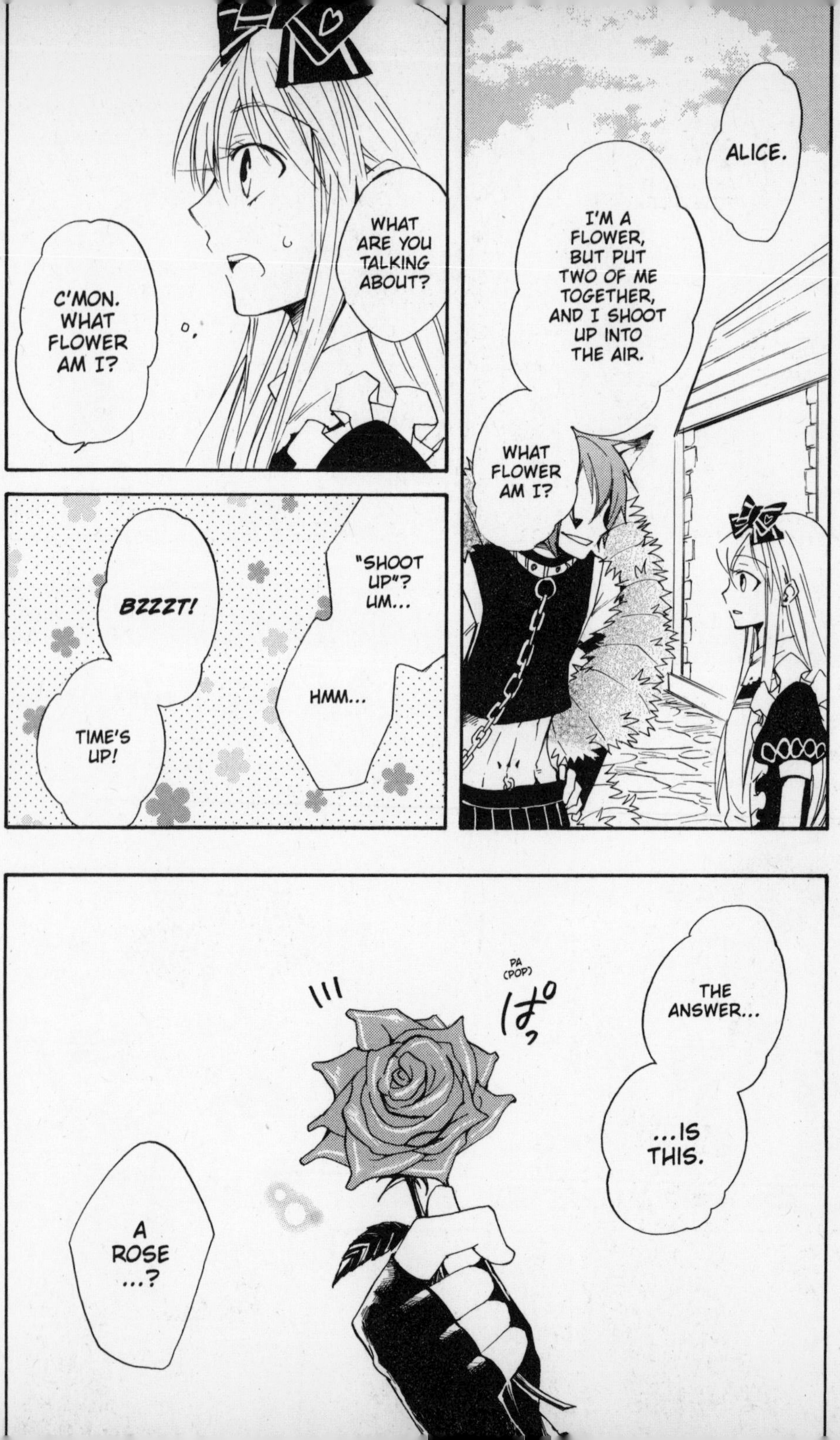
ALICE.
I'M A FLOWER, BUT PUT TWO OF ME TOGETHER, AND I SHOOT UP INTO THE AIR.
WHAT FLOWER AM I?
WHAT ARE YOU TALKING ABOUT?
C'MON. WHAT FLOWER AM I?
"SHOOT UP"? UM...
HMM...
BZZZT!
TIME'S UP!
THE ANSWER...
...IS THIS.
PA (POP)
ぱっ
A ROSE ...?

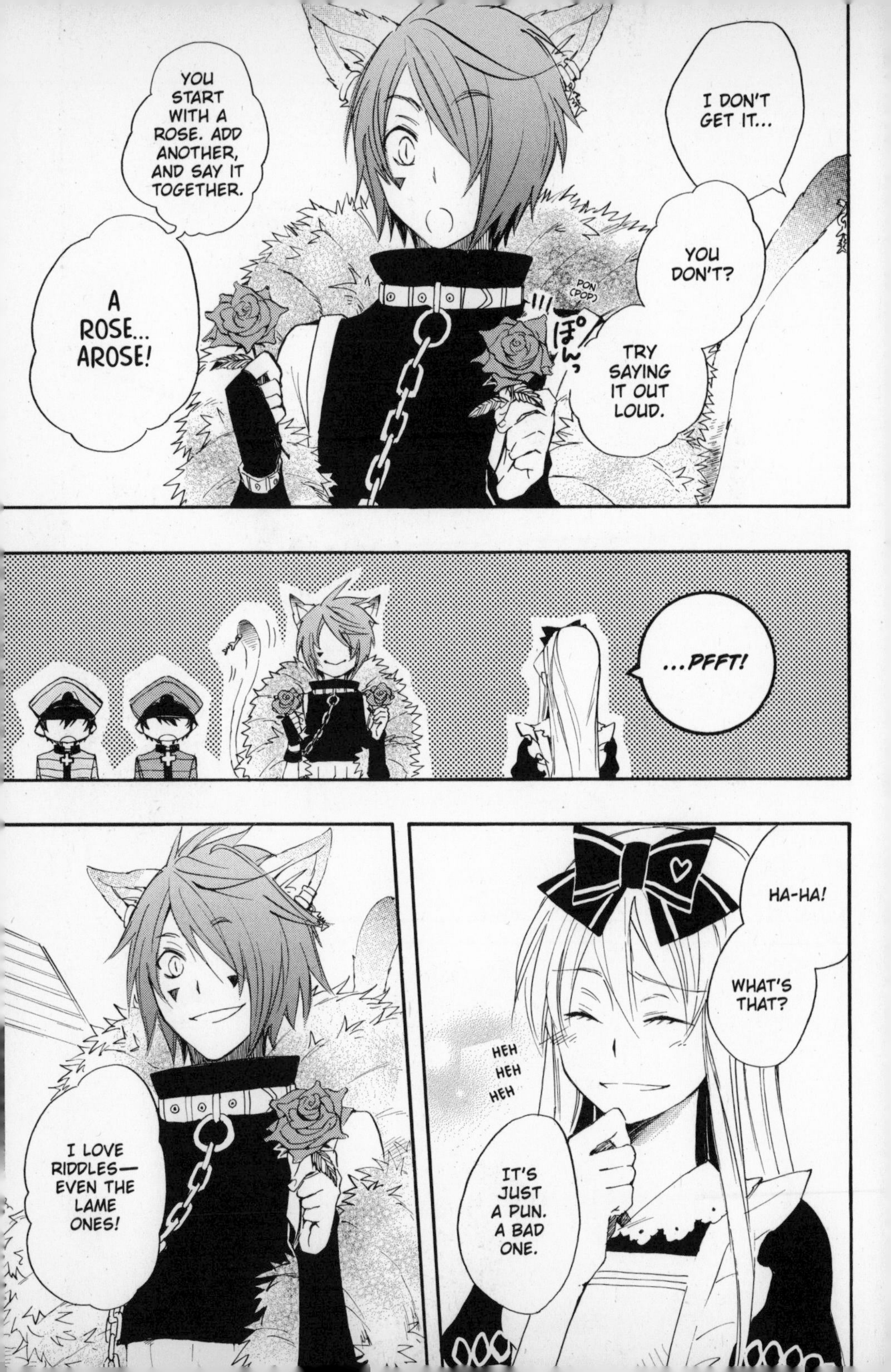
I DON'T GET IT...
YOU DON'T?
PON (POP)
ぽん
TRY SAYING IT OUT LOUD.
YOU START WITH A ROSE. ADD ANOTHER, AND SAY IT TOGETHER.
A ROSE... AROSE!
...PFFT!
HA-HA!
WHAT'S THAT?
HEH HEH HEH
IT'S JUST A PUN. A BAD ONE.
I LOVE RIDDLES—EVEN THE LAME ONES!

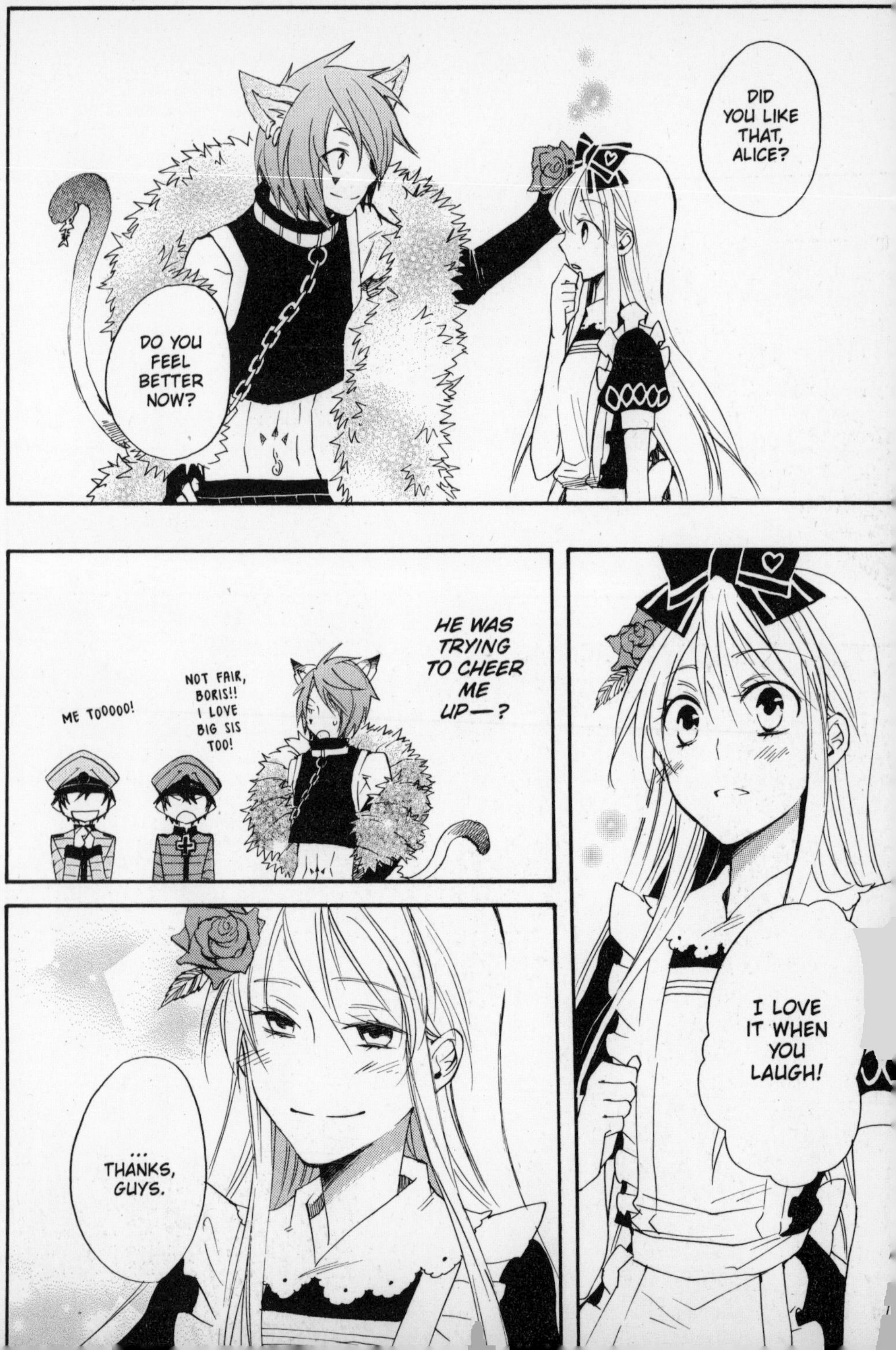
DID YOU LIKE THAT, ALICE?
DO YOU FEEL BETTER NOW?
I LOVE IT WHEN YOU LAUGH!
HE WAS TRYING TO CHEER ME UP—?
NOT FAIR, BORIS!! I LOVE BIG SIS TOO!
ME TOOOOO!
...THANKS, GUYS.

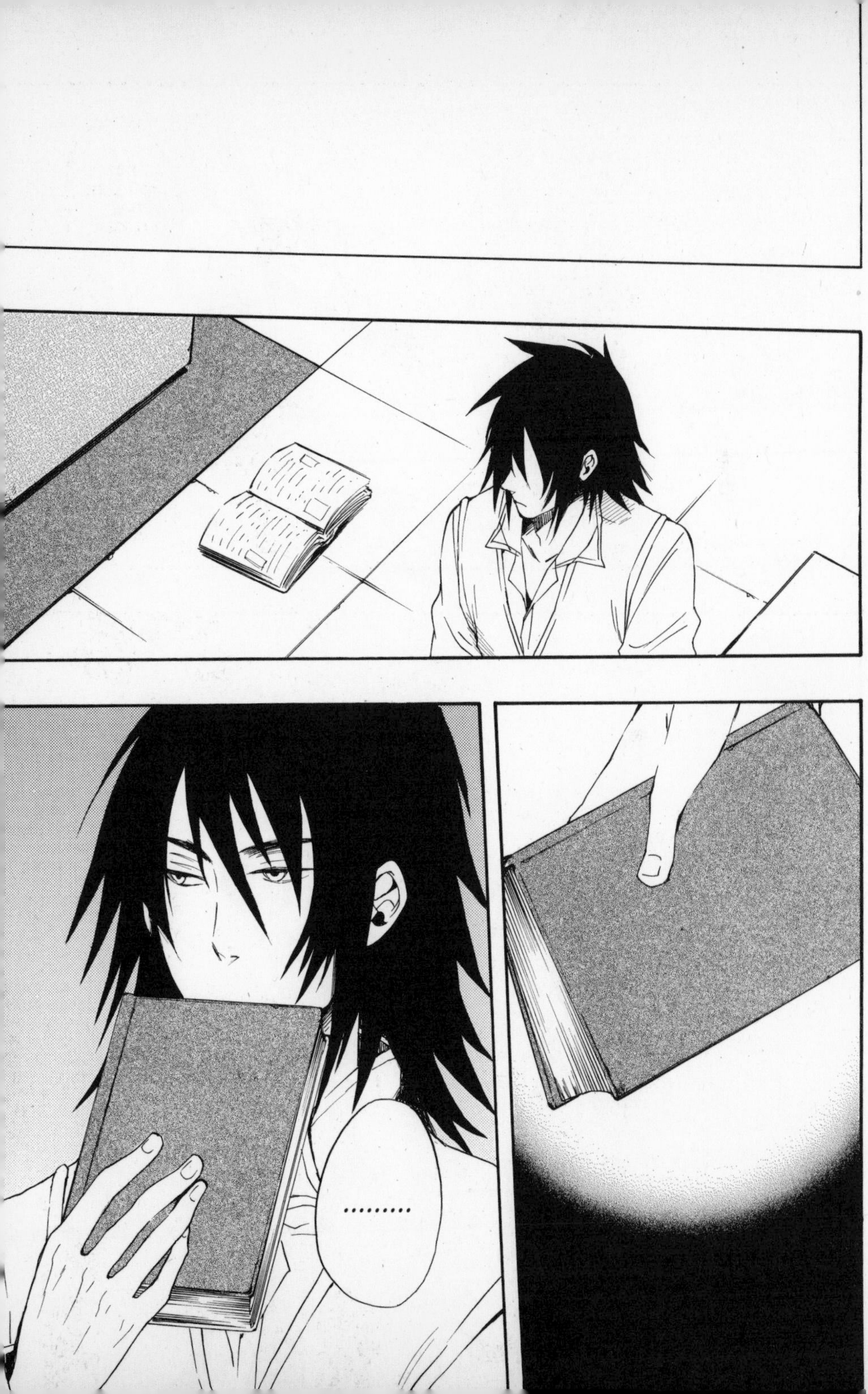
....

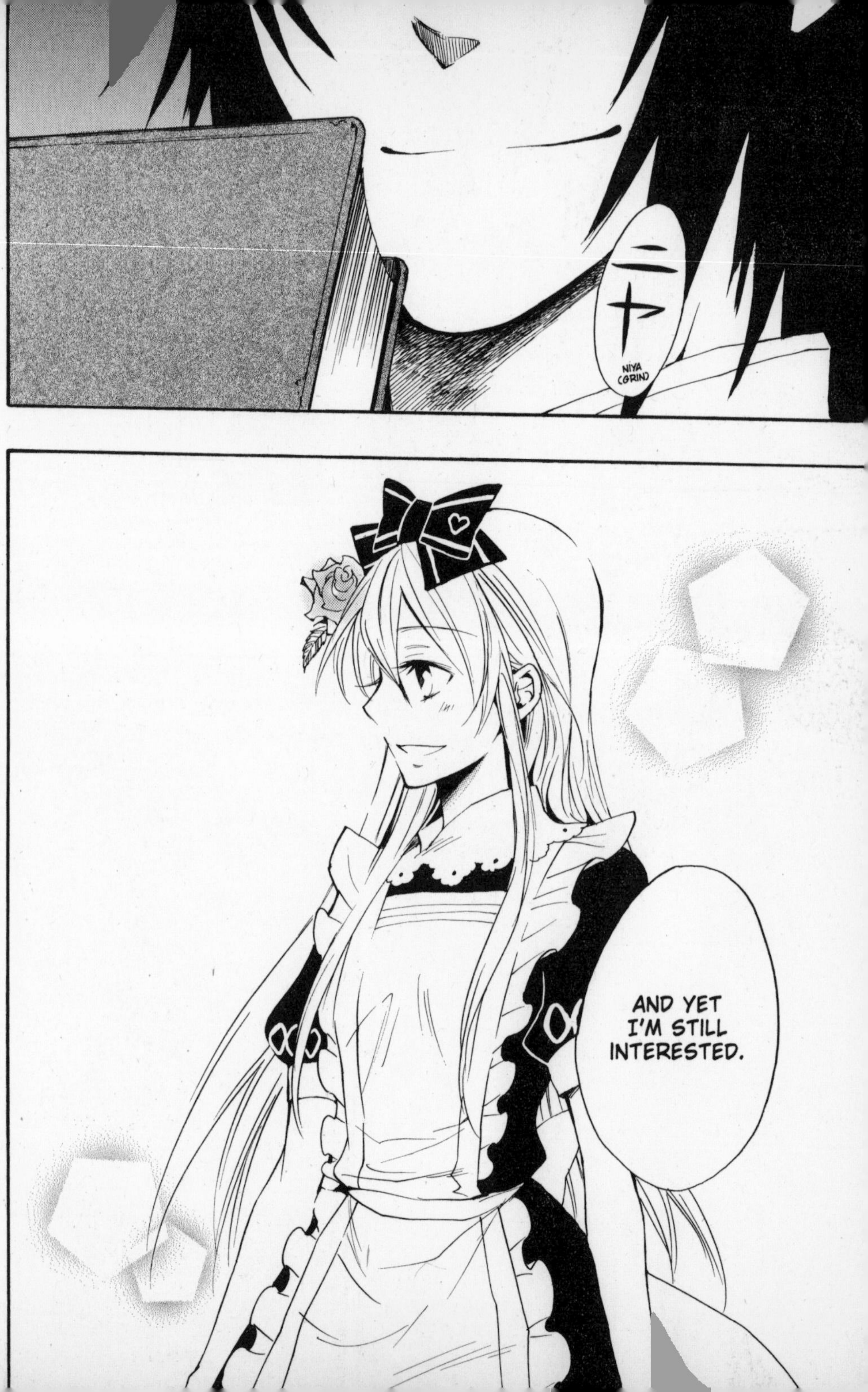
ニヤ
NIYA (GRIN)
AND YET I'M STILL INTERESTED.

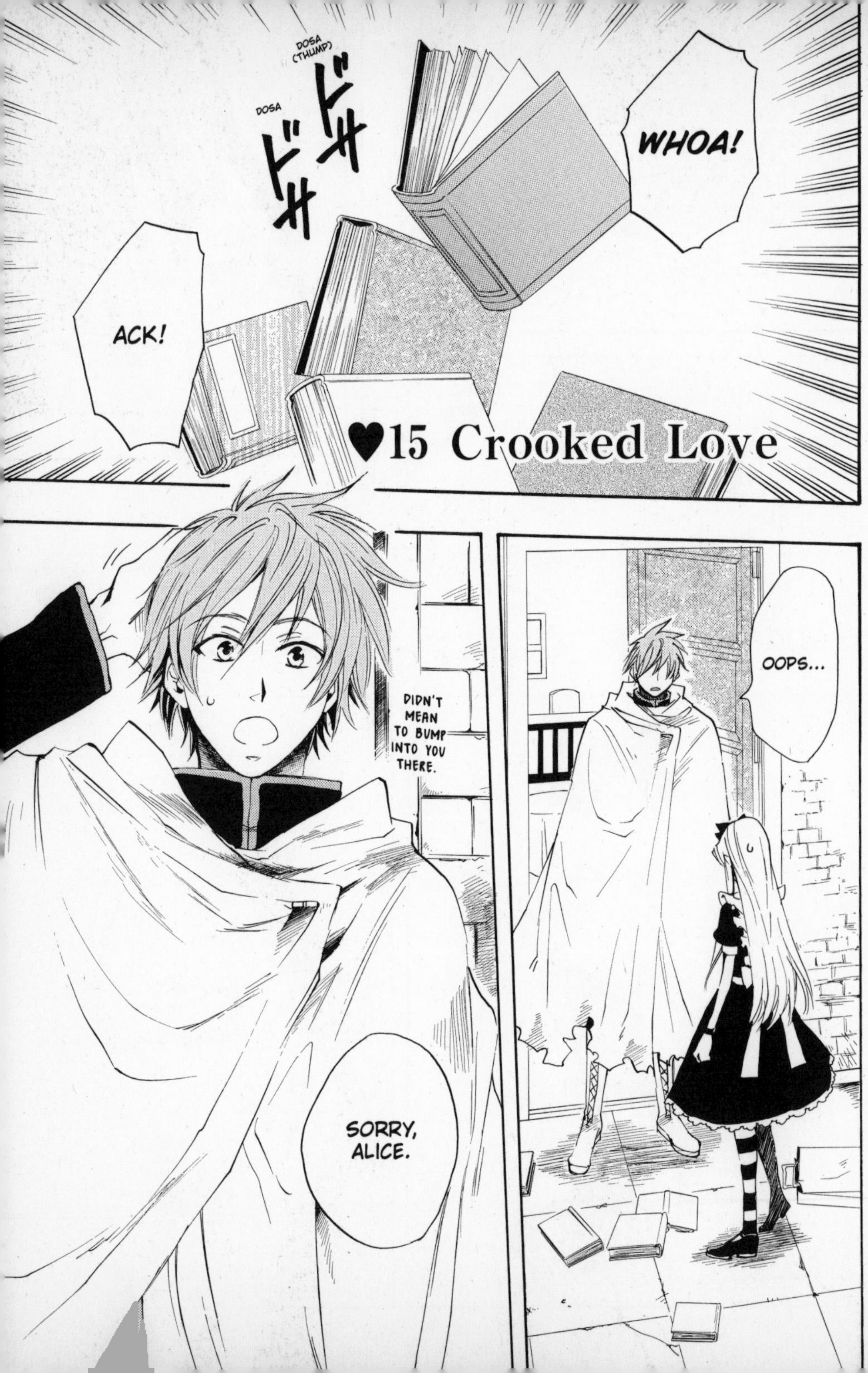
WHOA!
ドサ DOSA (THUMP)
ドサ DOSA
ACK!
♥15 Crooked Love
OOPS...
DIDN'T MEAN TO BUMP INTO YOU THERE.
SORRY, ALICE.

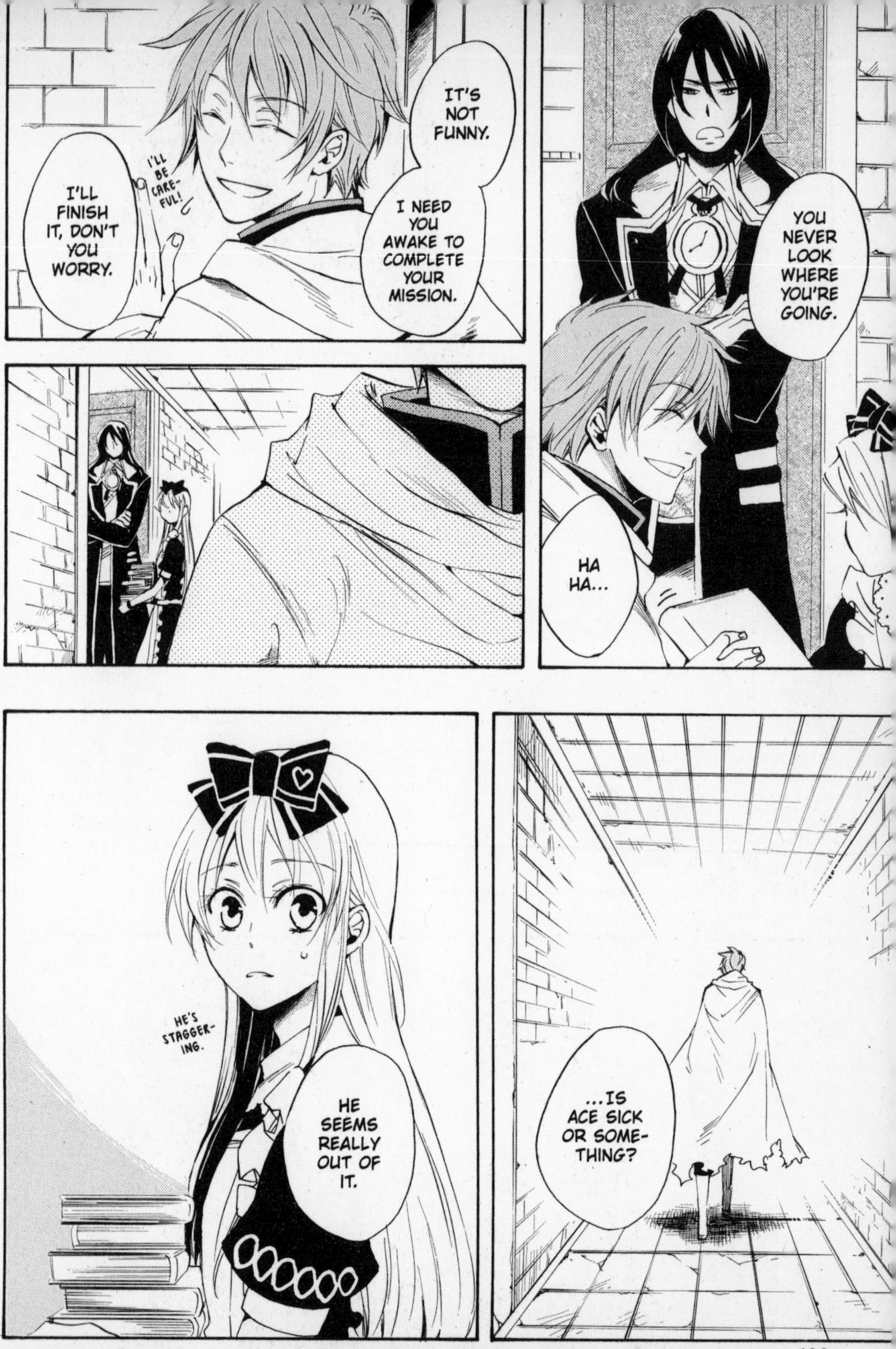
YOU NEVER LOOK WHERE YOU'RE GOING.
HA HA...
IT'S NOT FUNNY.
I NEED YOU AWAKE TO COMPLETE YOUR MISSION.
I'LL BE CARE-FUL!
I'LL FINISH IT, DON'T YOU WORRY.
...IS ACE SICK OR SOME-THING?
HE SEEMS REALLY OUT OF IT.
HE'S STAGGER-ING.

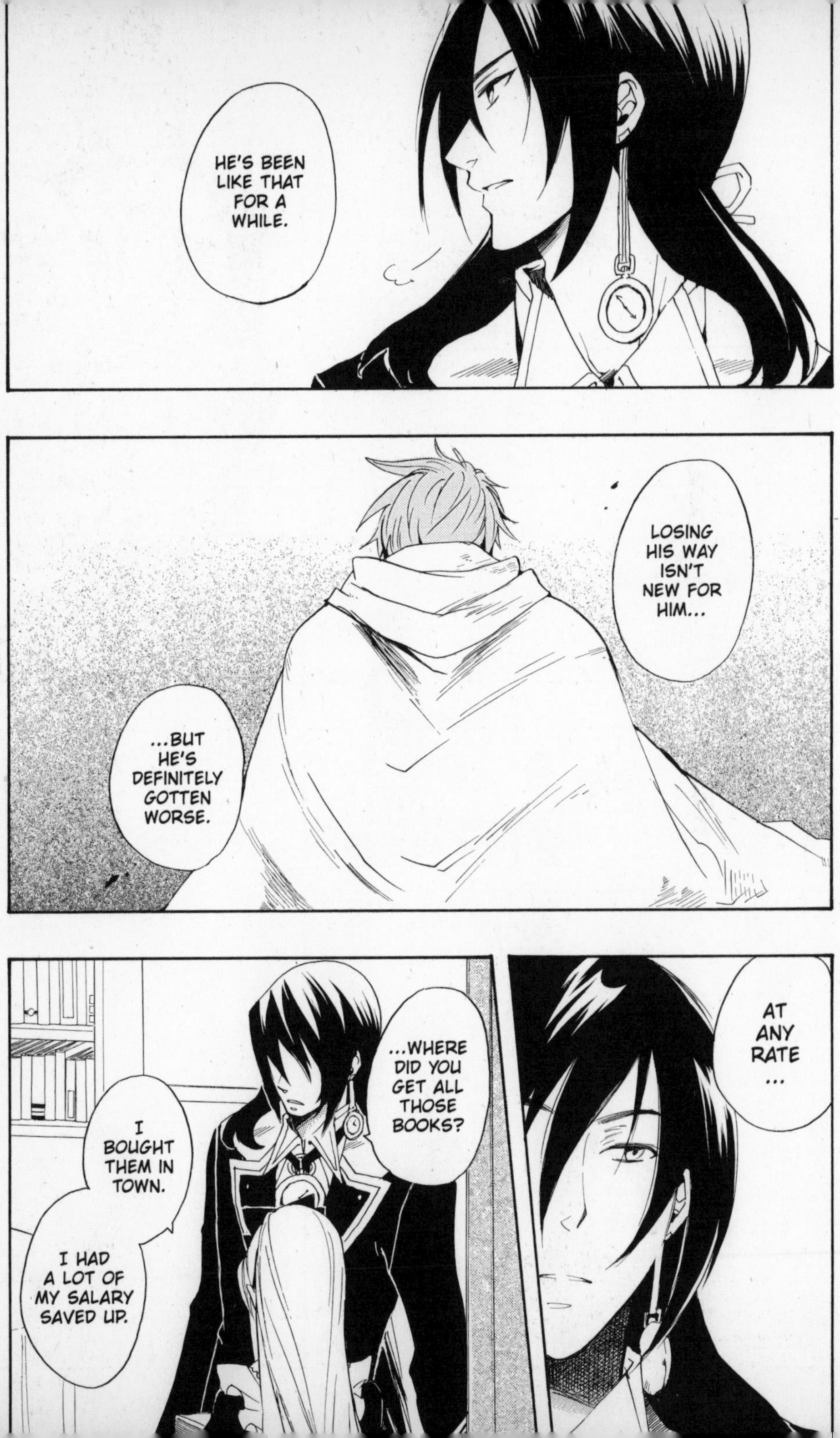
HE'S BEEN LIKE THAT FOR A WHILE.
LOSING HIS WAY ISN'T NEW FOR HIM...
...BUT HE'S DEFINITELY GOTTEN WORSE.
AT ANY RATE...
...WHERE DID YOU GET ALL THOSE BOOKS?
I BOUGHT THEM IN TOWN.
I HAD A LOT OF MY SALARY SAVED UP.

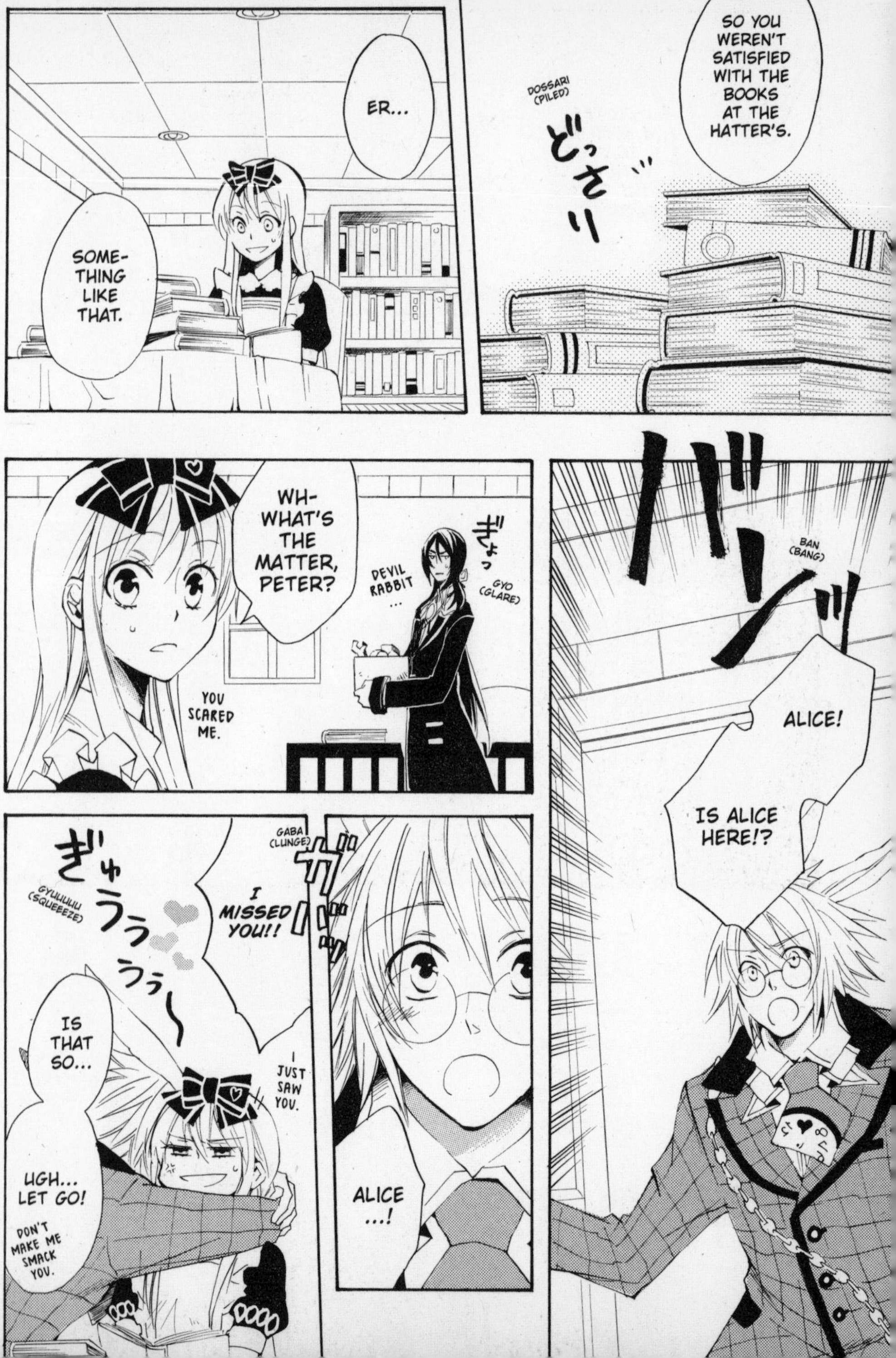
SO YOU WEREN'T SATISFIED WITH THE BOOKS AT THE HATTER'S.
どっさり
DOSSARI (PILED)
ER...
SOME-THING LIKE THAT.
バンッ
BAN (BANG)
ALICE!
IS ALICE HERE!?
WH-WHAT'S THE MATTER, PETER?
ぎょっ
GYO (GLARE)
DEVIL RABBIT ...
YOU SCARED ME.
ALICE ...!
ガバッ
GABA (LUNGE)
I MISSED YOU!!
ぎゅうううう~
GYUUUUU (SQUEEEZE)
IS THAT SO...
I JUST SAW YOU.
UGH... LET GO!
DON'T MAKE ME SMACK YOU.

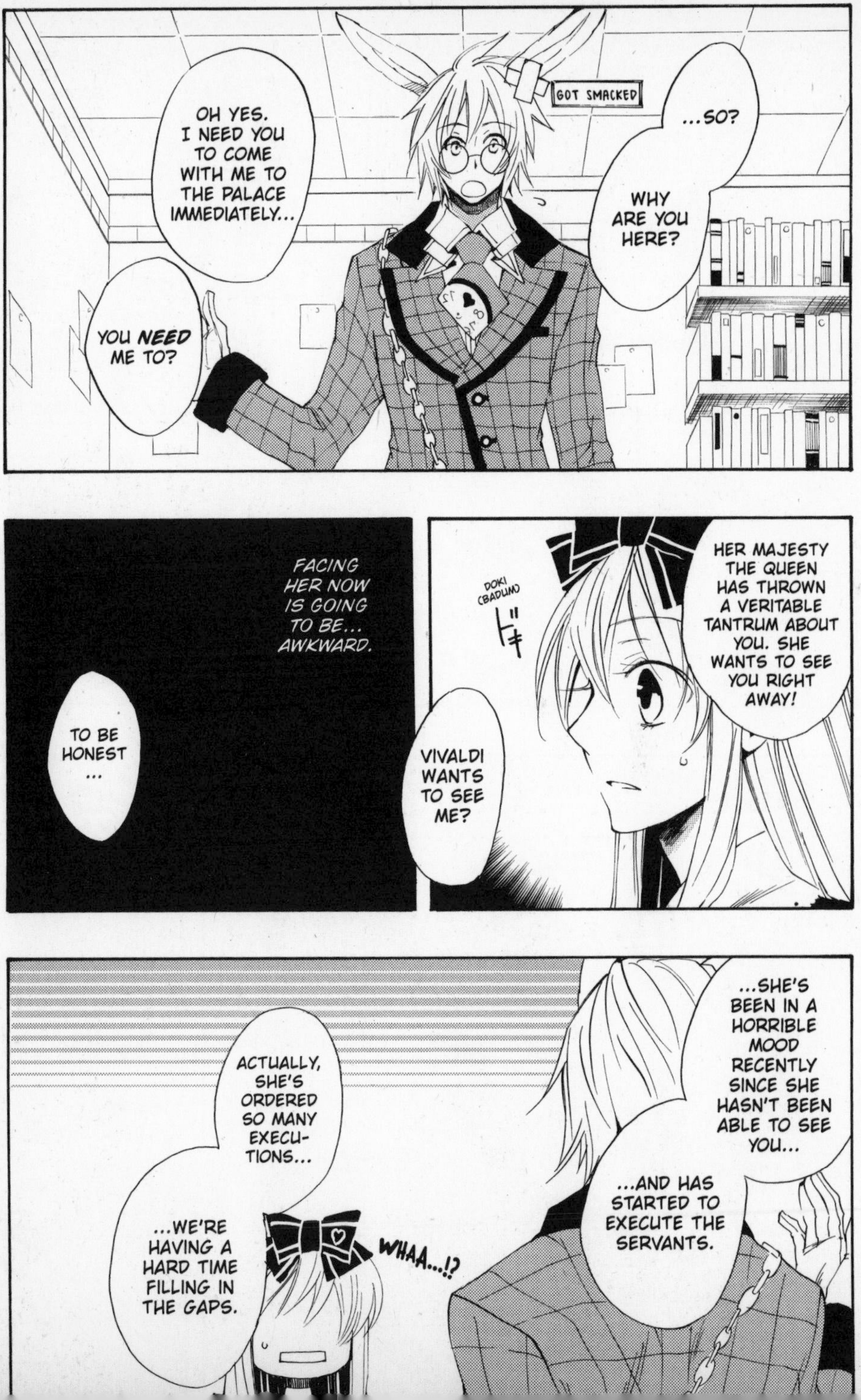
...SO?
WHY ARE YOU HERE?
GOT SMACKED
OH YES. I NEED YOU TO COME WITH ME TO THE PALACE IMMEDIATELY...
YOU NEED ME TO?
HER MAJESTY THE QUEEN HAS THROWN A VERITABLE TANTRUM ABOUT YOU. SHE WANTS TO SEE YOU RIGHT AWAY!
DOKI (BADUM)
VIVALDI WANTS TO SEE ME?
FACING HER NOW IS GOING TO BE... AWKWARD.
TO BE HONEST ...
...SHE'S BEEN IN A HORRIBLE MOOD RECENTLY SINCE SHE HASN'T BEEN ABLE TO SEE YOU...
...AND HAS STARTED TO EXECUTE THE SERVANTS.
ACTUALLY, SHE'S ORDERED SO MANY EXECUTIONS...
WHAA...!?
...WE'RE HAVING A HARD TIME FILLING IN THE GAPS.

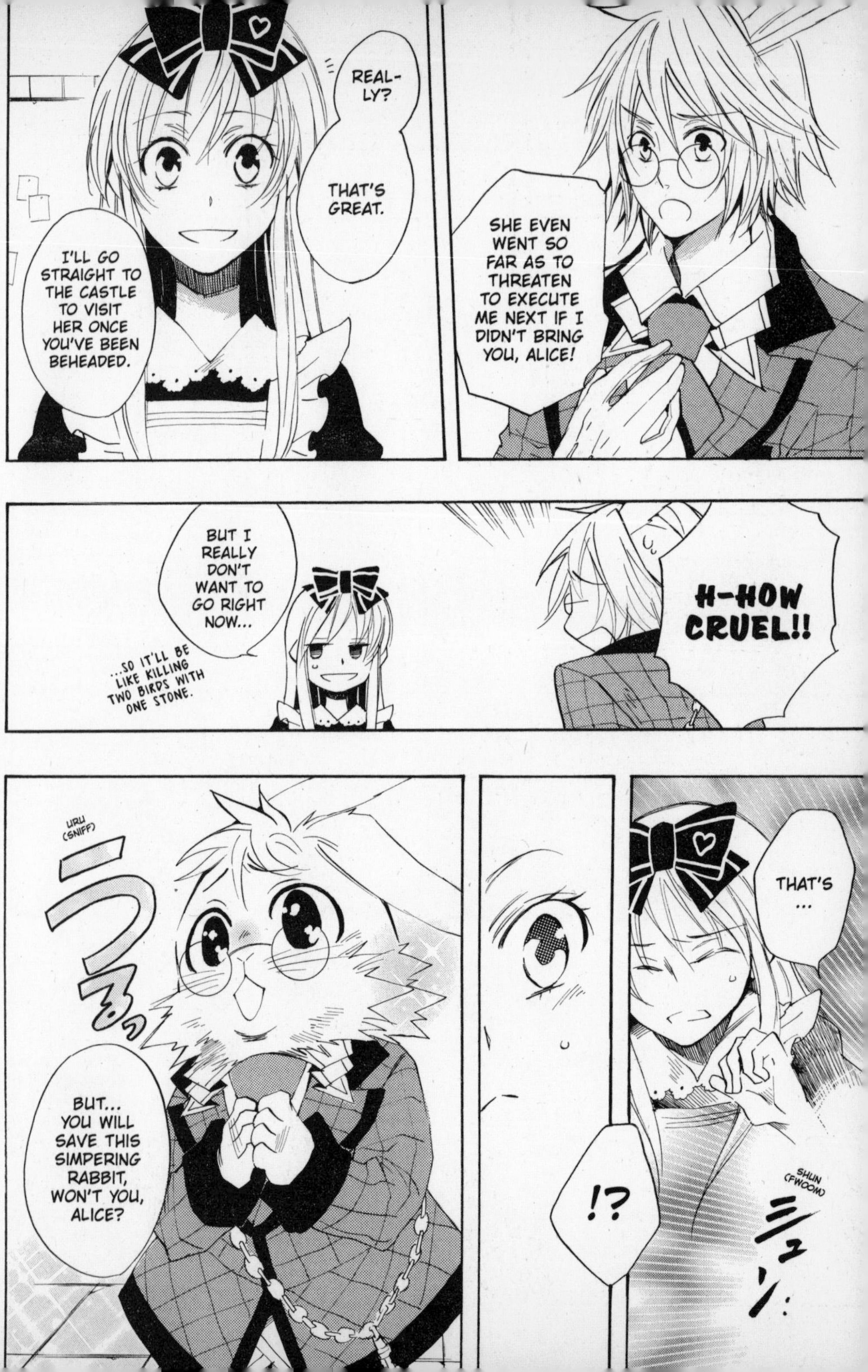
SHE EVEN WENT SO FAR AS TO THREATEN TO EXECUTE ME NEXT IF I DIDN'T BRING YOU, ALICE!
REAL-LY?
THAT'S GREAT.
I'LL GO STRAIGHT TO THE CASTLE TO VISIT HER ONCE YOU'VE BEEN BEHEADED.
H-HOW CRUEL!!
BUT I REALLY DON'T WANT TO GO RIGHT NOW...
...SO IT'LL BE LIKE KILLING TWO BIRDS WITH ONE STONE.
THAT'S ...
シュン
SHUN (FWOOM)
!?
うるっ
URU (SNIFF)
BUT... YOU WILL SAVE THIS SIMPERING RABBIT, WON'T YOU, ALICE?

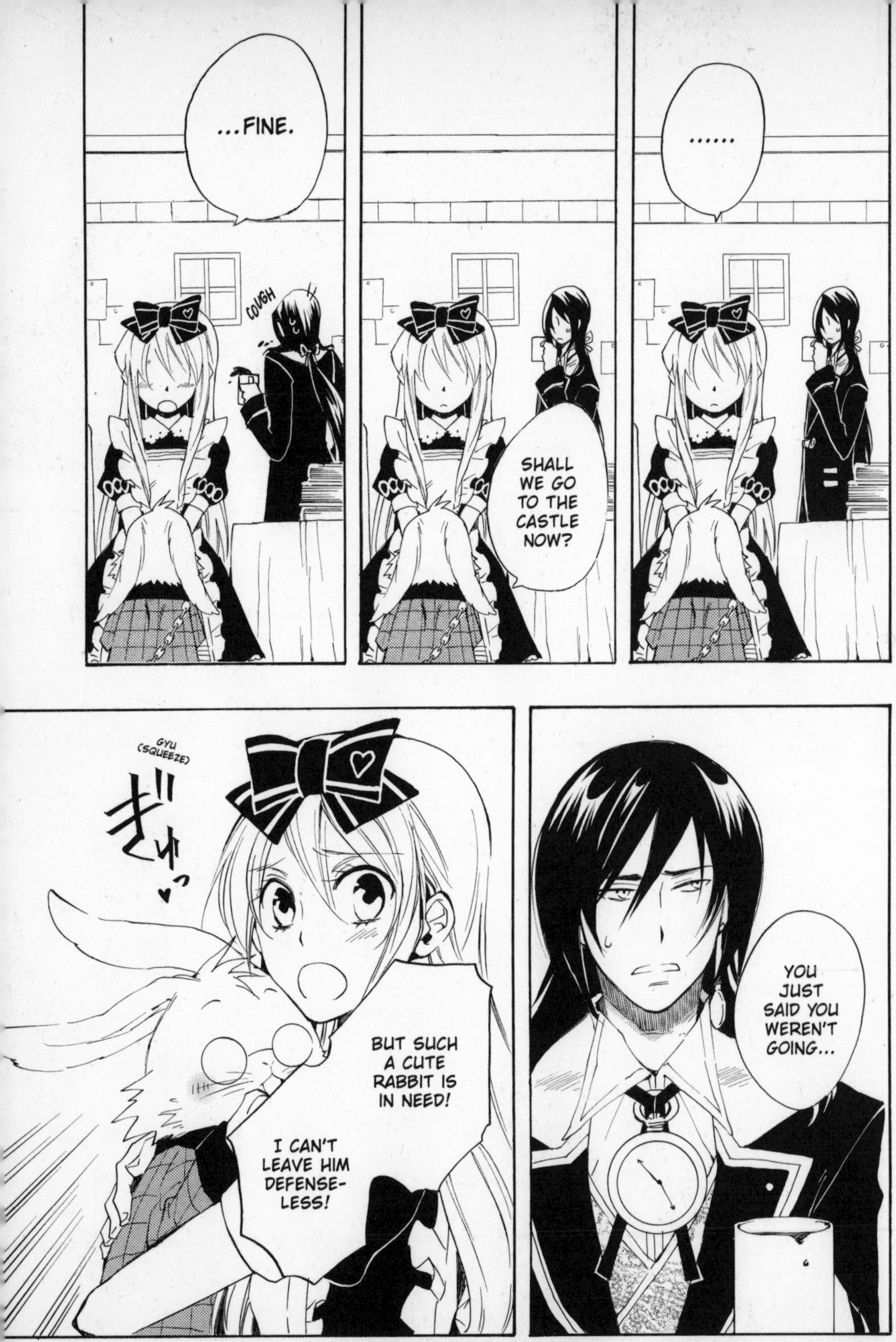
......
SHALL WE GO TO THE CASTLE NOW?
...FINE.
COUGH
YOU JUST SAID YOU WEREN'T GOING...
GYU (SQUEEZE)
ぎゅっ
BUT SUCH A CUTE RABBIT IS IN NEED!
I CAN'T LEAVE HIM DEFENSE-LESS!

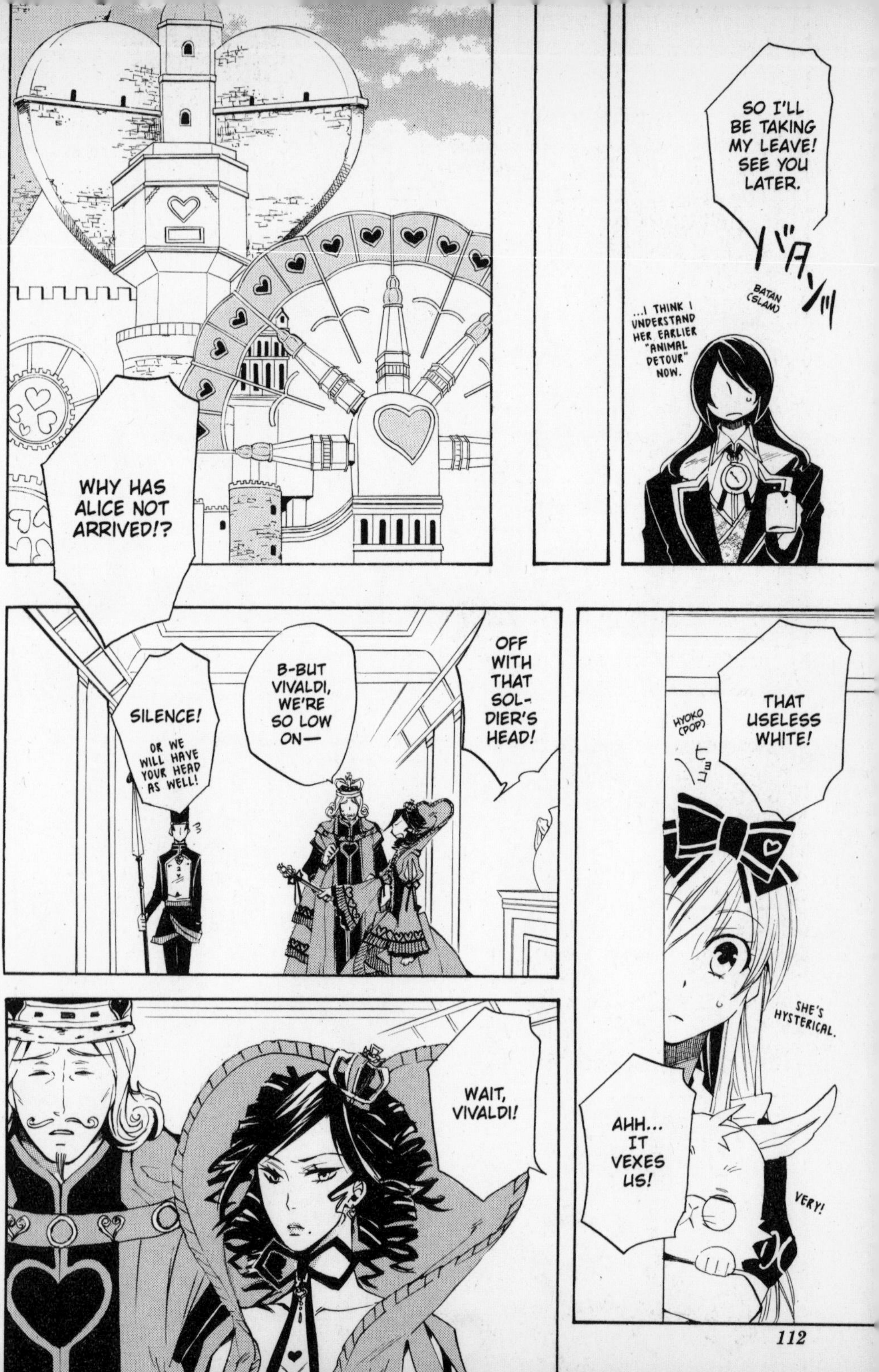
SO I'LL BE TAKING MY LEAVE! SEE YOU LATER.
バタンッ
BATAN (SLAM)
...I THINK I UNDERSTAND HER EARLIER "ANIMAL DETOUR" NOW.
WHY HAS ALICE NOT ARRIVED!?
THAT USELESS WHITE!
HYOKO (POP)
ヒョコ
SHE'S HYSTERICAL.
AHH... IT VEXES US!
VERY!
OFF WITH THAT SOL-DIER'S HEAD!
B-BUT VIVALDI, WE'RE SO LOW ON—
SILENCE!
OR WE WILL HAVE YOUR HEAD AS WELL!
WAIT, VIVALDI!

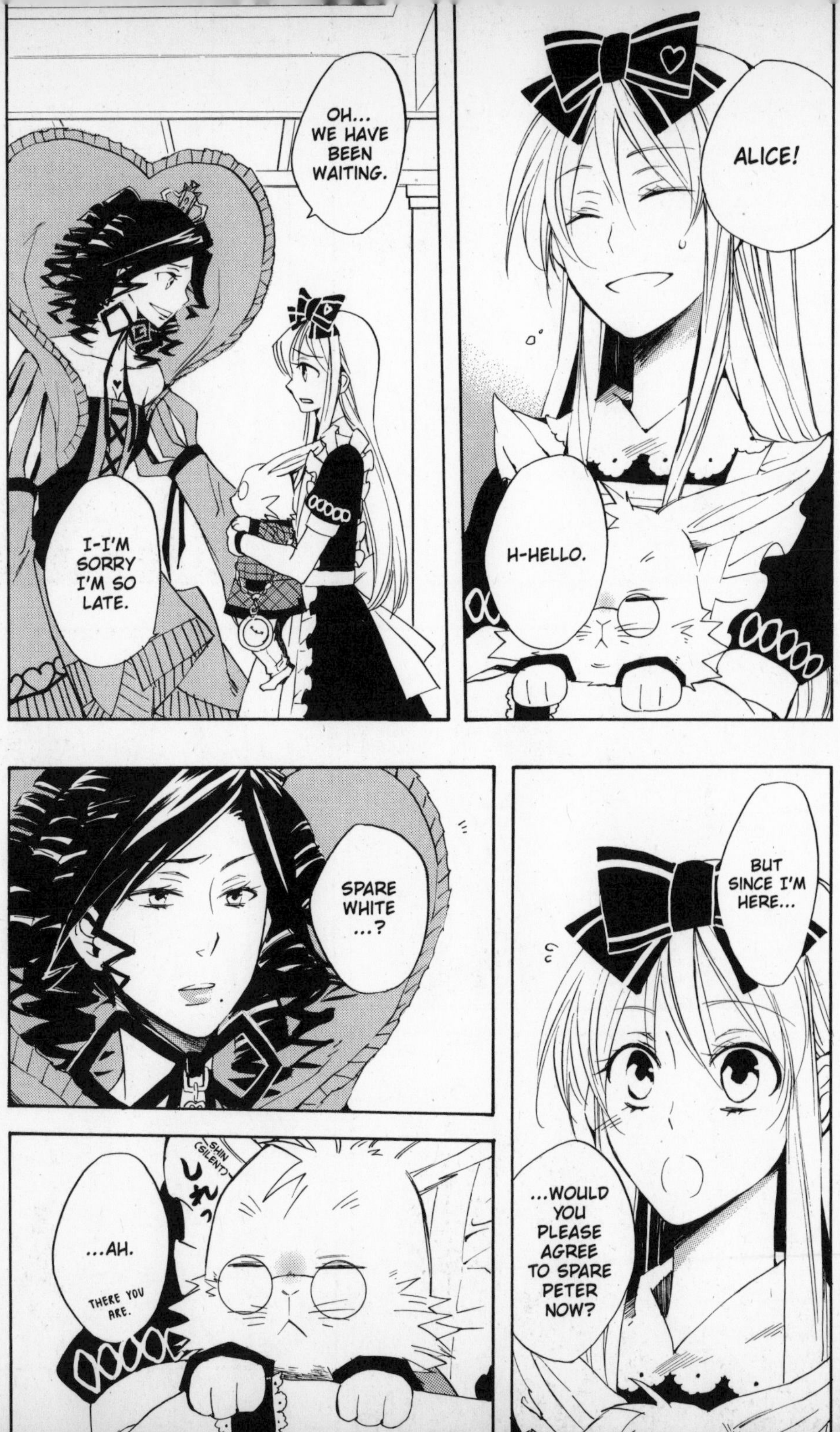
ALICE!
H-HELLO.
OH... WE HAVE BEEN WAITING.
I-I'M SORRY I'M SO LATE.
BUT SINCE I'M HERE...
...WOULD YOU PLEASE AGREE TO SPARE PETER NOW?
SPARE WHITE ...?
SHIN (SILENT)
しれっ
...AH.
THERE YOU ARE.

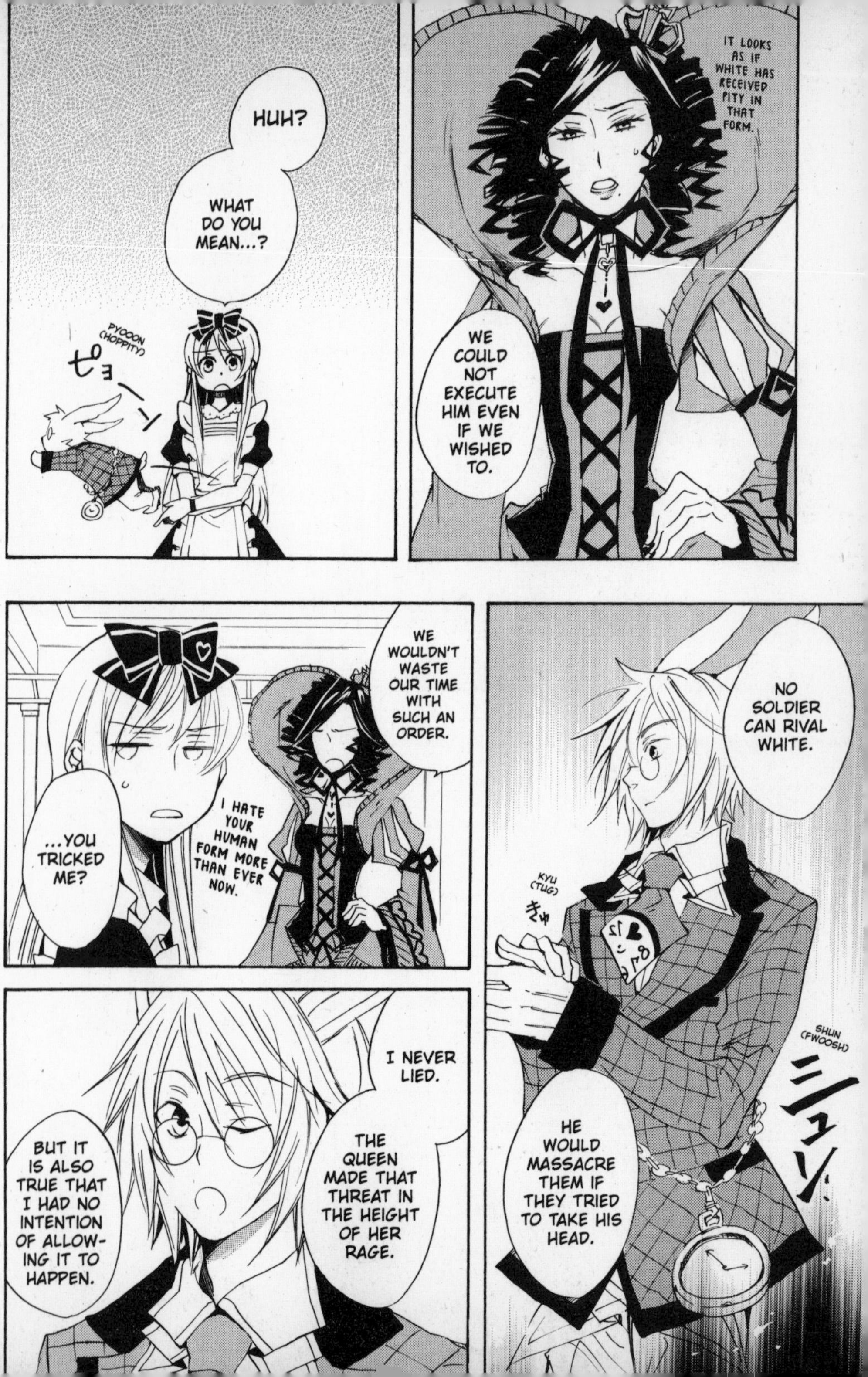
IT LOOKS AS IF WHITE HAS RECEIVED PITY IN THAT FORM.
WE COULD NOT EXECUTE HIM EVEN IF WE WISHED TO.
HUH?
WHAT DO YOU MEAN...?
ピョーン
PYOOON (HOPPITY)
NO SOLDIER CAN RIVAL WHITE.
きゅ
KYU (TUG)
HE WOULD MASSACRE THEM IF THEY TRIED TO TAKE HIS HEAD.
シュン
SHUN (FWOOSH)
WE WOULDN'T WASTE OUR TIME WITH SUCH AN ORDER.
I HATE YOUR HUMAN FORM MORE THAN EVER NOW.
...YOU TRICKED ME?
I NEVER LIED.
THE QUEEN MADE THAT THREAT IN THE HEIGHT OF HER RAGE.
BUT IT IS ALSO TRUE THAT I HAD NO INTENTION OF ALLOW-ING IT TO HAPPEN.

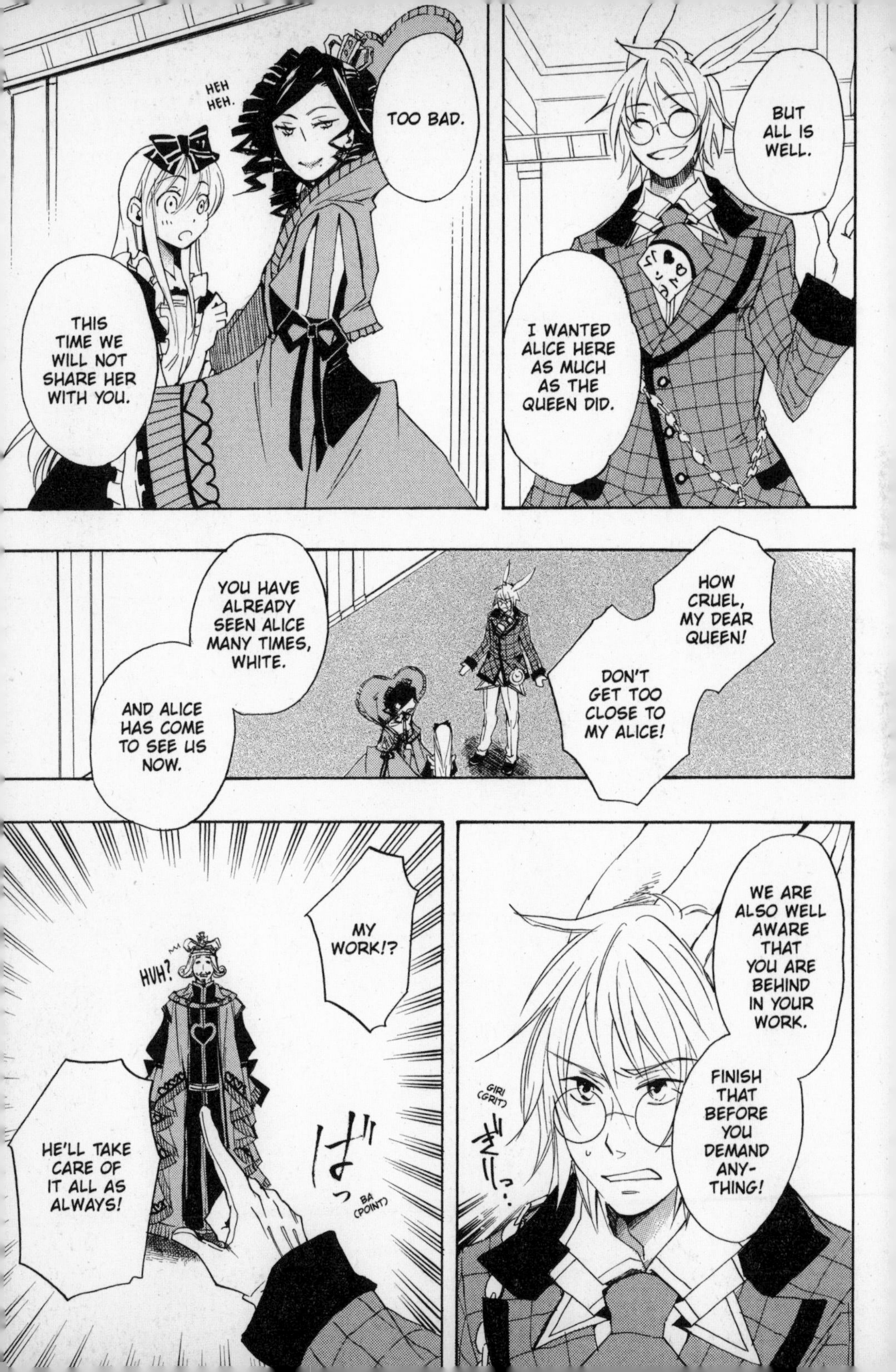
BUT ALL IS WELL.
I WANTED ALICE HERE AS MUCH AS THE QUEEN DID.
TOO BAD.
HEH HEH.
THIS TIME WE WILL NOT SHARE HER WITH YOU.
HOW CRUEL, MY DEAR QUEEN!
DON'T GET TOO CLOSE TO MY ALICE!
YOU HAVE ALREADY SEEN ALICE MANY TIMES, WHITE.
AND ALICE HAS COME TO SEE US NOW.
WE ARE ALSO WELL AWARE THAT YOU ARE BEHIND IN YOUR WORK.
FINISH THAT BEFORE YOU DEMAND ANY-THING!
GIRI (GRIT)
MY WORK!?
HUH?
BA (POINT)
HE'LL TAKE CARE OF IT ALL AS ALWAYS!

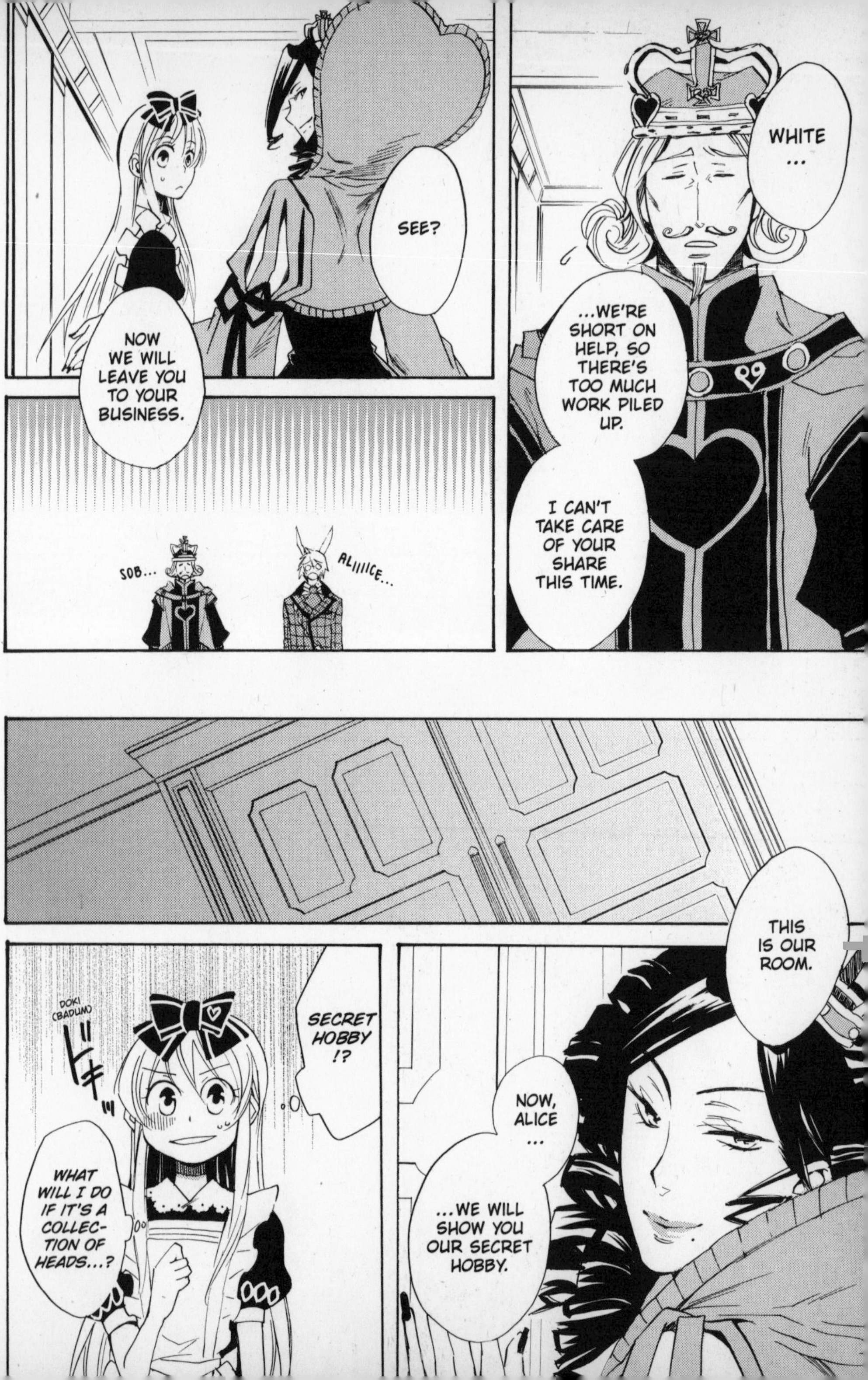
WHITE ...
...WE'RE SHORT ON HELP, SO THERE'S TOO MUCH WORK PILED UP.
I CAN'T TAKE CARE OF YOUR SHARE THIS TIME.
SEE?
NOW WE WILL LEAVE YOU TO YOUR BUSINESS.
ALIIIICE...
SOB...
THIS IS OUR ROOM.
NOW, ALICE ...
...WE WILL SHOW YOU OUR SECRET HOBBY.
SECRET HOBBY !?
DOKI (BADUM)
ドキッ
WHAT WILL I DO IF IT'S A COLLEC-TION OF HEADS...?

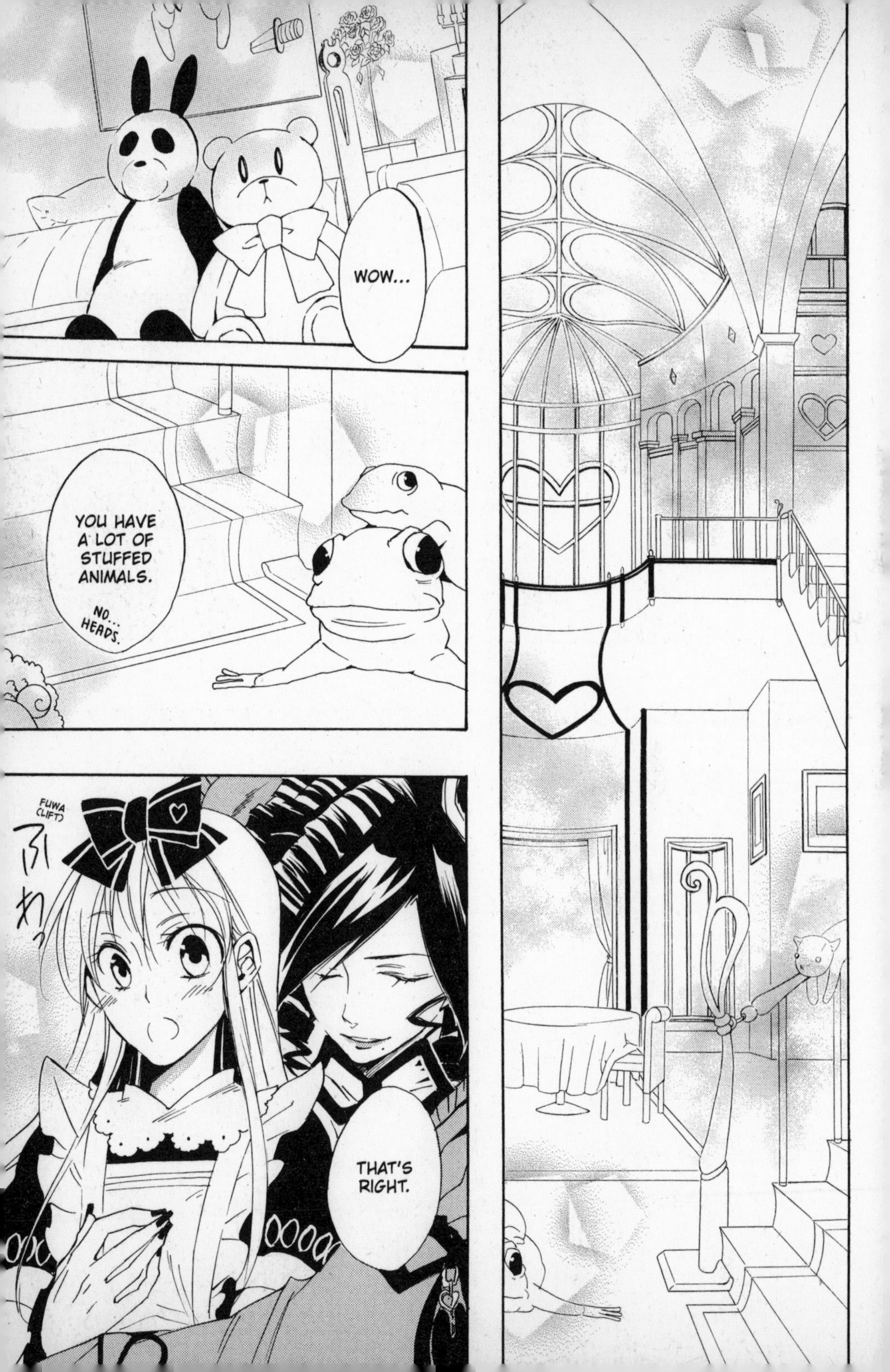
WOW...
YOU HAVE A LOT OF STUFFED ANIMALS.
NO... HEADS.
FUWA (LIFT)
ふわっ
THAT'S RIGHT.

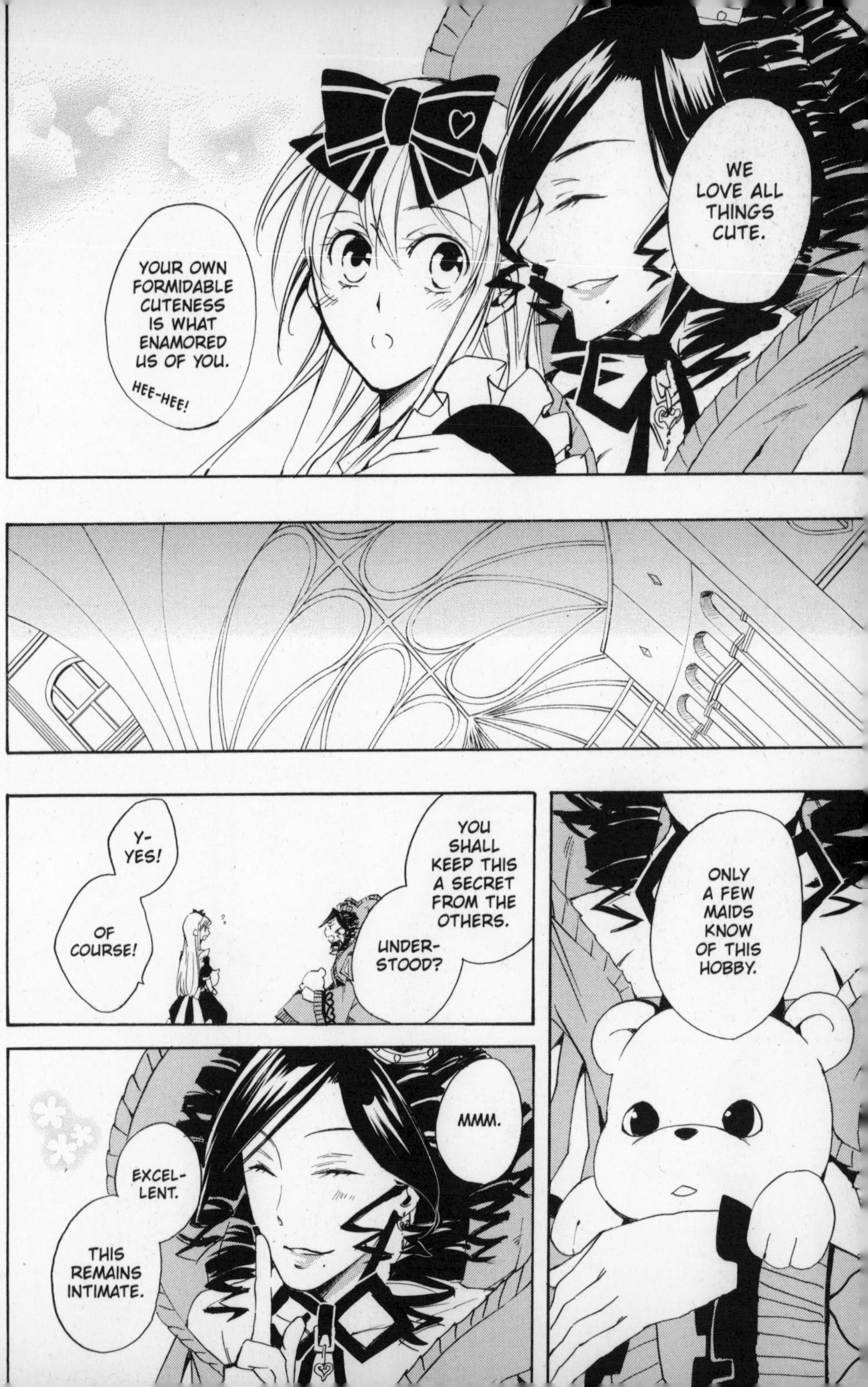

WE LOVE ALL THINGS CUTE.
YOUR OWN FORMIDABLE CUTENESS IS WHAT ENAMORED US OF YOU.
HEE-HEE!
ONLY A FEW MAIDS KNOW OF THIS HOBBY.
YOU SHALL KEEP THIS A SECRET FROM THE OTHERS.
UNDER-STOOD?
Y-YES!
OF COURSE!
MMM.
EXCEL-LENT.
THIS REMAINS INTIMATE.

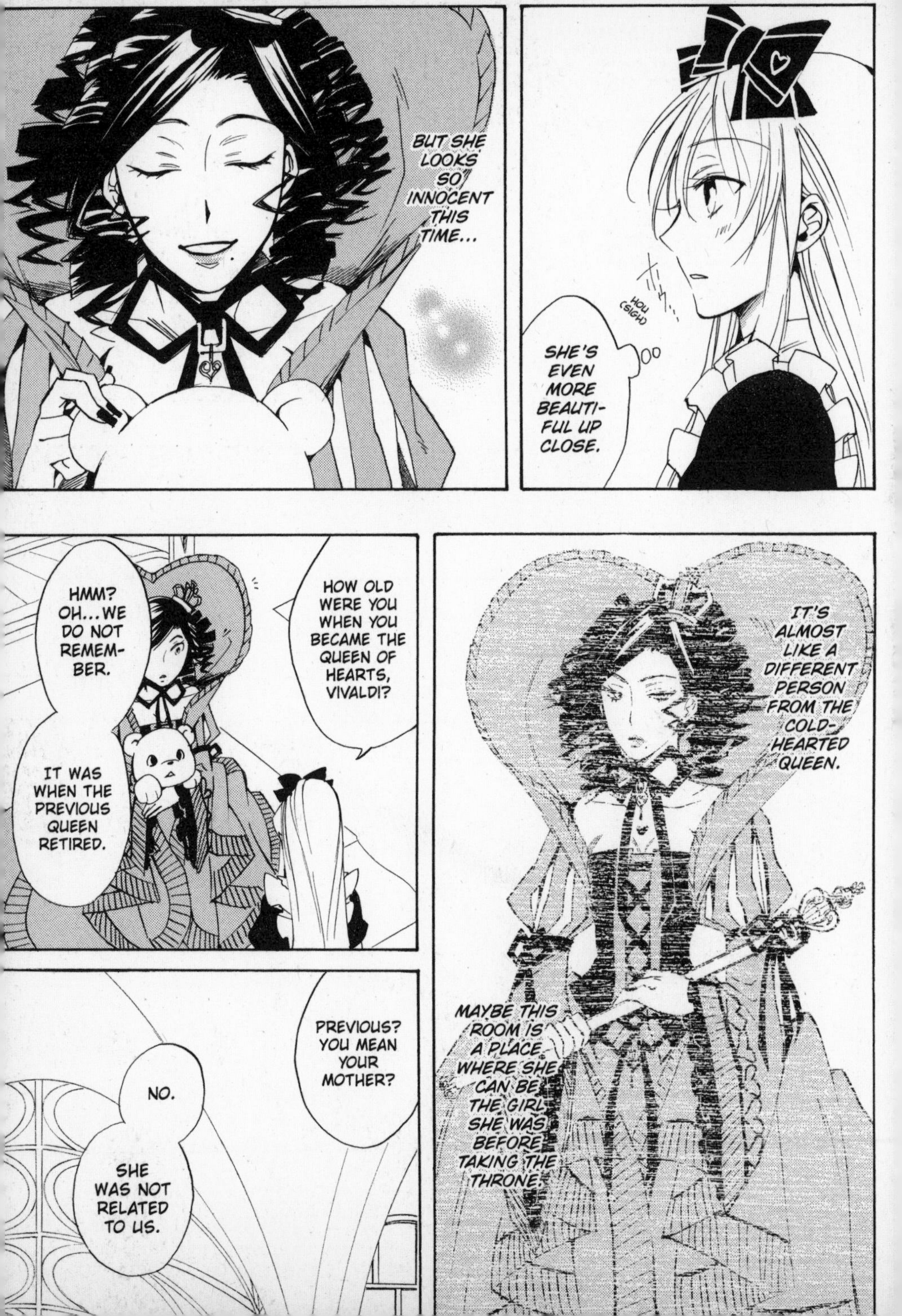
HOU (SIGH)
SHE'S EVEN MORE BEAUTI-FUL UP CLOSE.
BUT SHE LOOKS SO INNOCENT THIS TIME...
IT'S ALMOST LIKE A DIFFERENT PERSON FROM THE COLD-HEARTED QUEEN.
MAYBE THIS ROOM IS A PLACE WHERE SHE CAN BE THE GIRL SHE WAS BEFORE TAKING THE THRONE.
HOW OLD WERE YOU WHEN YOU BECAME THE QUEEN OF HEARTS, VIVALDI?
HMM? OH...WE DO NOT REMEM-BER.
IT WAS WHEN THE PREVIOUS QUEEN RETIRED.
PREVIOUS? YOU MEAN YOUR MOTHER?
NO.
SHE WAS NOT RELATED TO US.

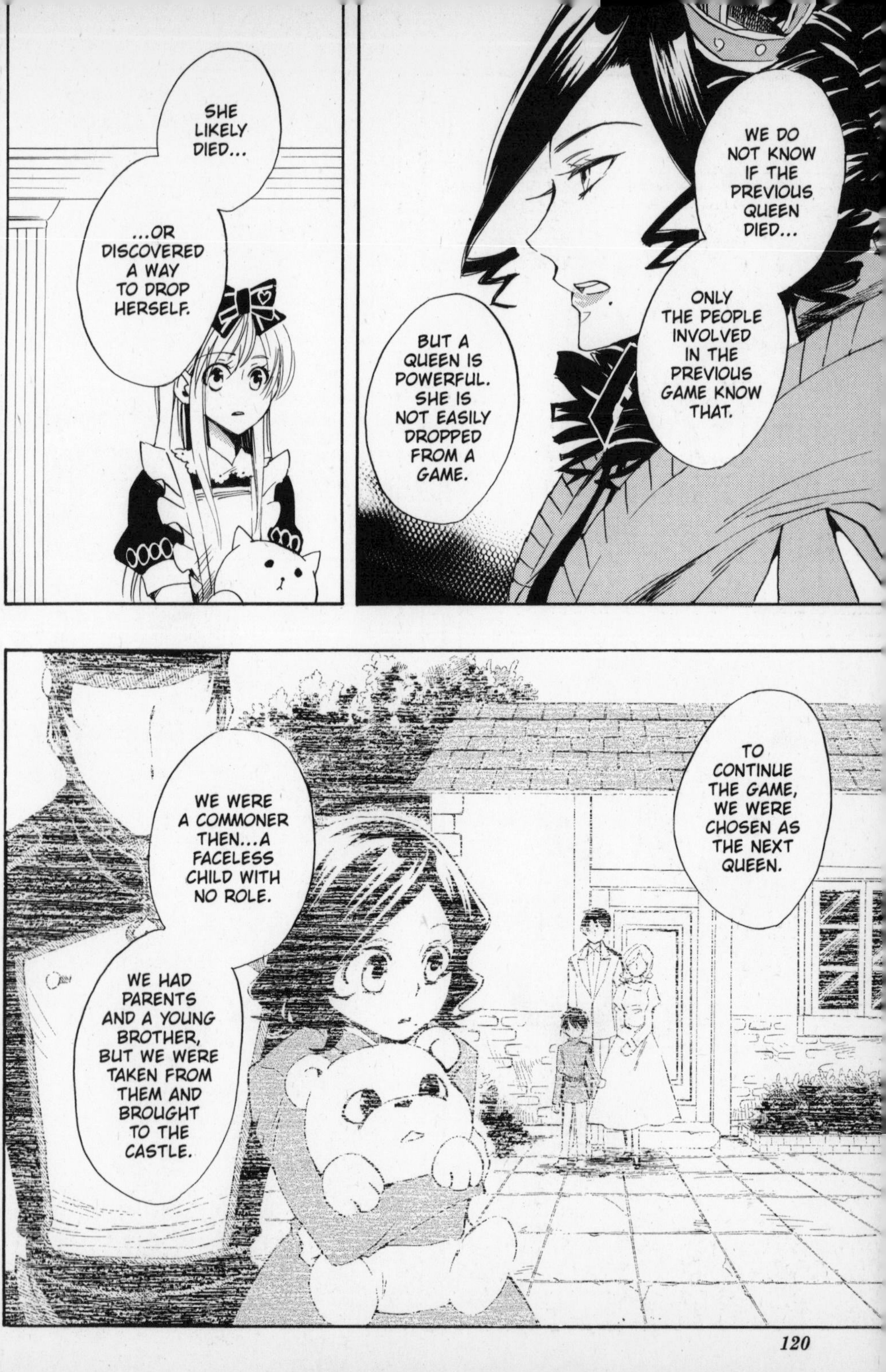
WE DO NOT KNOW IF THE PREVIOUS QUEEN DIED...
ONLY THE PEOPLE INVOLVED IN THE PREVIOUS GAME KNOW THAT.
BUT A QUEEN IS POWERFUL. SHE IS NOT EASILY DROPPED FROM A GAME.
SHE LIKELY DIED...
...OR DISCOVERED A WAY TO DROP HERSELF.
TO CONTINUE THE GAME, WE WERE CHOSEN AS THE NEXT QUEEN.
WE WERE A COMMONER THEN...A FACELESS CHILD WITH NO ROLE.
WE HAD PARENTS AND A YOUNG BROTHER, BUT WE WERE TAKEN FROM THEM AND BROUGHT TO THE CASTLE.

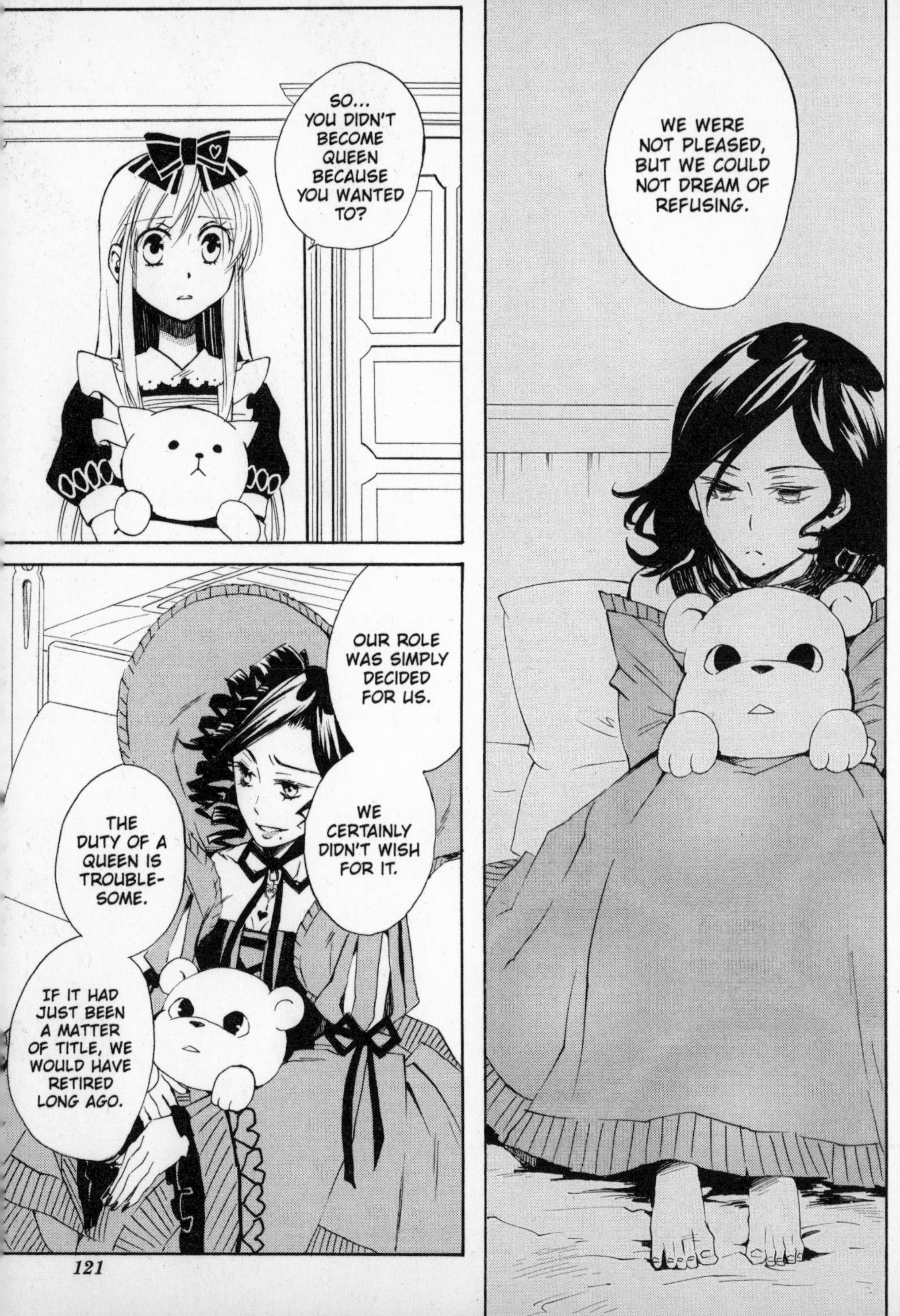
WE WERE NOT PLEASED, BUT WE COULD NOT DREAM OF REFUSING.
SO... YOU DIDN'T BECOME QUEEN BECAUSE YOU WANTED TO?
OUR ROLE WAS SIMPLY DECIDED FOR US.
WE CERTAINLY DIDN'T WISH FOR IT.
THE DUTY OF A QUEEN IS TROUBLE-SOME.
IF IT HAD JUST BEEN A MATTER OF TITLE, WE WOULD HAVE RETIRED LONG AGO.

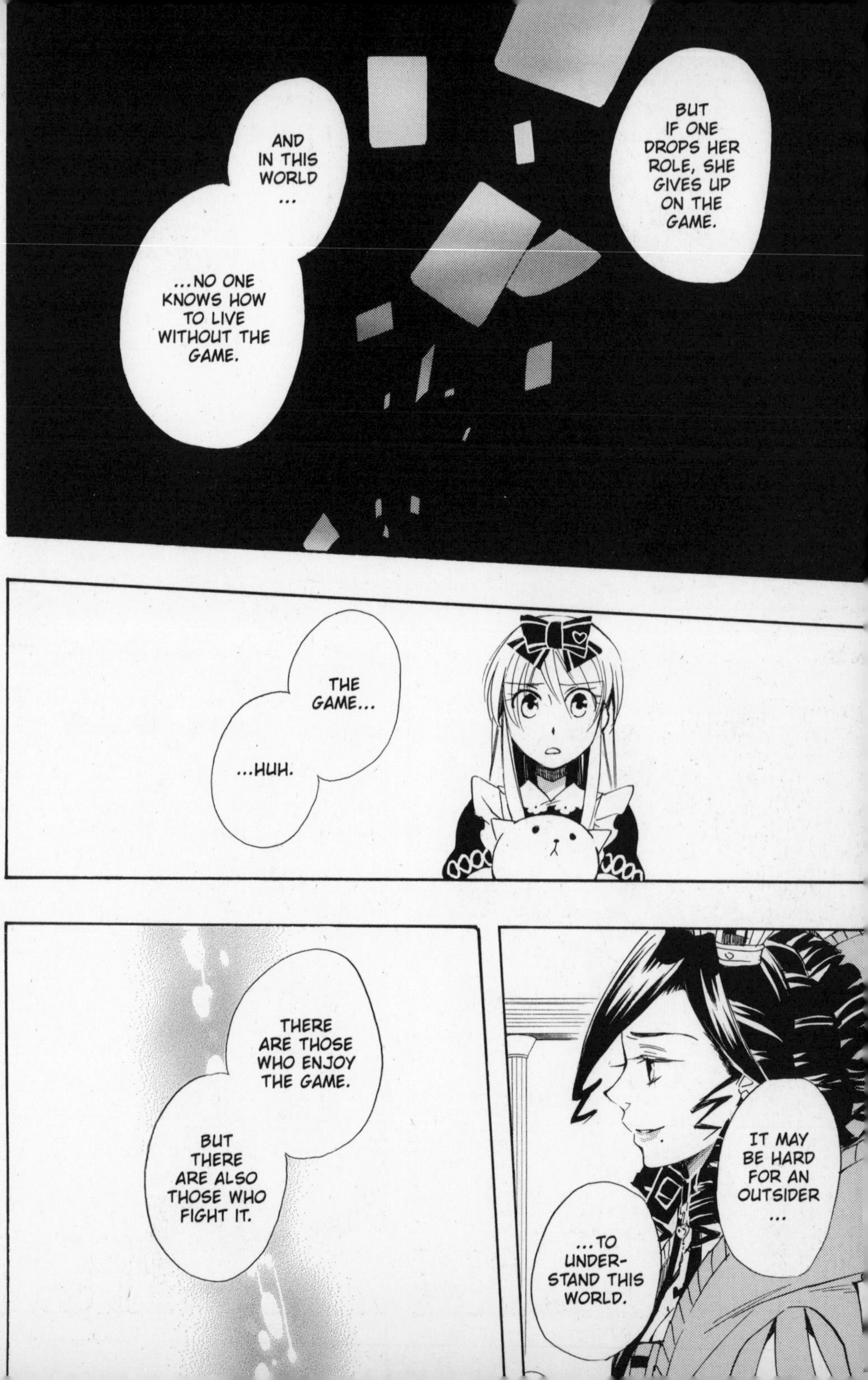
BUT IF ONE DROPS HER ROLE, SHE GIVES UP ON THE GAME.
AND IN THIS WORLD...
...NO ONE KNOWS HOW TO LIVE WITHOUT THE GAME.
THE GAME...
...HUH.
IT MAY BE HARD FOR AN OUTSIDER...
...TO UNDER-STAND THIS WORLD.
THERE ARE THOSE WHO ENJOY THE GAME.
BUT THERE ARE ALSO THOSE WHO FIGHT IT.

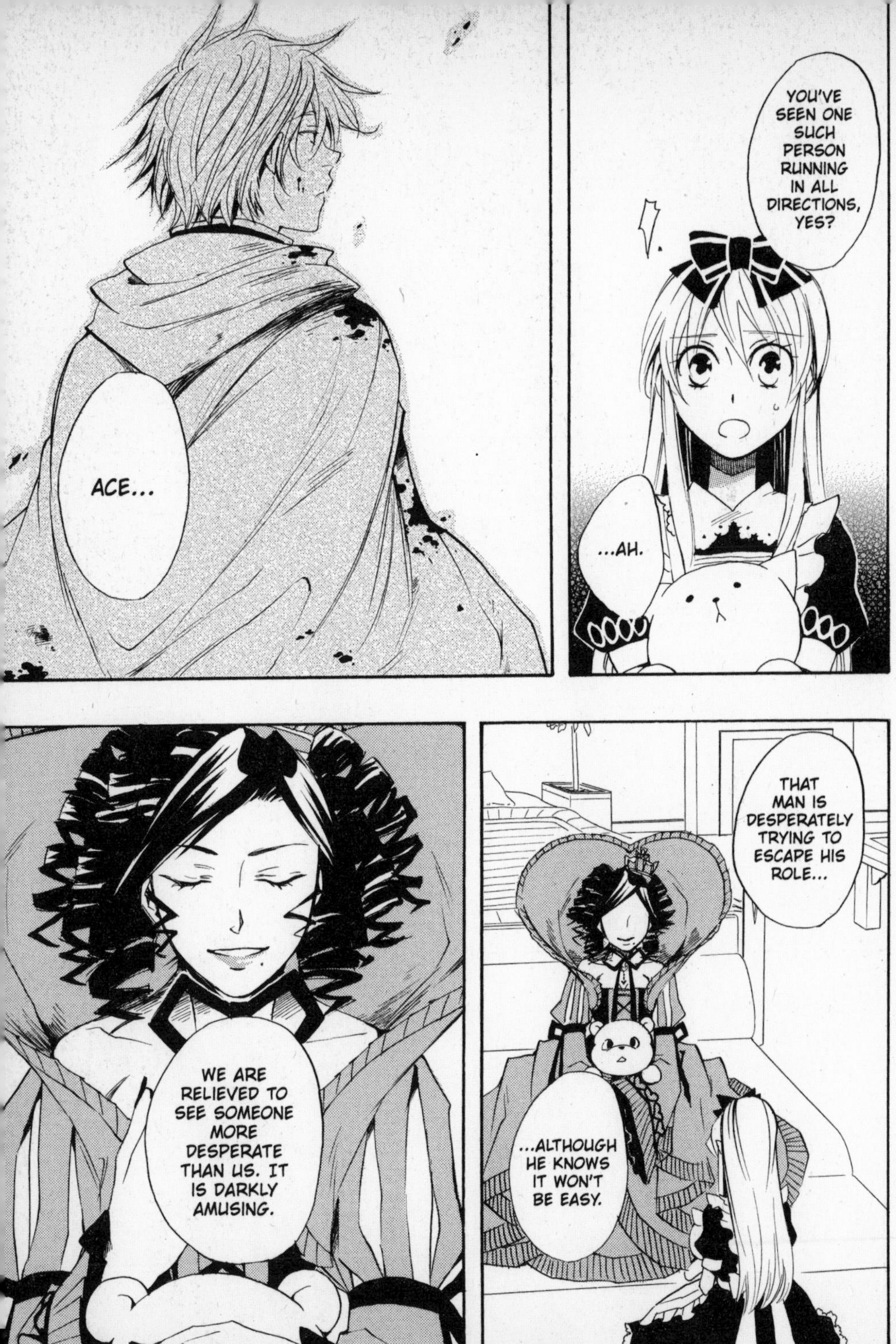
YOU'VE SEEN ONE SUCH PERSON RUNNING IN ALL DIRECTIONS, YES?
...AH.
ACE...
THAT MAN IS DESPERATELY TRYING TO ESCAPE HIS ROLE...
...ALTHOUGH HE KNOWS IT WON'T BE EASY.
WE ARE RELIEVED TO SEE SOMEONE MORE DESPERATE THAN US. IT IS DARKLY AMUSING.

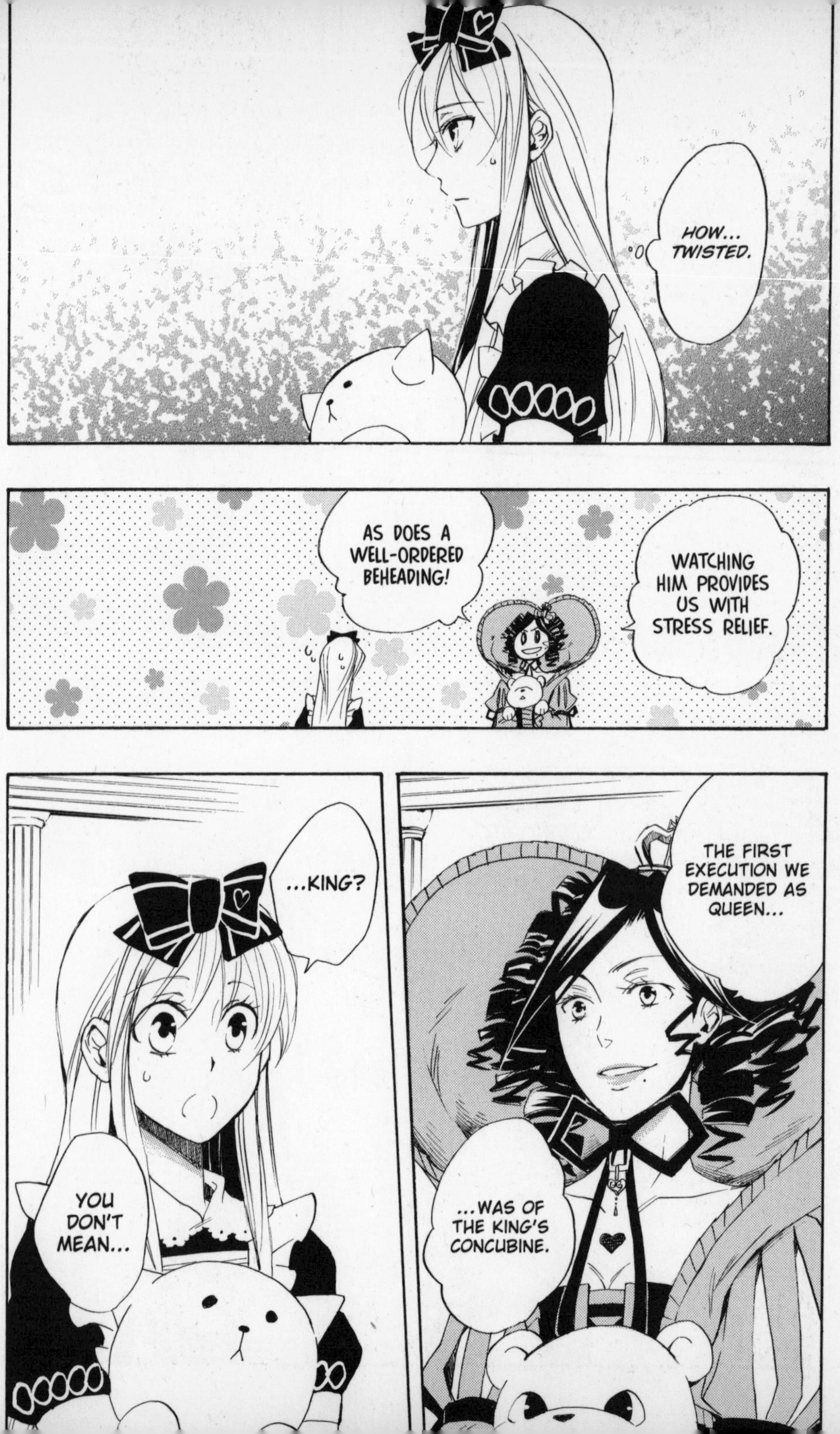
HOW... TWISTED.
WATCHING HIM PROVIDES US WITH STRESS RELIEF.
AS DOES A WELL-ORDERED BEHEADING!
THE FIRST EXECUTION WE DEMANDED AS QUEEN...
...WAS OF THE KING'S CONCUBINE.
...KING?
YOU DON'T MEAN...

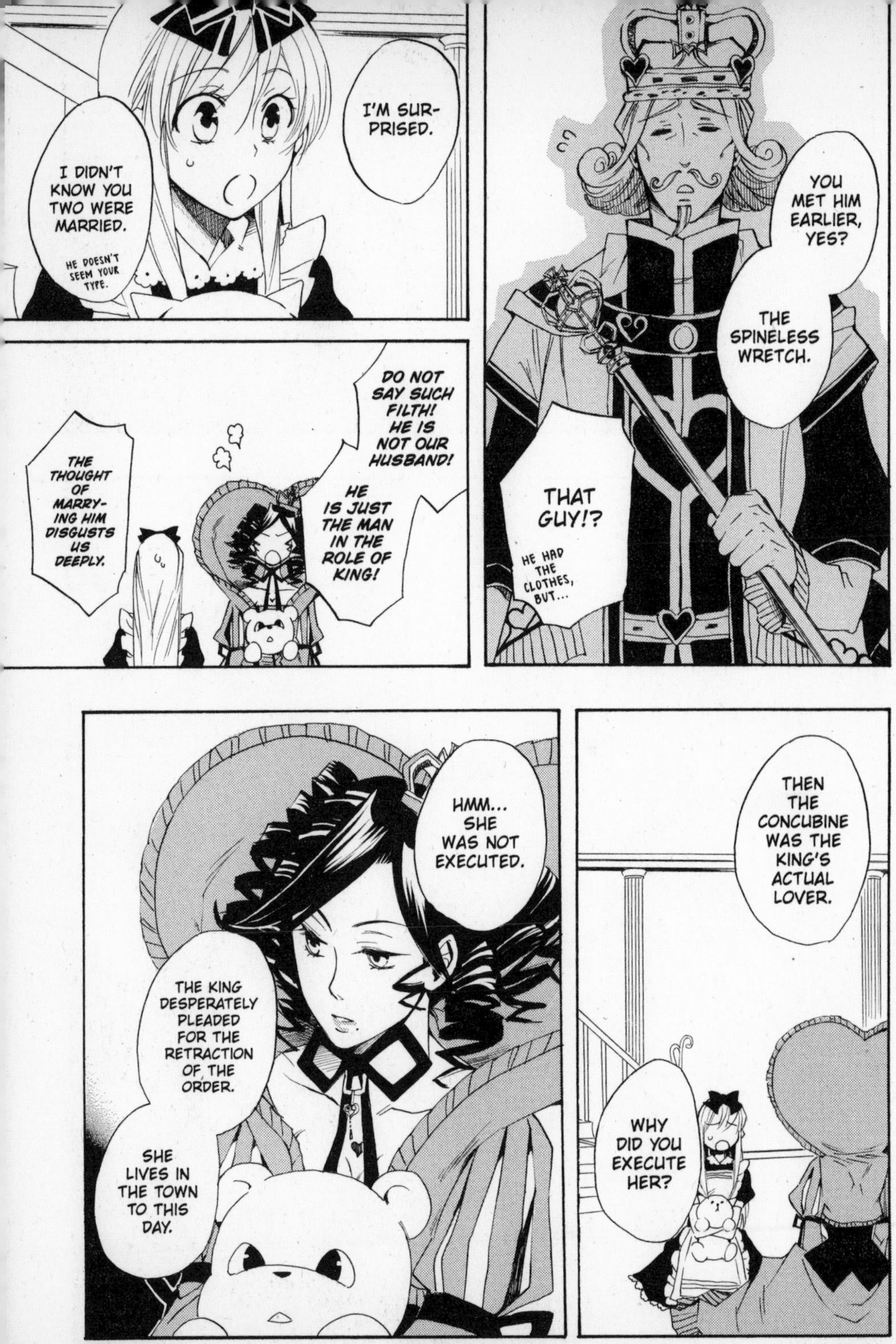
YOU MET HIM EARLIER, YES?
THE SPINELESS WRETCH.
THAT GUY!?
HE HAD THE CLOTHES, BUT...
I'M SURPRISED.
I DIDN'T KNOW YOU TWO WERE MARRIED.
HE DOESN'T SEEM YOUR TYPE.
DO NOT SAY SUCH FILTH! HE IS NOT OUR HUSBAND!
HE IS JUST THE MAN IN THE ROLE OF KING!
THE THOUGHT OF MARRYING HIM DISGUSTS US DEEPLY.
THEN THE CONCUBINE WAS THE KING'S ACTUAL LOVER.
WHY DID YOU EXECUTE HER?
HMM... SHE WAS NOT EXECUTED.
THE KING DESPERATELY PLEADED FOR THE RETRACTION OF THE ORDER.
SHE LIVES IN THE TOWN TO THIS DAY.

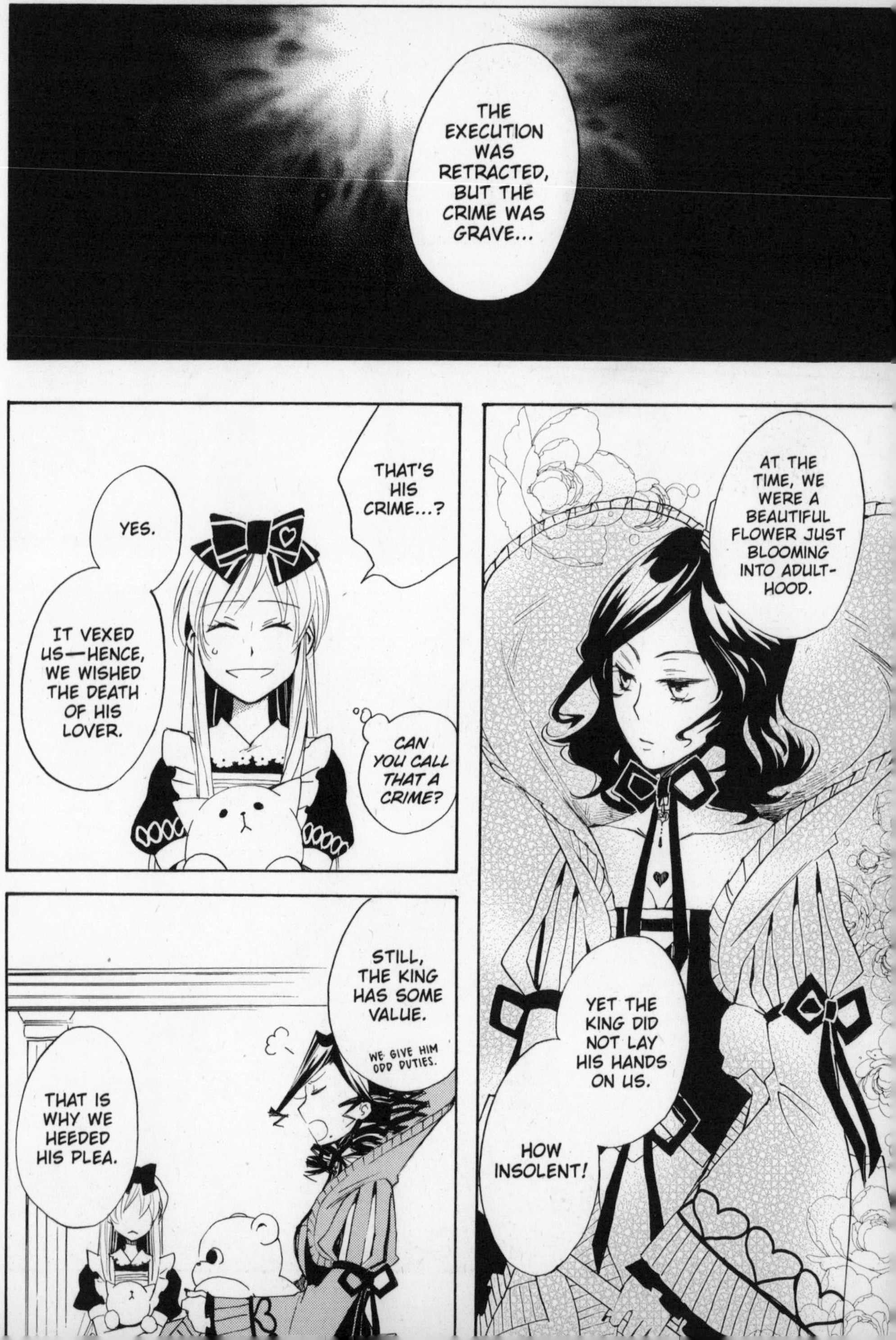
THE EXECUTION WAS RETRACTED, BUT THE CRIME WAS GRAVE...
AT THE TIME, WE WERE A BEAUTIFUL FLOWER JUST BLOOMING INTO ADULT-HOOD.
YET THE KING DID NOT LAY HIS HANDS ON US.
HOW INSOLENT!
THAT'S HIS CRIME...?
YES.
IT VEXED US—HENCE, WE WISHED THE DEATH OF HIS LOVER.
CAN YOU CALL THAT A CRIME?
STILL, THE KING HAS SOME VALUE.
WE GIVE HIM ODD DUTIES.
THAT IS WHY WE HEEDED HIS PLEA.

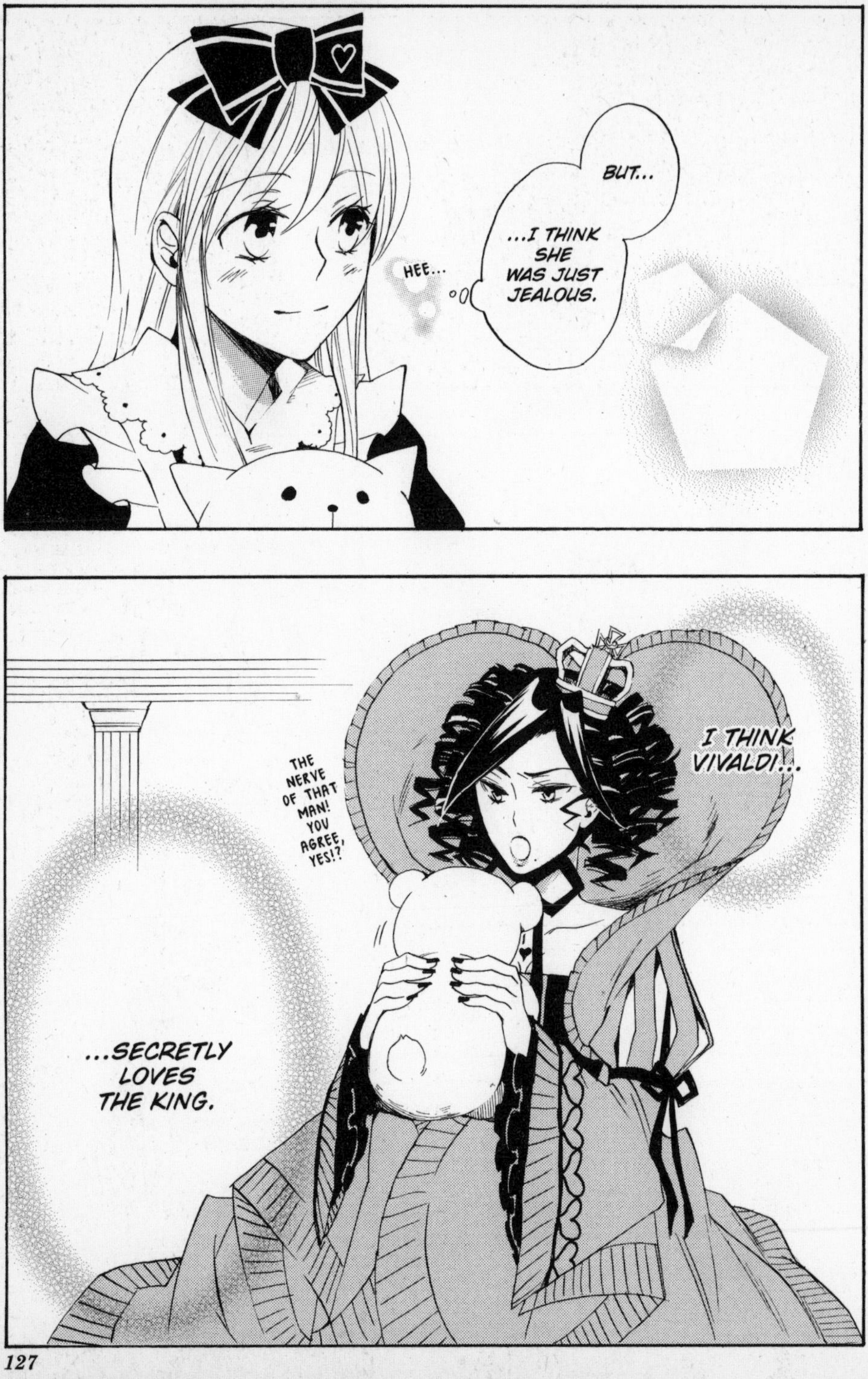
BUT...
...I THINK SHE WAS JUST JEALOUS.
HEE...
I THINK VIVALDI...
THE NERVE OF THAT MAN! YOU AGREE, YES!?
...SECRETLY LOVES THE KING.

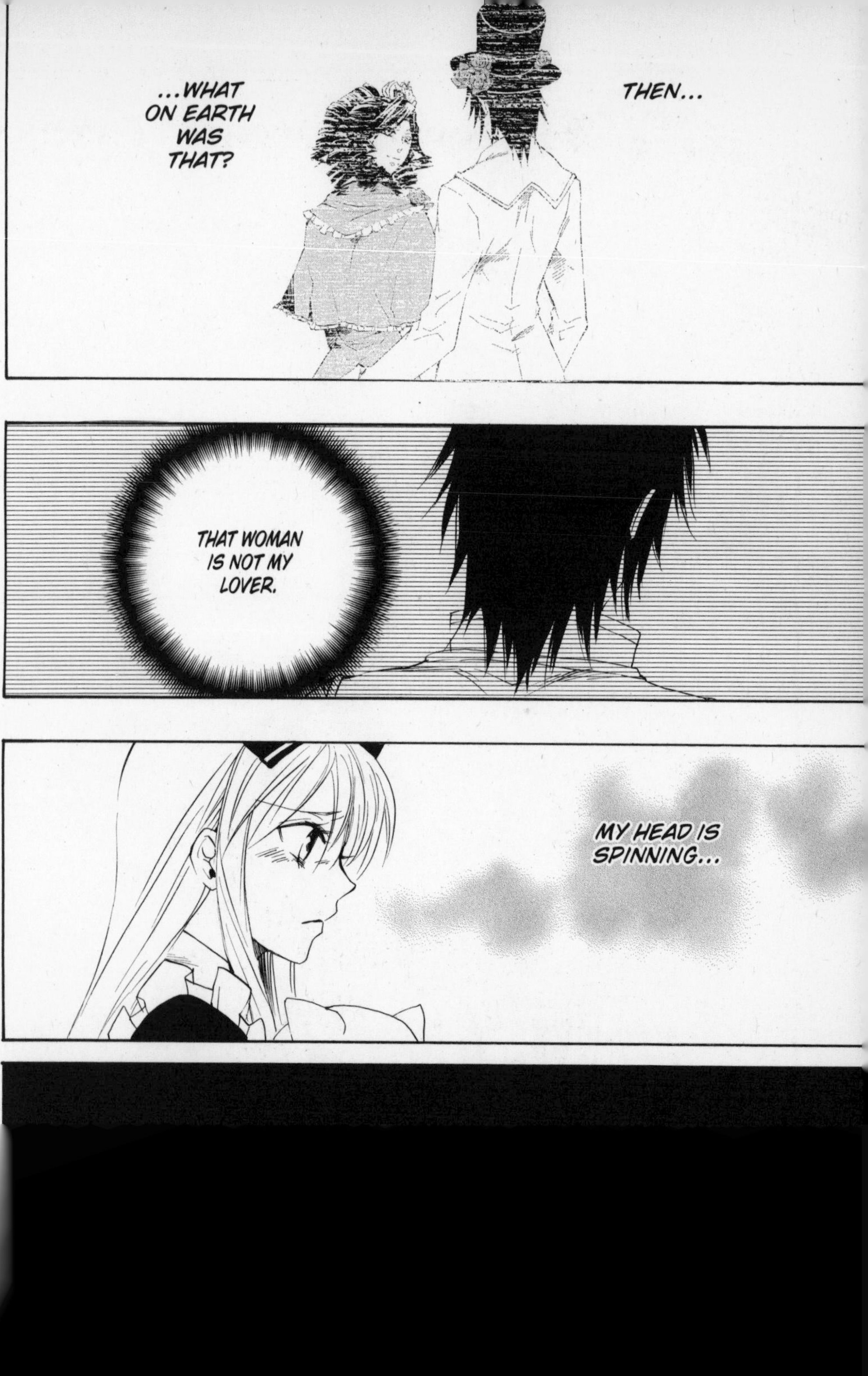
THEN...
...WHAT ON EARTH WAS THAT?
THAT WOMAN IS NOT MY LOVER.
MY HEAD IS SPINNING...

♥16 Sweet Dream Taste

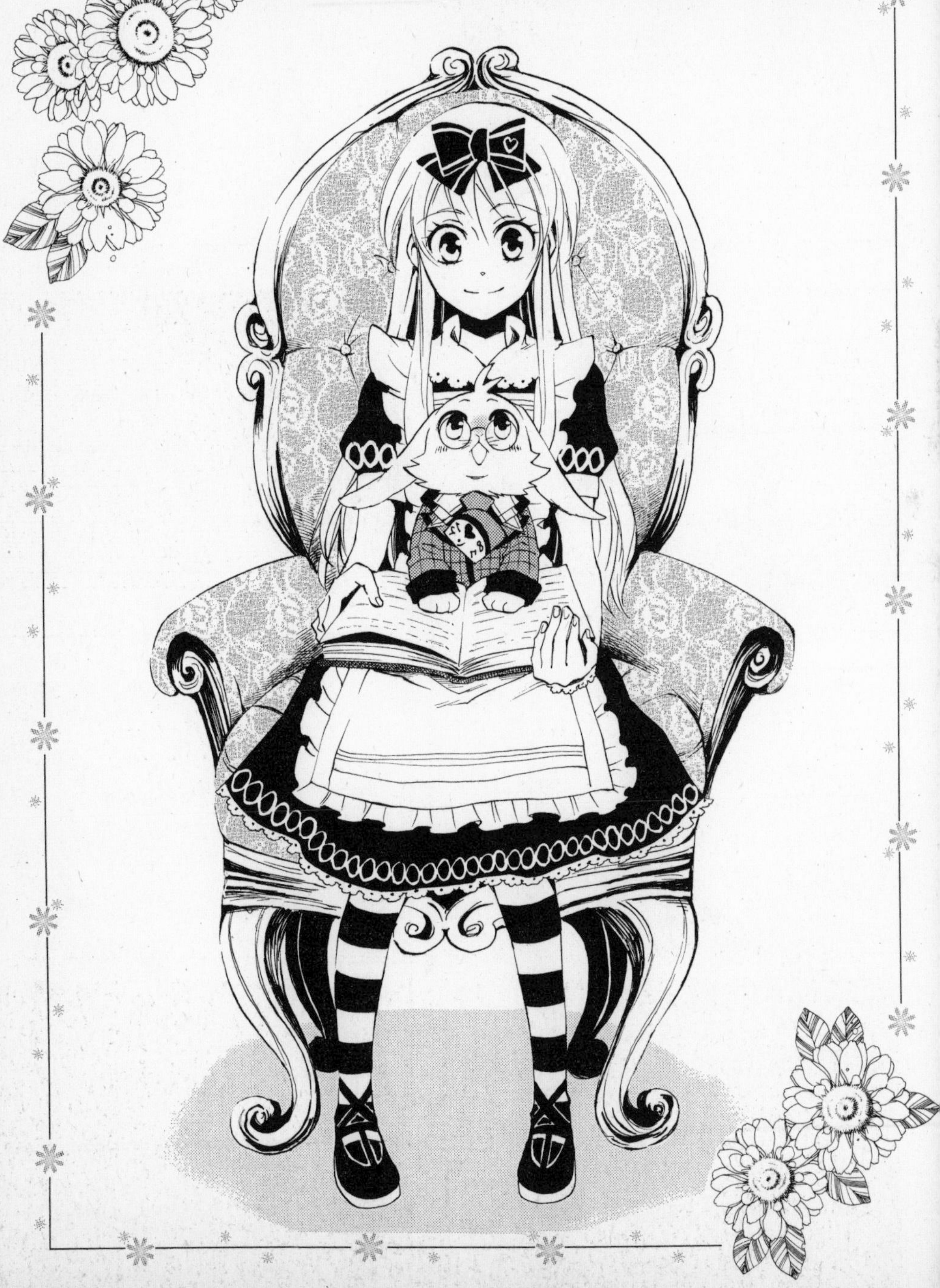

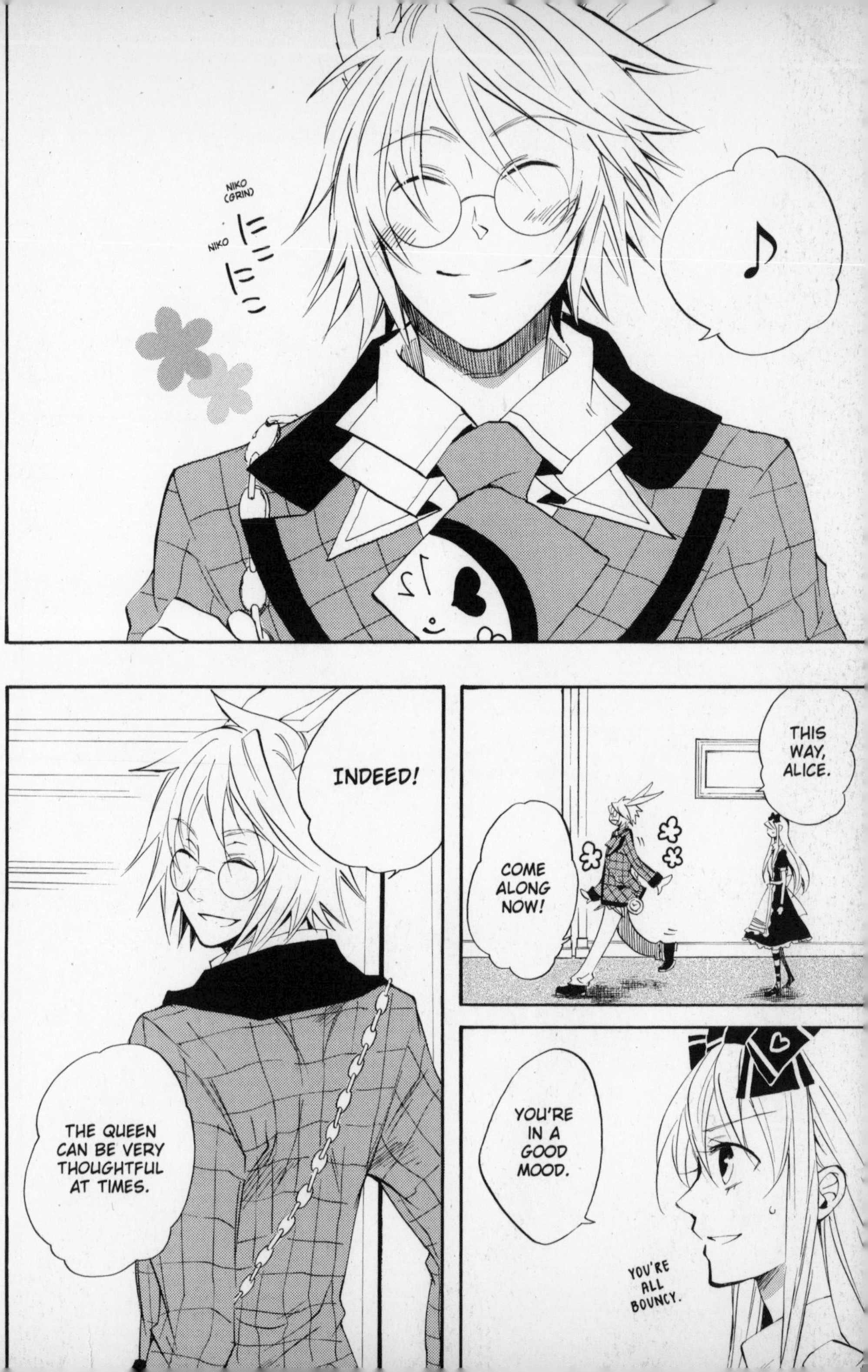
NIKO (GRIN)
NIKO
にこにこ
♪
THIS WAY, ALICE.
COME ALONG NOW!
YOU'RE IN A GOOD MOOD.
YOU'RE ALL BOUNCY.
INDEED!
THE QUEEN CAN BE VERY THOUGHTFUL AT TIMES.

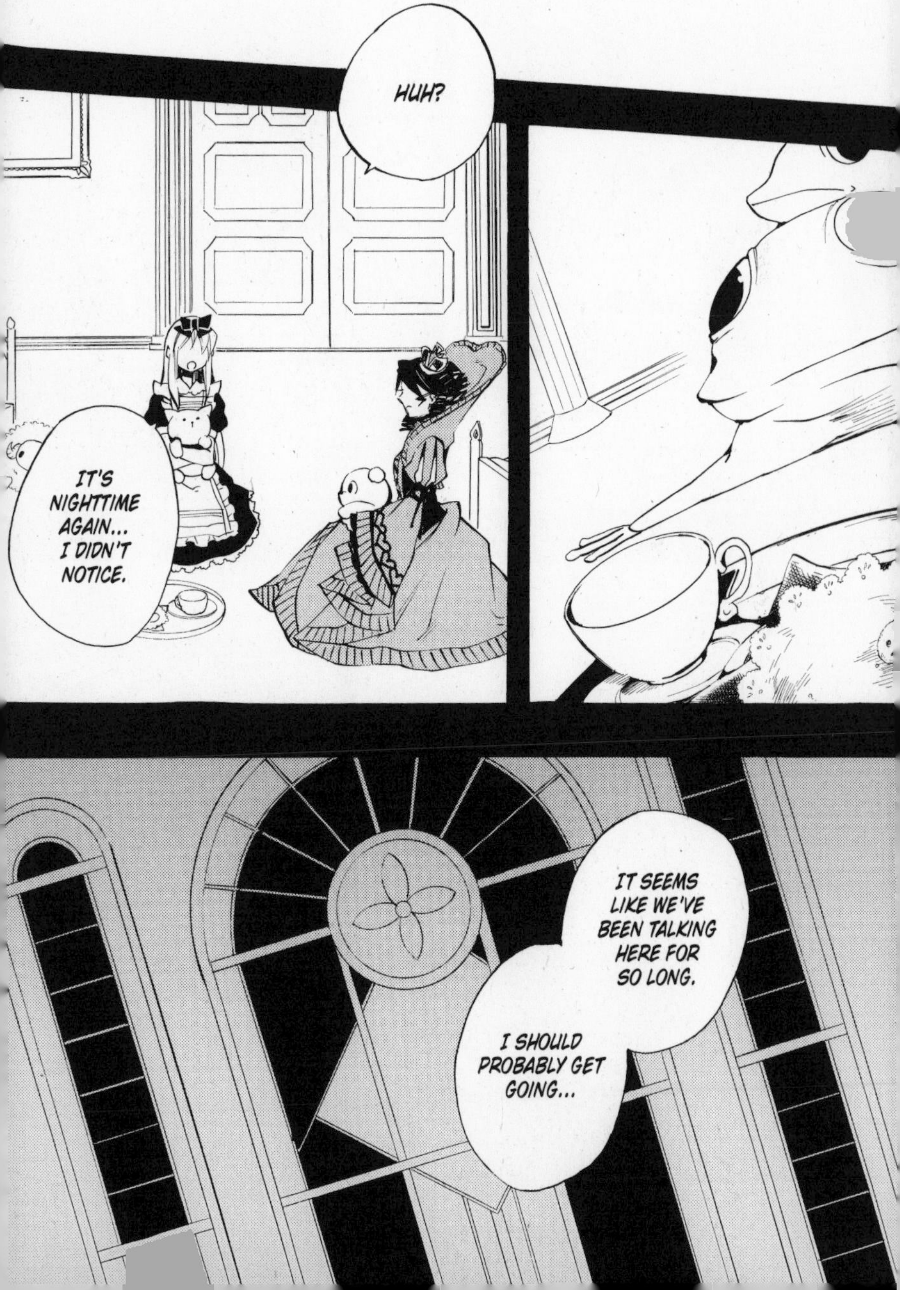
HUH?
IT'S NIGHTTIME AGAIN... I DIDN'T NOTICE.
IT SEEMS LIKE WE'VE BEEN TALKING HERE FOR SO LONG.
I SHOULD PROBABLY GET GOING...

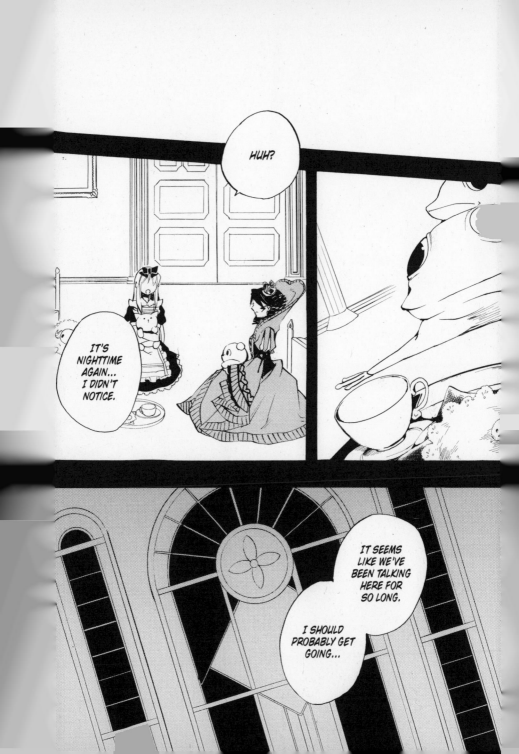

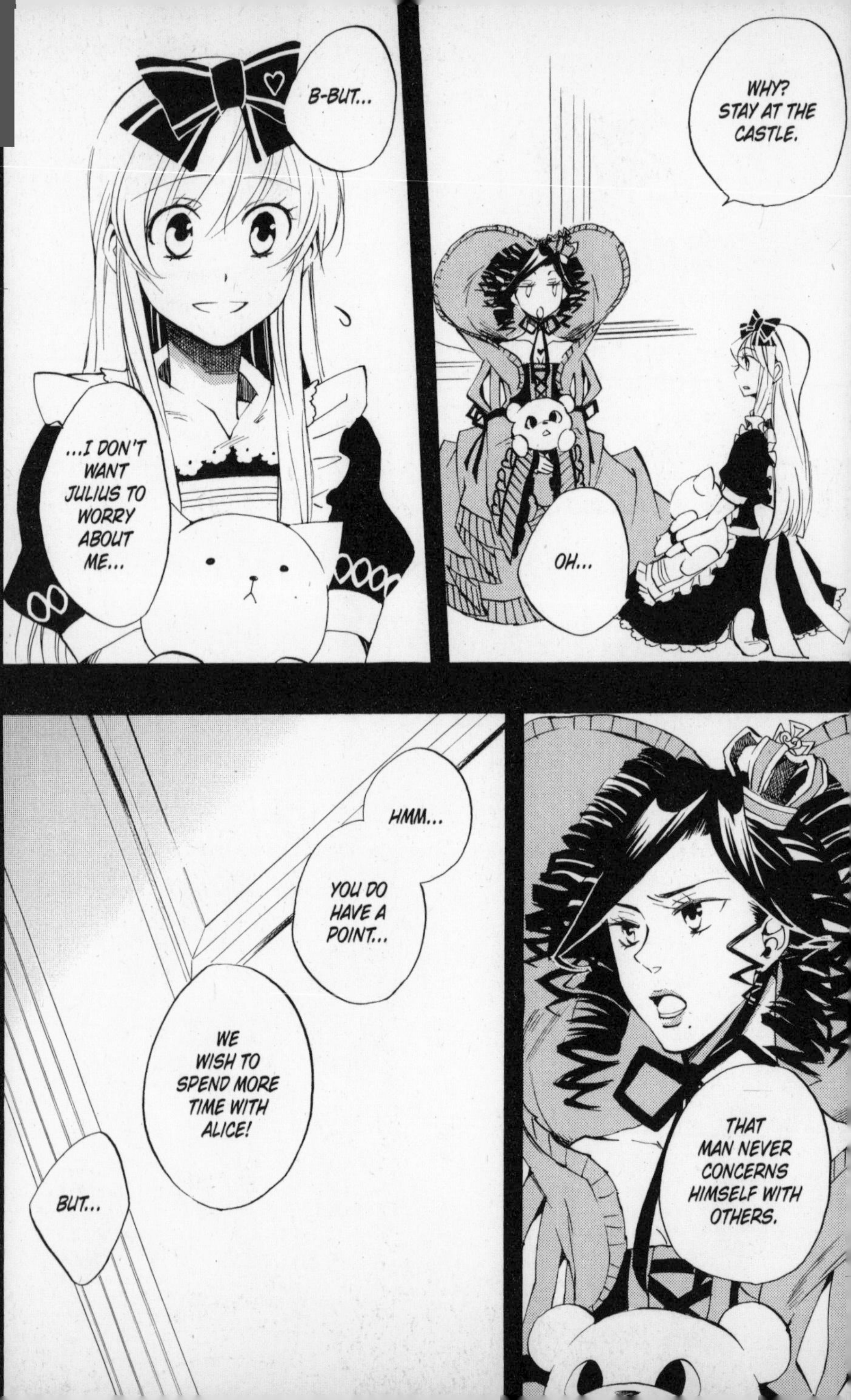
WHY? STAY AT THE CASTLE.
OH...
B-BUT...
...I DON'T WANT JULIUS TO WORRY ABOUT ME...
THAT MAN NEVER CONCERNS HIMSELF WITH OTHERS.
HMM...
YOU DO HAVE A POINT...
WE WISH TO SPEND MORE TIME WITH ALICE!
BUT...

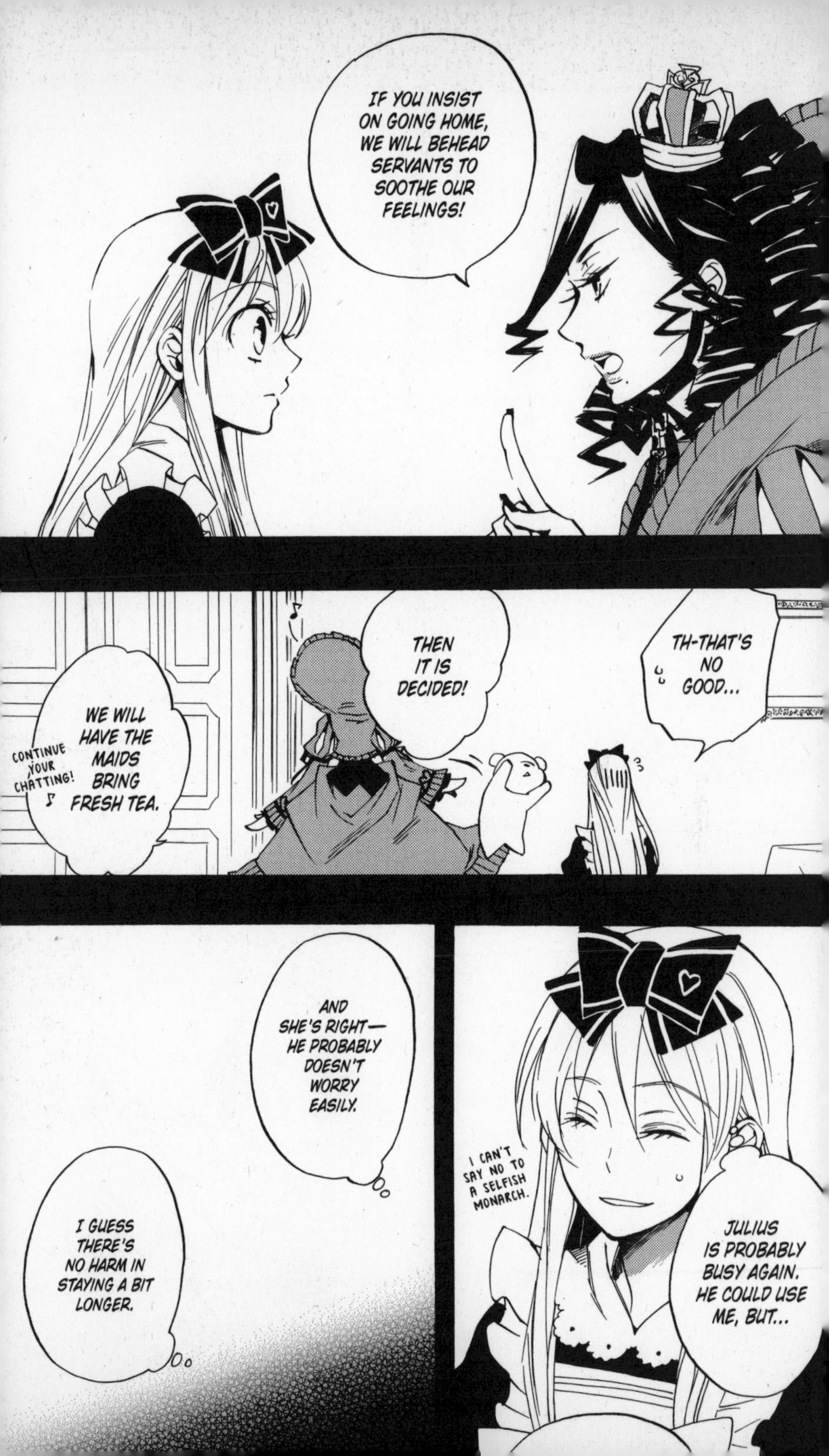
IF YOU INSIST ON GOING HOME, WE WILL BEHEAD SERVANTS TO SOOTHE OUR FEELINGS!
TH-THAT'S NO GOOD...
THEN IT IS DECIDED!
WE WILL HAVE THE MAIDS BRING FRESH TEA.
CONTINUE YOUR CHATTING! ♪
JULIUS IS PROBABLY BUSY AGAIN. HE COULD USE ME, BUT...
I CAN'T SAY NO TO A SELFISH MONARCH.
AND SHE'S RIGHT— HE PROBABLY DOESN'T WORRY EASILY.
I GUESS THERE'S NO HARM IN STAYING A BIT LONGER.

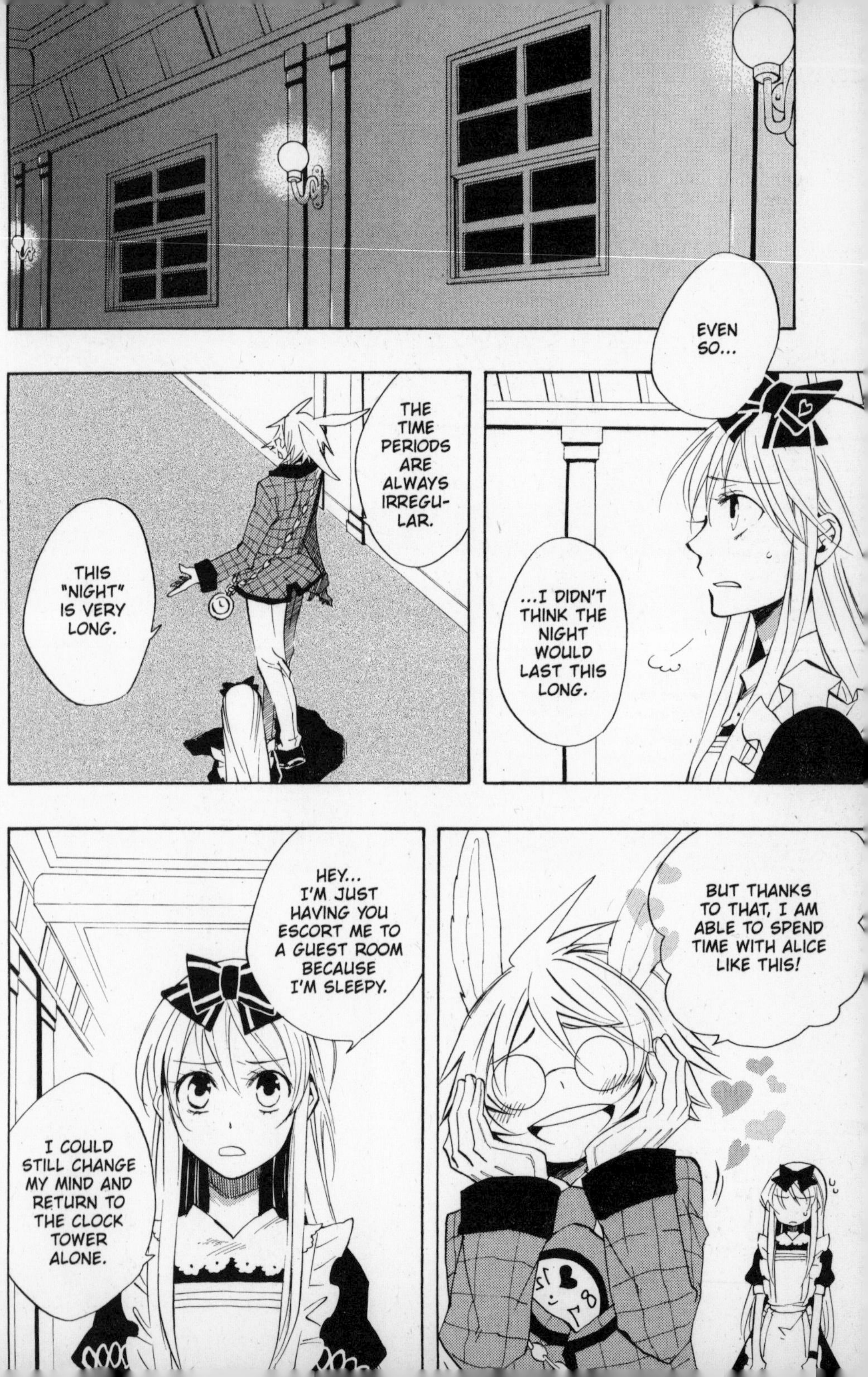
EVEN SO...
...I DIDN'T THINK THE NIGHT WOULD LAST THIS LONG.
THE TIME PERIODS ARE ALWAYS IRREGULAR.
THIS "NIGHT" IS VERY LONG.
BUT THANKS TO THAT, I AM ABLE TO SPEND TIME WITH ALICE LIKE THIS!
HEY... I'M JUST HAVING YOU ESCORT ME TO A GUEST ROOM BECAUSE I'M SLEEPY.
I COULD STILL CHANGE MY MIND AND RETURN TO THE CLOCK TOWER ALONE.

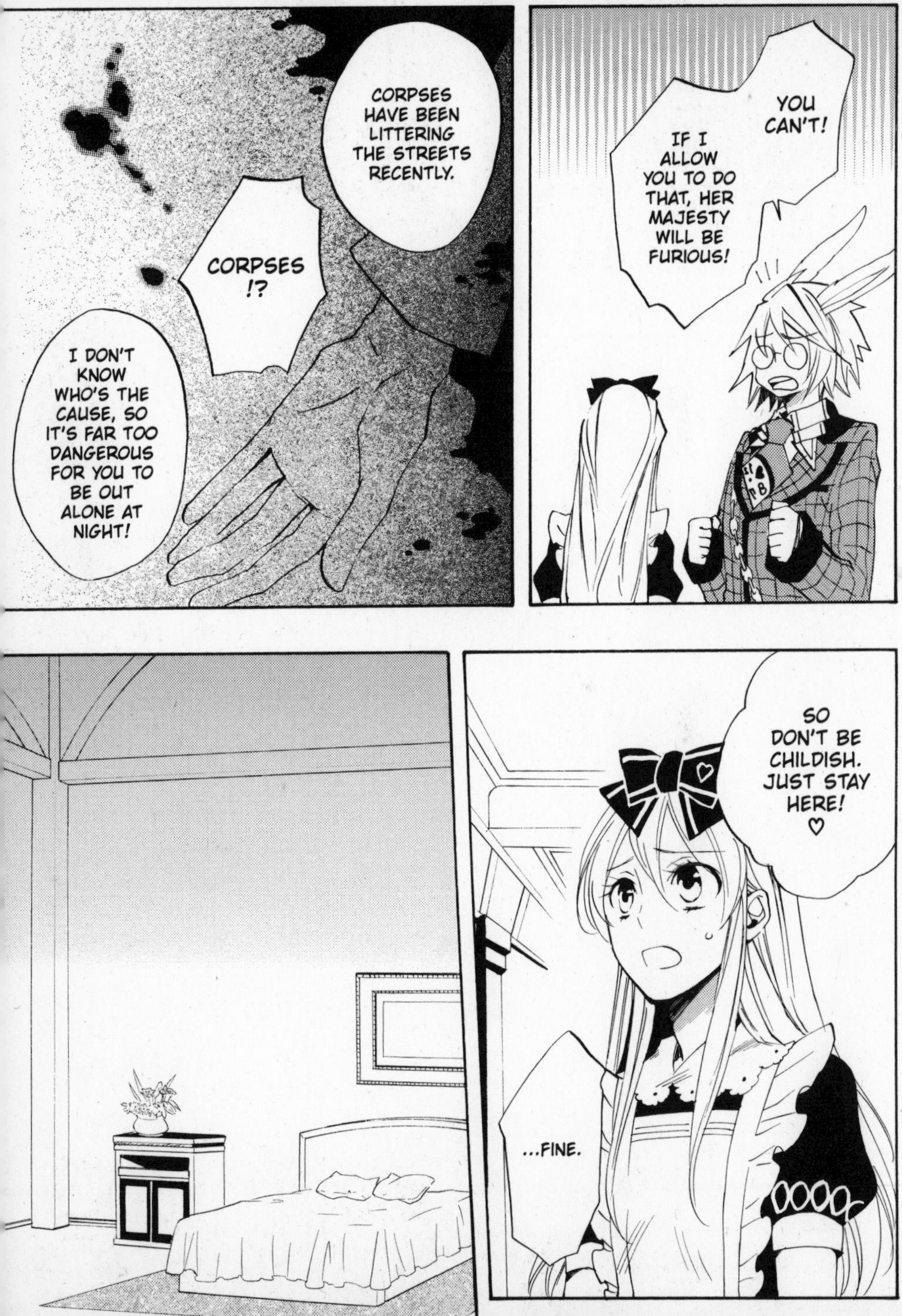
YOU CAN'T!
IF I ALLOW YOU TO DO THAT, HER MAJESTY WILL BE FURIOUS!
CORPSES HAVE BEEN LITTERING THE STREETS RECENTLY.
CORPSES!?
I DON'T KNOW WHO'S THE CAUSE, SO IT'S FAR TOO DANGEROUS FOR YOU TO BE OUT ALONE AT NIGHT!
SO DON'T BE CHILDISH. JUST STAY HERE! ♡
...FINE.

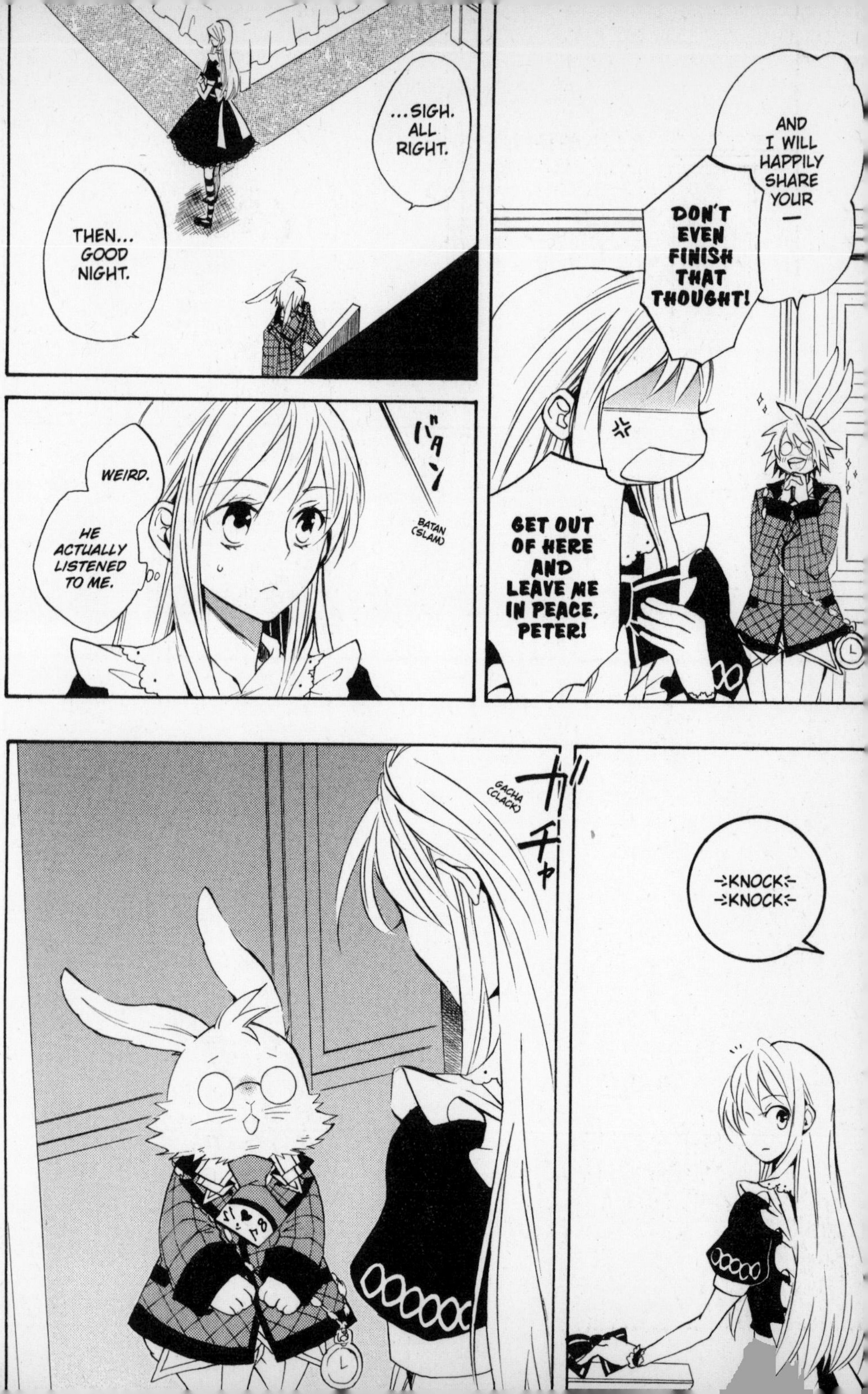
AND I WILL HAPPILY SHARE YOUR—
DON'T EVEN FINISH THAT THOUGHT!
GET OUT OF HERE AND LEAVE ME IN PEACE, PETER!
...SIGH. ALL RIGHT.
THEN... GOOD NIGHT.
バタン
BATAN (SLAM)
WEIRD.
HE ACTUALLY LISTENED TO ME.
KNOCK KNOCK
ガチャ
GACHA (CLACK)

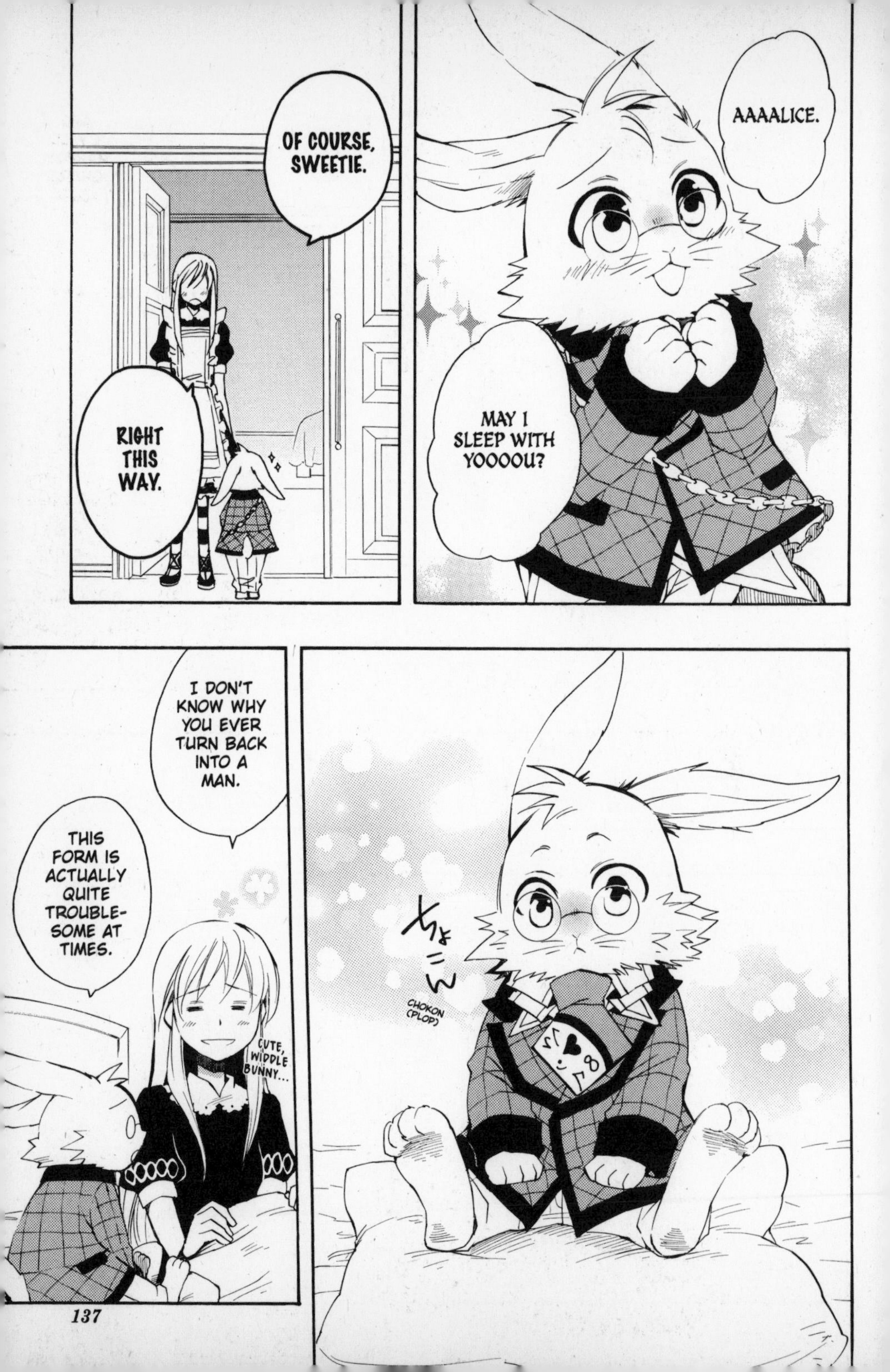
AAAALICE.
MAY I SLEEP WITH YOOOOU?
OF COURSE, SWEETIE.
RIGHT THIS WAY.
CHOKON (PLOP)
I DON'T KNOW WHY YOU EVER TURN BACK INTO A MAN.
THIS FORM IS ACTUALLY QUITE TROUBLE-SOME AT TIMES.
CUTE, WIDDLE BUNNY...

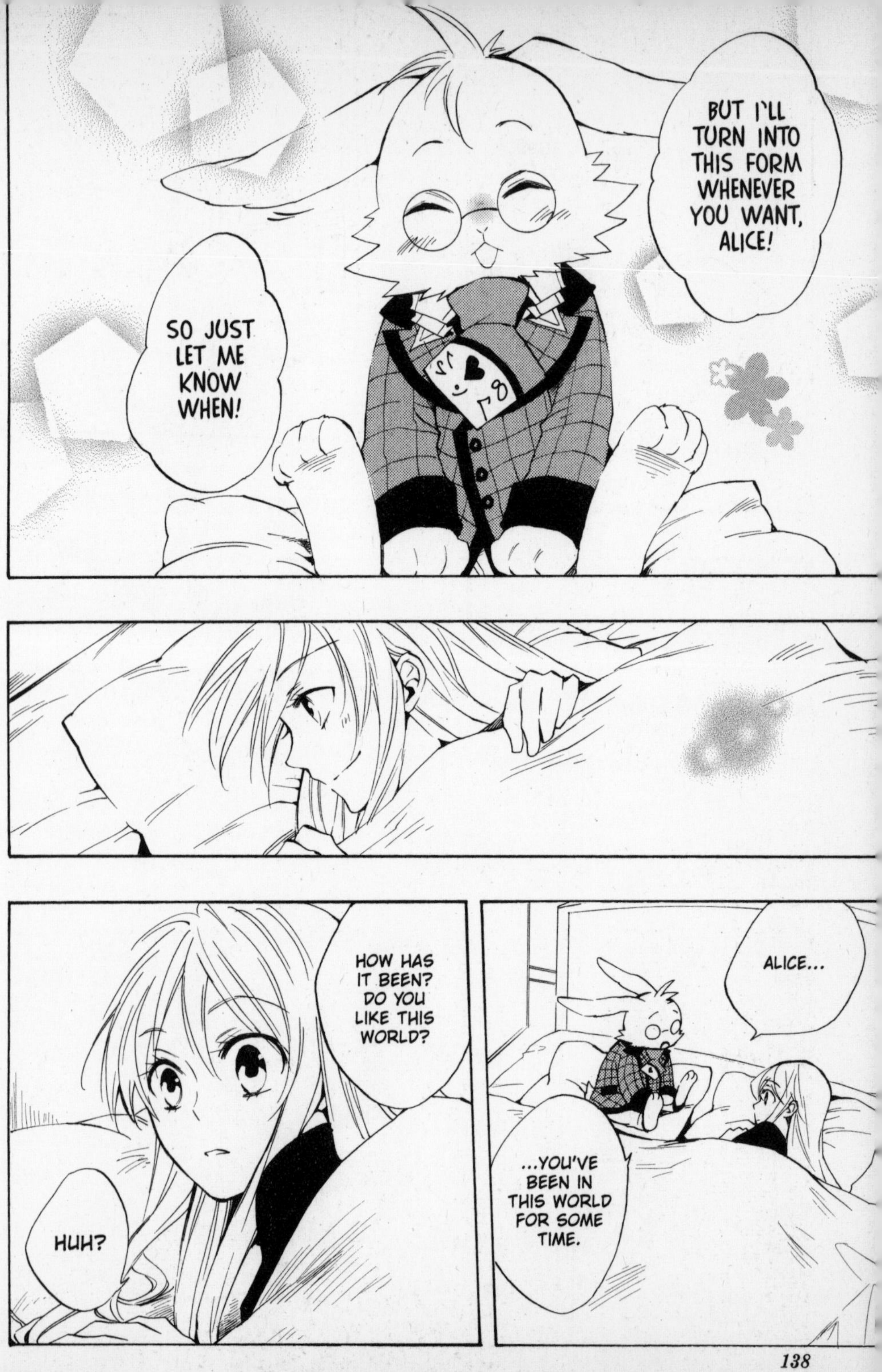
BUT I'LL TURN INTO THIS FORM WHENEVER YOU WANT, ALICE!
SO JUST LET ME KNOW WHEN!
ALICE...
...YOU'VE BEEN IN THIS WORLD FOR SOME TIME.
HOW HAS IT BEEN? DO YOU LIKE THIS WORLD?
HUH?

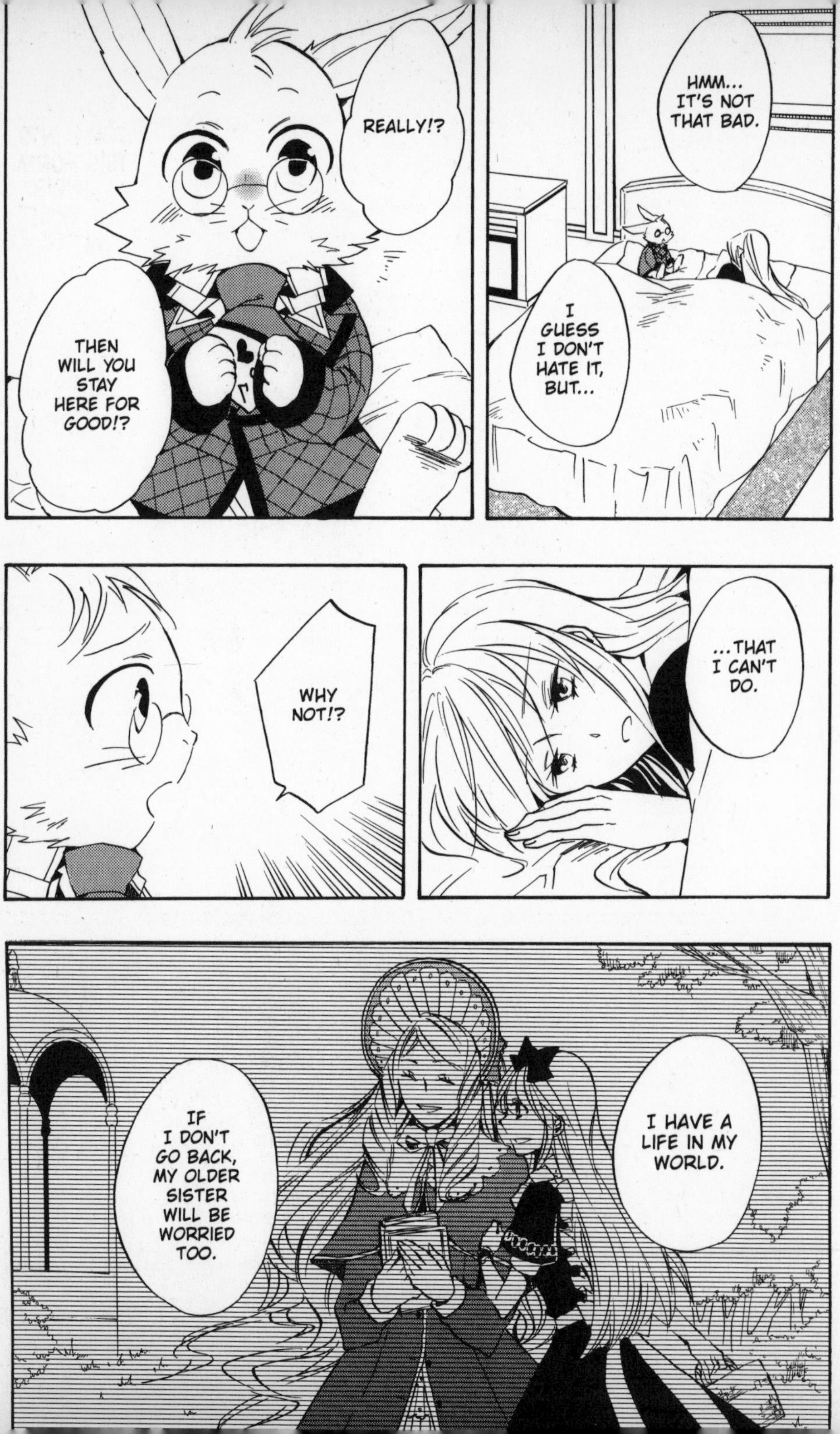
HMM... IT'S NOT THAT BAD.
I GUESS I DON'T HATE IT, BUT...
REALLY!?
THEN WILL YOU STAY HERE FOR GOOD!?
...THAT I CAN'T DO.
WHY NOT!?
I HAVE A LIFE IN MY WORLD.
IF I DON'T GO BACK, MY OLDER SISTER WILL BE WORRIED TOO.

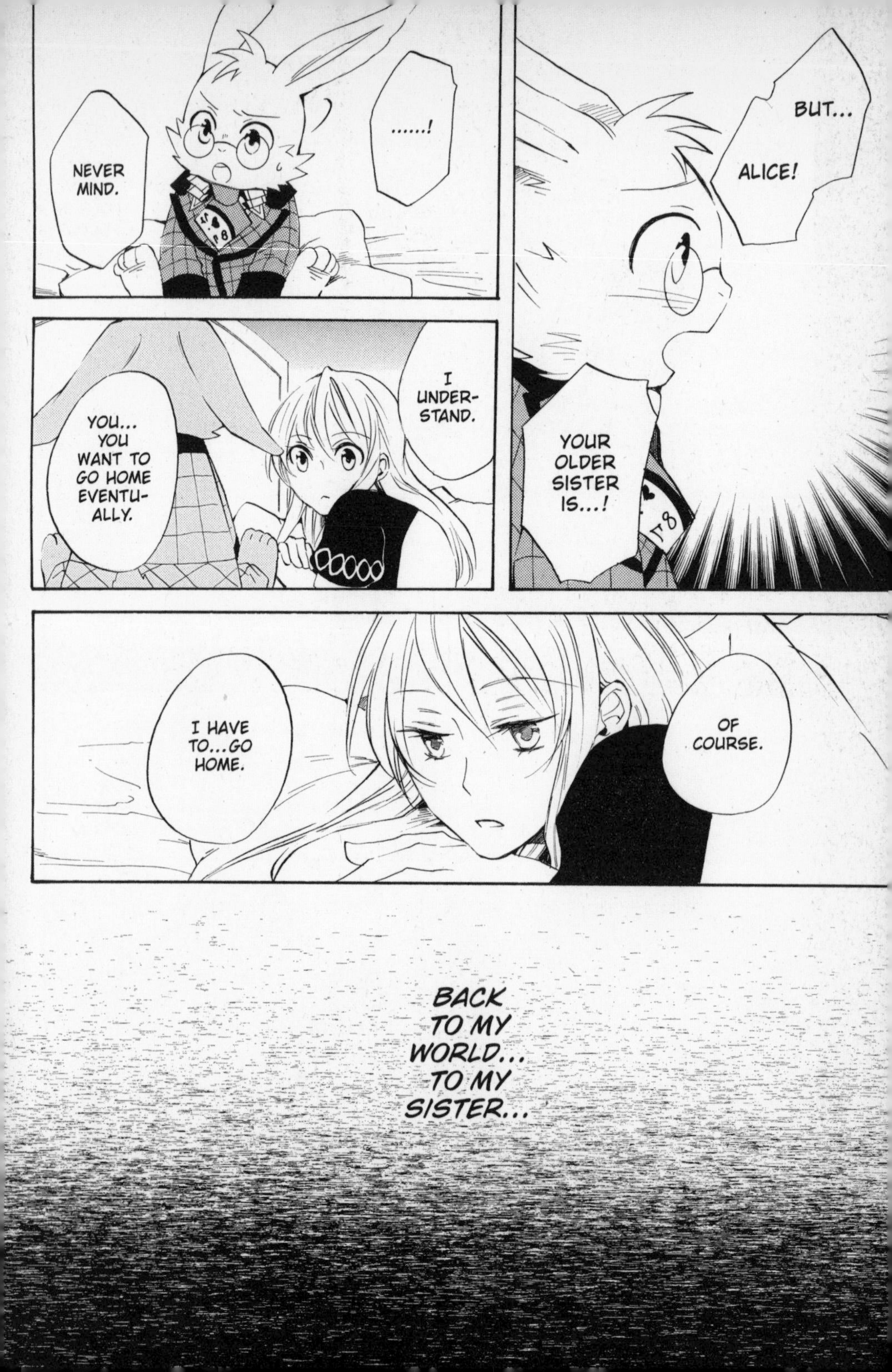
BUT...
ALICE!
YOUR OLDER SISTER IS...!
......!
NEVER MIND.
I UNDERSTAND.
YOU... YOU WANT TO GO HOME EVENTU-ALLY.
OF COURSE.
I HAVE TO...GO HOME.
BACK TO MY WORLD... TO MY SISTER...

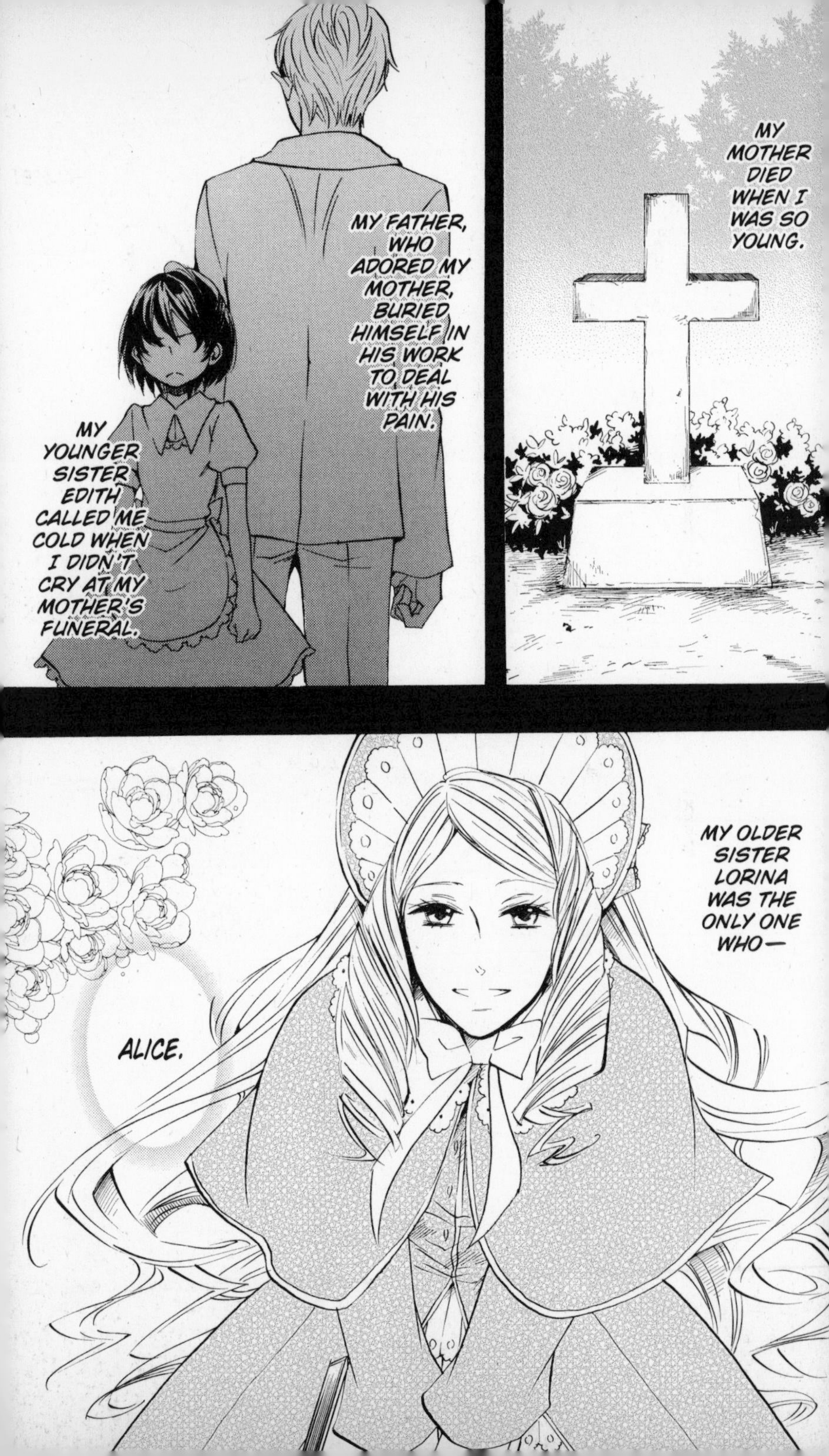
MY MOTHER DIED WHEN I WAS SO YOUNG.
MY FATHER, WHO ADORED MY MOTHER, BURIED HIMSELF IN HIS WORK TO DEAL WITH HIS PAIN.
MY YOUNGER SISTER EDITH CALLED ME COLD WHEN I DIDN'T CRY AT MY MOTHER'S FUNERAL.
MY OLDER SISTER LORINA WAS THE ONLY ONE WHO—
ALICE.

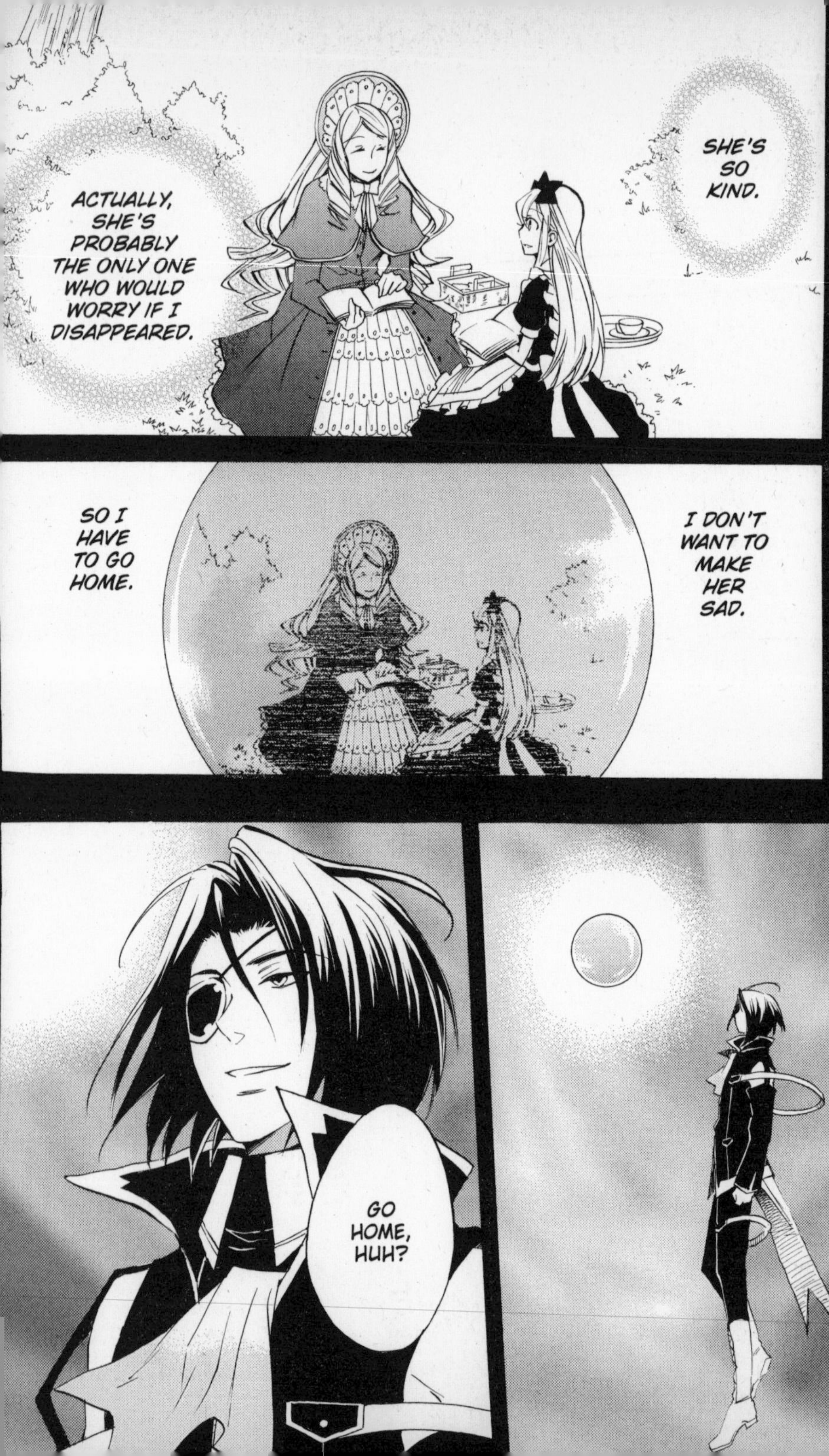
SHE'S SO KIND.
ACTUALLY, SHE'S PROBABLY THE ONLY ONE WHO WOULD WORRY IF I DISAPPEARED.
I DON'T WANT TO MAKE HER SAD.
SO I HAVE TO GO HOME.
GO HOME, HUH?

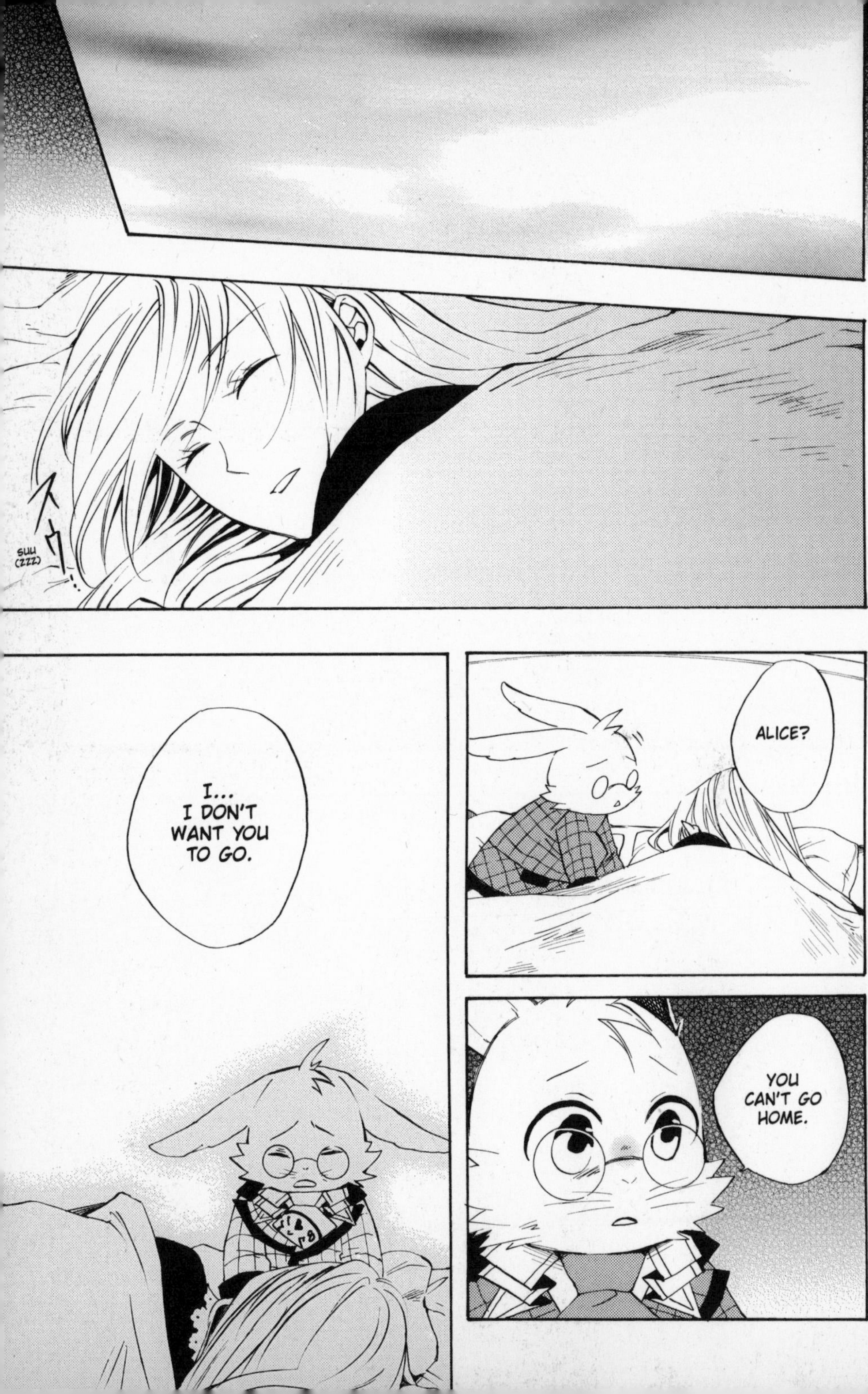
SUU (ZZZ)
ALICE?
YOU CAN'T GO HOME.
I... I DON'T WANT YOU TO GO.

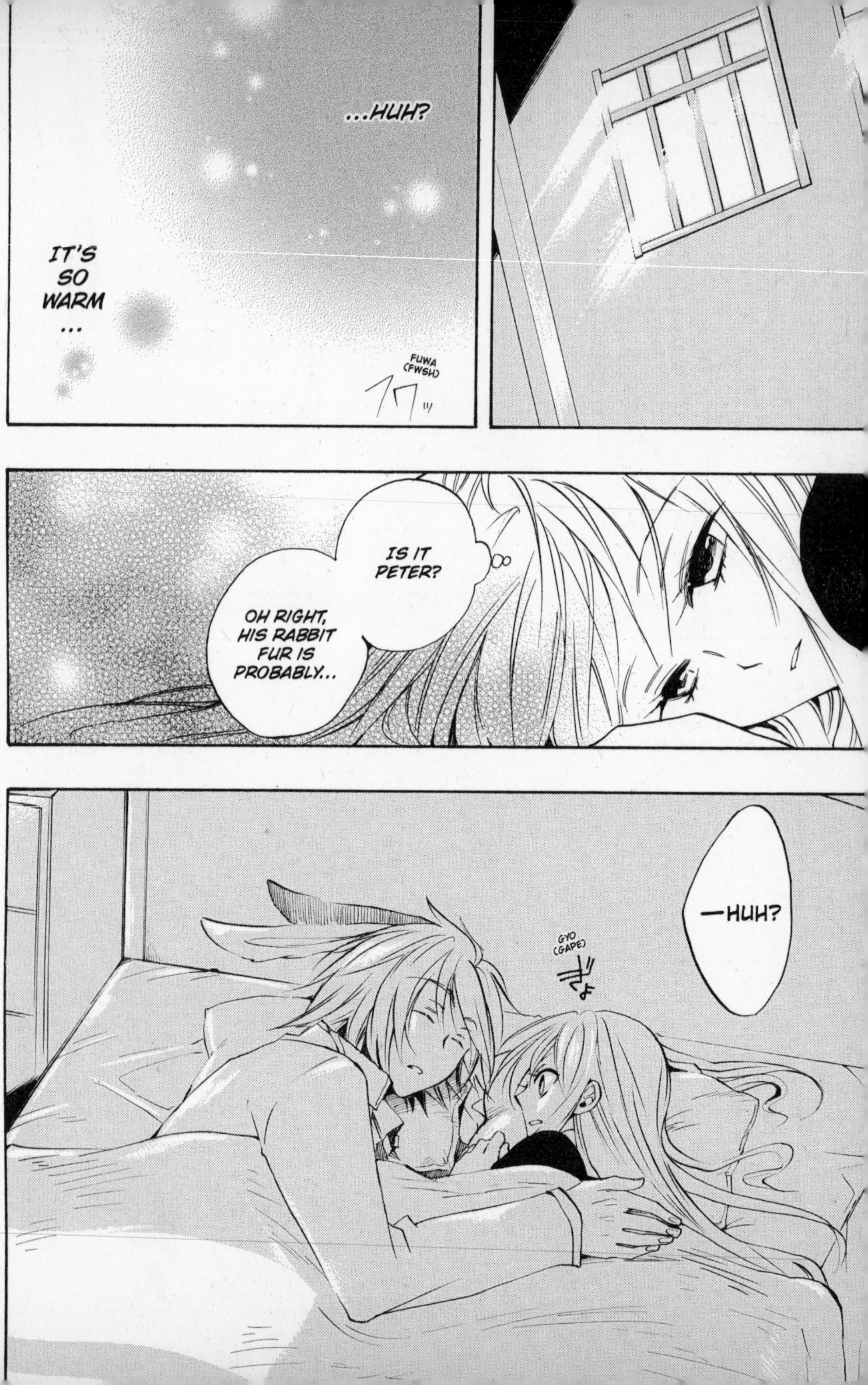
...HUH?
IT'S SO WARM ...
FUWA (FWSH)
IS IT PETER?
OH RIGHT, HIS RABBIT FUR IS PROBABLY...
—HUH?
GYO (GAPE)

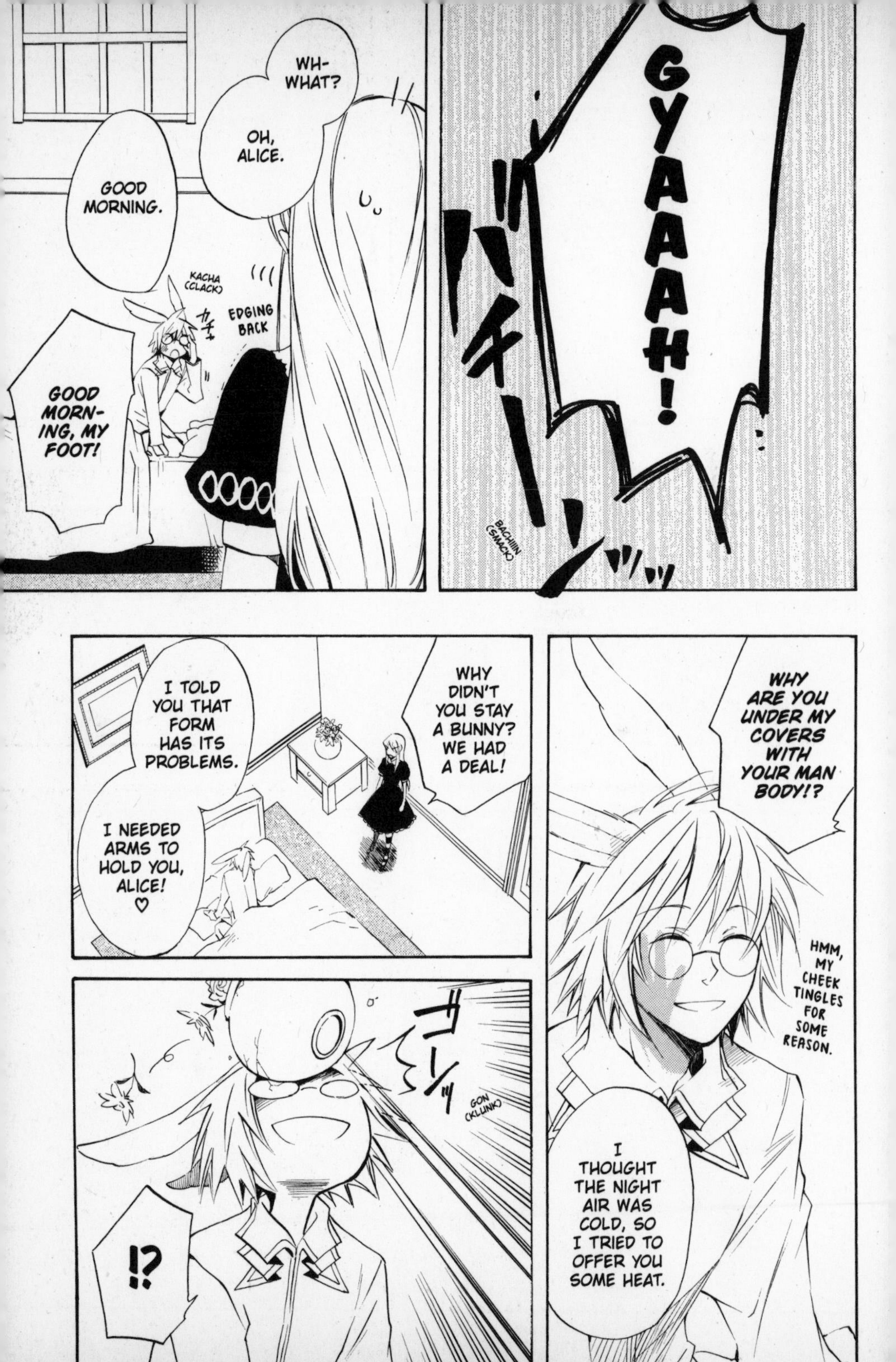
GYAAAH!
BACHIIN (SMACK)
WH-WHAT?
OH, ALICE.
GOOD MORNING.
EDGING BACK
KACHA (CLACK)
GOOD MORNING, MY FOOT!
WHY ARE YOU UNDER MY COVERS WITH YOUR MAN BODY!?
HMM, MY CHEEK TINGLES FOR SOME REASON.
I THOUGHT THE NIGHT AIR WAS COLD, SO I TRIED TO OFFER YOU SOME HEAT.
WHY DIDN'T YOU STAY A BUNNY? WE HAD A DEAL!
I TOLD YOU THAT FORM HAS ITS PROBLEMS.
I NEEDED ARMS TO HOLD YOU, ALICE! ♡
GON (KLUNK)
!?

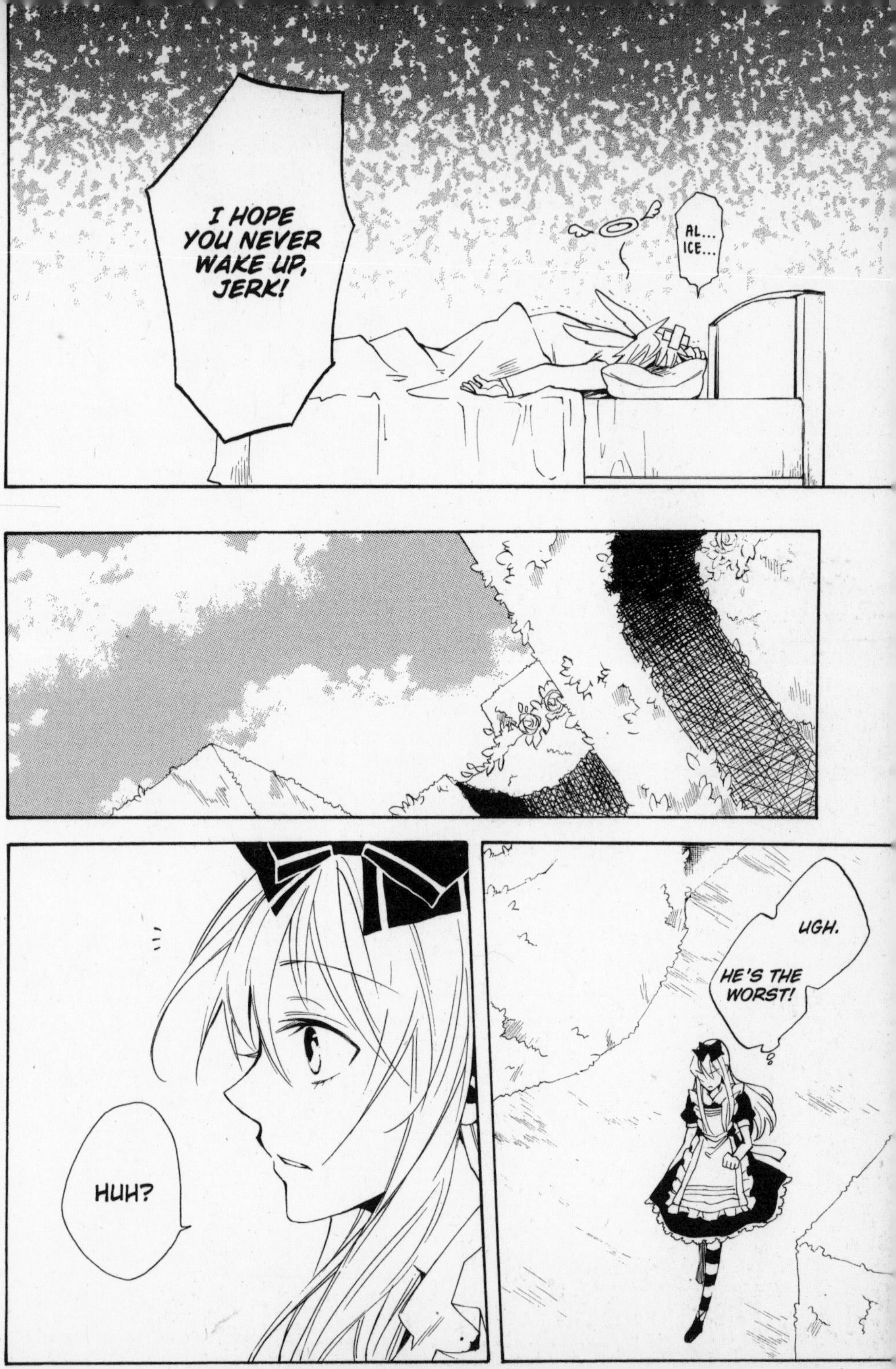
AL... ICE...
I HOPE YOU NEVER WAKE UP, JERK!
UGH.
HE'S THE WORST!
HUH?

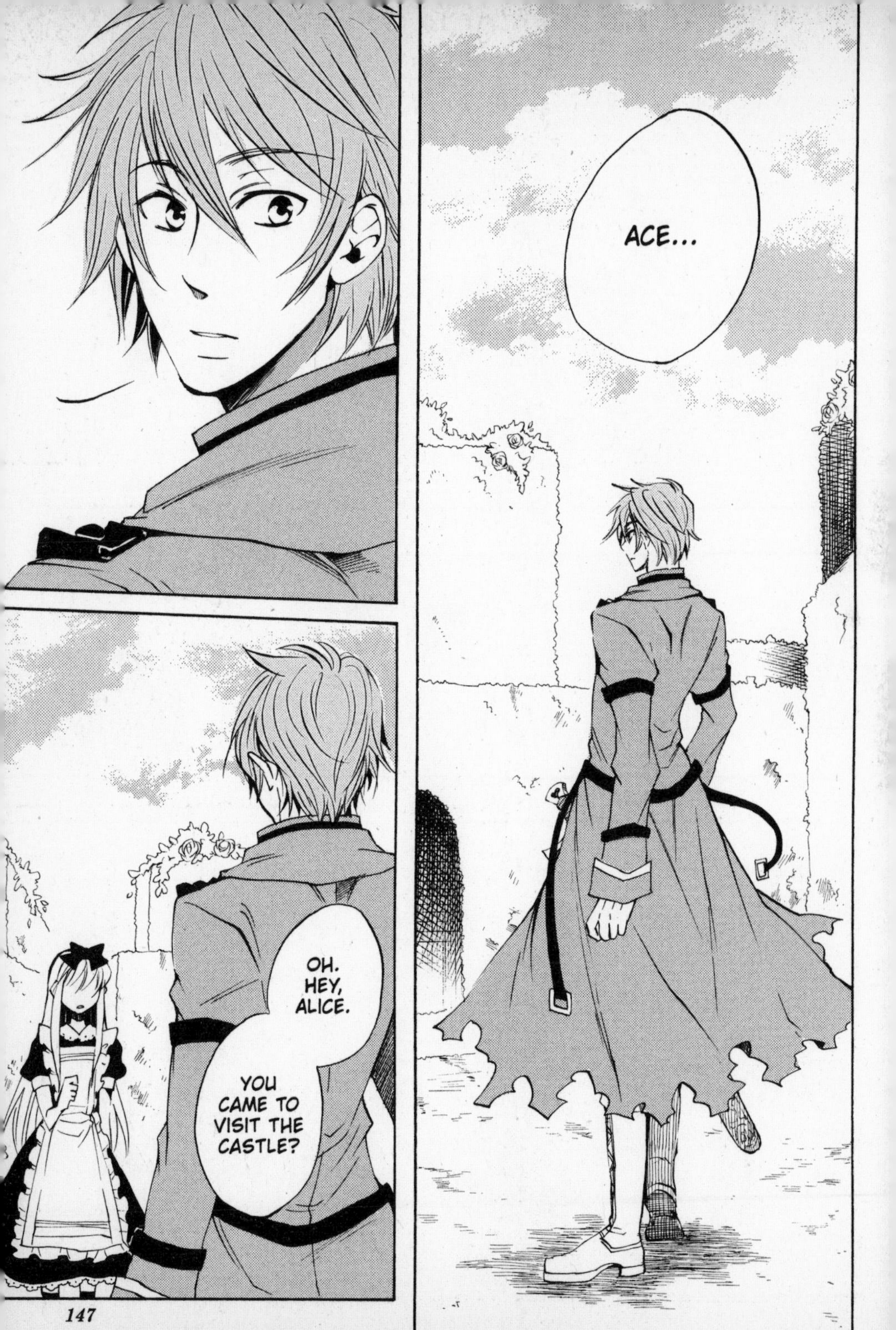
ACE...
OH. HEY, ALICE.
YOU CAME TO VISIT THE CASTLE?

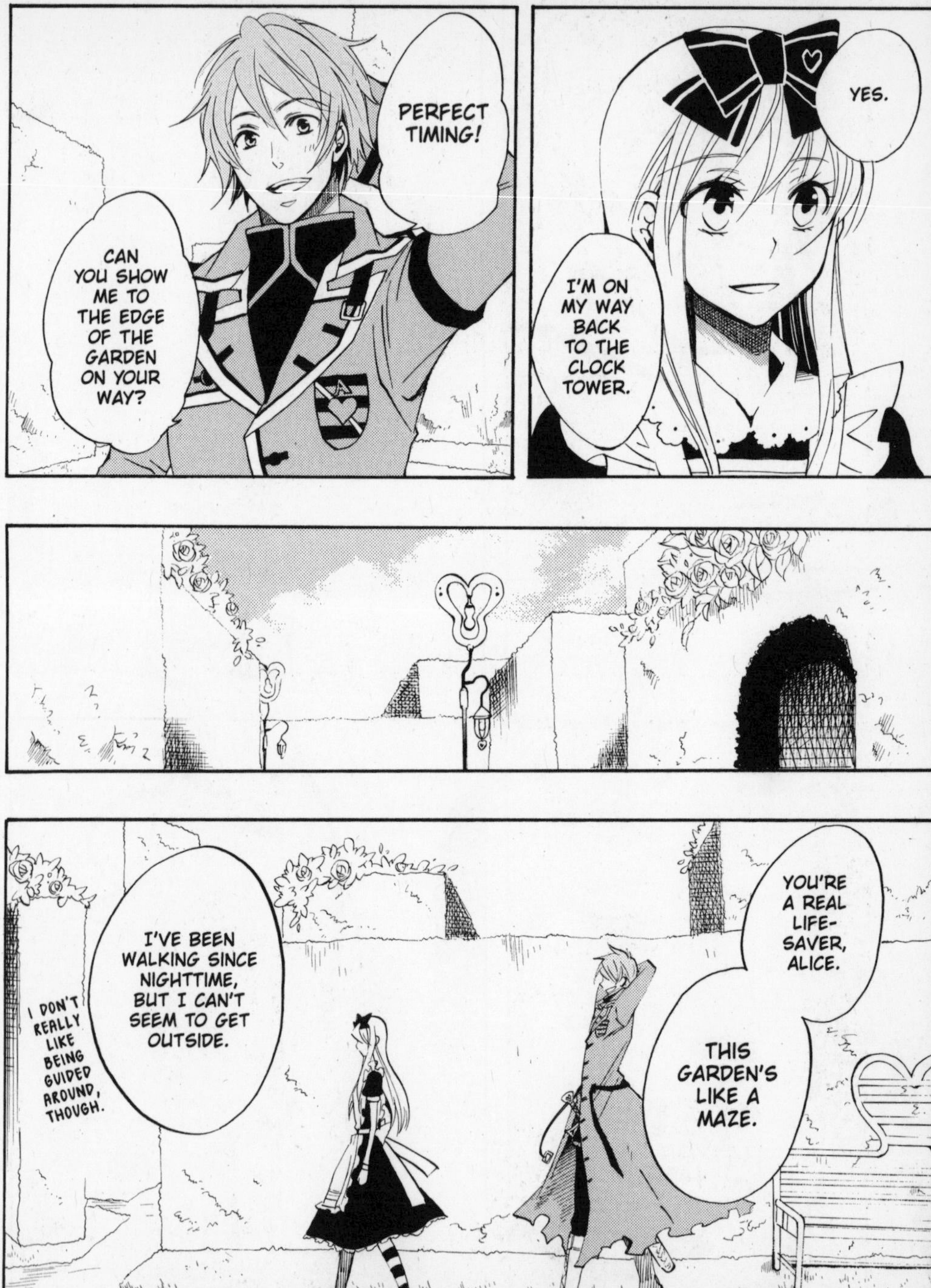
YES.
I'M ON MY WAY BACK TO THE CLOCK TOWER.
PERFECT TIMING!
CAN YOU SHOW ME TO THE EDGE OF THE GARDEN ON YOUR WAY?
YOU'RE A REAL LIFE-SAVER, ALICE.
THIS GARDEN'S LIKE A MAZE.
I'VE BEEN WALKING SINCE NIGHTTIME, BUT I CAN'T SEEM TO GET OUTSIDE.
I DON'T REALLY LIKE BEING GUIDED AROUND, THOUGH.

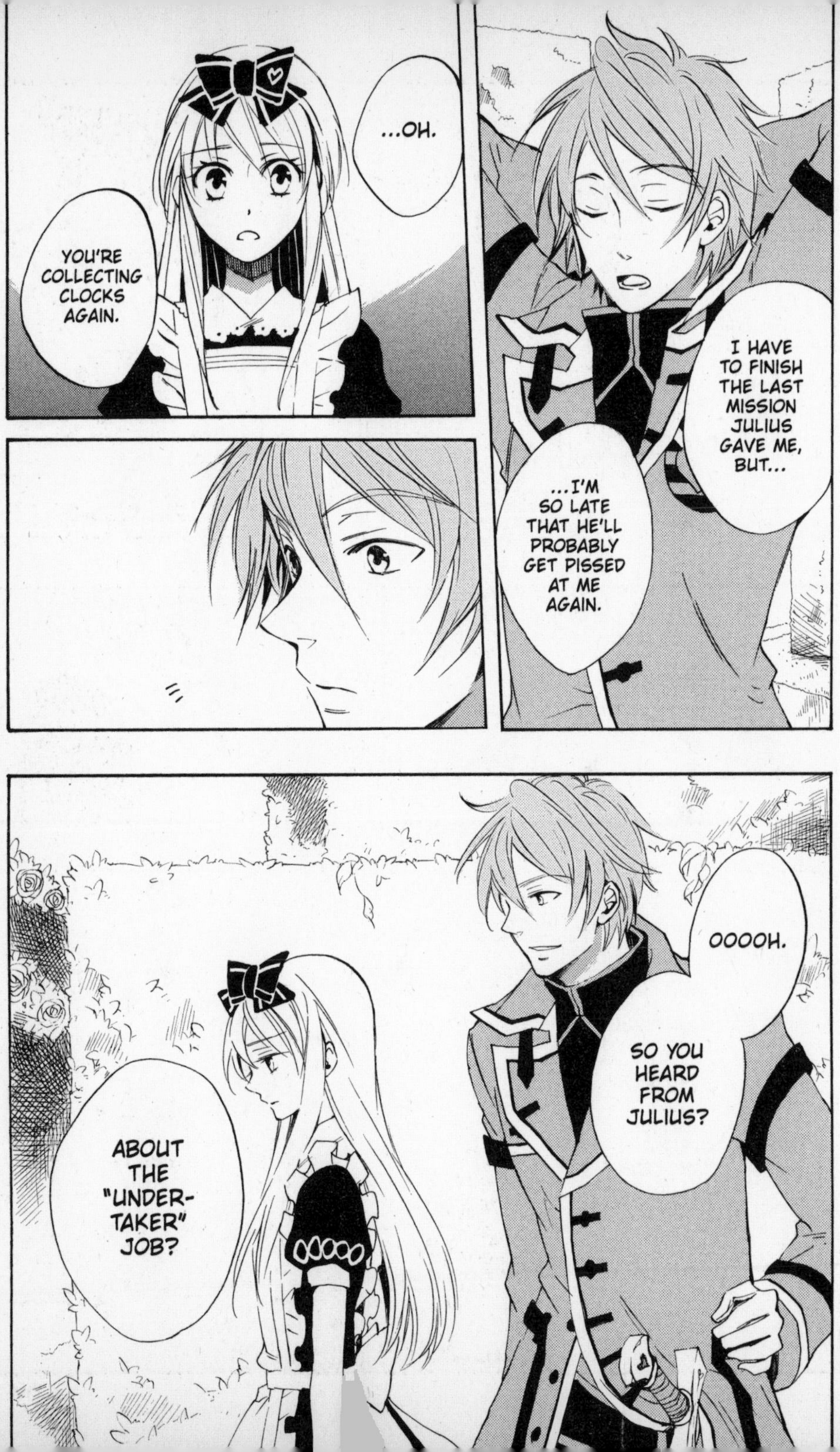
I HAVE TO FINISH THE LAST MISSION JULIUS GAVE ME, BUT...
...I'M SO LATE THAT HE'LL PROBABLY GET PISSED AT ME AGAIN.
...OH.
YOU'RE COLLECTING CLOCKS AGAIN.
OOOOH.
SO YOU HEARD FROM JULIUS?
ABOUT THE "UNDER-TAKER" JOB?

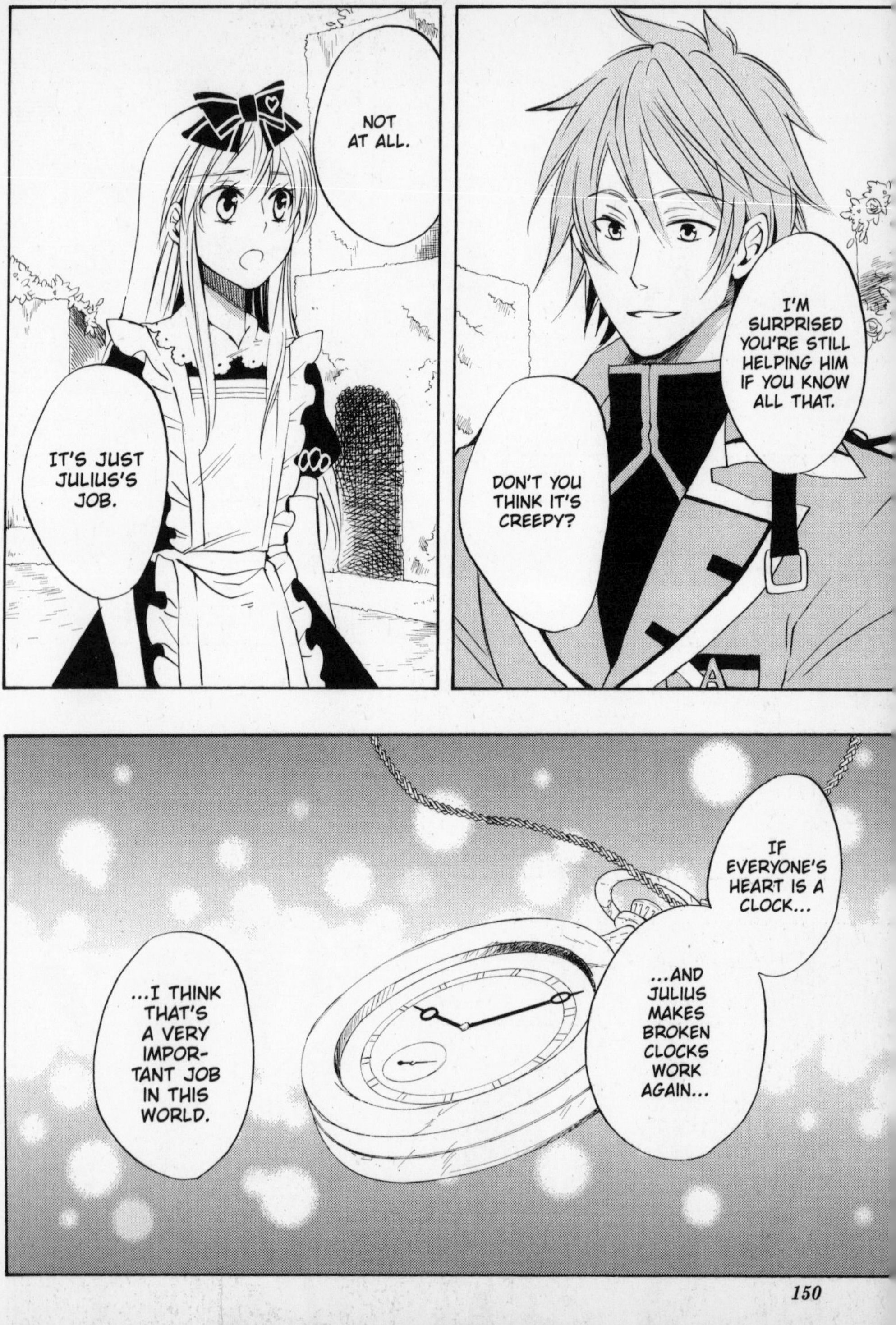
I'M SURPRISED YOU'RE STILL HELPING HIM IF YOU KNOW ALL THAT.
DON'T YOU THINK IT'S CREEPY?
NOT AT ALL.
IT'S JUST JULIUS'S JOB.
IF EVERYONE'S HEART IS A CLOCK...
...AND JULIUS MAKES BROKEN CLOCKS WORK AGAIN...
...I THINK THAT'S A VERY IMPOR-TANT JOB IN THIS WORLD.

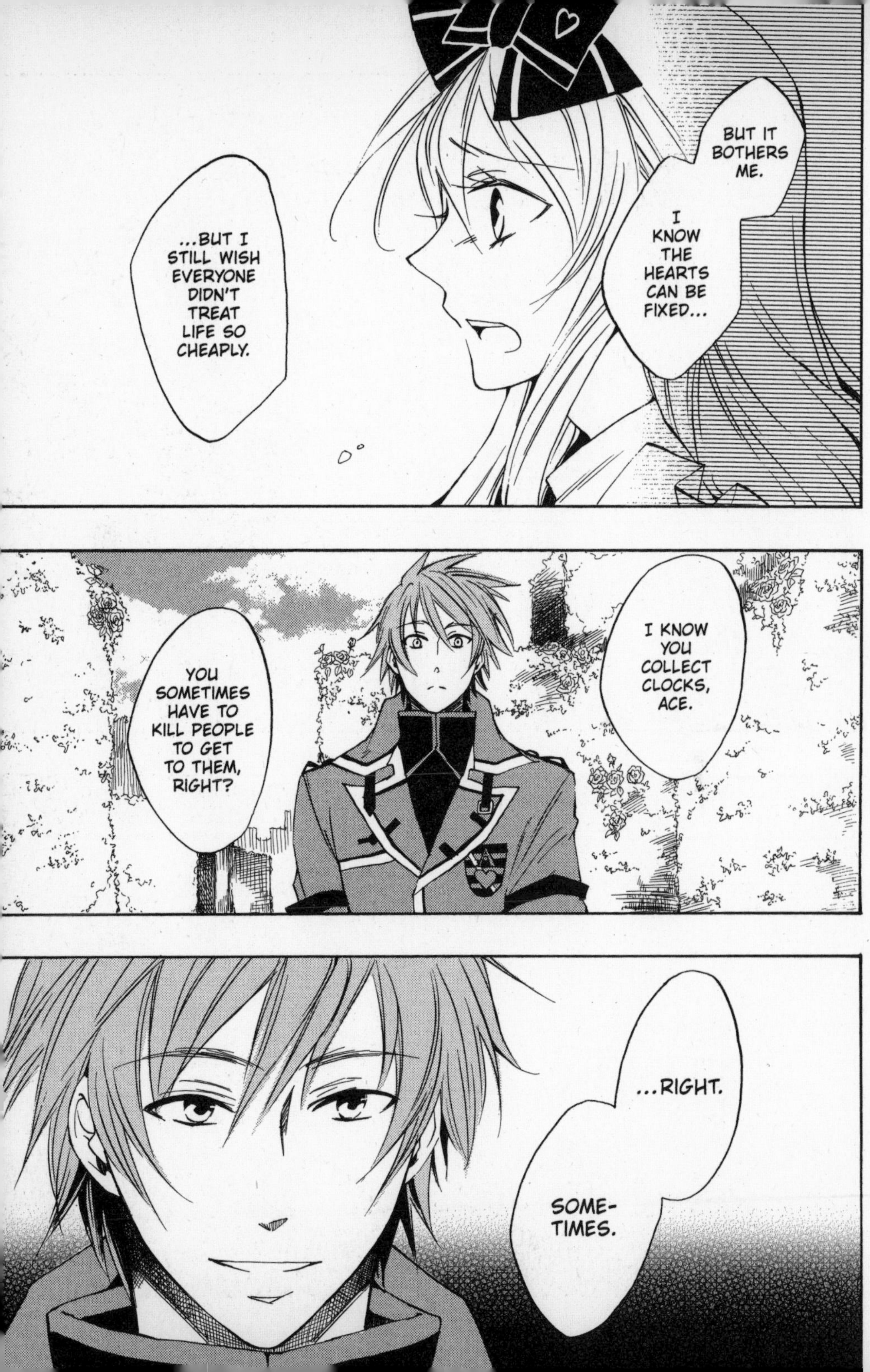
BUT IT BOTHERS ME.
I KNOW THE HEARTS CAN BE FIXED...
...BUT I STILL WISH EVERYONE DIDN'T TREAT LIFE SO CHEAPLY.
I KNOW YOU COLLECT CLOCKS, ACE.
YOU SOMETIMES HAVE TO KILL PEOPLE TO GET TO THEM, RIGHT?
...RIGHT.
SOME-TIMES.

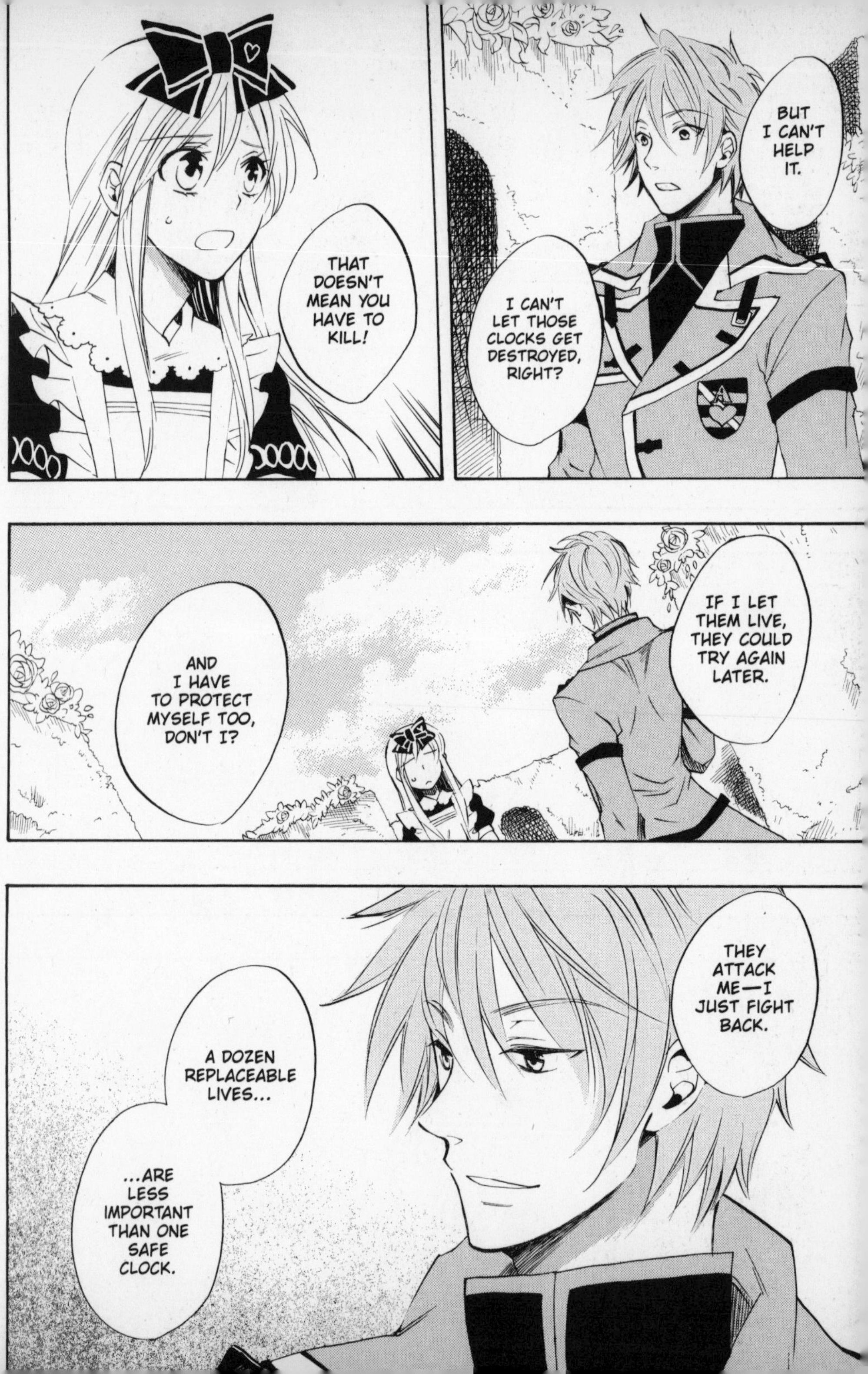
BUT I CAN'T HELP IT.
I CAN'T LET THOSE CLOCKS GET DESTROYED, RIGHT?
THAT DOESN'T MEAN YOU HAVE TO KILL!
IF I LET THEM LIVE, THEY COULD TRY AGAIN LATER.
AND I HAVE TO PROTECT MYSELF TOO, DON'T I?
THEY ATTACK ME—I JUST FIGHT BACK.
A DOZEN REPLACEABLE LIVES...
...ARE LESS IMPORTANT THAN ONE SAFE CLOCK.

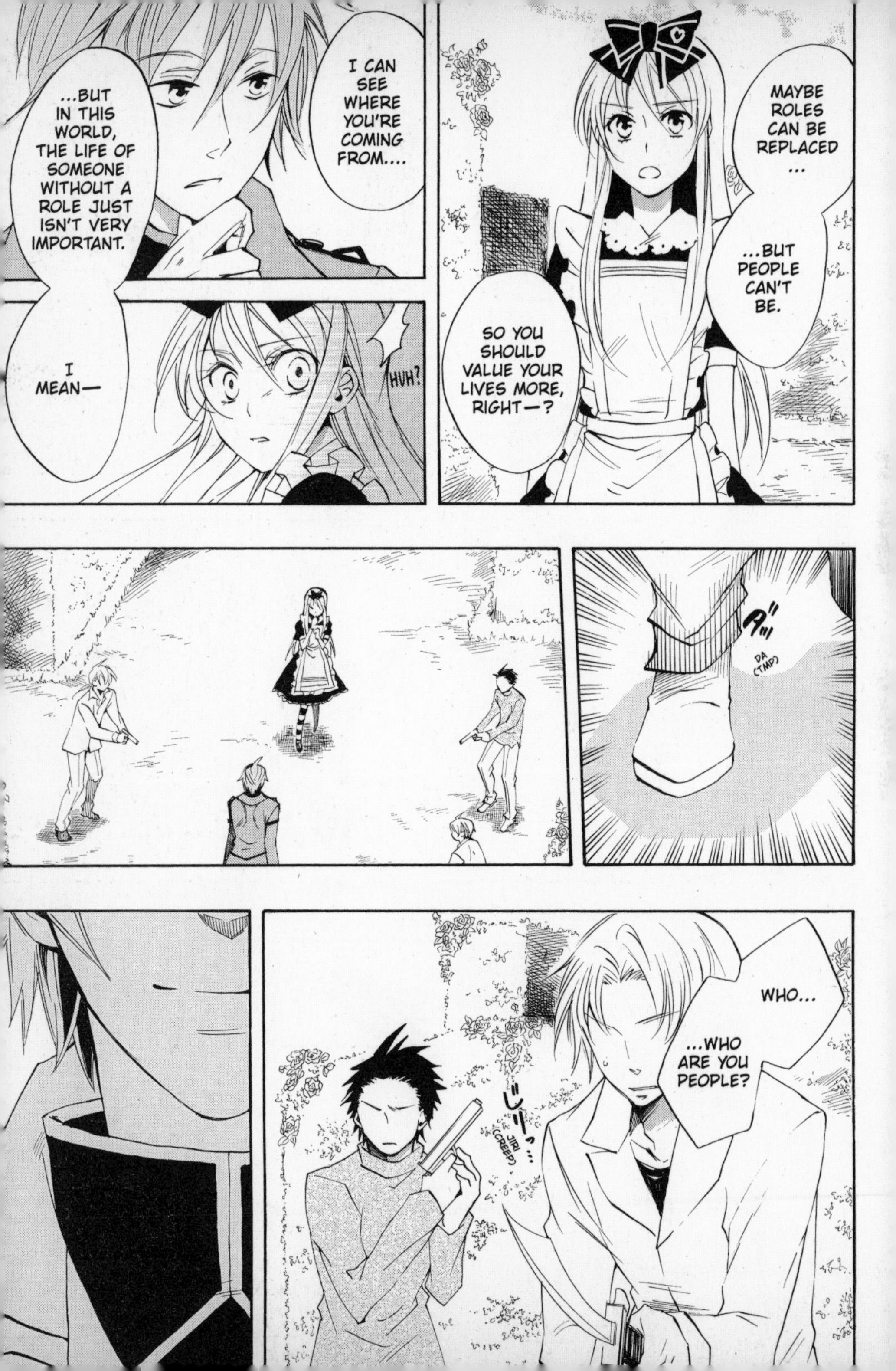
MAYBE ROLES CAN BE REPLACED ...
...BUT PEOPLE CAN'T BE.
SO YOU SHOULD VALUE YOUR LIVES MORE, RIGHT—?
I CAN SEE WHERE YOU'RE COMING FROM....
...BUT IN THIS WORLD, THE LIFE OF SOMEONE WITHOUT A ROLE JUST ISN'T VERY IMPORTANT.
HUH?
I MEAN—
DA (TMP)
WHO...
...WHO ARE YOU PEOPLE?
JIRI (CREEP)

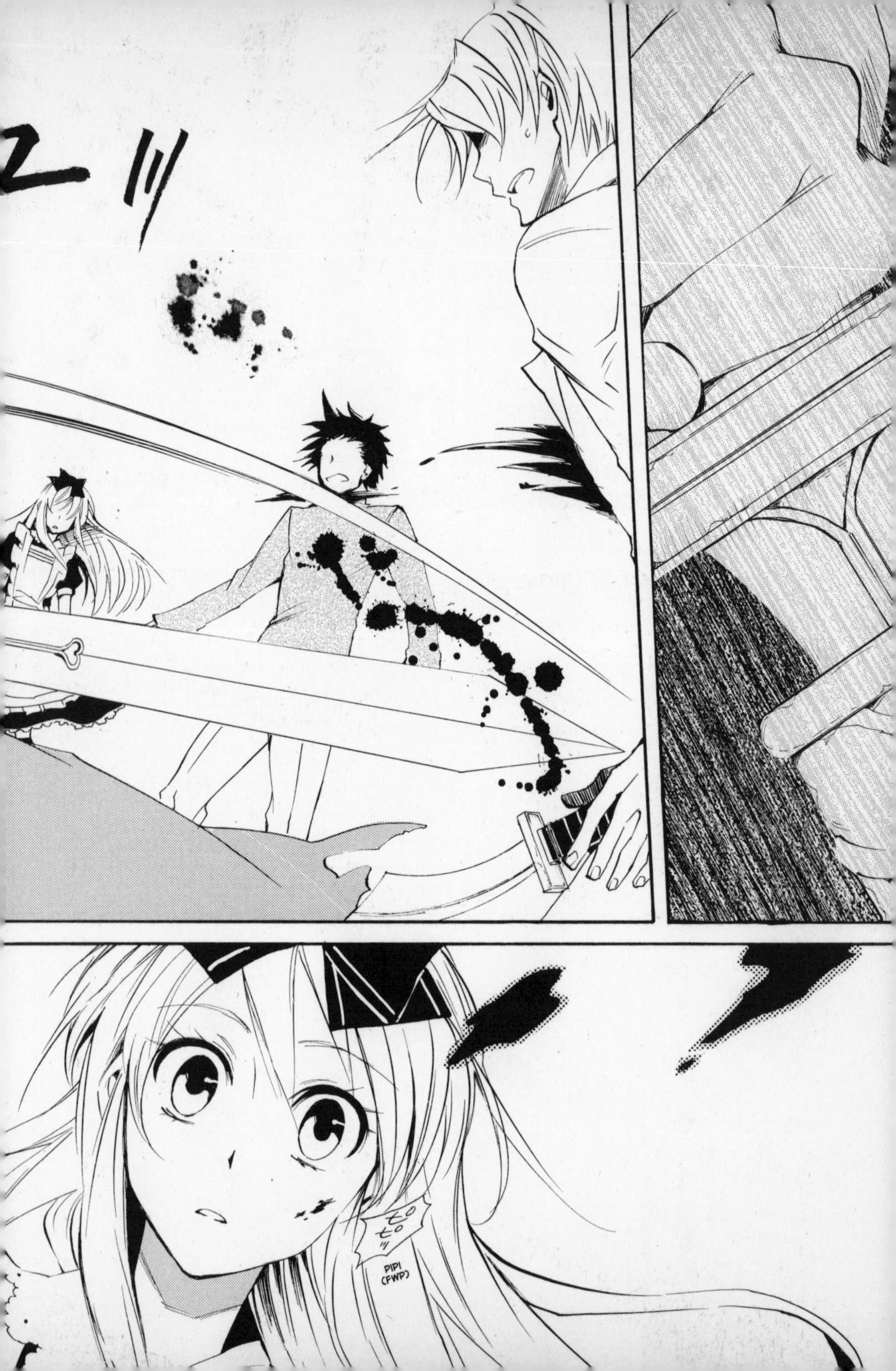
ピピッ
PIPI
(FWP)

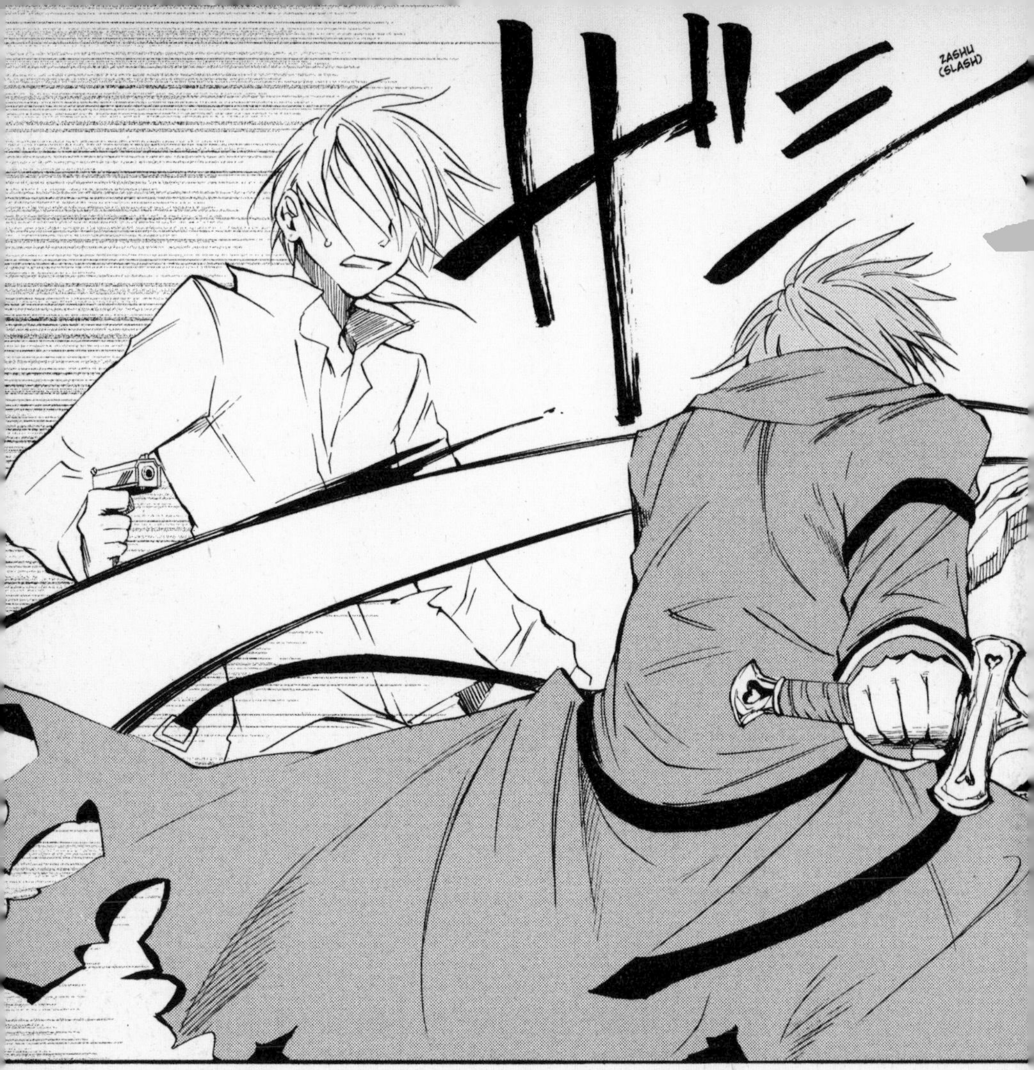
ザシュ
ZASHU (SLASH)
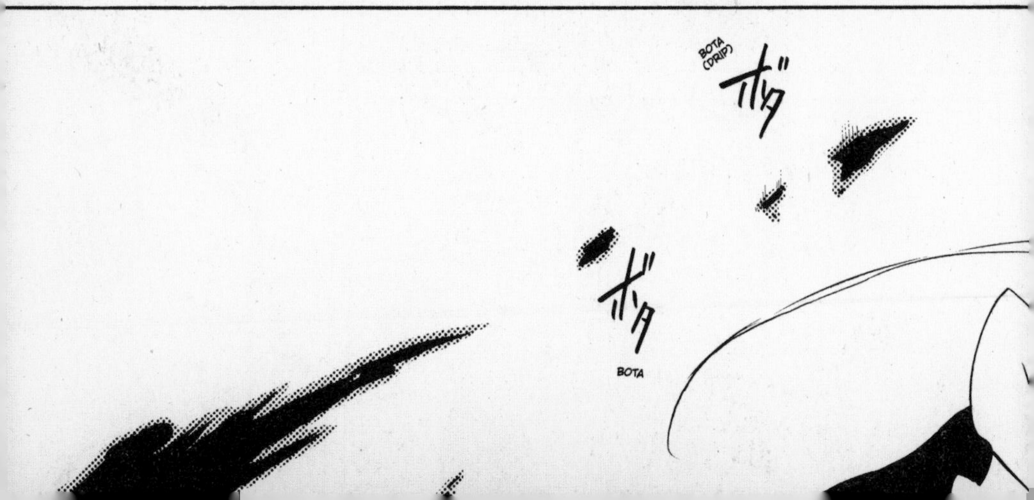
ボタ
BOTA (DRIP)
ボタ
BOTA

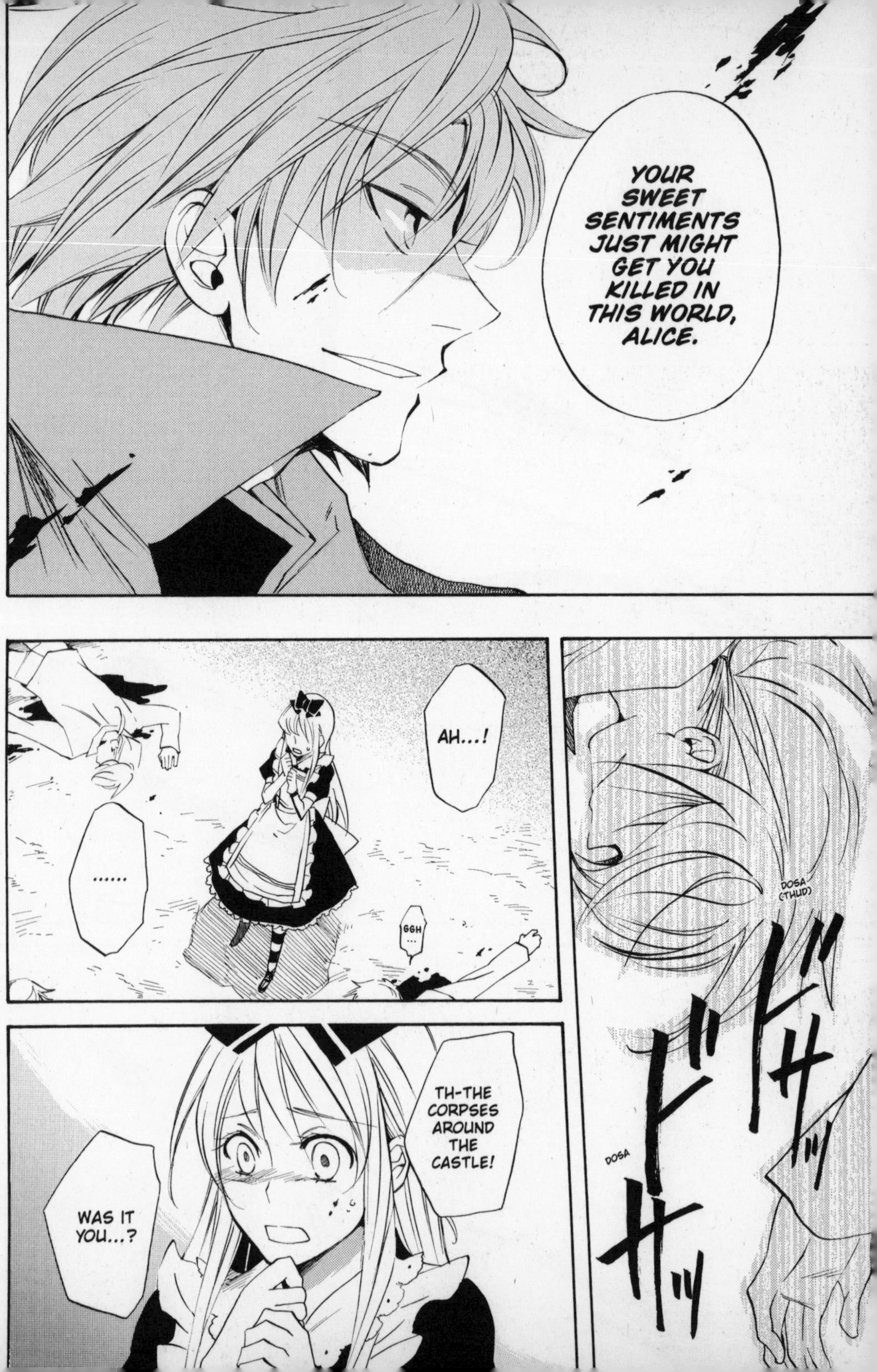
YOUR SWEET SENTIMENTS JUST MIGHT GET YOU KILLED IN THIS WORLD, ALICE.
DOSA (THUD)
ドサッ
DOSA
ドサッ
AH...!
......
GGH ...
TH-THE CORPSES AROUND THE CASTLE!
WAS IT YOU...?

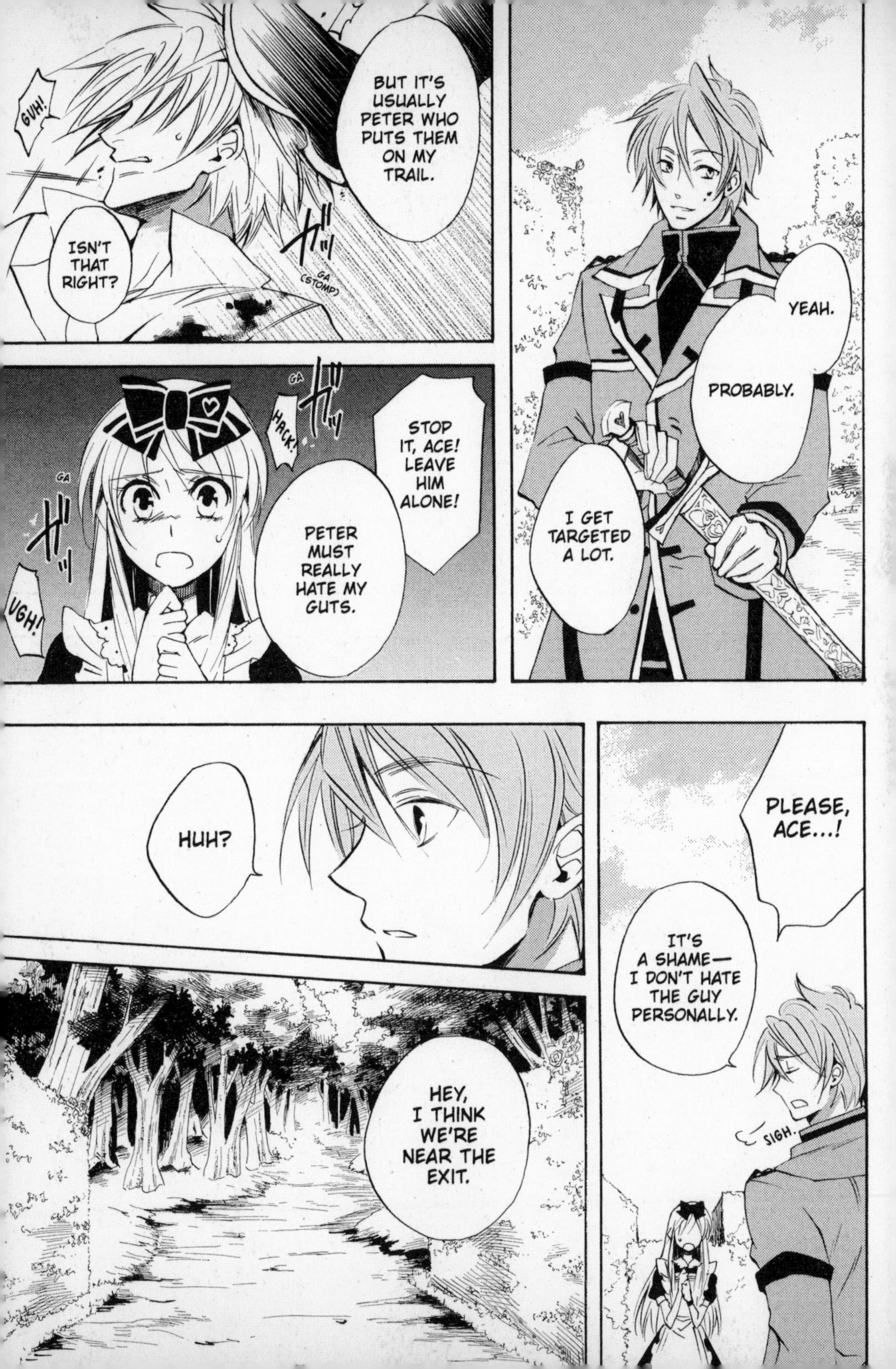
YEAH.
PROBABLY.
I GET TARGETED A LOT.
BUT IT'S USUALLY PETER WHO PUTS THEM ON MY TRAIL.
ISN'T THAT RIGHT?
GUH!
ガッ
GA (STOMP)
STOP IT, ACE! LEAVE HIM ALONE!
GA ガッ
HACK!
PETER MUST REALLY HATE MY GUTS.
GA ガッ
UGH!
PLEASE, ACE...!
IT'S A SHAME— I DON'T HATE THE GUY PERSONALLY.
SIGH.
HUH?
HEY, I THINK WE'RE NEAR THE EXIT.

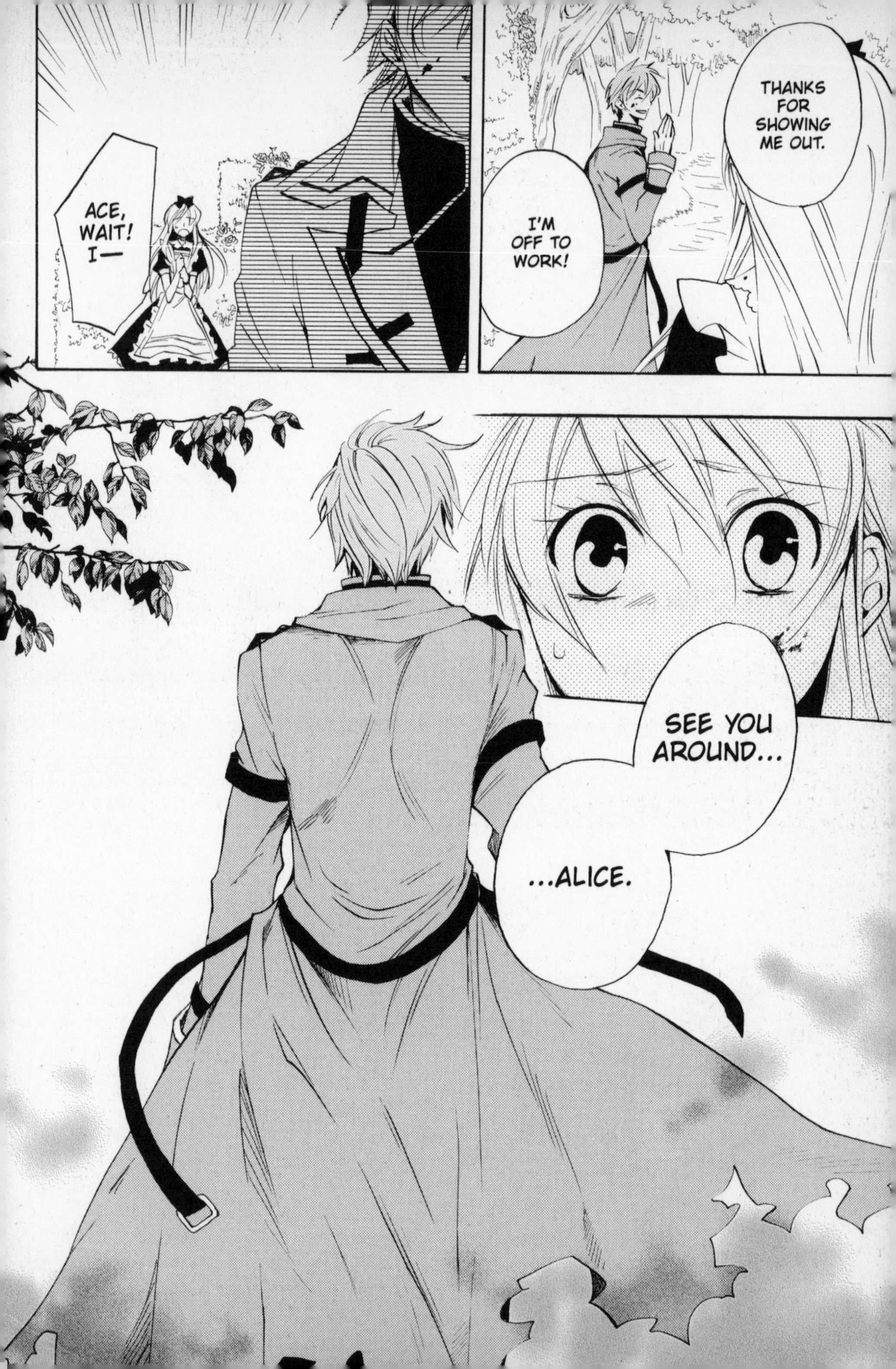
THANKS FOR SHOWING ME OUT.
I'M OFF TO WORK!
ACE, WAIT! I—
SEE YOU AROUND...
...ALICE.

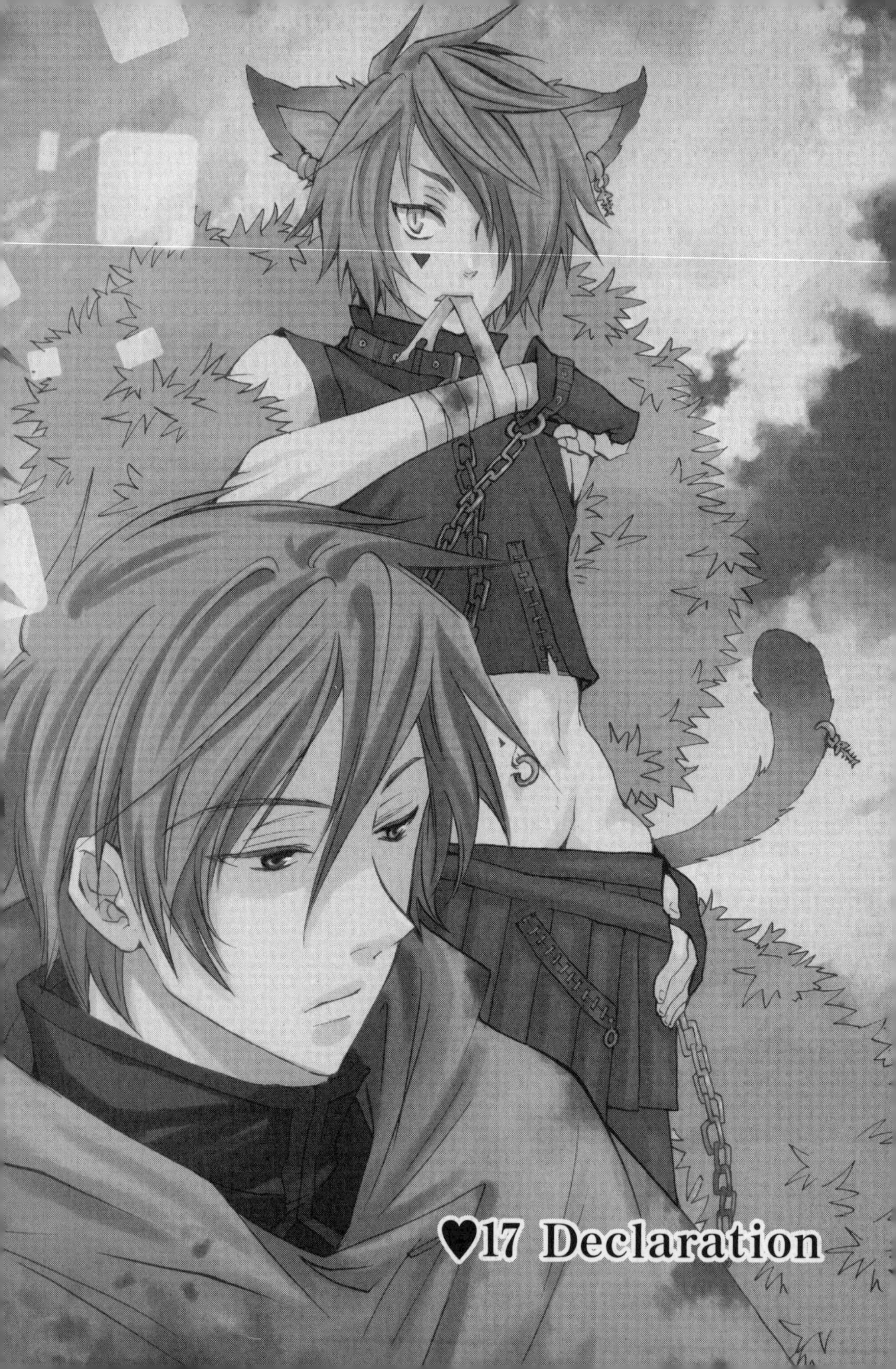

♥17 Declaration

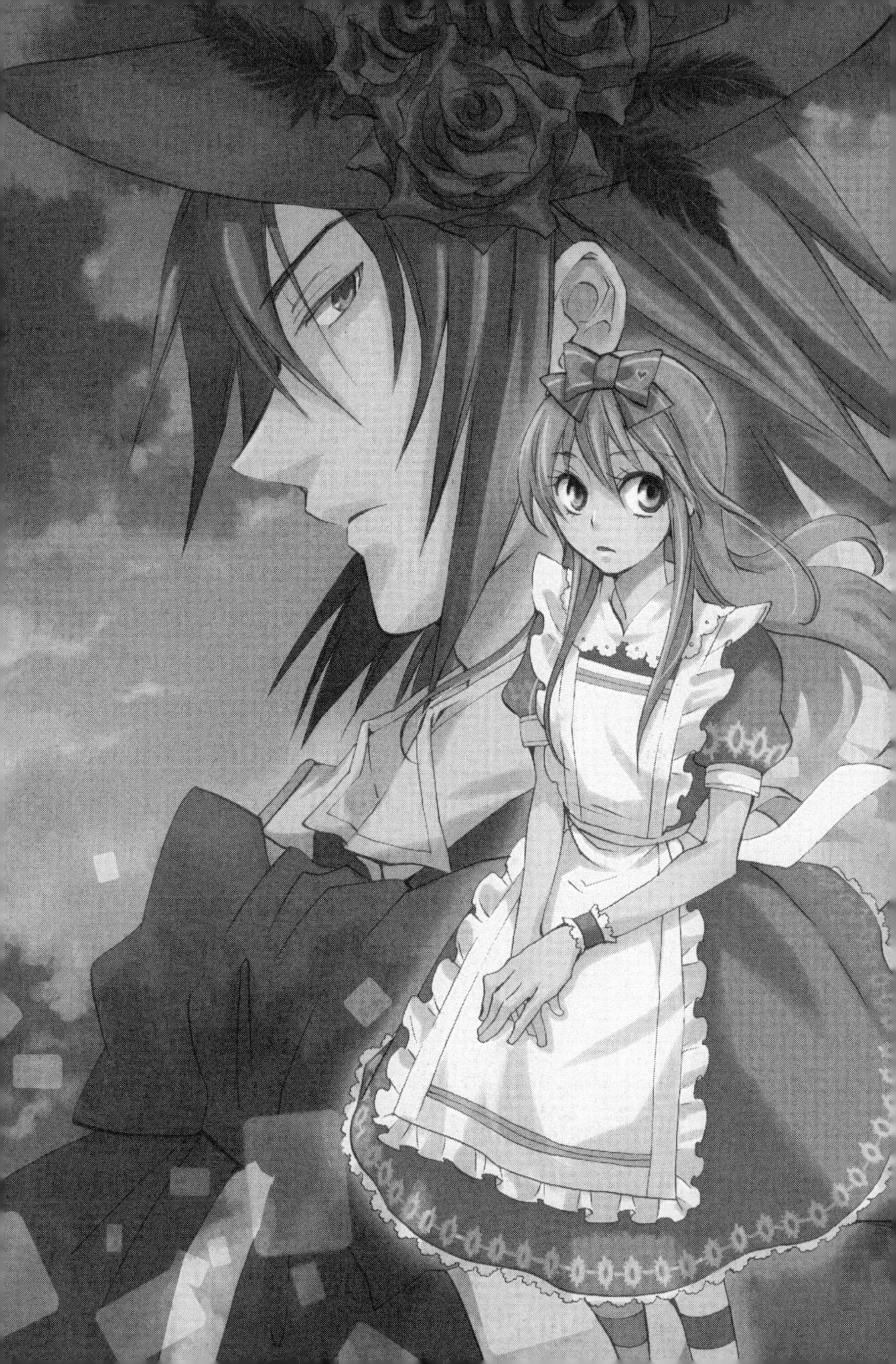

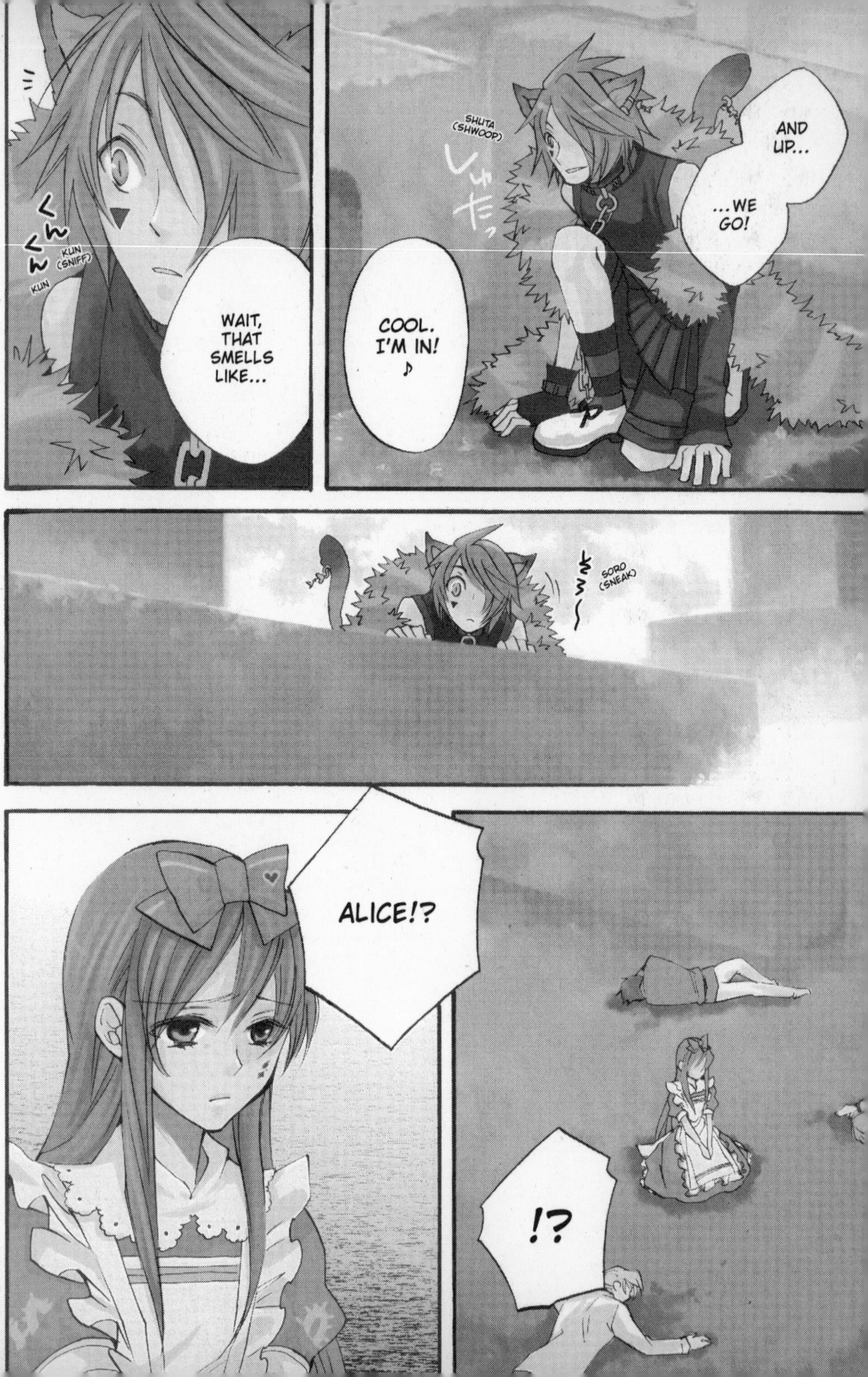
AND UP...
...WE GO!
しゅたっ
SHUTA (SHWOOP)
COOL. I'M IN! ♪
くんくん
KUN KUN (SNIFF)
WAIT, THAT SMELLS LIKE...
そろ〜
SORO (SNEAK)
!?
ALICE!?

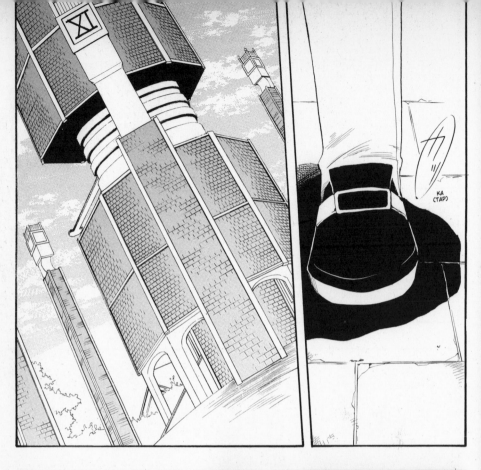

KA
(TAP)

...HMMM.

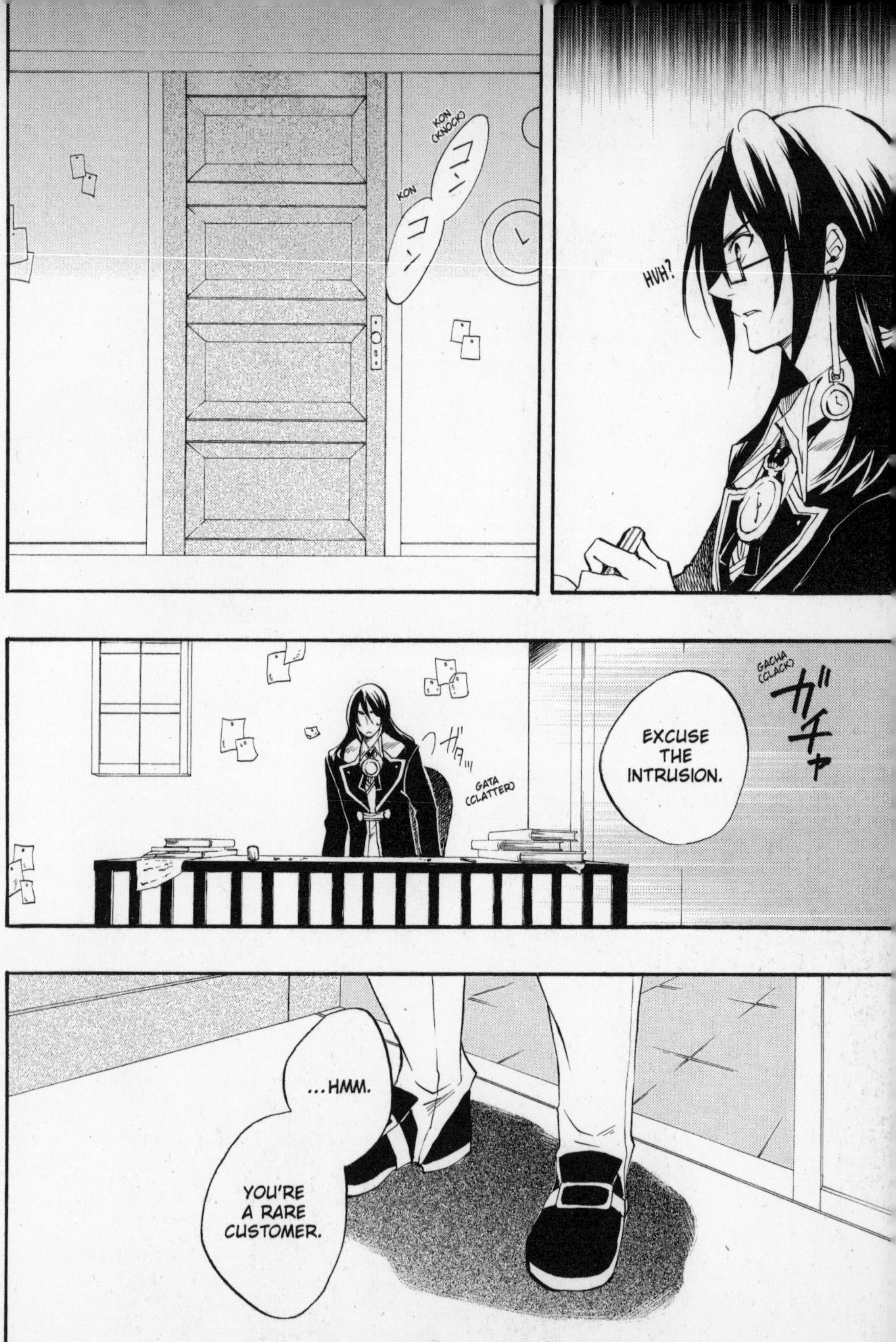
HUH?
KON (KNOCK)
コン
KON
コン
GACHA (CLACK)
ガチャ
EXCUSE THE INTRUSION.
ガタッ
GATA (CLATTER)
...HMM.
YOU'RE A RARE CUSTOMER.

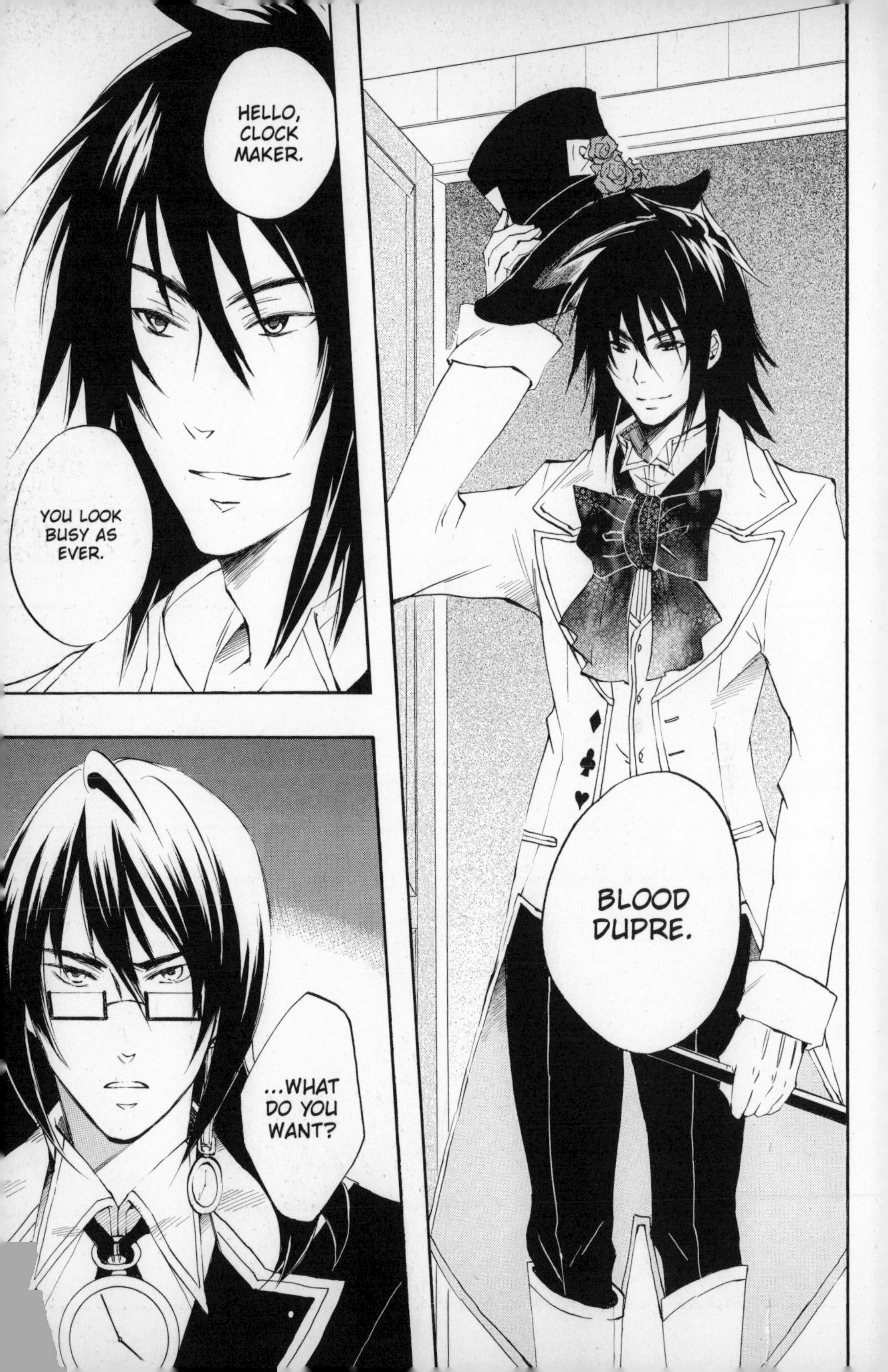
BLOOD DUPRE.
HELLO, CLOCK MAKER.
YOU LOOK BUSY AS EVER.
...WHAT DO YOU WANT?

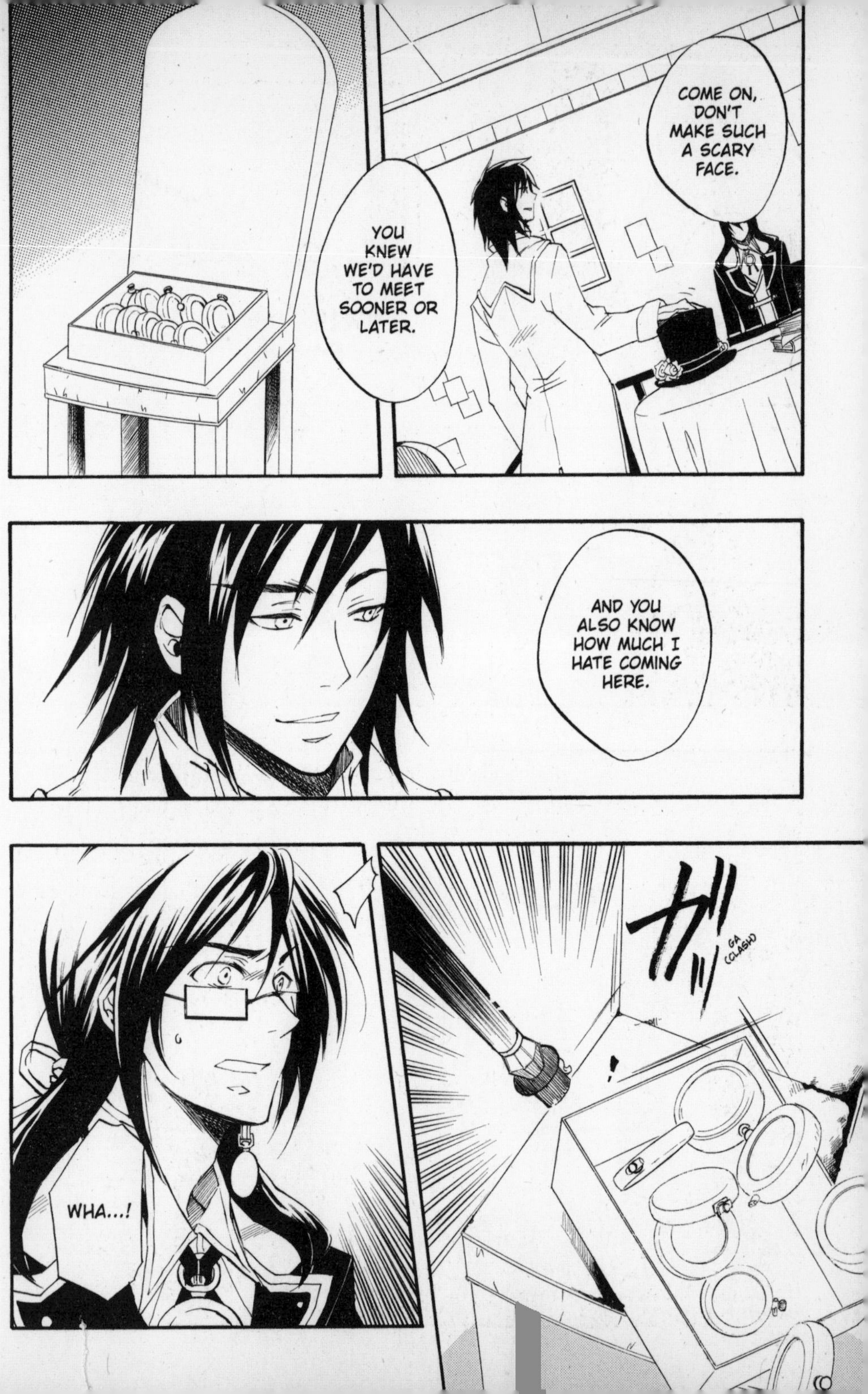
COME ON, DON'T MAKE SUCH A SCARY FACE.
YOU KNEW WE'D HAVE TO MEET SOONER OR LATER.
AND YOU ALSO KNOW HOW MUCH I HATE COMING HERE.
GA (CLASH)
WHA...!

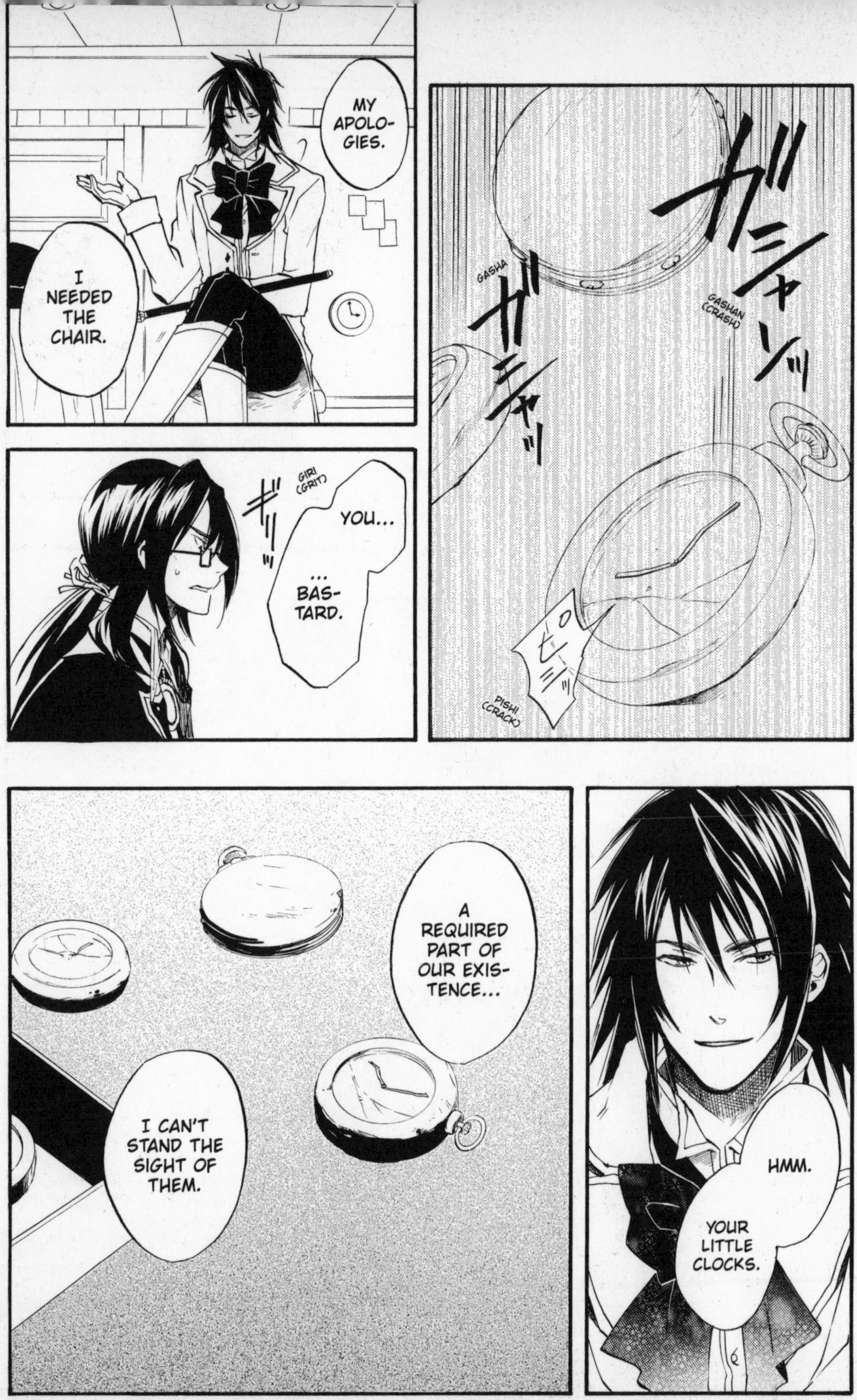
GASHAN (CRASH)
GASHA
PISHI (CRACK)
MY APOLO-GIES.
I NEEDED THE CHAIR.
GIRI (GRIT)
YOU...
... BAS-TARD.
HMM.
YOUR LITTLE CLOCKS.
A REQUIRED PART OF OUR EXIS-TENCE...
I CAN'T STAND THE SIGHT OF THEM.

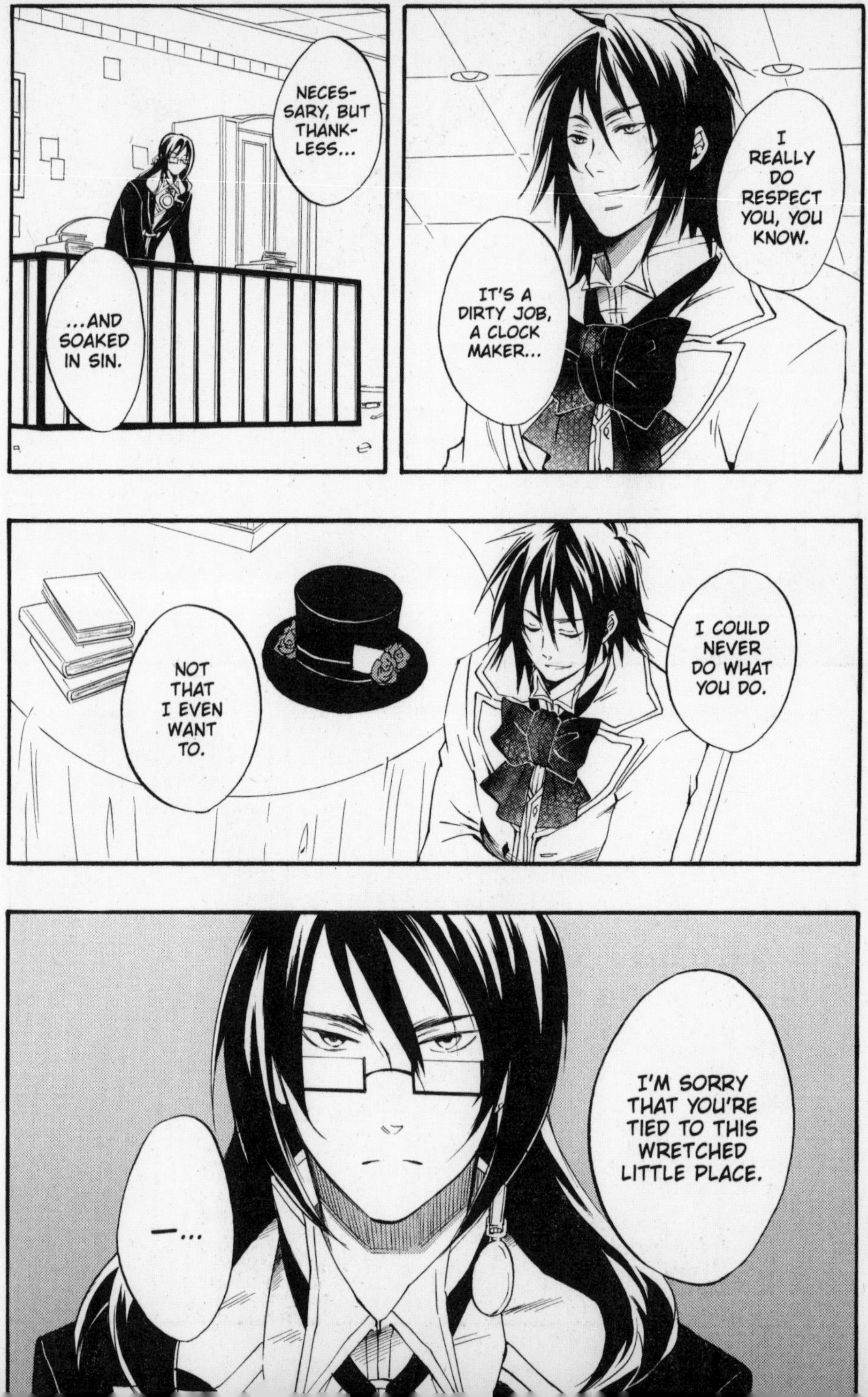
I REALLY DO RESPECT YOU, YOU KNOW.
IT'S A DIRTY JOB, A CLOCK MAKER...
NECES-SARY, BUT THANK-LESS...
...AND SOAKED IN SIN.
I COULD NEVER DO WHAT YOU DO.
NOT THAT I EVEN WANT TO.
I'M SORRY THAT YOU'RE TIED TO THIS WRETCHED LITTLE PLACE.
—...

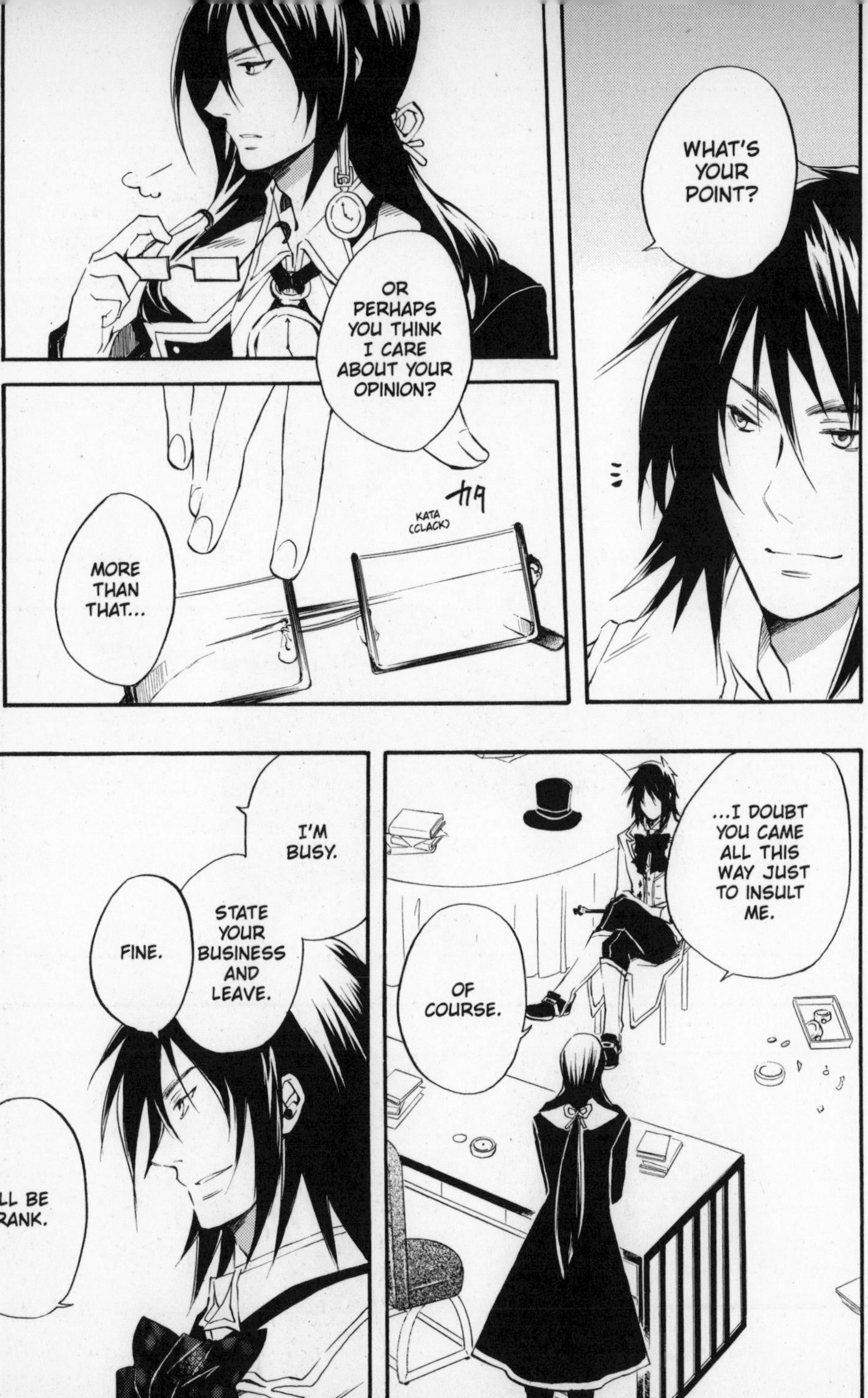
WHAT'S YOUR POINT?
OR PERHAPS YOU THINK I CARE ABOUT YOUR OPINION?
カタ
KATA (CLACK)
MORE THAN THAT...
...I DOUBT YOU CAME ALL THIS WAY JUST TO INSULT ME.
OF COURSE.
I'M BUSY.
STATE YOUR BUSINESS AND LEAVE.
FINE.
I'LL BE FRANK.

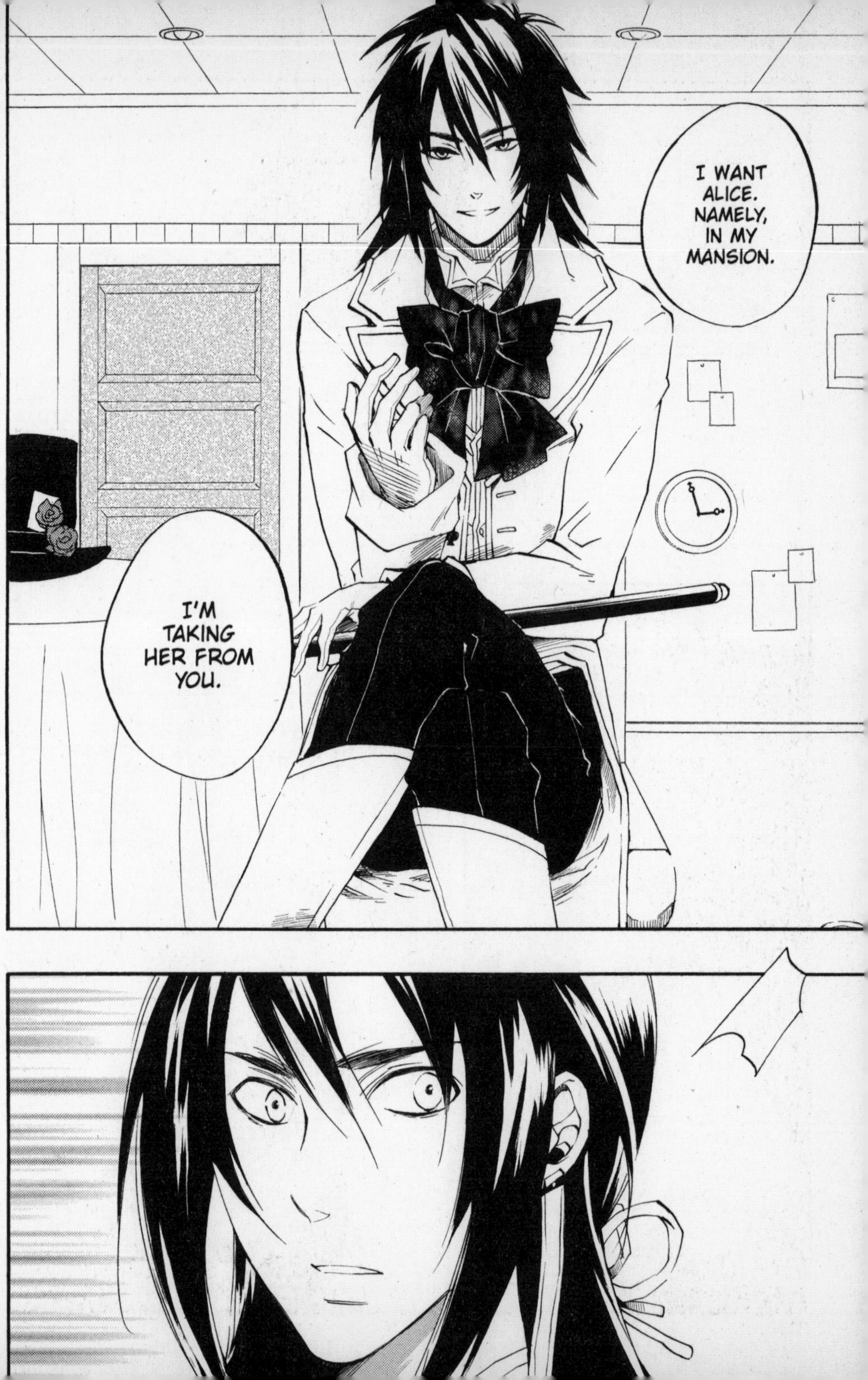
I WANT ALICE. NAMELY, IN MY MANSION.
I'M TAKING HER FROM YOU.

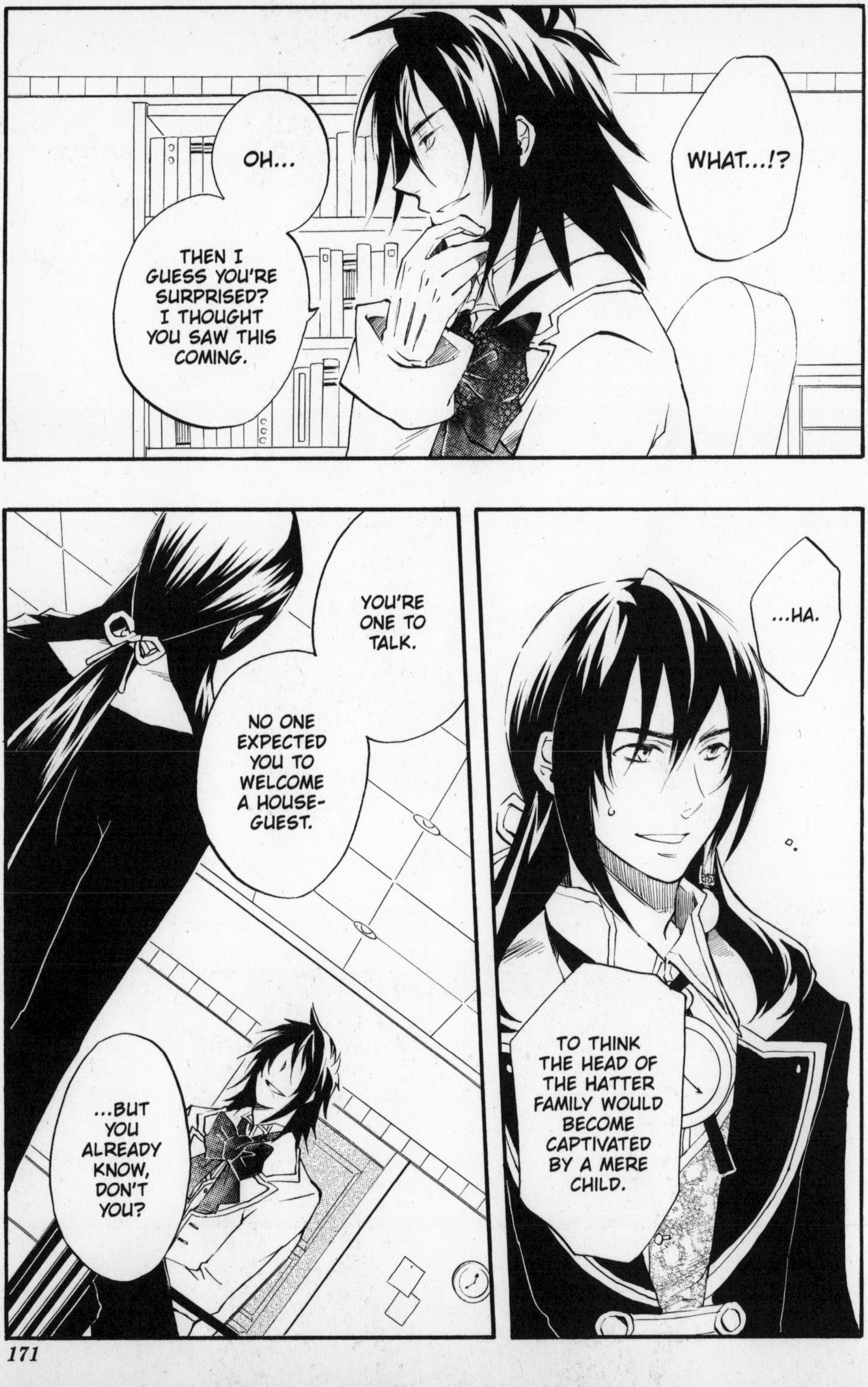
WHAT...!?
OH...
THEN I GUESS YOU'RE SURPRISED? I THOUGHT YOU SAW THIS COMING.
...HA.
TO THINK THE HEAD OF THE HATTER FAMILY WOULD BECOME CAPTIVATED BY A MERE CHILD.
YOU'RE ONE TO TALK.
NO ONE EXPECTED YOU TO WELCOME A HOUSE-GUEST.
...BUT YOU ALREADY KNOW, DON'T YOU?

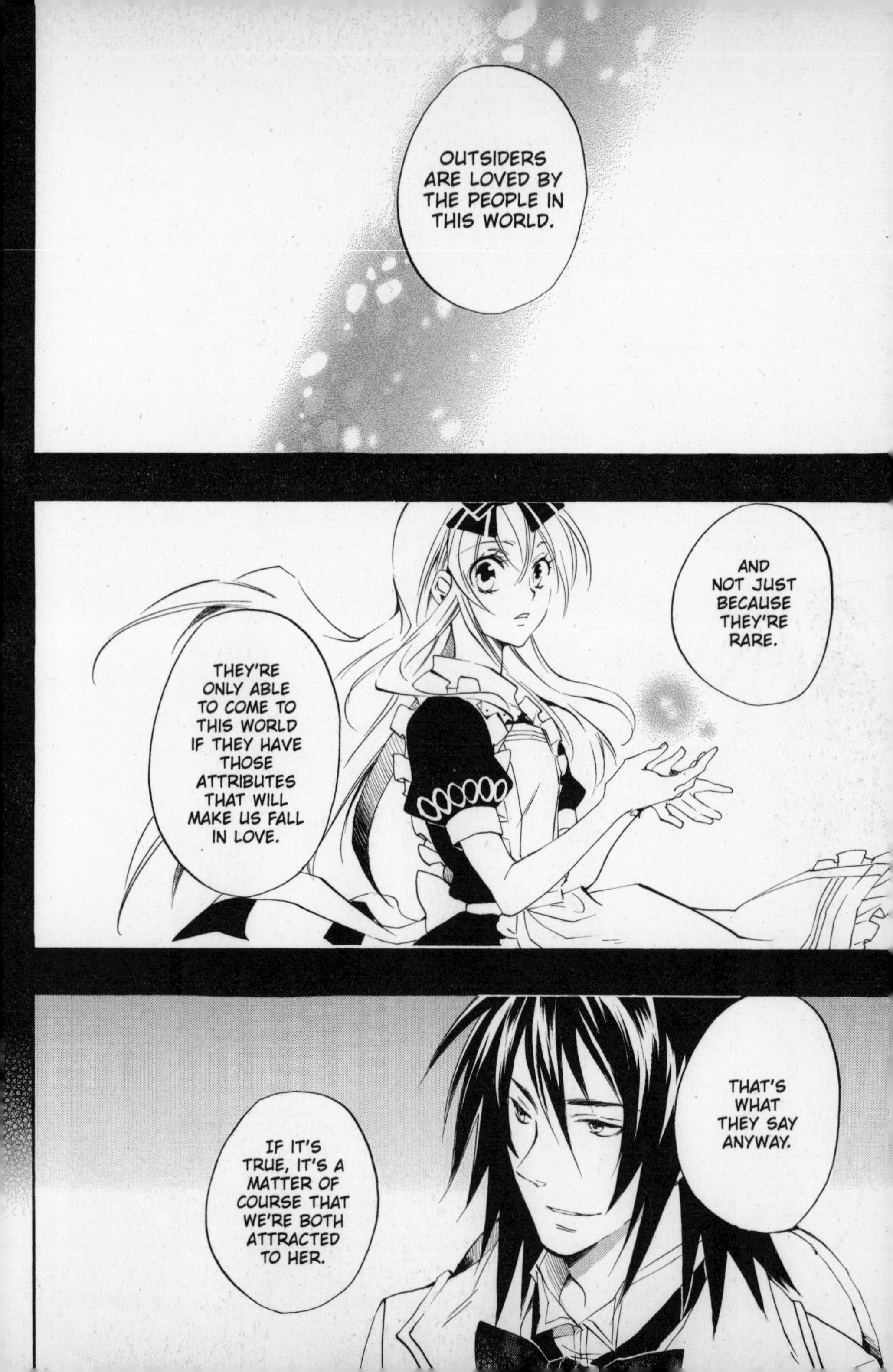
OUTSIDERS ARE LOVED BY THE PEOPLE IN THIS WORLD.
AND NOT JUST BECAUSE THEY'RE RARE.
THEY'RE ONLY ABLE TO COME TO THIS WORLD IF THEY HAVE THOSE ATTRIBUTES THAT WILL MAKE US FALL IN LOVE.
THAT'S WHAT THEY SAY ANYWAY.
IF IT'S TRUE, IT'S A MATTER OF COURSE THAT WE'RE BOTH ATTRACTED TO HER.

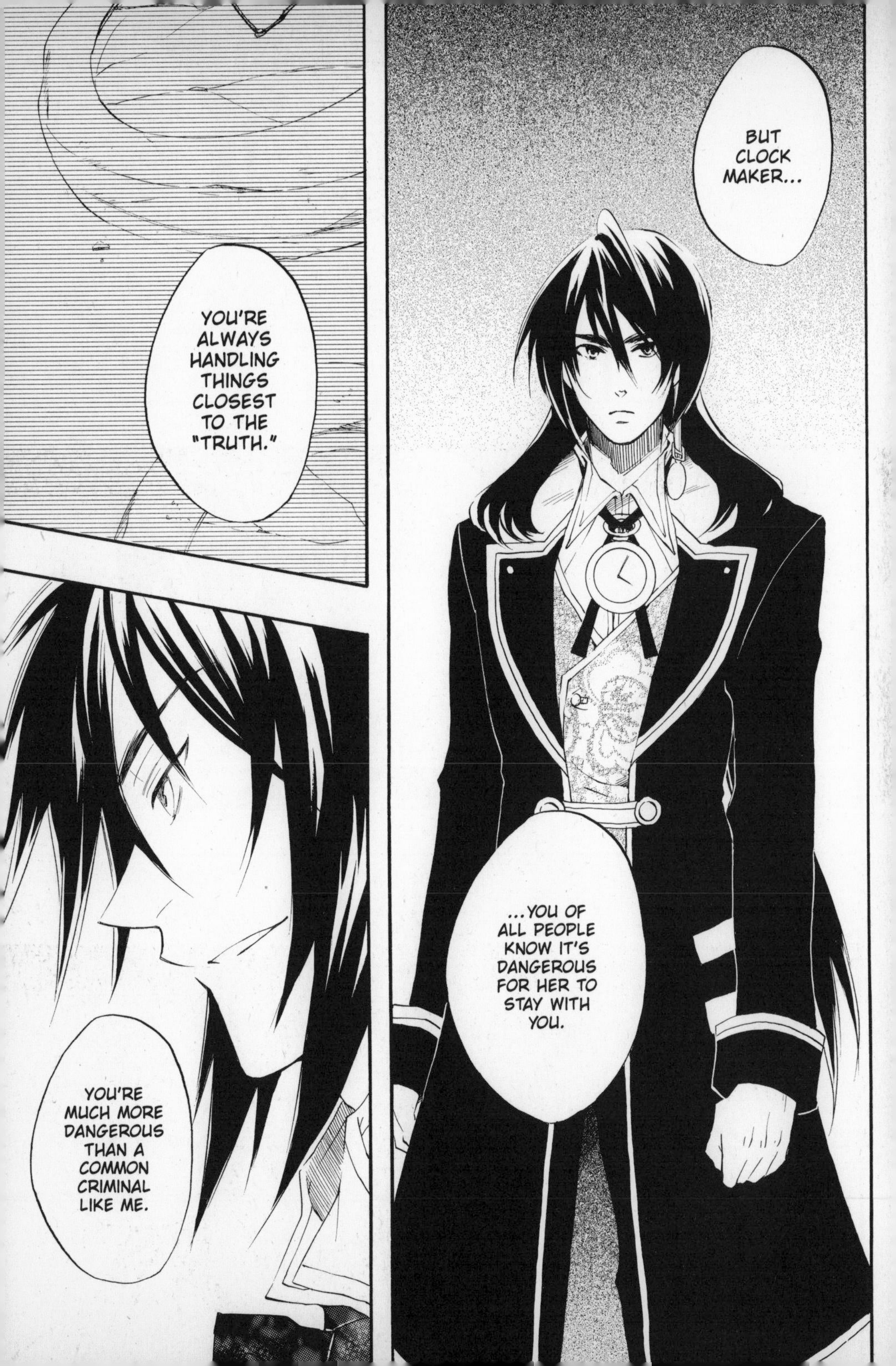
BUT CLOCK MAKER...
...YOU OF ALL PEOPLE KNOW IT'S DANGEROUS FOR HER TO STAY WITH YOU.
YOU'RE ALWAYS HANDLING THINGS CLOSEST TO THE "TRUTH."
YOU'RE MUCH MORE DANGEROUS THAN A COMMON CRIMINAL LIKE ME.

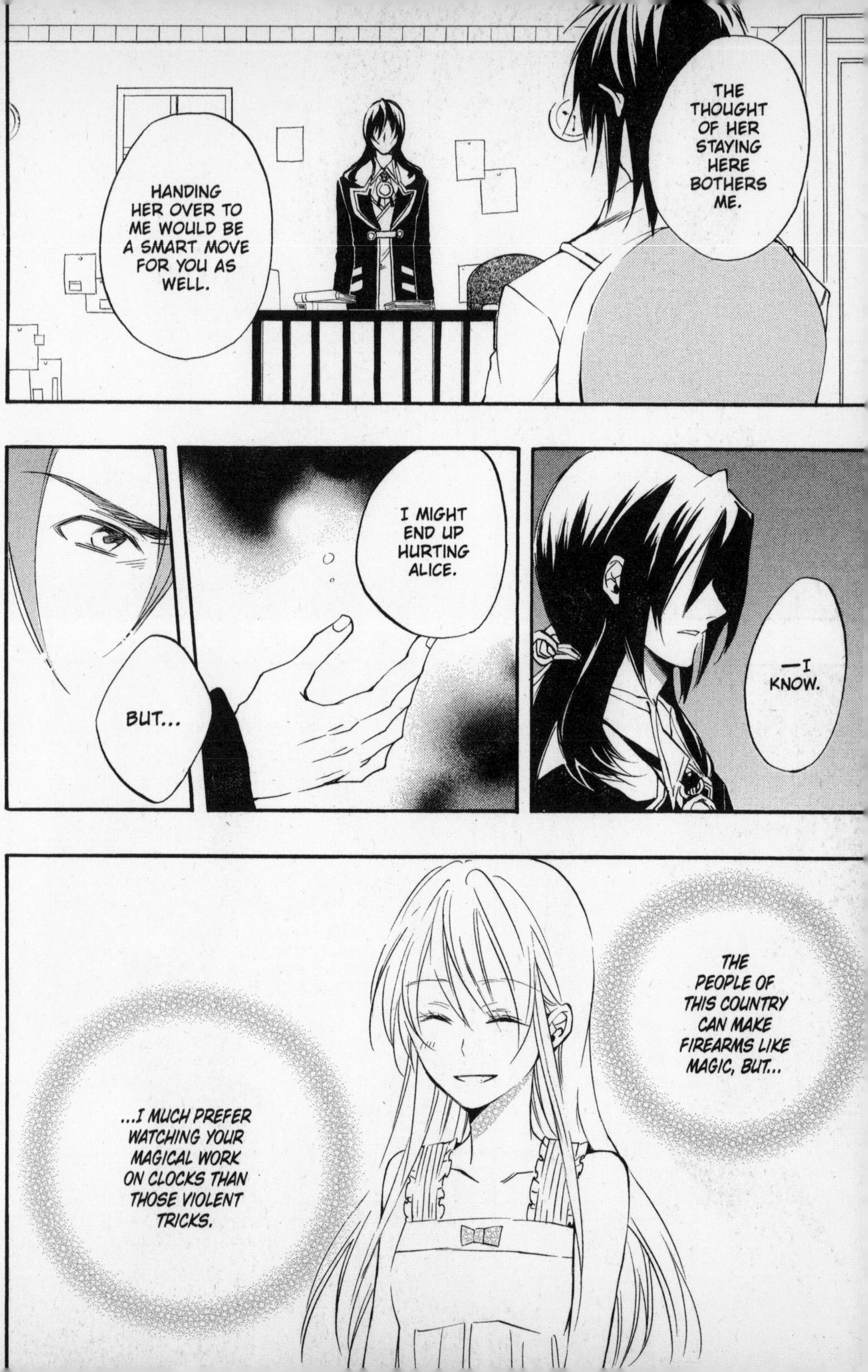
THE THOUGHT OF HER STAYING HERE BOTHERS ME.
HANDING HER OVER TO ME WOULD BE A SMART MOVE FOR YOU AS WELL.
—I KNOW.
I MIGHT END UP HURTING ALICE.
BUT...
THE PEOPLE OF THIS COUNTRY CAN MAKE FIREARMS LIKE MAGIC, BUT...
...I MUCH PREFER WATCHING YOUR MAGICAL WORK ON CLOCKS THAN THOSE VIOLENT TRICKS.

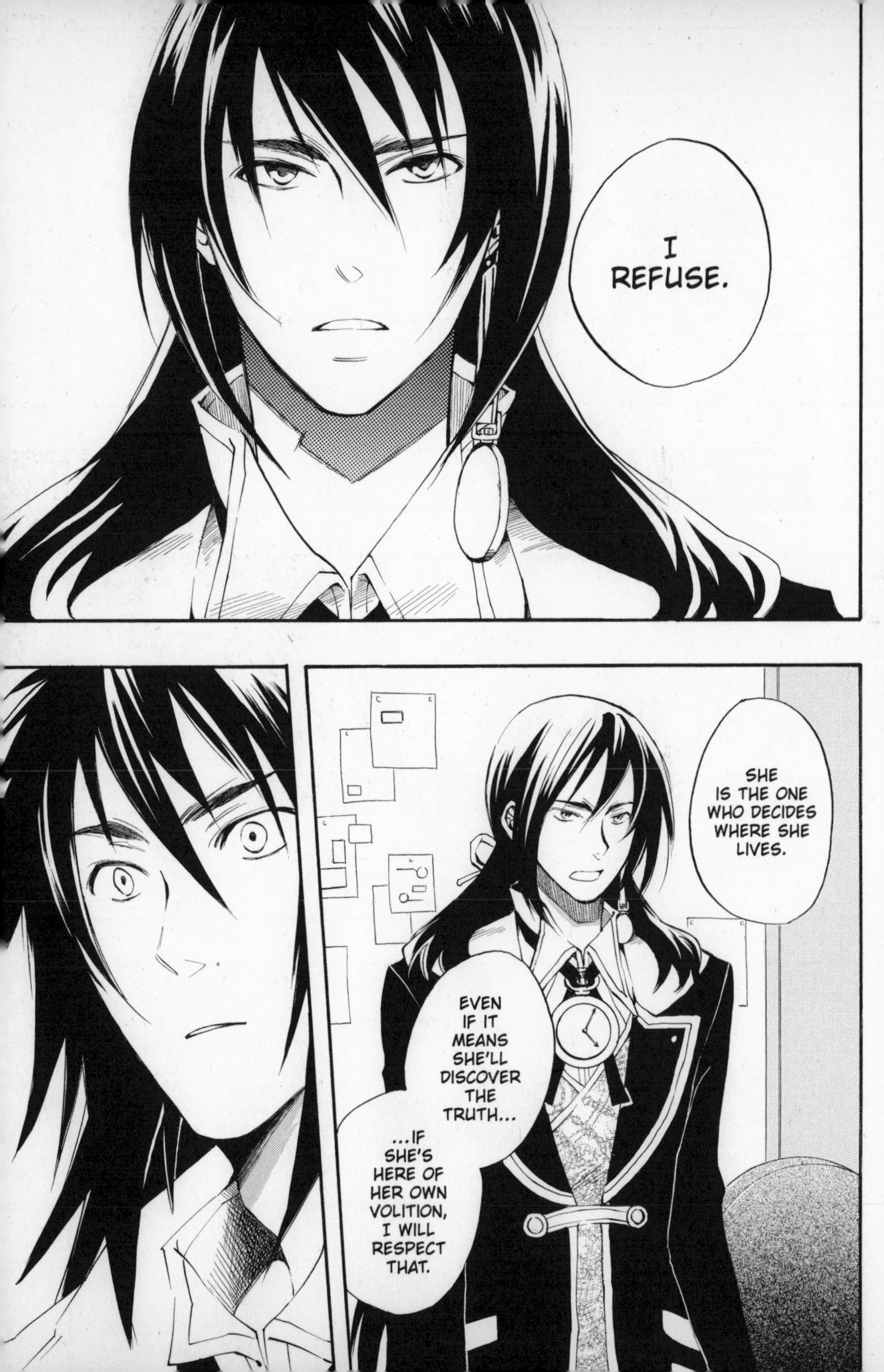
I REFUSE.
SHE IS THE ONE WHO DECIDES WHERE SHE LIVES.
EVEN IF IT MEANS SHE'LL DISCOVER THE TRUTH...
...IF SHE'S HERE OF HER OWN VOLITION, I WILL RESPECT THAT.

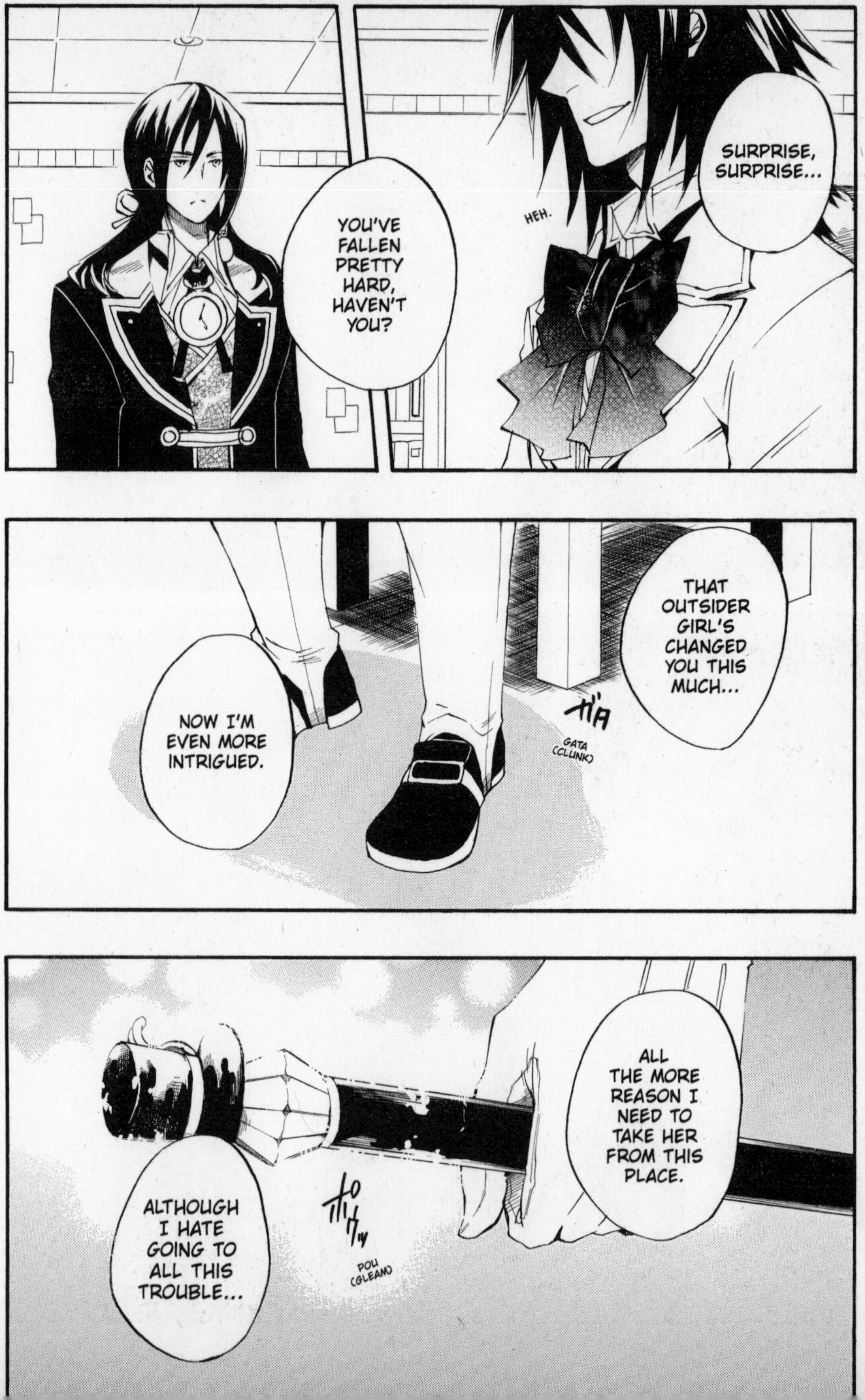
SURPRISE, SURPRISE...
HEH.
YOU'VE FALLEN PRETTY HARD, HAVEN'T YOU?
THAT OUTSIDER GIRL'S CHANGED YOU THIS MUCH...
GATA (CLUNK)
NOW I'M EVEN MORE INTRIGUED.
ALL THE MORE REASON I NEED TO TAKE HER FROM THIS PLACE.
POU (GLEAM)
ALTHOUGH I HATE GOING TO ALL THIS TROUBLE...

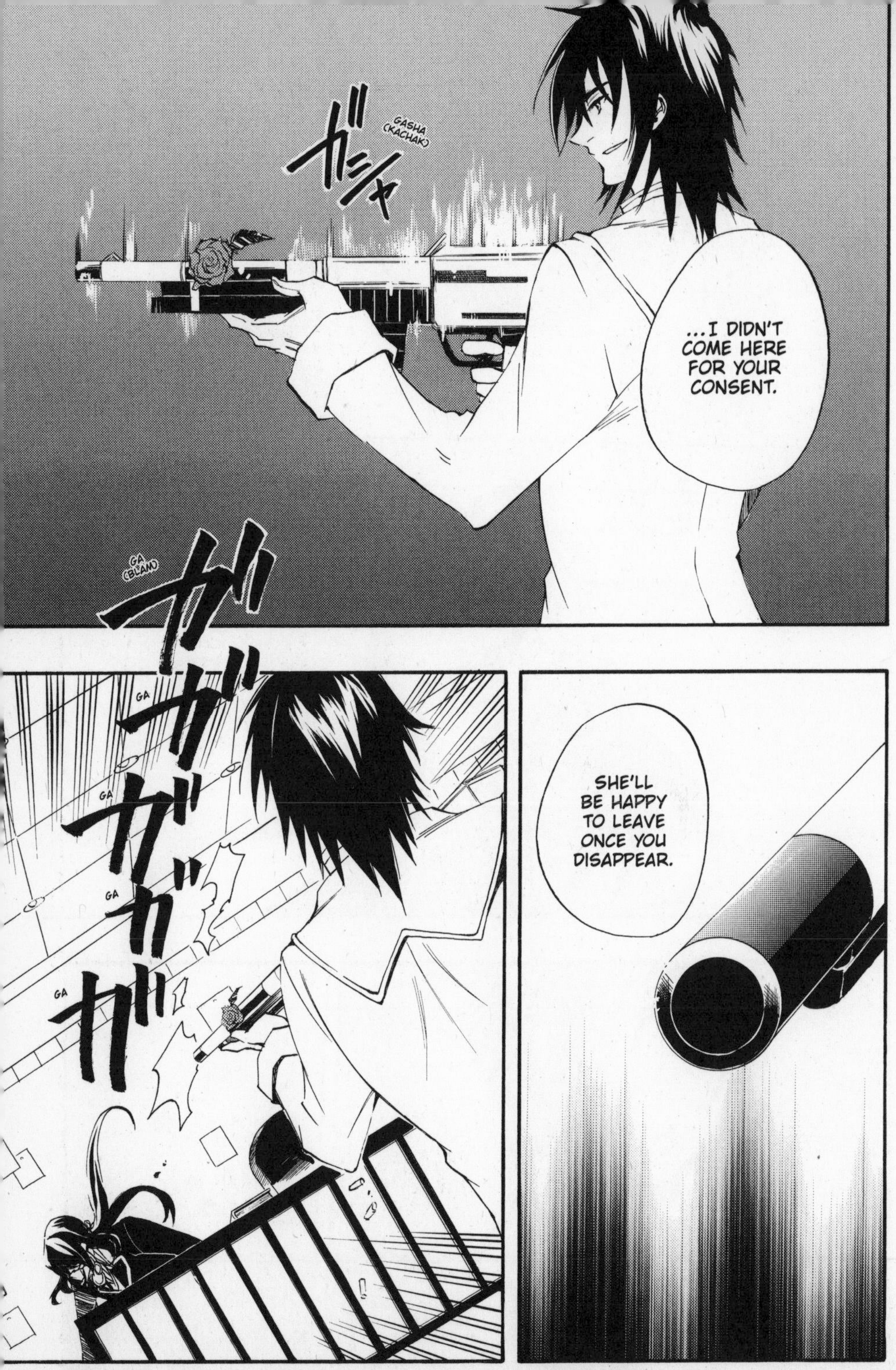

ガシャ
GASHA (KACHAK)
...I DIDN'T COME HERE FOR YOUR CONSENT.
SHE'LL BE HAPPY TO LEAVE ONCE YOU DISAPPEAR.
ガガガガガ
GA (BLAM)
GA
GA
GA
GA

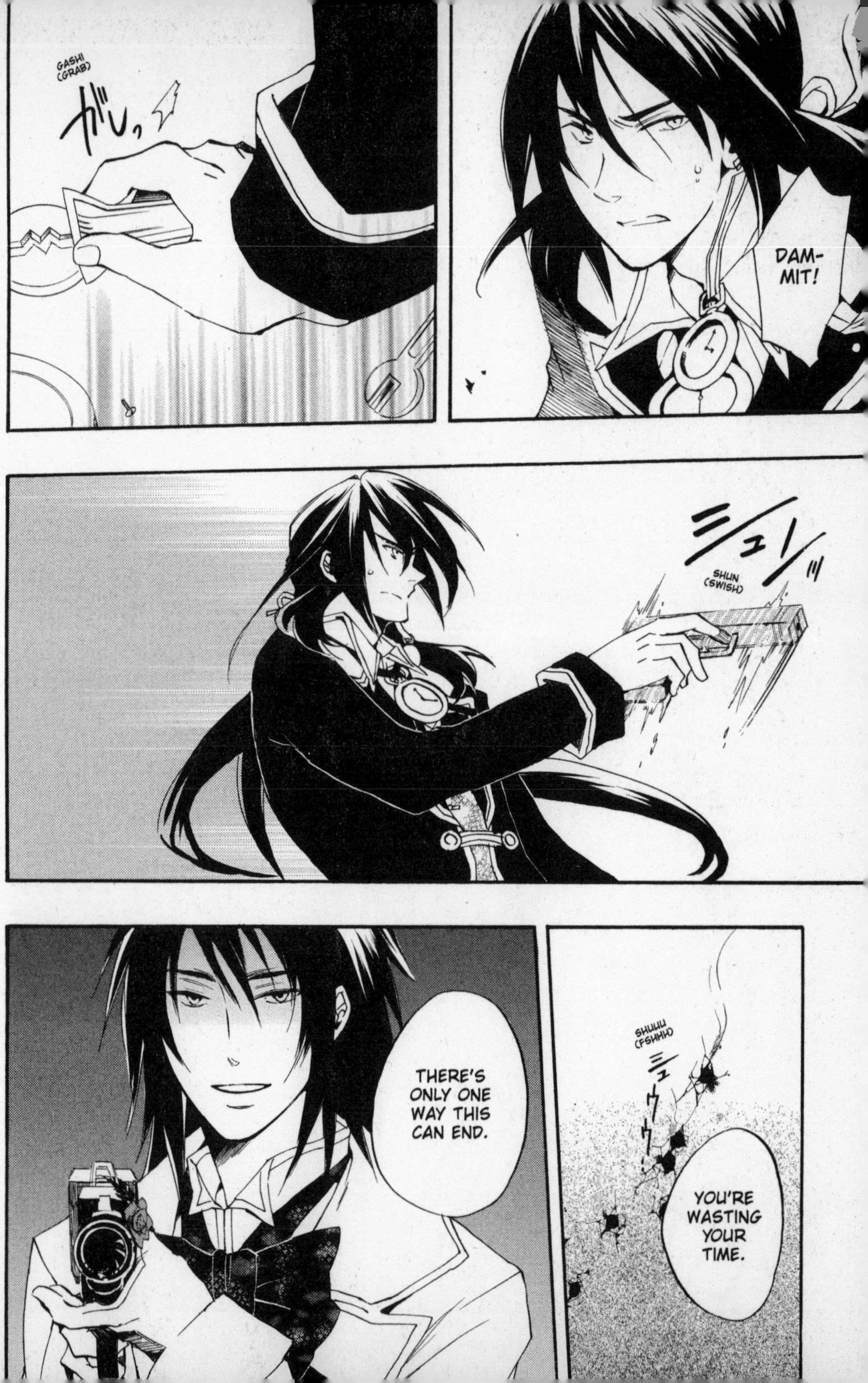
DAM-MIT!
GASHI (GRAB)
SHUN (SWISH)
SHUUU (FSHHH)
YOU'RE WASTING YOUR TIME.
THERE'S ONLY ONE WAY THIS CAN END.

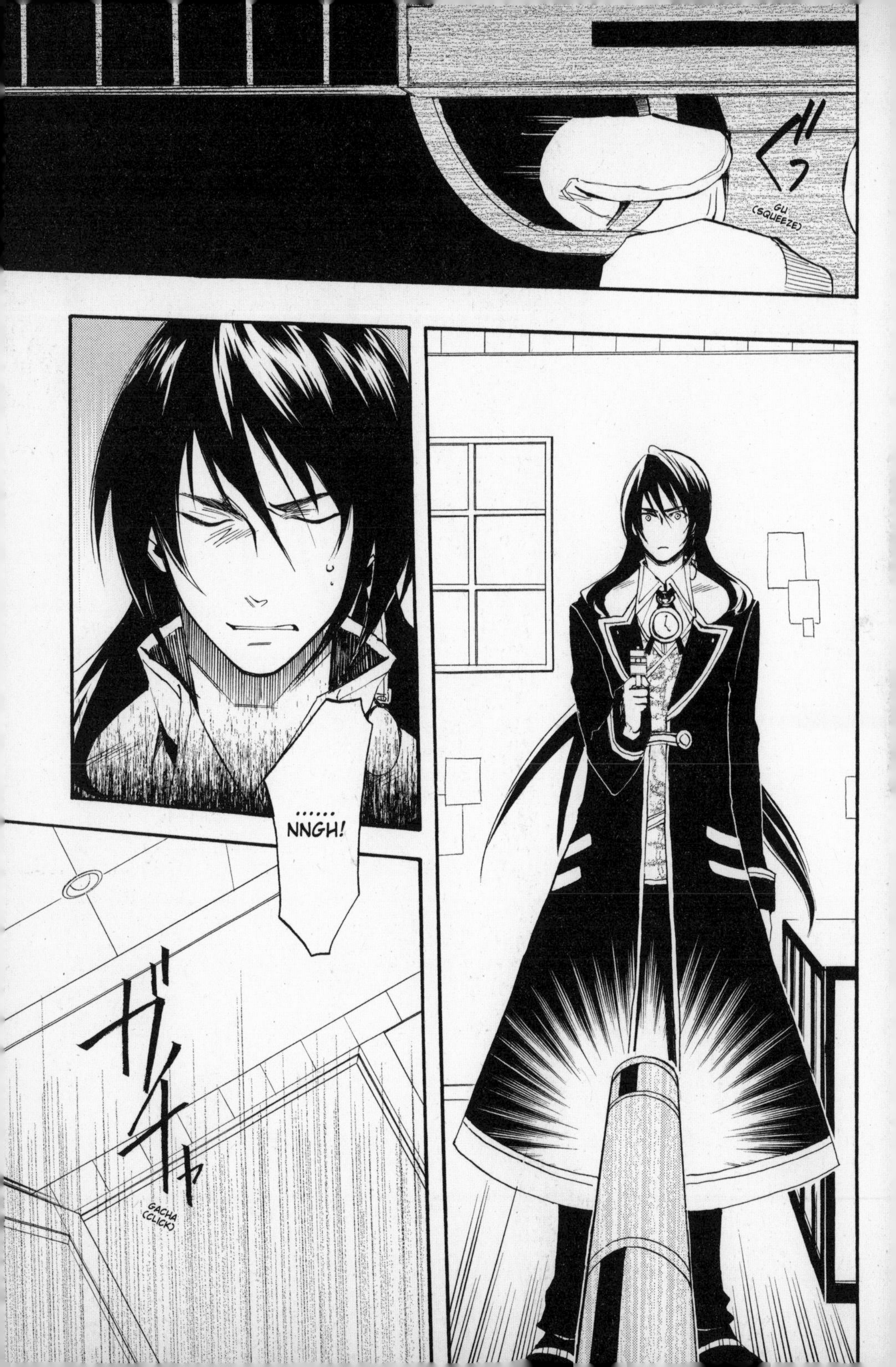
GU
(SQUEEZE)
......
NNGH!
GACHA
(CLICK)

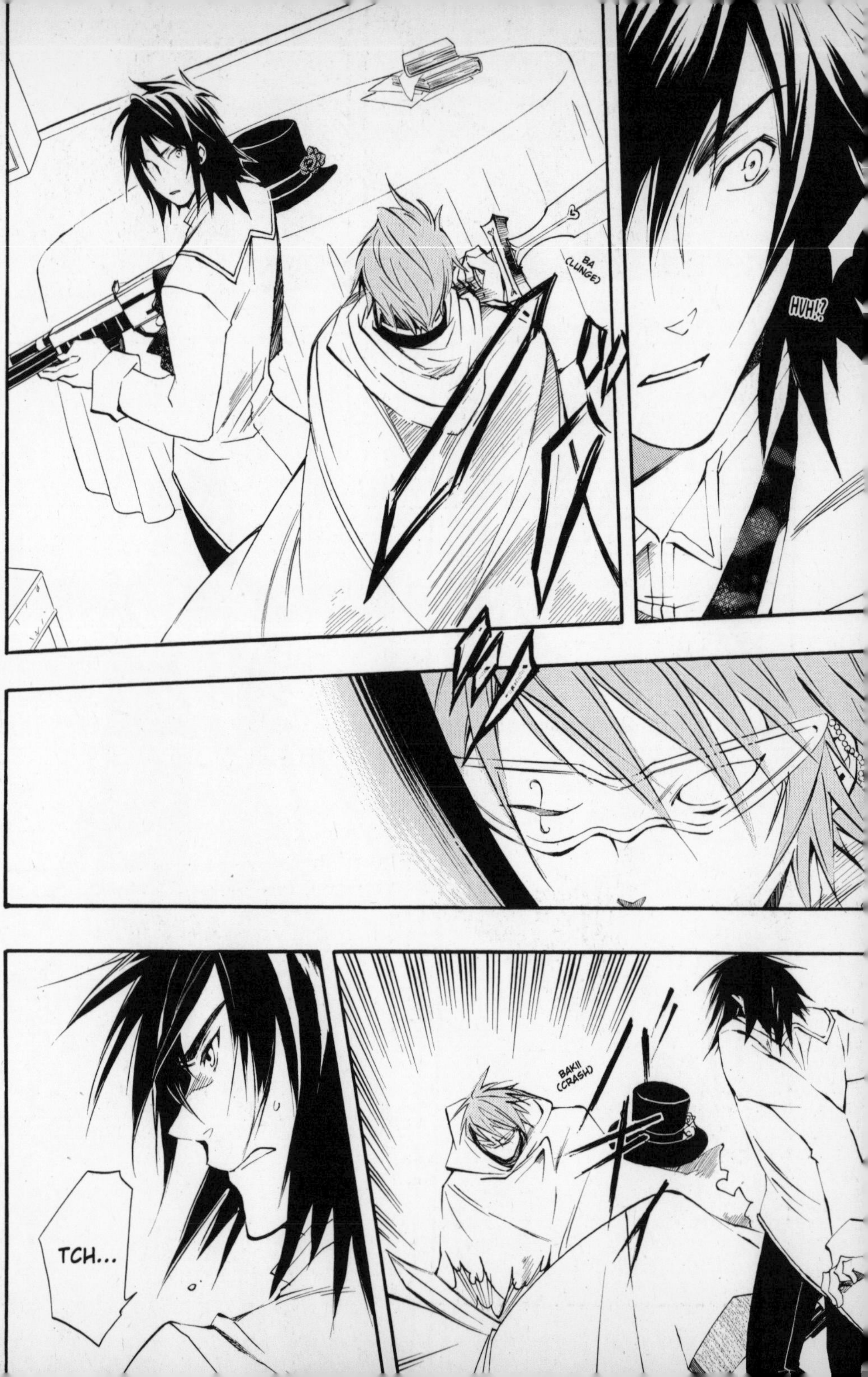
HUH!?
BA
(LUNGE)
BAKII
(CRASH)
TCH...

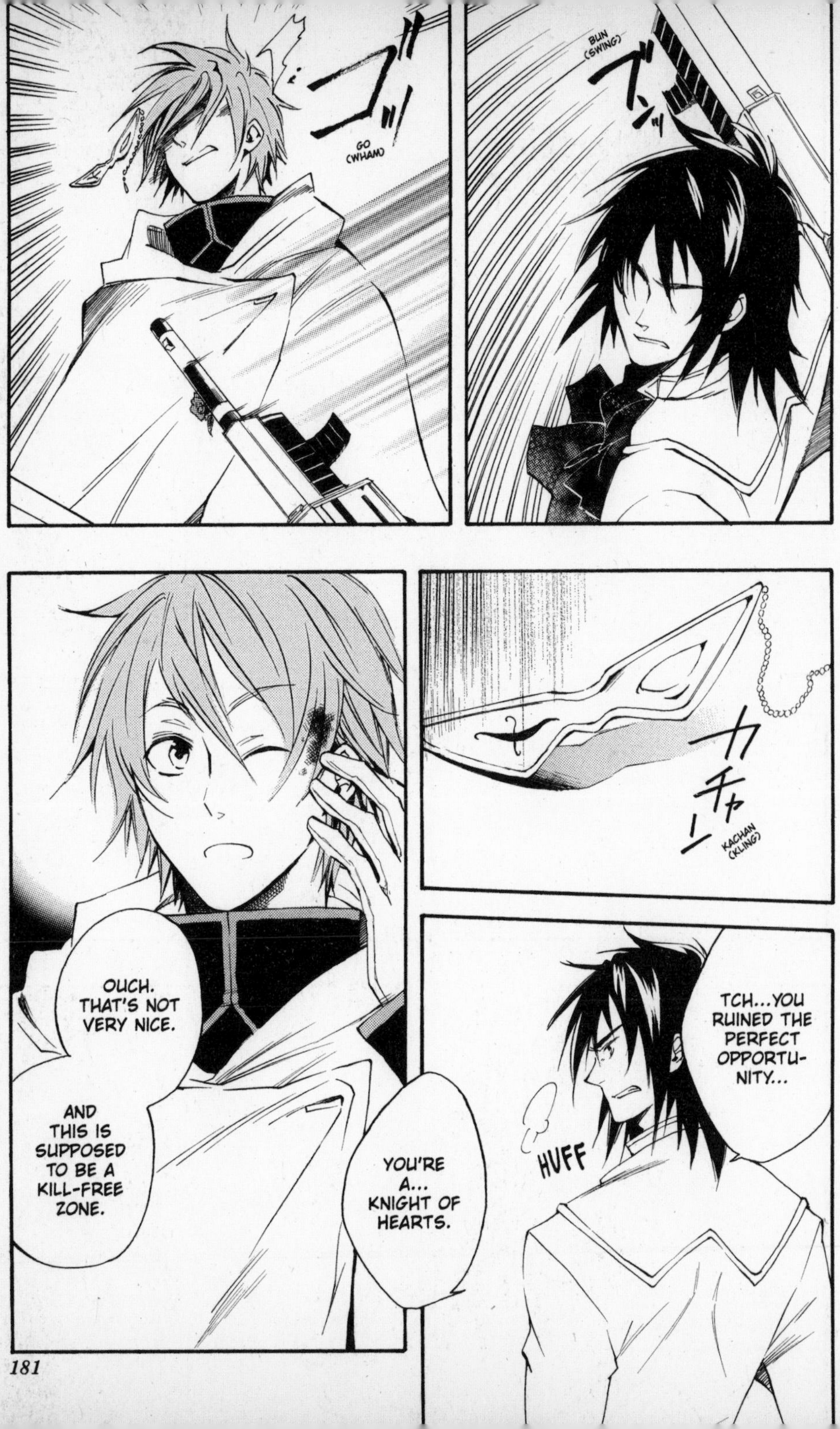
BUN (SWING)
GO (WHAM)
KACHAN (KLING)
TCH...YOU RUINED THE PERFECT OPPORTU-NITY...
HUFF
OUCH. THAT'S NOT VERY NICE.
AND THIS IS SUPPOSED TO BE A KILL-FREE ZONE.
YOU'RE A... KNIGHT OF HEARTS.

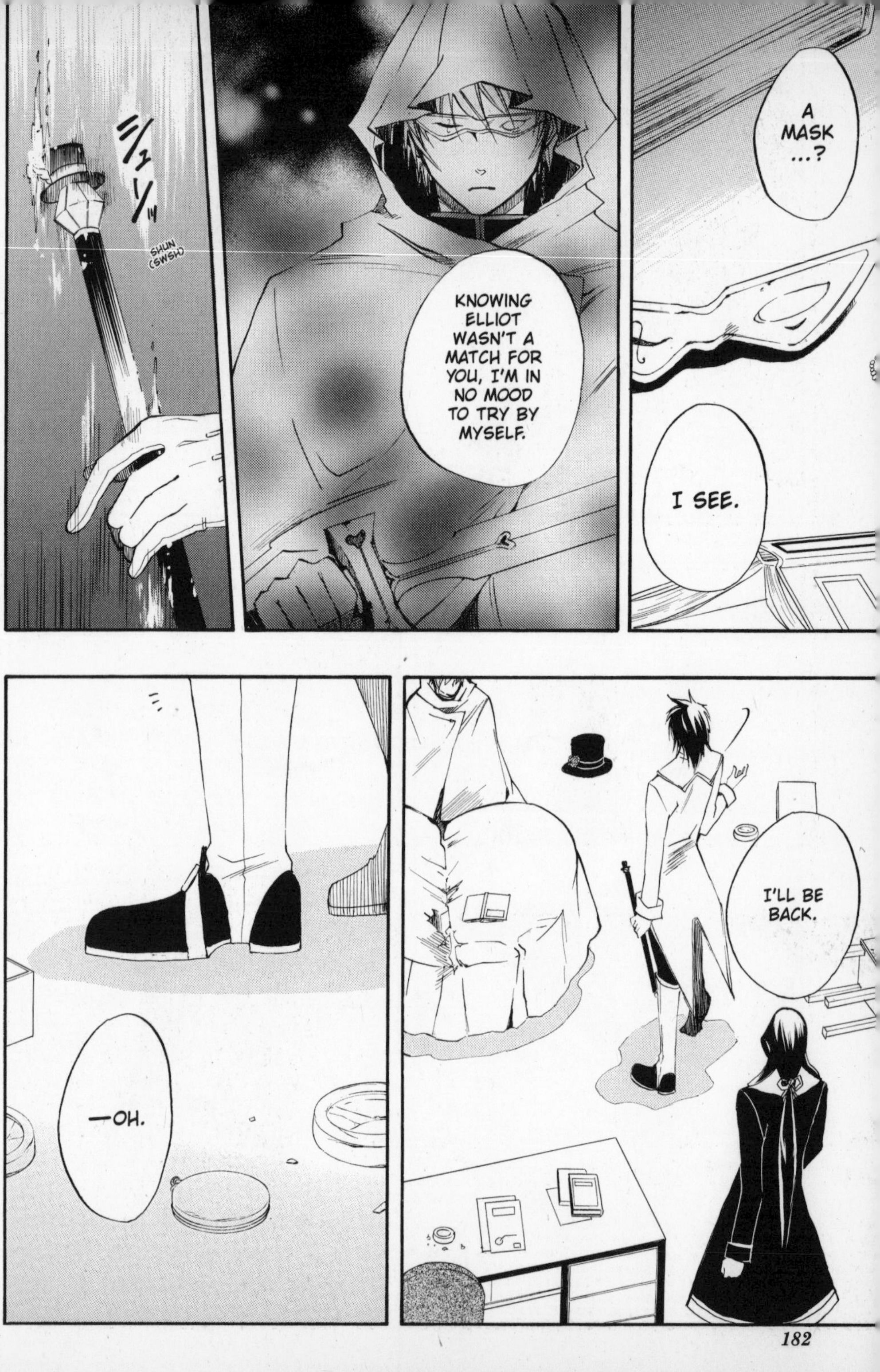
A MASK ...?
I SEE.
KNOWING ELLIOT WASN'T A MATCH FOR YOU, I'M IN NO MOOD TO TRY BY MYSELF.
SHUN (SWSH)
I'LL BE BACK.
—OH.

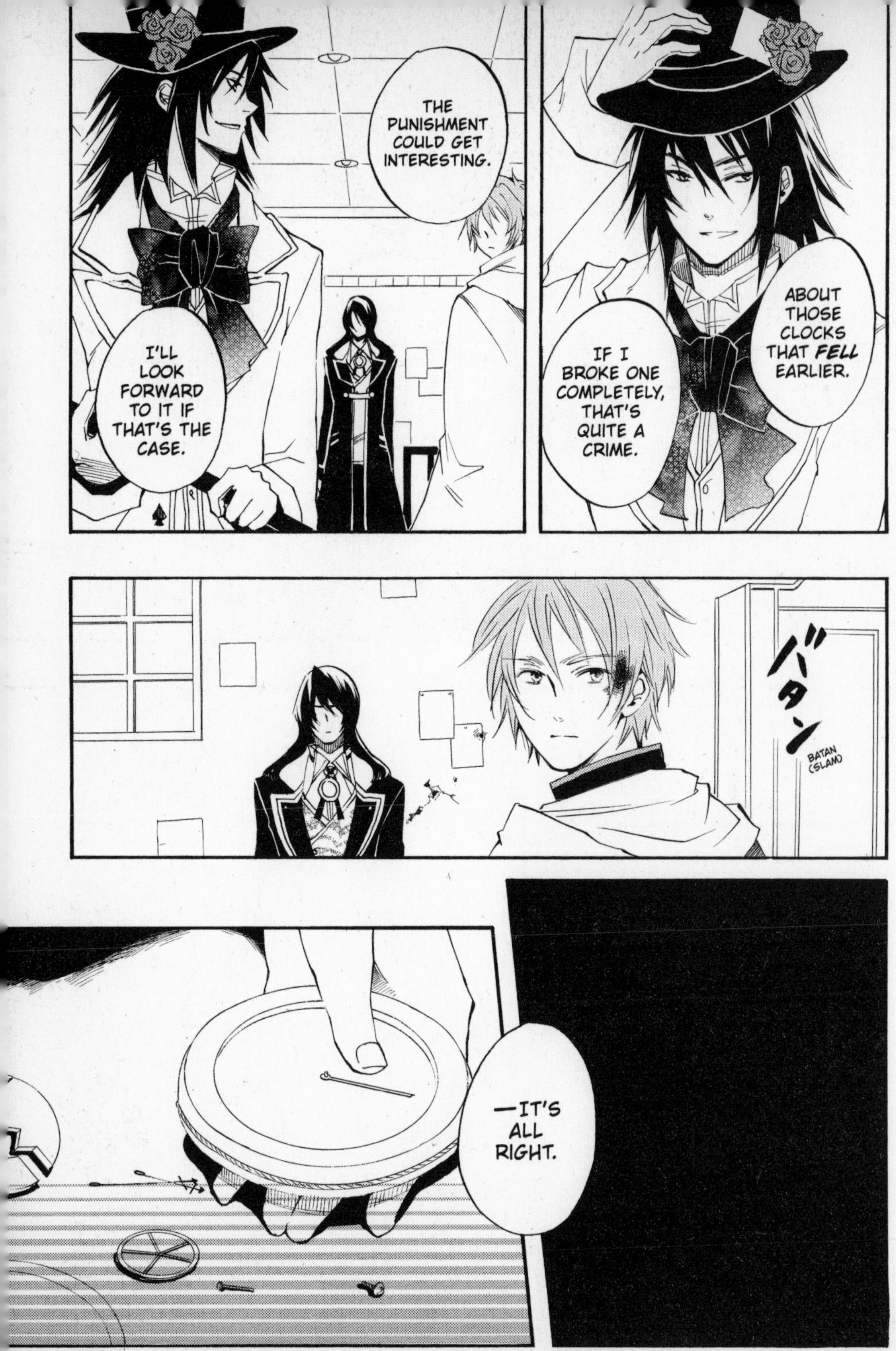
ABOUT THOSE CLOCKS THAT FELL EARLIER.
IF I BROKE ONE COMPLETELY, THAT'S QUITE A CRIME.
THE PUNISHMENT COULD GET INTERESTING.
I'LL LOOK FORWARD TO IT IF THAT'S THE CASE.
バタン
BATAN (SLAM)
—IT'S ALL RIGHT.

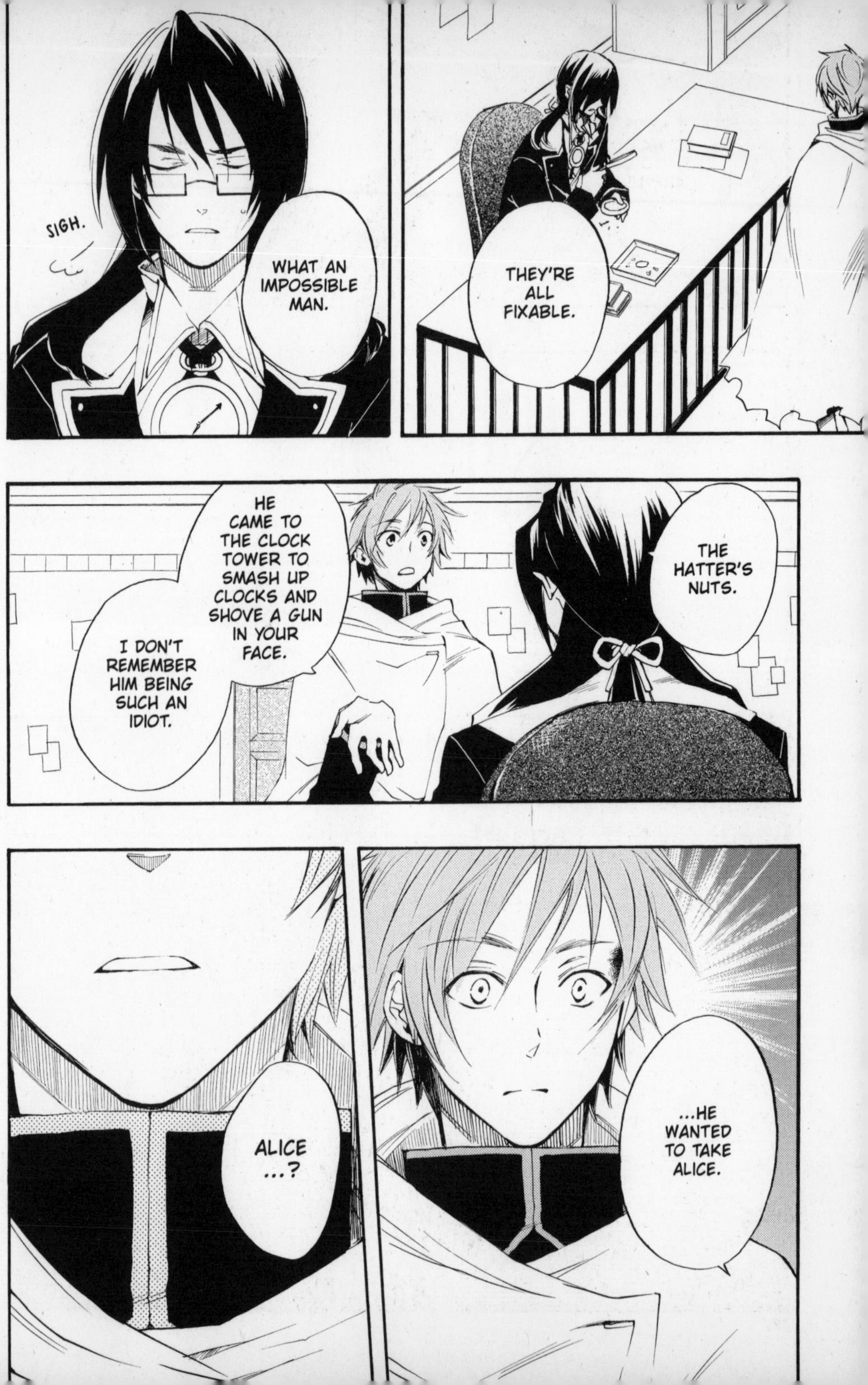
THEY'RE ALL FIXABLE.
WHAT AN IMPOSSIBLE MAN.
SIGH.
THE HATTER'S NUTS.
HE CAME TO THE CLOCK TOWER TO SMASH UP CLOCKS AND SHOVE A GUN IN YOUR FACE.
I DON'T REMEMBER HIM BEING SUCH AN IDIOT.
...HE WANTED TO TAKE ALICE.
ALICE ...?

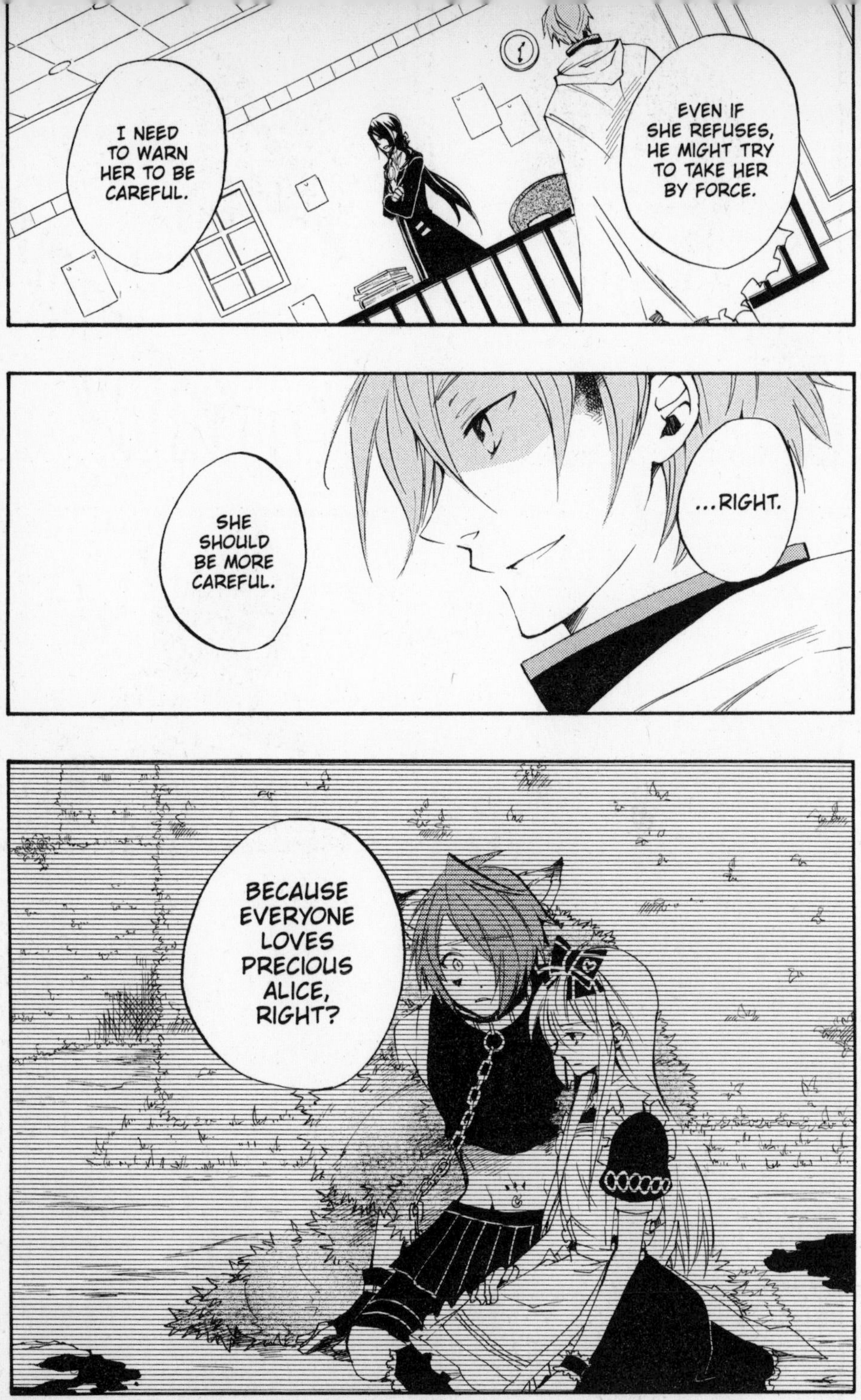
EVEN IF SHE REFUSES, HE MIGHT TRY TO TAKE HER BY FORCE.
I NEED TO WARN HER TO BE CAREFUL.
...RIGHT.
SHE SHOULD BE MORE CAREFUL.
BECAUSE EVERYONE LOVES PRECIOUS ALICE, RIGHT?

ALICE IN THE COUNTRY OF HEARTS

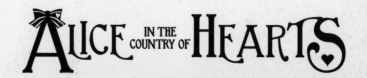

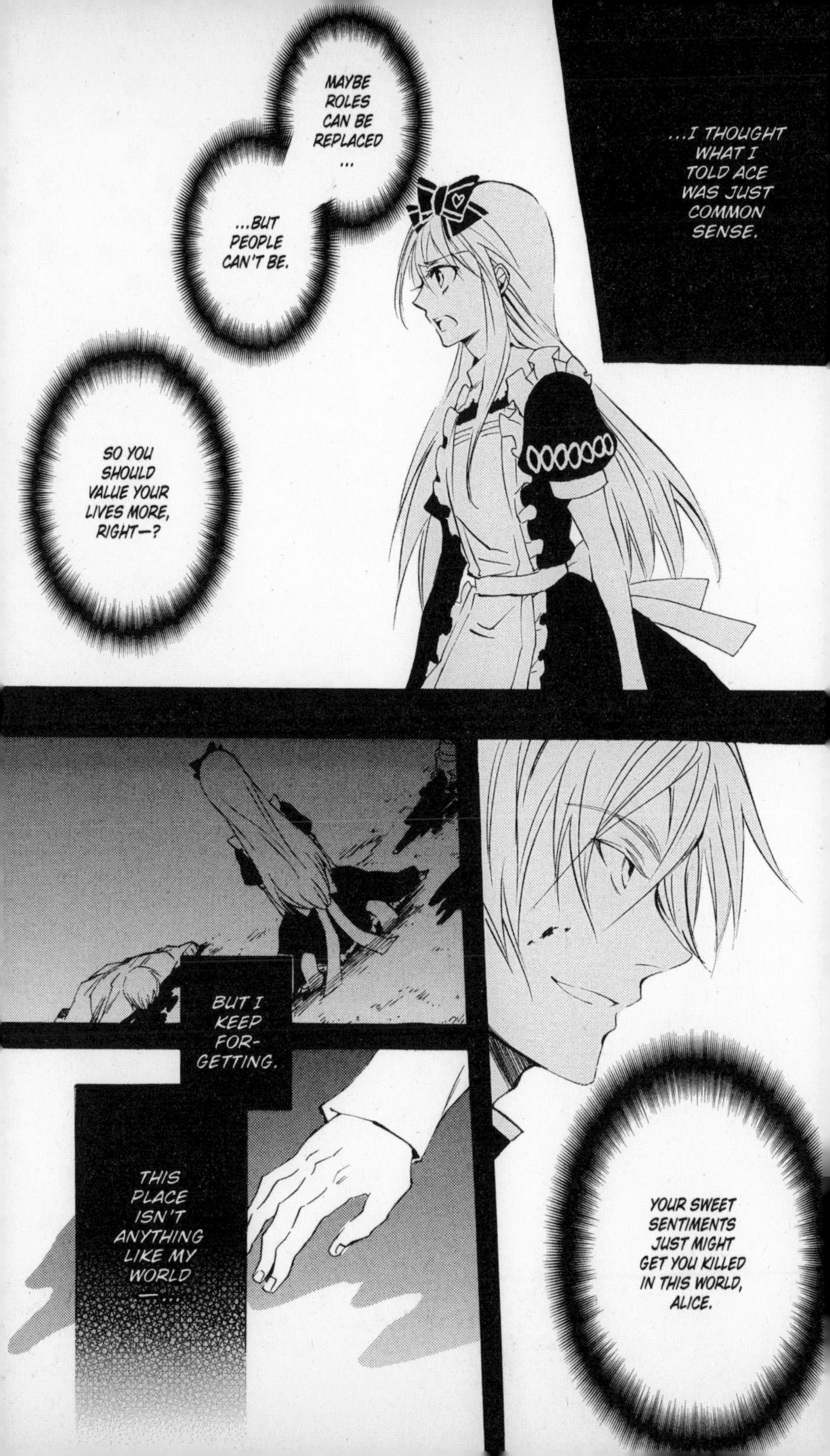
...I THOUGHT WHAT I TOLD ACE WAS JUST COMMON SENSE.
MAYBE ROLES CAN BE REPLACED ...
...BUT PEOPLE CAN'T BE.
SO YOU SHOULD VALUE YOUR LIVES MORE, RIGHT—?
YOUR SWEET SENTIMENTS JUST MIGHT GET YOU KILLED IN THIS WORLD, ALICE.
BUT I KEEP FOR-GETTING.
THIS PLACE ISN'T ANYTHING LIKE MY WORLD—...

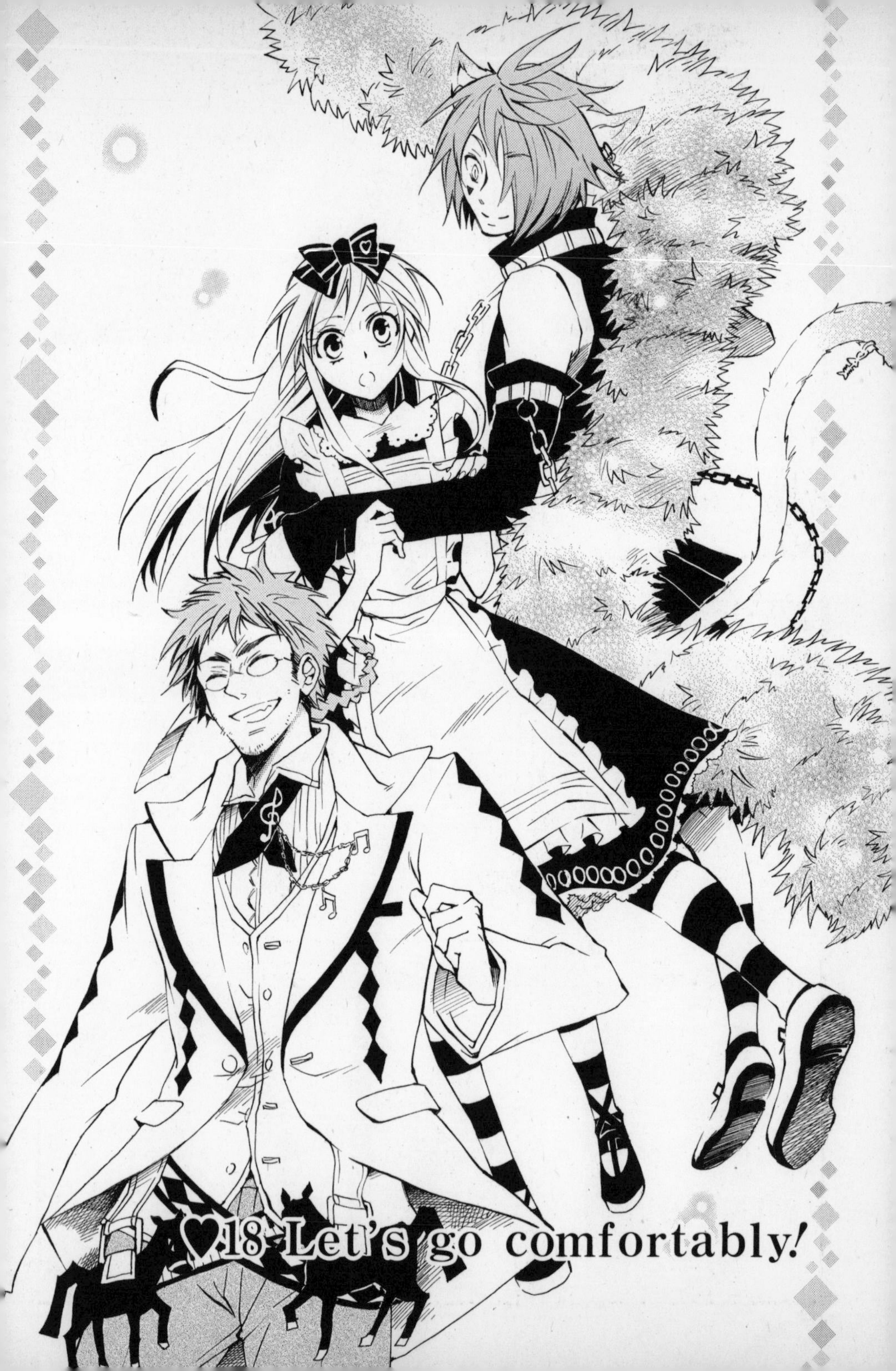
♡18 Let's go comfortably!

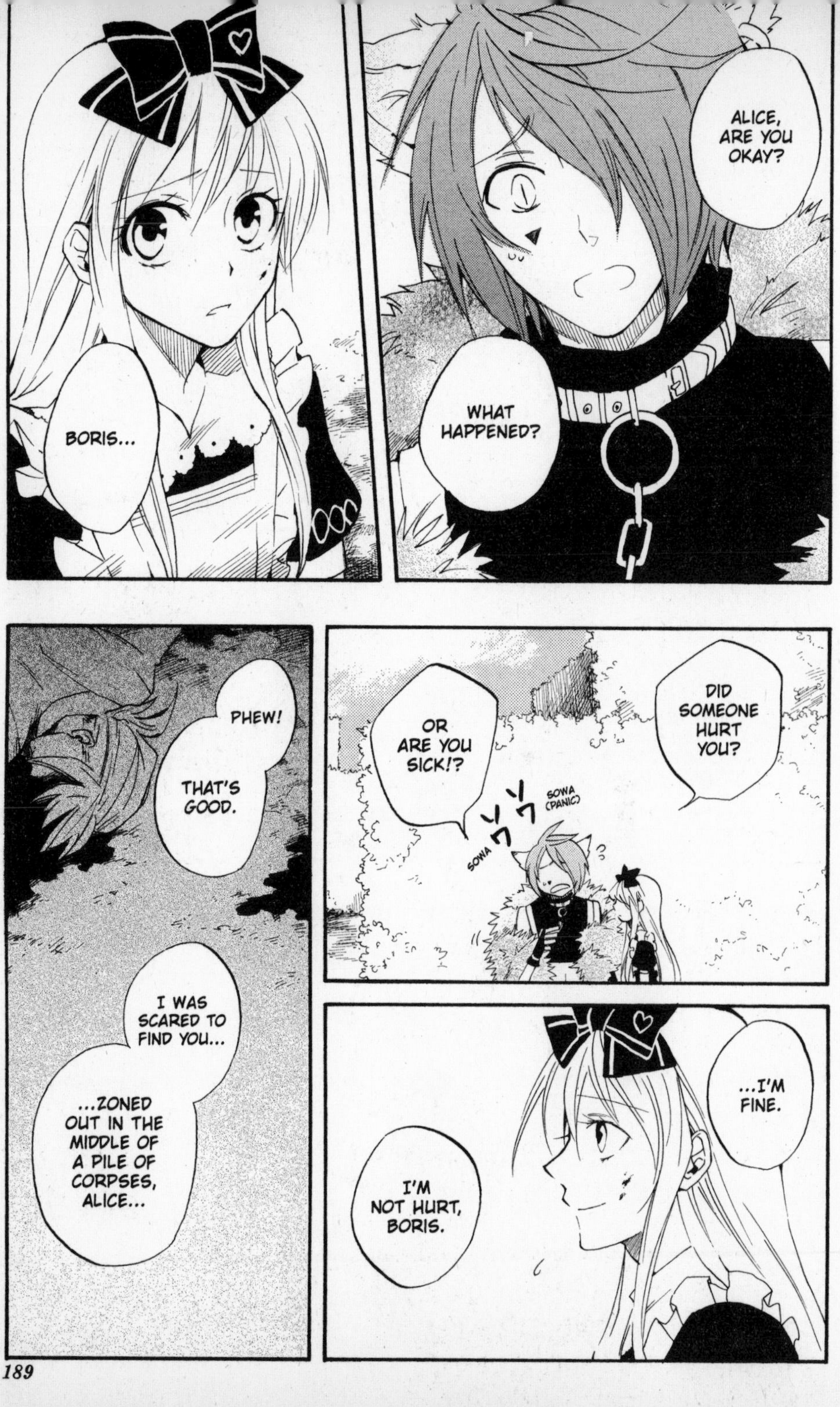
ALICE, ARE YOU OKAY?
WHAT HAPPENED?
BORIS...
DID SOMEONE HURT YOU?
OR ARE YOU SICK!?
SOWA (PANIC)
SOWA
...I'M FINE.
I'M NOT HURT, BORIS.
PHEW!
THAT'S GOOD.
I WAS SCARED TO FIND YOU...
...ZONED OUT IN THE MIDDLE OF A PILE OF CORPSES, ALICE...

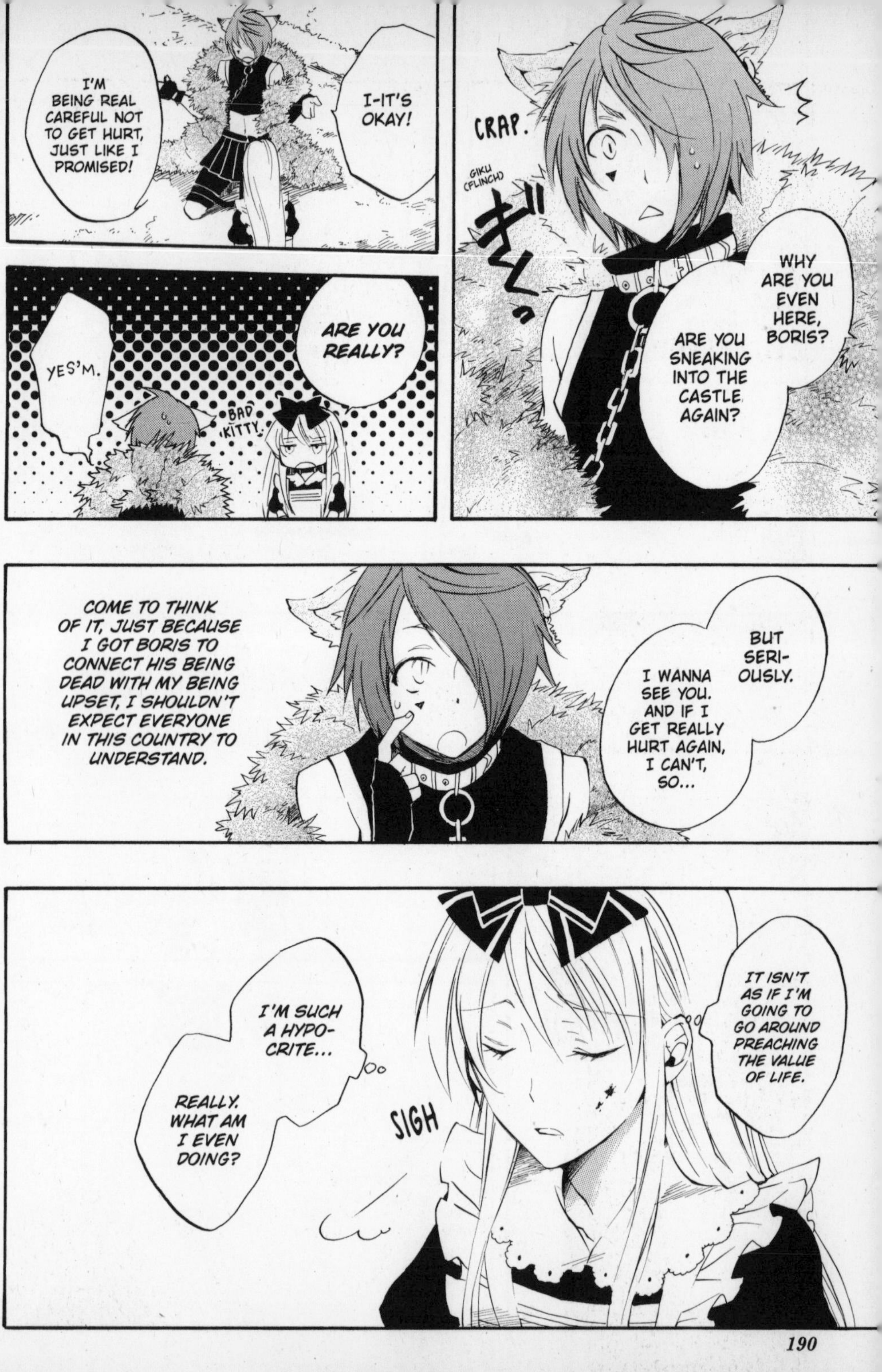
CRAP.
GIKU (FLINCH)
WHY ARE YOU EVEN HERE, BORIS?
ARE YOU SNEAKING INTO THE CASTLE AGAIN?
I-IT'S OKAY!
I'M BEING REAL CAREFUL NOT TO GET HURT, JUST LIKE I PROMISED!
ARE YOU REALLY?
BAD KITTY.
YES'M.
BUT SERI-OUSLY.
I WANNA SEE YOU. AND IF I GET REALLY HURT AGAIN, I CAN'T, SO...
COME TO THINK OF IT, JUST BECAUSE I GOT BORIS TO CONNECT HIS BEING DEAD WITH MY BEING UPSET, I SHOULDN'T EXPECT EVERYONE IN THIS COUNTRY TO UNDERSTAND.
IT ISN'T AS IF I'M GOING TO GO AROUND PREACHING THE VALUE OF LIFE.
SIGH
I'M SUCH A HYPO-CRITE...
REALLY. WHAT AM I EVEN DOING?

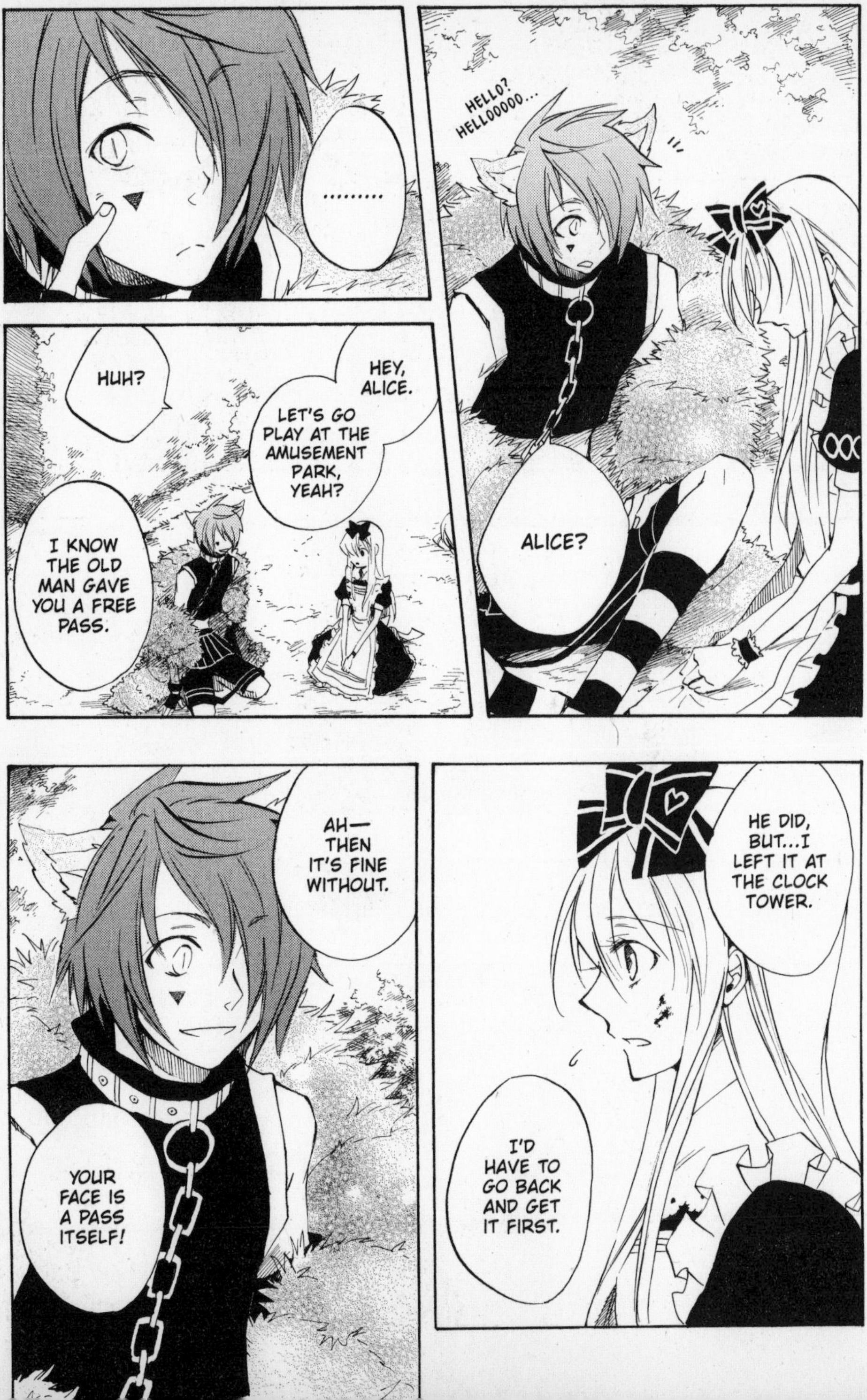
HELLO? HELLOOOOO...
ALICE?
....
HEY, ALICE.
LET'S GO PLAY AT THE AMUSEMENT PARK, YEAH?
HUH?
I KNOW THE OLD MAN GAVE YOU A FREE PASS.
HE DID, BUT...I LEFT IT AT THE CLOCK TOWER.
I'D HAVE TO GO BACK AND GET IT FIRST.
AH— THEN IT'S FINE WITHOUT.
YOUR FACE IS A PASS ITSELF!

GASP!

I DON'T KNOW...

IT'S FINE, IT'S FINE.

YURA (FLICKER)

THEY'LL KNOW YOU HAVE A FREE PASS ANYWAY.

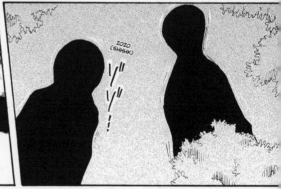

ZOZO (SHHHK)

YOU SHOULDN'T LINGER HERE TOO LONG.

C'MON, LET'S GO.

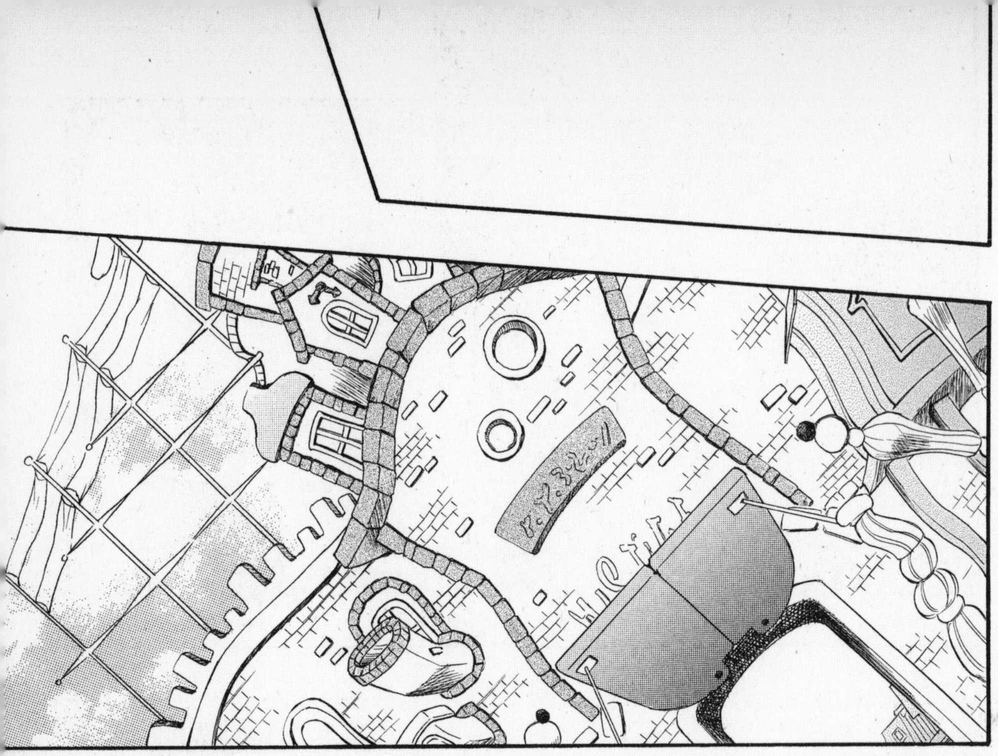

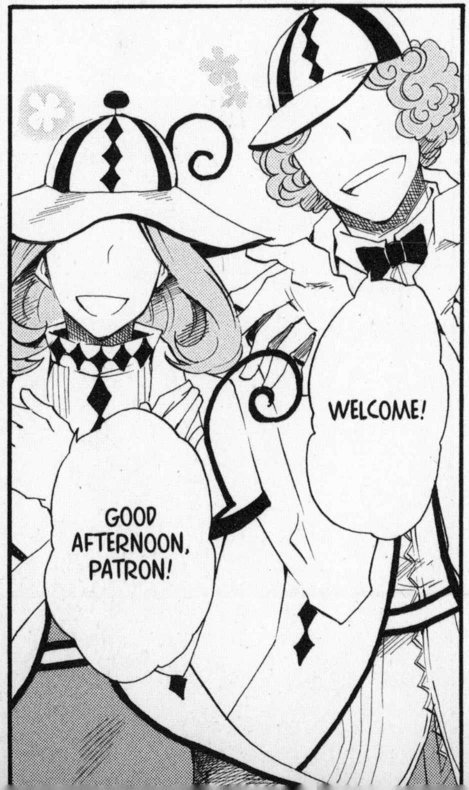
WELCOME!
GOOD AFTERNOON, PATRON!

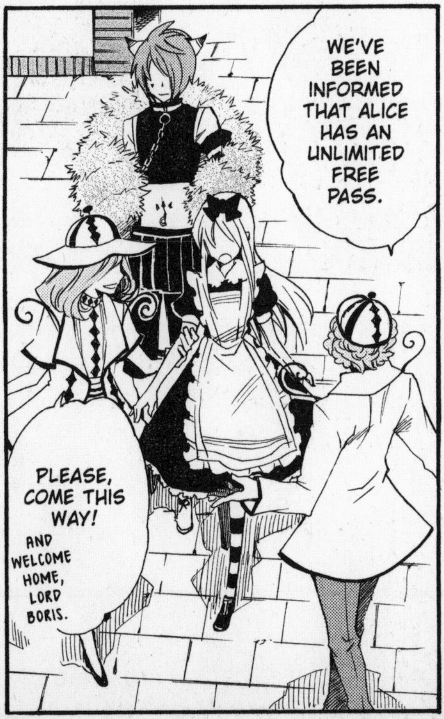
WE'VE BEEN INFORMED THAT ALICE HAS AN UNLIMITED FREE PASS.
PLEASE, COME THIS WAY!
AND WELCOME HOME, LORD BORIS.

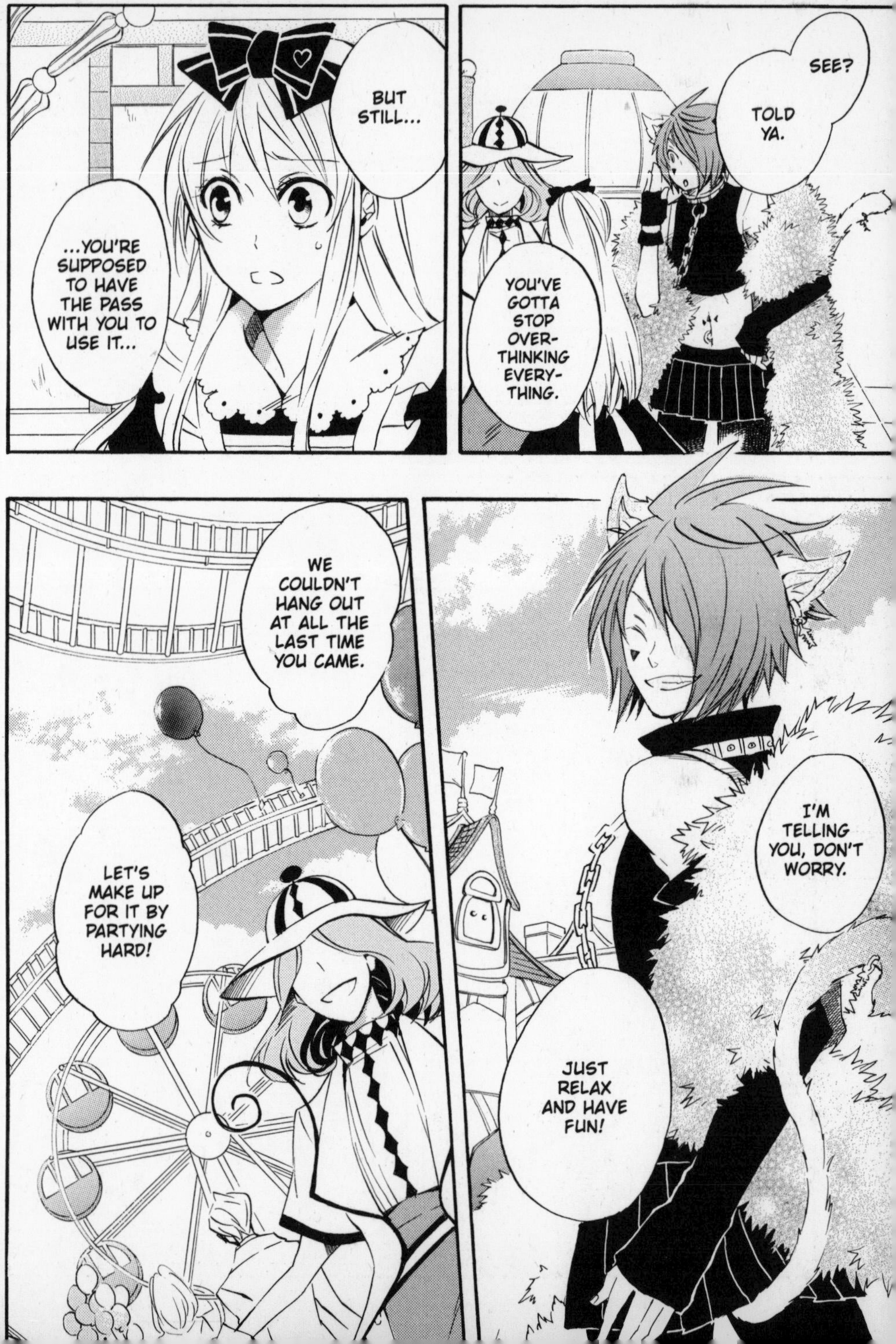
SEE?
TOLD YA.
YOU'VE GOTTA STOP OVER-THINKING EVERY-THING.
BUT STILL...
...YOU'RE SUPPOSED TO HAVE THE PASS WITH YOU TO USE IT...
I'M TELLING YOU, DON'T WORRY.
JUST RELAX AND HAVE FUN!
WE COULDN'T HANG OUT AT ALL THE LAST TIME YOU CAME.
LET'S MAKE UP FOR IT BY PARTYING HARD!

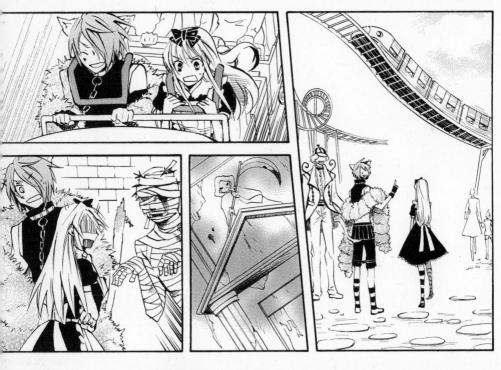

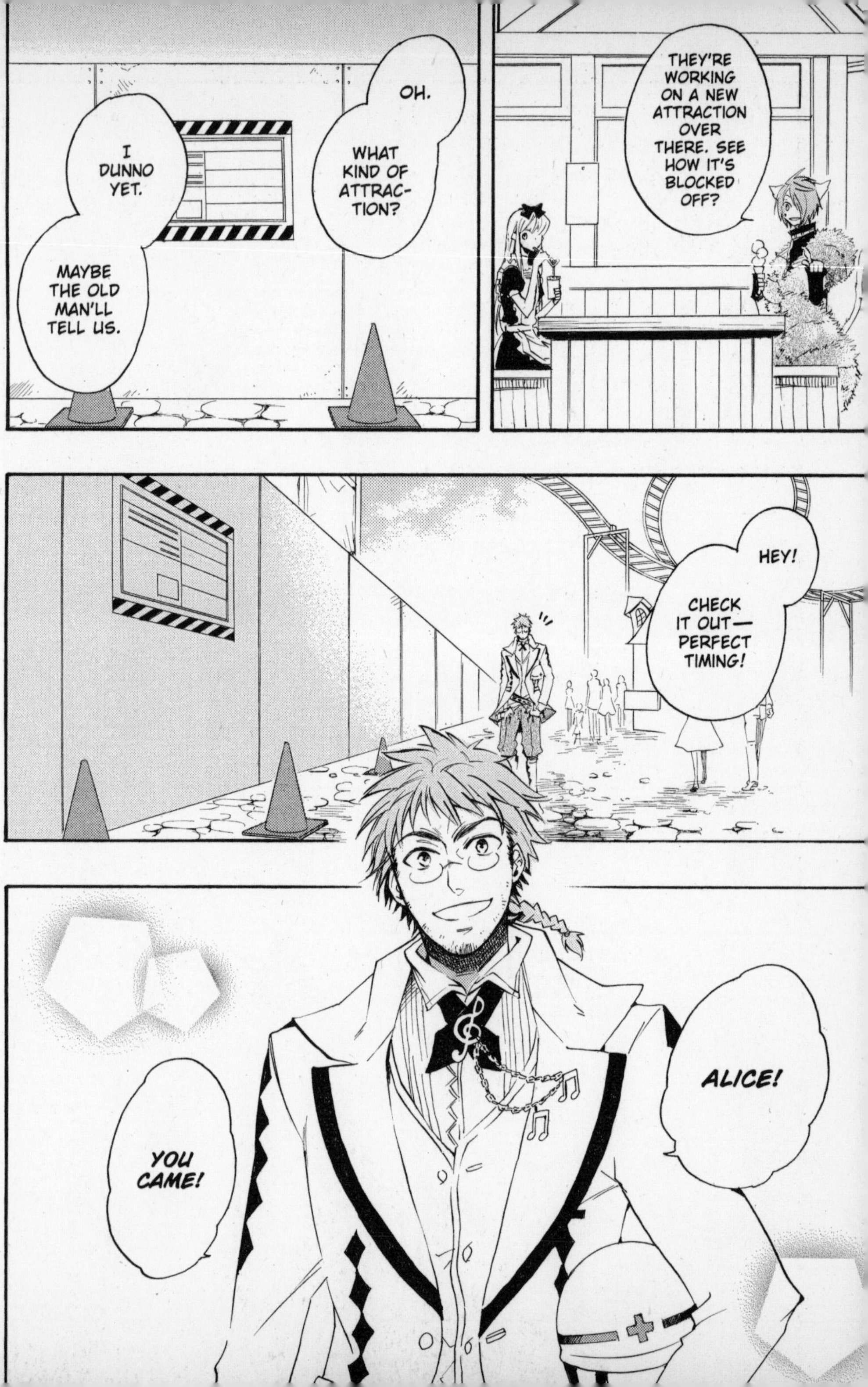
THEY'RE WORKING ON A NEW ATTRACTION OVER THERE. SEE HOW IT'S BLOCKED OFF?
OH.
WHAT KIND OF ATTRAC-TION?
I DUNNO YET.
MAYBE THE OLD MAN'LL TELL US.
HEY!
CHECK IT OUT—PERFECT TIMING!
ALICE!
YOU CAME!

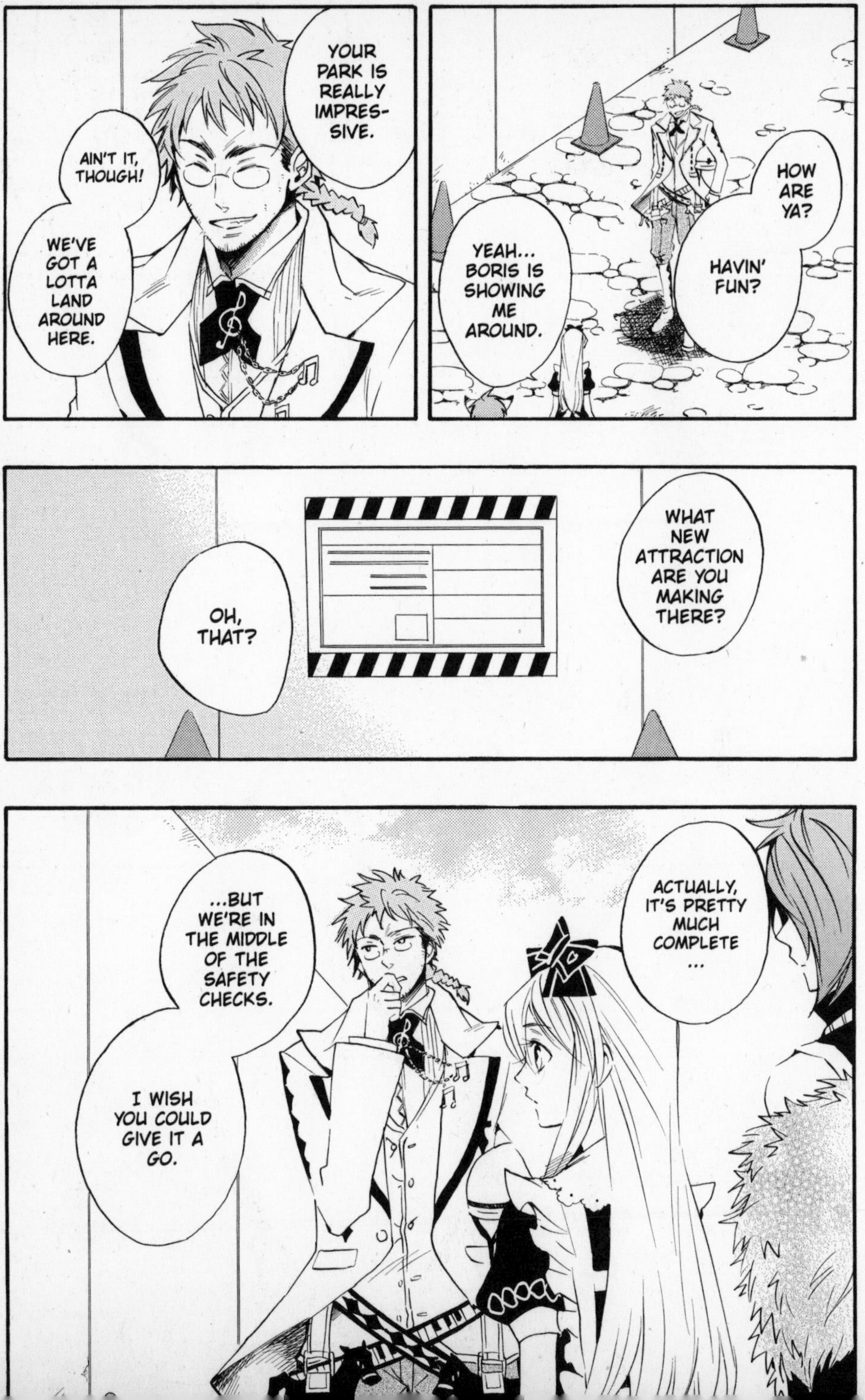
HOW ARE YA?
HAVIN' FUN?
YEAH... BORIS IS SHOWING ME AROUND.
YOUR PARK IS REALLY IMPRES-SIVE.
AIN'T IT, THOUGH!
WE'VE GOT A LOTTA LAND AROUND HERE.
WHAT NEW ATTRACTION ARE YOU MAKING THERE?
OH, THAT?
ACTUALLY, IT'S PRETTY MUCH COMPLETE ...
...BUT WE'RE IN THE MIDDLE OF THE SAFETY CHECKS.
I WISH YOU COULD GIVE IT A GO.

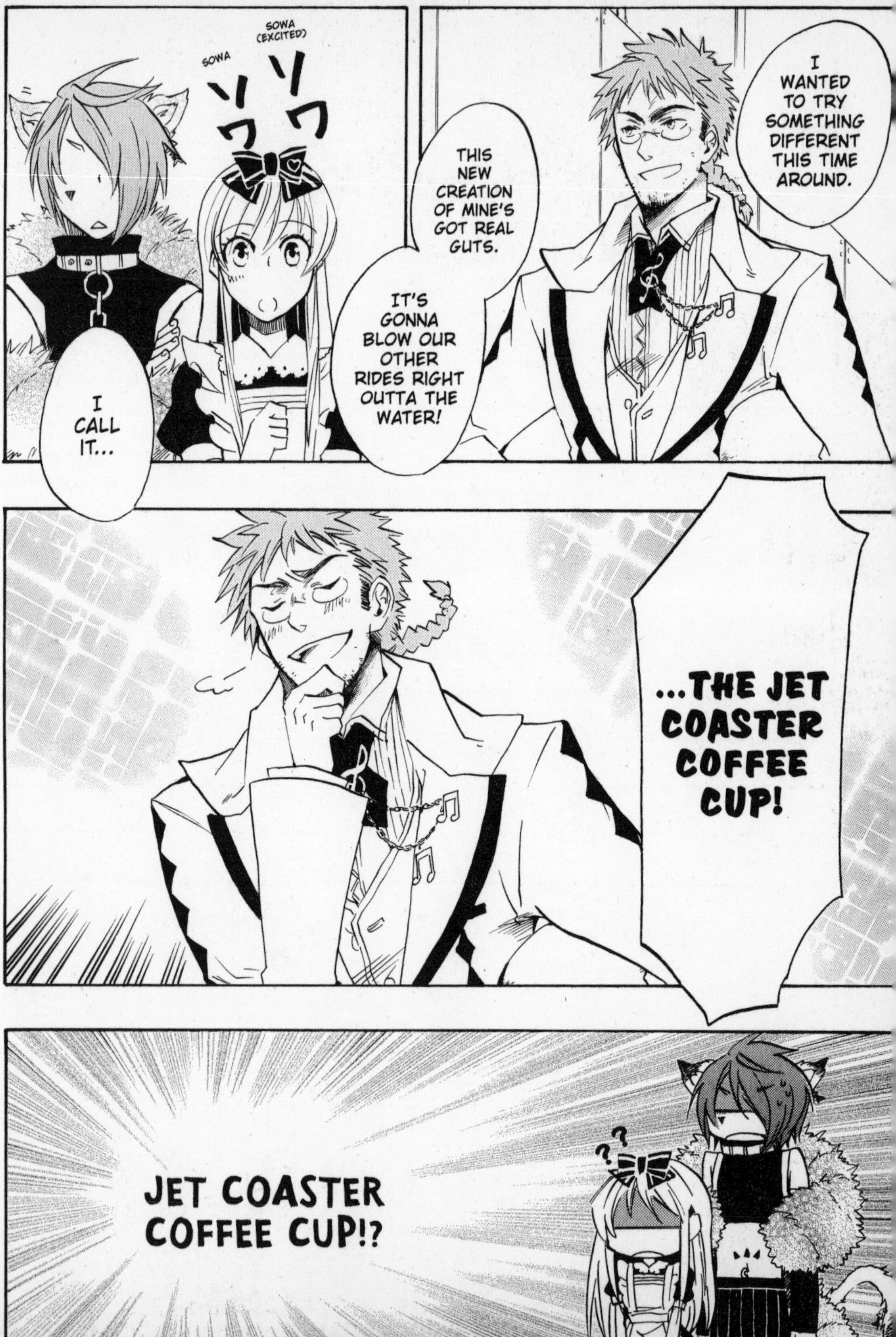
I WANTED TO TRY SOMETHING DIFFERENT THIS TIME AROUND.
THIS NEW CREATION OF MINE'S GOT REAL GUTS.
IT'S GONNA BLOW OUR OTHER RIDES RIGHT OUTTA THE WATER!
ソワ
SOWA (EXCITED)
ソワ
SOWA
I CALL IT...
...THE JET COASTER COFFEE CUP!
JET COASTER COFFEE CUP!?

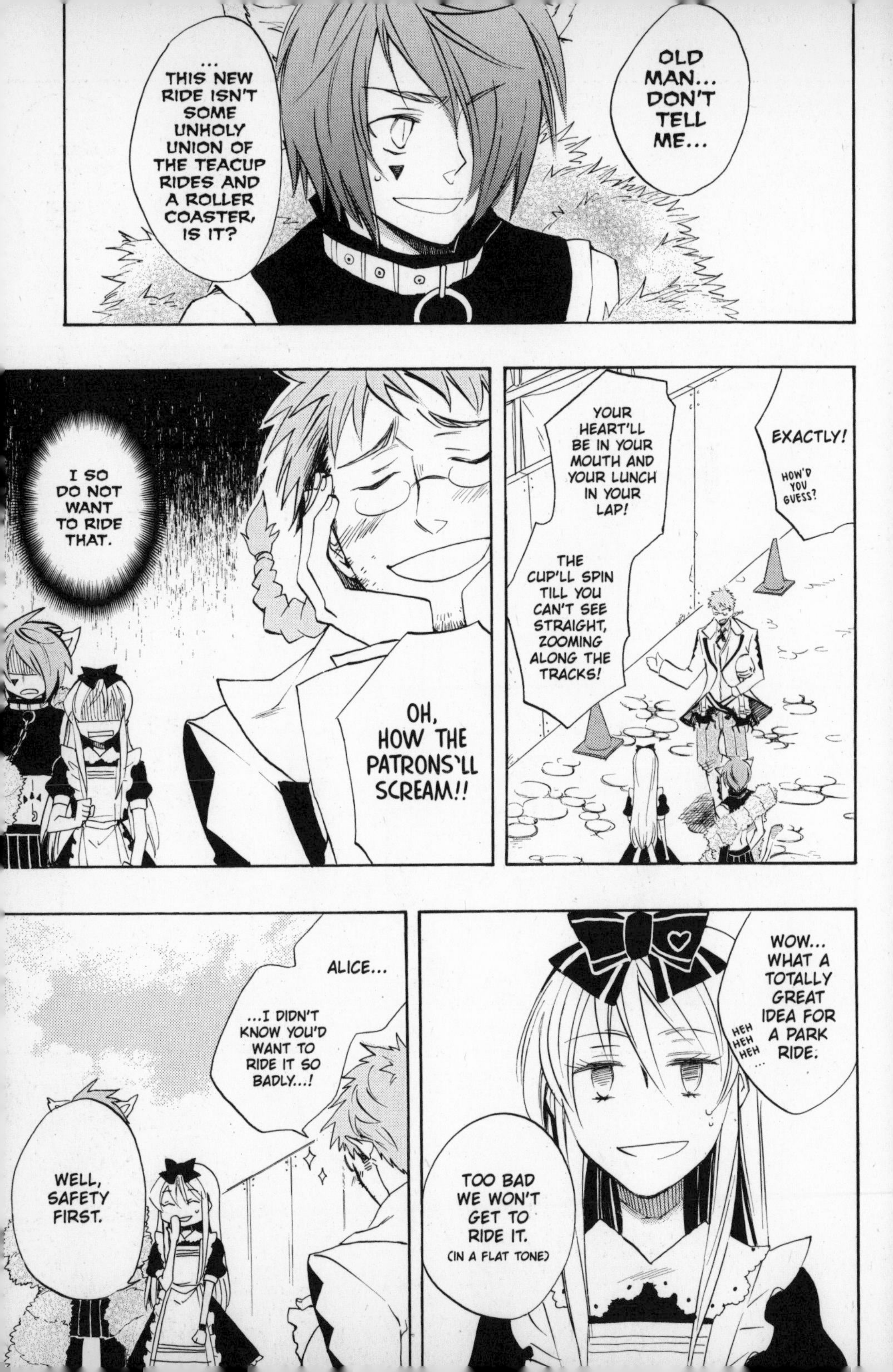
OLD MAN... DON'T TELL ME...
...THIS NEW RIDE ISN'T SOME UNHOLY UNION OF THE TEACUP RIDES AND A ROLLER COASTER, IS IT?
EXACTLY!
HOW'D YOU GUESS?
YOUR HEART'LL BE IN YOUR MOUTH AND YOUR LUNCH IN YOUR LAP!
THE CUP'LL SPIN TILL YOU CAN'T SEE STRAIGHT, ZOOMING ALONG THE TRACKS!
OH, HOW THE PATRONS'LL SCREAM!!
I SO DO NOT WANT TO RIDE THAT.
WOW... WHAT A TOTALLY GREAT IDEA FOR A PARK RIDE.
HEH HEH HEH...
TOO BAD WE WON'T GET TO RIDE IT.
(IN A FLAT TONE)
ALICE...
...I DIDN'T KNOW YOU'D WANT TO RIDE IT SO BADLY...!
WELL, SAFETY FIRST.

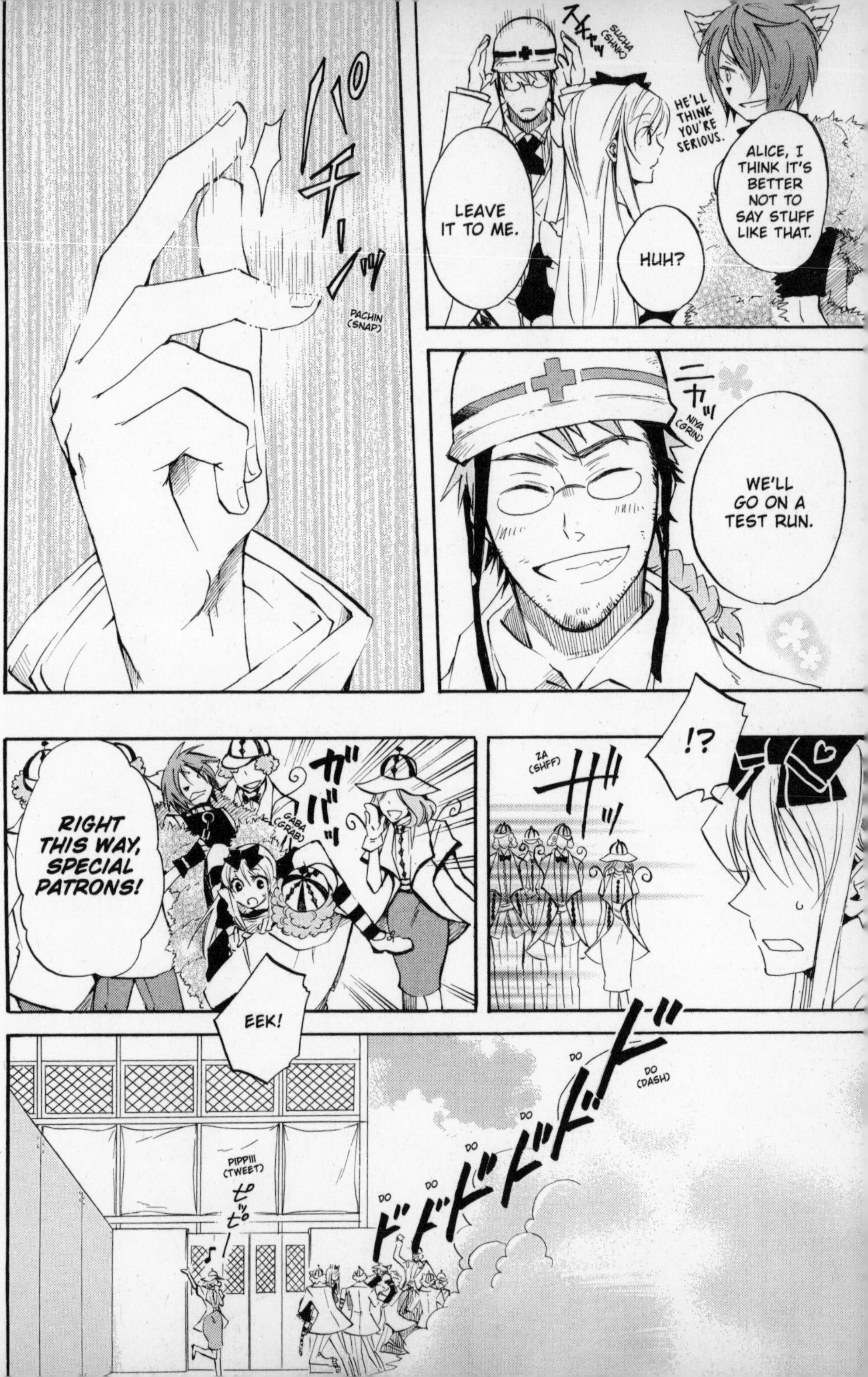
SUCHA (SHNK)
ALICE, I THINK IT'S BETTER NOT TO SAY STUFF LIKE THAT.
HE'LL THINK YOU'RE SERIOUS.
HUH?
LEAVE IT TO ME.
NIYA (GRIN)
WE'LL GO ON A TEST RUN.
PACHIN (SNAP)
!?
ZA (SHFF)
GABA (GRAB)
RIGHT THIS WAY, SPECIAL PATRONS!
EEK!
DO
DO (DASH)
DO
DO
DO
DO
PIPPIII (TWEET)

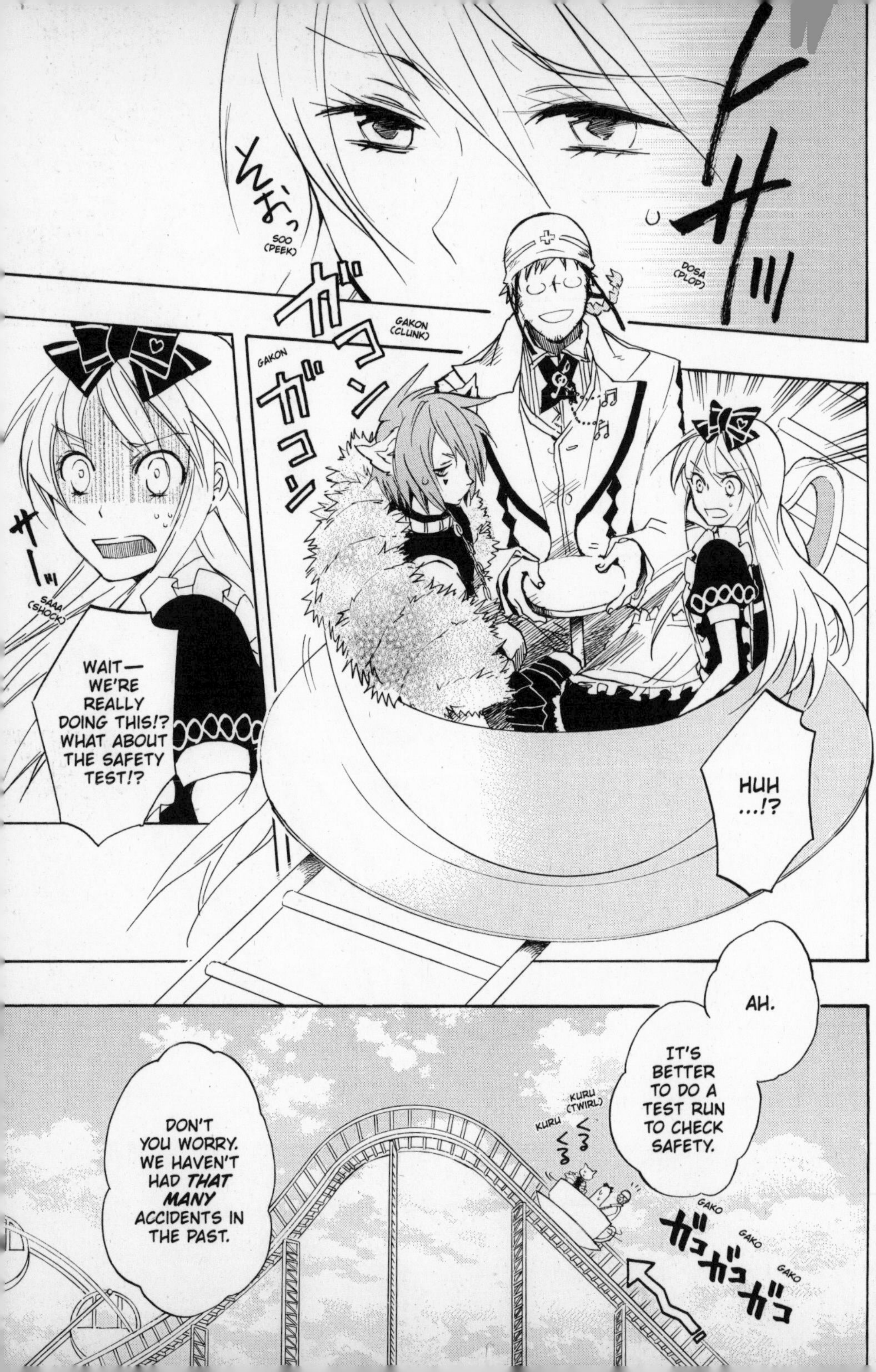
DOSA (PLOP)
SOO (PEEK)
GAKON (CLUNK)
GAKON
HUH ...!?
SAAA (SHOCK)
WAIT— WE'RE REALLY DOING THIS!? WHAT ABOUT THE SAFETY TEST!?
AH.
IT'S BETTER TO DO A TEST RUN TO CHECK SAFETY.
KURU (TWIRL)
KURU
GAKO
GAKO
GAKO
DON'T YOU WORRY. WE HAVEN'T HAD ***THAT MANY*** ACCIDENTS IN THE PAST.

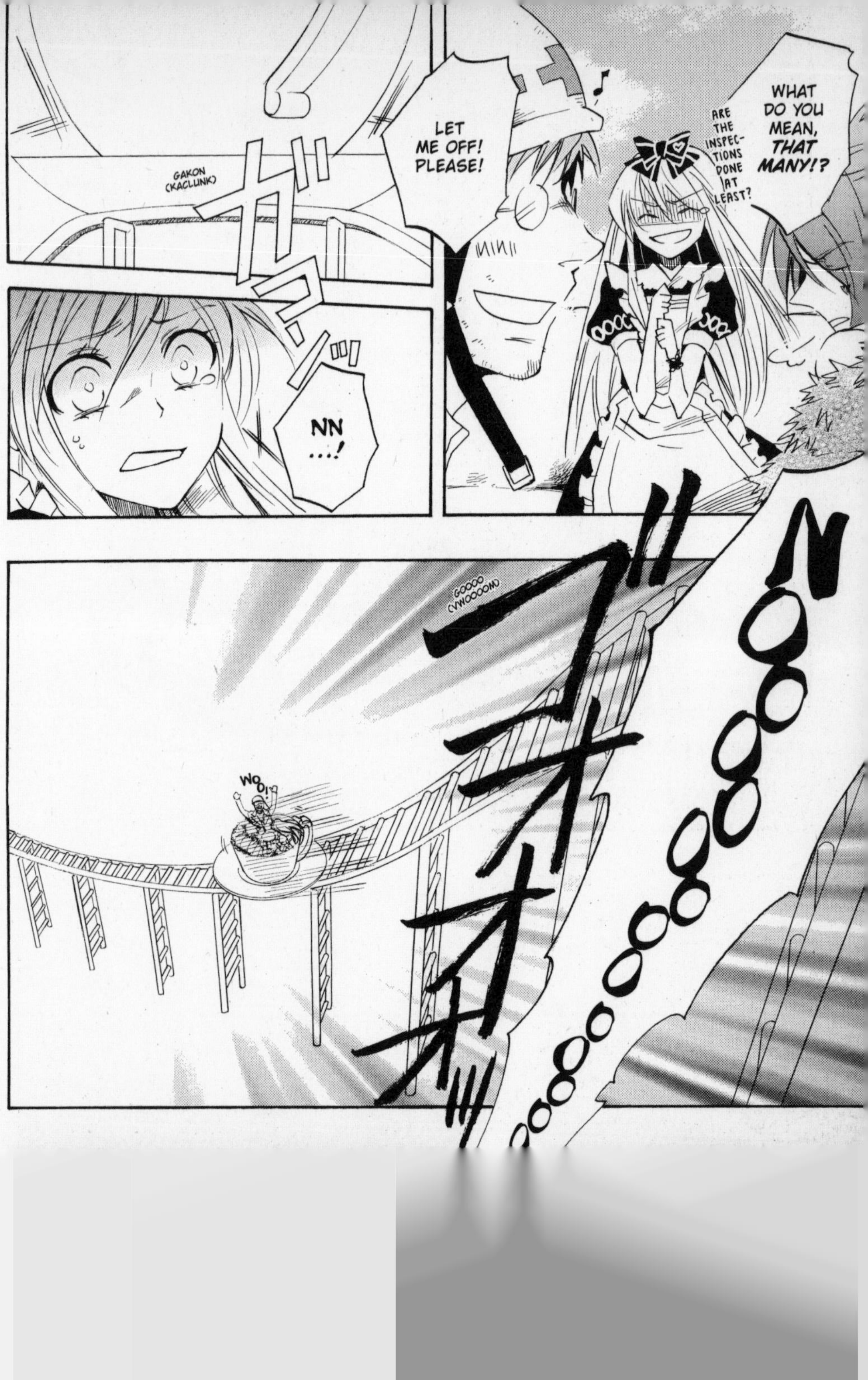
WHAT DO YOU MEAN, THAT MANY!?
ARE THE INSPECTIONS DONE AT LEAST?
LET ME OFF! PLEASE!
GAKON (KACLUNK)
NN ...!
GOOOO (VWOOOOM)
WOO!
NOOOOOOOOOOOOOOOOO

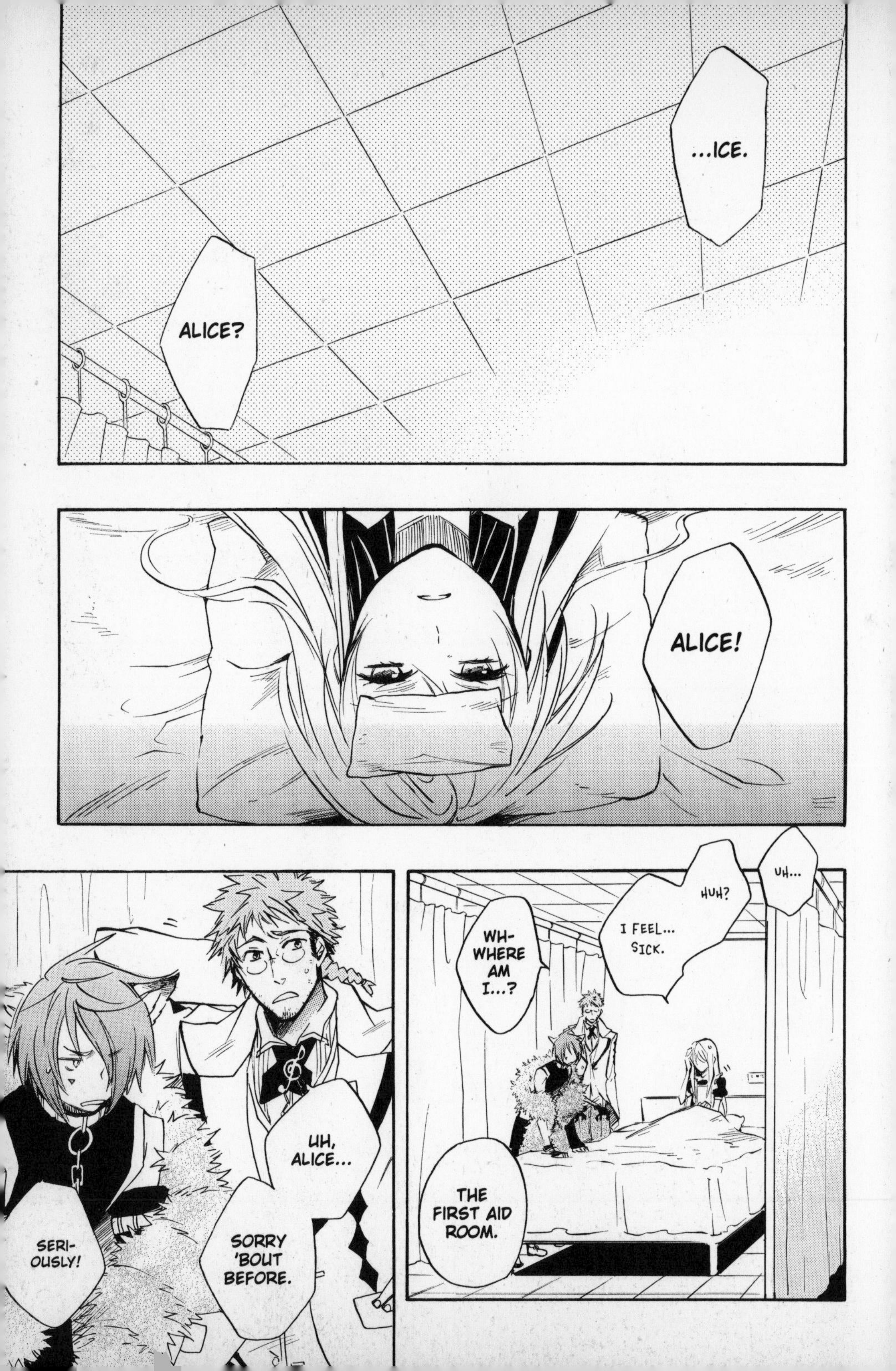
...ICE.
ALICE?
ALICE!
UH...
HUH?
I FEEL... SICK.
WH- WHERE AM I...?
THE FIRST AID ROOM.
UH, ALICE...
SORRY 'BOUT BEFORE.
SERI-OUSLY!

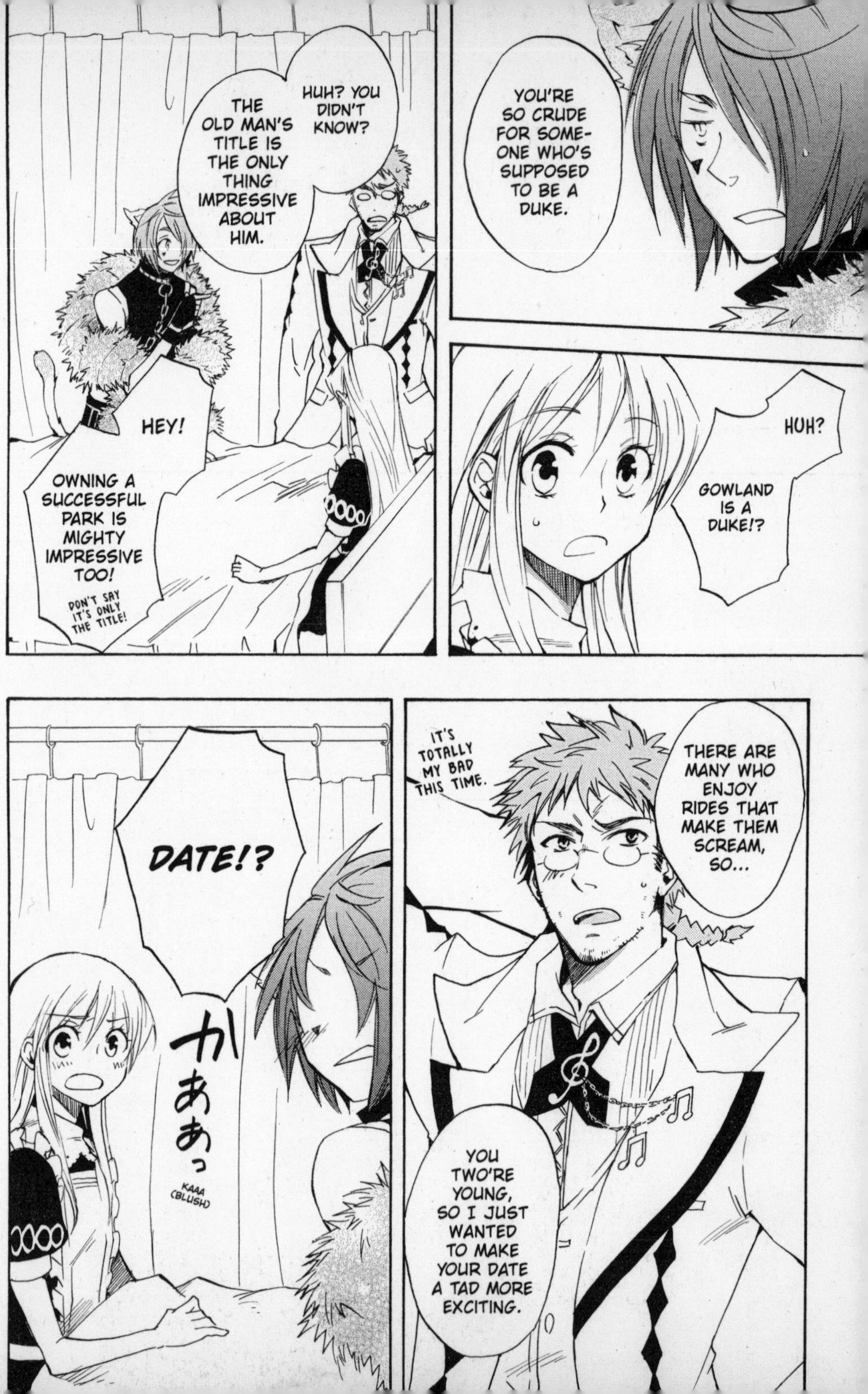
YOU'RE SO CRUDE FOR SOME-ONE WHO'S SUPPOSED TO BE A DUKE.
HUH?
GOWLAND IS A DUKE!?
HUH? YOU DIDN'T KNOW?
THE OLD MAN'S TITLE IS THE ONLY THING IMPRESSIVE ABOUT HIM.
HEY!
OWNING A SUCCESSFUL PARK IS MIGHTY IMPRESSIVE TOO!
DON'T SAY IT'S ONLY THE TITLE!
THERE ARE MANY WHO ENJOY RIDES THAT MAKE THEM SCREAM, SO...
IT'S TOTALLY MY BAD THIS TIME.
YOU TWO'RE YOUNG, SO I JUST WANTED TO MAKE YOUR DATE A TAD MORE EXCITING.
DATE!?
かぁあっ
KAAA (BLUSH)

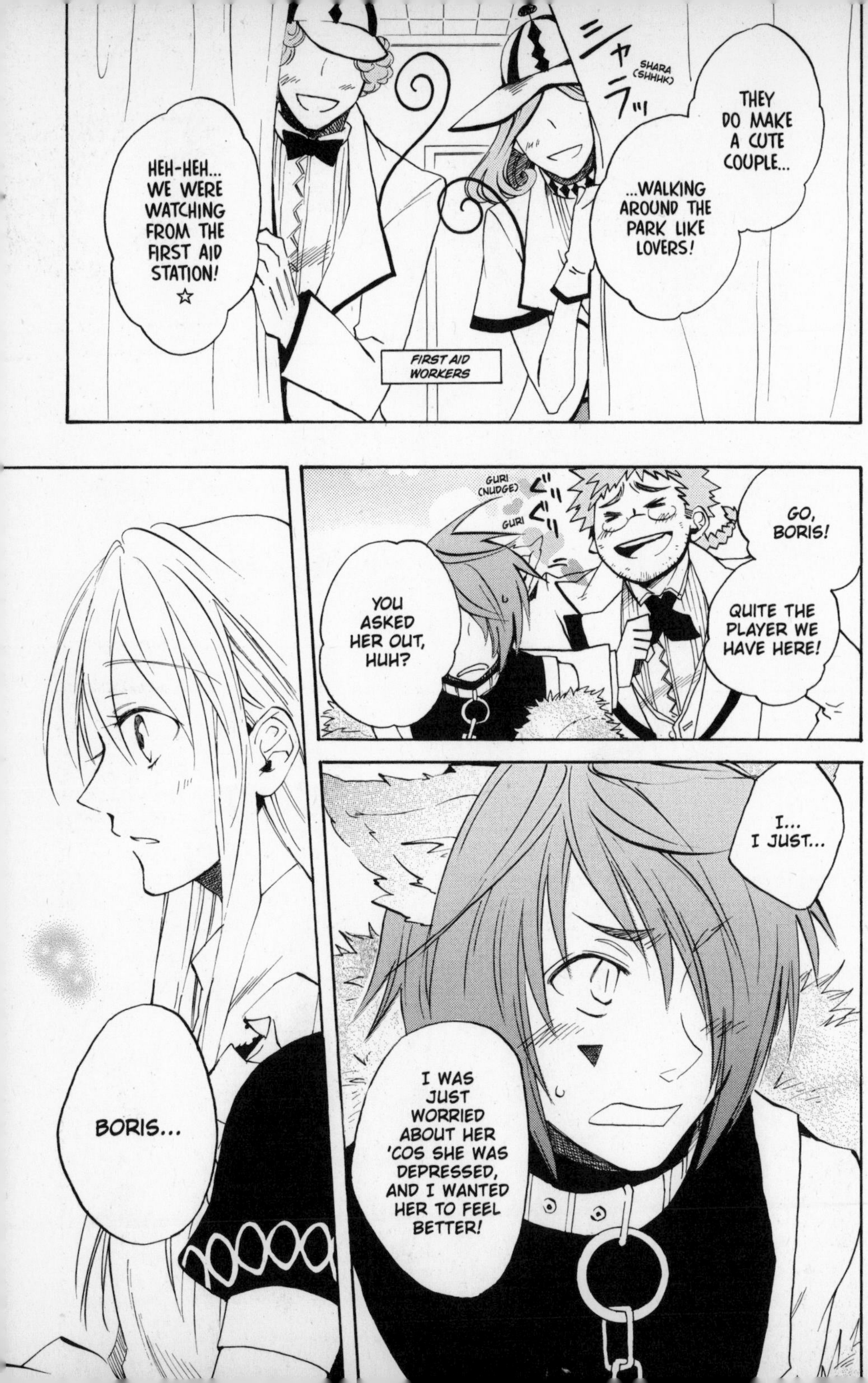
SHARA (SHHHK)
THEY DO MAKE A CUTE COUPLE...
...WALKING AROUND THE PARK LIKE LOVERS!
HEH-HEH... WE WERE WATCHING FROM THE FIRST AID STATION! ☆
FIRST AID WORKERS
GO, BORIS!
QUITE THE PLAYER WE HAVE HERE!
GURI (NUDGE)
GURI
YOU ASKED HER OUT, HUH?
I... I JUST...
I WAS JUST WORRIED ABOUT HER 'COS SHE WAS DEPRESSED, AND I WANTED HER TO FEEL BETTER!
BORIS...

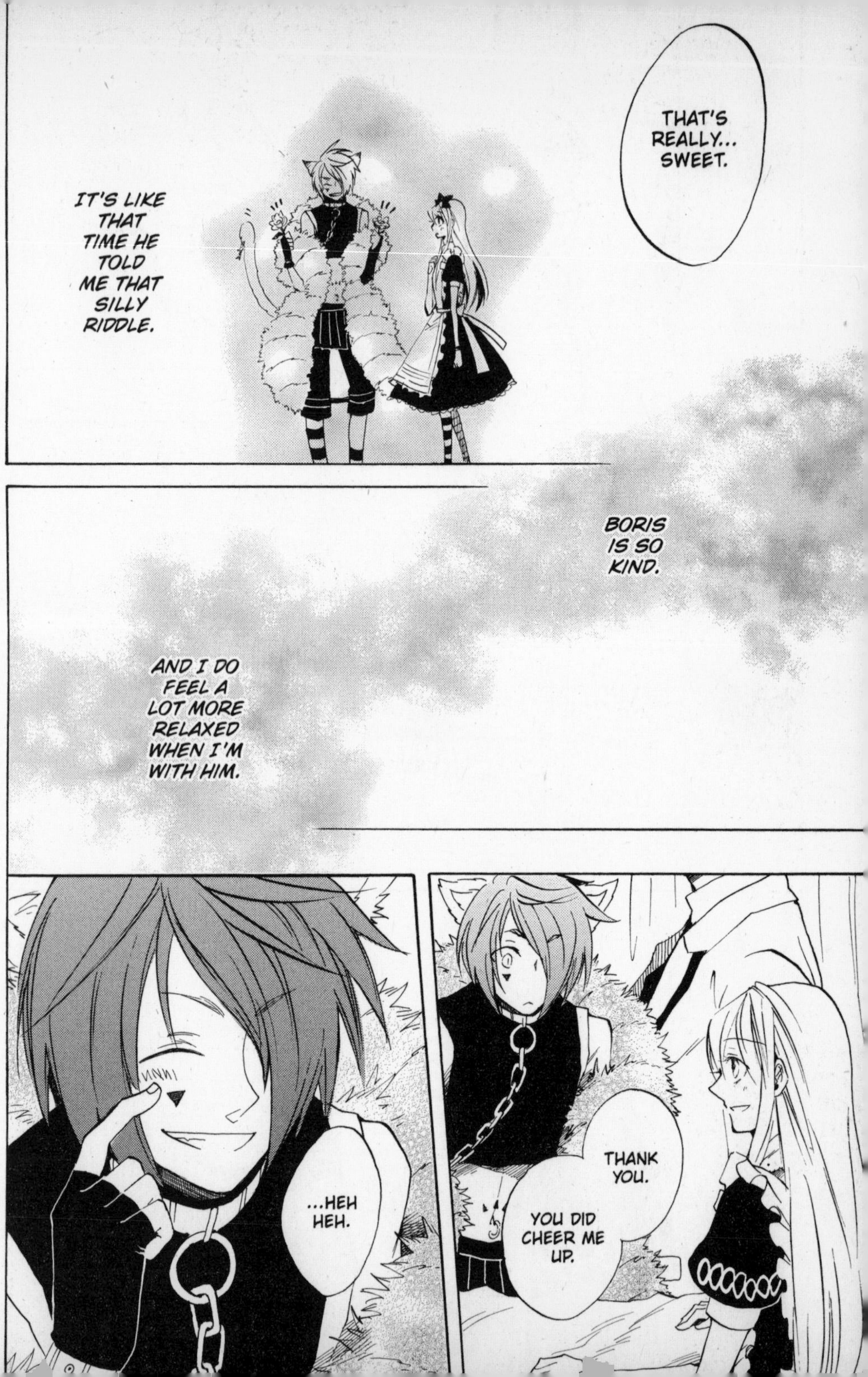
THAT'S REALLY... SWEET.
IT'S LIKE THAT TIME HE TOLD ME THAT SILLY RIDDLE.
BORIS IS SO KIND.
AND I DO FEEL A LOT MORE RELAXED WHEN I'M WITH HIM.
THANK YOU.
YOU DID CHEER ME UP.
...HEH HEH.

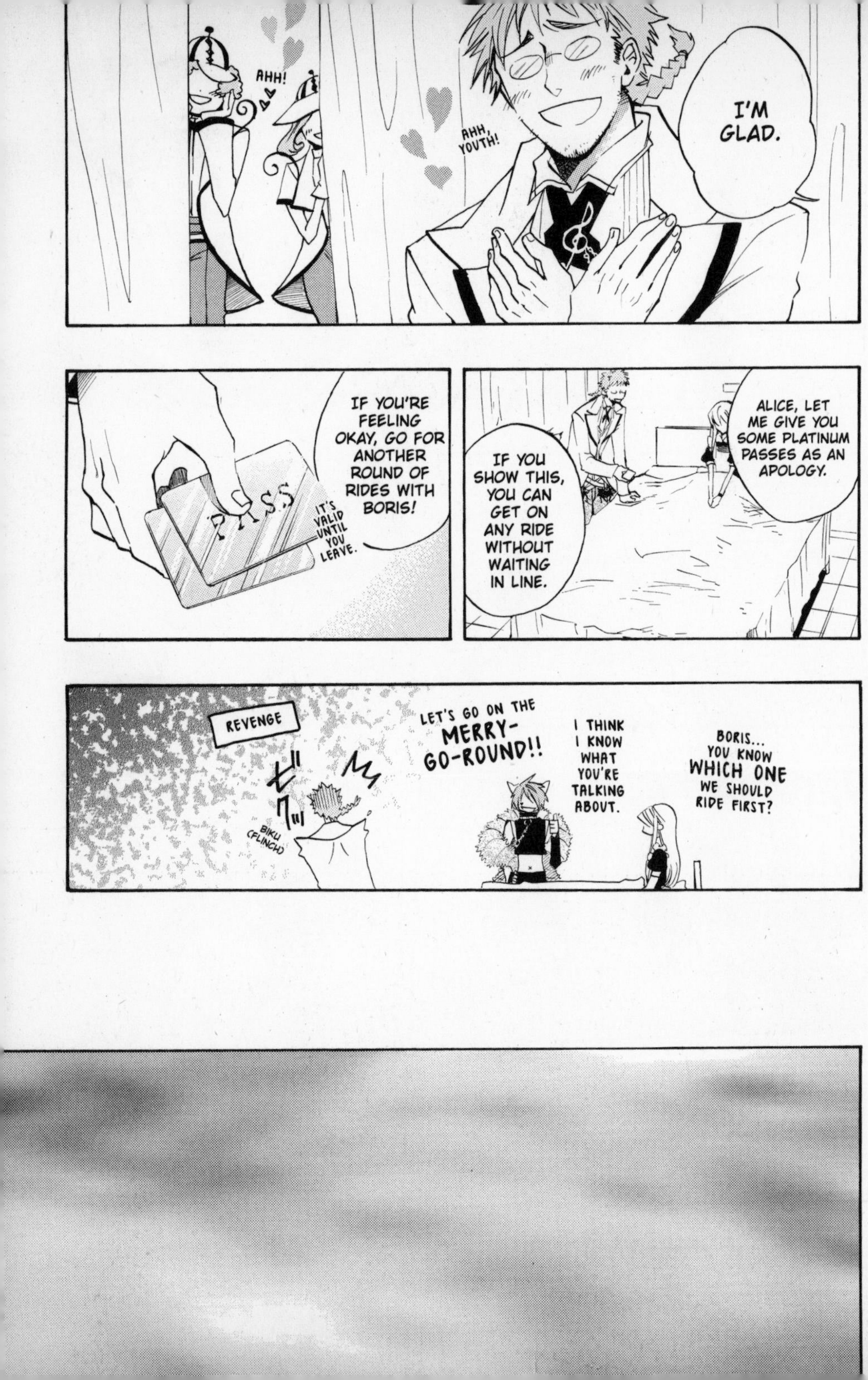
I'M GLAD.
AHH, YOUTH!
AHH!
ALICE, LET ME GIVE YOU SOME PLATINUM PASSES AS AN APOLOGY.
IF YOU SHOW THIS, YOU CAN GET ON ANY RIDE WITHOUT WAITING IN LINE.
IF YOU'RE FEELING OKAY, GO FOR ANOTHER ROUND OF RIDES WITH BORIS!
IT'S VALID UNTIL YOU LEAVE.
PASS
BORIS... YOU KNOW WHICH ONE WE SHOULD RIDE FIRST?
I THINK I KNOW WHAT YOU'RE TALKING ABOUT.
LET'S GO ON THE MERRY-GO-ROUND!!
BIKU (FLINCH)
REVENGE

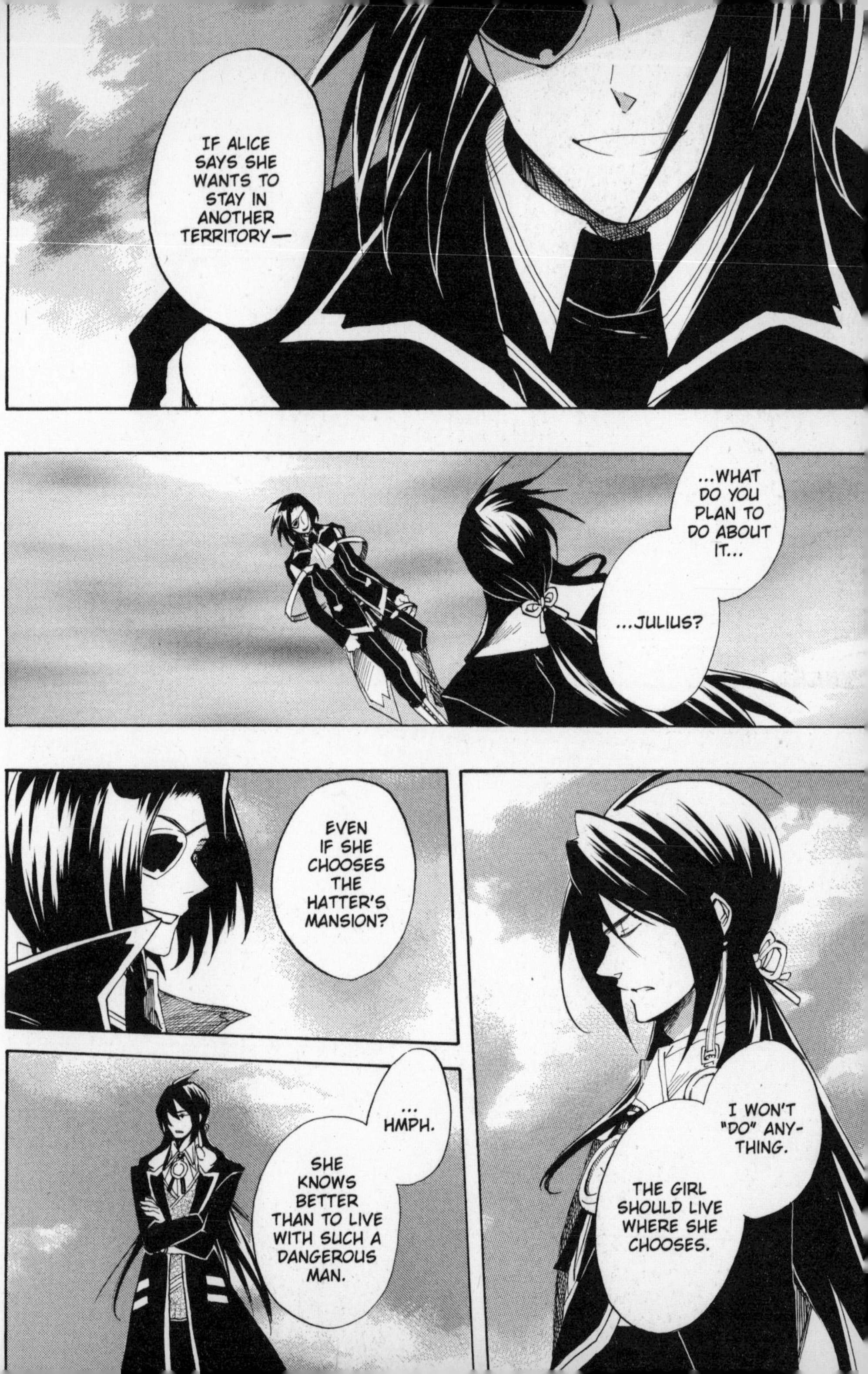
IF ALICE SAYS SHE WANTS TO STAY IN ANOTHER TERRITORY—
...WHAT DO YOU PLAN TO DO ABOUT IT...
...JULIUS?
I WON'T "DO" ANY-THING.
THE GIRL SHOULD LIVE WHERE SHE CHOOSES.
EVEN IF SHE CHOOSES THE HATTER'S MANSION?
... HMPH.
SHE KNOWS BETTER THAN TO LIVE WITH SUCH A DANGEROUS MAN.

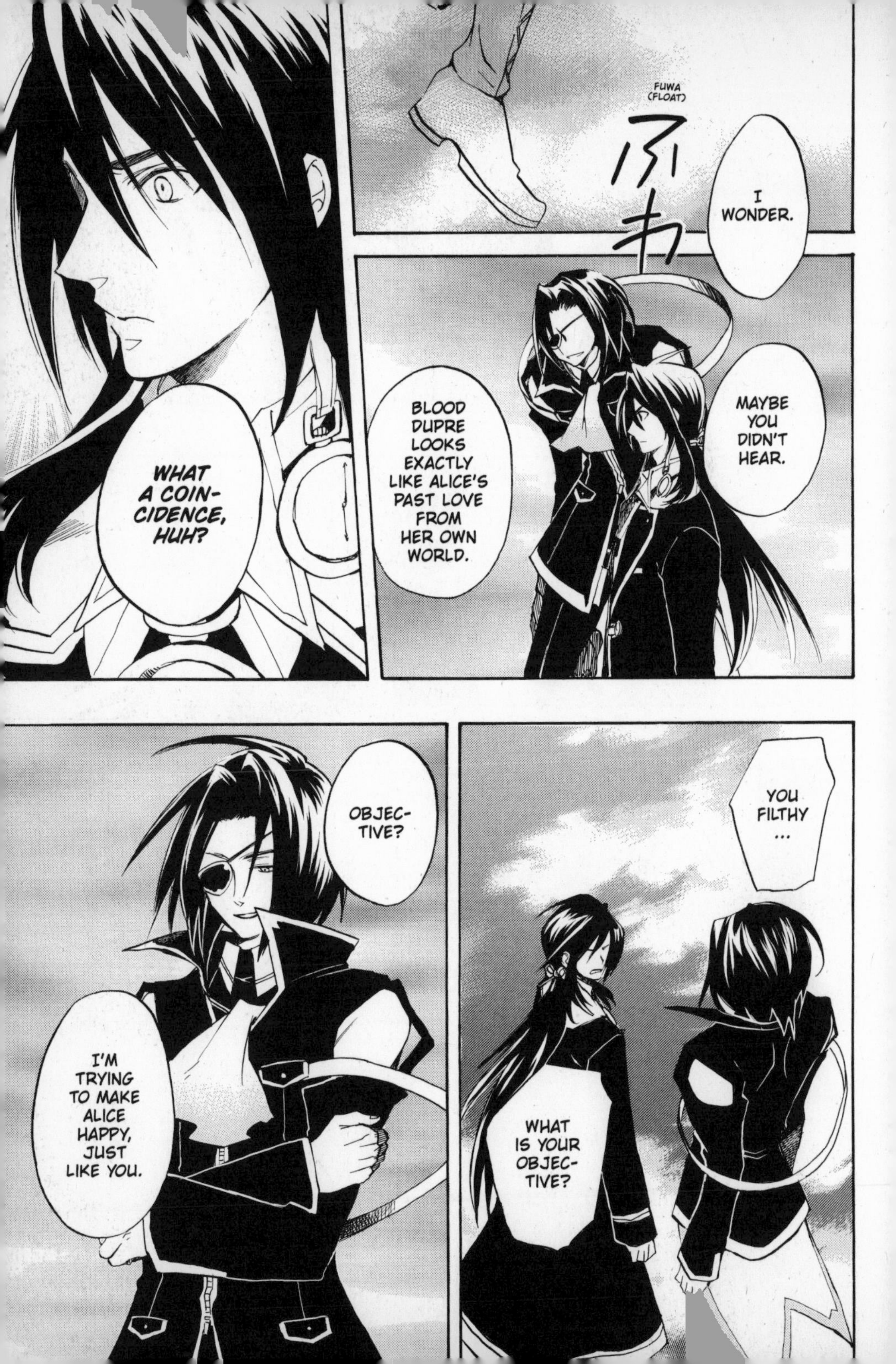
FUWA (FLOAT)
ふわ
I WONDER.
MAYBE YOU DIDN'T HEAR.
BLOOD DUPRE LOOKS EXACTLY LIKE ALICE'S PAST LOVE FROM HER OWN WORLD.
WHAT A COINCIDENCE, HUH?
YOU FILTHY ...
WHAT IS YOUR OBJECTIVE?
OBJECTIVE?
I'M TRYING TO MAKE ALICE HAPPY, JUST LIKE YOU.

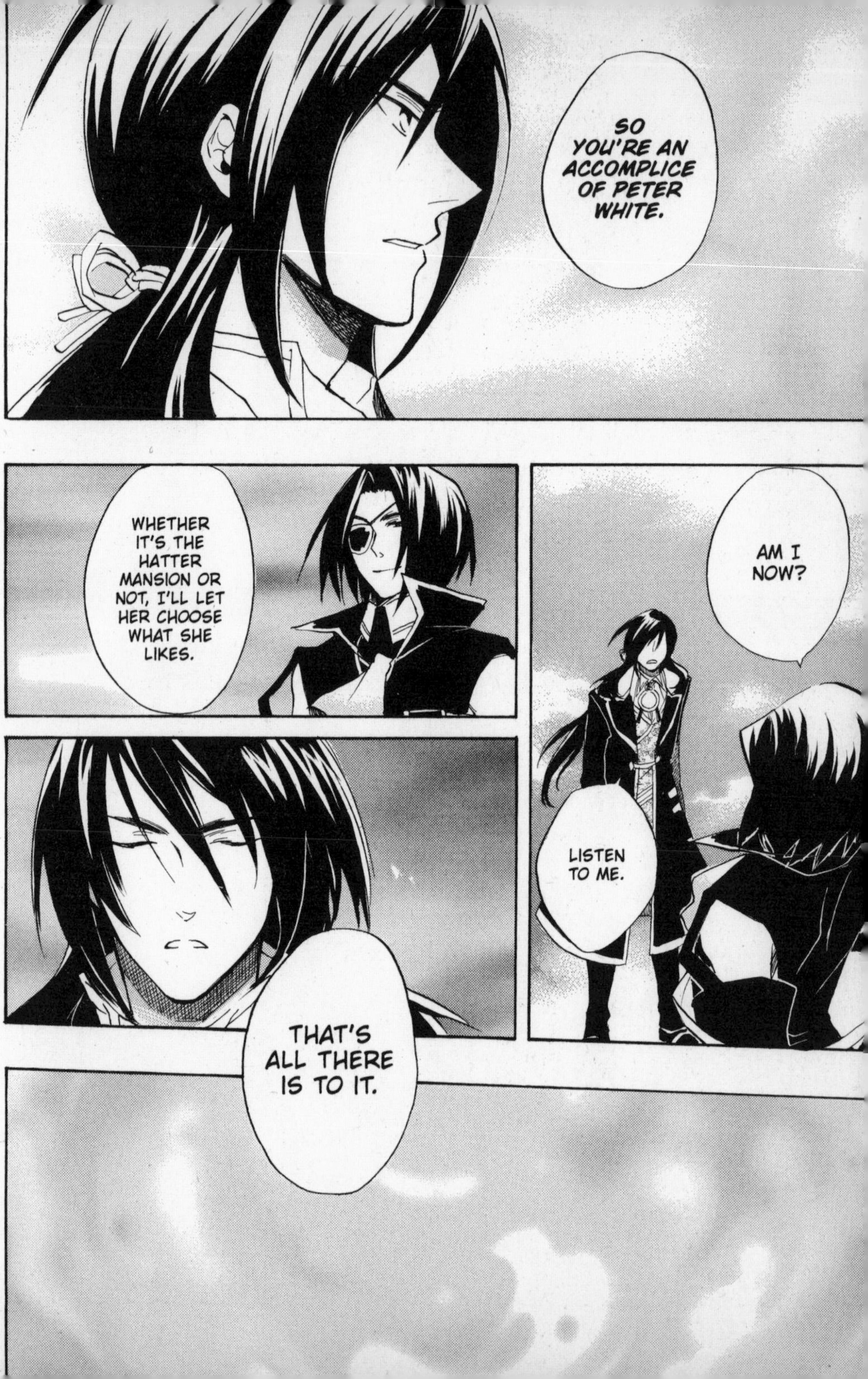
SO YOU'RE AN ACCOMPLICE OF PETER WHITE.
AM I NOW?
LISTEN TO ME.
WHETHER IT'S THE HATTER MANSION OR NOT, I'LL LET HER CHOOSE WHAT SHE LIKES.
THAT'S ALL THERE IS TO IT.

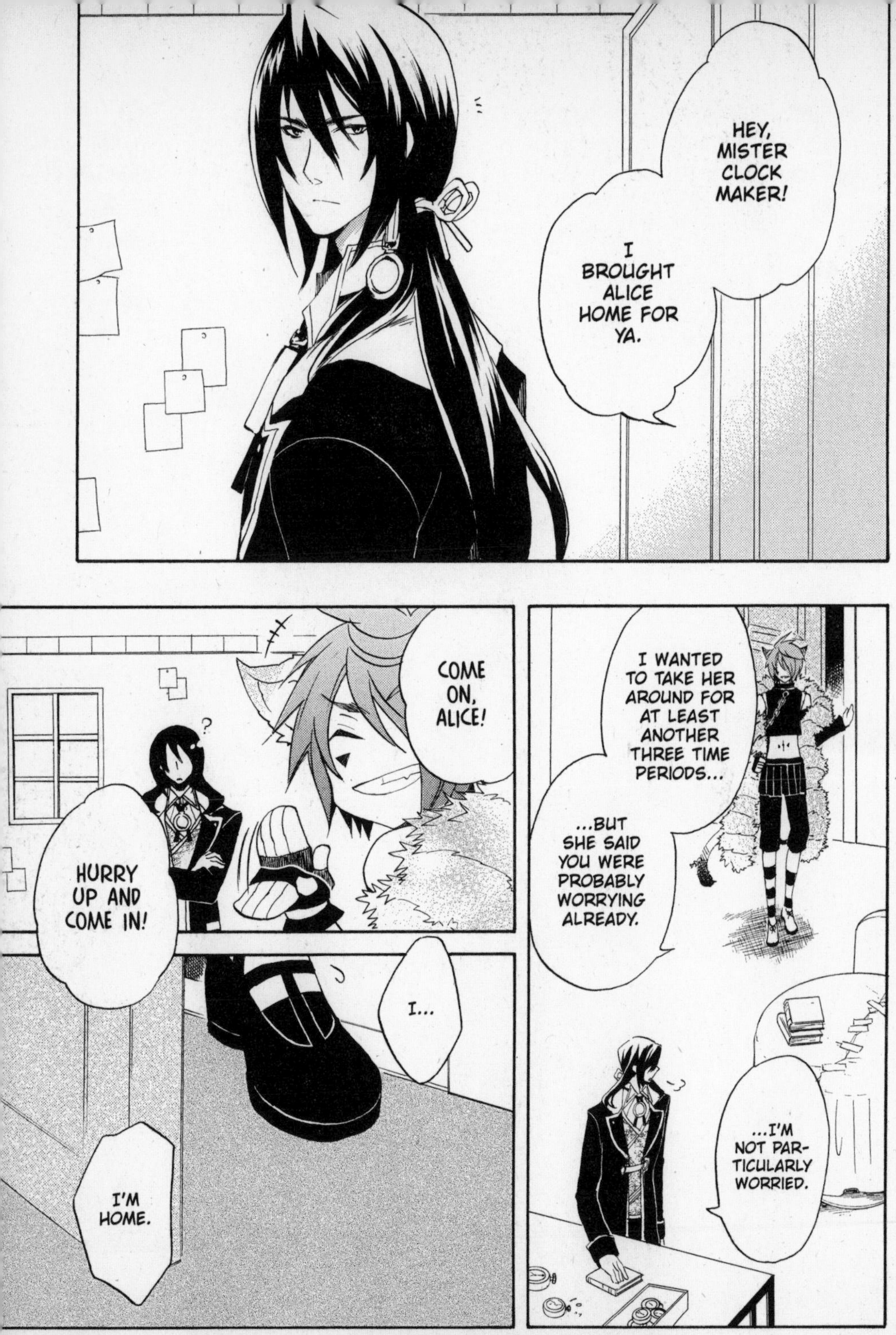
HEY, MISTER CLOCK MAKER!
I BROUGHT ALICE HOME FOR YA.
I WANTED TO TAKE HER AROUND FOR AT LEAST ANOTHER THREE TIME PERIODS...
...BUT SHE SAID YOU WERE PROBABLY WORRYING ALREADY.
...I'M NOT PAR-TICULARLY WORRIED.
COME ON, ALICE!
HURRY UP AND COME IN!
I...
I'M HOME.

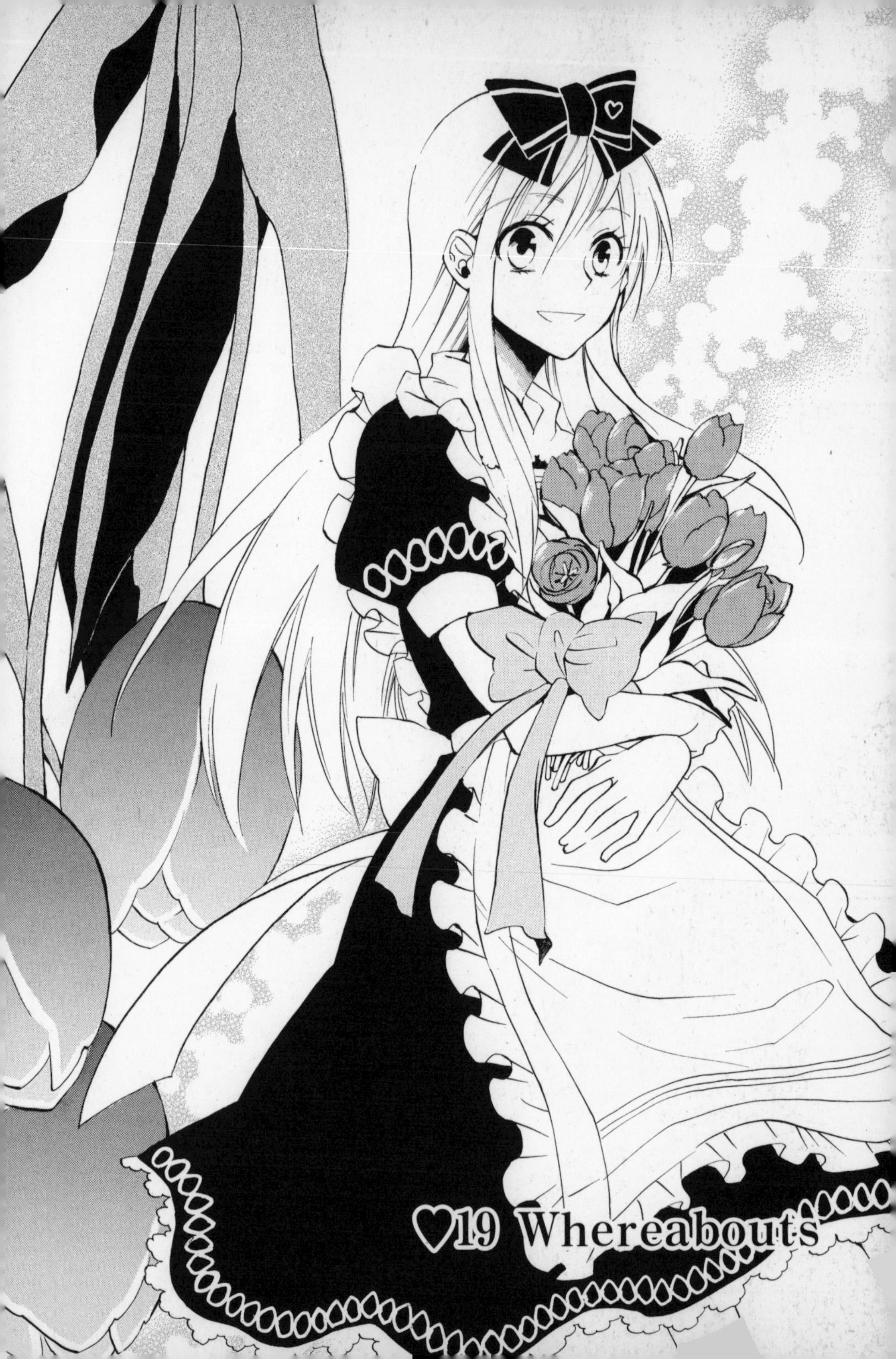
♡19 Whereabouts

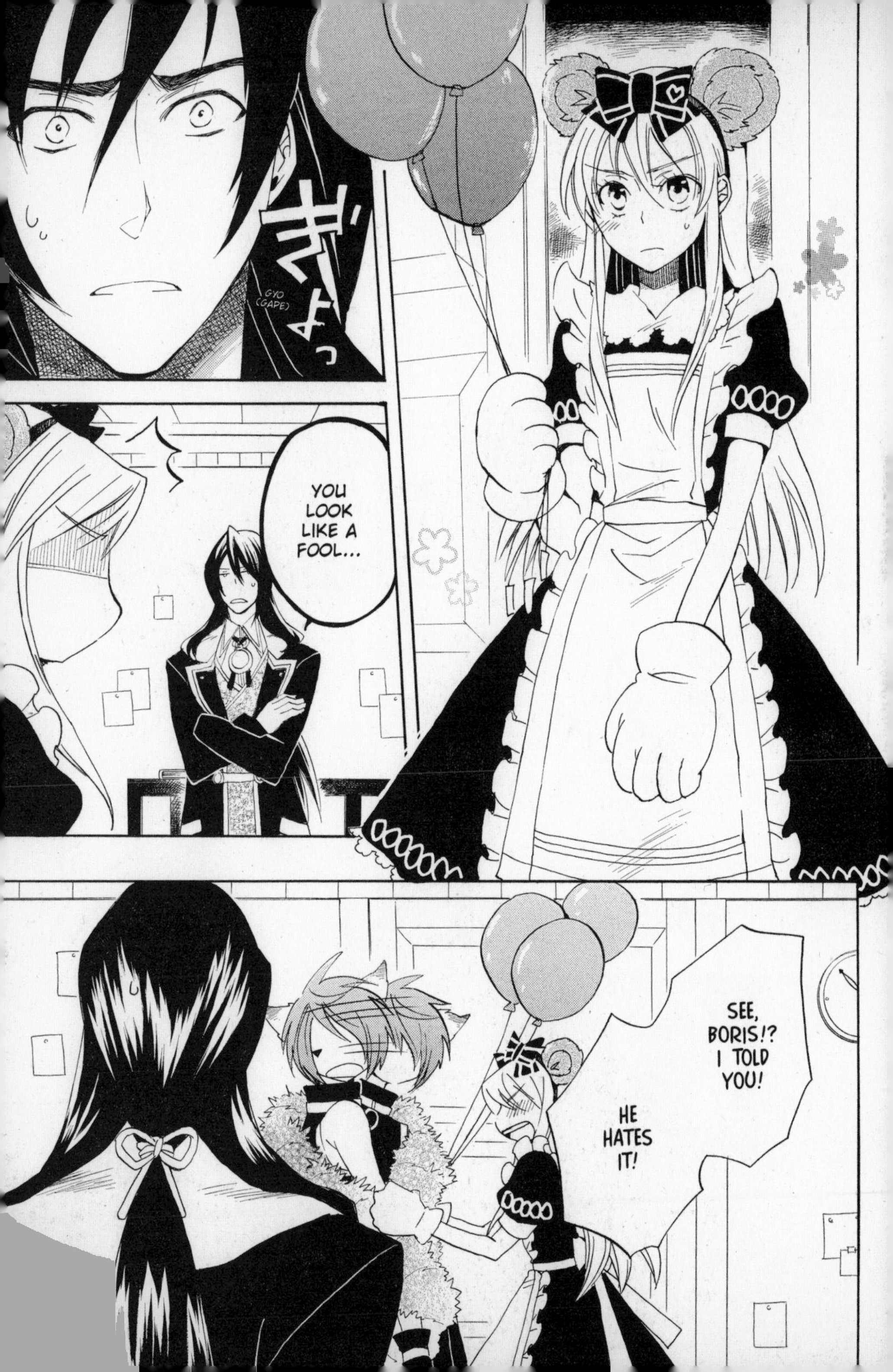
ぎょっ
GYO (GAPE)
YOU LOOK LIKE A FOOL...
SEE, BORIS!? I TOLD YOU!
HE HATES IT!

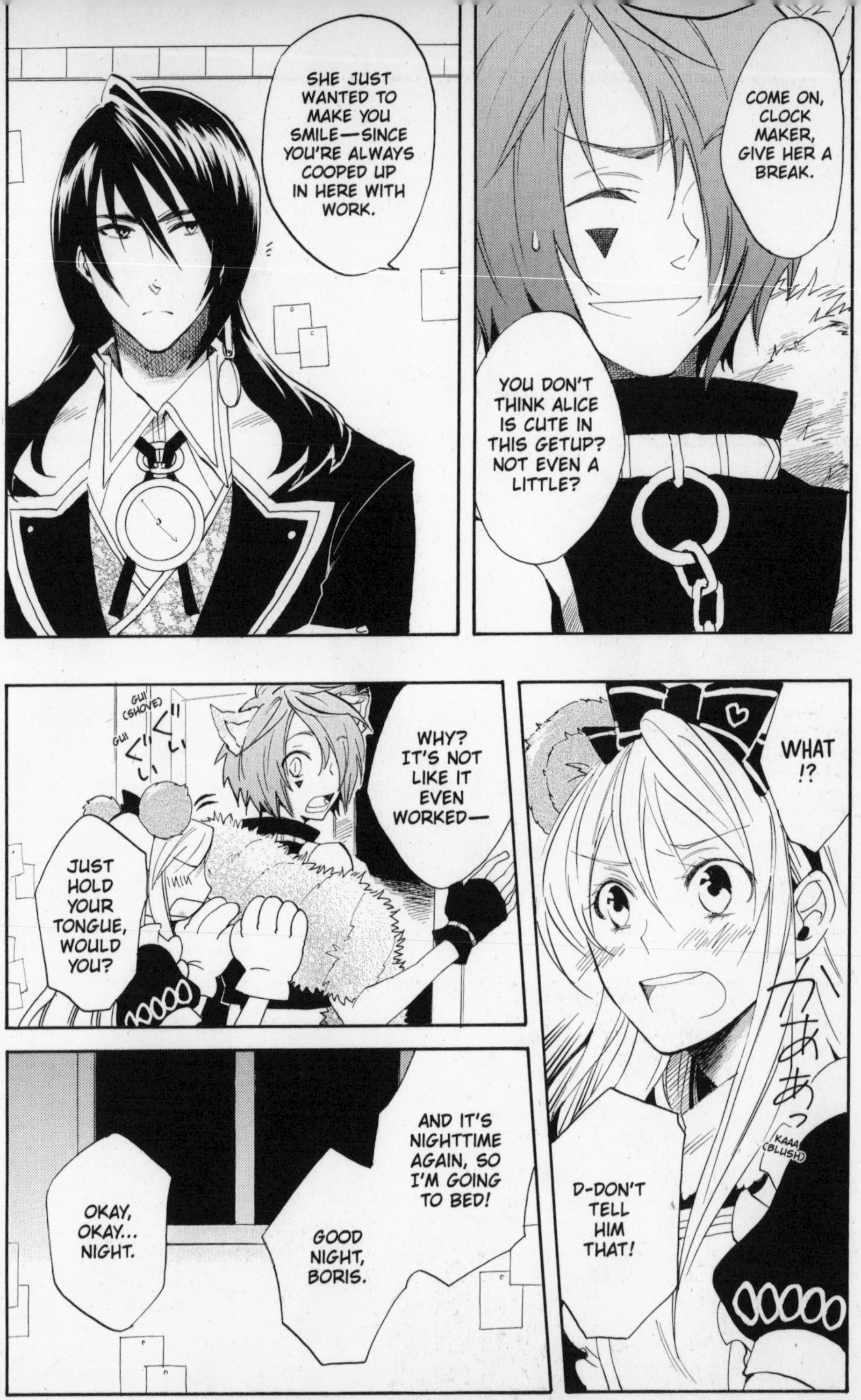
COME ON, CLOCK MAKER, GIVE HER A BREAK.
YOU DON'T THINK ALICE IS CUTE IN THIS GETUP? NOT EVEN A LITTLE?
SHE JUST WANTED TO MAKE YOU SMILE—SINCE YOU'RE ALWAYS COOPED UP IN HERE WITH WORK.
WHAT!?
KAAA (BLUSH)
D-DON'T TELL HIM THAT!
WHY? IT'S NOT LIKE IT EVEN WORKED—
GUI (SHOVE)
GUI
JUST HOLD YOUR TONGUE, WOULD YOU?
AND IT'S NIGHTTIME AGAIN, SO I'M GOING TO BED!
GOOD NIGHT, BORIS.
OKAY, OKAY... NIGHT.

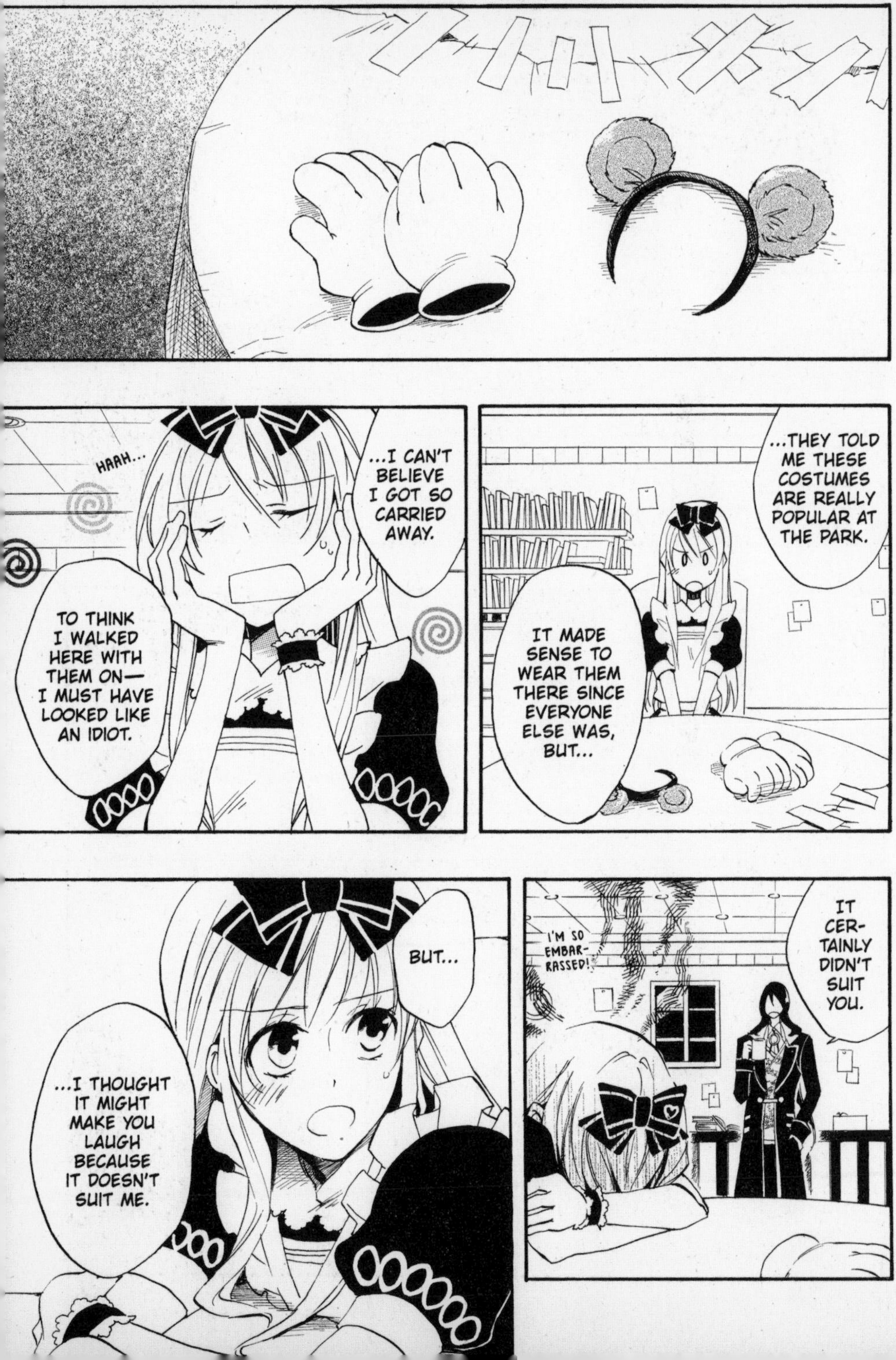
...THEY TOLD ME THESE COSTUMES ARE REALLY POPULAR AT THE PARK.
IT MADE SENSE TO WEAR THEM THERE SINCE EVERYONE ELSE WAS, BUT...
...I CAN'T BELIEVE I GOT SO CARRIED AWAY.
HAAH...
TO THINK I WALKED HERE WITH THEM ON— I MUST HAVE LOOKED LIKE AN IDIOT.
IT CER-TAINLY DIDN'T SUIT YOU.
I'M SO EMBAR-RASSED!
BUT...
...I THOUGHT IT MIGHT MAKE YOU LAUGH BECAUSE IT DOESN'T SUIT ME.

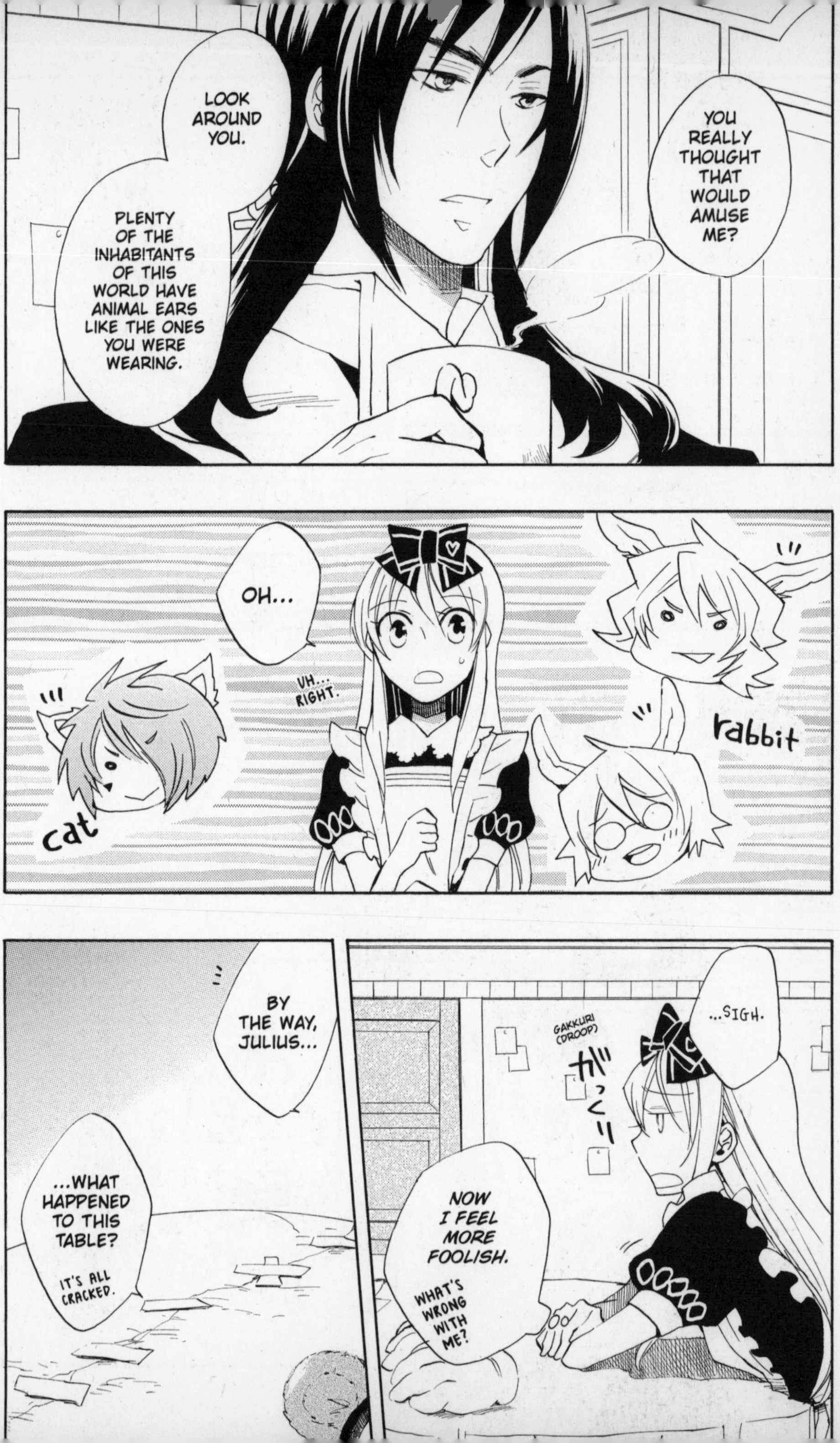
YOU REALLY THOUGHT THAT WOULD AMUSE ME?
LOOK AROUND YOU.
PLENTY OF THE INHABITANTS OF THIS WORLD HAVE ANIMAL EARS LIKE THE ONES YOU WERE WEARING.
OH...
UH... RIGHT.
rabbit
cat
...SIGH.
GAKKURI (DROOP)
がっくり
NOW I FEEL MORE FOOLISH.
WHAT'S WRONG WITH ME?
BY THE WAY, JULIUS...
...WHAT HAPPENED TO THIS TABLE?
IT'S ALL CRACKED.

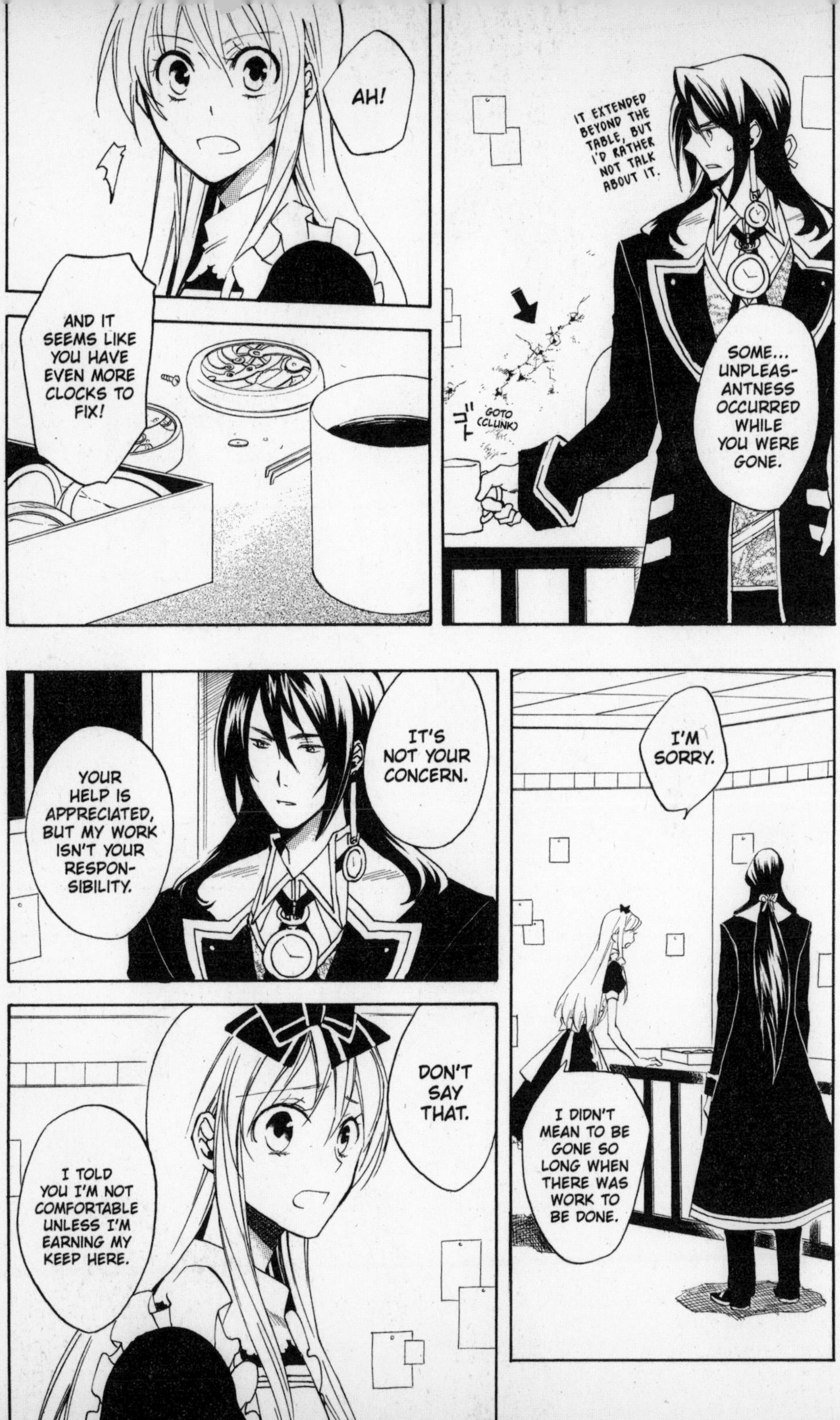
IT EXTENDED BEYOND THE TABLE, BUT I'D RATHER NOT TALK ABOUT IT.
GOTO (CLUNK)
SOME... UNPLEAS-ANTNESS OCCURRED WHILE YOU WERE GONE.
AH!
AND IT SEEMS LIKE YOU HAVE EVEN MORE CLOCKS TO FIX!
I'M SORRY.
I DIDN'T MEAN TO BE GONE SO LONG WHEN THERE WAS WORK TO BE DONE.
IT'S NOT YOUR CONCERN.
YOUR HELP IS APPRECIATED, BUT MY WORK ISN'T YOUR RESPON-SIBILITY.
DON'T SAY THAT.
I TOLD YOU I'M NOT COMFORTABLE UNLESS I'M EARNING MY KEEP HERE.

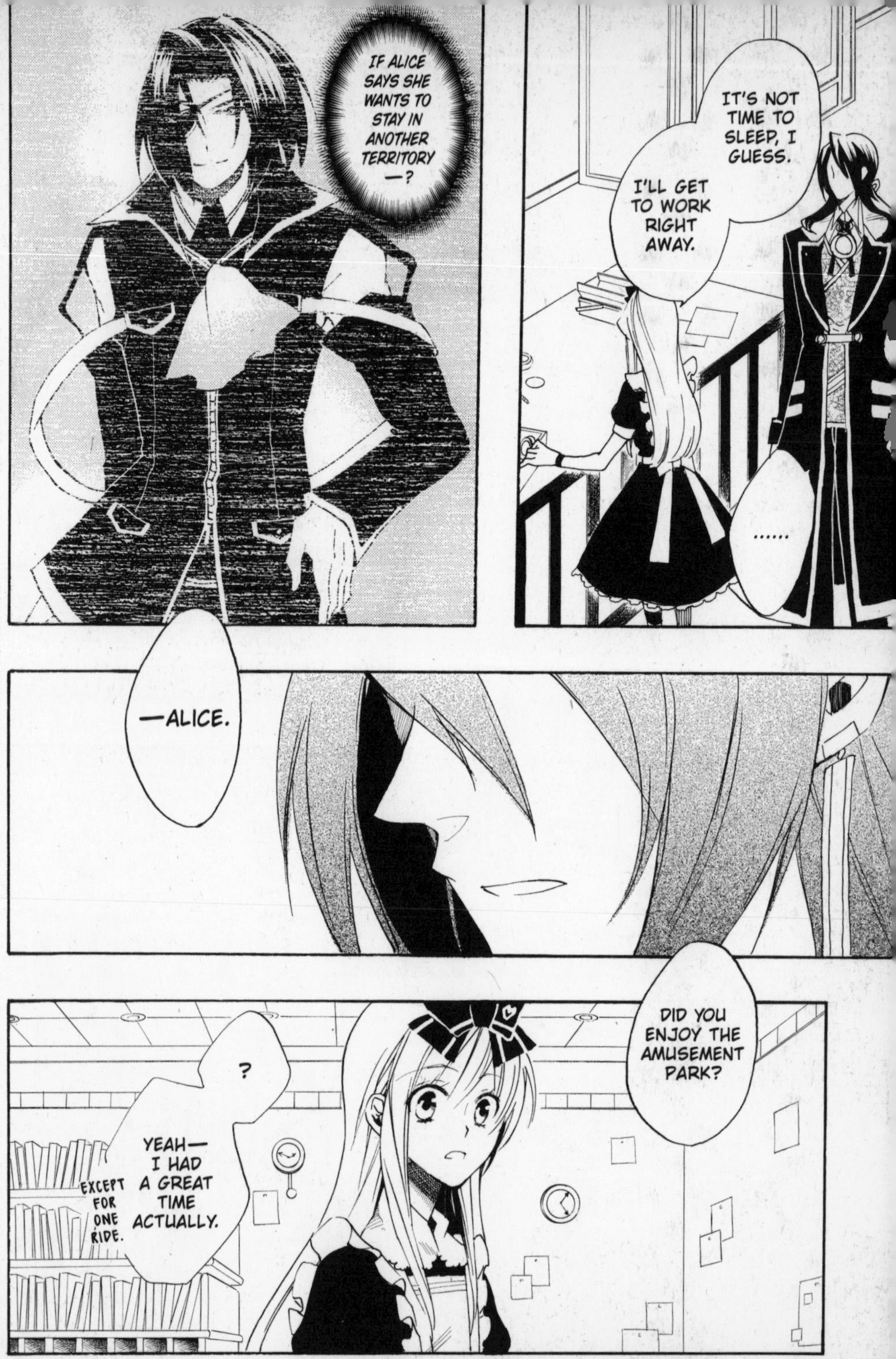
IT'S NOT TIME TO SLEEP, I GUESS.
I'LL GET TO WORK RIGHT AWAY.
......
IF ALICE SAYS SHE WANTS TO STAY IN ANOTHER TERRITORY—?
—ALICE.
DID YOU ENJOY THE AMUSEMENT PARK?
?
YEAH— I HAD A GREAT TIME ACTUALLY.
EXCEPT FOR ONE RIDE.

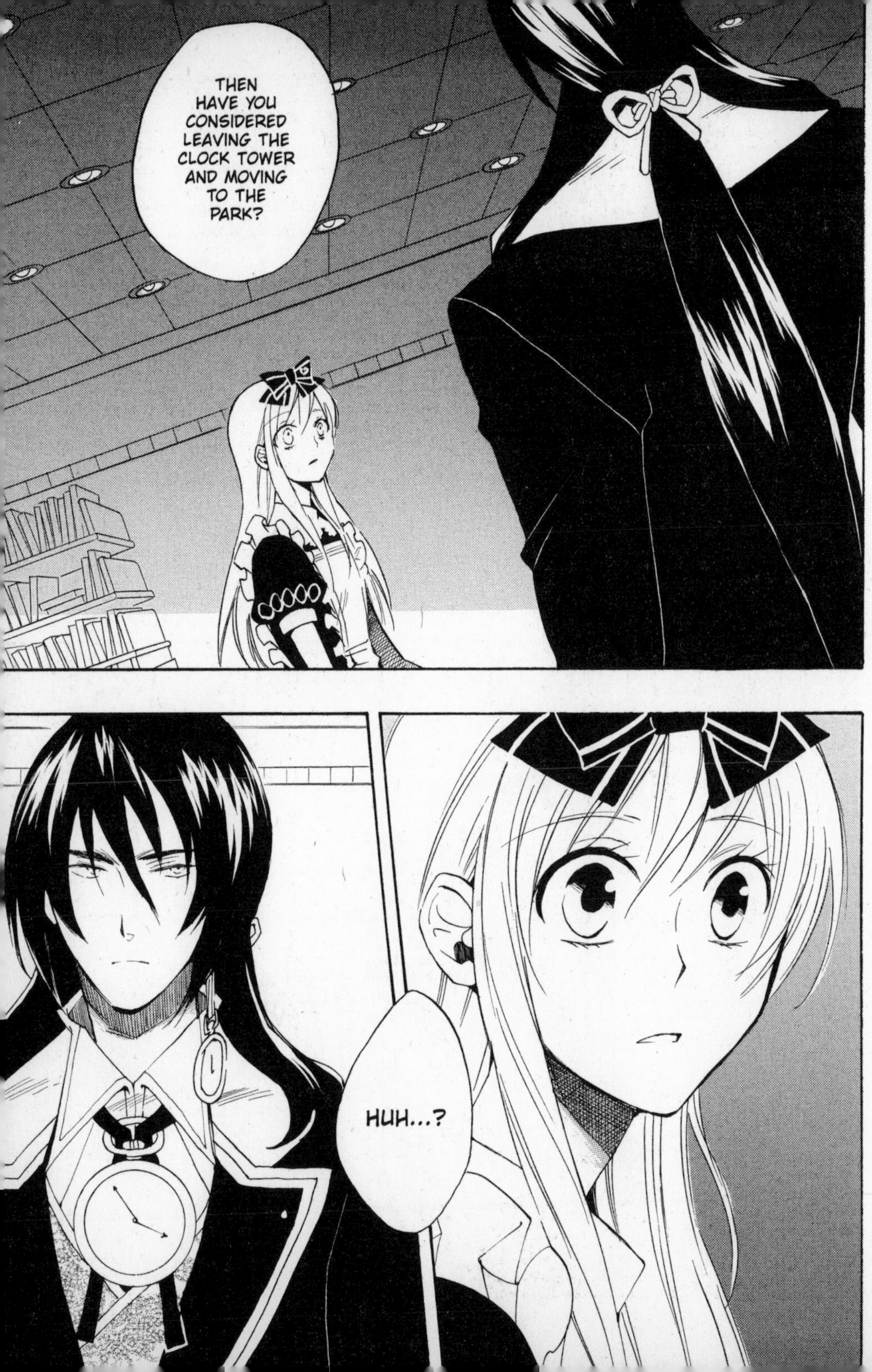
THEN HAVE YOU CONSIDERED LEAVING THE CLOCK TOWER AND MOVING TO THE PARK?
HUH...?

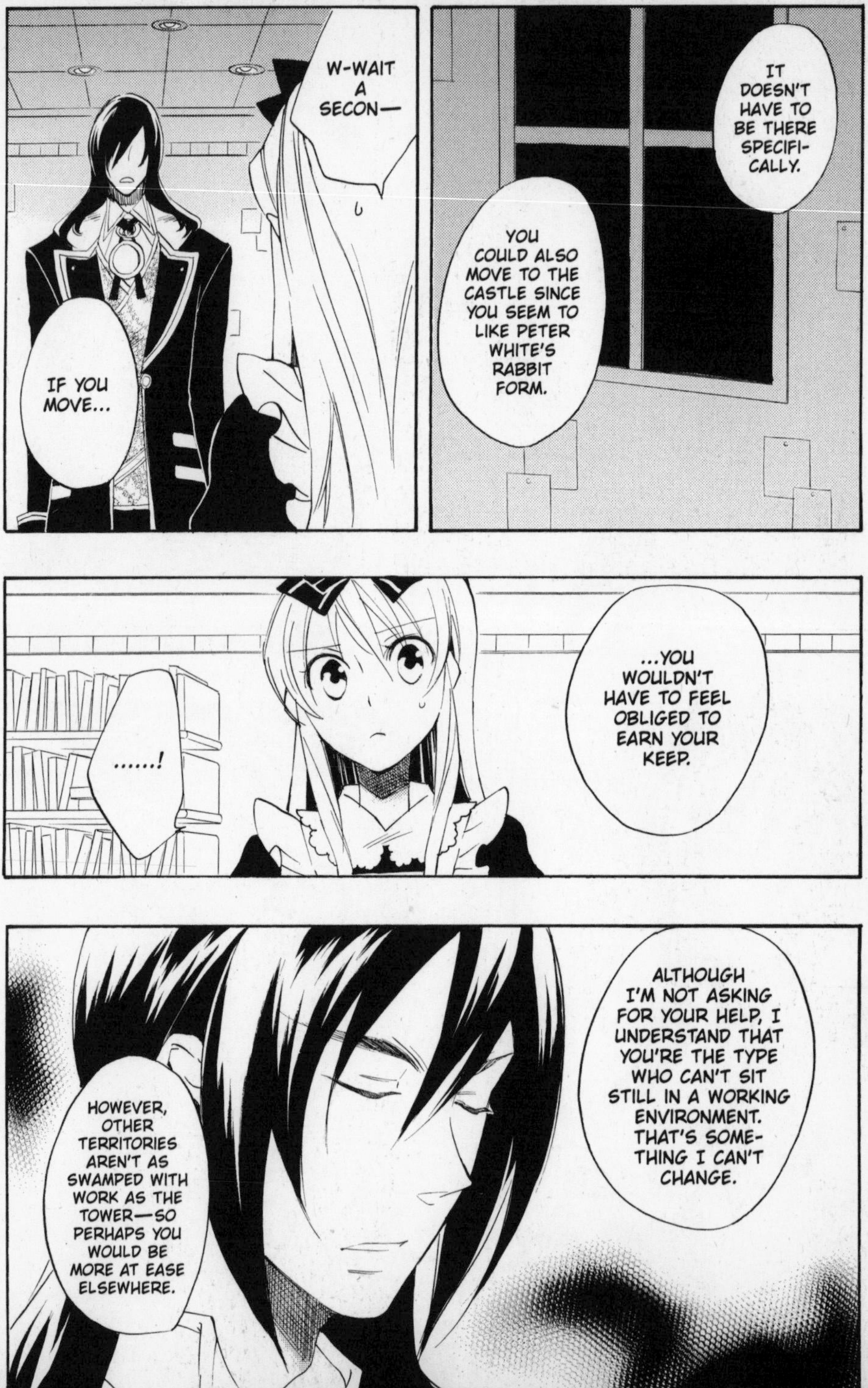
IT DOESN'T HAVE TO BE THERE SPECIFI-CALLY.
YOU COULD ALSO MOVE TO THE CASTLE SINCE YOU SEEM TO LIKE PETER WHITE'S RABBIT FORM.
W-WAIT A SECON—
IF YOU MOVE...
...YOU WOULDN'T HAVE TO FEEL OBLIGED TO EARN YOUR KEEP.
......!
ALTHOUGH I'M NOT ASKING FOR YOUR HELP, I UNDERSTAND THAT YOU'RE THE TYPE WHO CAN'T SIT STILL IN A WORKING ENVIRONMENT. THAT'S SOME-THING I CAN'T CHANGE.
HOWEVER, OTHER TERRITORIES AREN'T AS SWAMPED WITH WORK AS THE TOWER—SO PERHAPS YOU WOULD BE MORE AT EASE ELSEWHERE.

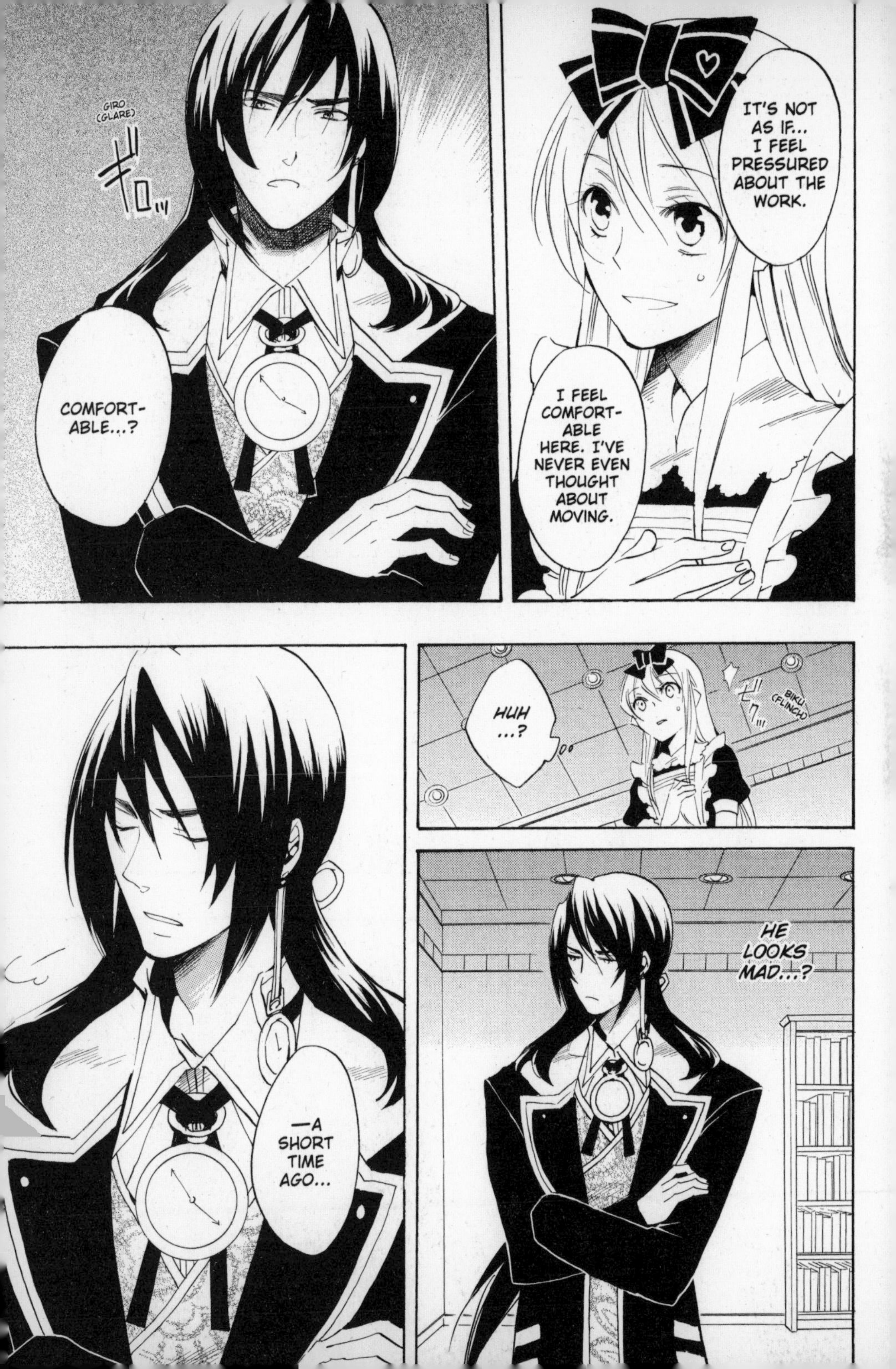

IT'S NOT AS IF... I FEEL PRESSURED ABOUT THE WORK.
I FEEL COMFORTABLE HERE. I'VE NEVER EVEN THOUGHT ABOUT MOVING.
GIRO (GLARE)
ギロッ
COMFORTABLE...?
HUH ...?
BIKU (FLINCH)
ビクッ
HE LOOKS MAD...?
—A SHORT TIME AGO...

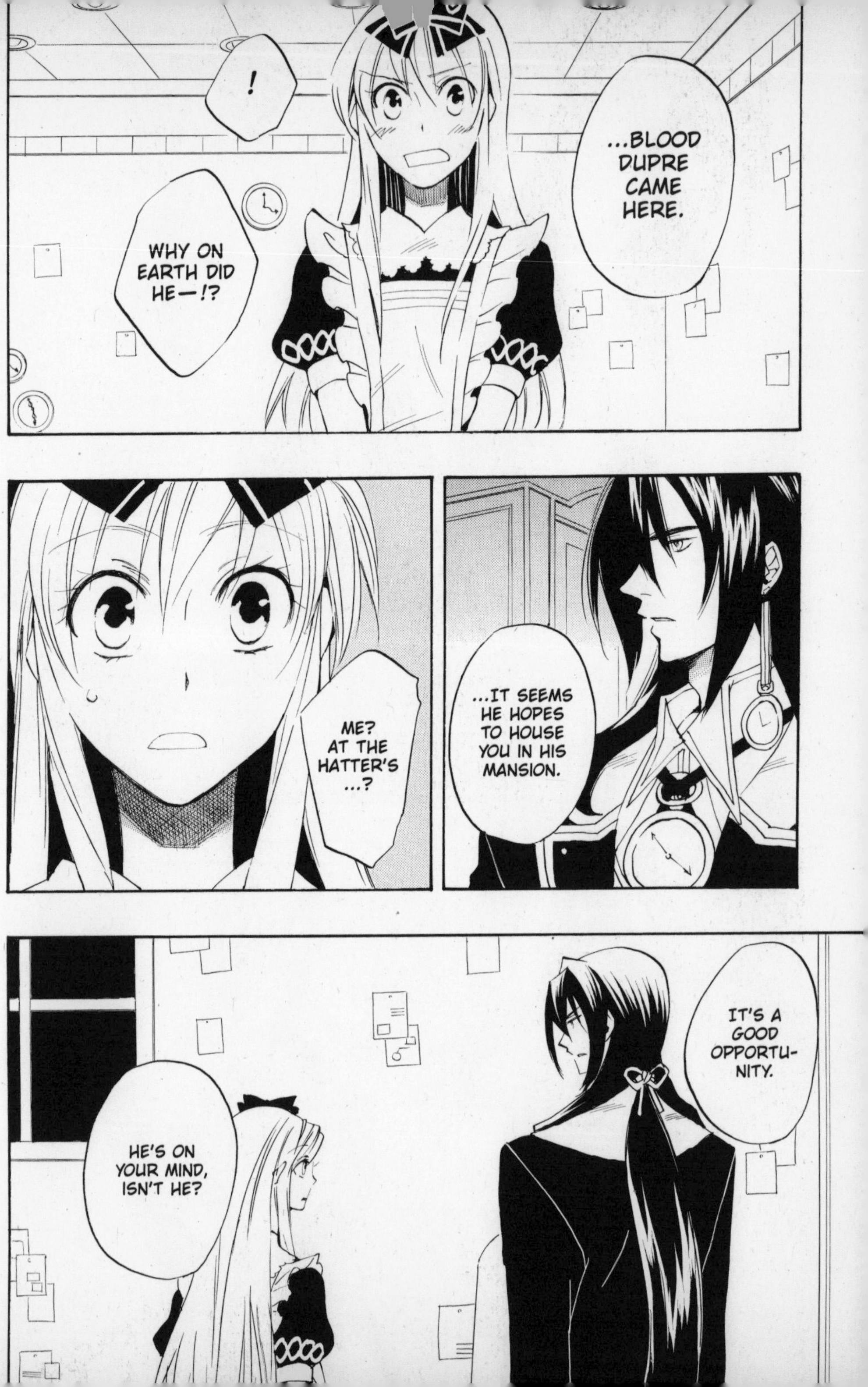
...BLOOD DUPRE CAME HERE.
!
WHY ON EARTH DID HE—!?
...IT SEEMS HE HOPES TO HOUSE YOU IN HIS MANSION.
ME? AT THE HATTER'S ...?
IT'S A GOOD OPPORTUNITY.
HE'S ON YOUR MIND, ISN'T HE?

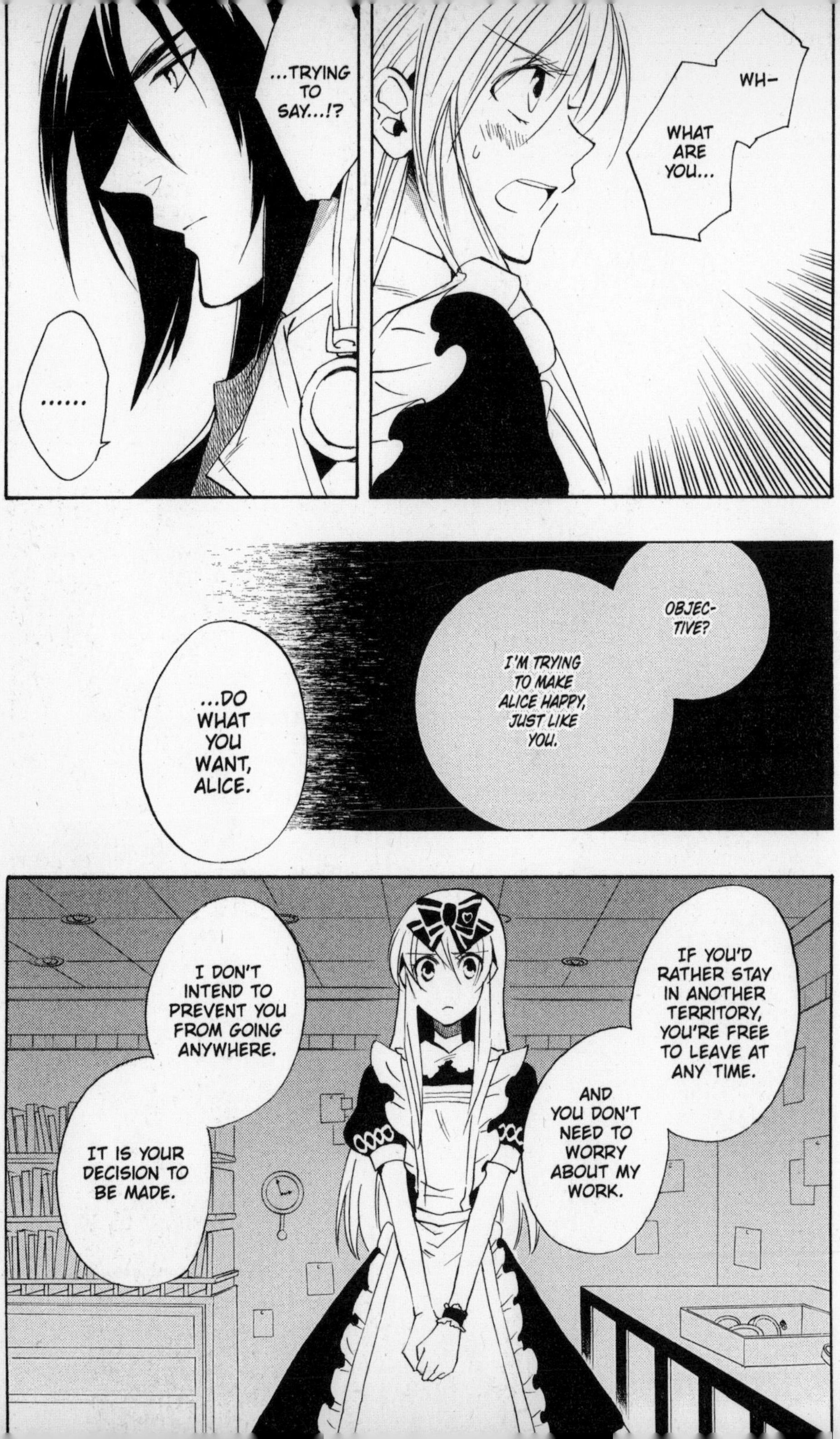
WH-
WHAT ARE YOU...
...TRYING TO SAY...!?
......
OBJECTIVE?
I'M TRYING TO MAKE ALICE HAPPY, JUST LIKE YOU.
...DO WHAT YOU WANT, ALICE.
IF YOU'D RATHER STAY IN ANOTHER TERRITORY, YOU'RE FREE TO LEAVE AT ANY TIME.
AND YOU DON'T NEED TO WORRY ABOUT MY WORK.
I DON'T INTEND TO PREVENT YOU FROM GOING ANYWHERE.
IT IS YOUR DECISION TO BE MADE.

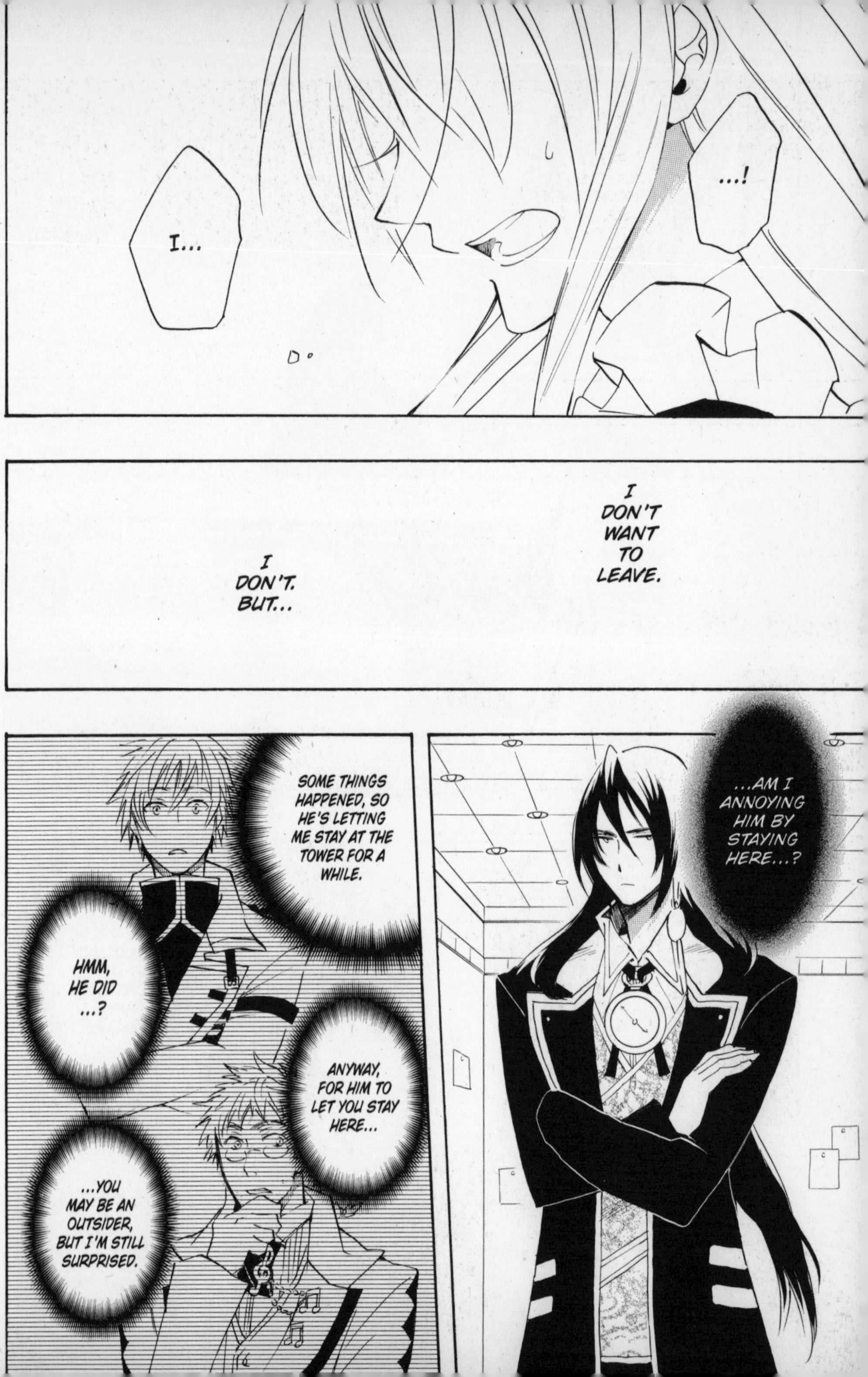
...!
I...
I DON'T WANT TO LEAVE.
I DON'T. BUT...
...AM I ANNOYING HIM BY STAYING HERE...?
SOME THINGS HAPPENED, SO HE'S LETTING ME STAY AT THE TOWER FOR A WHILE.
HMM, HE DID ...?
ANYWAY, FOR HIM TO LET YOU STAY HERE...
...YOU MAY BE AN OUTSIDER, BUT I'M STILL SURPRISED.

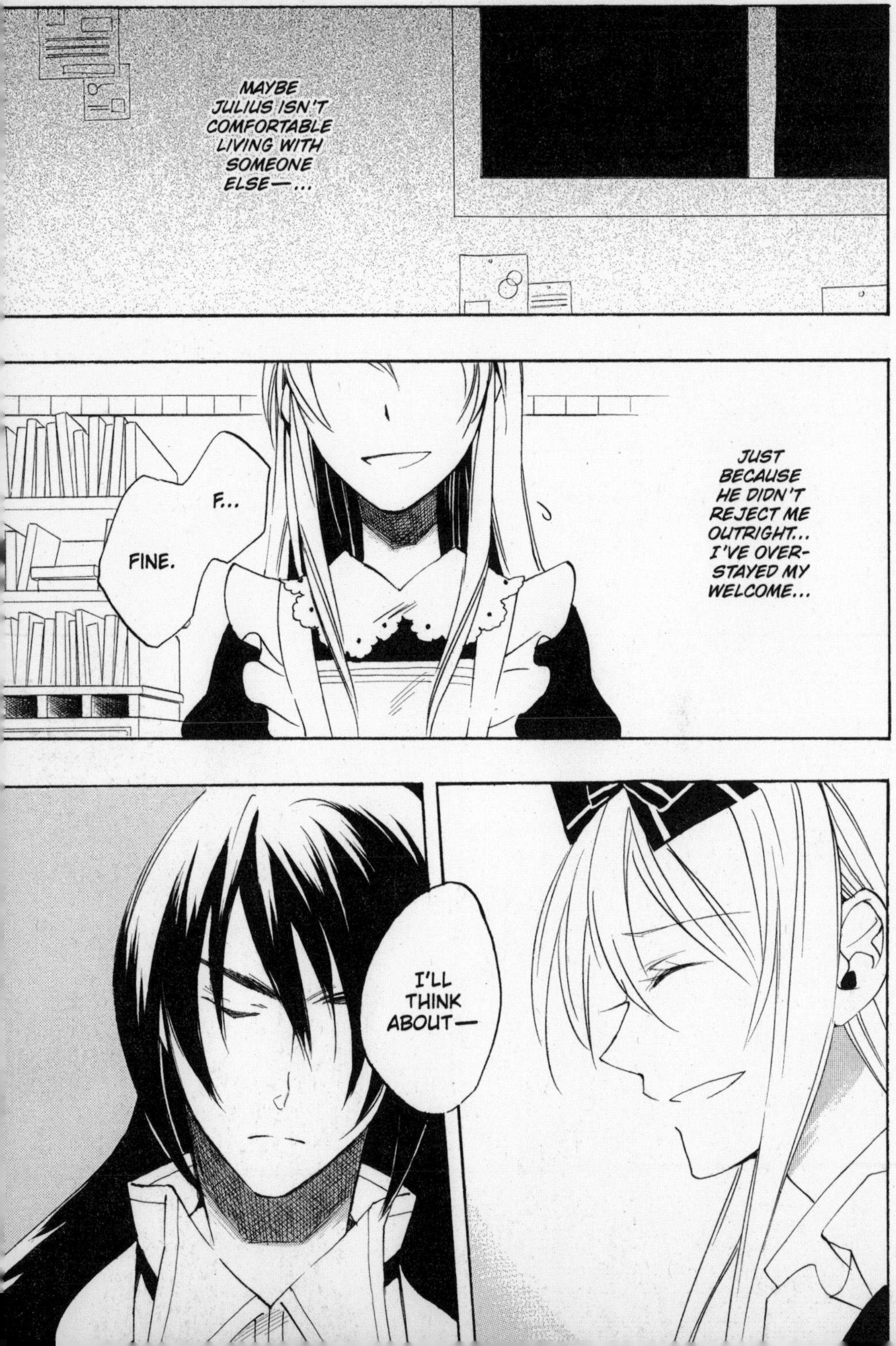
MAYBE JULIUS ISN'T COMFORTABLE LIVING WITH SOMEONE ELSE—...
JUST BECAUSE HE DIDN'T REJECT ME OUTRIGHT... I'VE OVER-STAYED MY WELCOME...
F...
FINE.
I'LL THINK ABOUT—

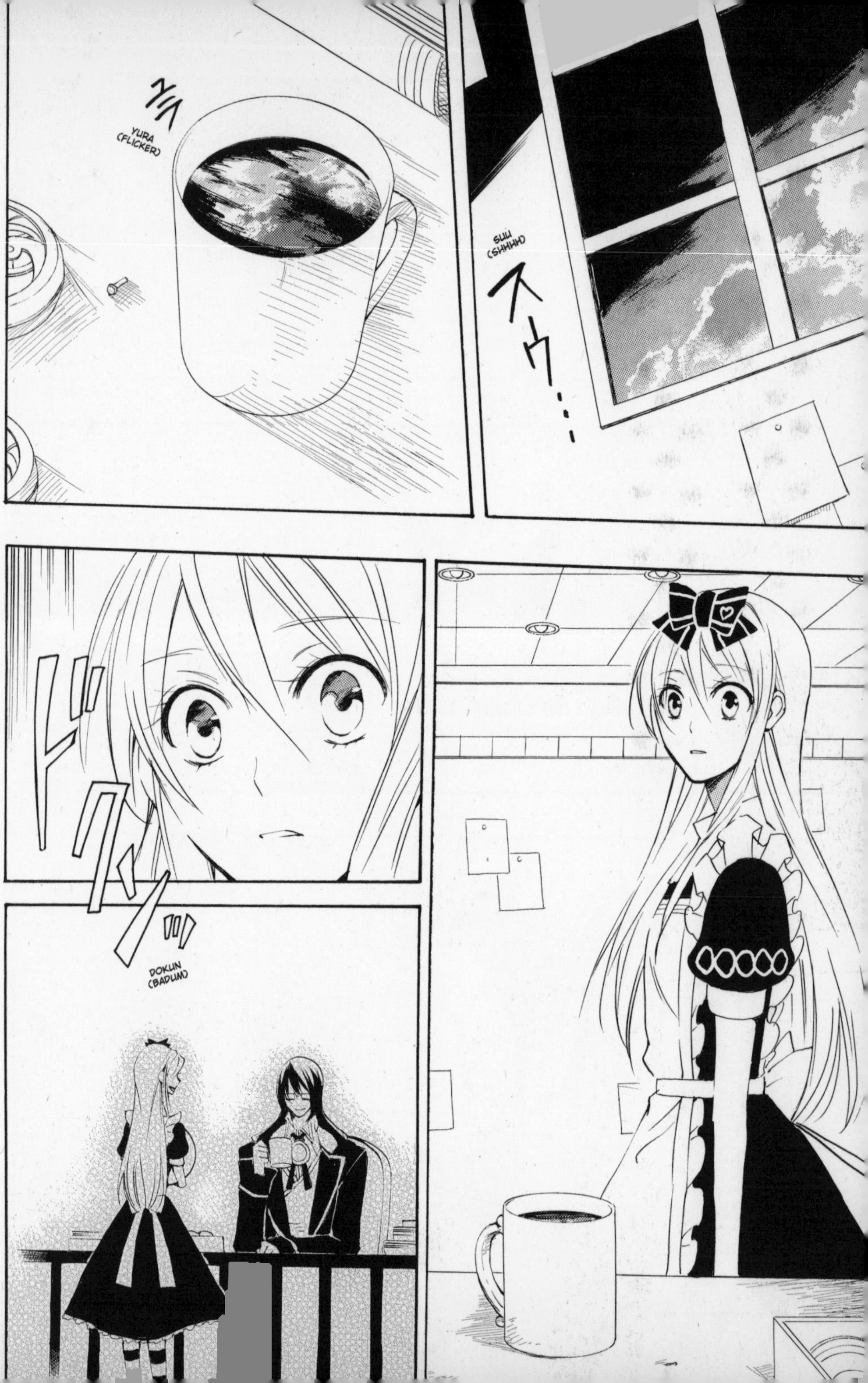
SUU (SHHHH)
YURA (FLICKER)
DOKUN (BADUM)

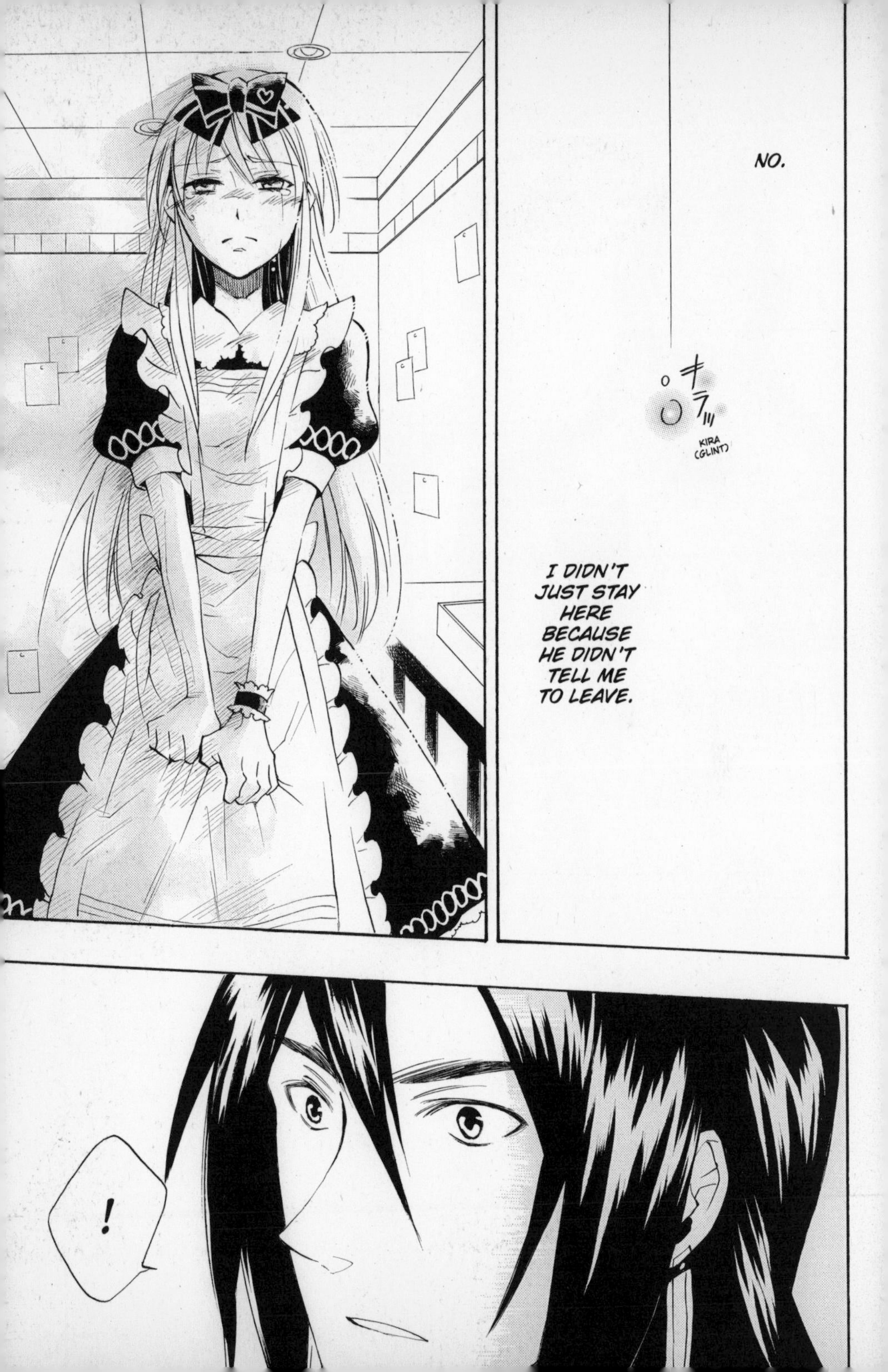
NO.
キラ
KIRA (GLINT)
I DIDN'T JUST STAY HERE BECAUSE HE DIDN'T TELL ME TO LEAVE.
!

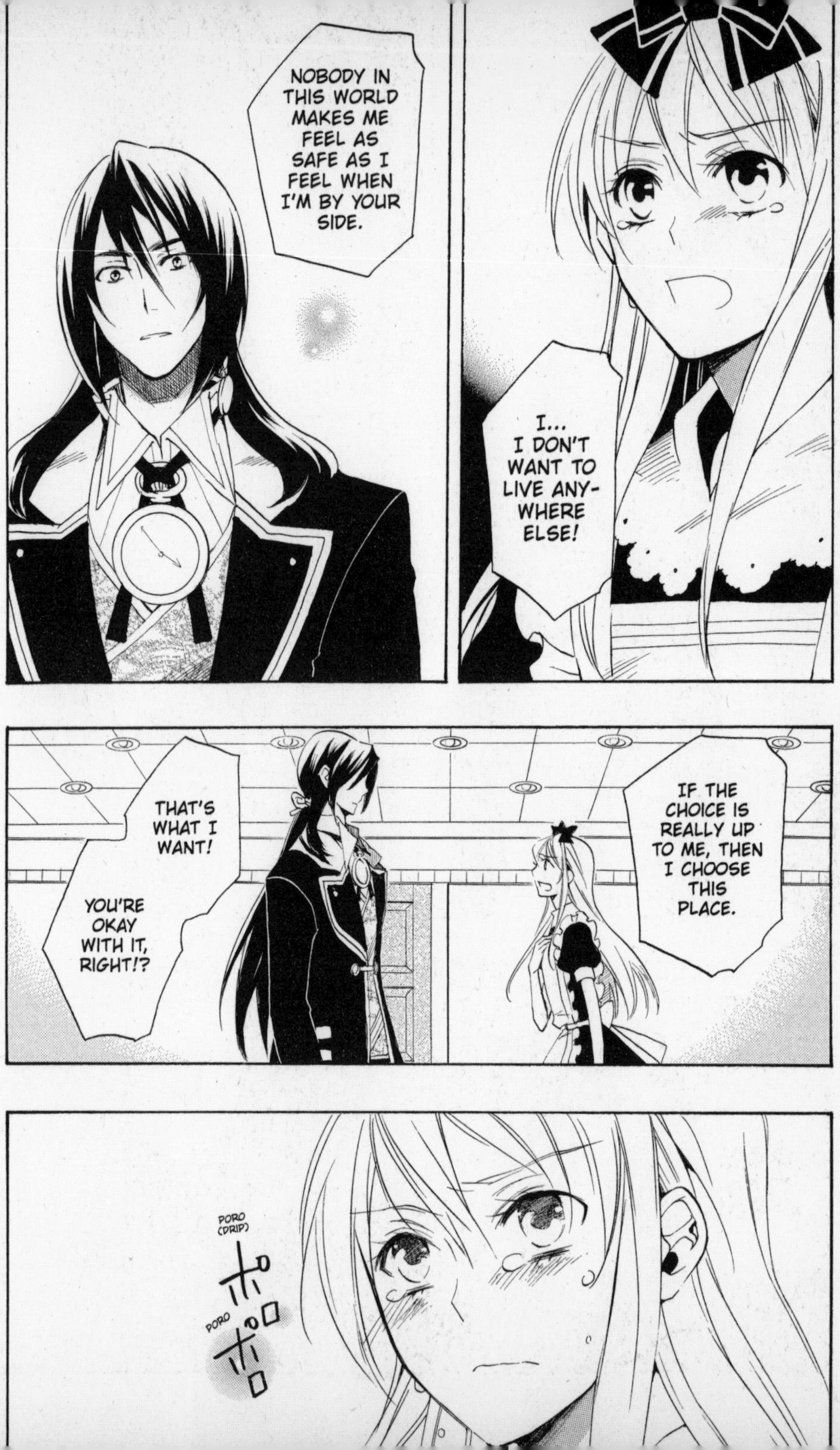
I... I DON'T WANT TO LIVE ANY-WHERE ELSE!
NOBODY IN THIS WORLD MAKES ME FEEL AS SAFE AS I FEEL WHEN I'M BY YOUR SIDE.
IF THE CHOICE IS REALLY UP TO ME, THEN I CHOOSE THIS PLACE.
THAT'S WHAT I WANT!
YOU'RE OKAY WITH IT, RIGHT!?
PORO (DRIP)
PORO

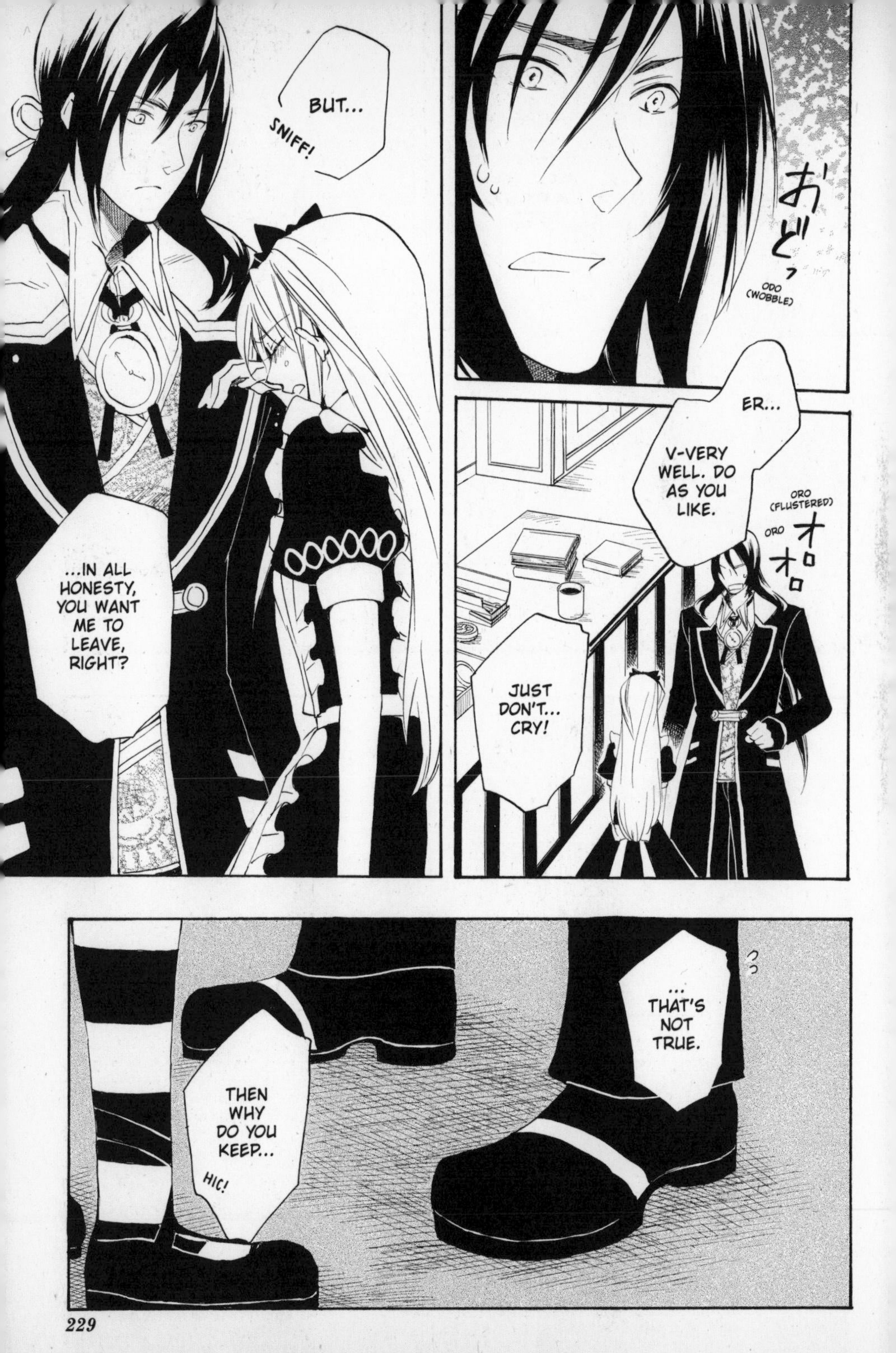

おどっ
ODO (WOBBLE)
ER...
V-VERY WELL. DO AS YOU LIKE.
ORO (FLUSTERED)
ORO
オロオロ
JUST DON'T... CRY!
BUT...
SNIFF!
...IN ALL HONESTY, YOU WANT ME TO LEAVE, RIGHT?
... THAT'S NOT TRUE.
THEN WHY DO YOU KEEP...
HIC!

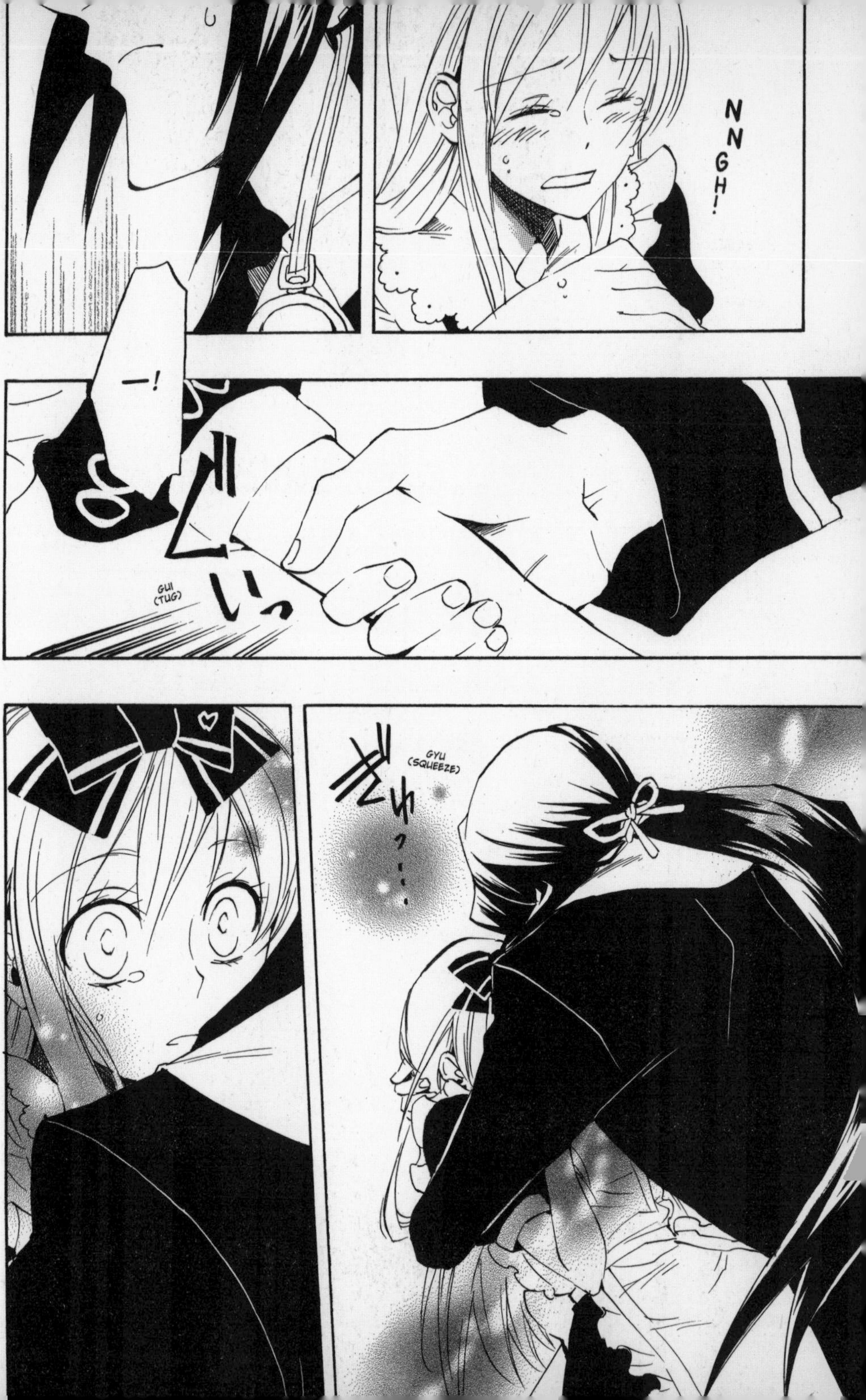
NNGH!
—!
GUI (TUG)
GYU (SQUEEZE)

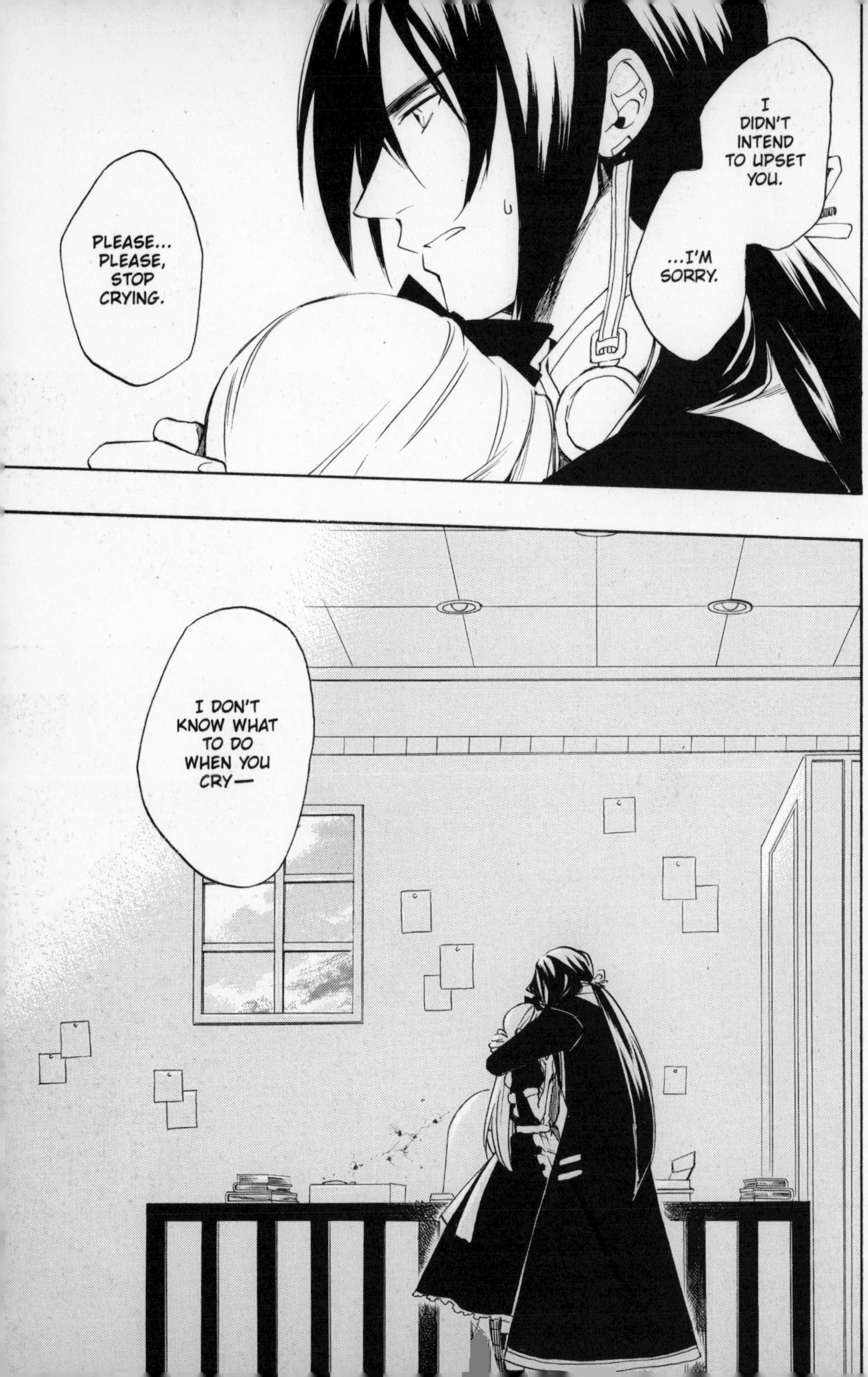
I DIDN'T INTEND TO UPSET YOU.
...I'M SORRY.
PLEASE... PLEASE, STOP CRYING.
I DON'T KNOW WHAT TO DO WHEN YOU CRY—

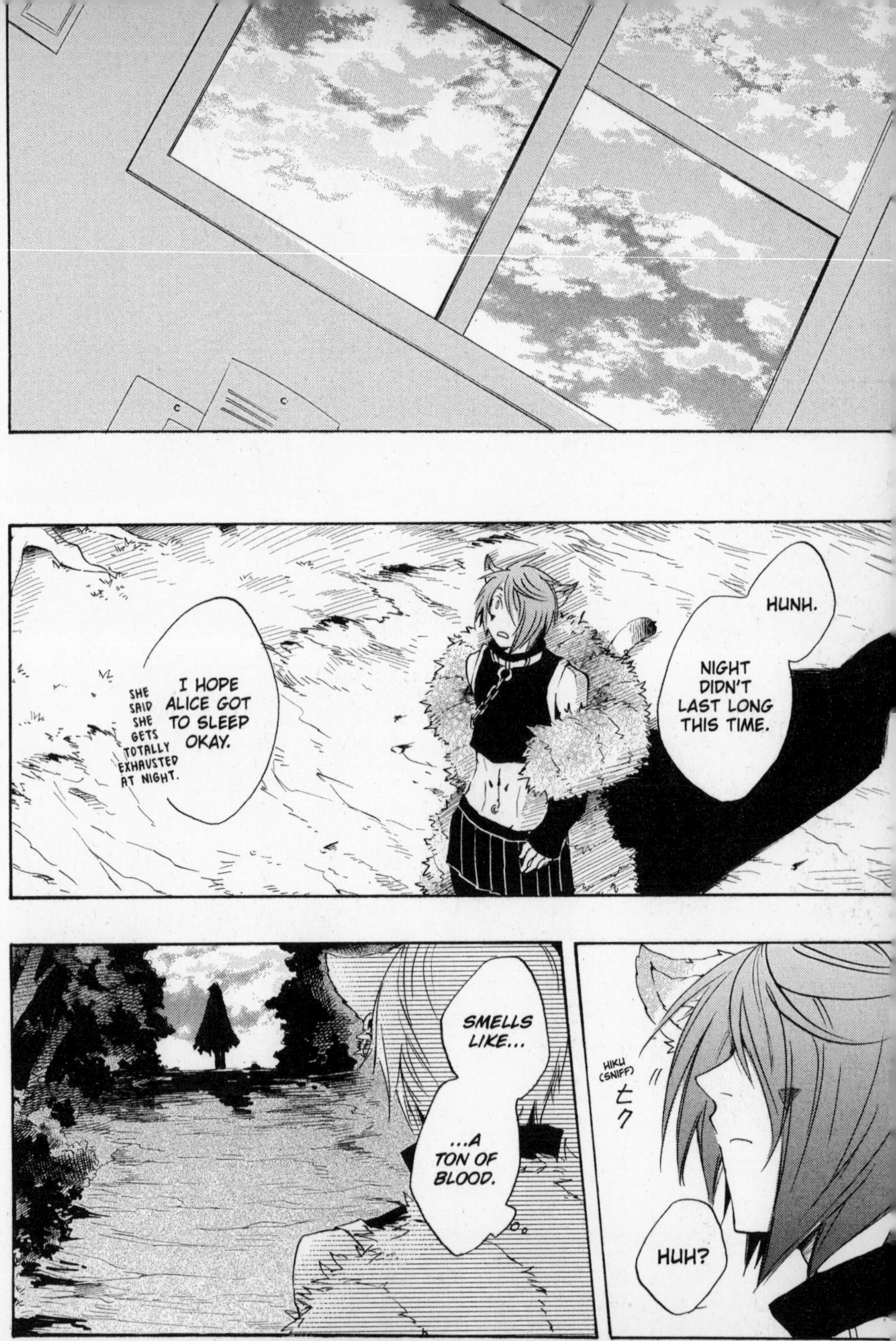
HUNH.
NIGHT DIDN'T LAST LONG THIS TIME.
I HOPE ALICE GOT TO SLEEP OKAY.
SHE SAID SHE GETS TOTALLY EXHAUSTED AT NIGHT.
HIKU (SNIFF)
ヒク
HUH?
SMELLS LIKE...
...A TON OF BLOOD.

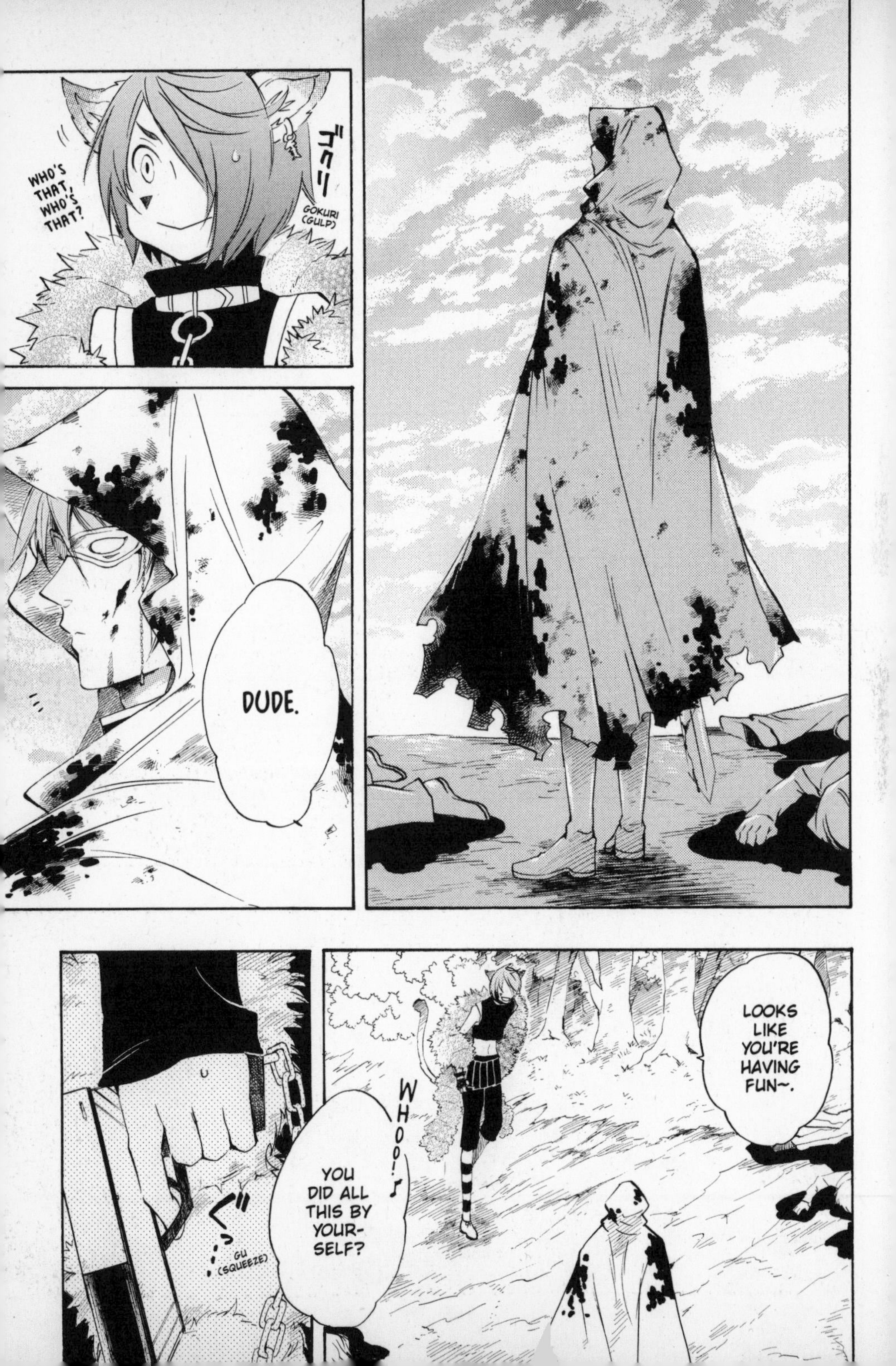
ゴクリ
GOKURI (GULP)
WHO'S THAT, WHO'S THAT?
DUDE.
LOOKS LIKE YOU'RE HAVING FUN~.
WHOO!♪
YOU DID ALL THIS BY YOURSELF?
ぐっ
GU (SQUEEZE)

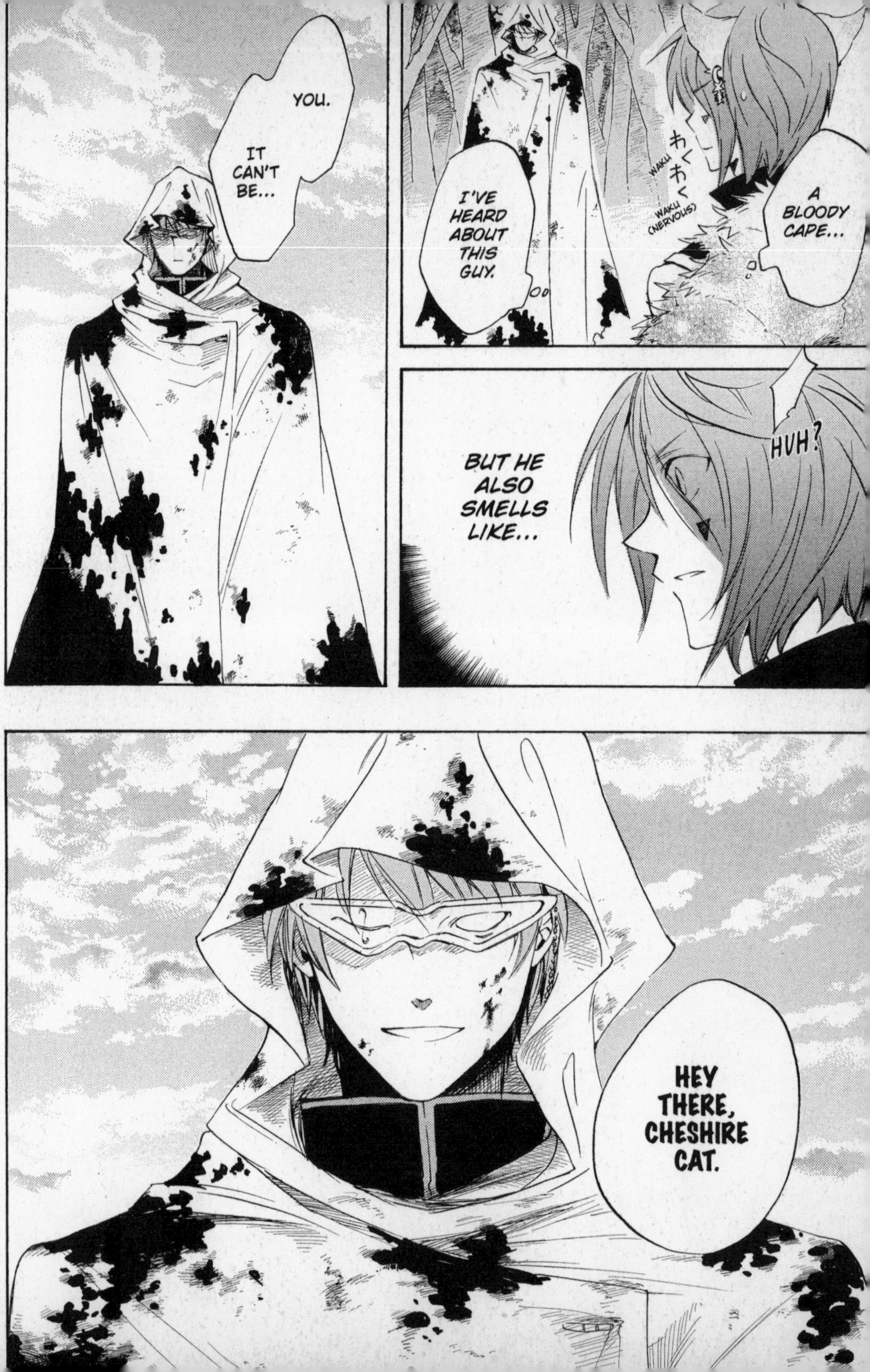
A BLOODY CAPE...
わくわく
WAKU WAKU (NERVOUS)
I'VE HEARD ABOUT THIS GUY.
HUH?
BUT HE ALSO SMELLS LIKE...
YOU.
IT CAN'T BE...
HEY THERE, CHESHIRE CAT.

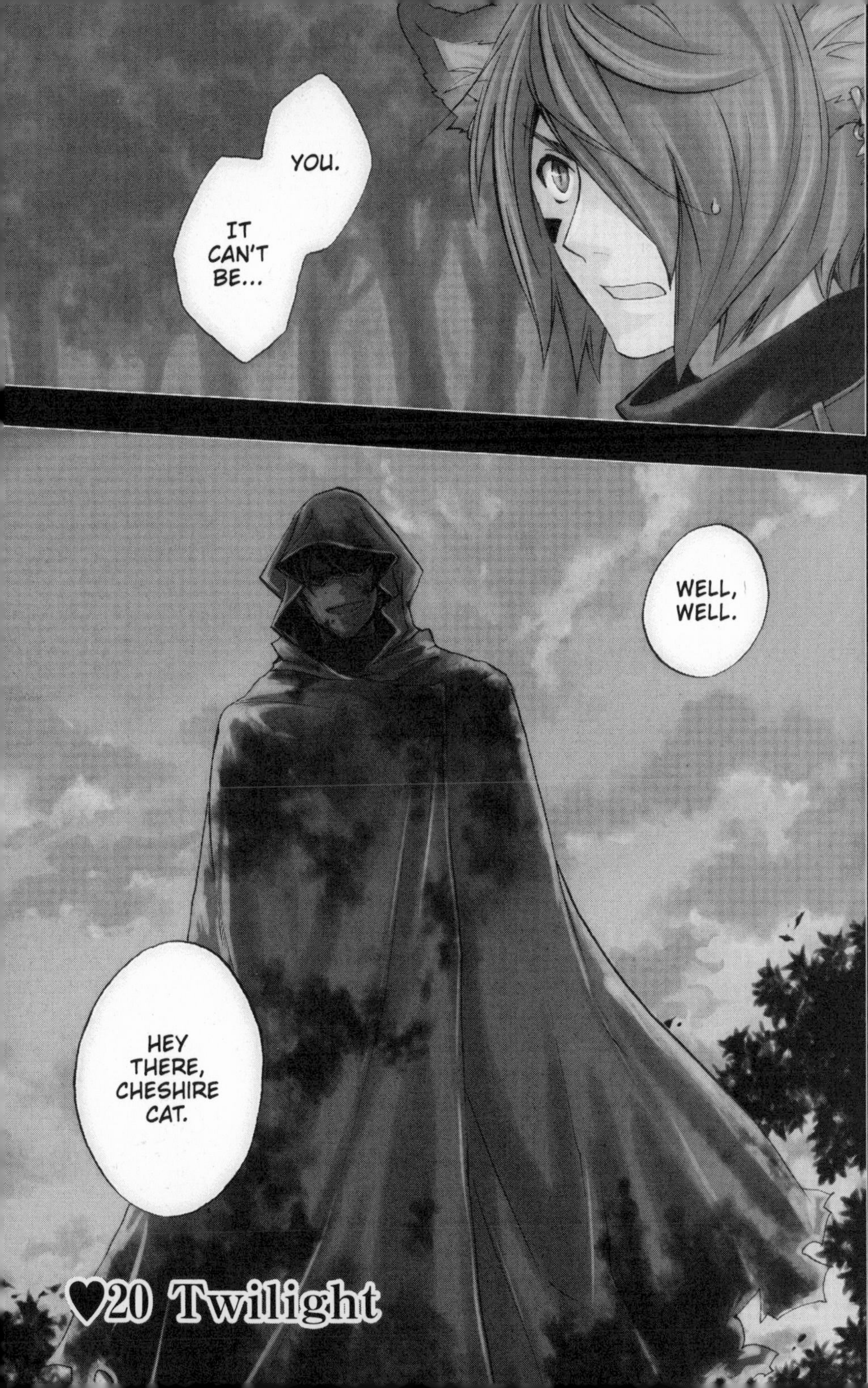
YOU.
IT CAN'T BE...
WELL, WELL.
HEY THERE, CHESHIRE CAT.

♥20 Twilight

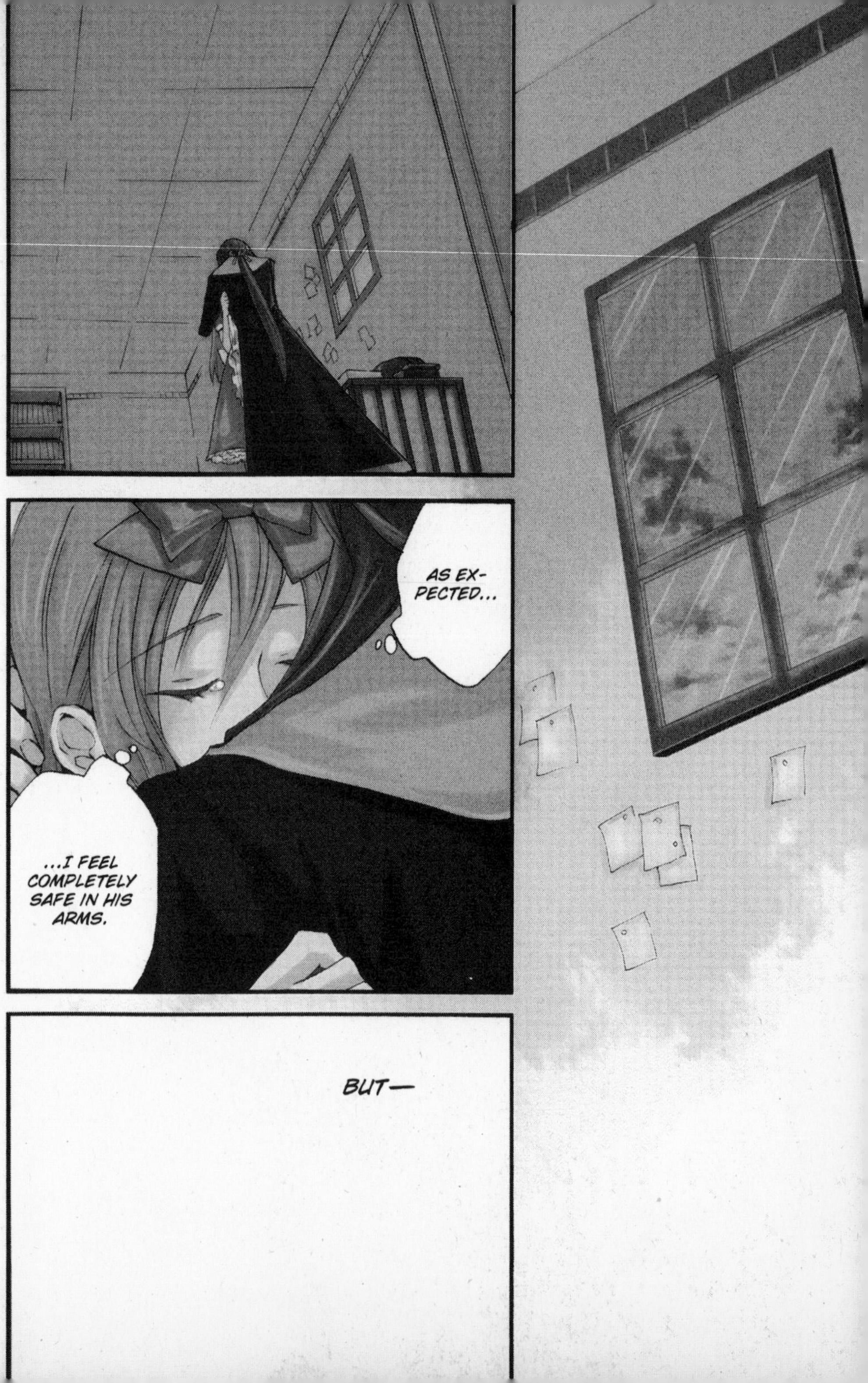
AS EX-
PECTED...
...I FEEL COMPLETELY SAFE IN HIS ARMS.
BUT—

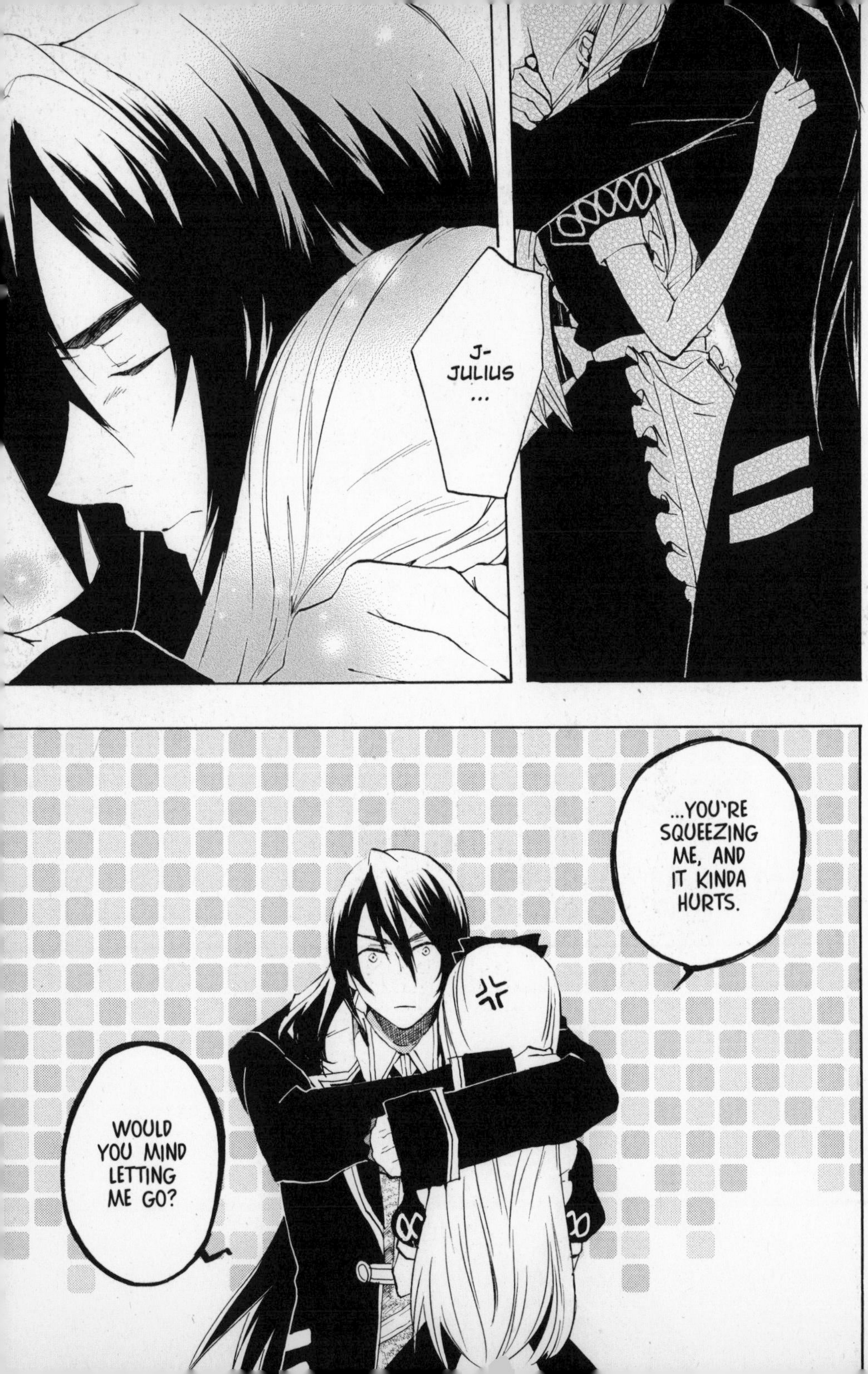
J-JULIUS...
...YOU'RE SQUEEZING ME, AND IT KINDA HURTS.
WOULD YOU MIND LETTING ME GO?

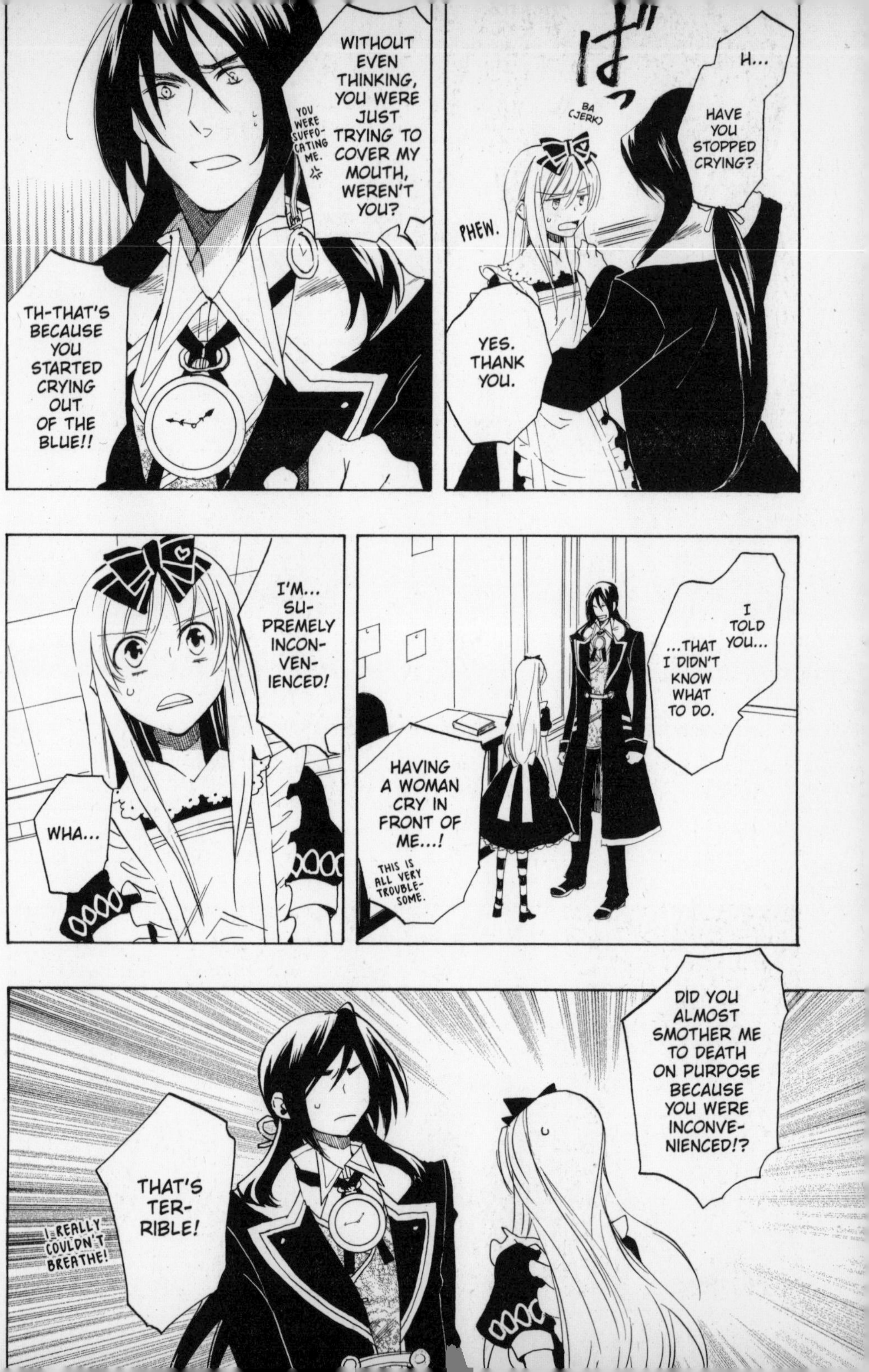
ばっ
BA (JERK)
H...
HAVE YOU STOPPED CRYING?
PHEW.
YES. THANK YOU.
WITHOUT EVEN THINKING, YOU WERE JUST TRYING TO COVER MY MOUTH, WEREN'T YOU?
YOU WERE SUFFOCATING ME.
TH-THAT'S BECAUSE YOU STARTED CRYING OUT OF THE BLUE!!
I TOLD YOU...
...THAT I DIDN'T KNOW WHAT TO DO.
HAVING A WOMAN CRY IN FRONT OF ME...!
THIS IS ALL VERY TROUBLESOME.
I'M... SUPREMELY INCONVENIENCED!
WHA...
DID YOU ALMOST SMOTHER ME TO DEATH ON PURPOSE BECAUSE YOU WERE INCONVENIENCED!?
THAT'S TERRIBLE!
I REALLY COULDN'T BREATHE!

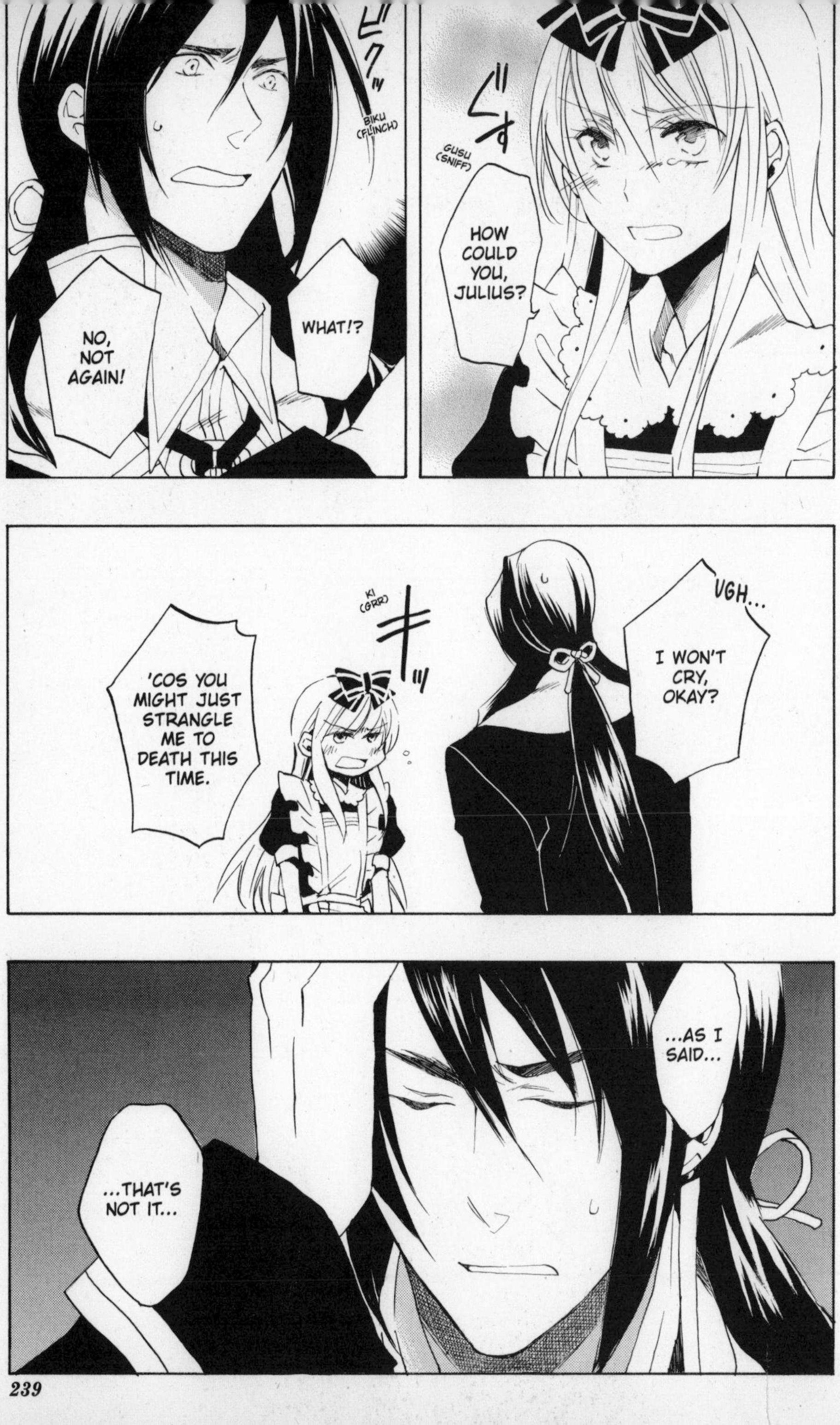
ぐす
GUSU (SNIFF)
HOW COULD YOU, JULIUS?
ビクッ
BIKU (FLINCH)
WHAT!?
NO, NOT AGAIN!
UGH...
I WON'T CRY, OKAY?
キッ
KI (GRR)
'COS YOU MIGHT JUST STRANGLE ME TO DEATH THIS TIME.
...AS I SAID...
...THAT'S NOT IT...

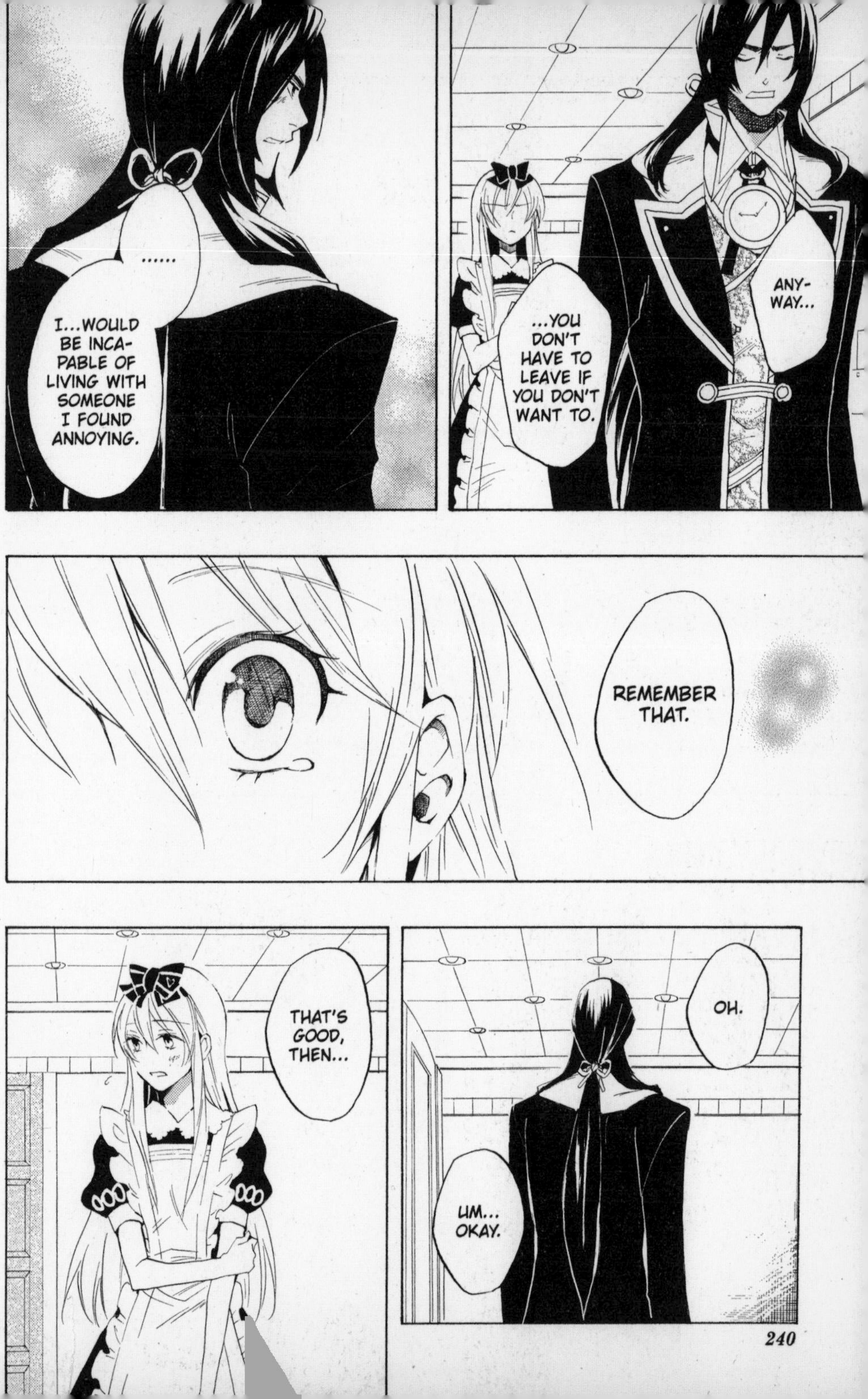
ANY-WAY...
...YOU DON'T HAVE TO LEAVE IF YOU DON'T WANT TO.
......
I...WOULD BE INCA-PABLE OF LIVING WITH SOMEONE I FOUND ANNOYING.
REMEMBER THAT.
OH.
UM... OKAY.
THAT'S GOOD, THEN...

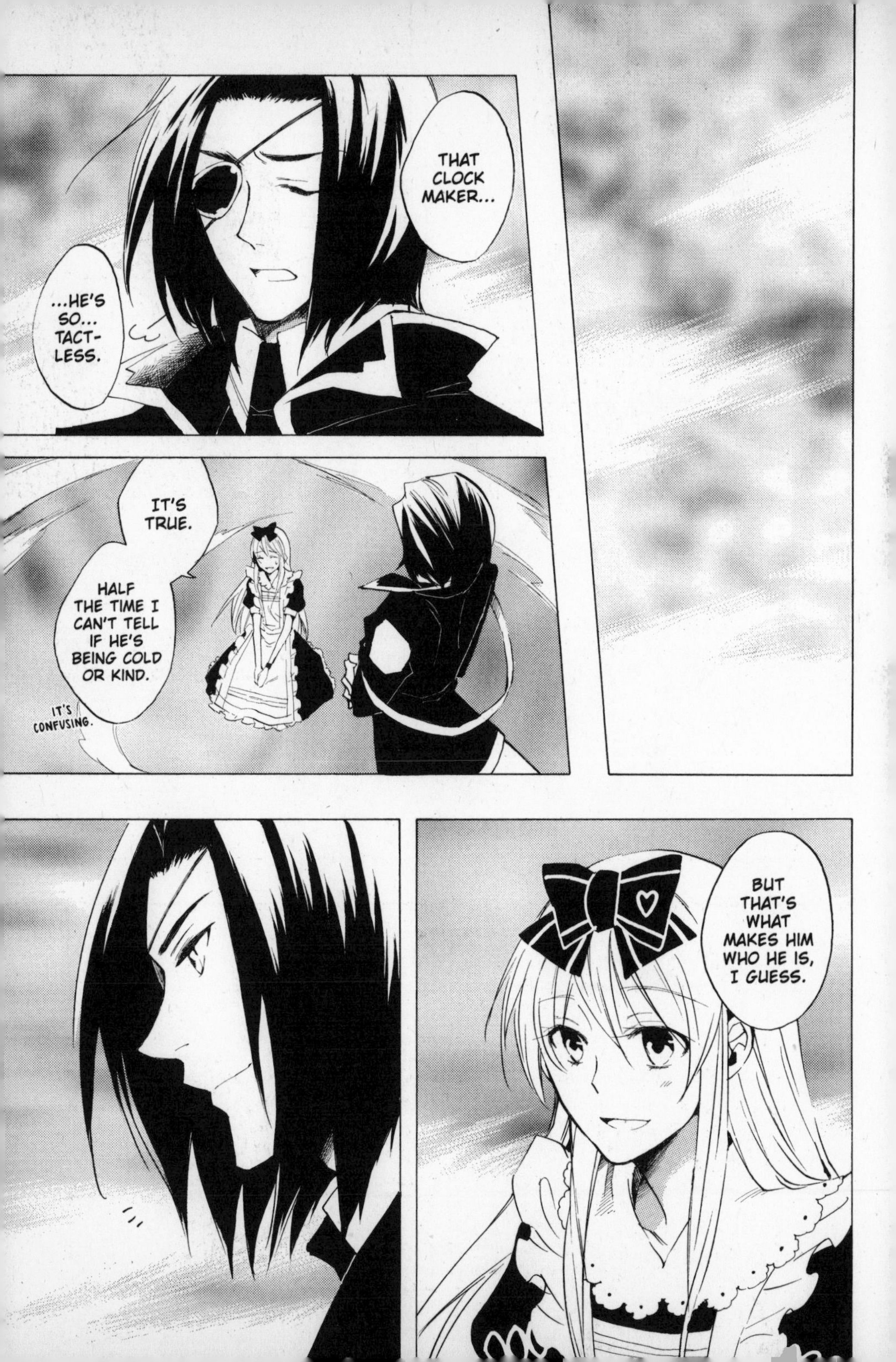
THAT CLOCK MAKER...
...HE'S SO... TACT-LESS.
IT'S TRUE.
HALF THE TIME I CAN'T TELL IF HE'S BEING COLD OR KIND.
IT'S CONFUSING.
BUT THAT'S WHAT MAKES HIM WHO HE IS, I GUESS.

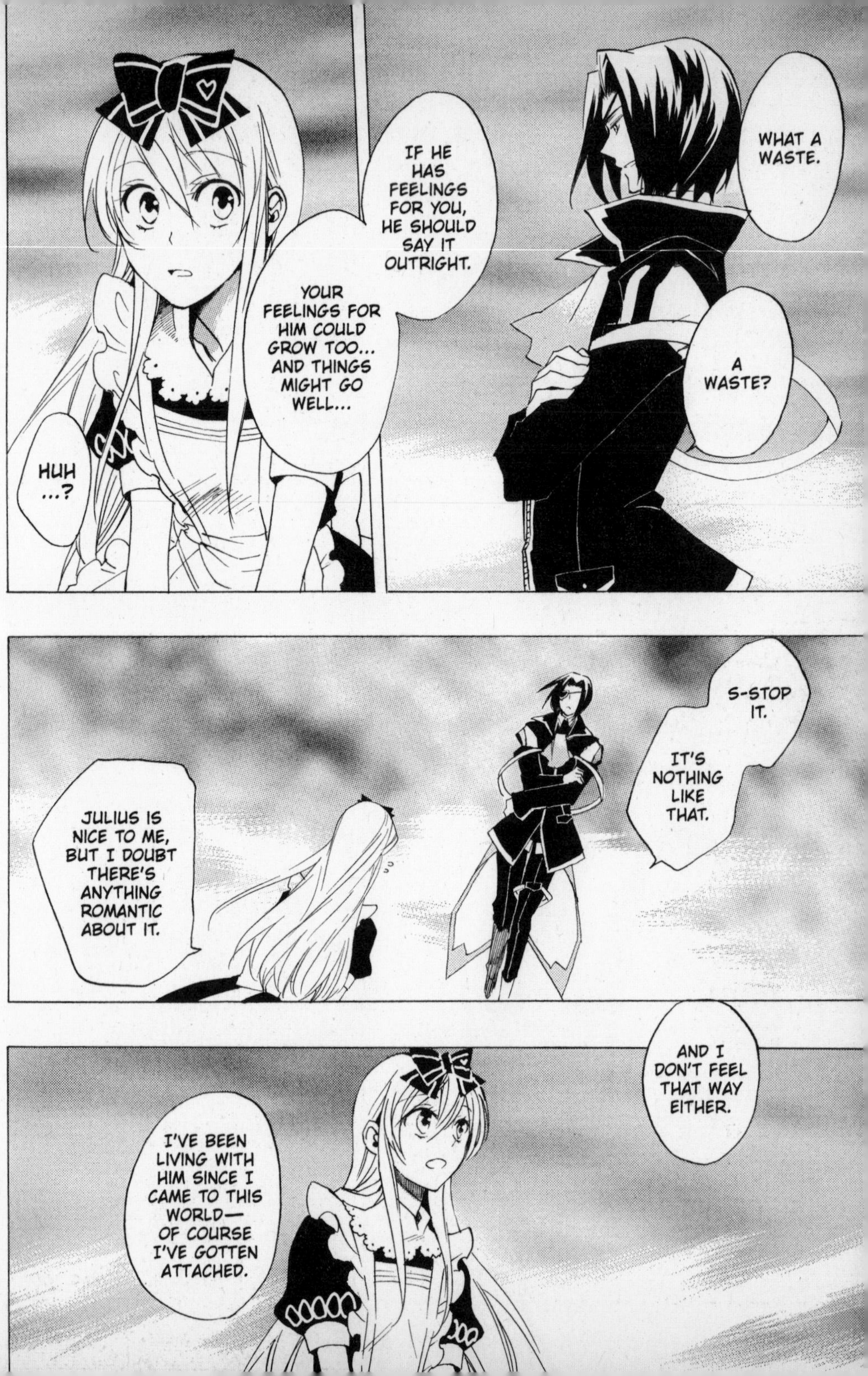
WHAT A WASTE.
A WASTE?
IF HE HAS FEELINGS FOR YOU, HE SHOULD SAY IT OUTRIGHT.
YOUR FEELINGS FOR HIM COULD GROW TOO... AND THINGS MIGHT GO WELL...
HUH ...?
S-STOP IT.
IT'S NOTHING LIKE THAT.
JULIUS IS NICE TO ME, BUT I DOUBT THERE'S ANYTHING ROMANTIC ABOUT IT.
AND I DON'T FEEL THAT WAY EITHER.
I'VE BEEN LIVING WITH HIM SINCE I CAME TO THIS WORLD— OF COURSE I'VE GOTTEN ATTACHED.

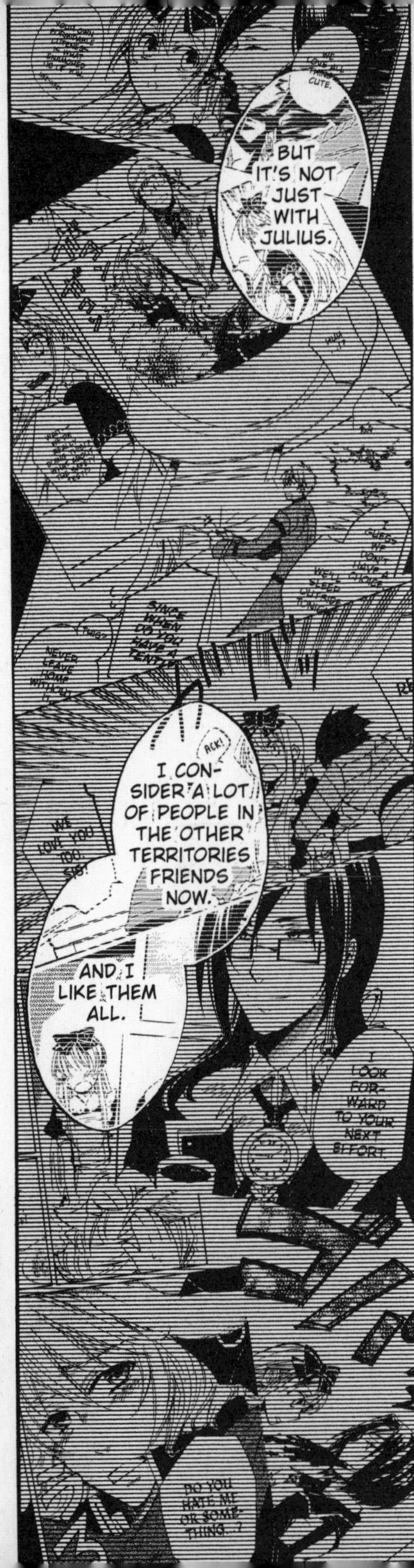
WE LOVE ALL THINGS CUTE.
BUT IT'S NOT JUST WITH JULIUS.
I GUESS WE DON'T HAVE A CHOICE.
WE'LL SLEEP OUTSIDE TONIGHT.
SINCE WHEN DO YOU HAVE A TENT?!
NEVER LEAVE HOME WITHOUT
ACK!
I CON-SIDER A LOT OF PEOPLE IN THE OTHER TERRITORIES FRIENDS NOW.
WE LOVE YOU TOO, SIS!
AND I LIKE THEM ALL.
I LOOK FOR-WARD TO YOUR NEXT EFFORT.
DO YOU HATE ME OR SOME-THING...?

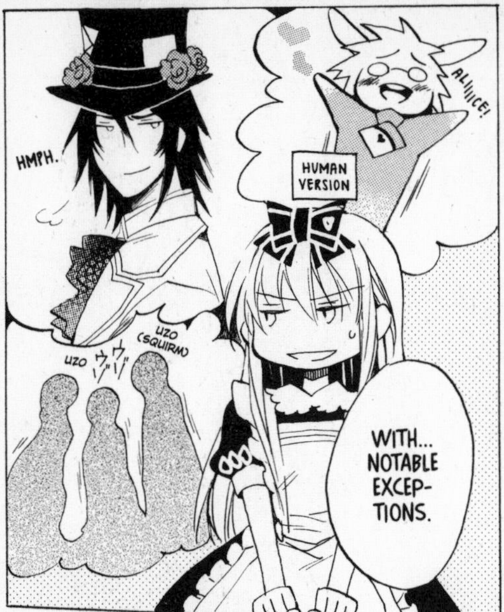
ALI-I-I-ICE!
HUMAN VERSION
HMPH.
UZO (SQUIRM)
UZO
WITH... NOTABLE EXCEP-TIONS.

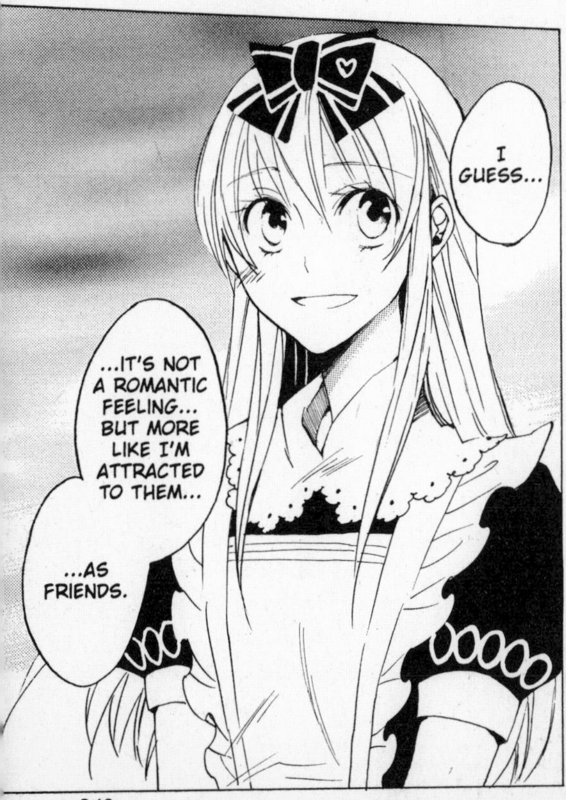
I GUESS...
...IT'S NOT A ROMANTIC FEELING... BUT MORE LIKE I'M ATTRACTED TO THEM...
...AS FRIENDS.

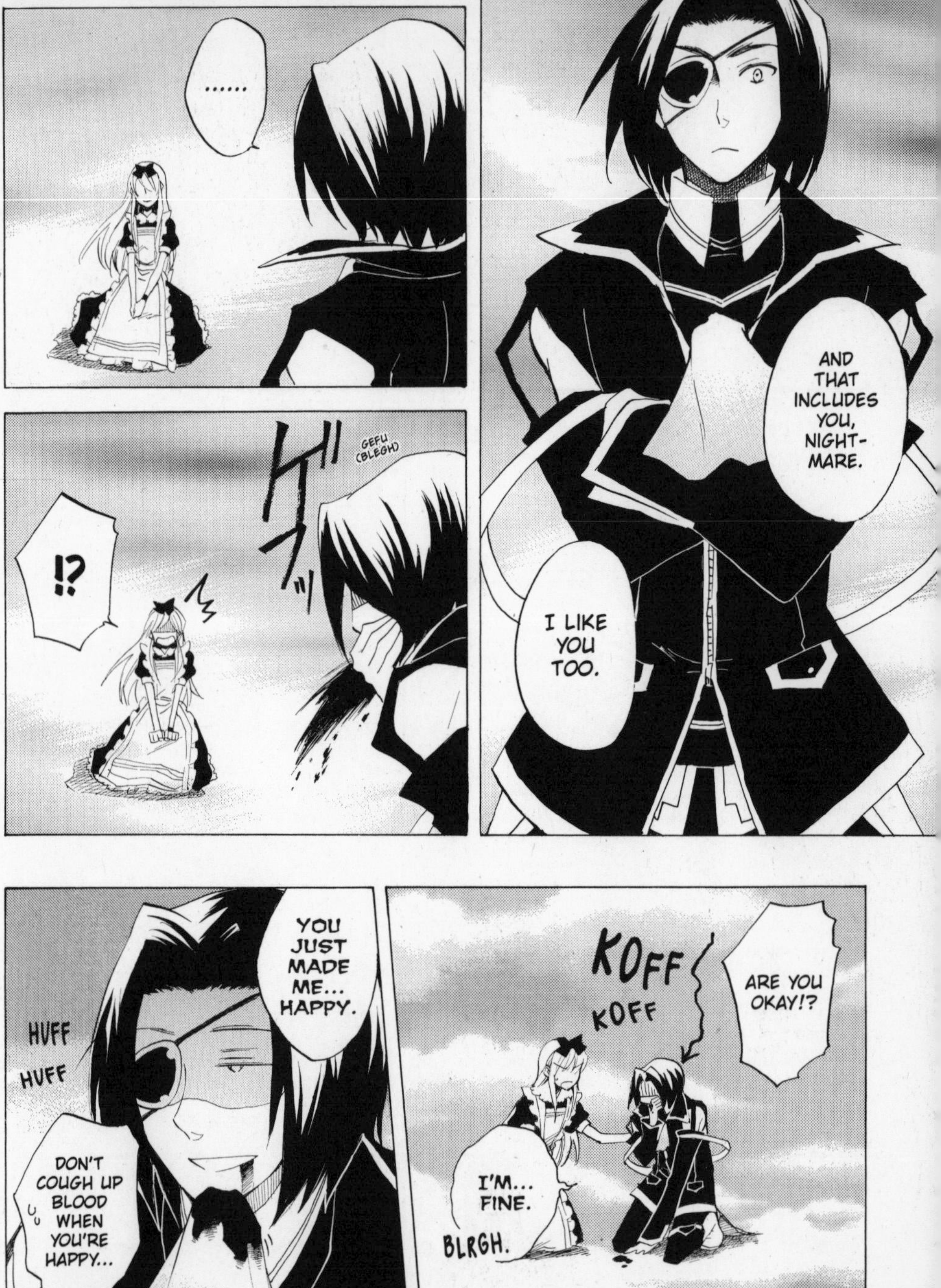
AND THAT INCLUDES YOU, NIGHT-MARE.
I LIKE YOU TOO.
......
GEFU (BLEGH)
!?
ARE YOU OKAY!?
KOFF
KOFF
I'M... FINE.
BLRGH.
YOU JUST MADE ME... HAPPY.
HUFF
HUFF
DON'T COUGH UP BLOOD WHEN YOU'RE HAPPY...

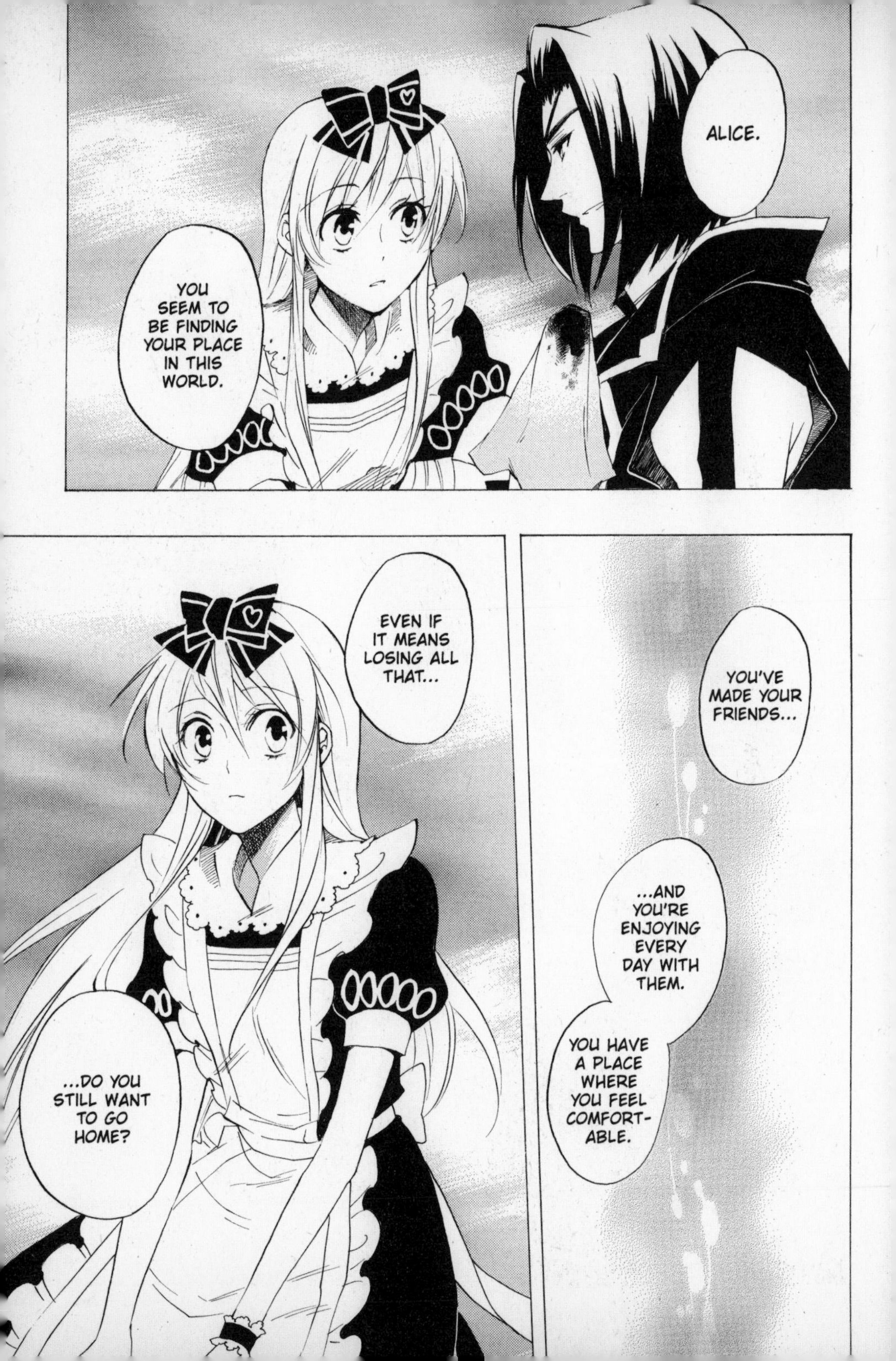
ALICE.
YOU SEEM TO BE FINDING YOUR PLACE IN THIS WORLD.
YOU'VE MADE YOUR FRIENDS...
...AND YOU'RE ENJOYING EVERY DAY WITH THEM.
YOU HAVE A PLACE WHERE YOU FEEL COMFORT-ABLE.
EVEN IF IT MEANS LOSING ALL THAT...
...DO YOU STILL WANT TO GO HOME?

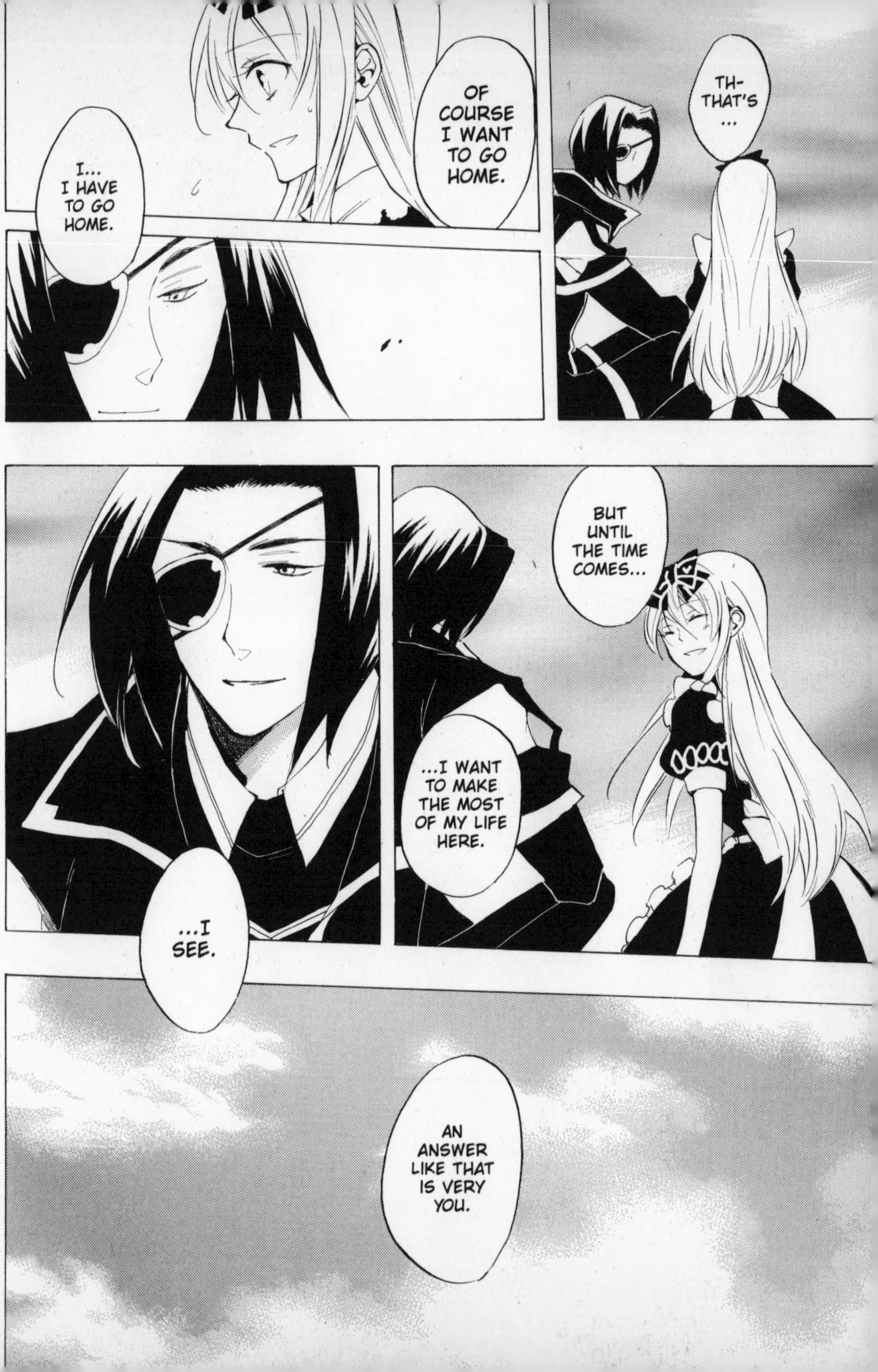
TH-THAT'S ...
OF COURSE I WANT TO GO HOME.
I... I HAVE TO GO HOME.
BUT UNTIL THE TIME COMES...
...I WANT TO MAKE THE MOST OF MY LIFE HERE.
...I SEE.
AN ANSWER LIKE THAT IS VERY YOU.

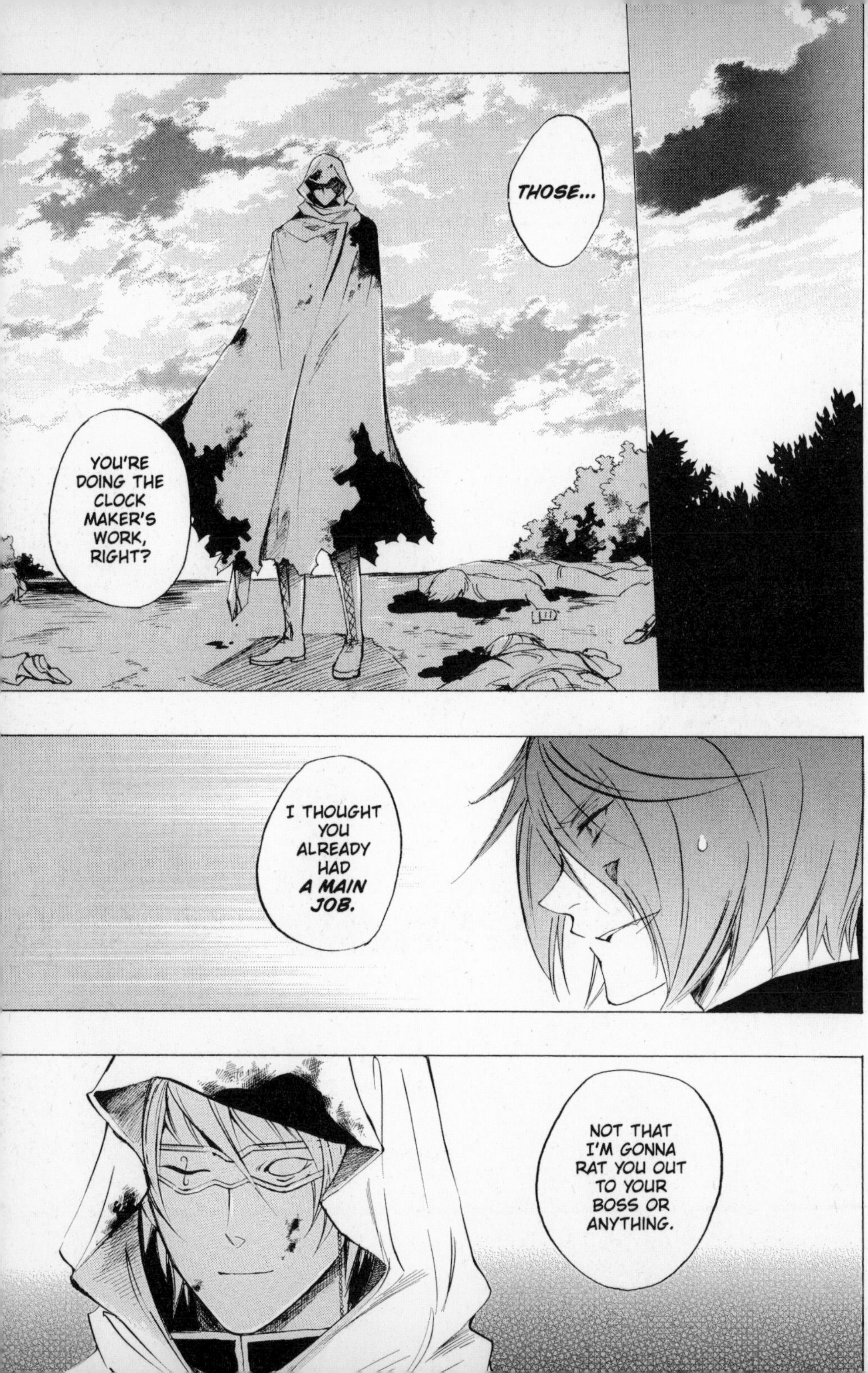
THOSE...
YOU'RE DOING THE CLOCK MAKER'S WORK, RIGHT?
I THOUGHT YOU ALREADY HAD A MAIN JOB.
NOT THAT I'M GONNA RAT YOU OUT TO YOUR BOSS OR ANYTHING.

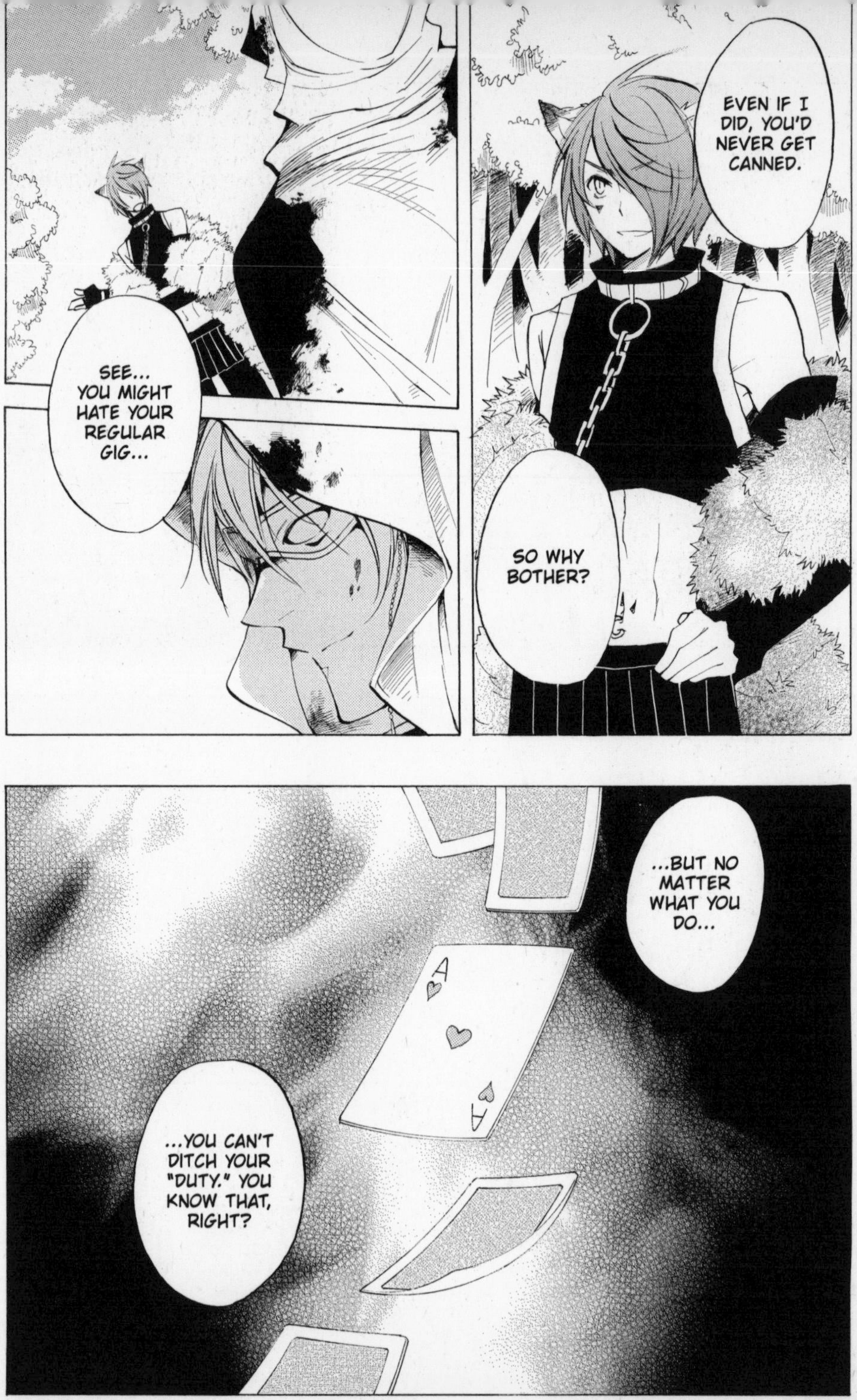
EVEN IF I DID, YOU'D NEVER GET CANNED.
SO WHY BOTHER?
SEE... YOU MIGHT HATE YOUR REGULAR GIG...
...BUT NO MATTER WHAT YOU DO...
...YOU CAN'T DITCH YOUR "DUTY." YOU KNOW THAT, RIGHT?

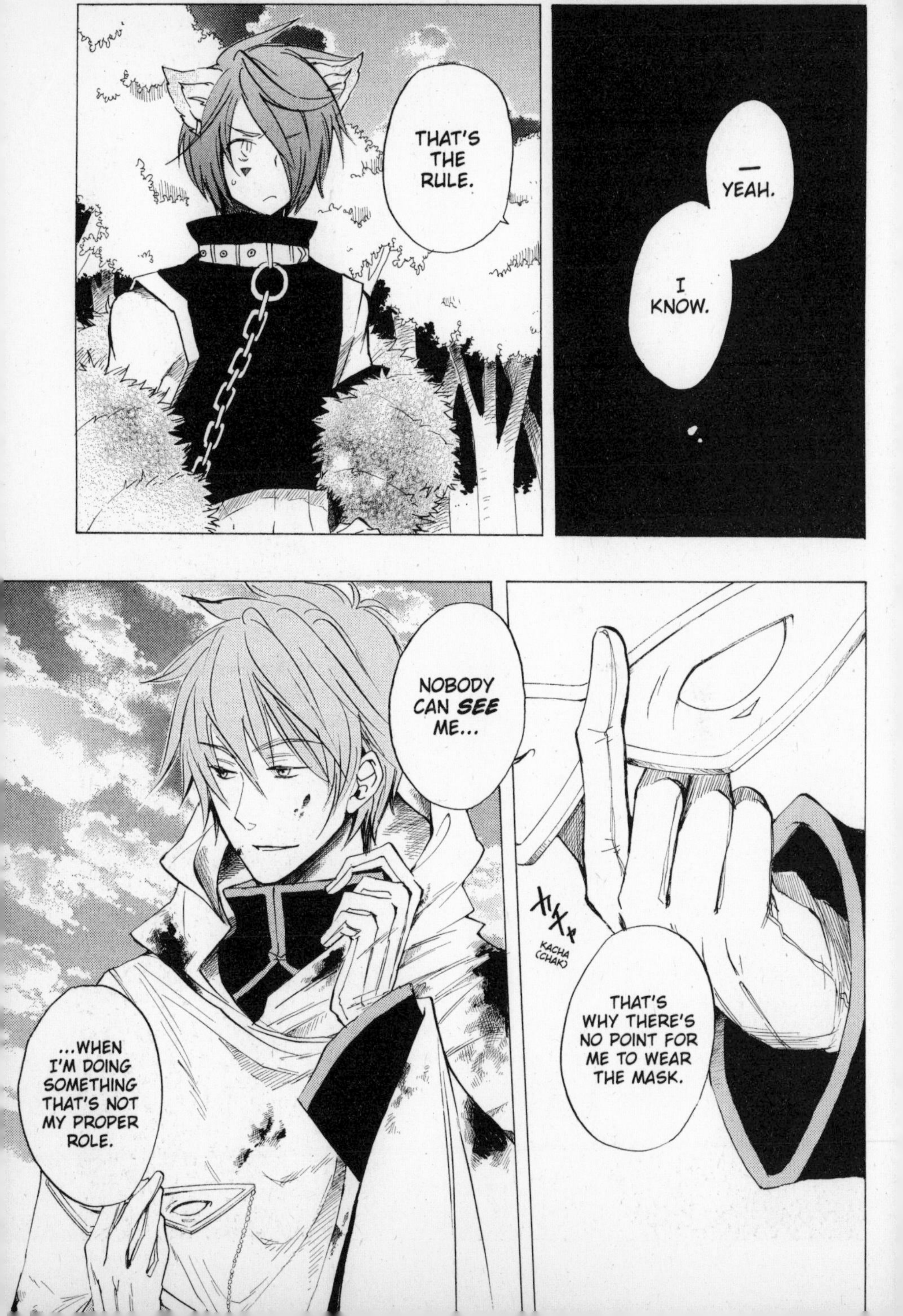
—YEAH.
I KNOW.
THAT'S THE RULE.
KACHA (CHAK)
THAT'S WHY THERE'S NO POINT FOR ME TO WEAR THE MASK.
NOBODY CAN SEE ME...
...WHEN I'M DOING SOMETHING THAT'S NOT MY PROPER ROLE.

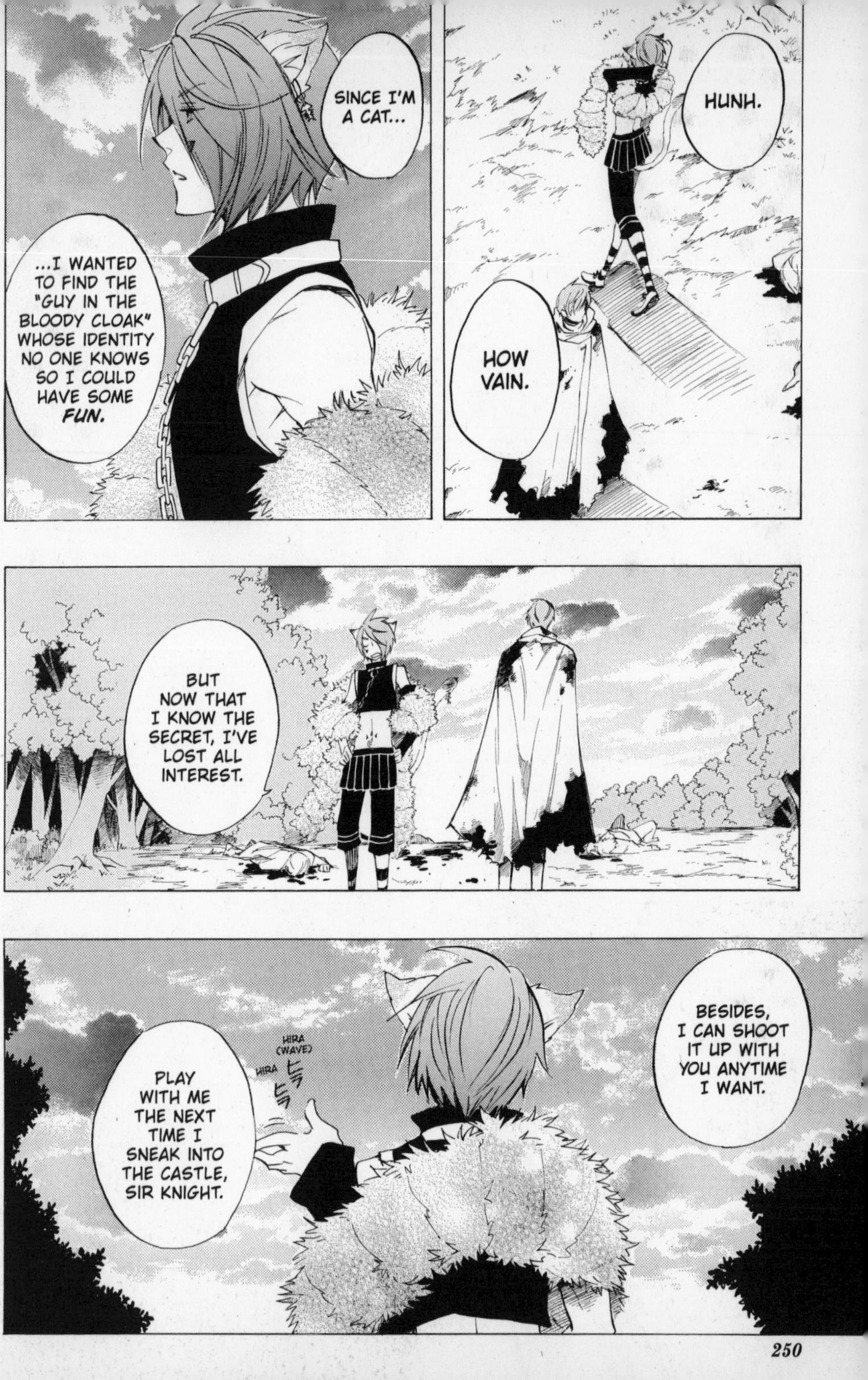
HUNH.
HOW VAIN.
SINCE I'M A CAT...
...I WANTED TO FIND THE "GUY IN THE BLOODY CLOAK" WHOSE IDENTITY NO ONE KNOWS SO I COULD HAVE SOME *FUN*.
BUT NOW THAT I KNOW THE SECRET, I'VE LOST ALL INTEREST.
BESIDES, I CAN SHOOT IT UP WITH YOU ANYTIME I WANT.
HIRA (WAVE) HIRA
PLAY WITH ME THE NEXT TIME I SNEAK INTO THE CASTLE, SIR KNIGHT.

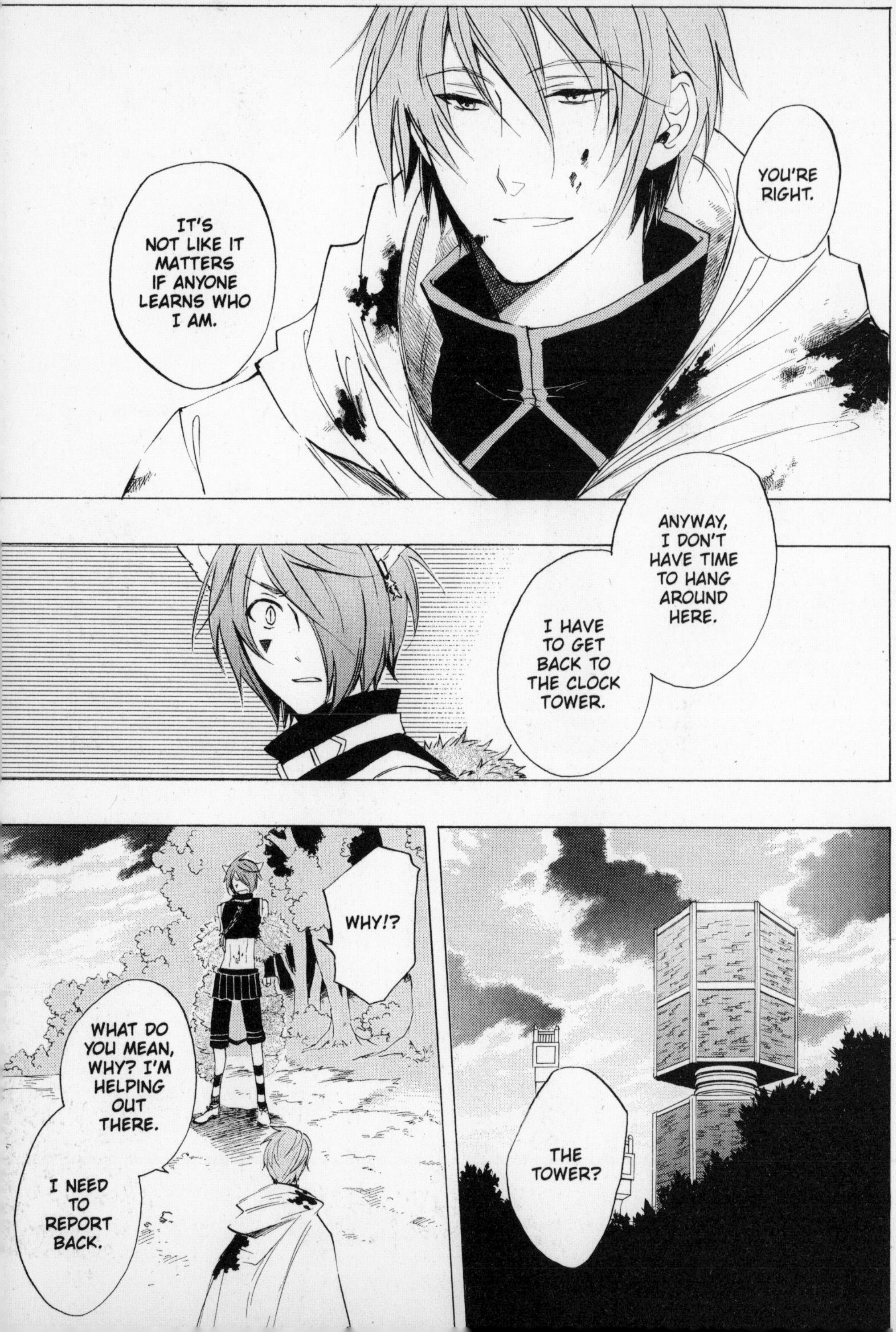
YOU'RE RIGHT.
IT'S NOT LIKE IT MATTERS IF ANYONE LEARNS WHO I AM.
ANYWAY, I DON'T HAVE TIME TO HANG AROUND HERE.
I HAVE TO GET BACK TO THE CLOCK TOWER.
THE TOWER?
WHY!?
WHAT DO YOU MEAN, WHY? I'M HELPING OUT THERE.
I NEED TO REPORT BACK.

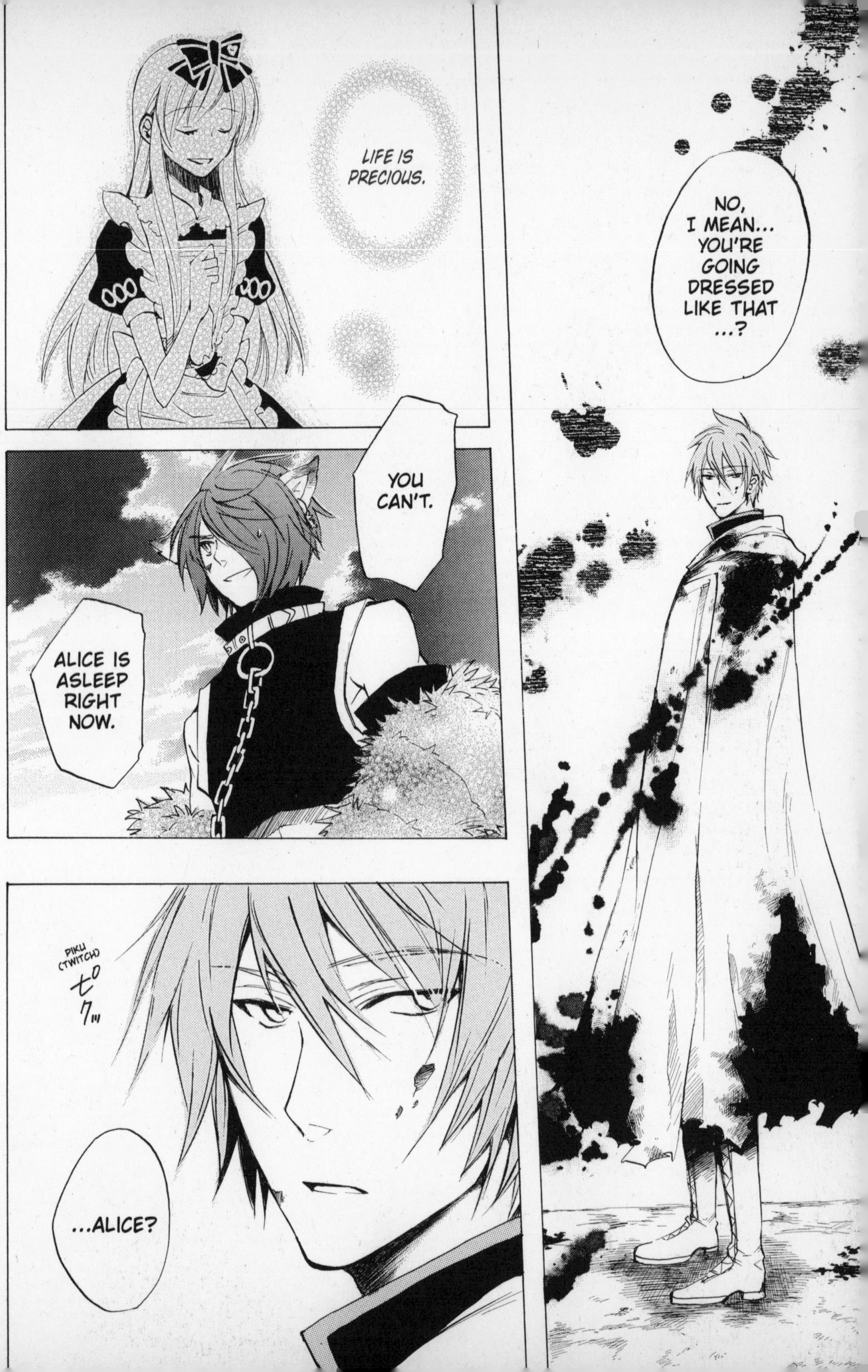
NO, I MEAN... YOU'RE GOING DRESSED LIKE THAT ...?
LIFE IS PRECIOUS.
YOU CAN'T.
ALICE IS ASLEEP RIGHT NOW.
PIKU (TWITCH)
ピク
...ALICE?

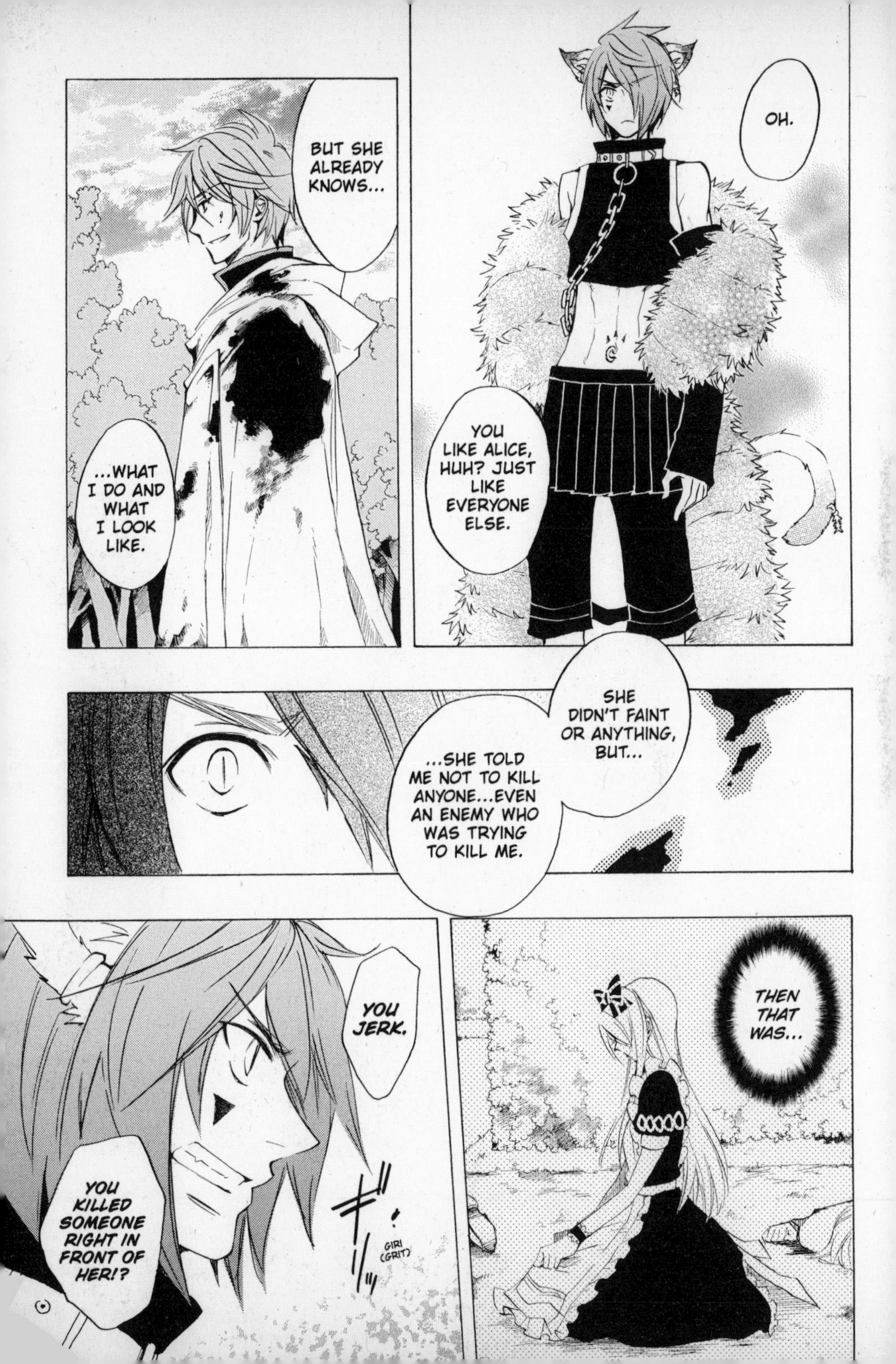
OH.
YOU LIKE ALICE, HUH? JUST LIKE EVERYONE ELSE.
BUT SHE ALREADY KNOWS...
...WHAT I DO AND WHAT I LOOK LIKE.
SHE DIDN'T FAINT OR ANYTHING, BUT...
...SHE TOLD ME NOT TO KILL ANYONE...EVEN AN ENEMY WHO WAS TRYING TO KILL ME.
THEN THAT WAS...
YOU JERK.
YOU KILLED SOMEONE RIGHT IN FRONT OF HER!?
GIRI (GRIT)

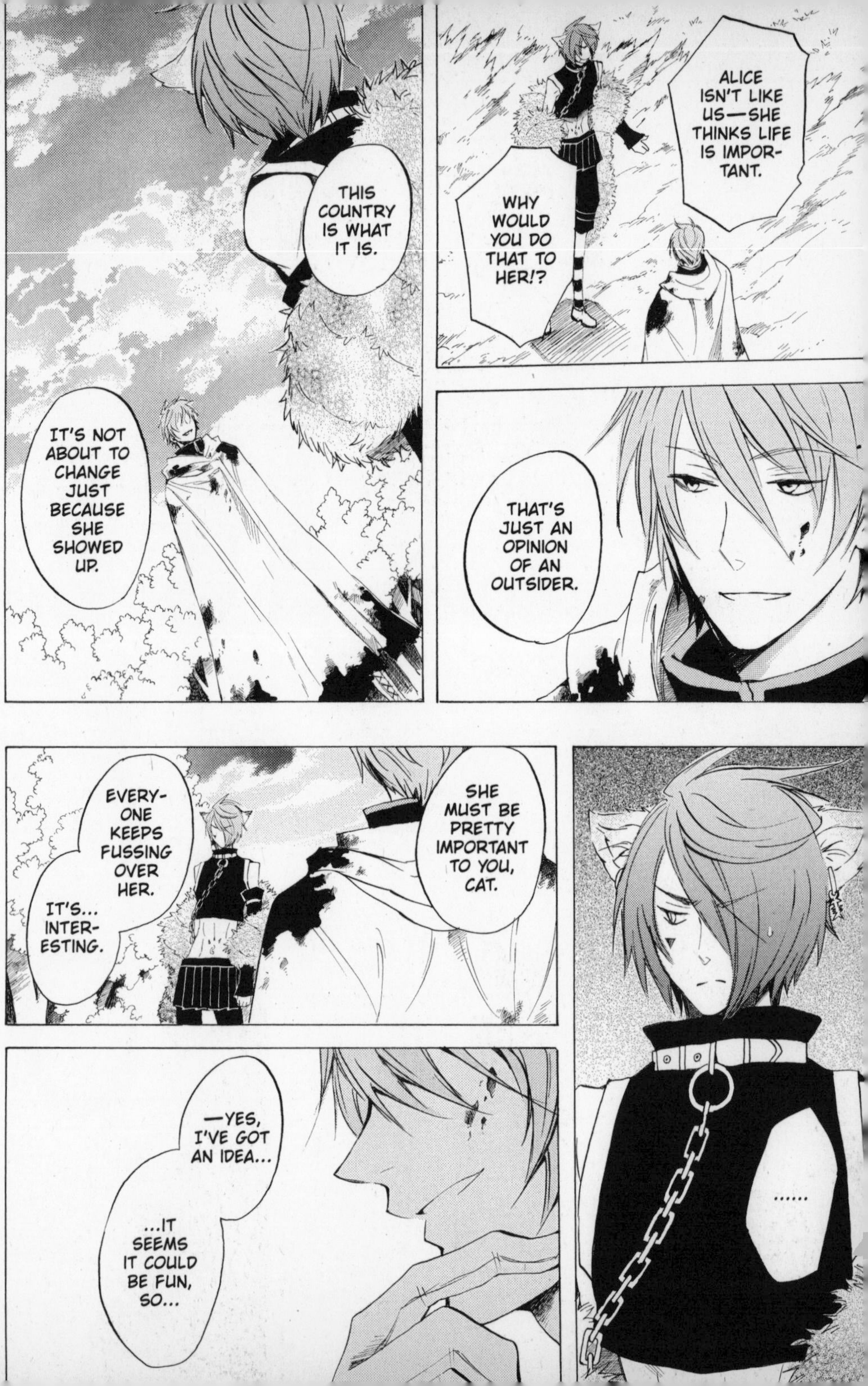

ALICE ISN'T LIKE US—SHE THINKS LIFE IS IMPORTANT.
WHY WOULD YOU DO THAT TO HER!?
THAT'S JUST AN OPINION OF AN OUTSIDER.
THIS COUNTRY IS WHAT IT IS.
IT'S NOT ABOUT TO CHANGE JUST BECAUSE SHE SHOWED UP.
......
SHE MUST BE PRETTY IMPORTANT TO YOU, CAT.
EVERY-ONE KEEPS FUSSING OVER HER.
IT'S... INTER-ESTING.
—YES, I'VE GOT AN IDEA...
...IT SEEMS IT COULD BE FUN, SO...

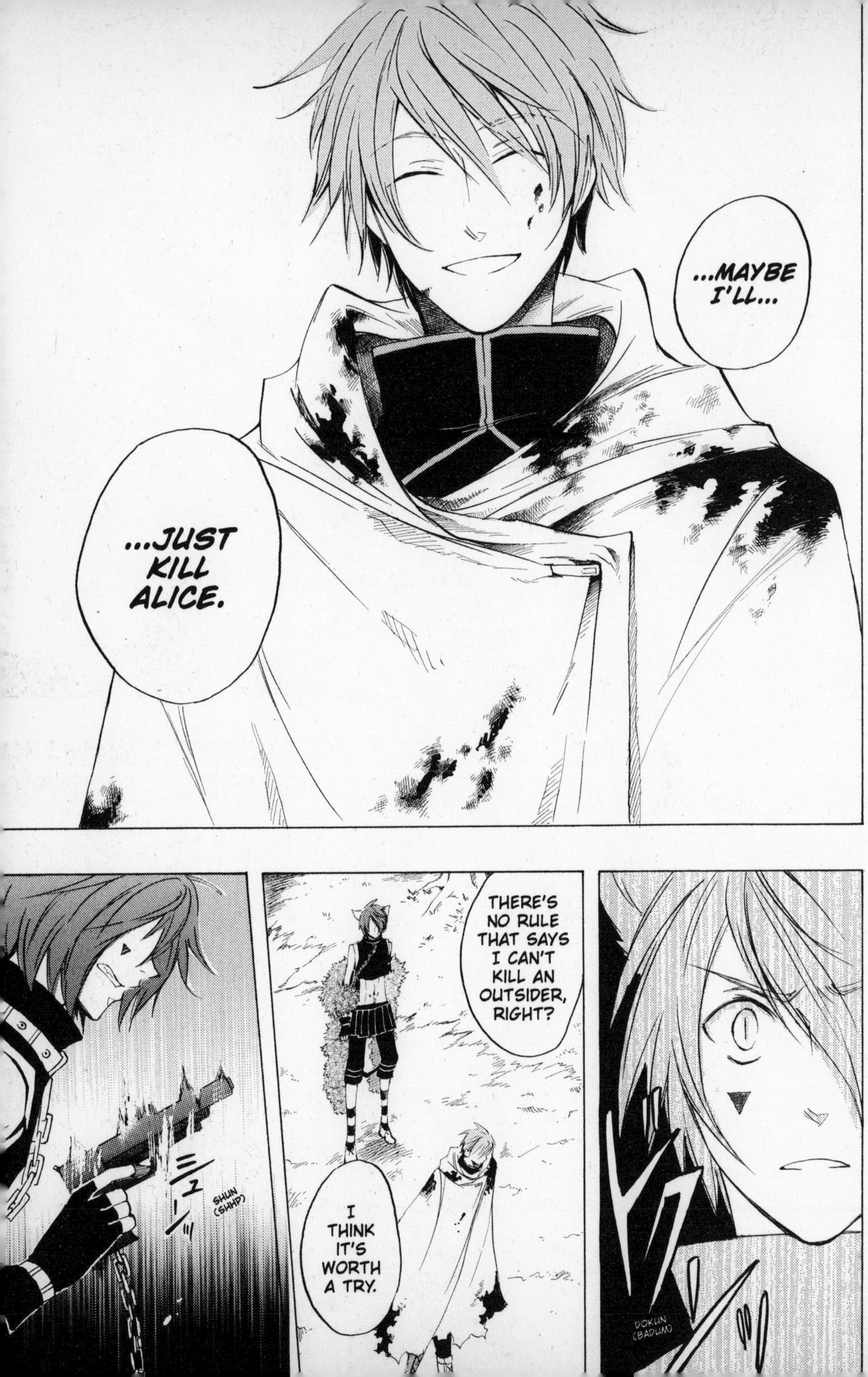
...MAYBE I'LL...
...JUST KILL ALICE.
DOKUN (BADUM)
THERE'S NO RULE THAT SAYS I CAN'T KILL AN OUTSIDER, RIGHT?
I THINK IT'S WORTH A TRY.
SHUN (SHHP)

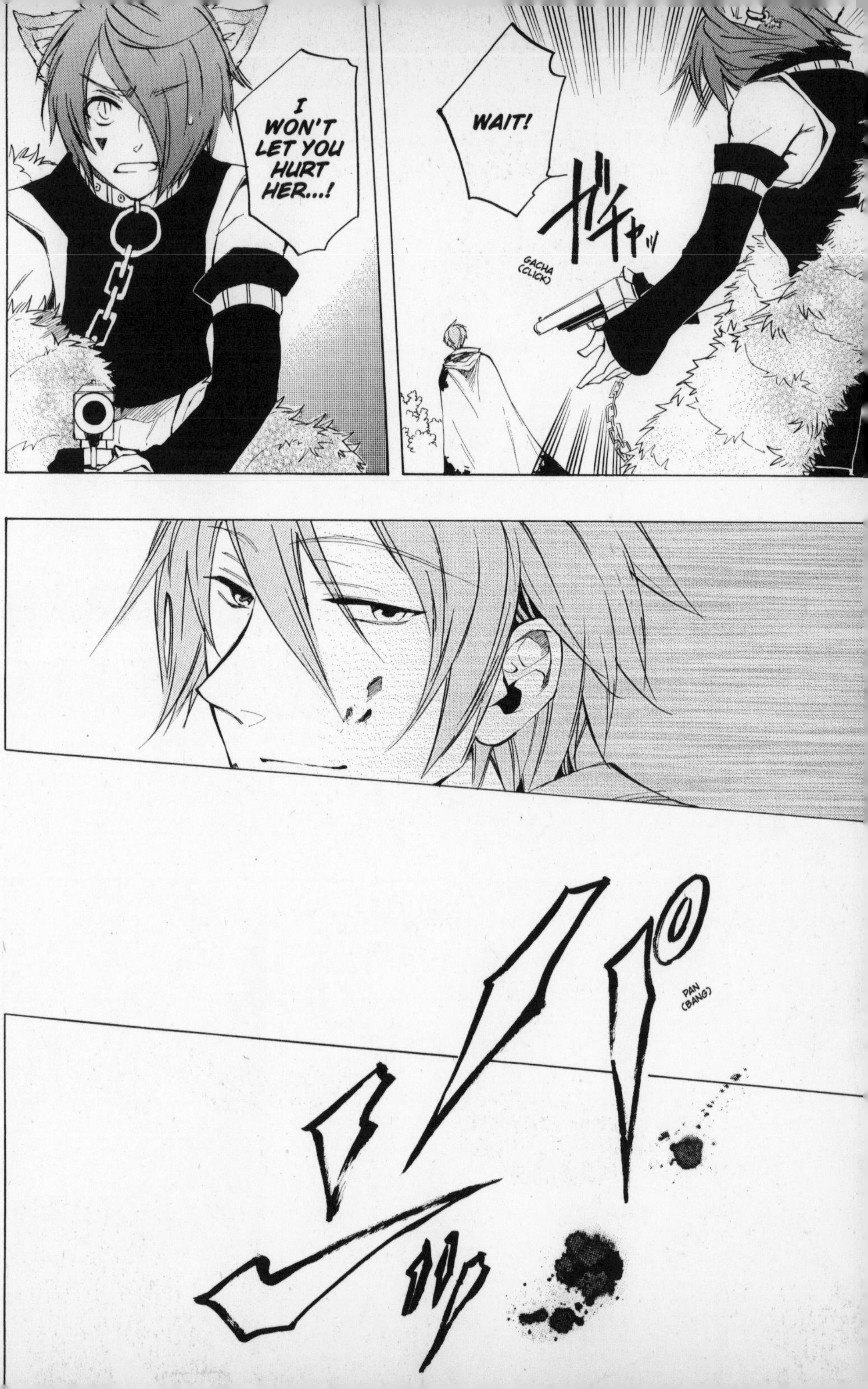
WAIT!
ガチャッ
GACHA (CLICK)
I WON'T LET YOU HURT HER...!
パン
PAN (BANG)

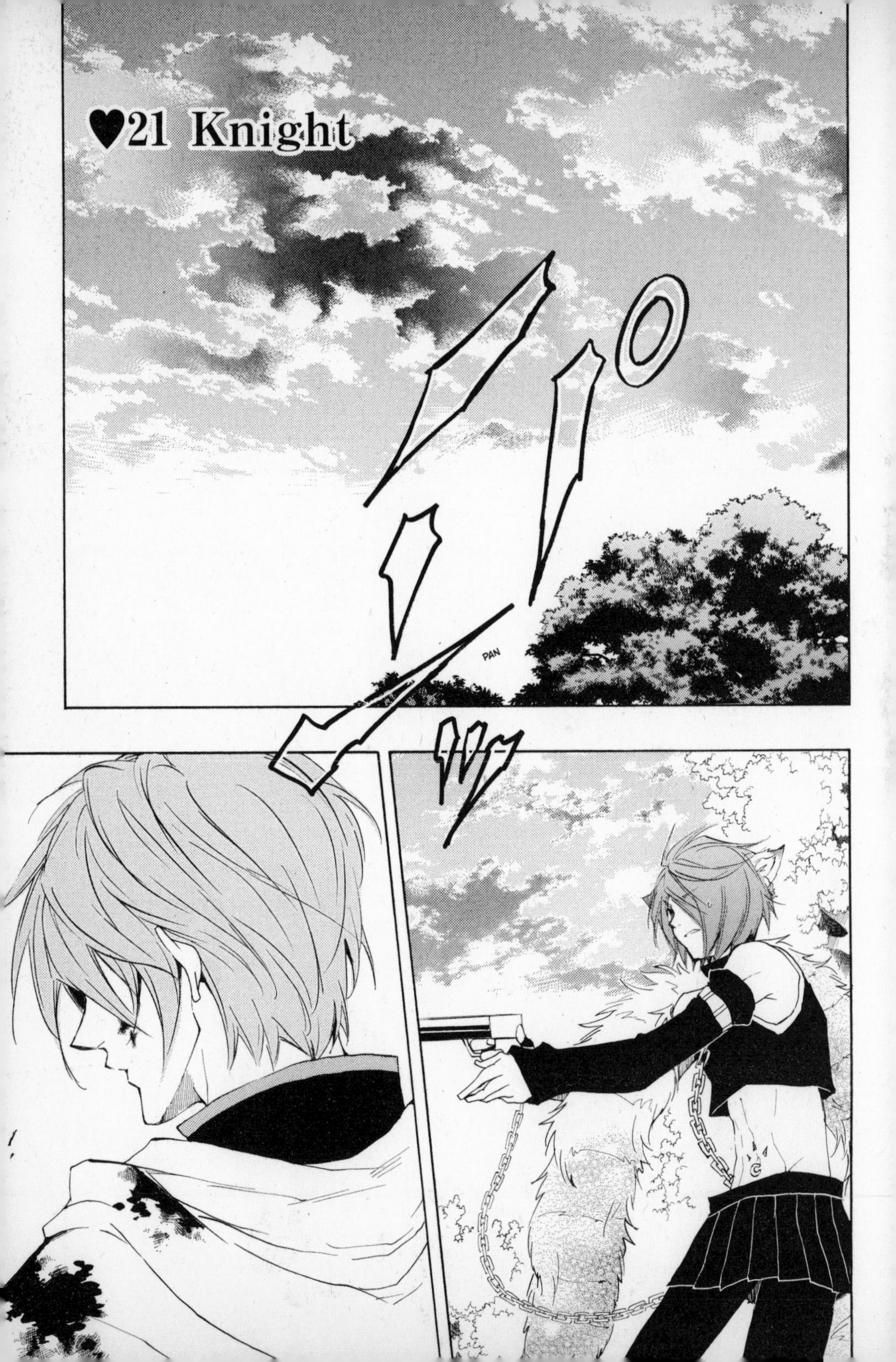
♥21 Knight
PAN

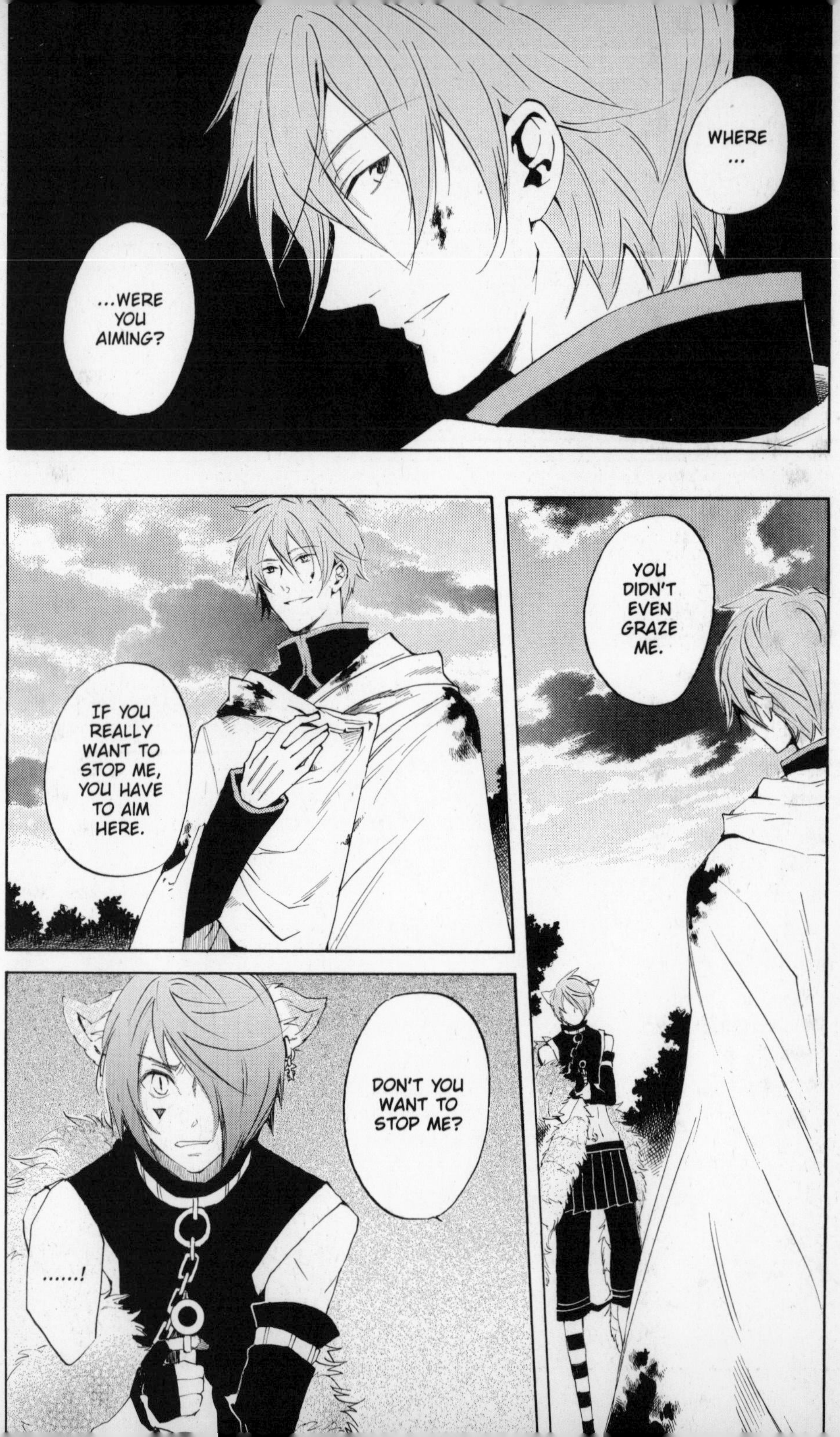
WHERE ...
...WERE YOU AIMING?
YOU DIDN'T EVEN GRAZE ME.
IF YOU REALLY WANT TO STOP ME, YOU HAVE TO AIM HERE.
DON'T YOU WANT TO STOP ME?
......!

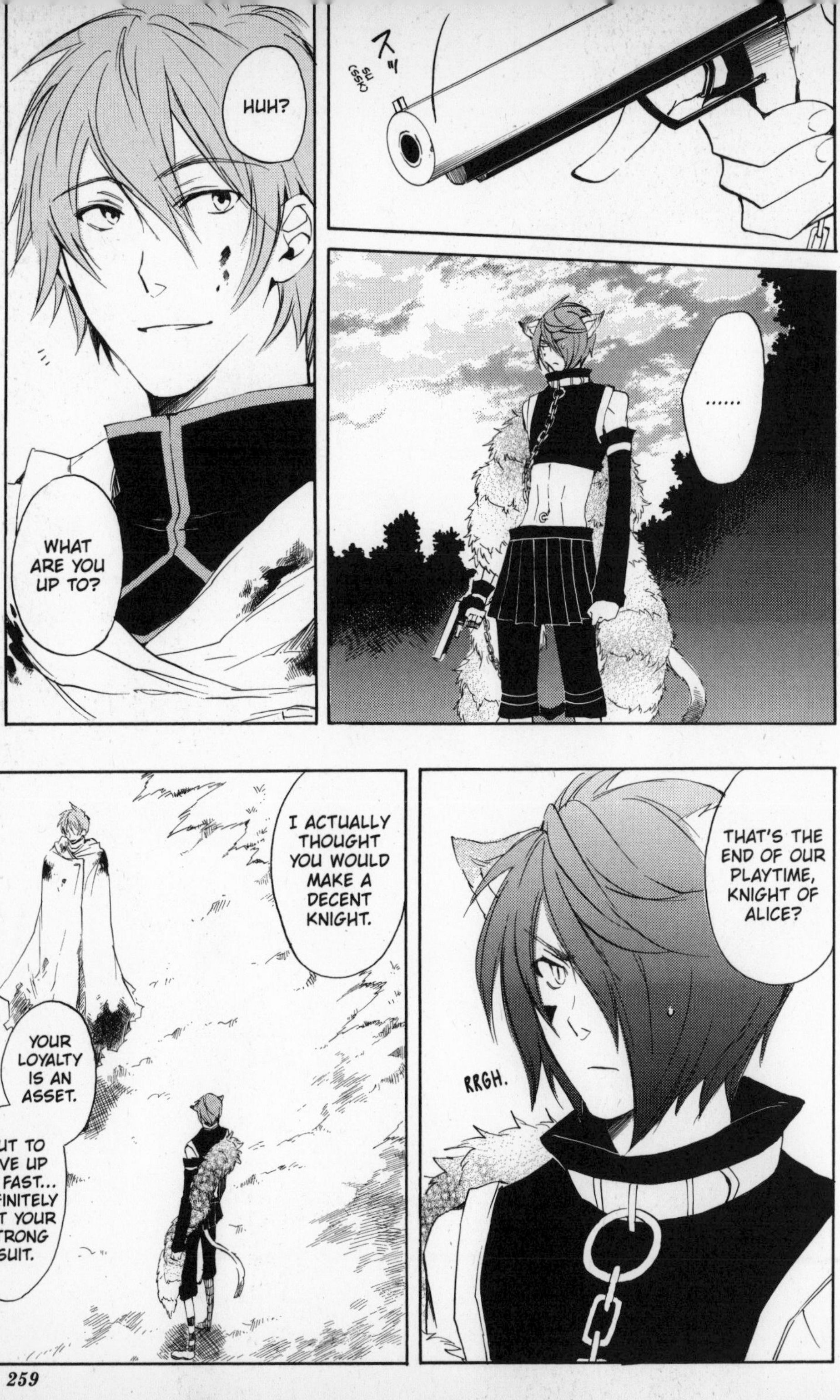
スッ
SU (SSK)
......
HUH?
WHAT ARE YOU UP TO?
THAT'S THE END OF OUR PLAYTIME, KNIGHT OF ALICE?
RRGH.
I ACTUALLY THOUGHT YOU WOULD MAKE A DECENT KNIGHT.
YOUR LOYALTY IS AN ASSET.
BUT TO GIVE UP SO FAST... DEFINITELY NOT YOUR STRONG SUIT.

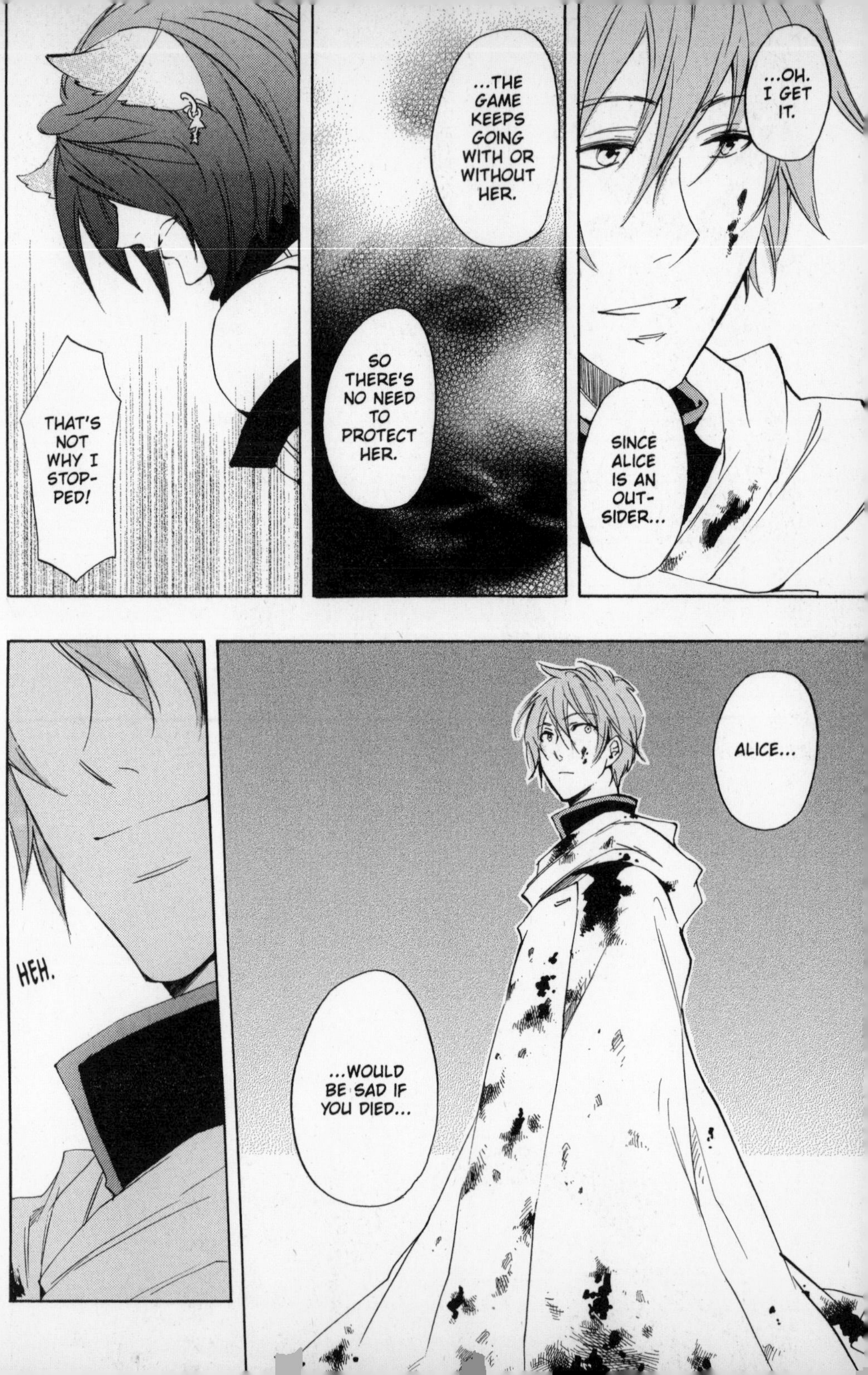
...OH. I GET IT.
SINCE ALICE IS AN OUTSIDER...
...THE GAME KEEPS GOING WITH OR WITHOUT HER.
SO THERE'S NO NEED TO PROTECT HER.
THAT'S NOT WHY I STOP-PED!
ALICE...
...WOULD BE SAD IF YOU DIED...
HEH.

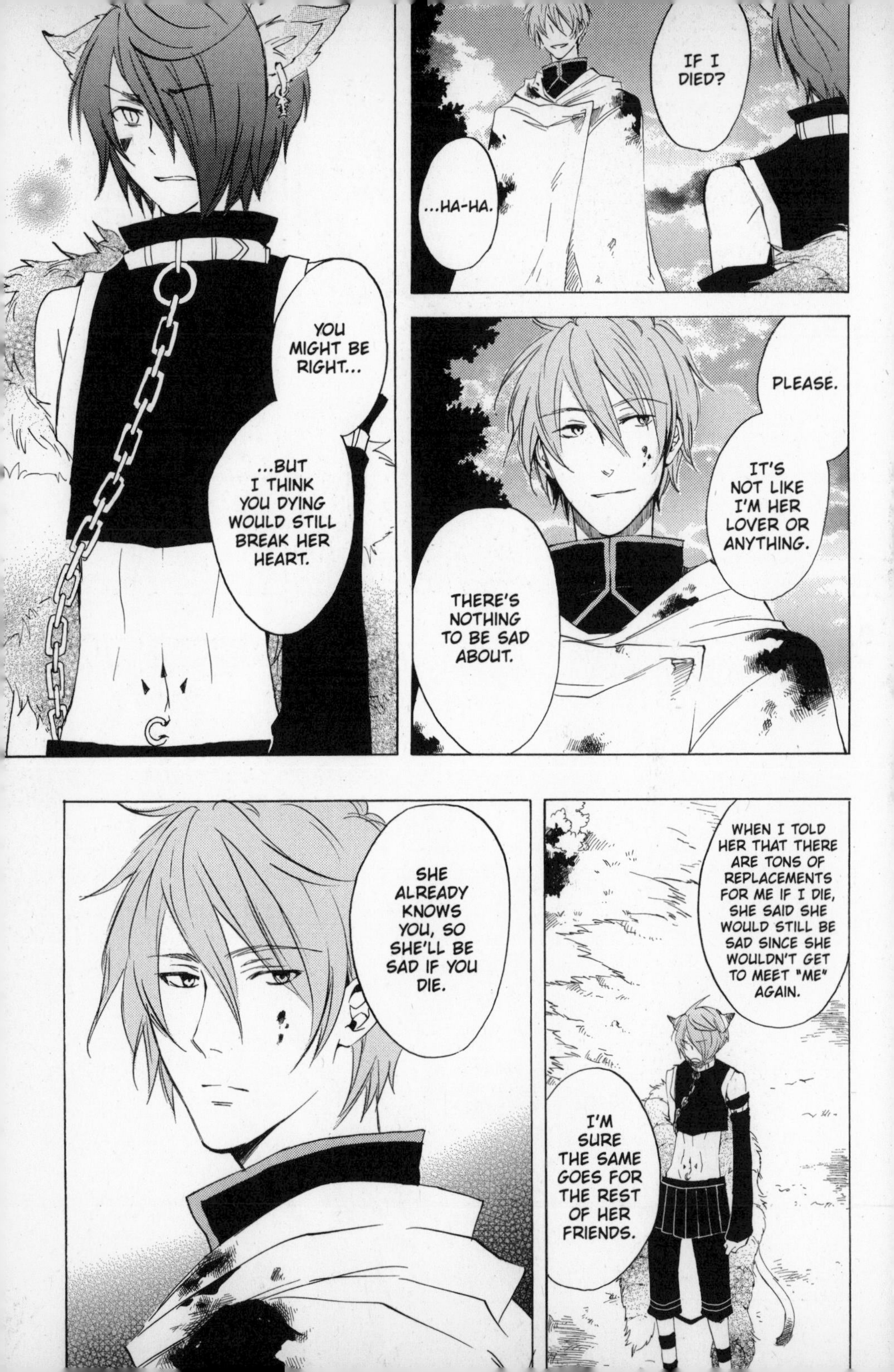
IF I DIED?
...HA-HA.
PLEASE.
IT'S NOT LIKE I'M HER LOVER OR ANYTHING.
THERE'S NOTHING TO BE SAD ABOUT.
YOU MIGHT BE RIGHT...
...BUT I THINK YOU DYING WOULD STILL BREAK HER HEART.
WHEN I TOLD HER THAT THERE ARE TONS OF REPLACEMENTS FOR ME IF I DIE, SHE SAID SHE WOULD STILL BE SAD SINCE SHE WOULDN'T GET TO MEET "ME" AGAIN.
I'M SURE THE SAME GOES FOR THE REST OF HER FRIENDS.
SHE ALREADY KNOWS YOU, SO SHE'LL BE SAD IF YOU DIE.

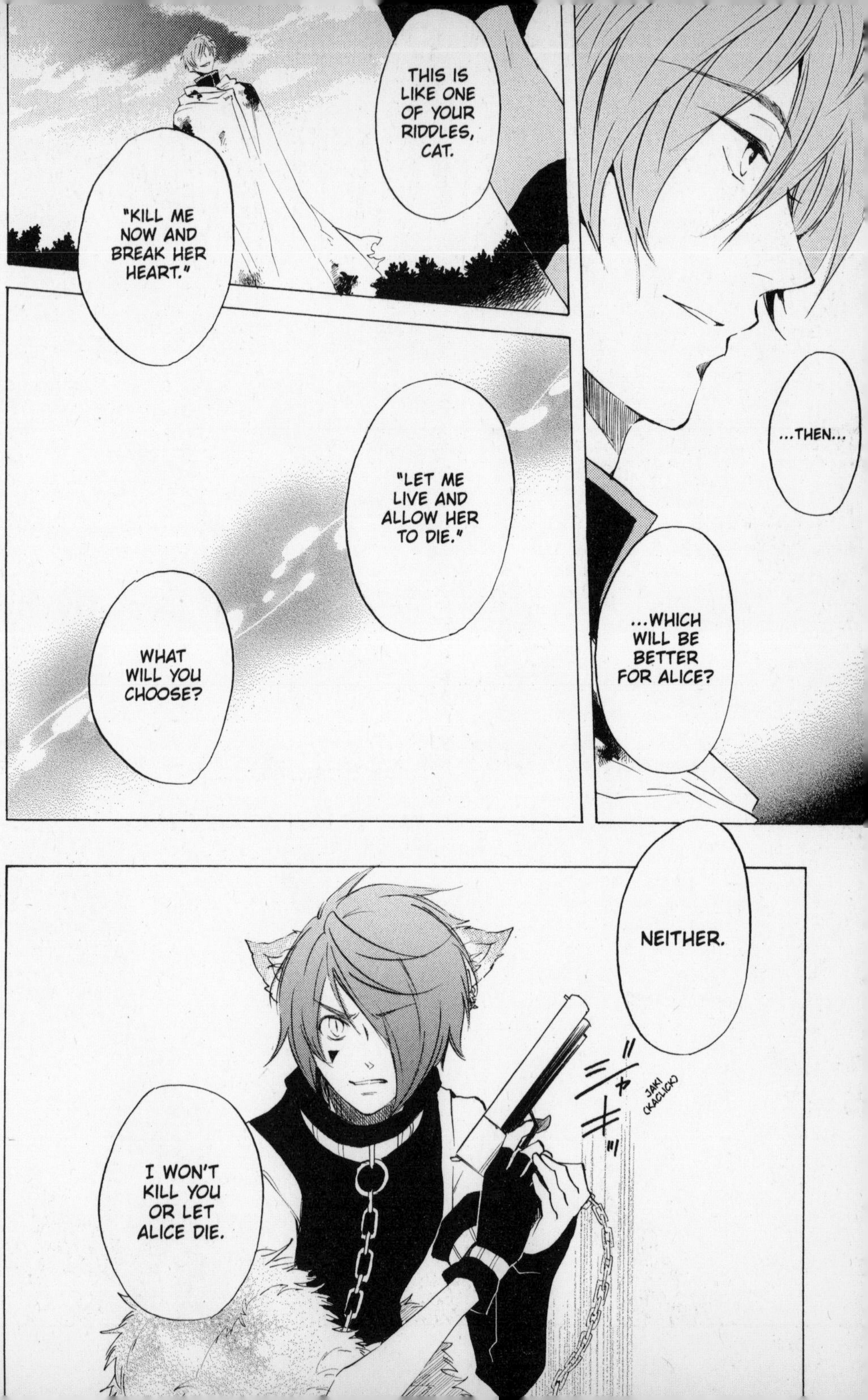
THIS IS LIKE ONE OF YOUR RIDDLES, CAT.
"KILL ME NOW AND BREAK HER HEART."
"LET ME LIVE AND ALLOW HER TO DIE."
WHAT WILL YOU CHOOSE?
...THEN...
...WHICH WILL BE BETTER FOR ALICE?
NEITHER.
JAKI (KACLICK)
I WON'T KILL YOU OR LET ALICE DIE.

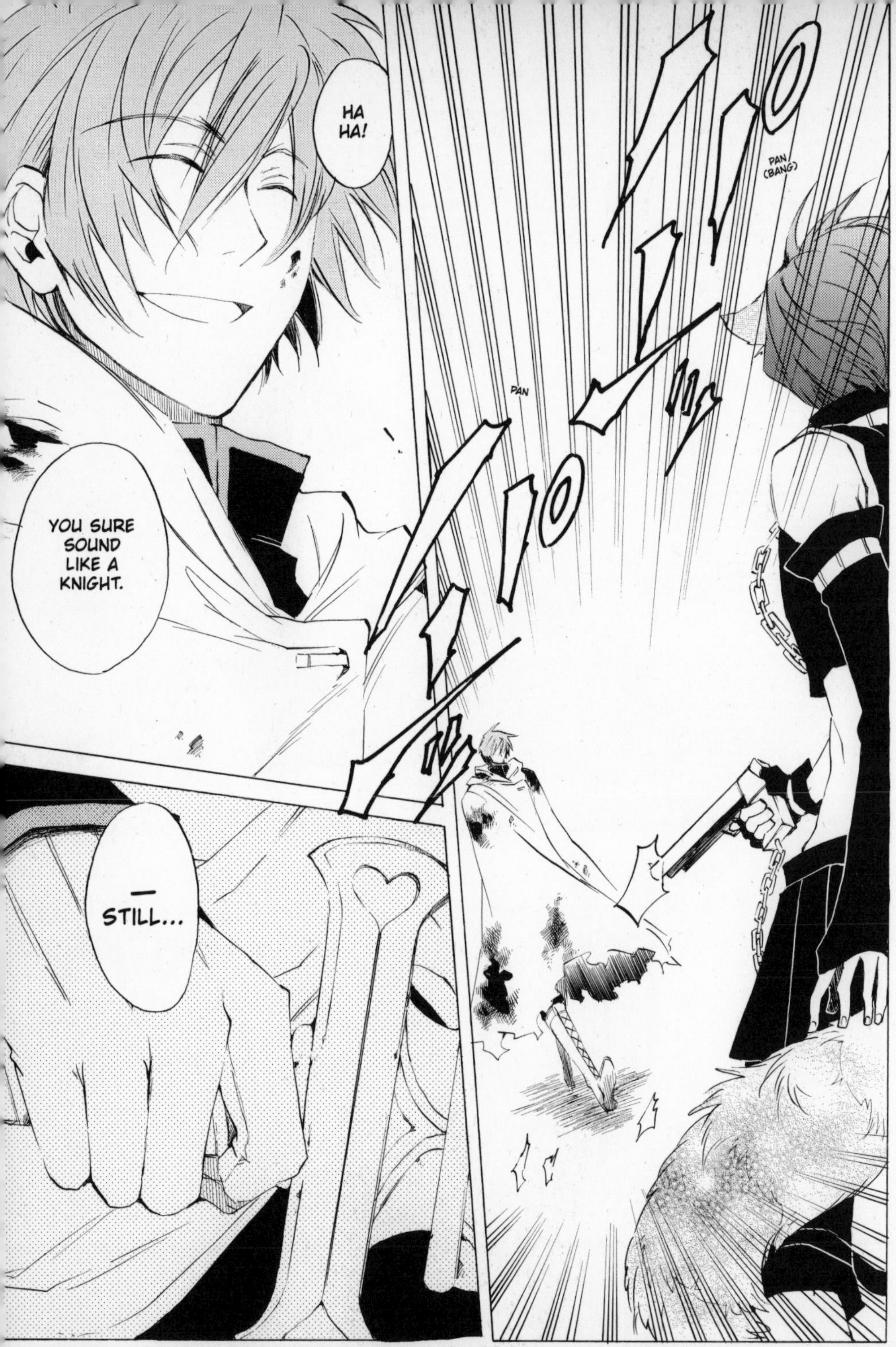
PAN
(BANG)
PAN
HA HA!
YOU SURE SOUND LIKE A KNIGHT.
— STILL...

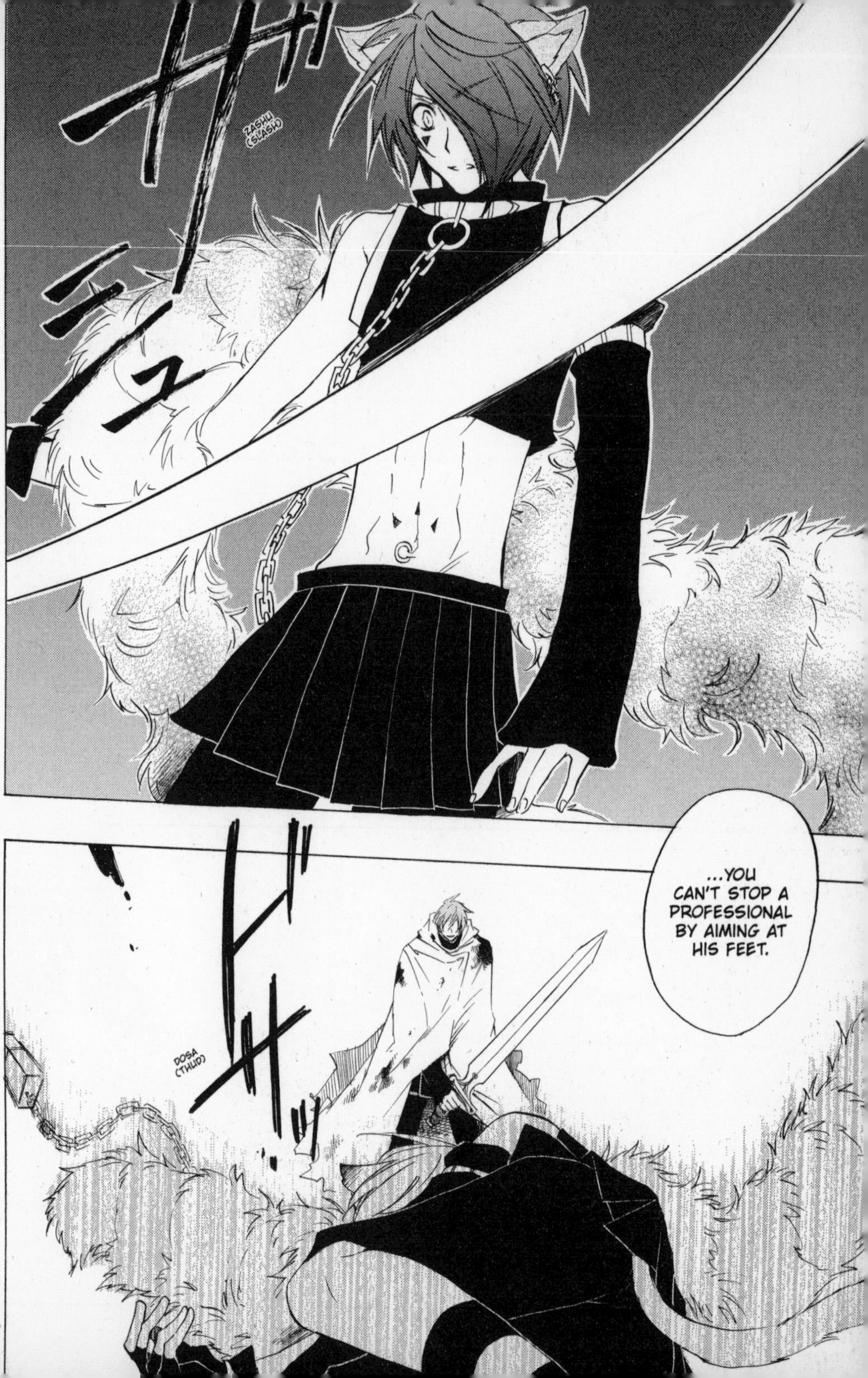
ZASHU (SLASH)
...YOU CAN'T STOP A PROFESSIONAL BY AIMING AT HIS FEET.
DOSA (THUD)

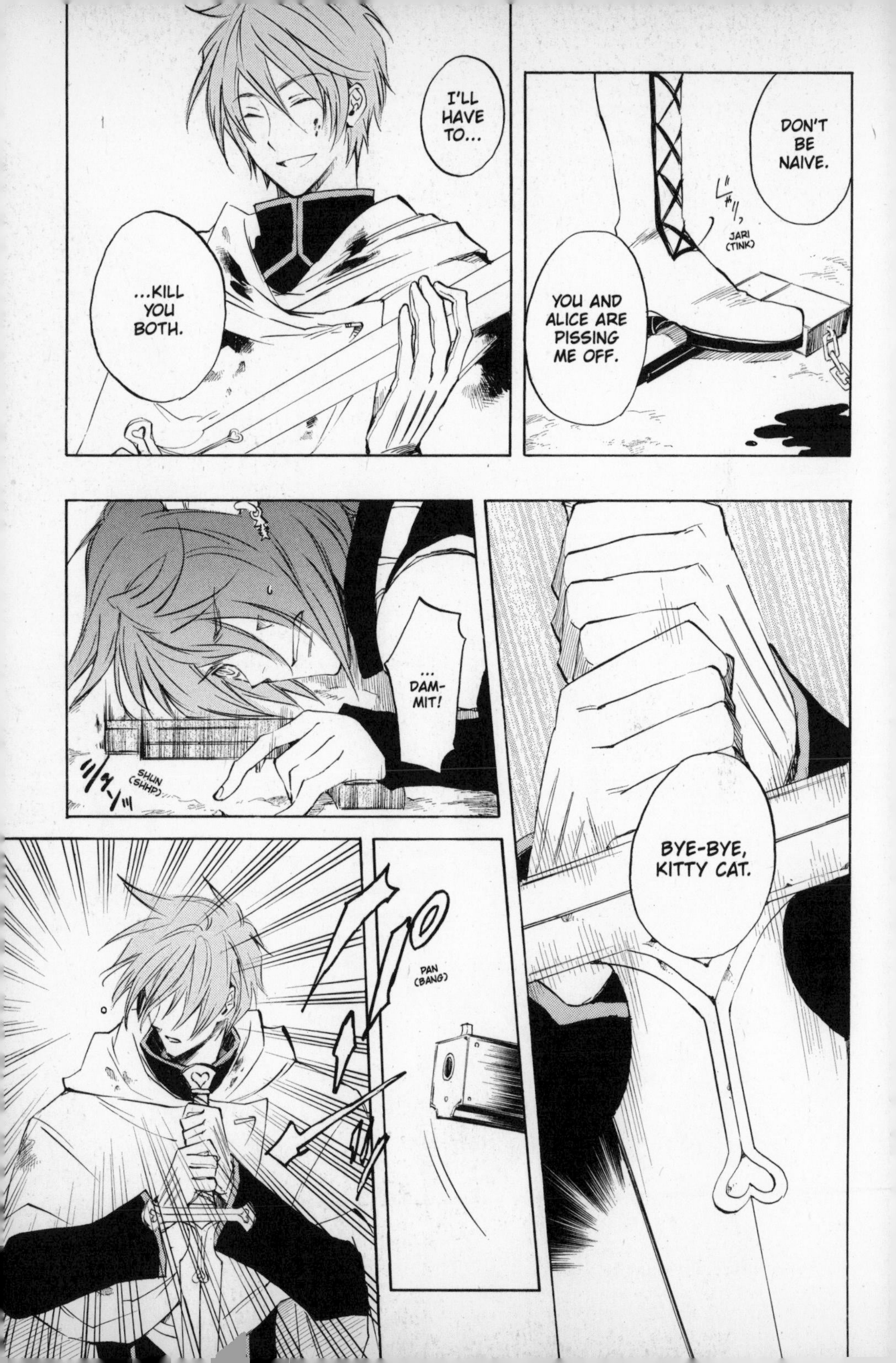
DON'T BE NAIVE.
JARI (TINK)
YOU AND ALICE ARE PISSING ME OFF.
I'LL HAVE TO...
...KILL YOU BOTH.
BYE-BYE, KITTY CAT.
...DAM-MIT!
SHUN (SHHP)
PAN (BANG)

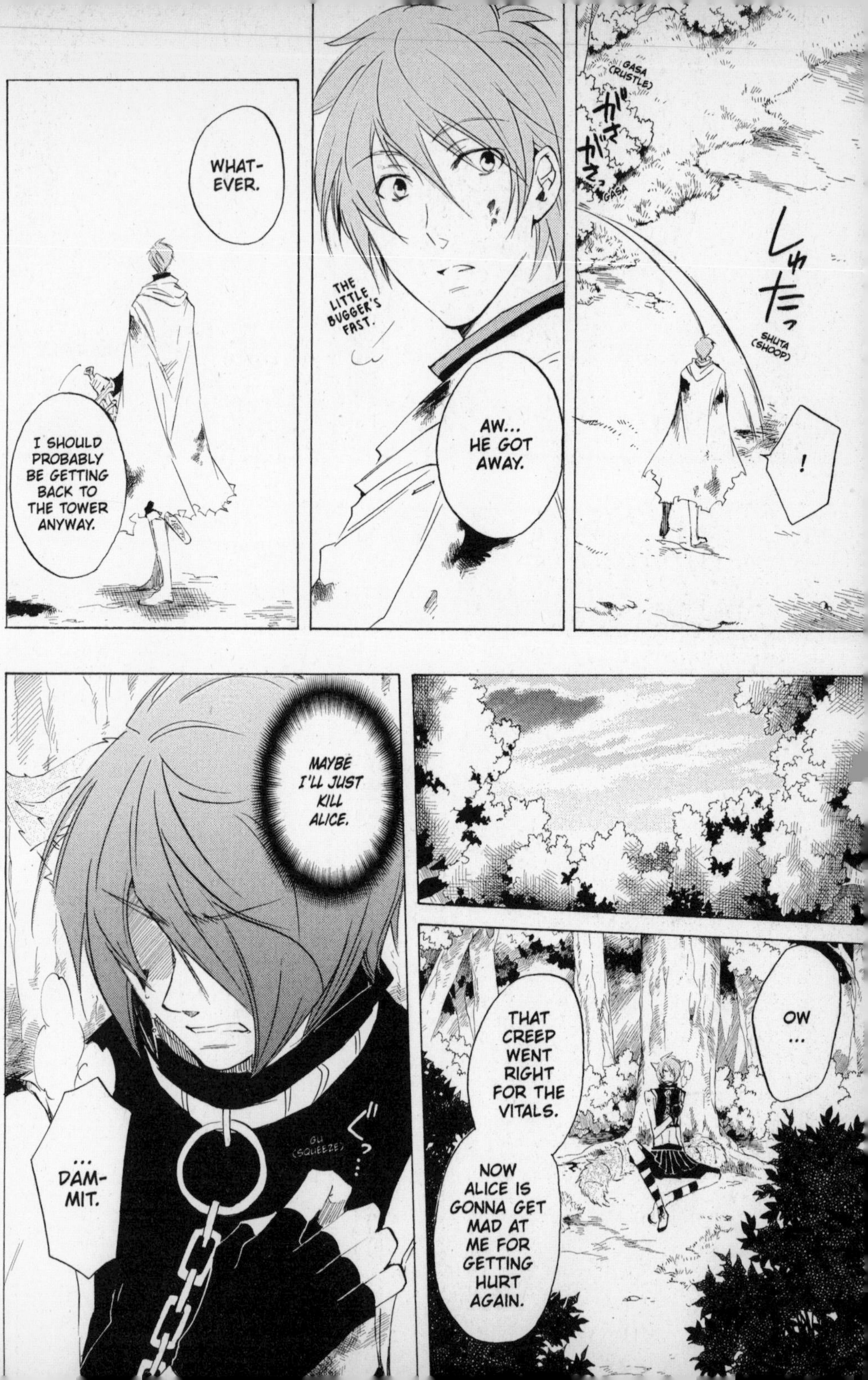
GASA (RUSTLE)
GASA
SHUTA (SHOOP)
!
THE LITTLE BUGGER'S FAST.
AW... HE GOT AWAY.
WHAT-EVER.
I SHOULD PROBABLY BE GETTING BACK TO THE TOWER ANYWAY.
OW ...
THAT CREEP WENT RIGHT FOR THE VITALS.
NOW ALICE IS GONNA GET MAD AT ME FOR GETTING HURT AGAIN.
MAYBE I'LL JUST KILL ALICE.
GU (SQUEEZE)
... DAM-MIT.

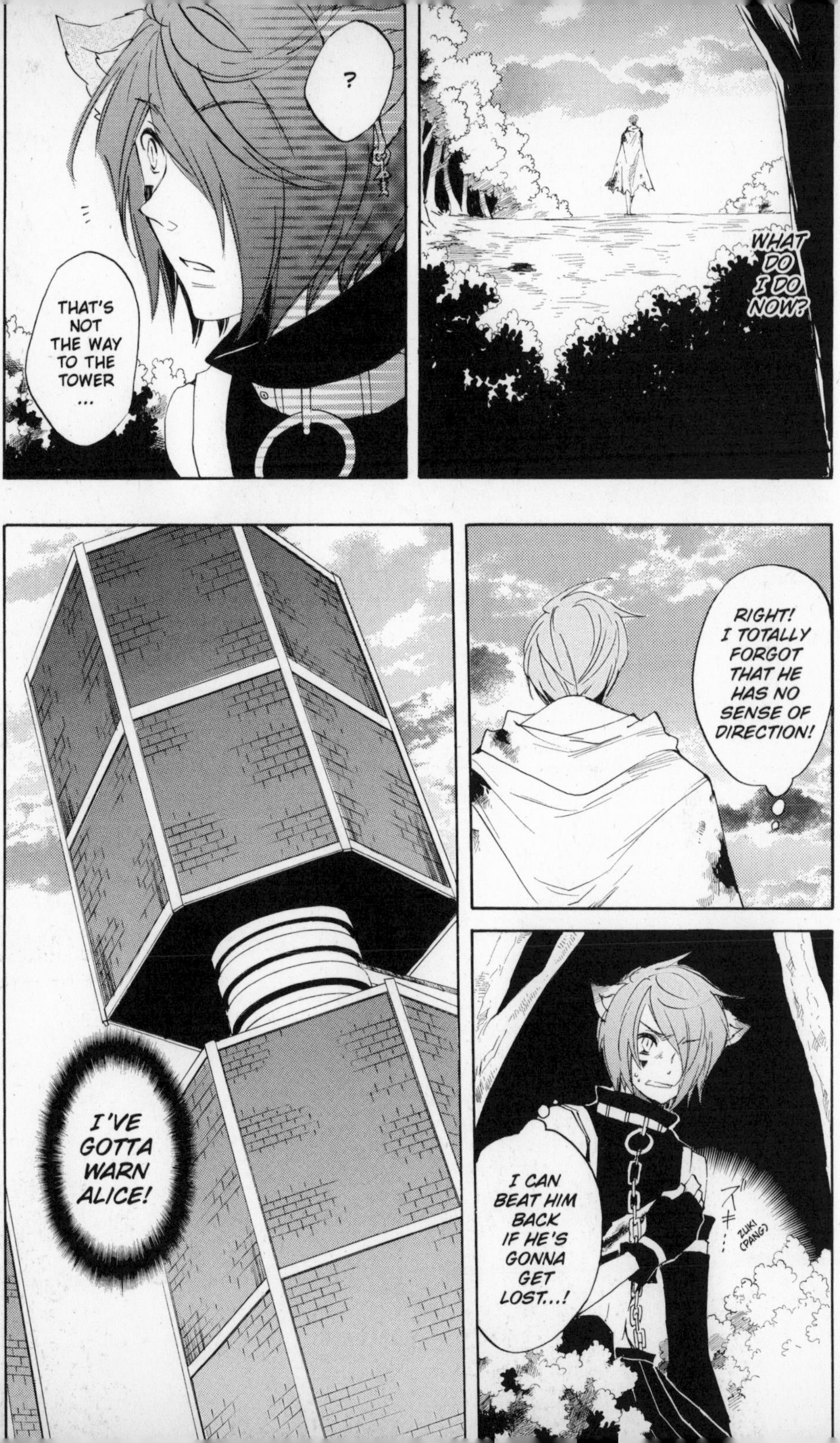
WHAT DO I DO NOW?
?
THAT'S NOT THE WAY TO THE TOWER...
RIGHT! I TOTALLY FORGOT THAT HE HAS NO SENSE OF DIRECTION!
I CAN BEAT HIM BACK IF HE'S GONNA GET LOST...!
ZUKI (PANG)
I'VE GOTTA WARN ALICE!

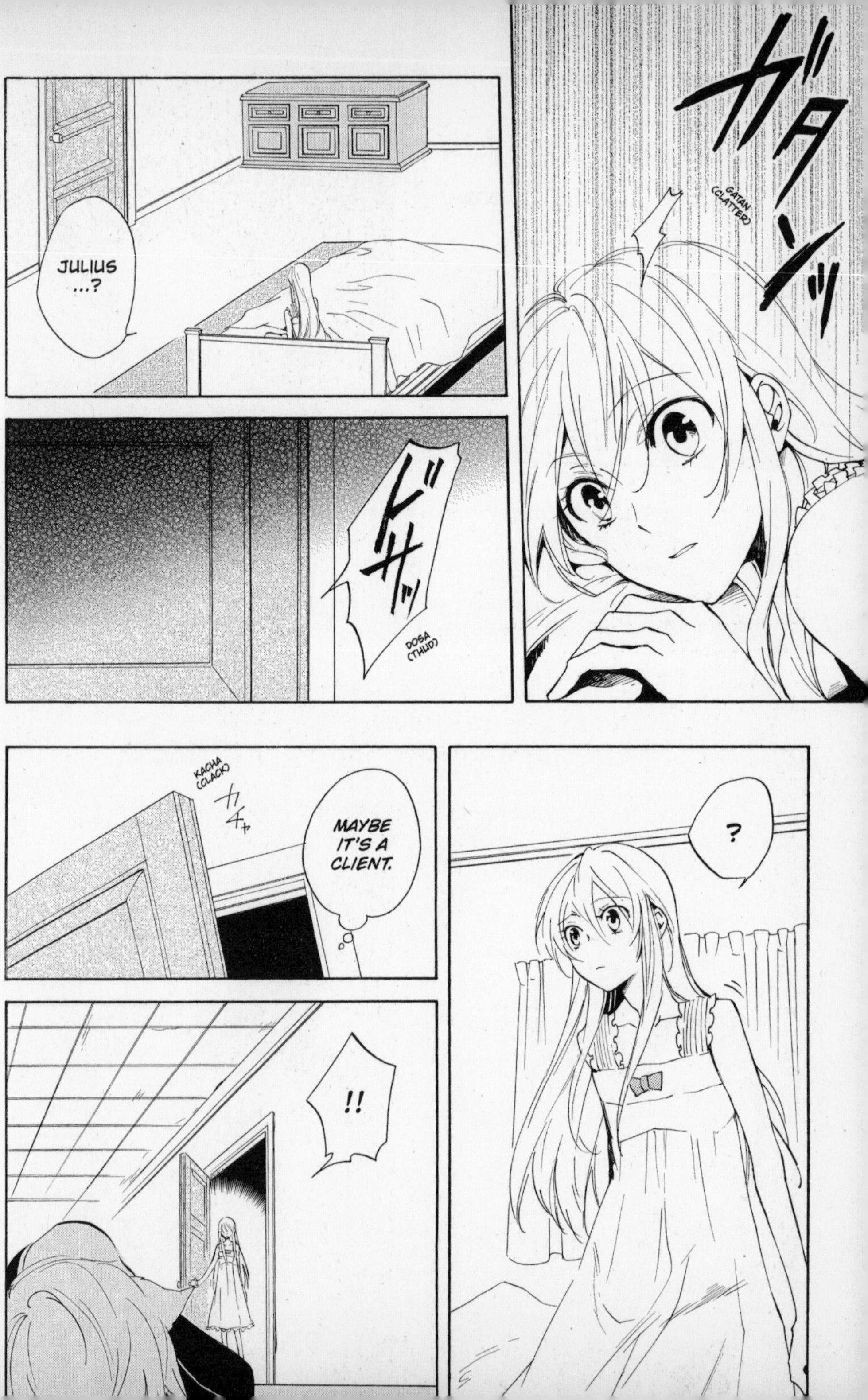

ガタンッ
GATAN (CLATTER)
JULIUS ...?
ドサッ
DOSA (THUD)
?
KACHA (CLACK)
カチャ
MAYBE IT'S A CLIENT.
!!

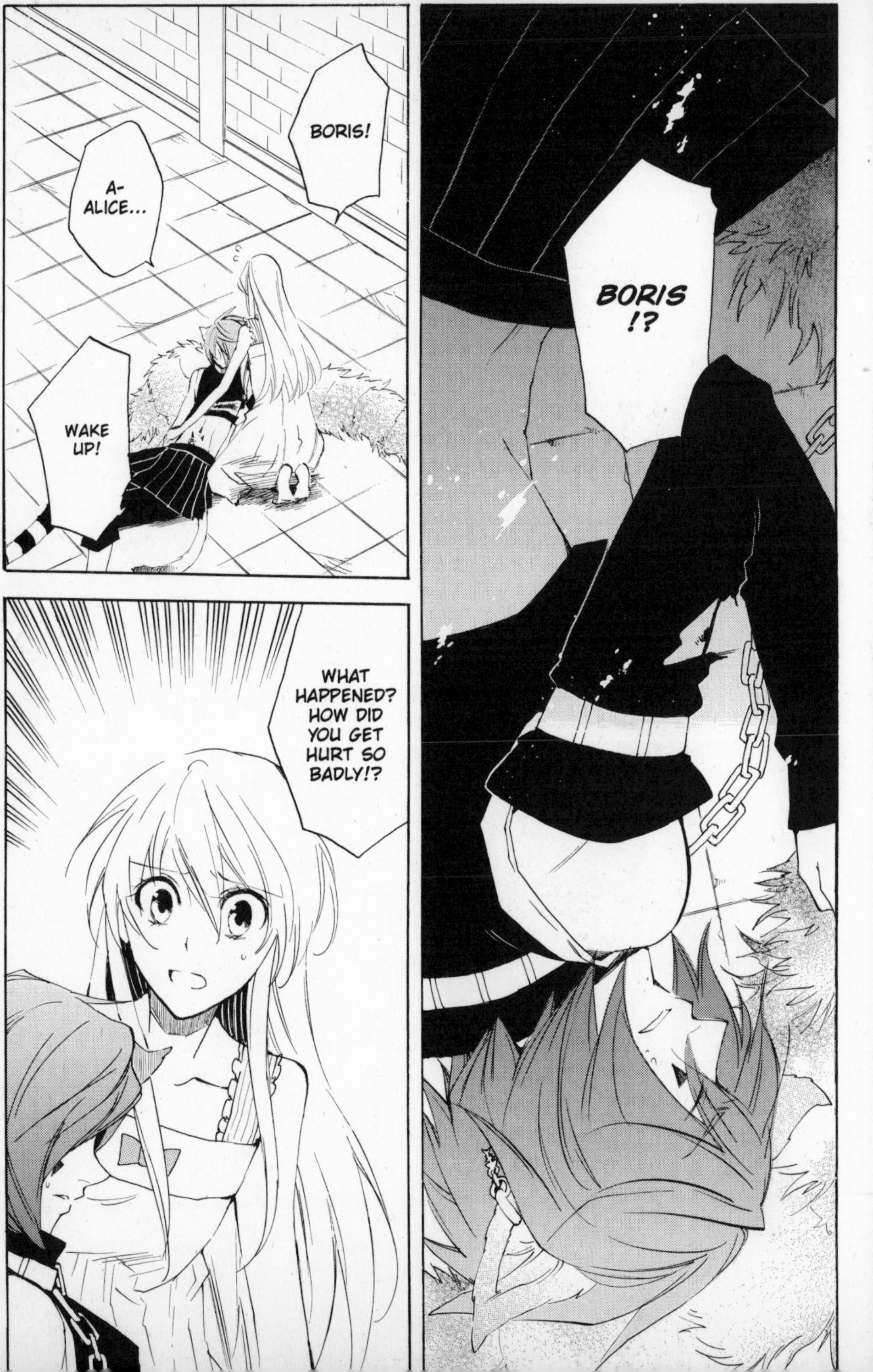
BORIS !?
BORIS!
A- ALICE...
WAKE UP!
WHAT HAPPENED? HOW DID YOU GET HURT SO BADLY!?

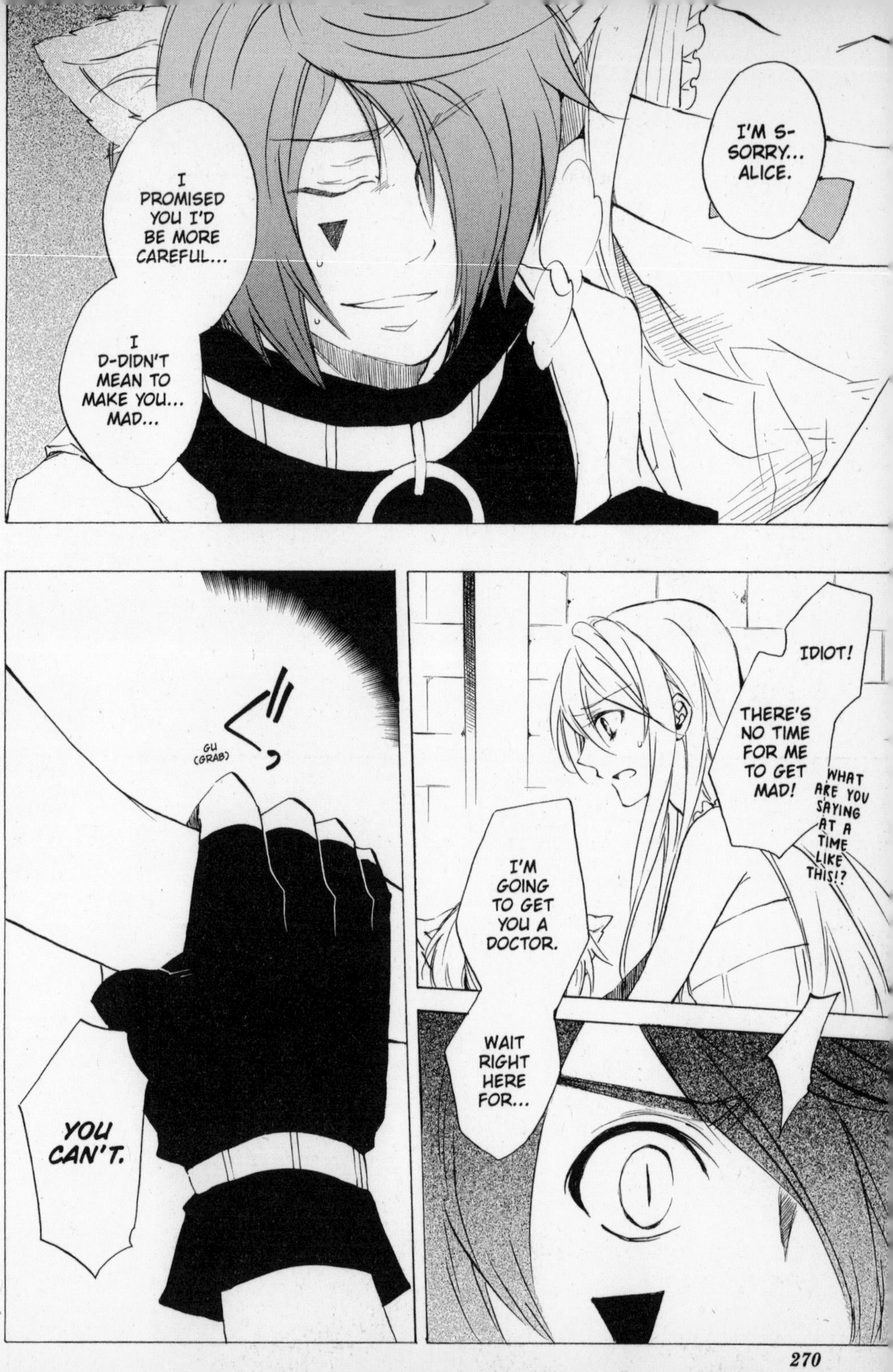
I'M S-SORRY... ALICE.
I PROMISED YOU I'D BE MORE CAREFUL...
I D-DIDN'T MEAN TO MAKE YOU... MAD...
IDIOT!
THERE'S NO TIME FOR ME TO GET MAD!
WHAT ARE YOU SAYING AT A TIME LIKE THIS!?
I'M GOING TO GET YOU A DOCTOR.
WAIT RIGHT HERE FOR...
GU (GRAB)
YOU CAN'T.

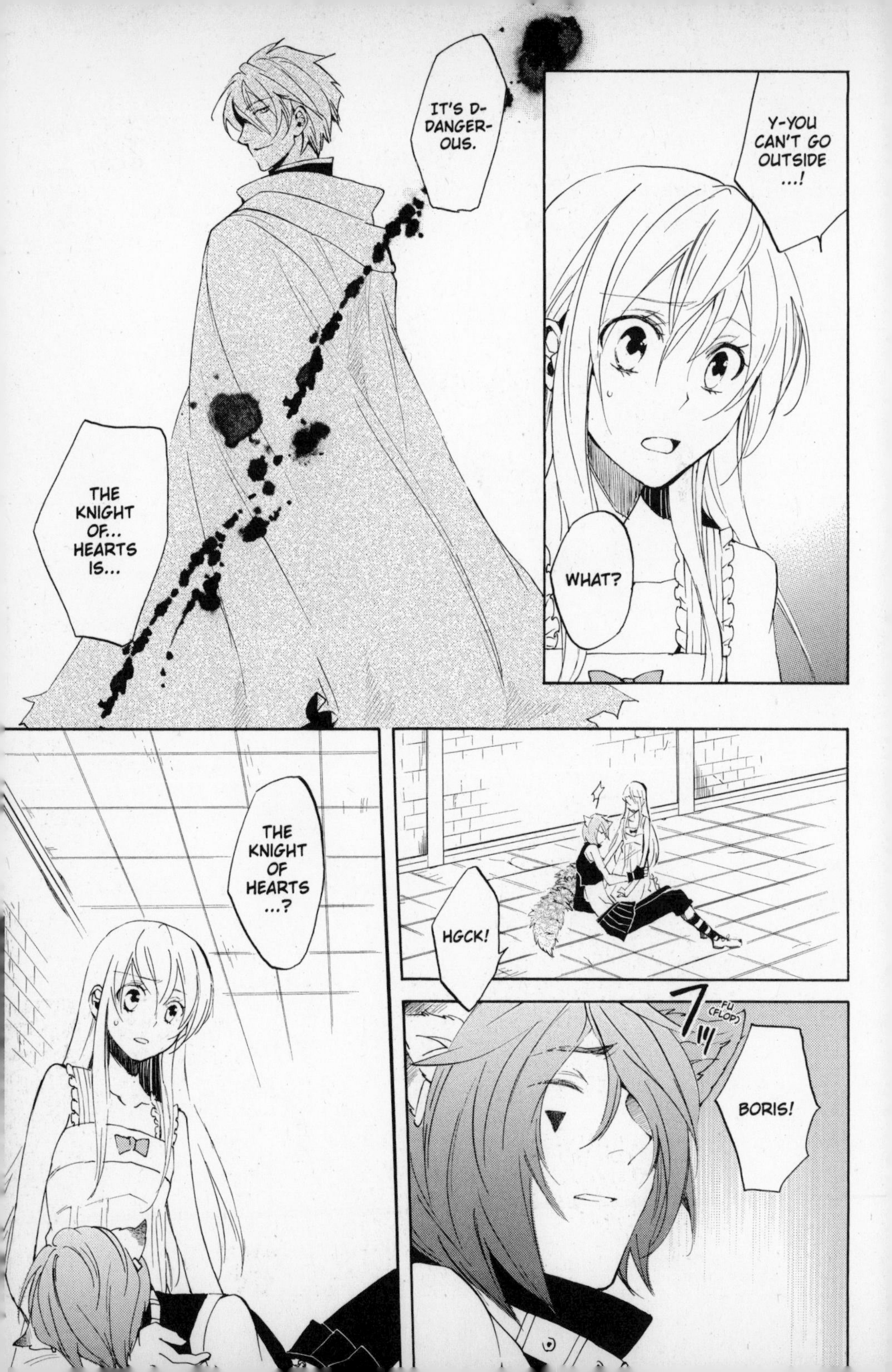
Y-YOU CAN'T GO OUTSIDE ...!
WHAT?
IT'S D-DANGER-OUS.
THE KNIGHT OF... HEARTS IS...
HGCK!
FU (FLOP)
BORIS!
THE KNIGHT OF HEARTS ...?

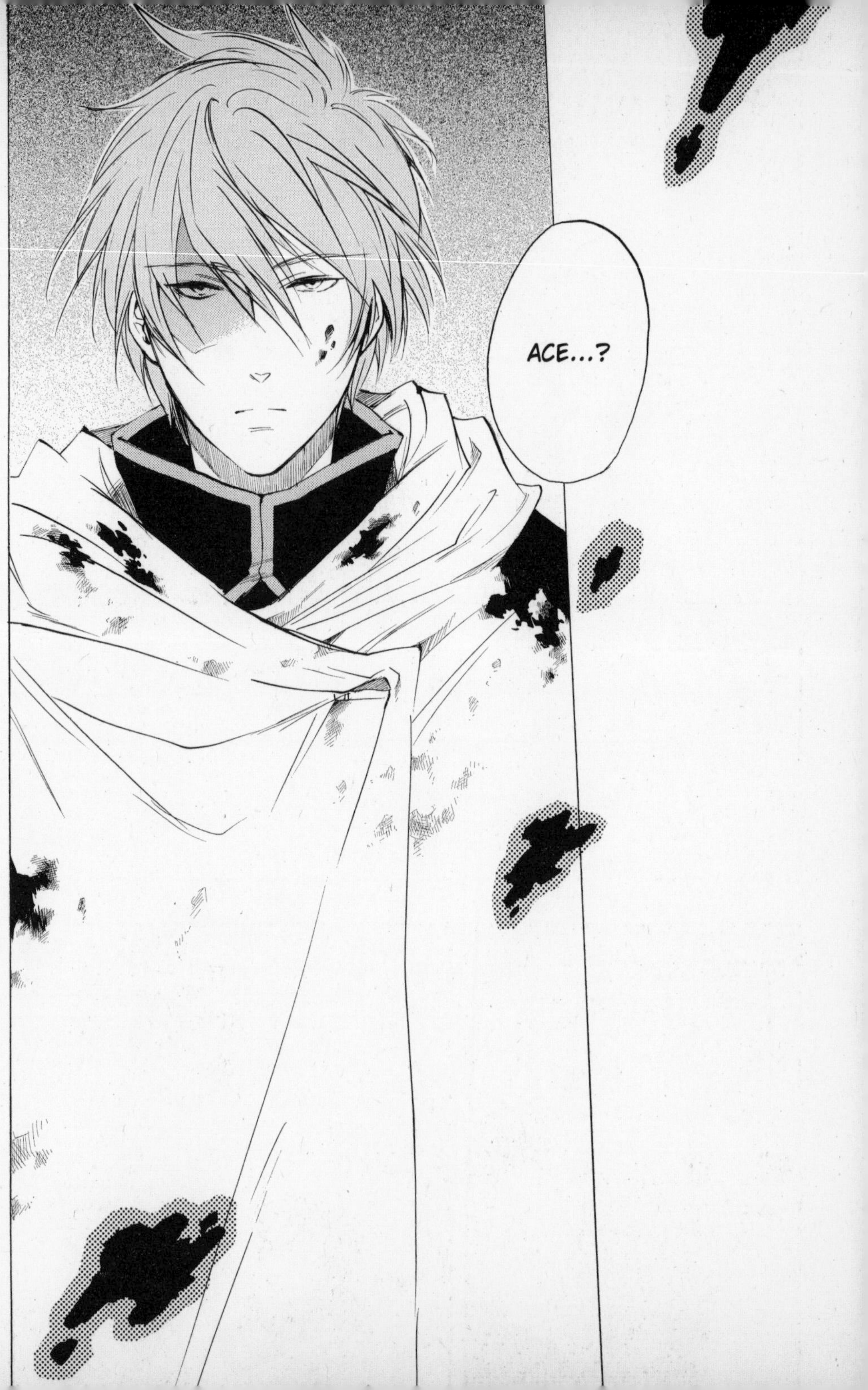
ACE...?

♥22 Coming Uneasiness

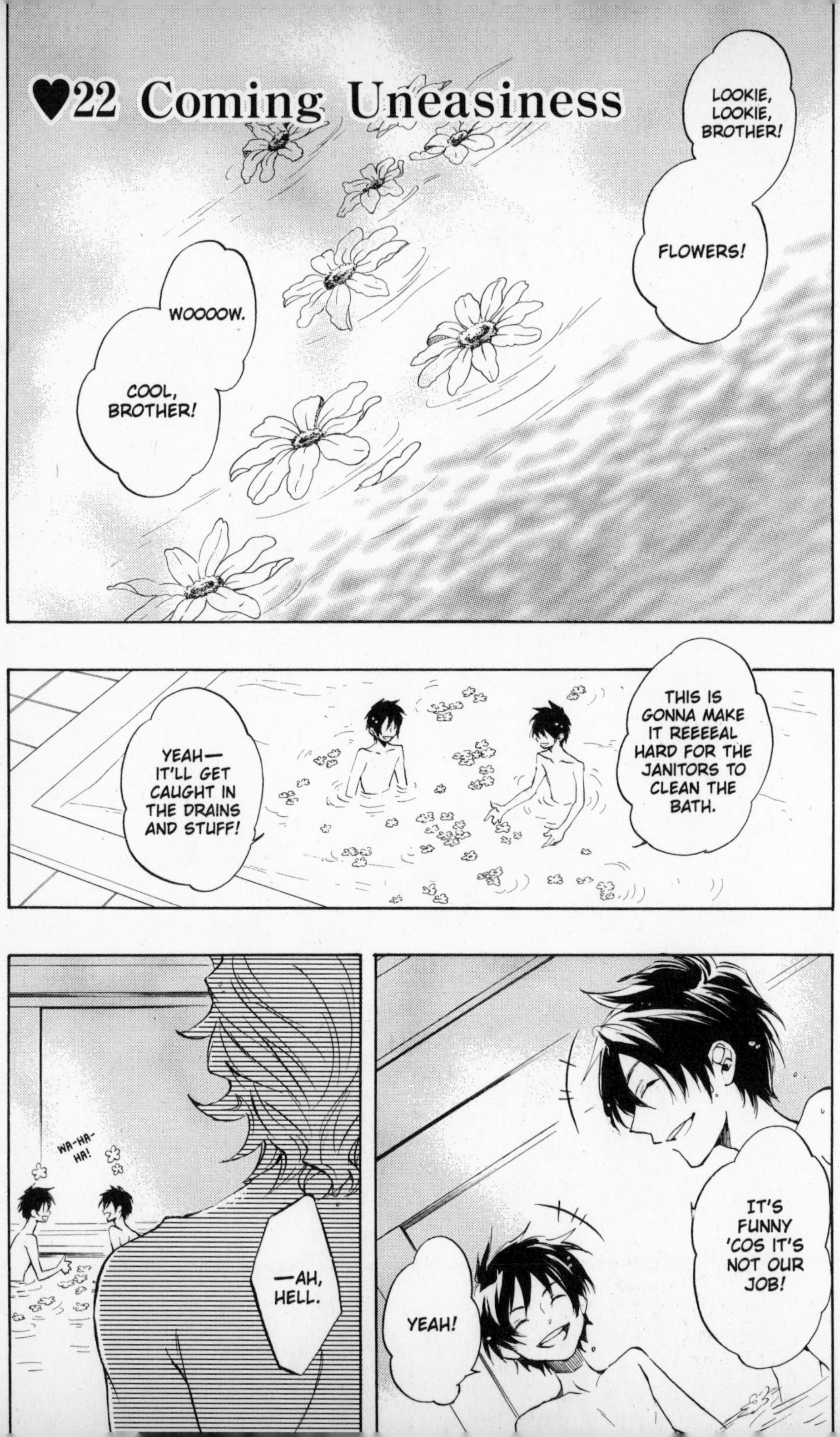
LOOKIE, LOOKIE, BROTHER! FLOWERS!
WOOOOW. COOL, BROTHER!
THIS IS GONNA MAKE IT REEEEAL HARD FOR THE JANITORS TO CLEAN THE BATH.
YEAH— IT'LL GET CAUGHT IN THE DRAINS AND STUFF!
IT'S FUNNY 'COS IT'S NOT OUR JOB!
YEAH!
WA-HA-HA!
—AH, HELL.

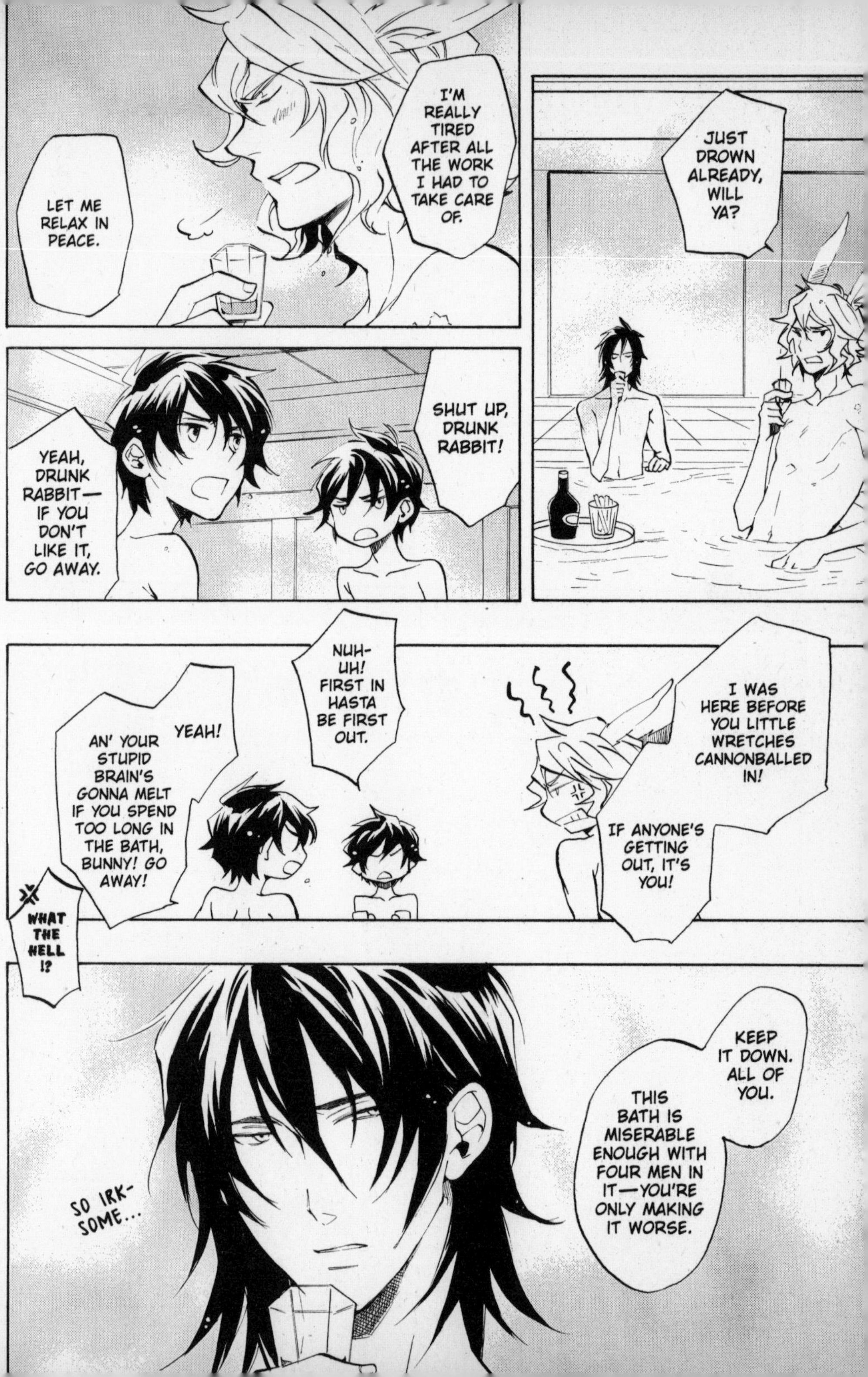
JUST DROWN ALREADY, WILL YA?
I'M REALLY TIRED AFTER ALL THE WORK I HAD TO TAKE CARE OF.
LET ME RELAX IN PEACE.
SHUT UP, DRUNK RABBIT!
YEAH, DRUNK RABBIT— IF YOU DON'T LIKE IT, GO AWAY.
I WAS HERE BEFORE YOU LITTLE WRETCHES CANNONBALLED IN!
IF ANYONE'S GETTING OUT, IT'S YOU!
NUH-UH! FIRST IN HASTA BE FIRST OUT.
YEAH!
AN' YOUR STUPID BRAIN'S GONNA MELT IF YOU SPEND TOO LONG IN THE BATH, BUNNY! GO AWAY!
WHAT THE HELL!?
KEEP IT DOWN. ALL OF YOU.
THIS BATH IS MISERABLE ENOUGH WITH FOUR MEN IN IT—YOU'RE ONLY MAKING IT WORSE.
SO IRK-SOME...

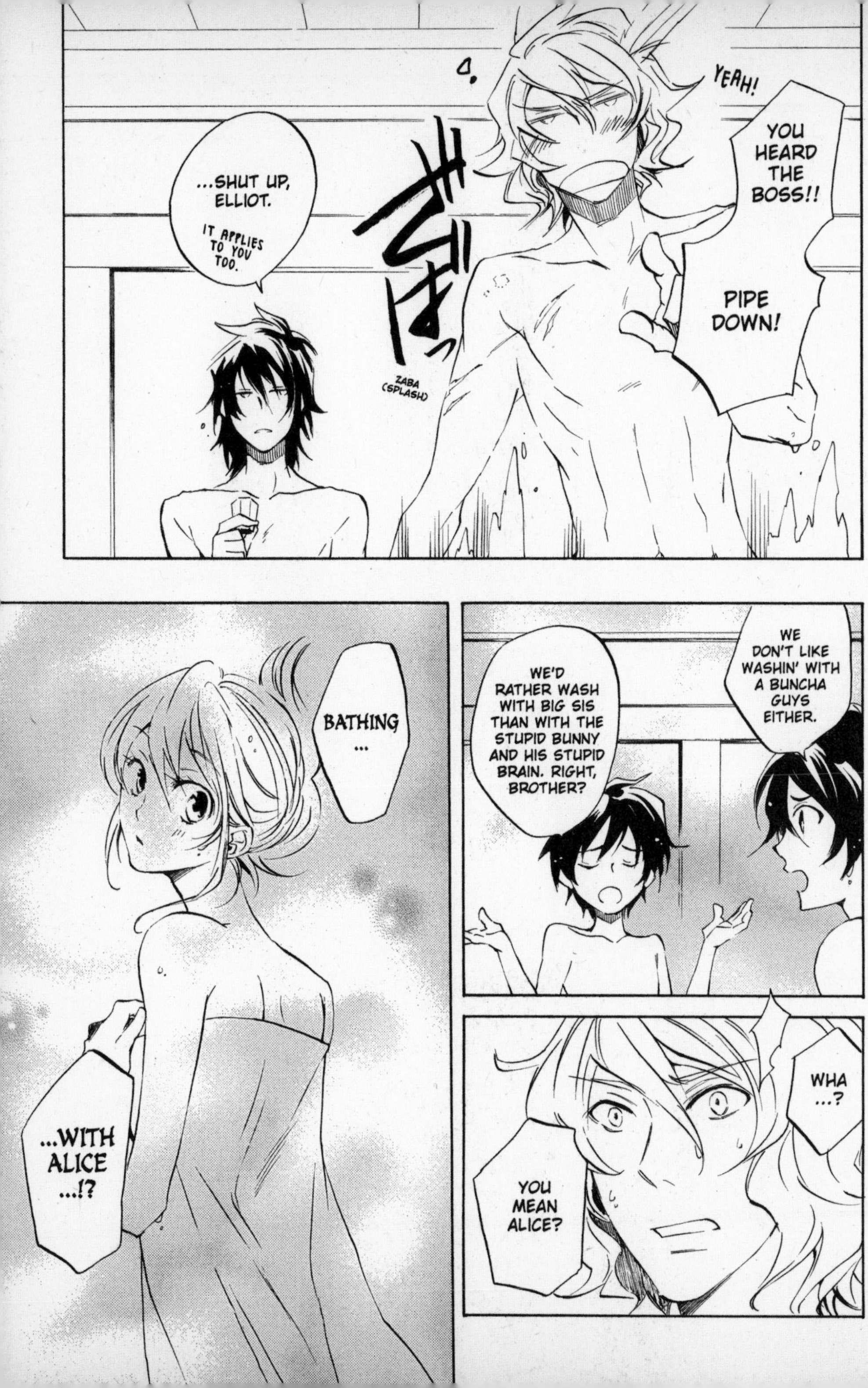
YEAH!
YOU HEARD THE BOSS!!
PIPE DOWN!
ZABA (SPLASH)
...SHUT UP, ELLIOT.
IT APPLIES TO YOU TOO.
WE DON'T LIKE WASHIN' WITH A BUNCHA GUYS EITHER.
WE'D RATHER WASH WITH BIG SIS THAN WITH THE STUPID BUNNY AND HIS STUPID BRAIN. RIGHT, BROTHER?
WHA ...?
YOU MEAN ALICE?
BATHING ...
...WITH ALICE ...!?

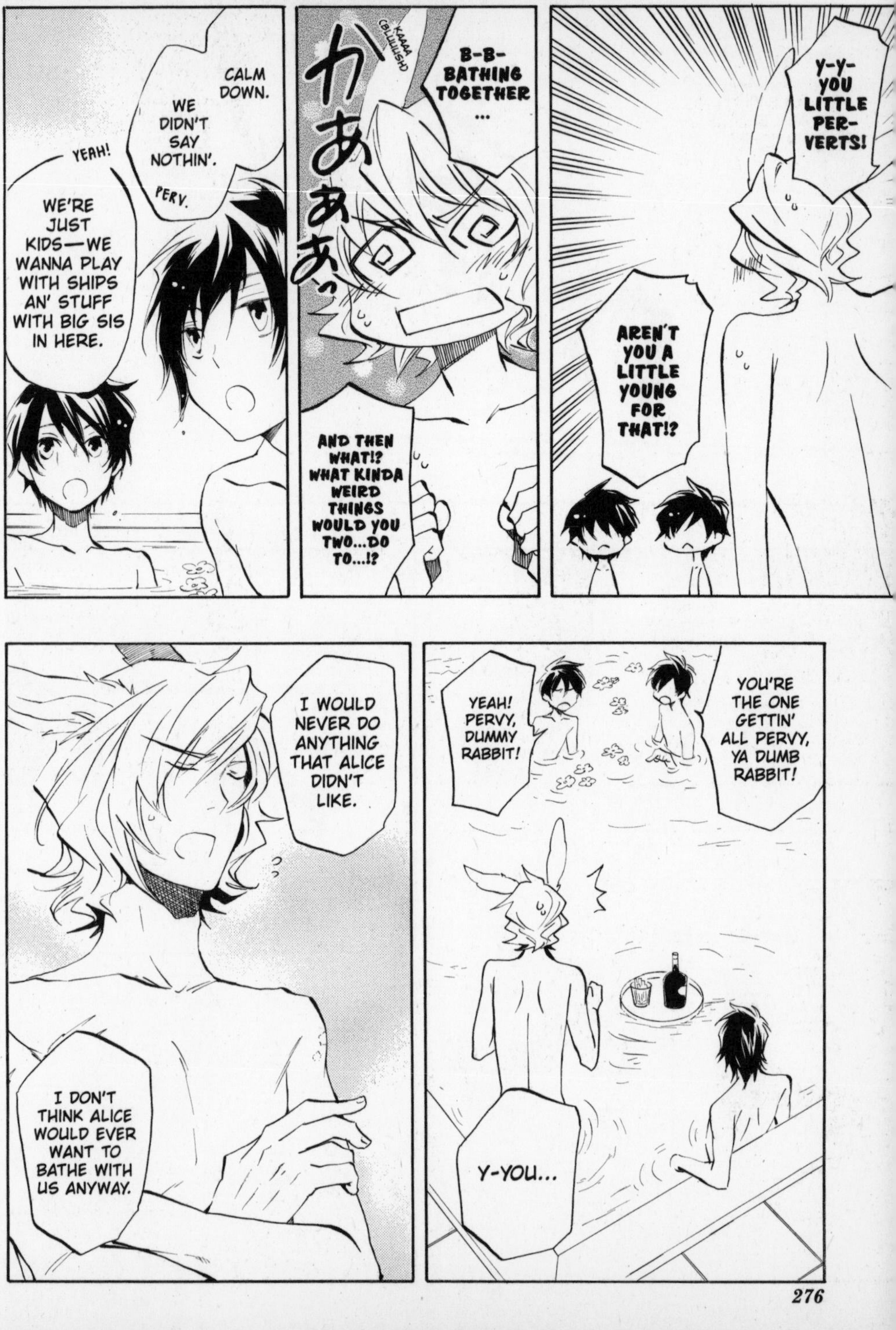
Y-Y-YOU LITTLE PER-VERTS!
AREN'T YOU A LITTLE YOUNG FOR THAT!?
B-B-BATHING TOGETHER...
かあああっ
KAAAA (BLUUUSH)
AND THEN WHAT!? WHAT KINDA WEIRD THINGS WOULD YOU TWO...DO TO...!?
CALM DOWN.
WE DIDN'T SAY NOTHIN'.
PERV.
YEAH!
WE'RE JUST KIDS—WE WANNA PLAY WITH SHIPS AN' STUFF WITH BIG SIS IN HERE.
YOU'RE THE ONE GETTIN' ALL PERVY, YA DUMB RABBIT!
YEAH! PERVY, DUMMY RABBIT!
Y-YOU...
I WOULD NEVER DO ANYTHING THAT ALICE DIDN'T LIKE.
I DON'T THINK ALICE WOULD EVER WANT TO BATHE WITH US ANYWAY.

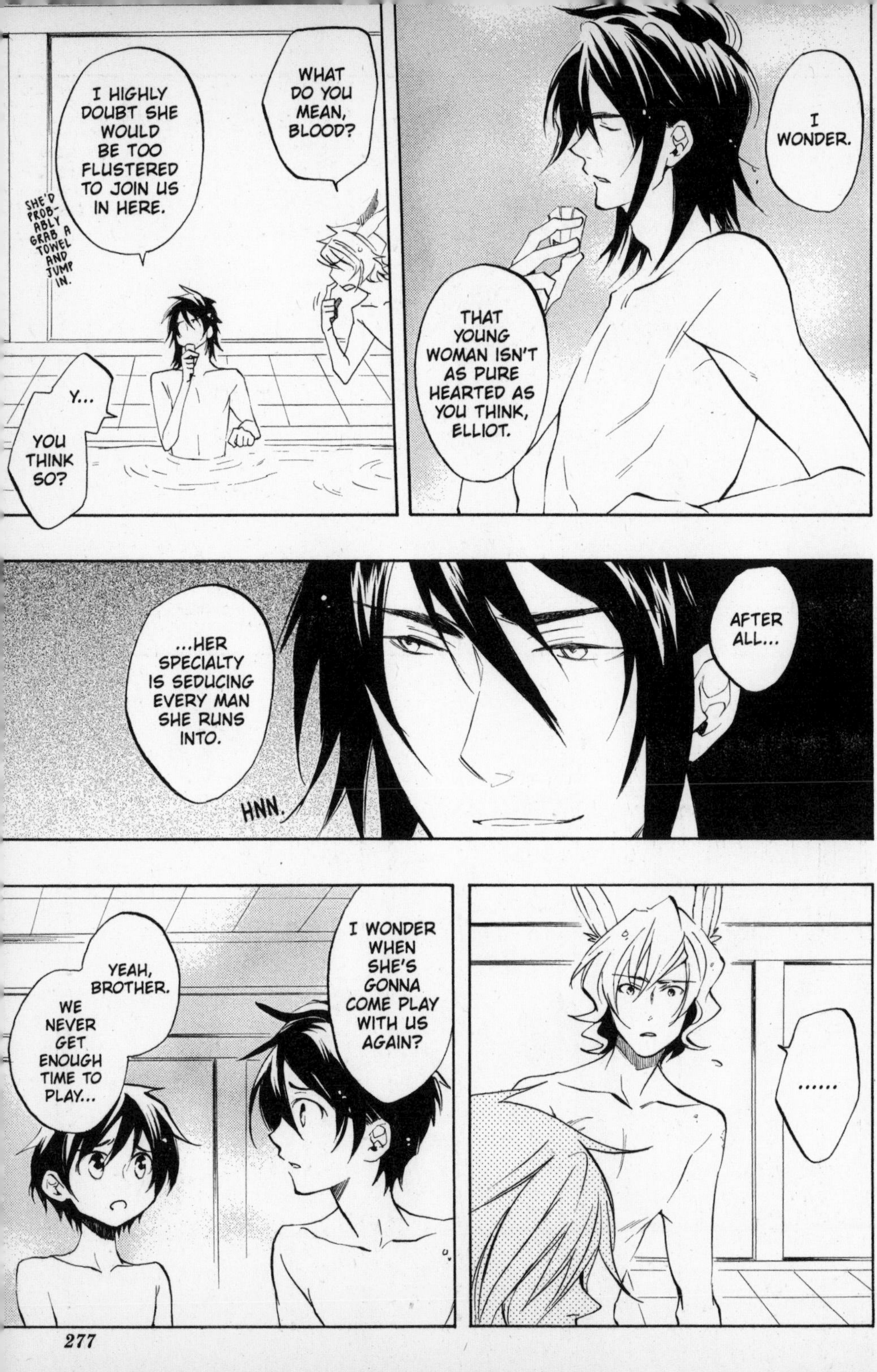
I WONDER.
THAT YOUNG WOMAN ISN'T AS PURE HEARTED AS YOU THINK, ELLIOT.
WHAT DO YOU MEAN, BLOOD?
I HIGHLY DOUBT SHE WOULD BE TOO FLUSTERED TO JOIN US IN HERE.
SHE'D PROBABLY GRAB A TOWEL AND JUMP IN.
Y...
YOU THINK SO?
AFTER ALL...
...HER SPECIALTY IS SEDUCING EVERY MAN SHE RUNS INTO.
HNN.
......
I WONDER WHEN SHE'S GONNA COME PLAY WITH US AGAIN?
YEAH, BROTHER.
WE NEVER GET ENOUGH TIME TO PLAY...

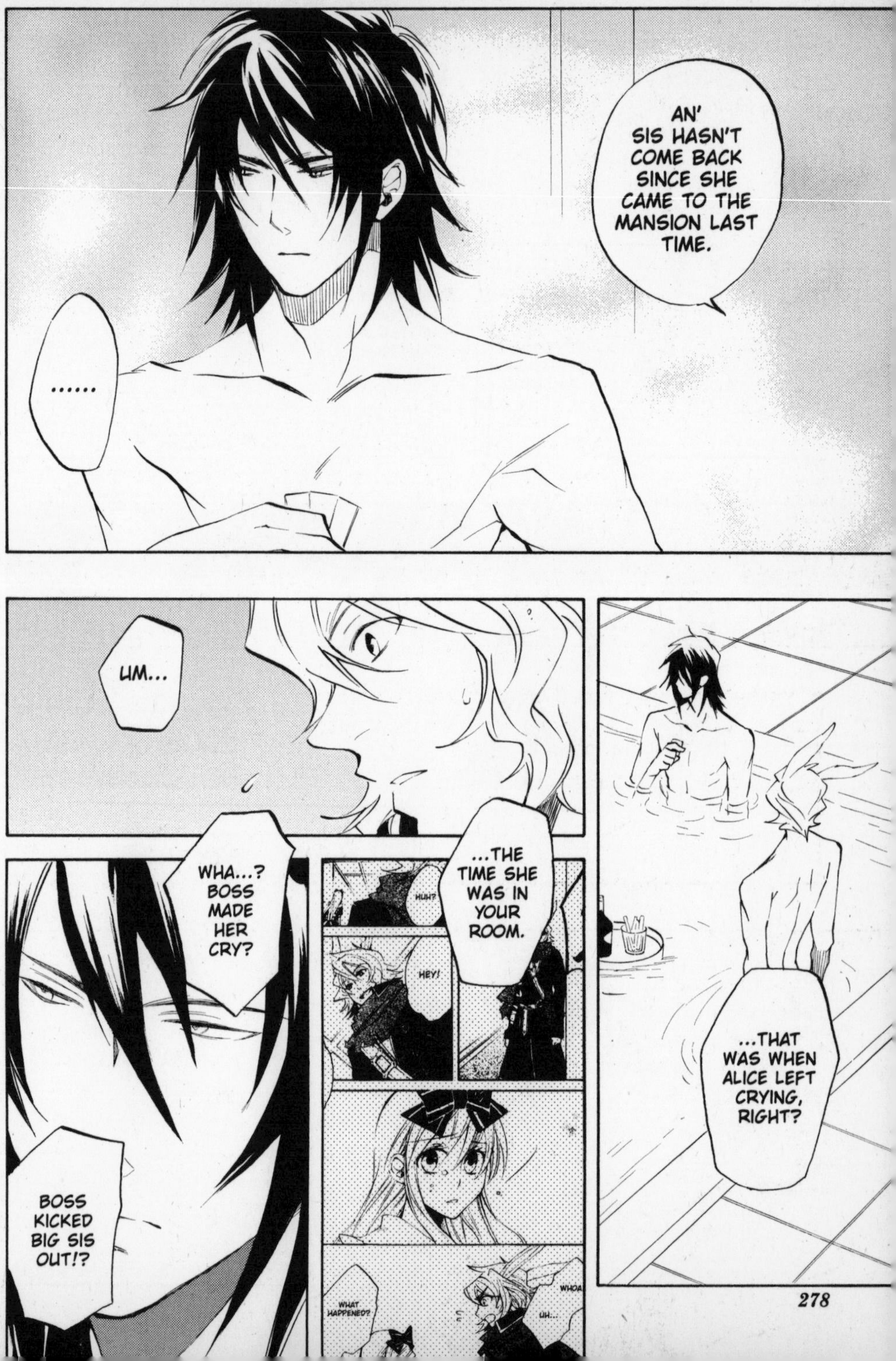
AN' SIS HASN'T COME BACK SINCE SHE CAME TO THE MANSION LAST TIME.
......
...THAT WAS WHEN ALICE LEFT CRYING, RIGHT?
UM...
...THE TIME SHE WAS IN YOUR ROOM.
HUH?
HEY!
WHOA
UH...
WHAT HAPPENED?
WHA...? BOSS MADE HER CRY?
BOSS KICKED BIG SIS OUT!?

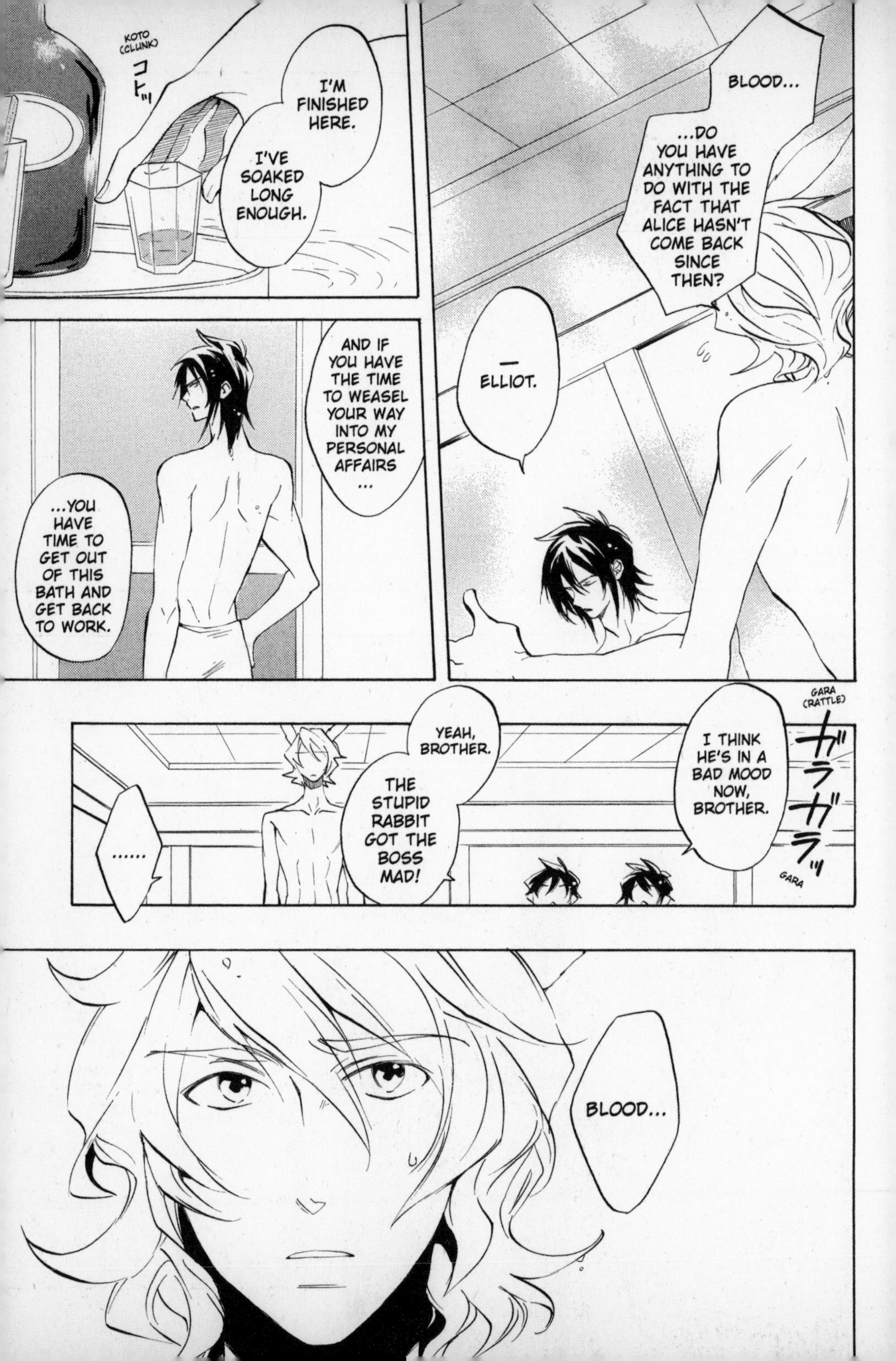
BLOOD...
...DO YOU HAVE ANYTHING TO DO WITH THE FACT THAT ALICE HASN'T COME BACK SINCE THEN?
—ELLIOT.
KOTO (CLUNK)
コトッ
I'M FINISHED HERE.
I'VE SOAKED LONG ENOUGH.
AND IF YOU HAVE THE TIME TO WEASEL YOUR WAY INTO MY PERSONAL AFFAIRS ...
...YOU HAVE TIME TO GET OUT OF THIS BATH AND GET BACK TO WORK.
GARA (RATTLE)
ガラガラッ
GARA
I THINK HE'S IN A BAD MOOD NOW, BROTHER.
YEAH, BROTHER.
THE STUPID RABBIT GOT THE BOSS MAD!
......
BLOOD...

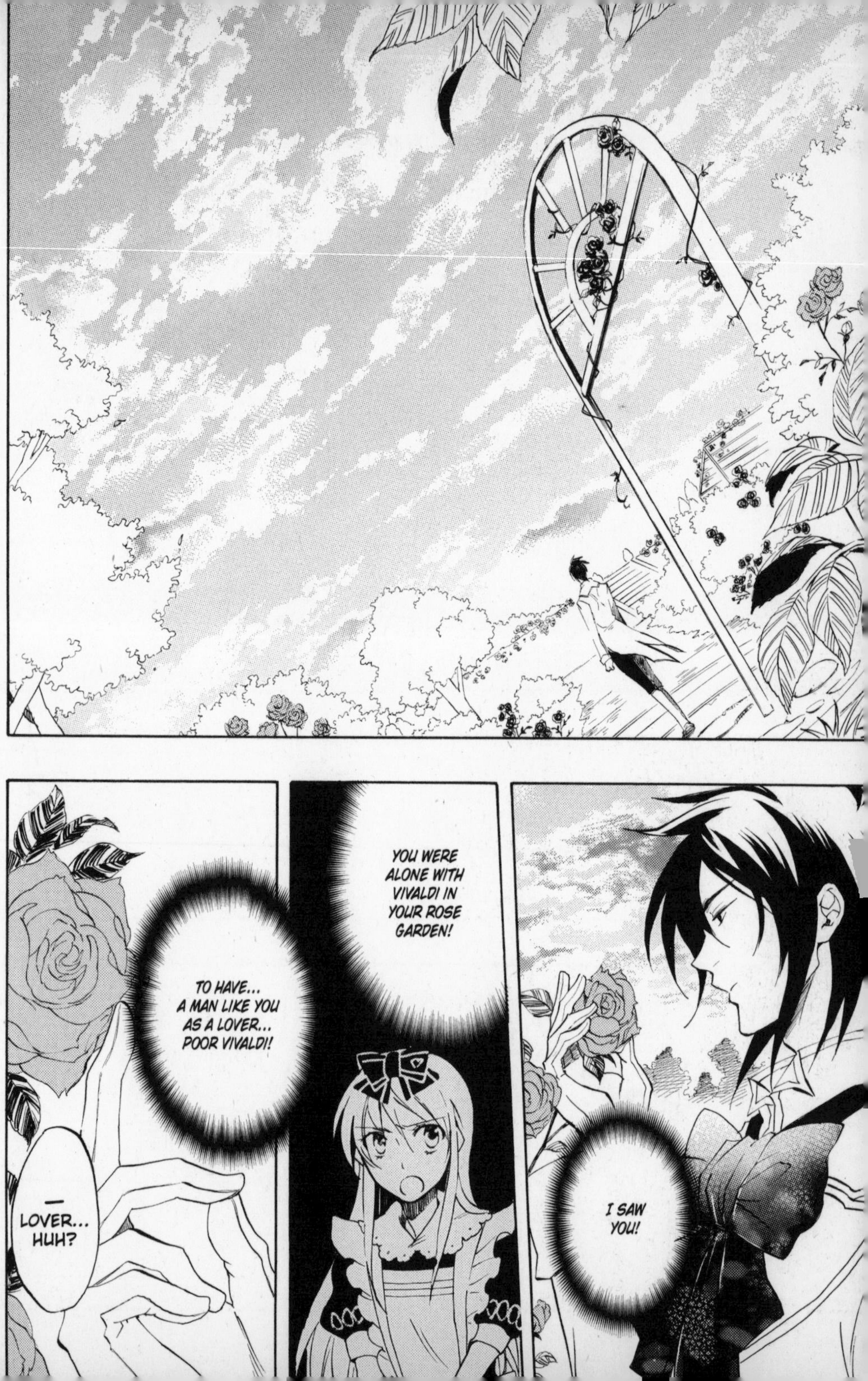
I SAW YOU!
YOU WERE ALONE WITH VIVALDI IN YOUR ROSE GARDEN!
TO HAVE... A MAN LIKE YOU AS A LOVER... POOR VIVALDI!
—LOVER... HUH?

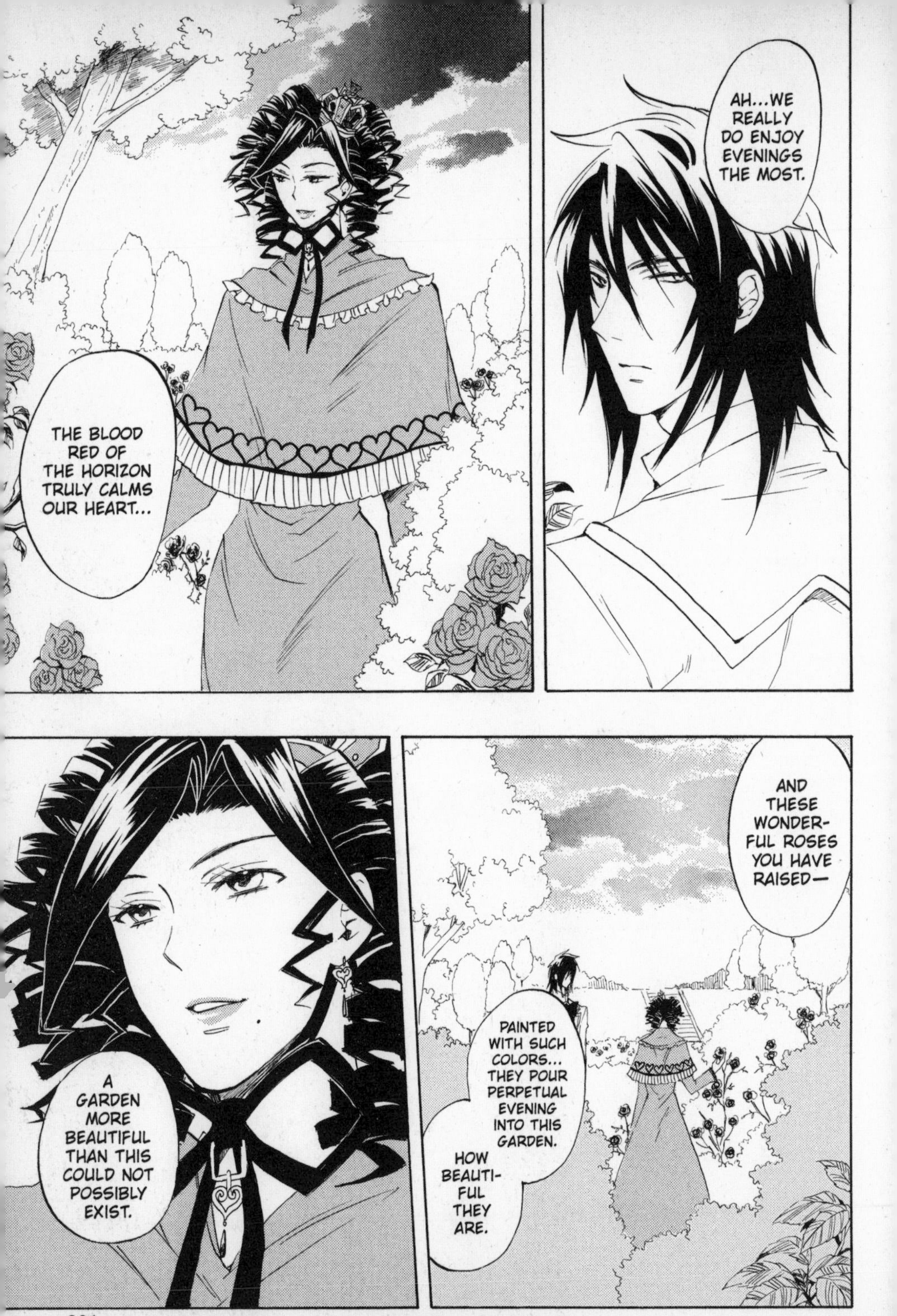
AH...WE REALLY DO ENJOY EVENINGS THE MOST.
THE BLOOD RED OF THE HORIZON TRULY CALMS OUR HEART...
AND THESE WONDER-FUL ROSES YOU HAVE RAISED—
PAINTED WITH SUCH COLORS... THEY POUR PERPETUAL EVENING INTO THIS GARDEN.
HOW BEAUTI-FUL THEY ARE.
A GARDEN MORE BEAUTIFUL THAN THIS COULD NOT POSSIBLY EXIST.

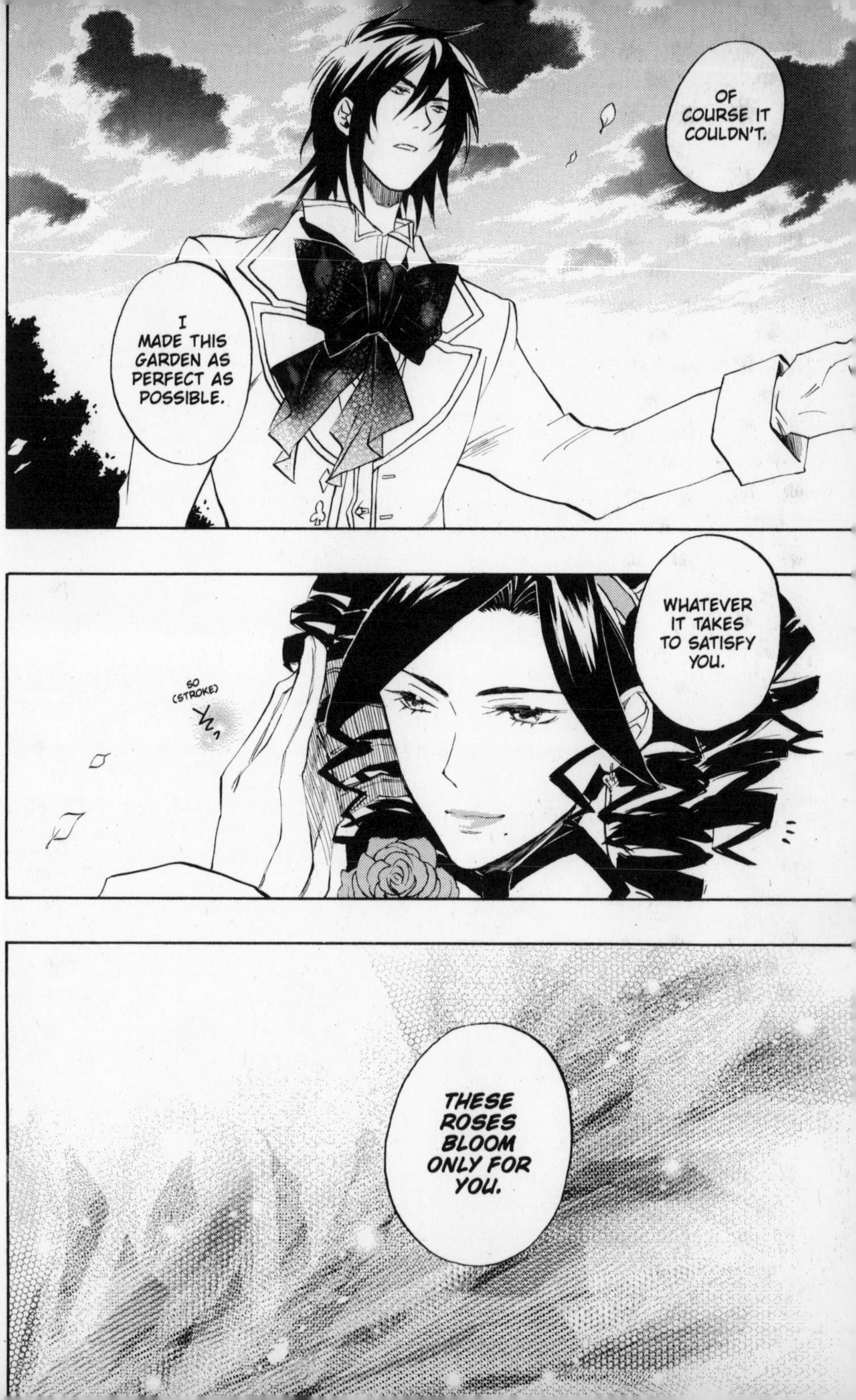
OF COURSE IT COULDN'T.
I MADE THIS GARDEN AS PERFECT AS POSSIBLE.
WHATEVER IT TAKES TO SATISFY YOU.
SO (STROKE)
THESE ROSES BLOOM ONLY FOR YOU.

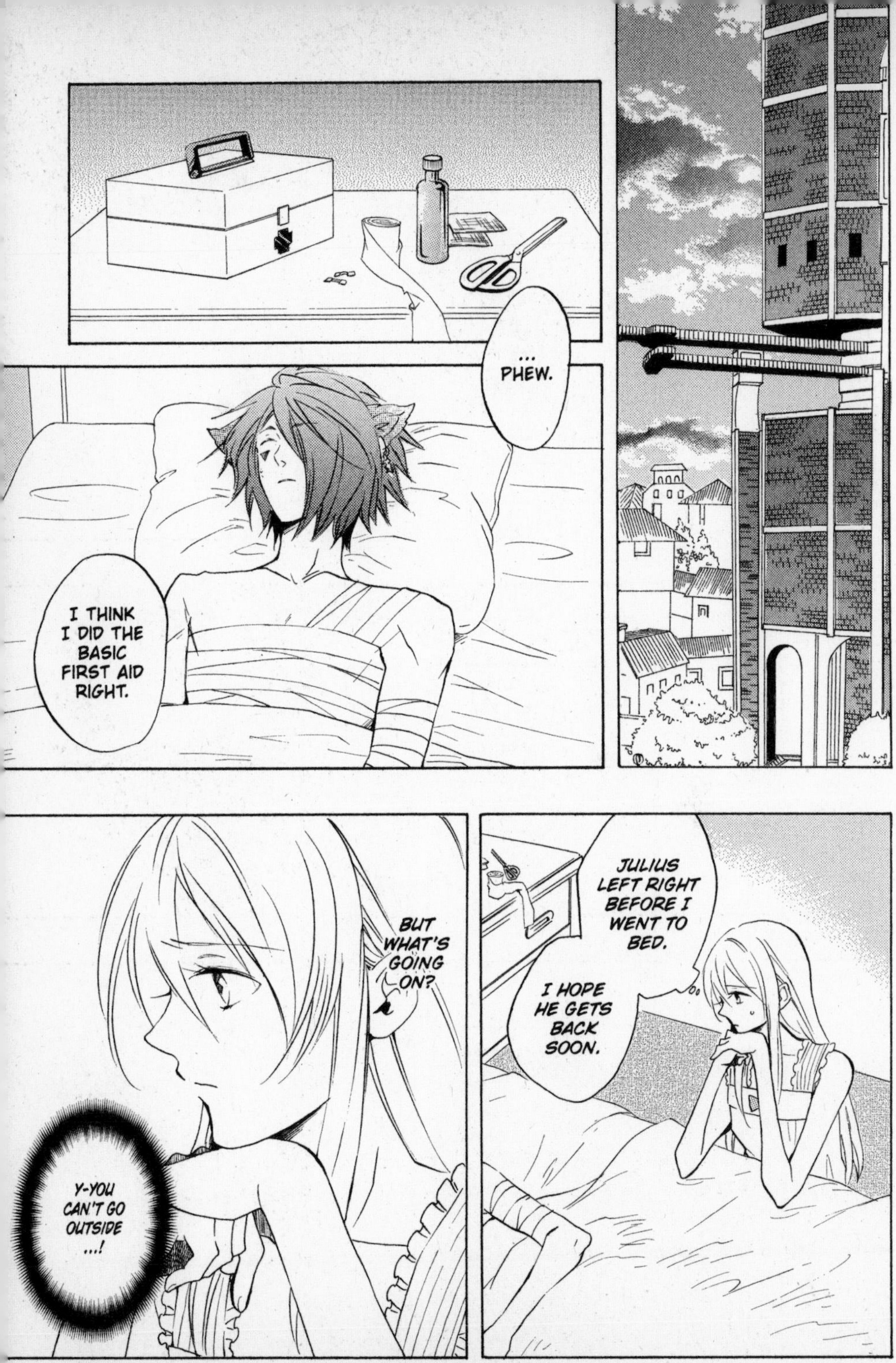
...PHEW.
I THINK I DID THE BASIC FIRST AID RIGHT.
JULIUS LEFT RIGHT BEFORE I WENT TO BED.
I HOPE HE GETS BACK SOON.
BUT WHAT'S GOING ON?
Y-YOU CAN'T GO OUTSIDE ...!

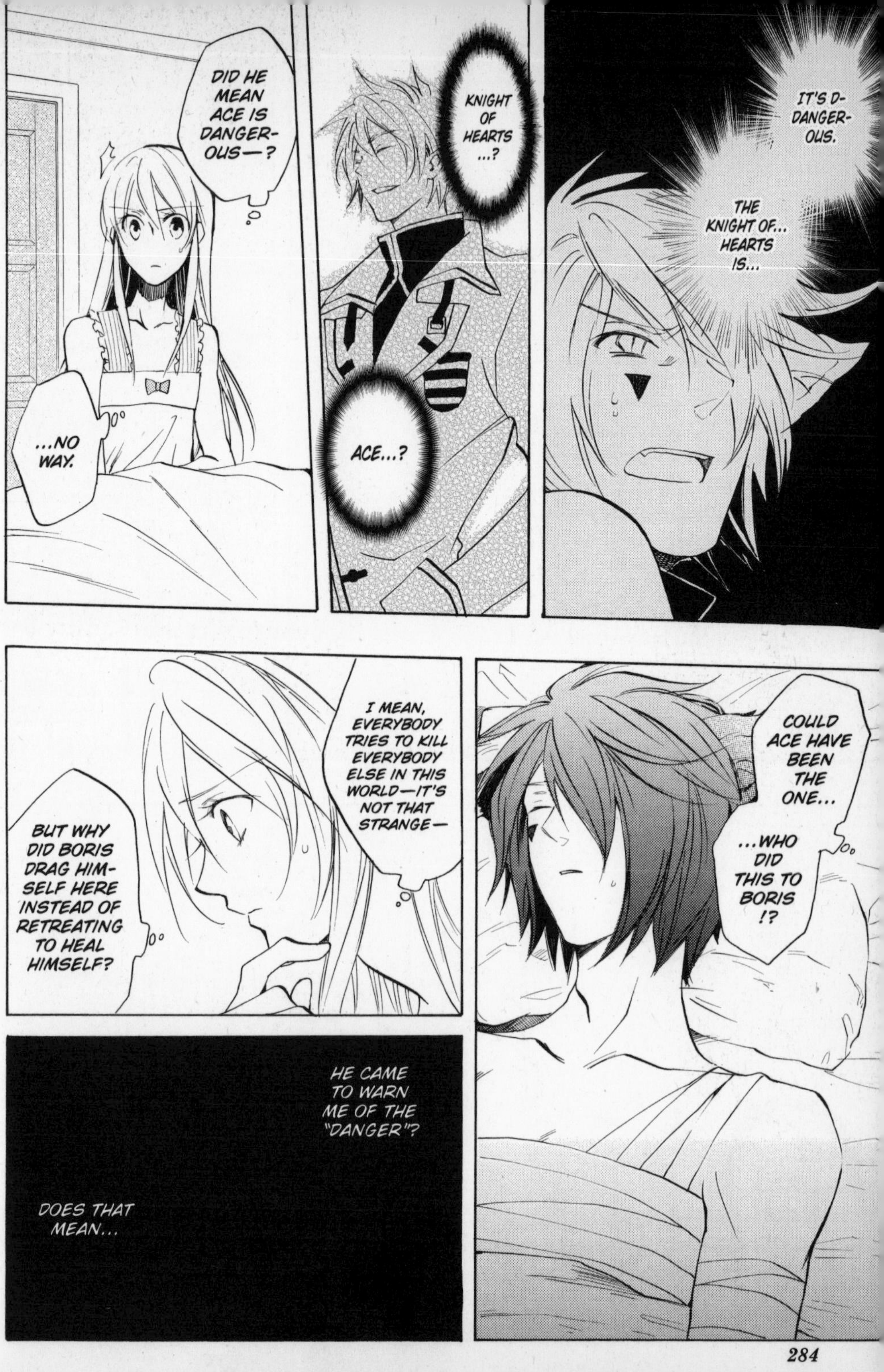
IT'S D-DANGEROUS.
THE KNIGHT OF... HEARTS IS...
KNIGHT OF HEARTS ...?
ACE...?
DID HE MEAN ACE IS DANGEROUS—?
...NO WAY.
COULD ACE HAVE BEEN THE ONE...
...WHO DID THIS TO BORIS !?
I MEAN, EVERYBODY TRIES TO KILL EVERYBODY ELSE IN THIS WORLD—IT'S NOT THAT STRANGE—
BUT WHY DID BORIS DRAG HIMSELF HERE INSTEAD OF RETREATING TO HEAL HIMSELF?
HE CAME TO WARN ME OF THE "DANGER"?
DOES THAT MEAN...

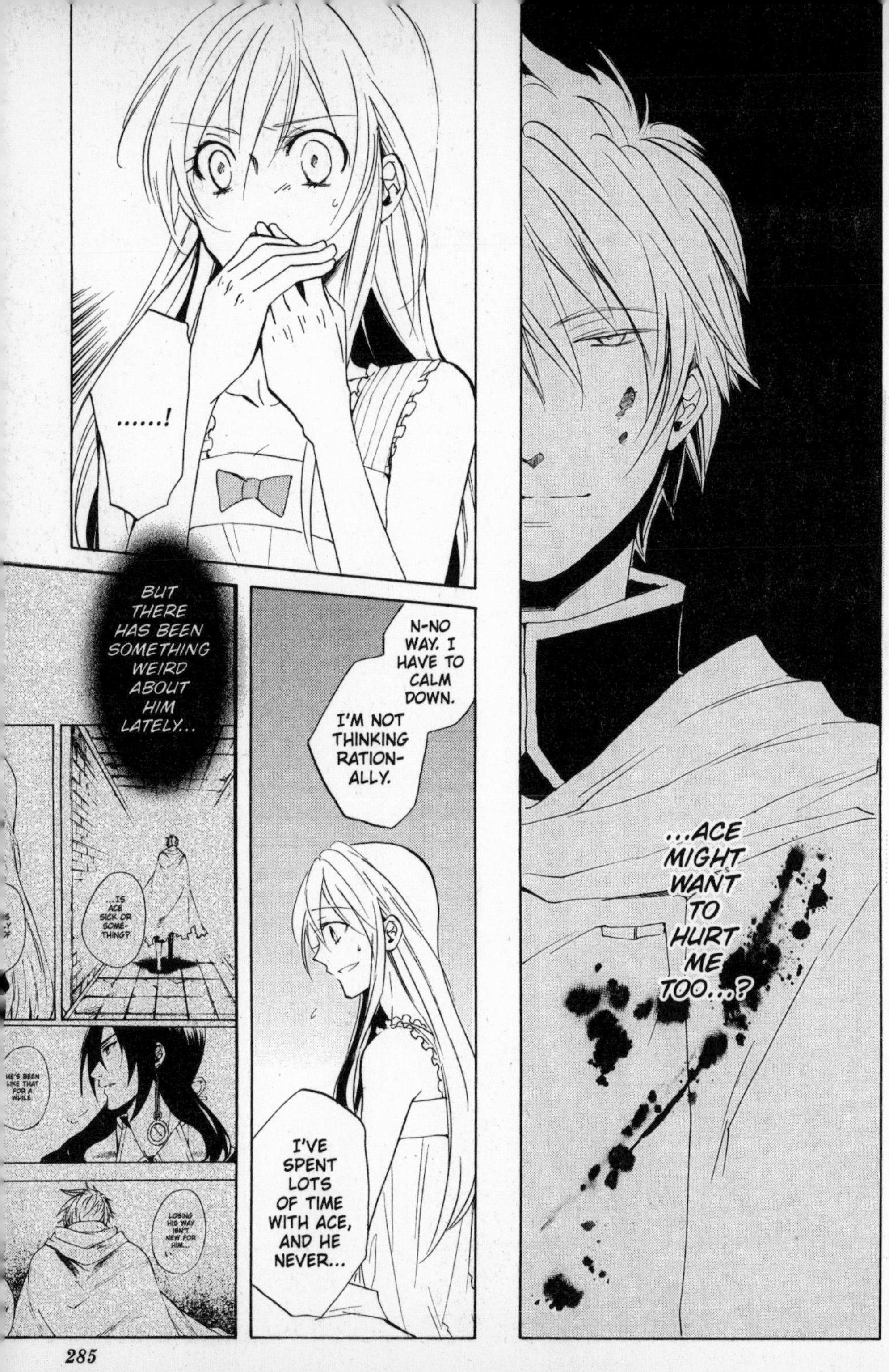

...ACE MIGHT WANT TO HURT ME TOO...?
......!
N-NO WAY. I HAVE TO CALM DOWN.
I'M NOT THINKING RATION-ALLY.
I'VE SPENT LOTS OF TIME WITH ACE, AND HE NEVER...
BUT THERE HAS BEEN SOMETHING WEIRD ABOUT HIM LATELY...
...IS ACE SICK OR SOME-THING?
HE'S BEEN LIKE THAT FOR A WHILE.
LOSING HIS WAY ISN'T NEW FOR HIM...

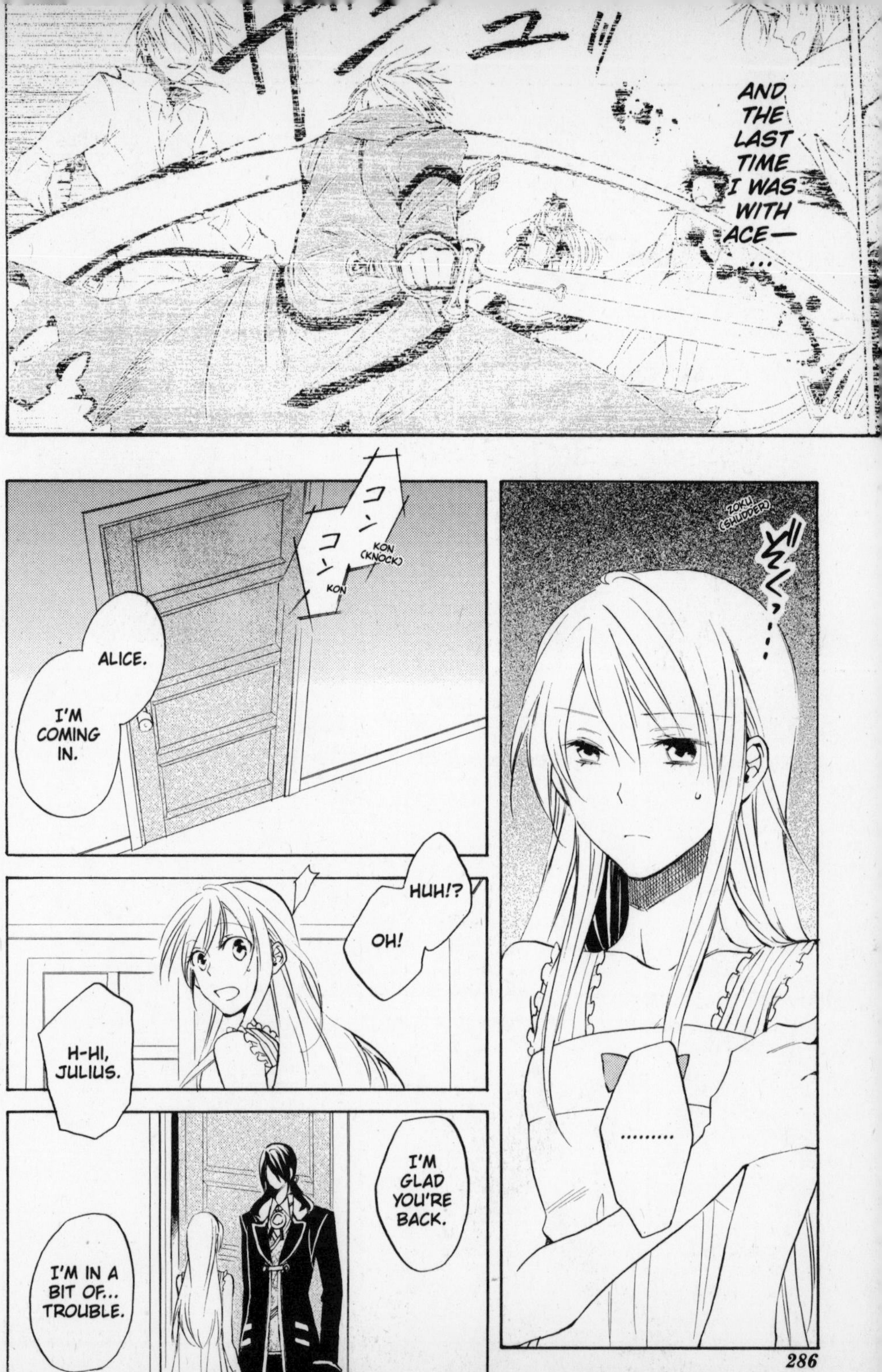
AND THE LAST TIME I WAS WITH ACE—...
ZOKU (SHUDDER)
....
コン
コン
KON (KNOCK)
KON
ALICE.
I'M COMING IN.
HUH!?
OH!
H-HI, JULIUS.
I'M GLAD YOU'RE BACK.
I'M IN A BIT OF... TROUBLE.

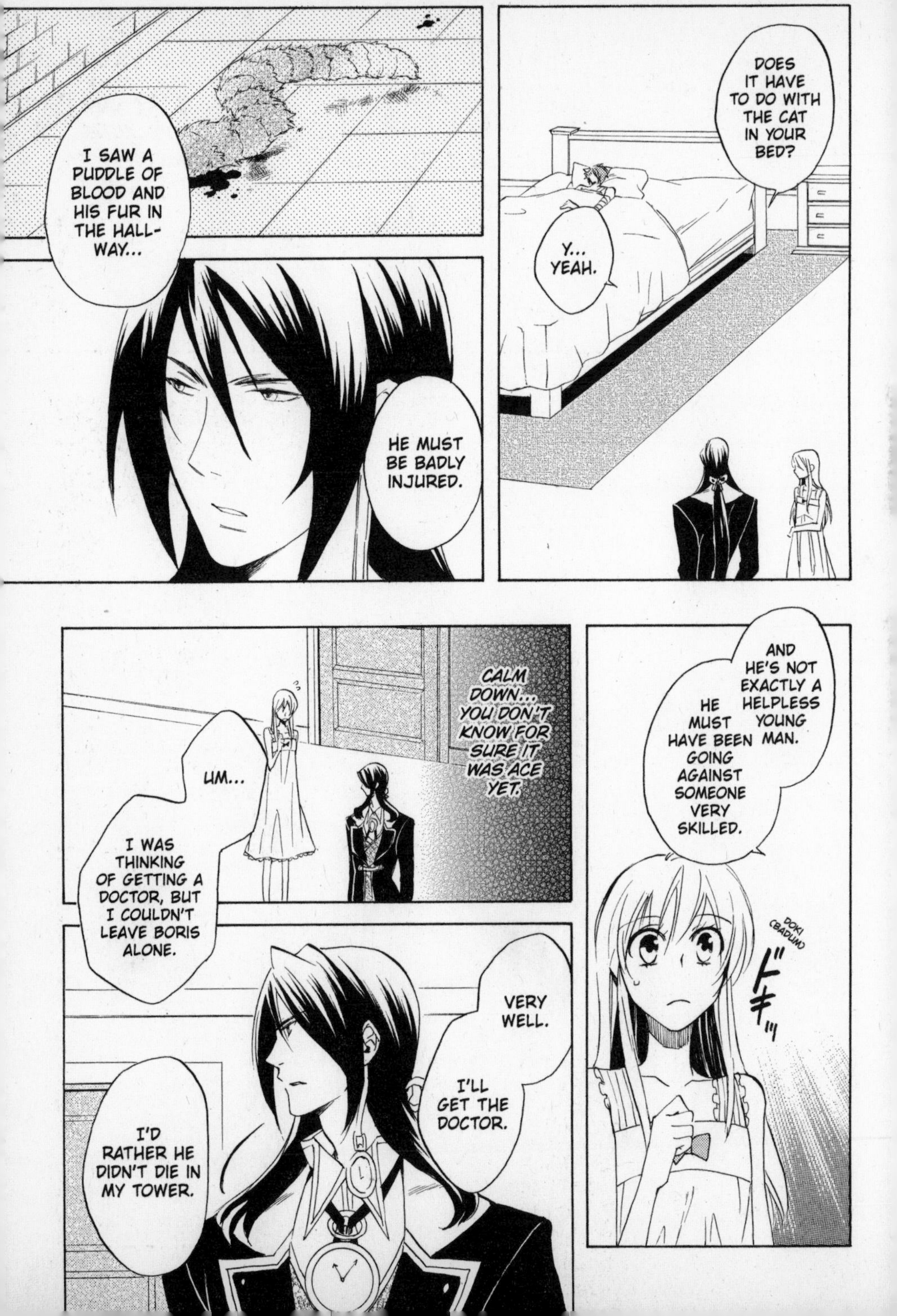
DOES IT HAVE TO DO WITH THE CAT IN YOUR BED?
Y... YEAH.
I SAW A PUDDLE OF BLOOD AND HIS FUR IN THE HALL-WAY...
HE MUST BE BADLY INJURED.
AND HE'S NOT EXACTLY A HELPLESS YOUNG MAN.
HE MUST HAVE BEEN GOING AGAINST SOMEONE VERY SKILLED.
DOKI (BADUM)
CALM DOWN... YOU DON'T KNOW FOR SURE IT WAS ACE YET.
UM...
I WAS THINKING OF GETTING A DOCTOR, BUT I COULDN'T LEAVE BORIS ALONE.
VERY WELL.
I'LL GET THE DOCTOR.
I'D RATHER HE DIDN'T DIE IN MY TOWER.

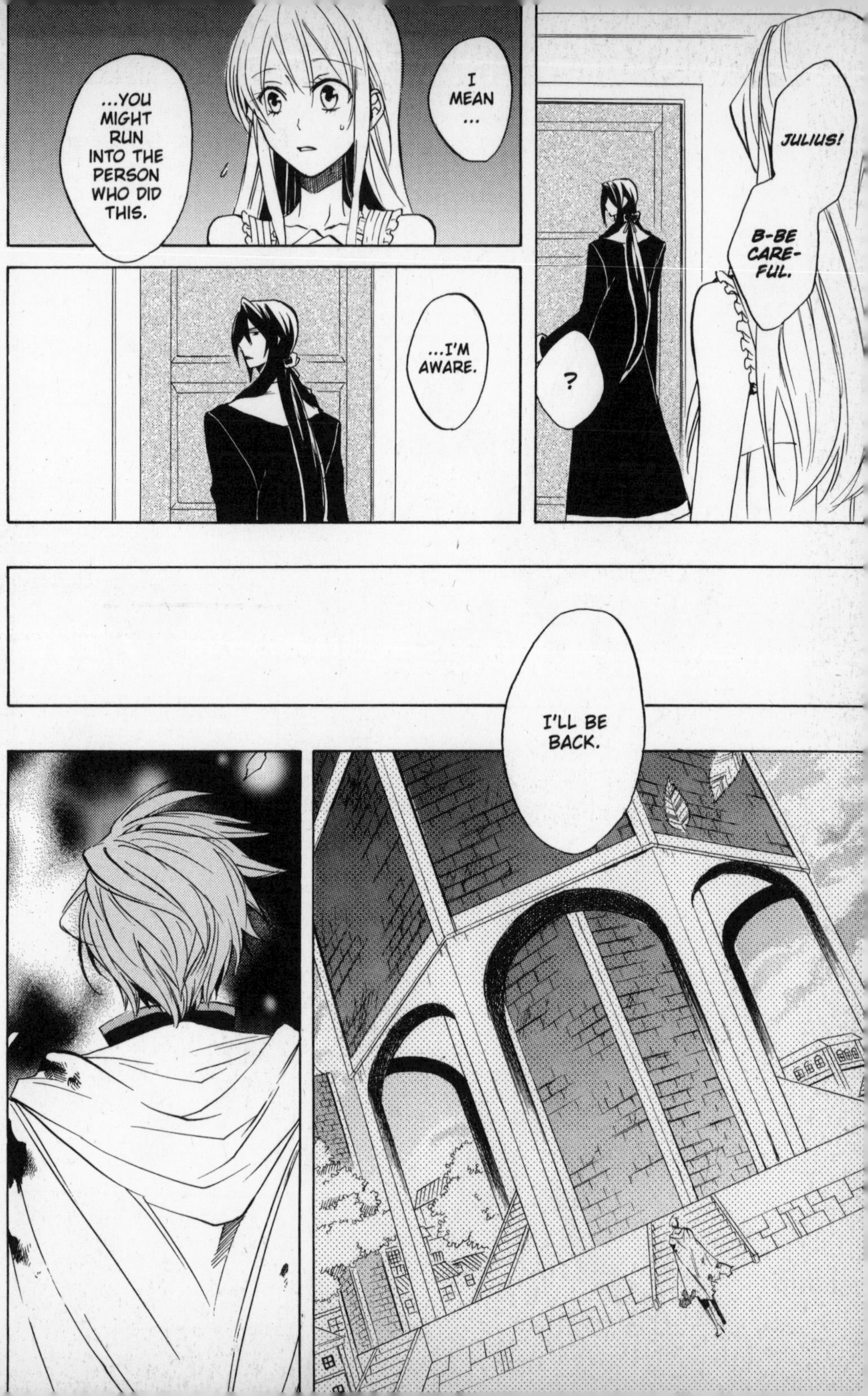
JULIUS!
B-BE CARE-FUL.
?
I MEAN …
…YOU MIGHT RUN INTO THE PERSON WHO DID THIS.
…I'M AWARE.
I'LL BE BACK.

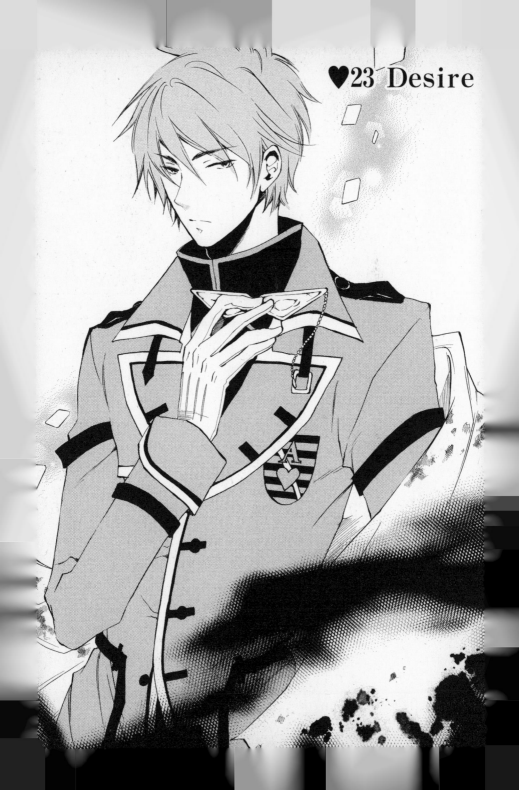

♥23 Desire

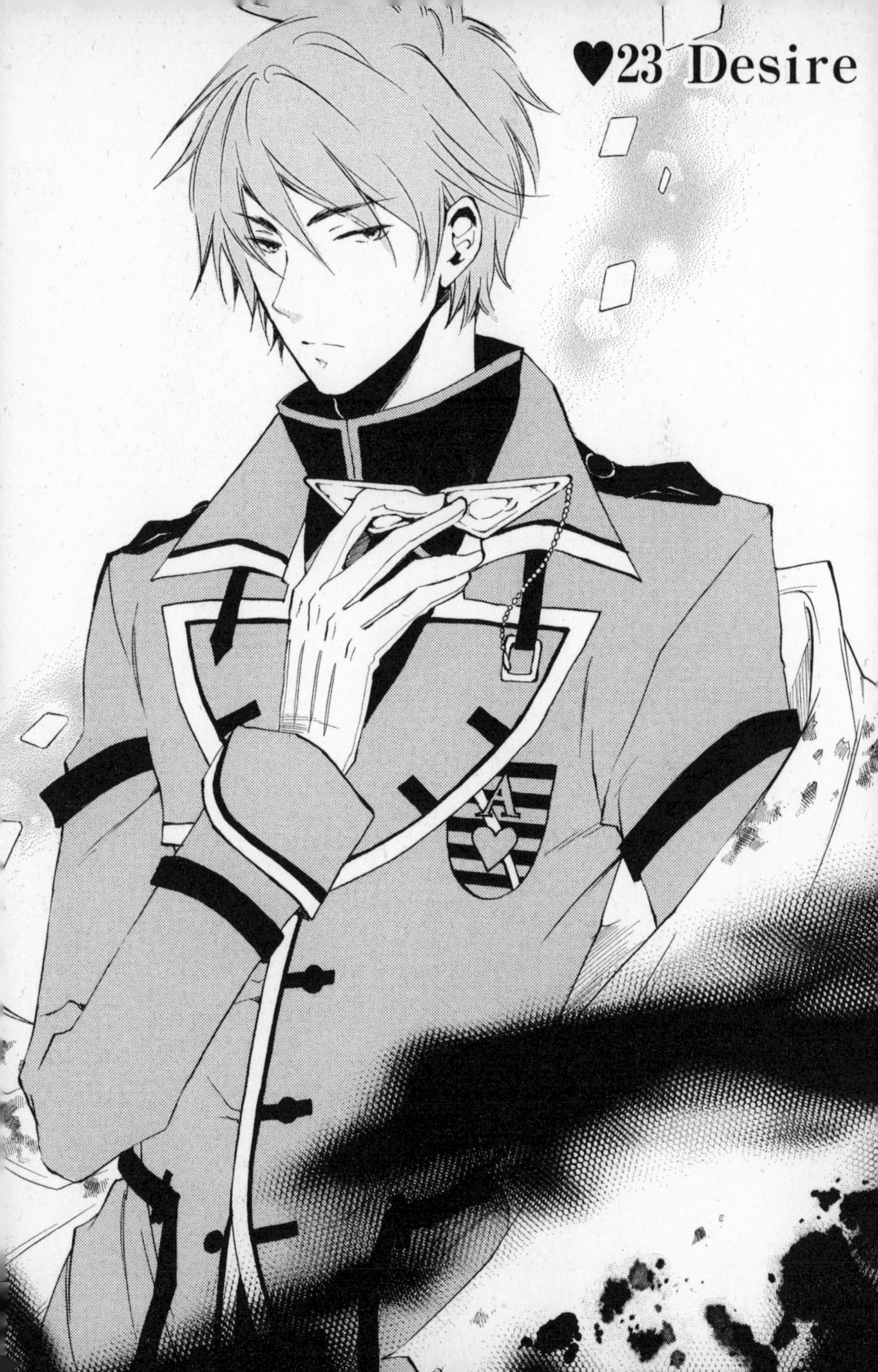

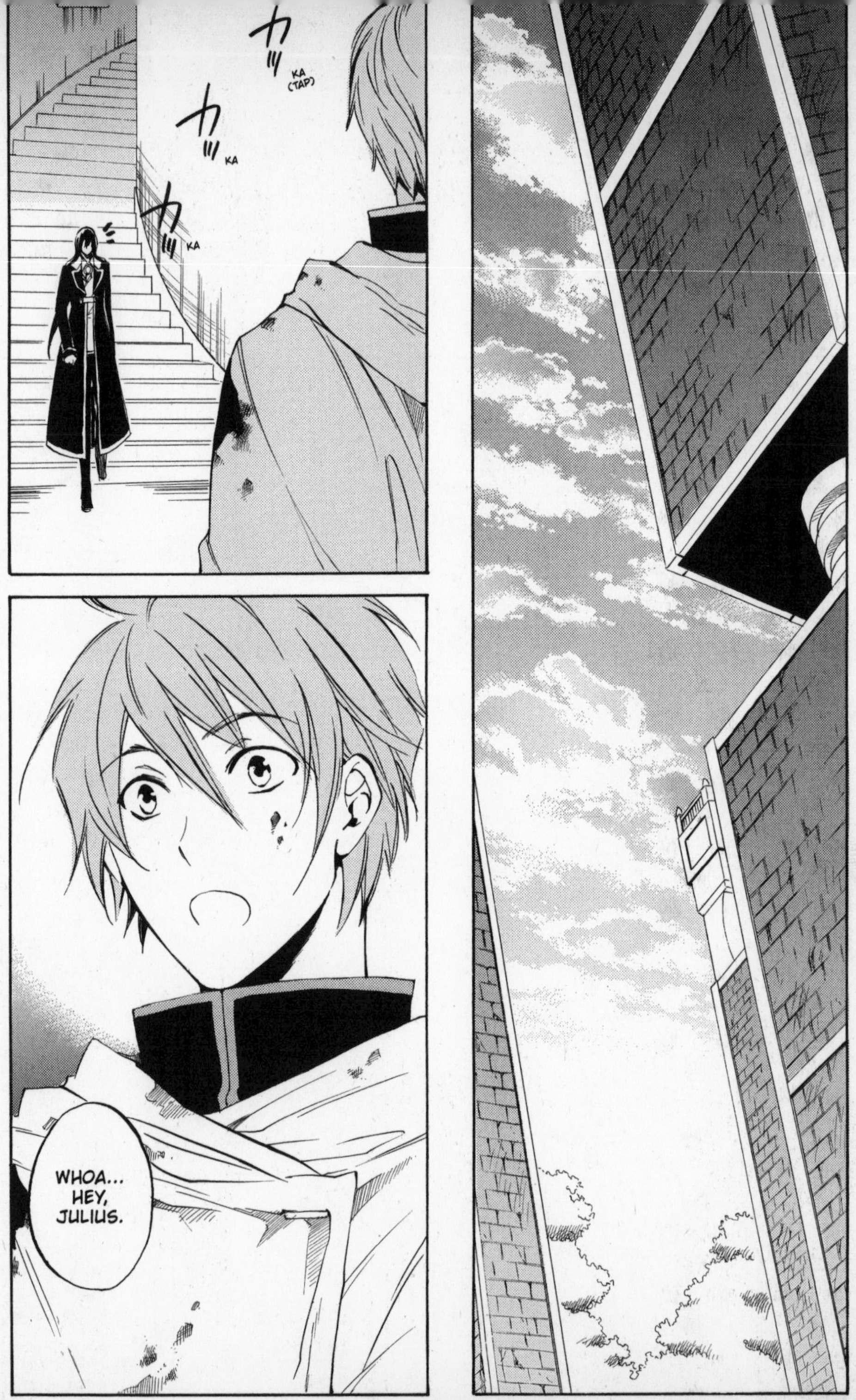
カッ
KA (TAP)
カッ
KA
カッ
KA
WHOA... HEY, JULIUS.

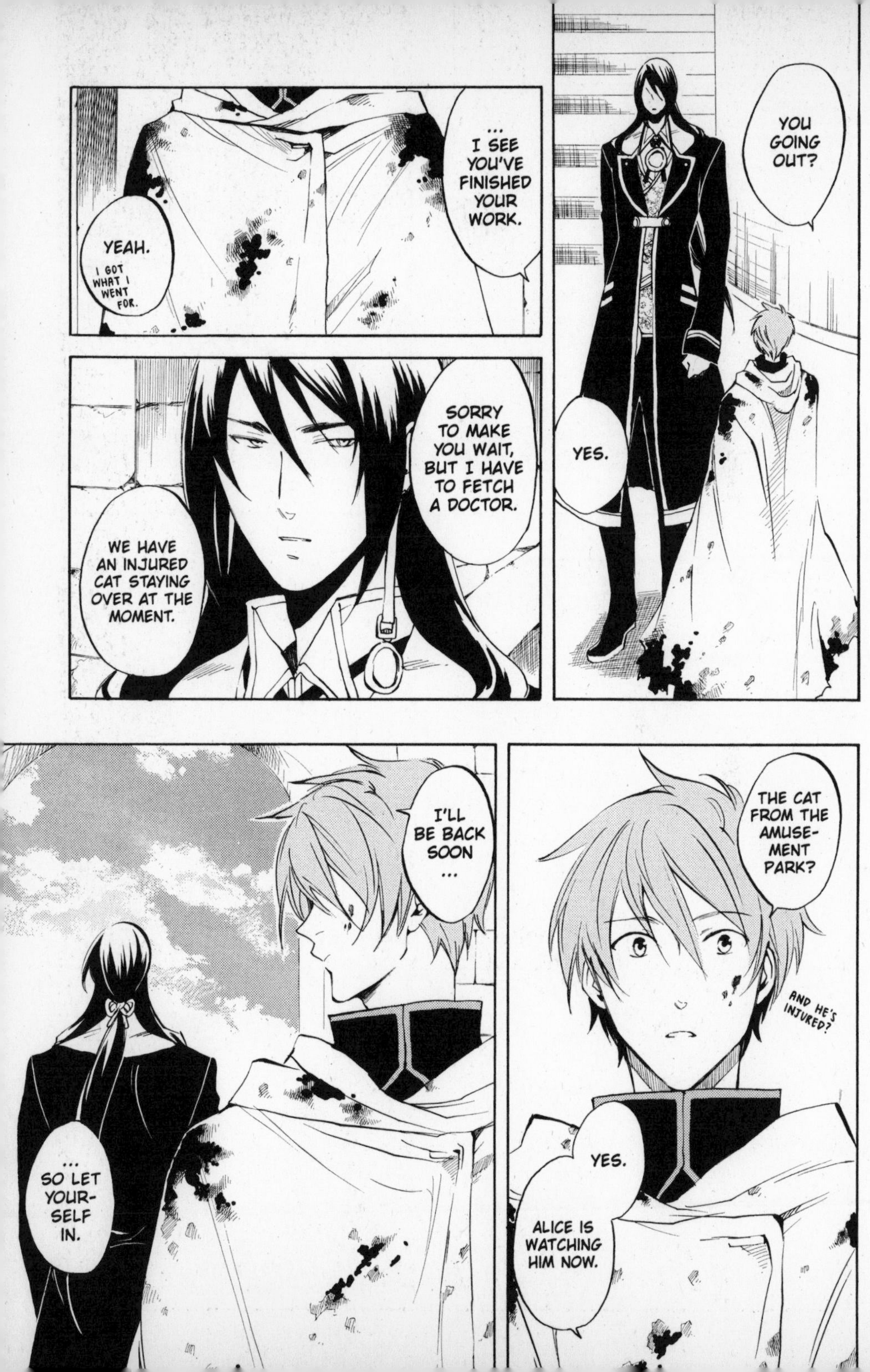
YOU GOING OUT?
YES.
... I SEE YOU'VE FINISHED YOUR WORK.
YEAH.
I GOT WHAT I WENT FOR.
SORRY TO MAKE YOU WAIT, BUT I HAVE TO FETCH A DOCTOR.
WE HAVE AN INJURED CAT STAYING OVER AT THE MOMENT.
THE CAT FROM THE AMUSE-MENT PARK?
AND HE'S INJURED?
YES.
ALICE IS WATCHING HIM NOW.
I'LL BE BACK SOON ...
... SO LET YOUR-SELF IN.

DON'T
MIND IF
I DO.

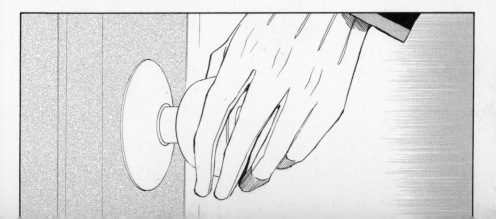

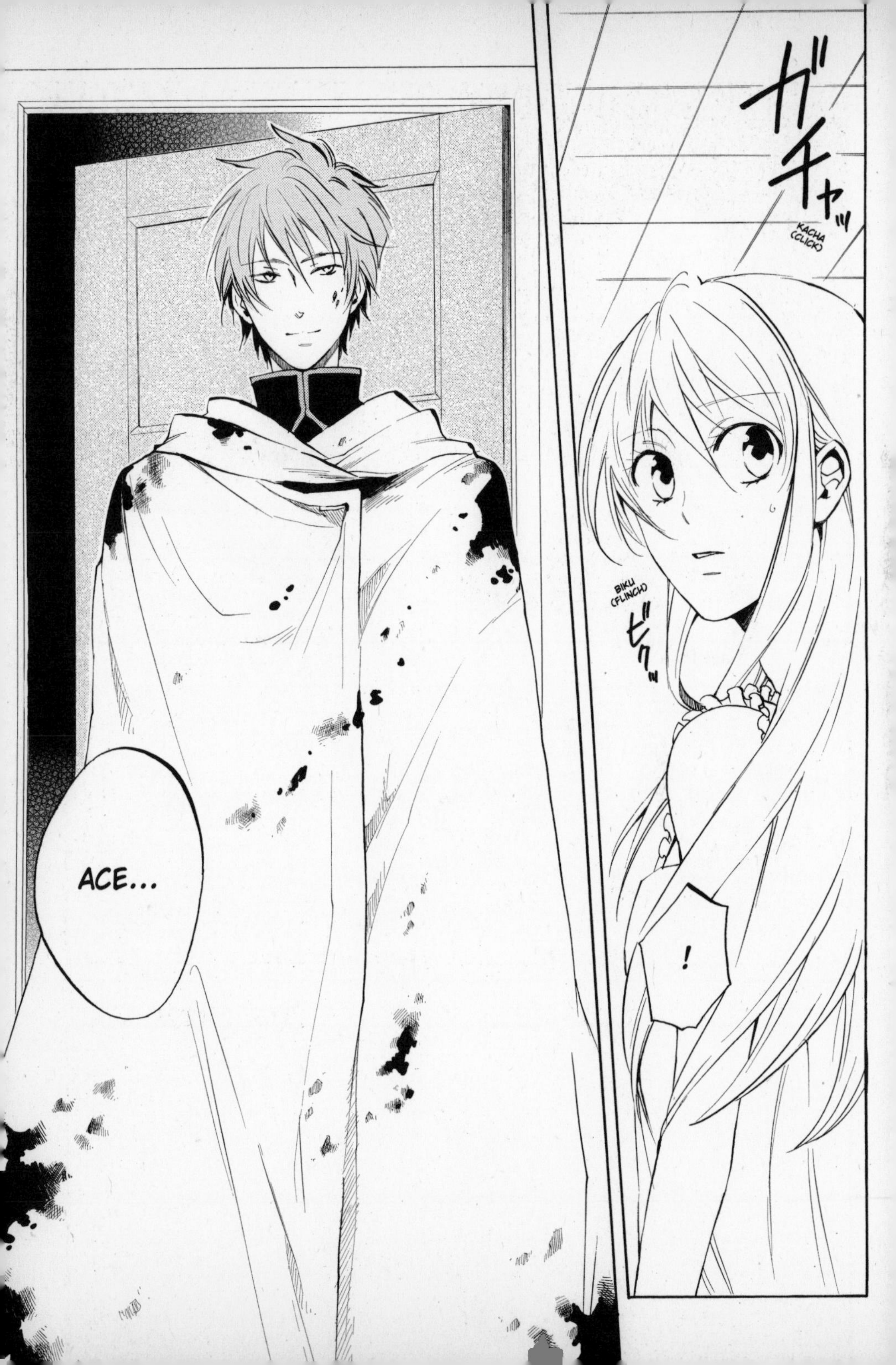
ガチャッ
KACHA (CLICK)
BIKU (FLINCH)
ビクッ
!
ACE...

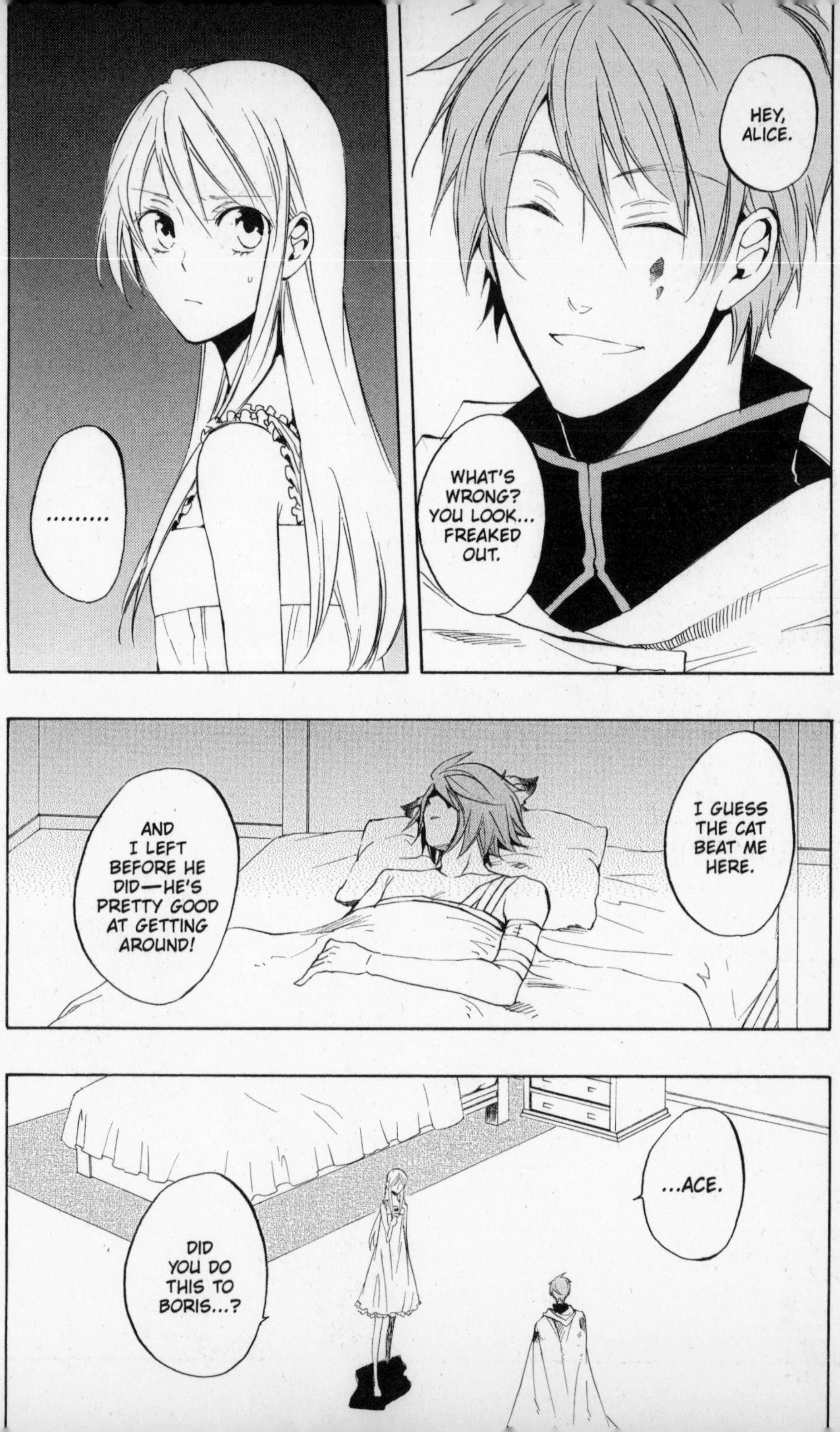
HEY, ALICE.
WHAT'S WRONG? YOU LOOK... FREAKED OUT.
....
I GUESS THE CAT BEAT ME HERE.
AND I LEFT BEFORE HE DID—HE'S PRETTY GOOD AT GETTING AROUND!
...ACE.
DID YOU DO THIS TO BORIS...?

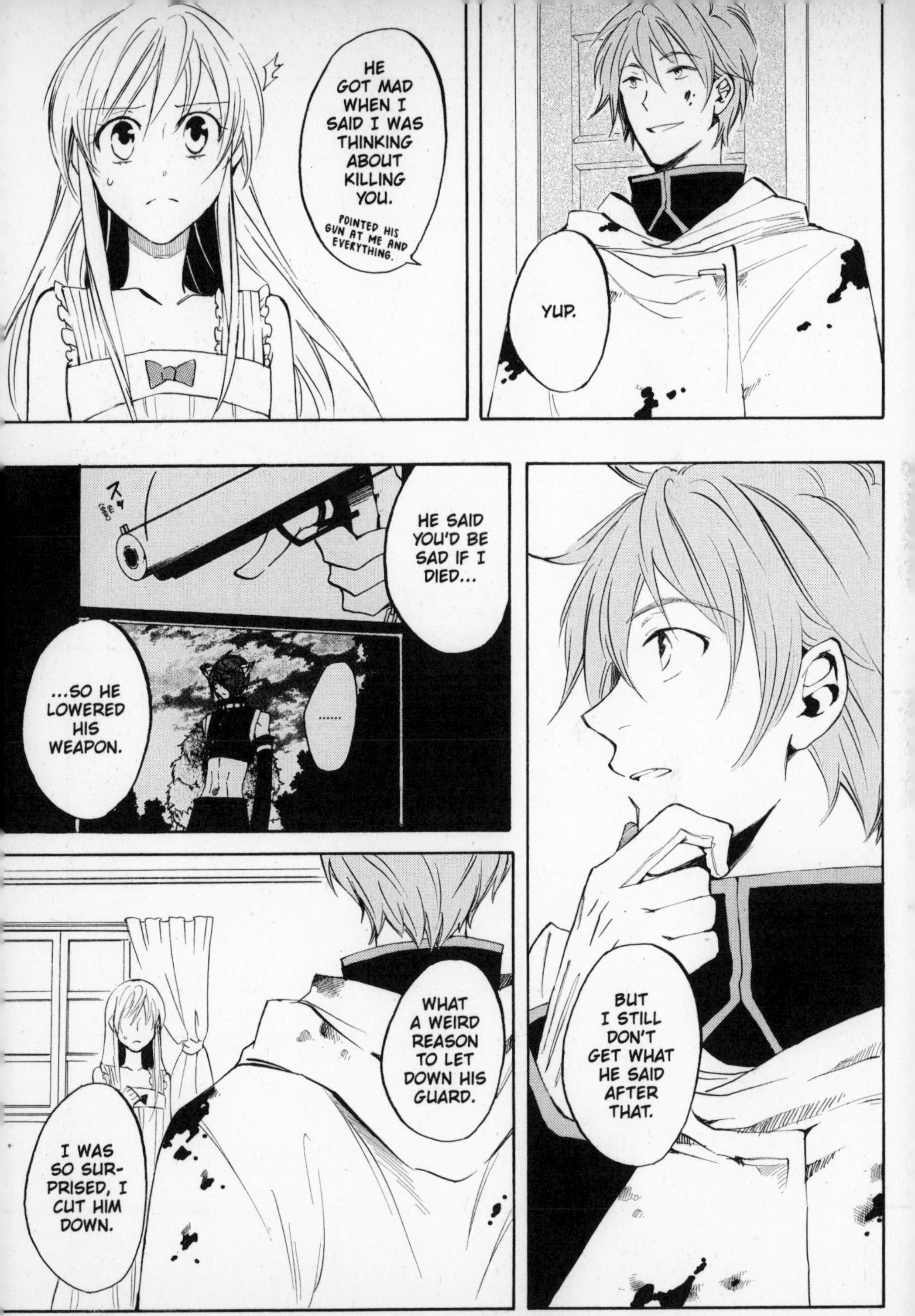
YUP.
HE GOT MAD WHEN I SAID I WAS THINKING ABOUT KILLING YOU.
POINTED HIS GUN AT ME AND EVERYTHING.
BUT I STILL DON'T GET WHAT HE SAID AFTER THAT.
HE SAID YOU'D BE SAD IF I DIED...
......
...SO HE LOWERED HIS WEAPON.
WHAT A WEIRD REASON TO LET DOWN HIS GUARD.
I WAS SO SURPRISED, I CUT HIM DOWN.

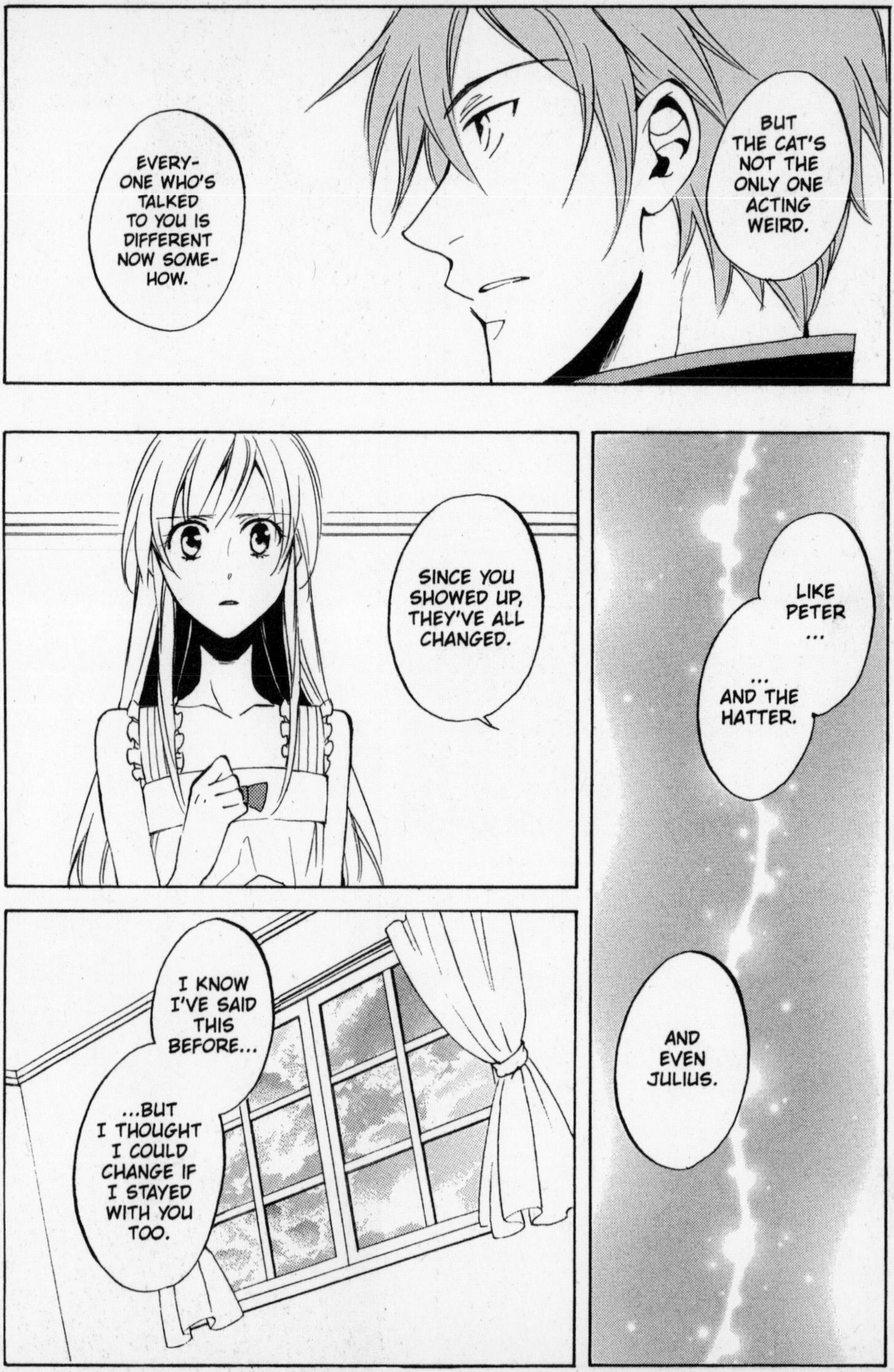
BUT THE CAT'S NOT THE ONLY ONE ACTING WEIRD.
EVERY-ONE WHO'S TALKED TO YOU IS DIFFERENT NOW SOME-HOW.
LIKE PETER...
...AND THE HATTER.
AND EVEN JULIUS.
SINCE YOU SHOWED UP, THEY'VE ALL CHANGED.
I KNOW I'VE SAID THIS BEFORE...
...BUT I THOUGHT I COULD CHANGE IF I STAYED WITH YOU TOO.

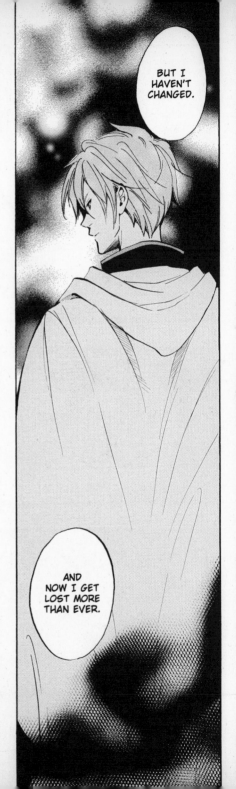

BUT I HAVEN'T CHANGED.

AND NOW I GET LOST MORE THAN EVER.

ALICE.

ACE...

DO YOU THINK I CAN CHANGE LIKE EVERYBODY ELSE?

DO... DO YOU WANT TO CHANGE?

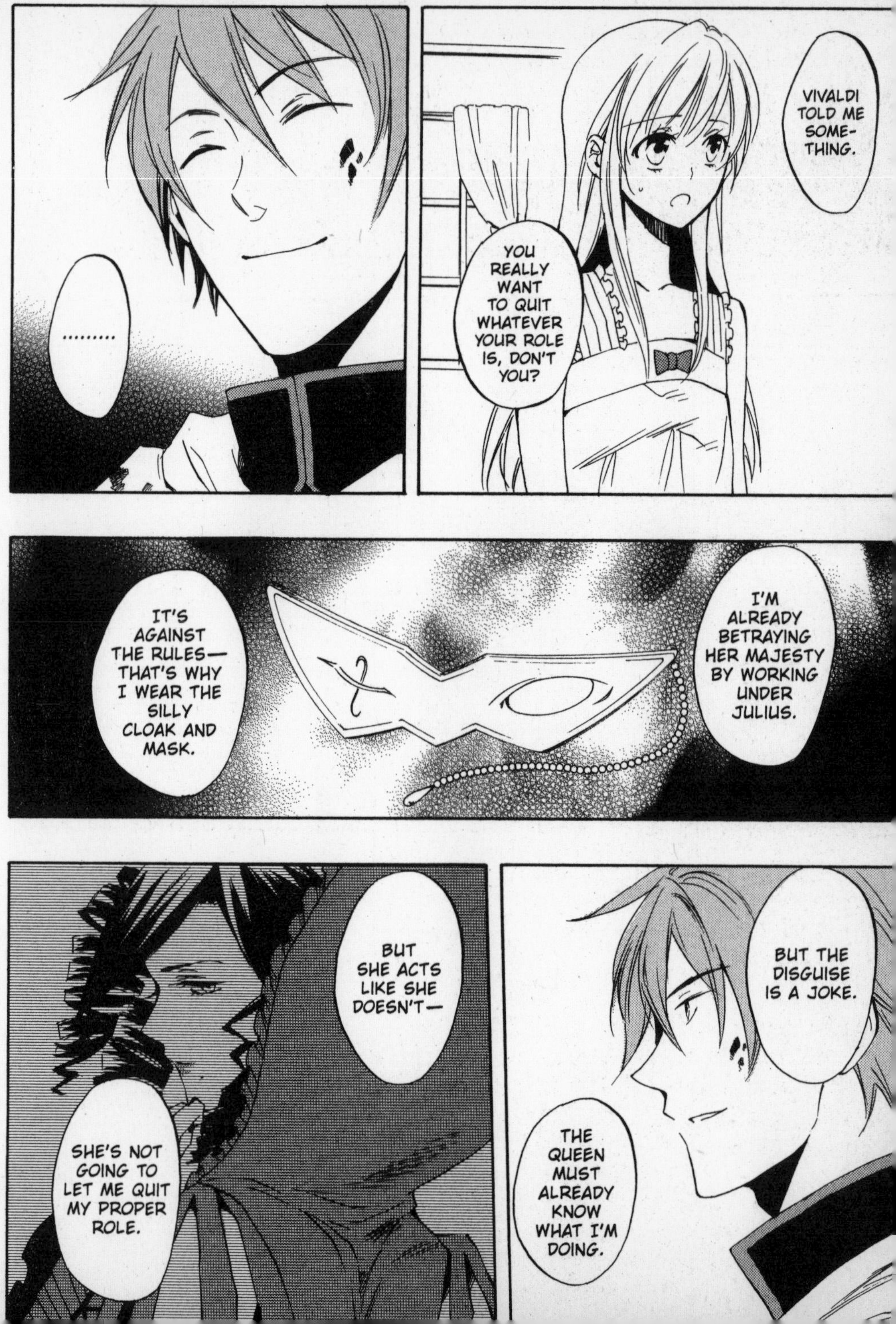
VIVALDI TOLD ME SOME-THING.
YOU REALLY WANT TO QUIT WHATEVER YOUR ROLE IS, DON'T YOU?
....
I'M ALREADY BETRAYING HER MAJESTY BY WORKING UNDER JULIUS.
IT'S AGAINST THE RULES— THAT'S WHY I WEAR THE SILLY CLOAK AND MASK.
BUT THE DISGUISE IS A JOKE.
THE QUEEN MUST ALREADY KNOW WHAT I'M DOING.
BUT SHE ACTS LIKE SHE DOESN'T—
SHE'S NOT GOING TO LET ME QUIT MY PROPER ROLE.

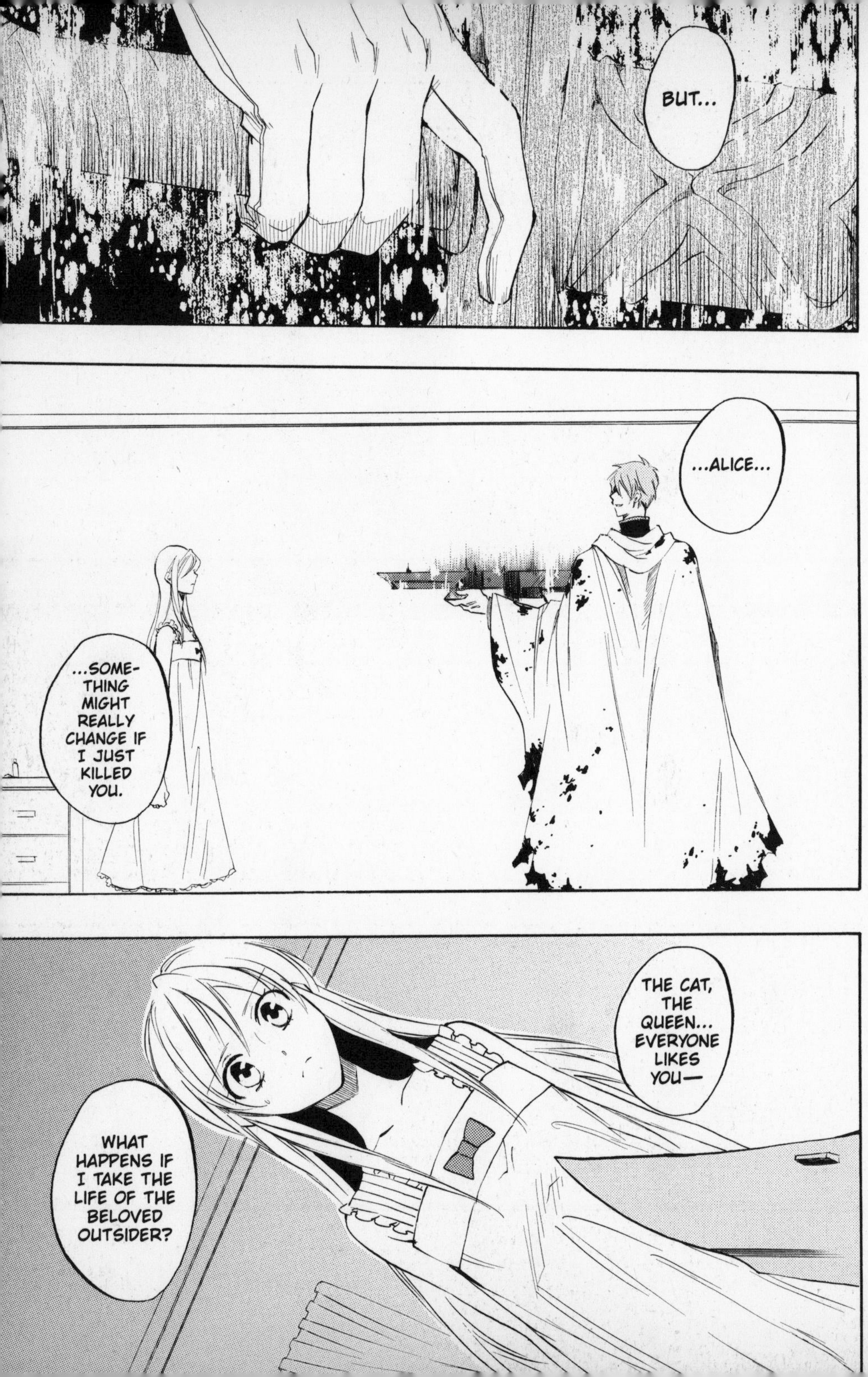
BUT...
...ALICE...
...SOME-THING MIGHT REALLY CHANGE IF I JUST KILLED YOU.
THE CAT, THE QUEEN... EVERYONE LIKES YOU—
WHAT HAPPENS IF I TAKE THE LIFE OF THE BELOVED OUTSIDER?

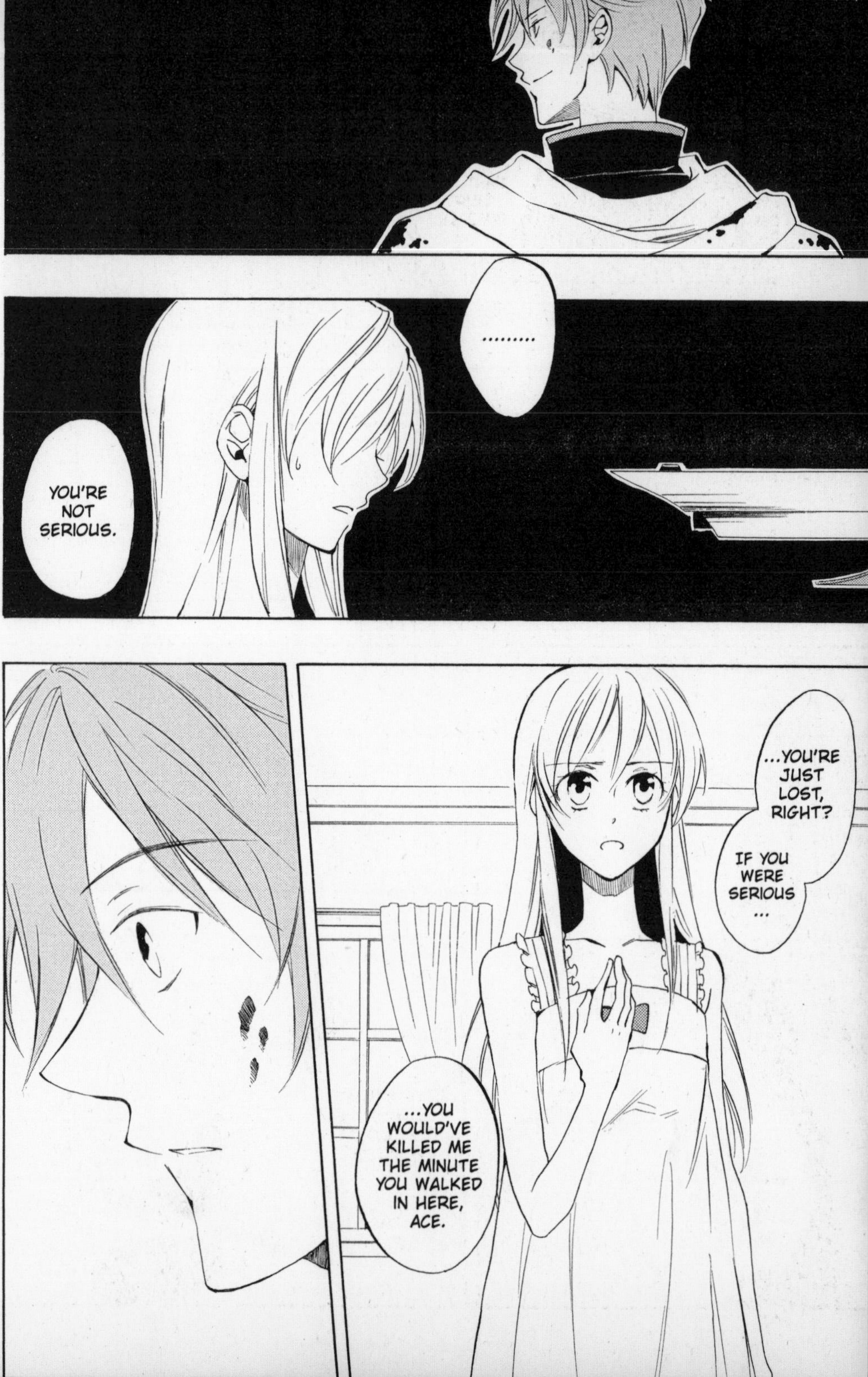
....
YOU'RE NOT SERIOUS.
...YOU'RE JUST LOST, RIGHT?
IF YOU WERE SERIOUS ...
...YOU WOULD'VE KILLED ME THE MINUTE YOU WALKED IN HERE, ACE.

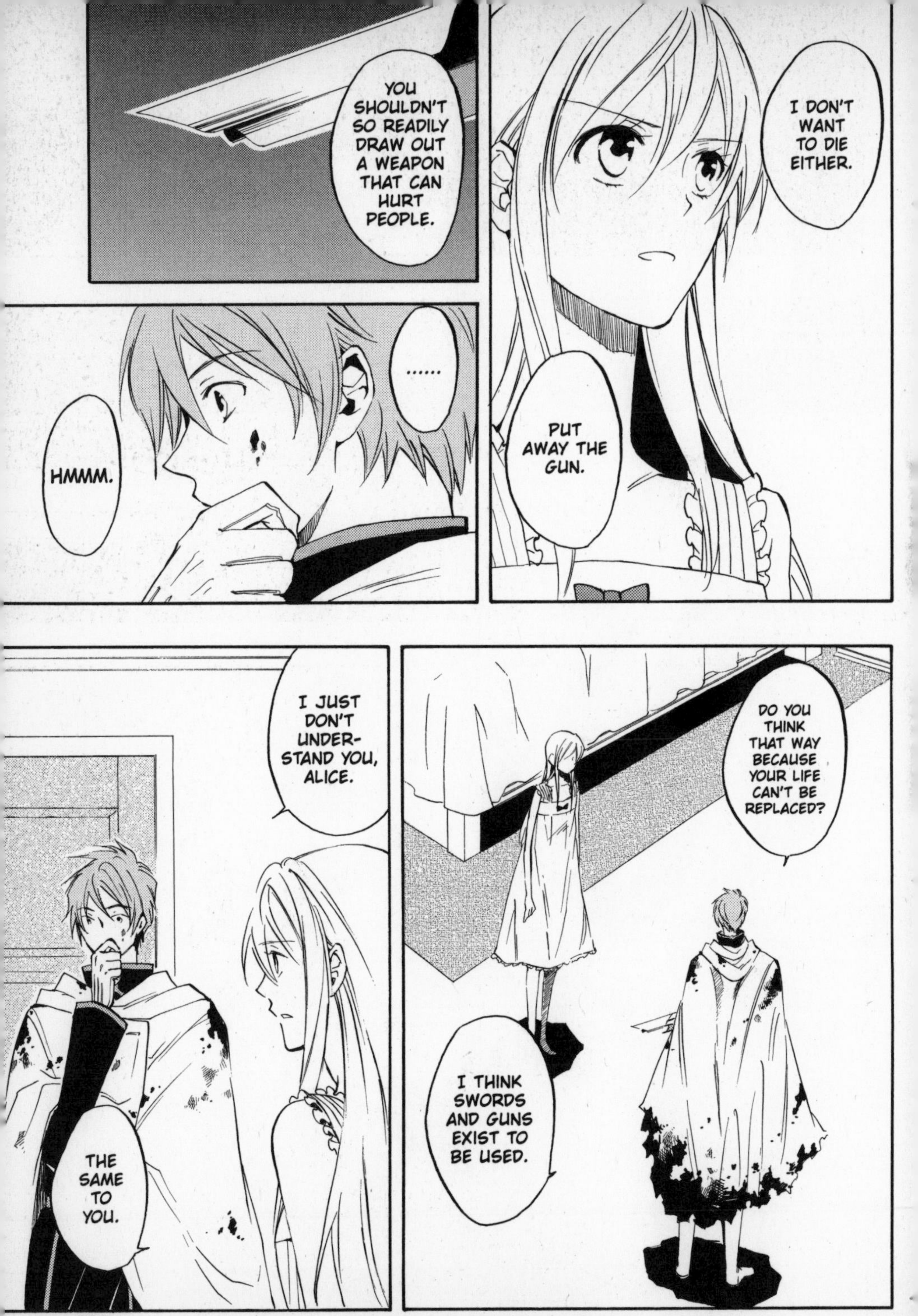
I DON'T WANT TO DIE EITHER.
PUT AWAY THE GUN.
YOU SHOULDN'T SO READILY DRAW OUT A WEAPON THAT CAN HURT PEOPLE.
......
HMMM.
DO YOU THINK THAT WAY BECAUSE YOUR LIFE CAN'T BE REPLACED?
I THINK SWORDS AND GUNS EXIST TO BE USED.
I JUST DON'T UNDER-STAND YOU, ALICE.
THE SAME TO YOU.

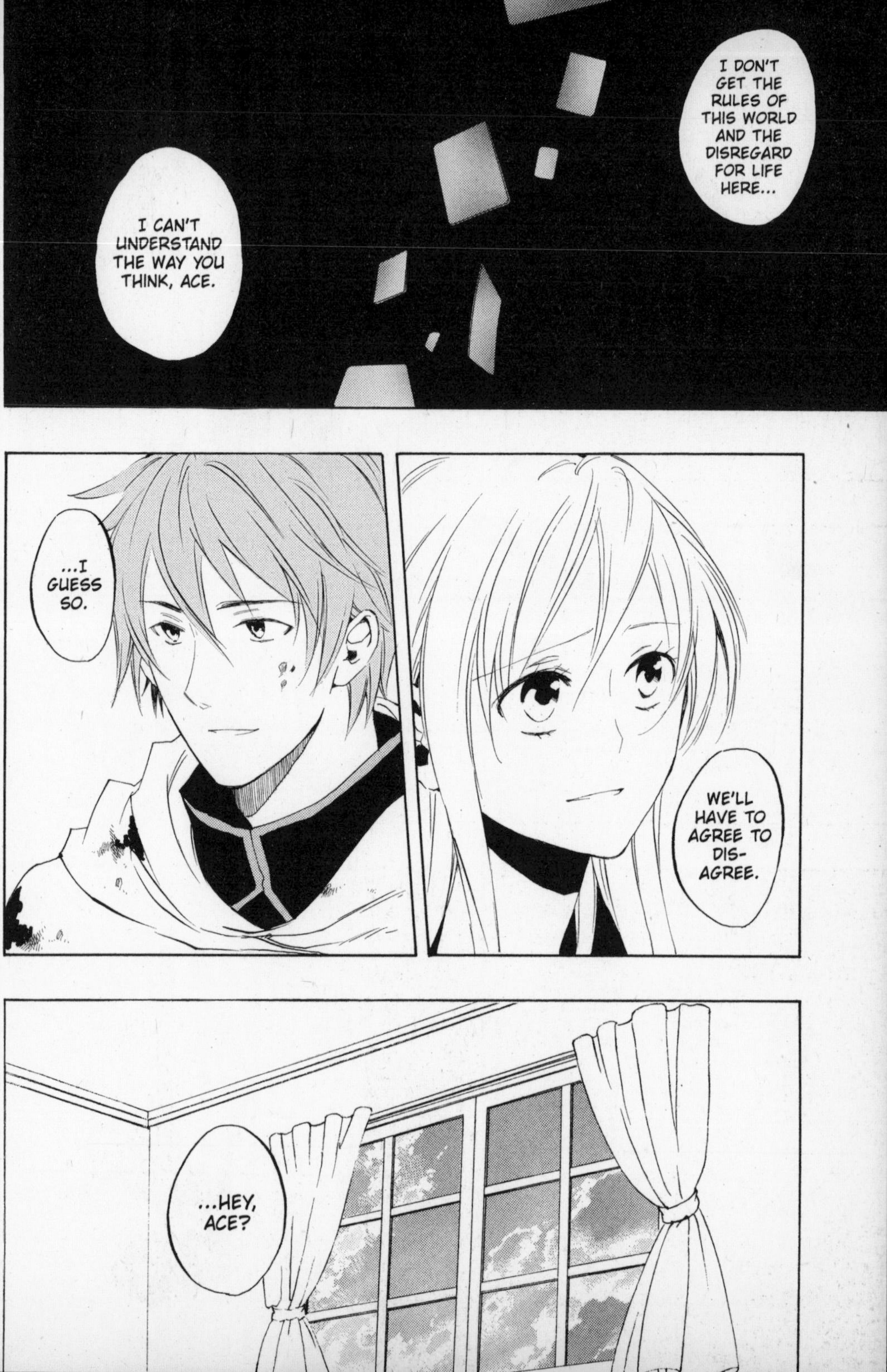
I DON'T GET THE RULES OF THIS WORLD AND THE DISREGARD FOR LIFE HERE...
I CAN'T UNDERSTAND THE WAY YOU THINK, ACE.
WE'LL HAVE TO AGREE TO DIS-AGREE.
...I GUESS SO.
...HEY, ACE?

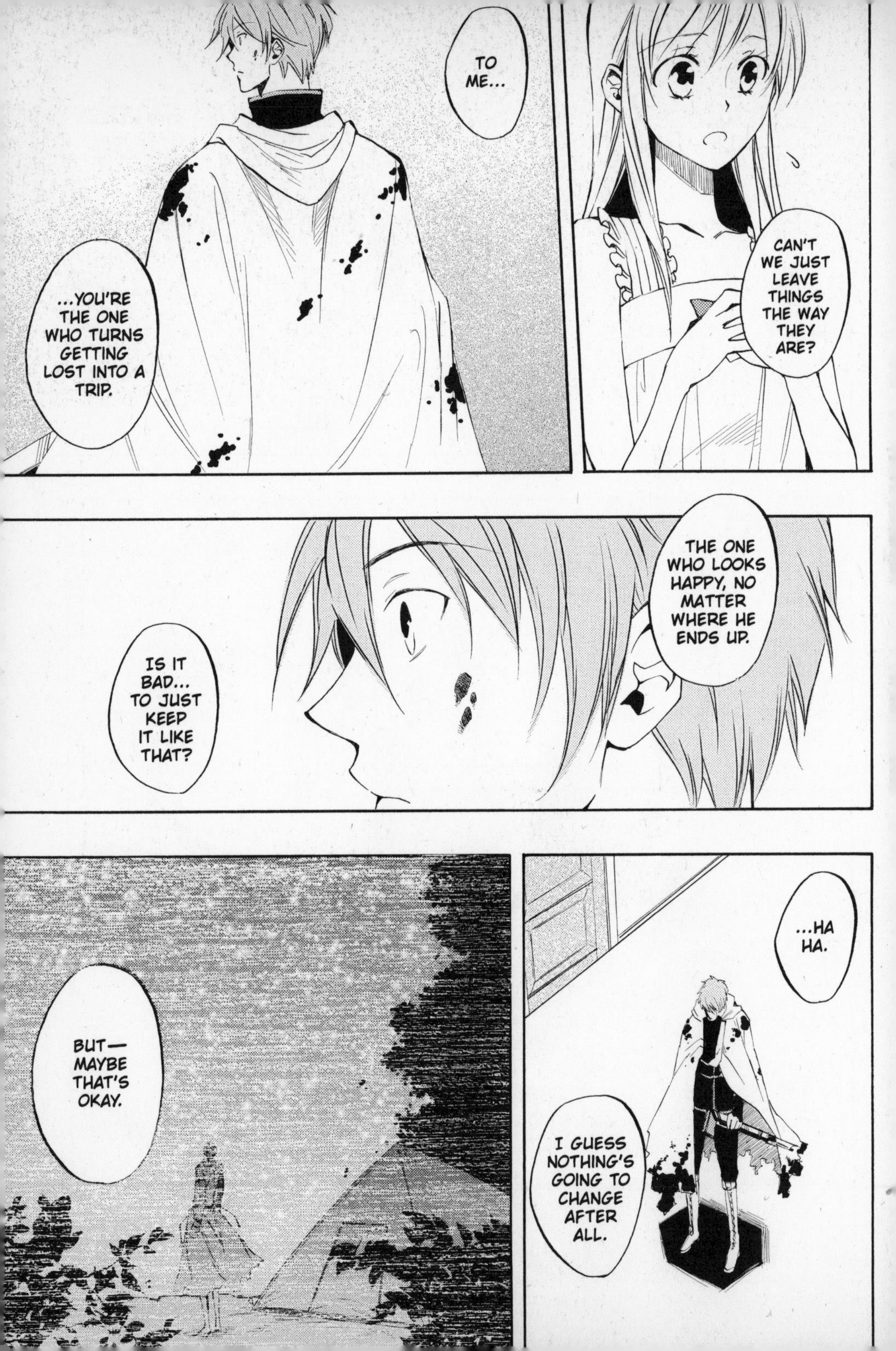
CAN'T WE JUST LEAVE THINGS THE WAY THEY ARE?
TO ME...
...YOU'RE THE ONE WHO TURNS GETTING LOST INTO A TRIP.
THE ONE WHO LOOKS HAPPY, NO MATTER WHERE HE ENDS UP.
IS IT BAD... TO JUST KEEP IT LIKE THAT?
...HA HA.
I GUESS NOTHING'S GOING TO CHANGE AFTER ALL.
BUT— MAYBE THAT'S OKAY.

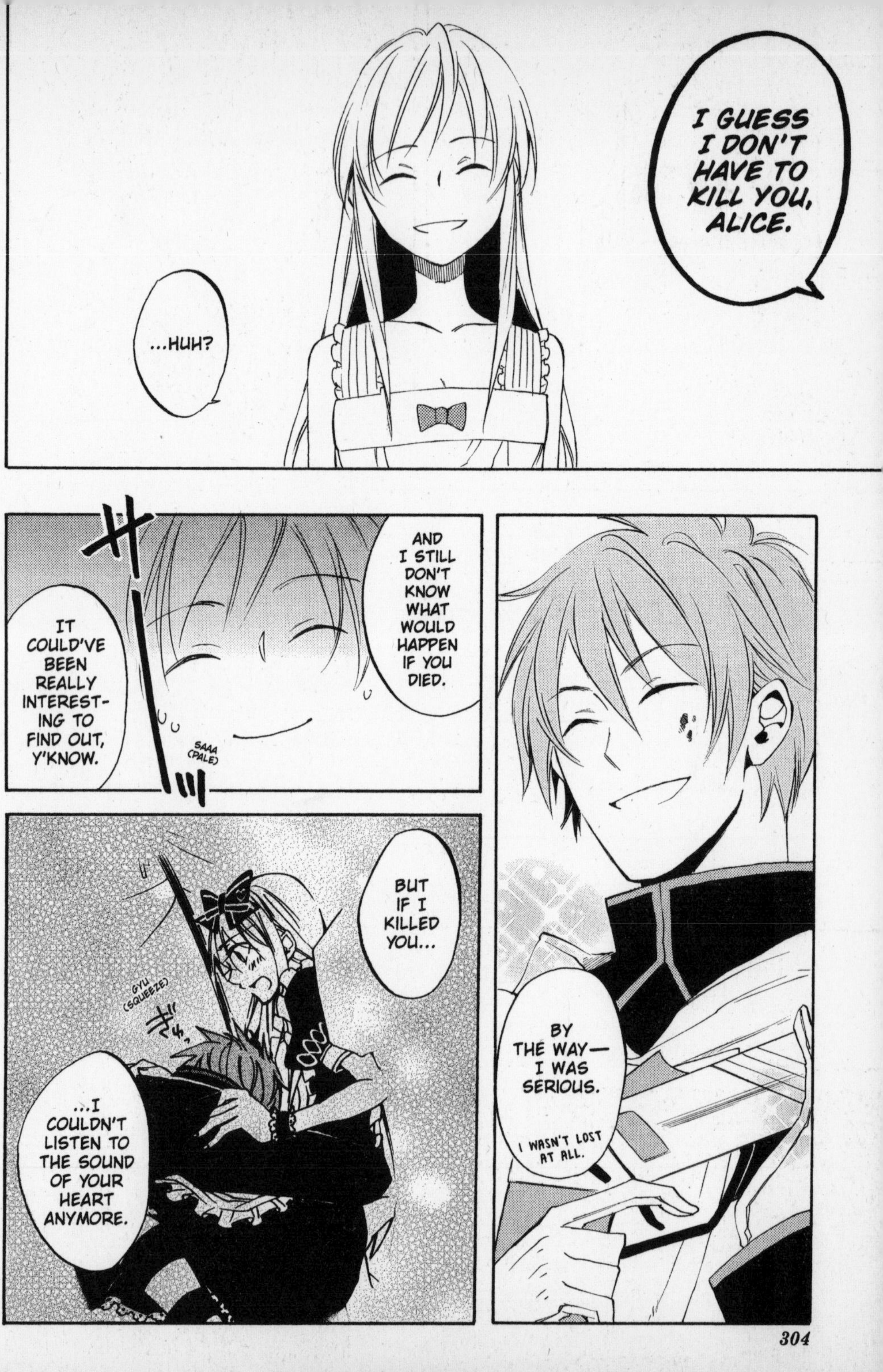
I GUESS I DON'T HAVE TO KILL YOU, ALICE.
...HUH?
BY THE WAY— I WAS SERIOUS.
I WASN'T LOST AT ALL.
AND I STILL DON'T KNOW WHAT WOULD HAPPEN IF YOU DIED.
IT COULD'VE BEEN REALLY INTEREST-ING TO FIND OUT, Y'KNOW.
SAAA (PALE)
BUT IF I KILLED YOU...
GYU (SQUEEZE)
...I COULDN'T LISTEN TO THE SOUND OF YOUR HEART ANYMORE.

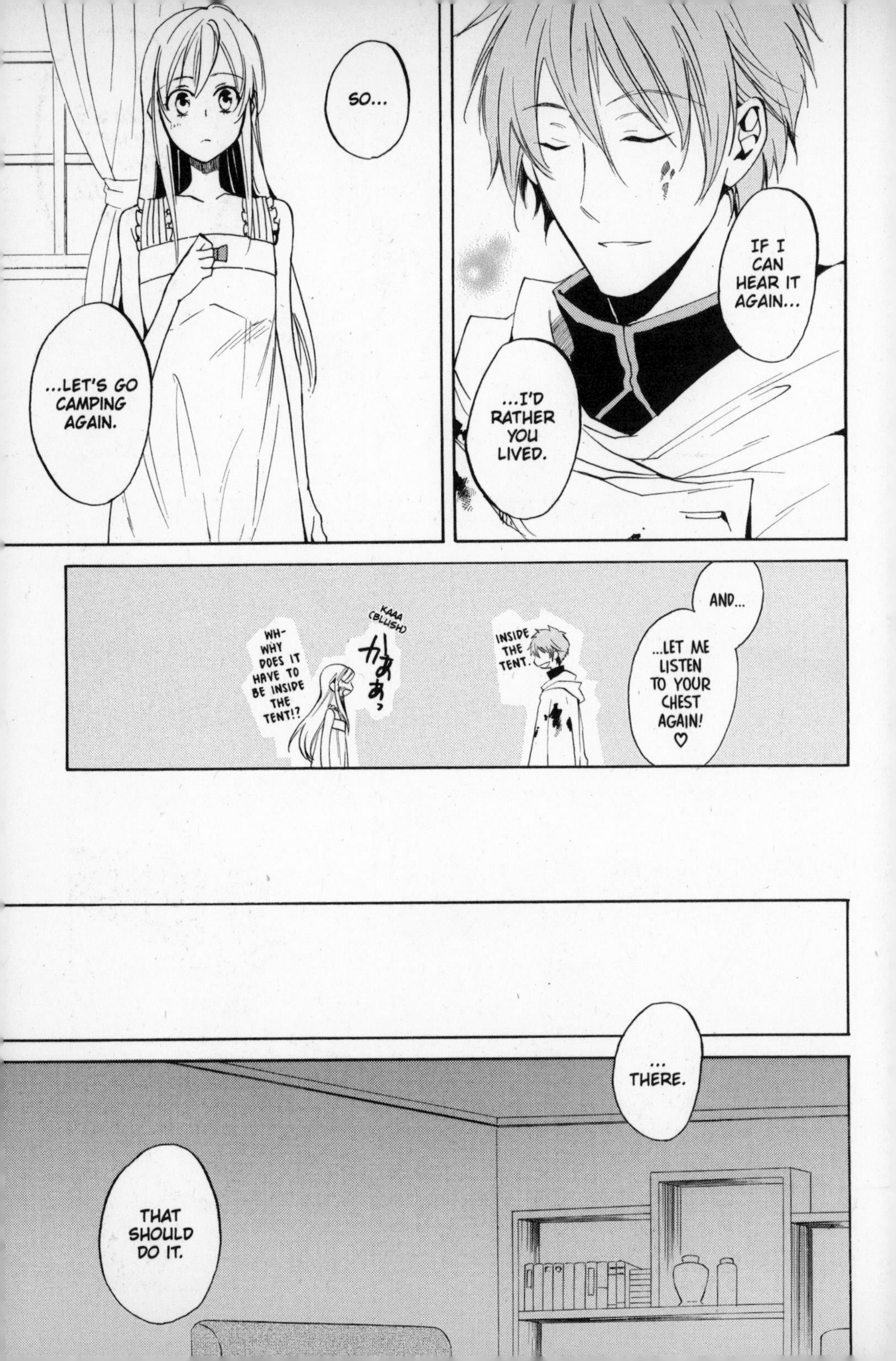
IF I CAN HEAR IT AGAIN...
...I'D RATHER YOU LIVED.
SO...
...LET'S GO CAMPING AGAIN.
AND...
...LET ME LISTEN TO YOUR CHEST AGAIN! ♡
INSIDE THE TENT.
KAAA (BLUSH)
かあっ
WH-WHY DOES IT HAVE TO BE INSIDE THE TENT!?
...THERE.
THAT SHOULD DO IT.

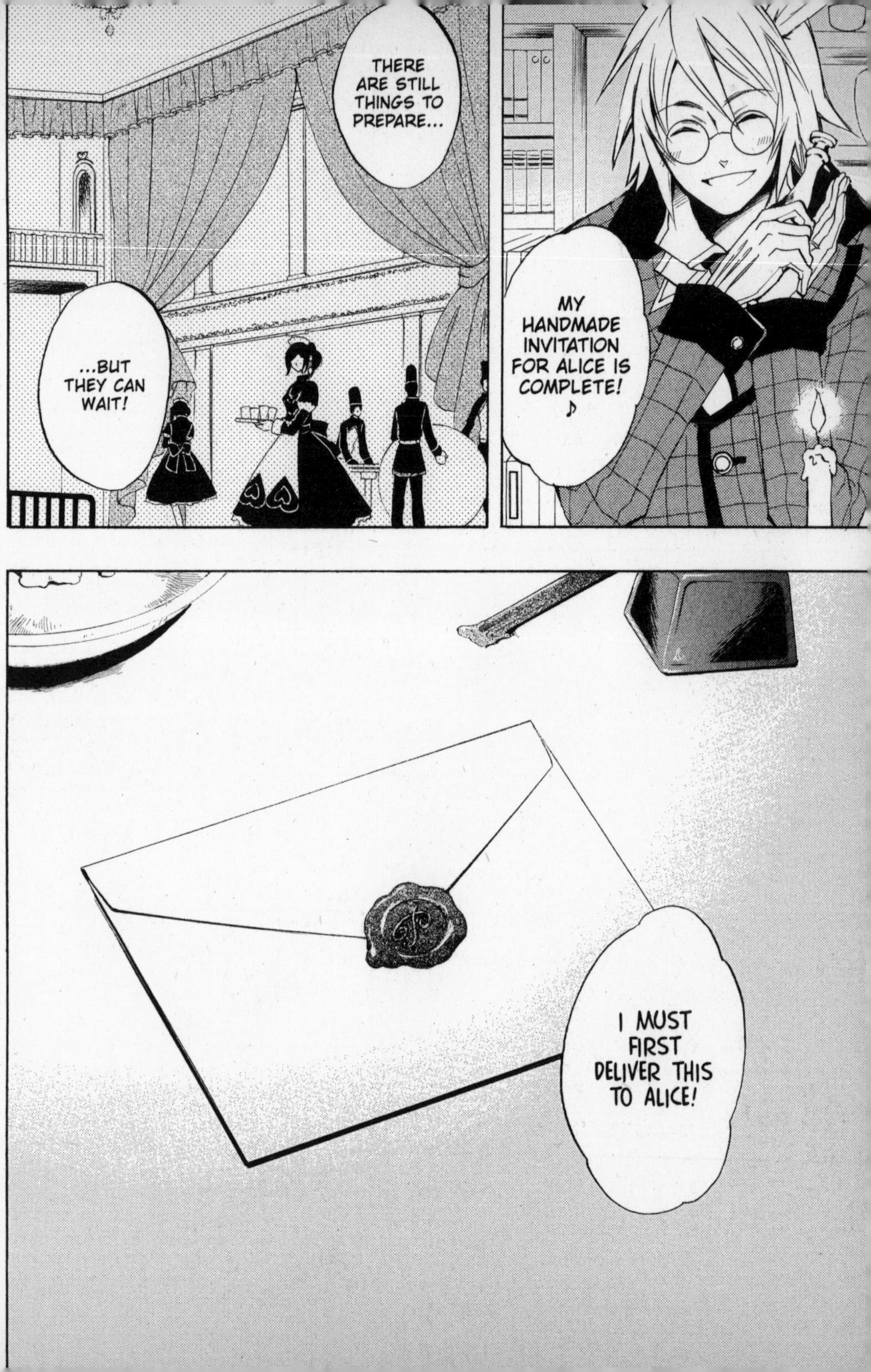
MY HANDMADE INVITATION FOR ALICE IS COMPLETE! ♪
THERE ARE STILL THINGS TO PREPARE...
...BUT THEY CAN WAIT!
I MUST FIRST DELIVER THIS TO ALICE!

♥24 Letter of Invitation

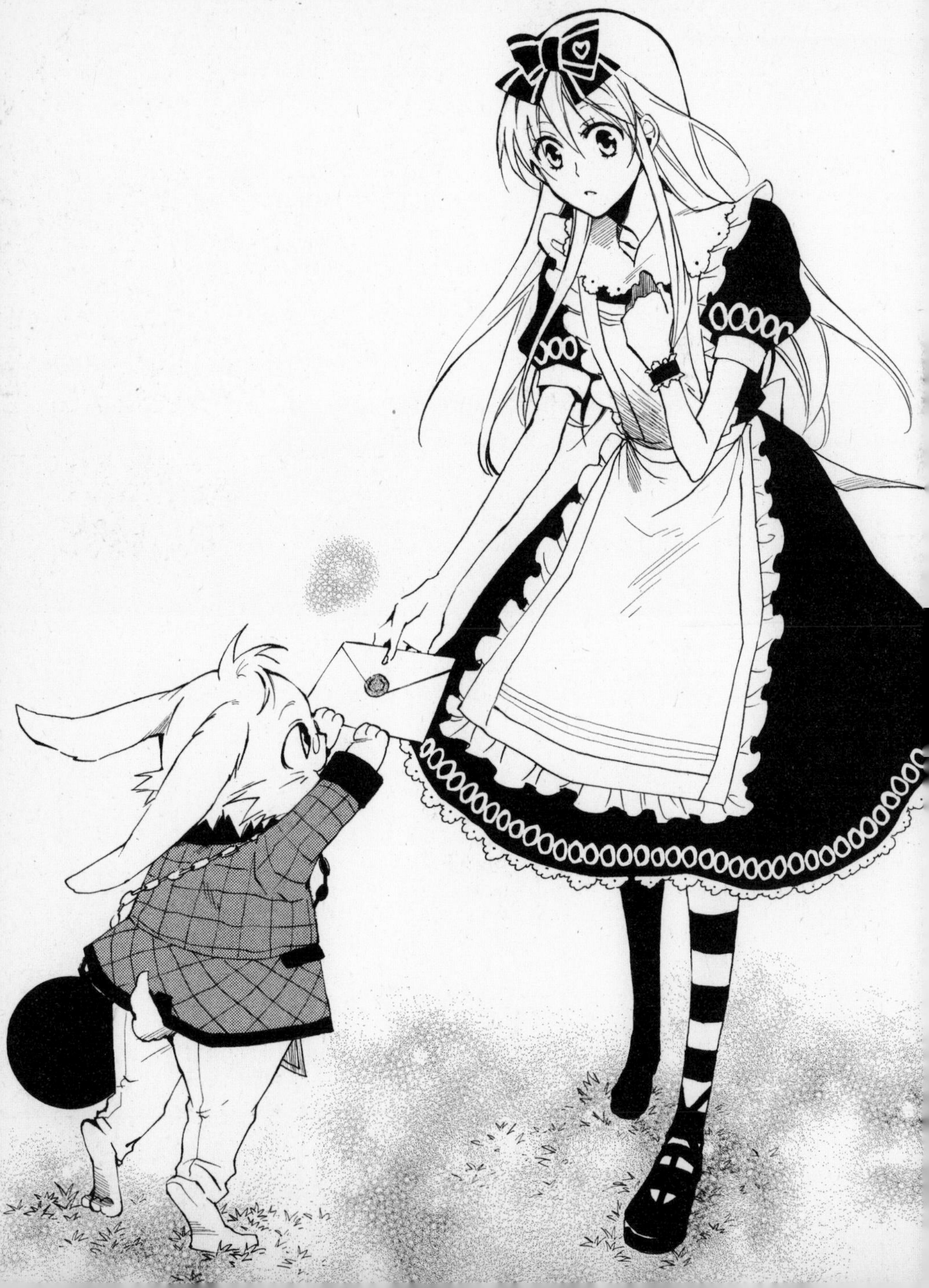

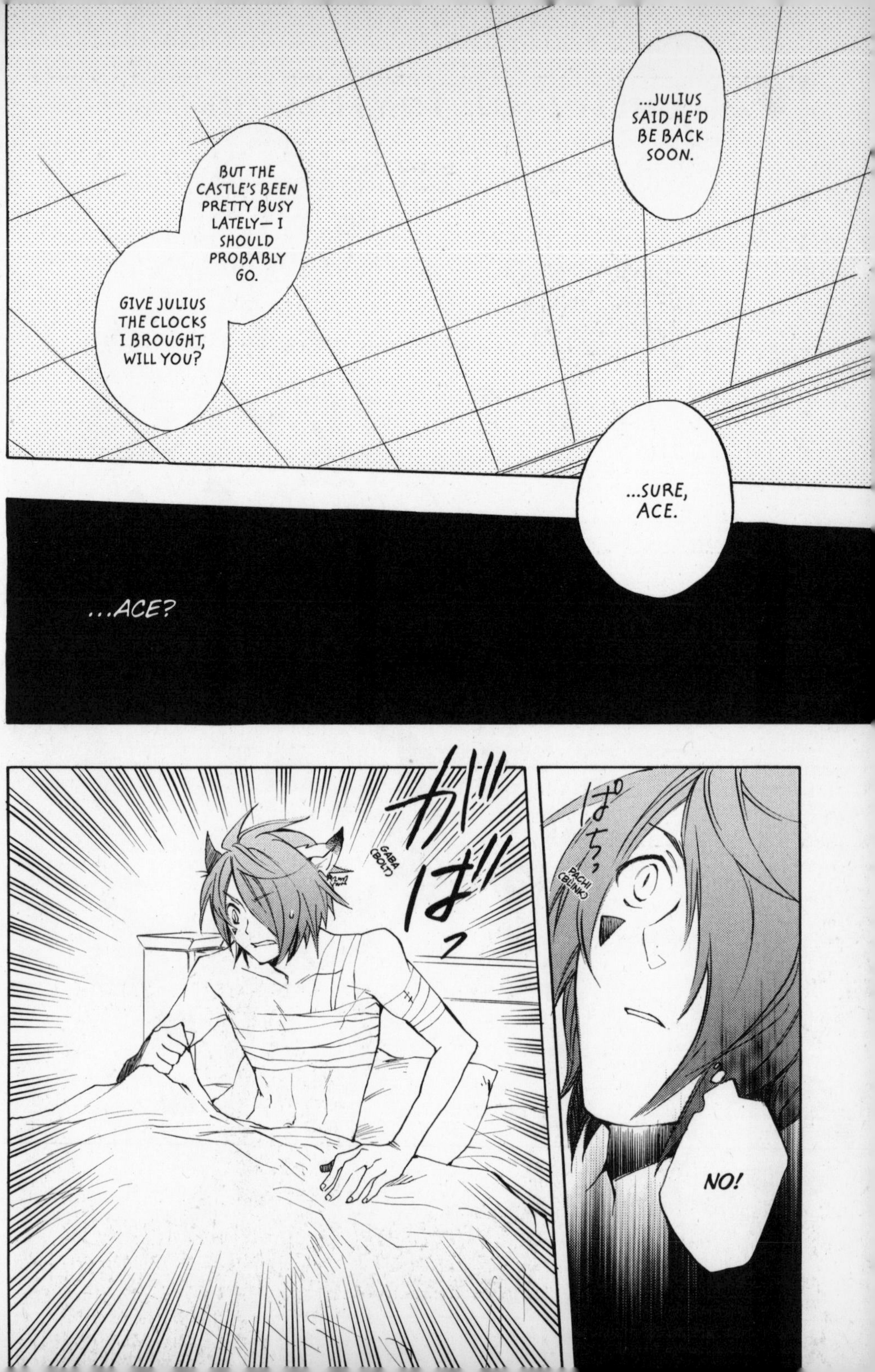
...JULIUS SAID HE'D BE BACK SOON.
BUT THE CASTLE'S BEEN PRETTY BUSY LATELY— I SHOULD PROBABLY GO.
GIVE JULIUS THE CLOCKS I BROUGHT, WILL YOU?
...SURE, ACE.
...ACE?
ぱち
PACHI (BLINK)
NO!
がばっ
GABA (BOLT)

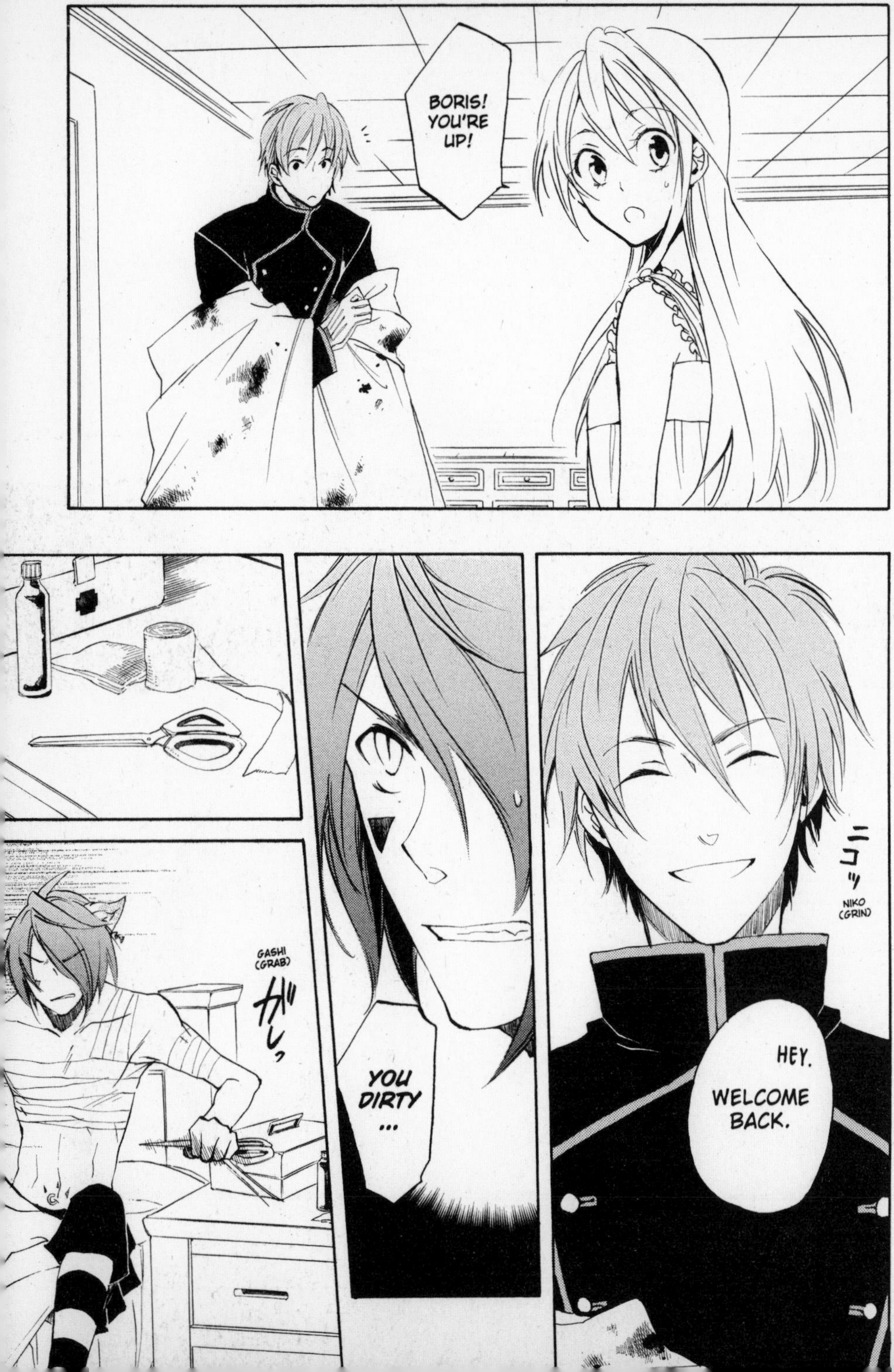
BORIS! YOU'RE UP!
ニコッ
NIKO (GRIN)
HEY.
WELCOME BACK.
YOU DIRTY ...
GASHI (GRAB)
がしっ

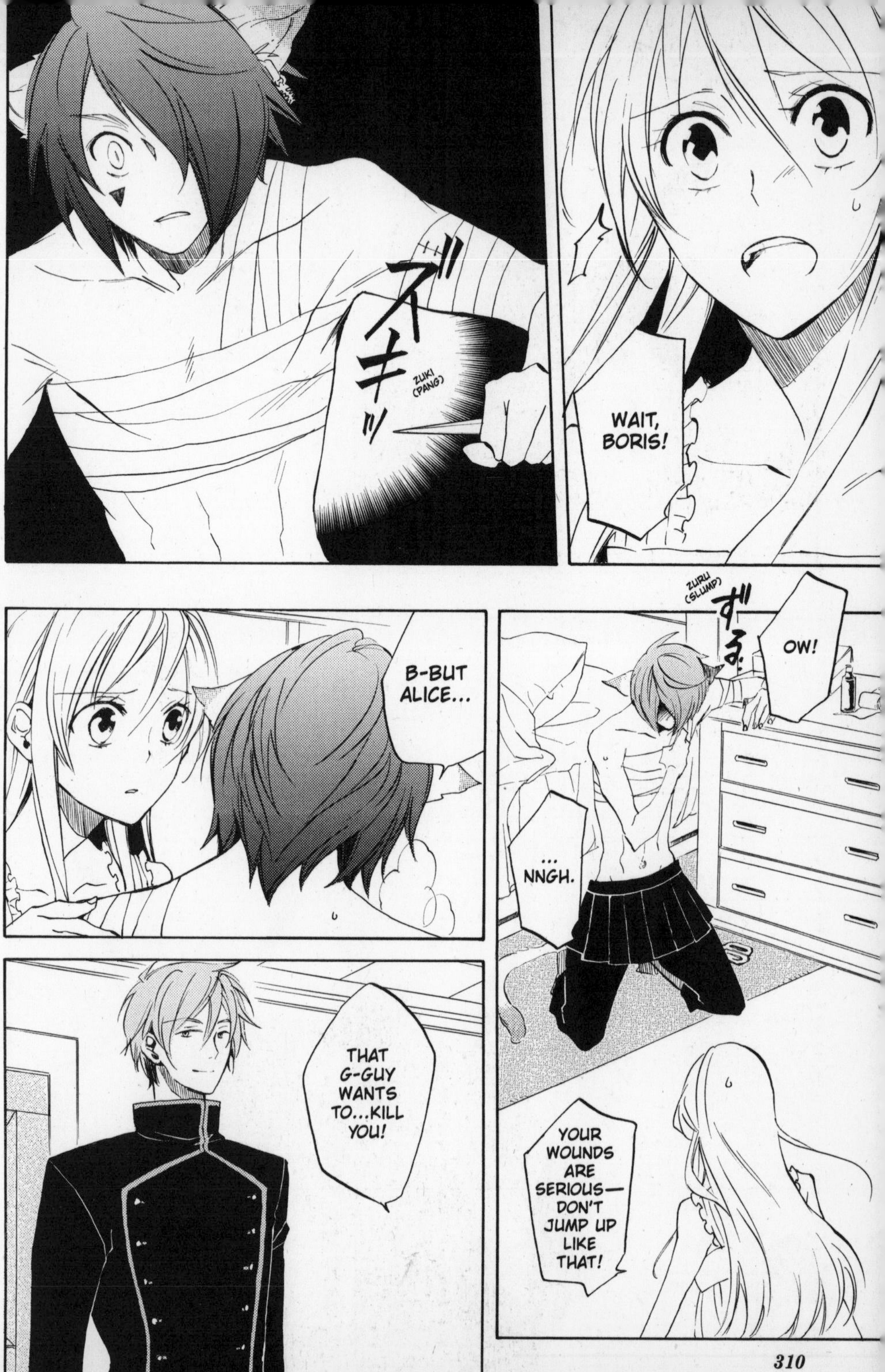
WAIT, BORIS!
ズキッ
ZUKI (PANG)
ずるっ
ZURU (SLUMP)
OW!
... NNGH.
YOUR WOUNDS ARE SERIOUS— DON'T JUMP UP LIKE THAT!
B-BUT ALICE...
THAT G-GUY WANTS TO...KILL YOU!

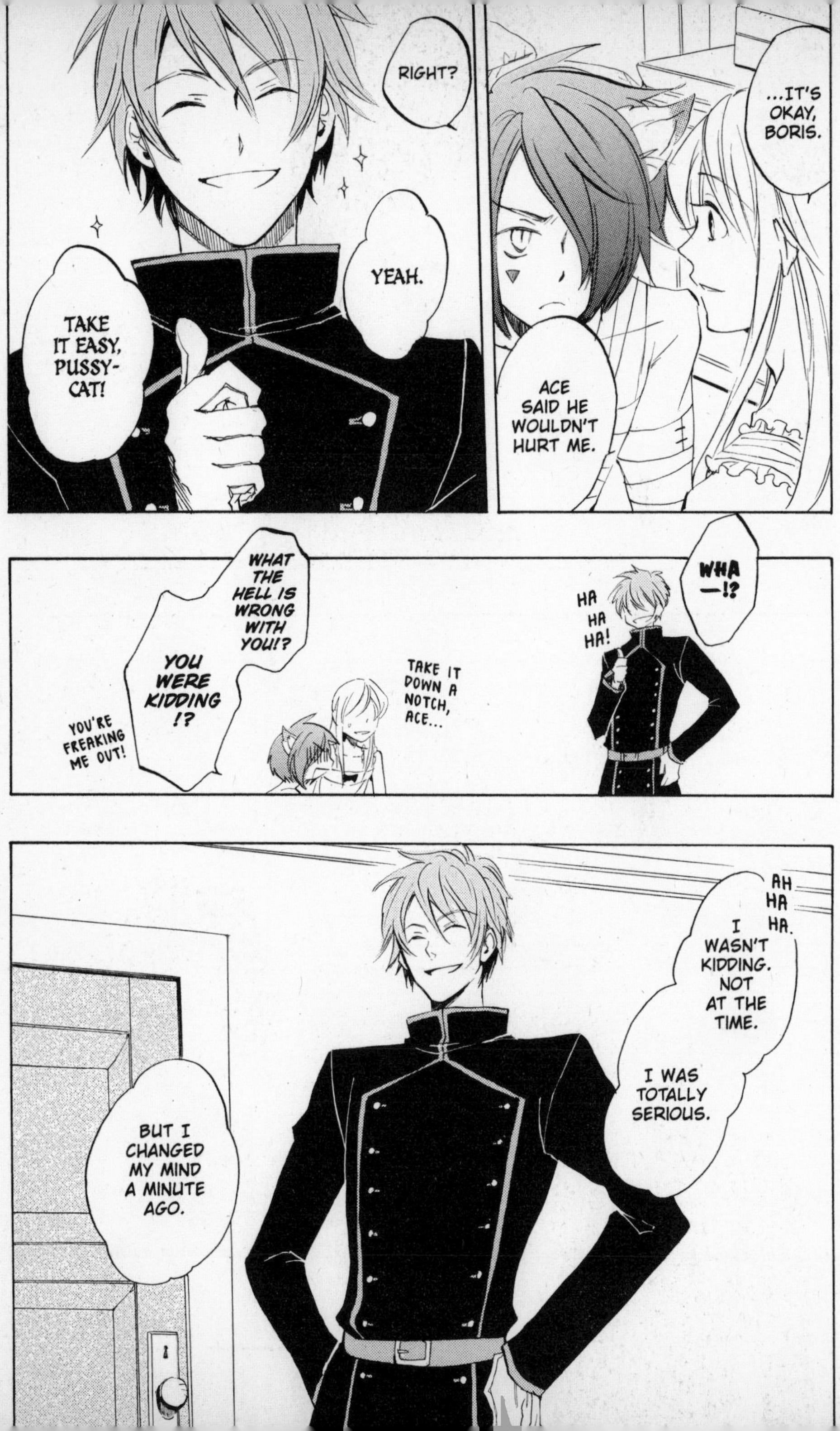
...IT'S OKAY, BORIS.
ACE SAID HE WOULDN'T HURT ME.
RIGHT?
YEAH.
TAKE IT EASY, PUSSY-CAT!
WHA—!?
HA HA HA!
WHAT THE HELL IS WRONG WITH YOU!?
TAKE IT DOWN A NOTCH, ACE...
YOU WERE KIDDING!?
YOU'RE FREAKING ME OUT!
AH HA HA.
I WASN'T KIDDING. NOT AT THE TIME.
I WAS TOTALLY SERIOUS.
BUT I CHANGED MY MIND A MINUTE AGO.

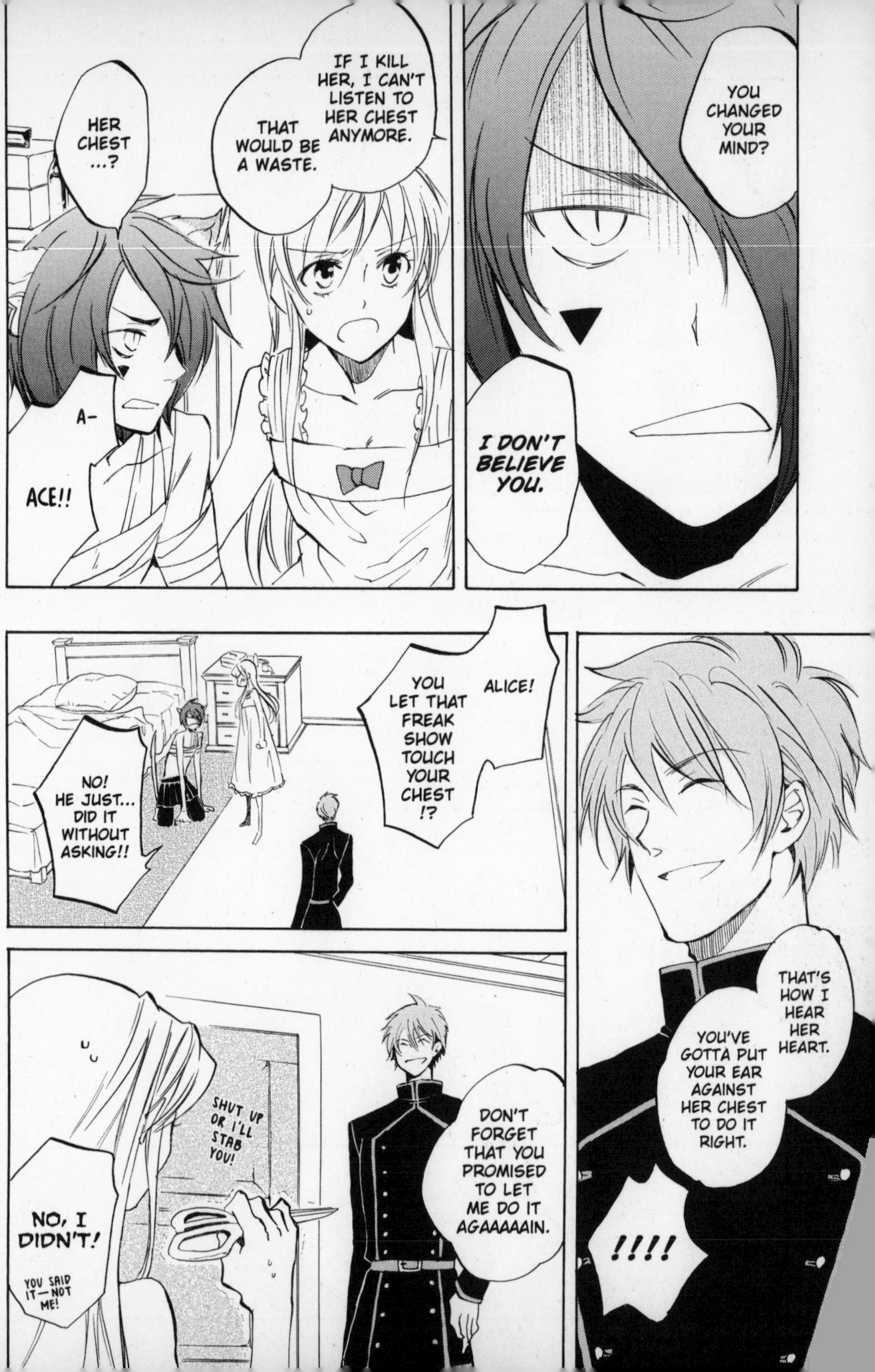
YOU CHANGED YOUR MIND?
I DON'T BELIEVE YOU.
IF I KILL HER, I CAN'T LISTEN TO HER CHEST ANYMORE.
THAT WOULD BE A WASTE.
HER CHEST ...?
A-
ACE!!
THAT'S HOW I HEAR HER HEART.
YOU'VE GOTTA PUT YOUR EAR AGAINST HER CHEST TO DO IT RIGHT.
!!!!
ALICE!
YOU LET THAT FREAK SHOW TOUCH YOUR CHEST!?
NO! HE JUST... DID IT WITHOUT ASKING!!
DON'T FORGET THAT YOU PROMISED TO LET ME DO IT AGAAAAAIN.
SHUT UP OR I'LL STAB YOU!
NO, I DIDN'T!
YOU SAID IT—NOT ME!

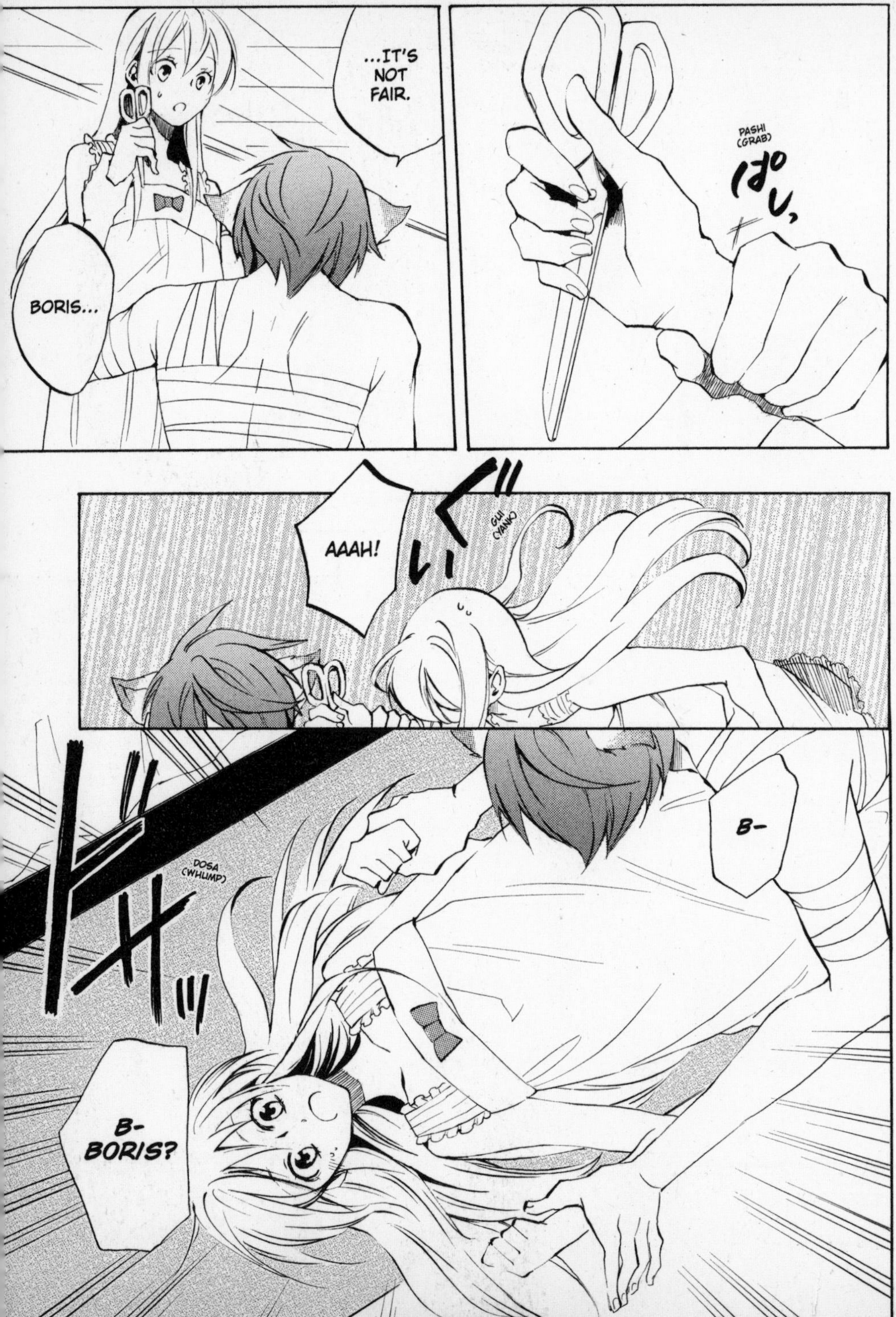
PASHI (GRAB)
ぱしっ
...IT'S NOT FAIR.
BORIS...
ぐい
GUI (YANK)
AAAH!
B-
ドサッ
DOSA (WHUMP)
B- BORIS?

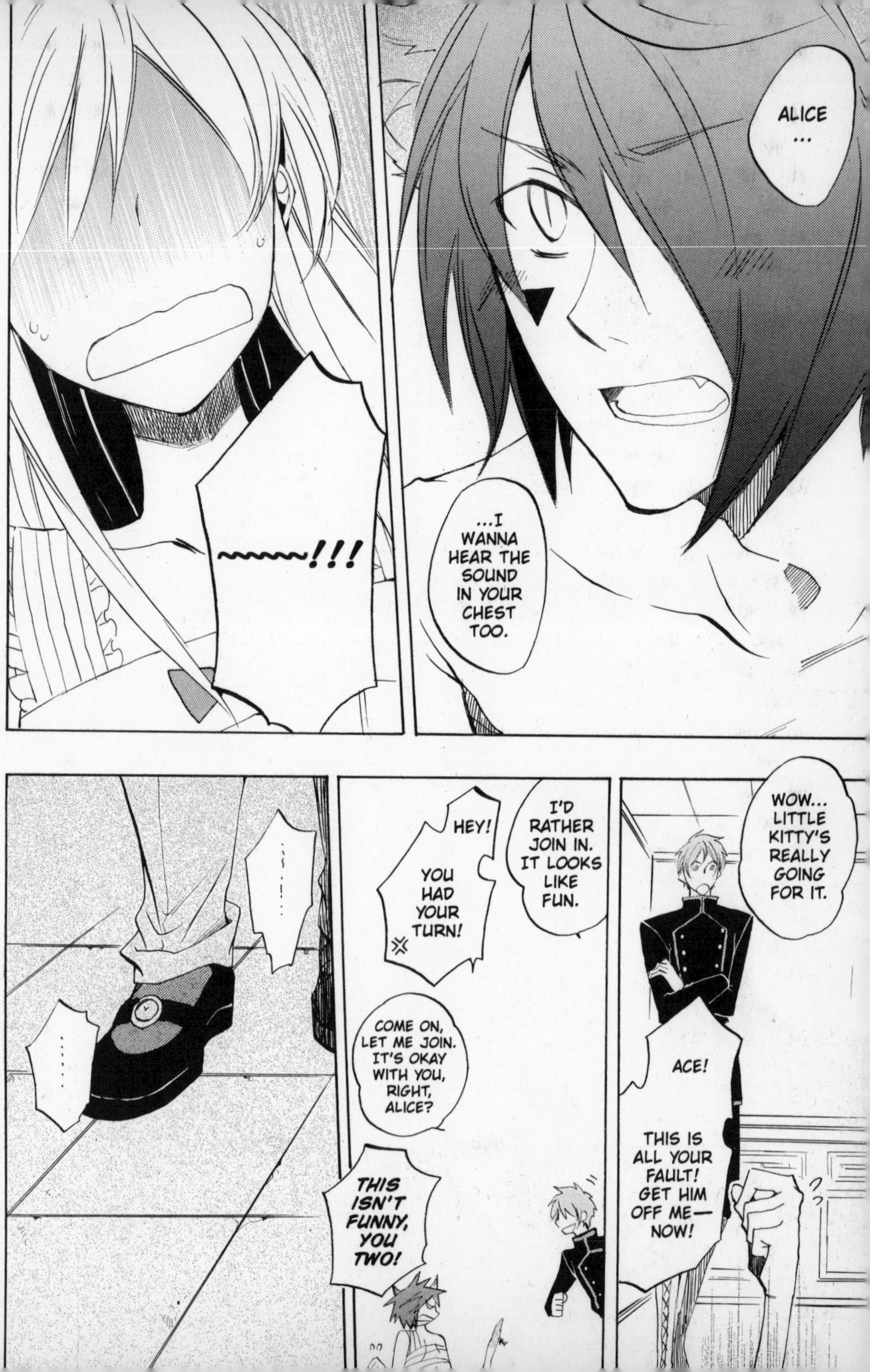
ALICE ...
...I WANNA HEAR THE SOUND IN YOUR CHEST TOO.
~~~~~!!!
WOW... LITTLE KITTY'S REALLY GOING FOR IT.
ACE!
THIS IS ALL YOUR FAULT! GET HIM OFF ME—NOW!
I'D RATHER JOIN IN. IT LOOKS LIKE FUN.
HEY!
YOU HAD YOUR TURN!
COME ON, LET ME JOIN. IT'S OKAY WITH YOU, RIGHT, ALICE?
THIS ISN'T FUNNY, YOU TWO!
...!...
......
~~~~~

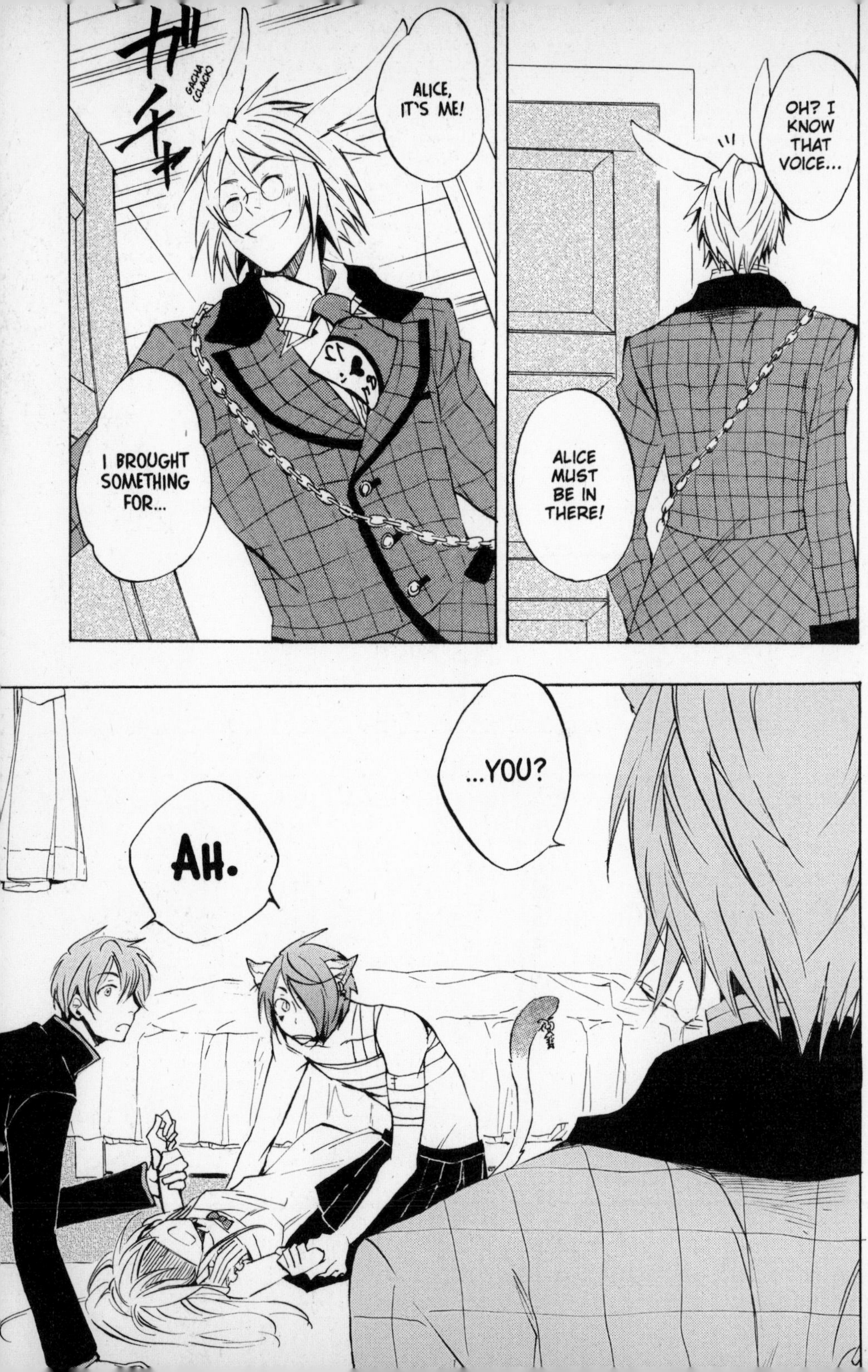
OH? I KNOW THAT VOICE...
ALICE MUST BE IN THERE!
ガチャ
GACHA (CLACK)
ALICE, IT'S ME!
I BROUGHT SOMETHING FOR...
...YOU?
AH.

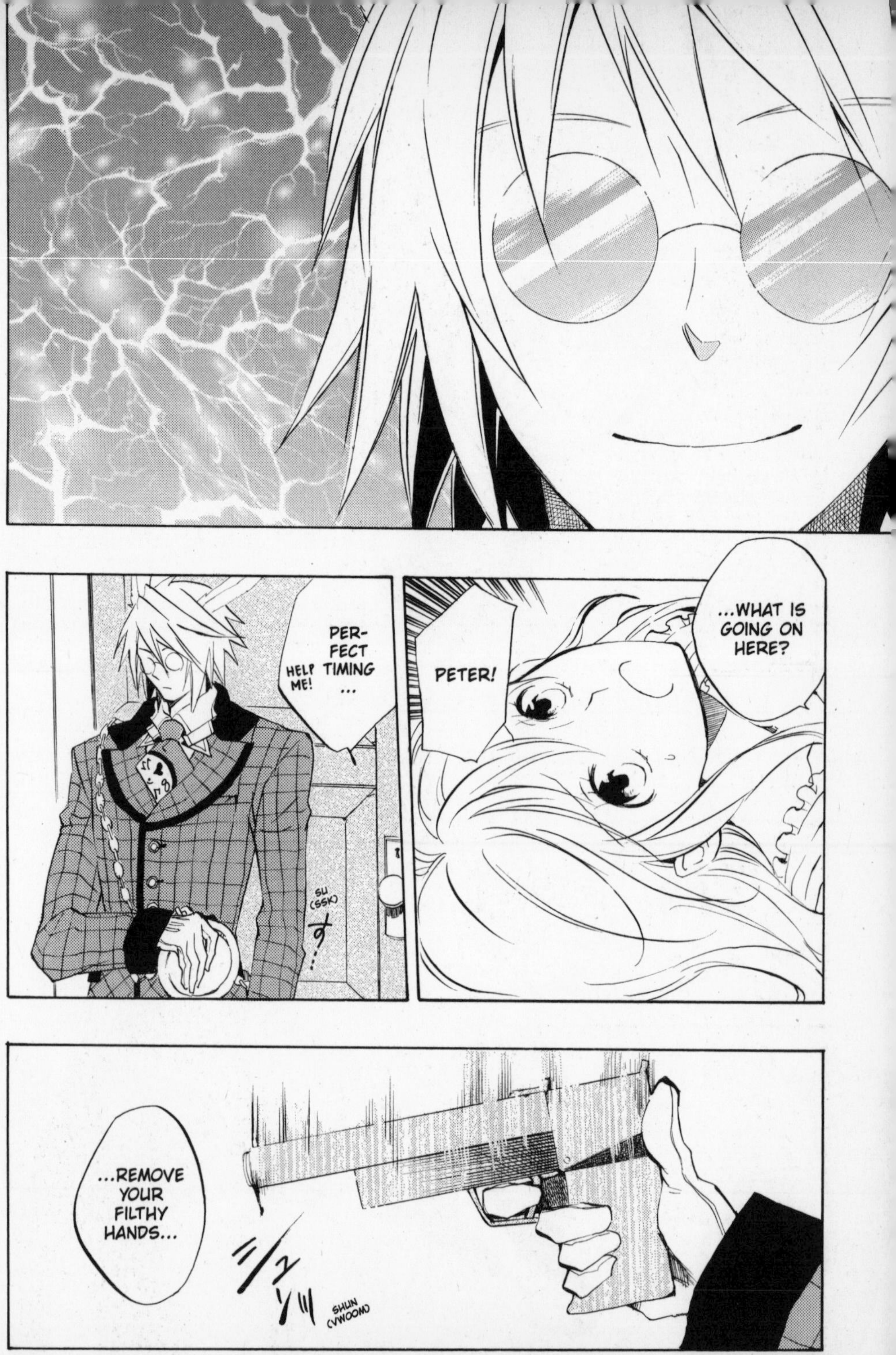
...WHAT IS GOING ON HERE?
PETER!
PER-FECT TIMING ...
HELP ME!
SU (SSK)
...REMOVE YOUR FILTHY HANDS...
SHUN (VWOOM)

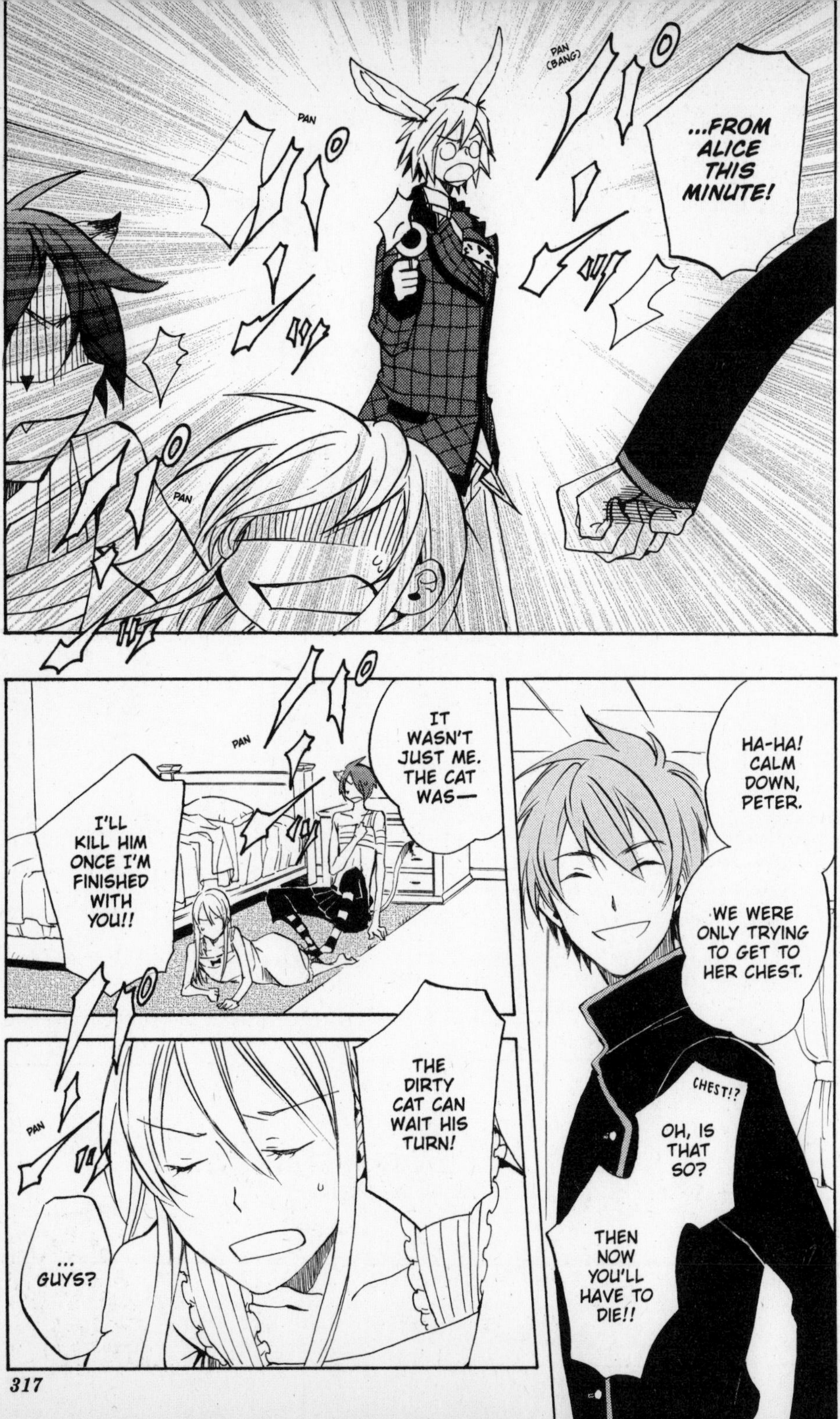
PAN (BANG)
...FROM ALICE THIS MINUTE!
PAN
PAN
HA-HA! CALM DOWN, PETER.
WE WERE ONLY TRYING TO GET TO HER CHEST.
CHEST!?
OH, IS THAT SO?
THEN NOW YOU'LL HAVE TO DIE!!
PAN
IT WASN'T JUST ME. THE CAT WAS—
I'LL KILL HIM ONCE I'M FINISHED WITH YOU!!
THE DIRTY CAT CAN WAIT HIS TURN!
PAN
...GUYS?

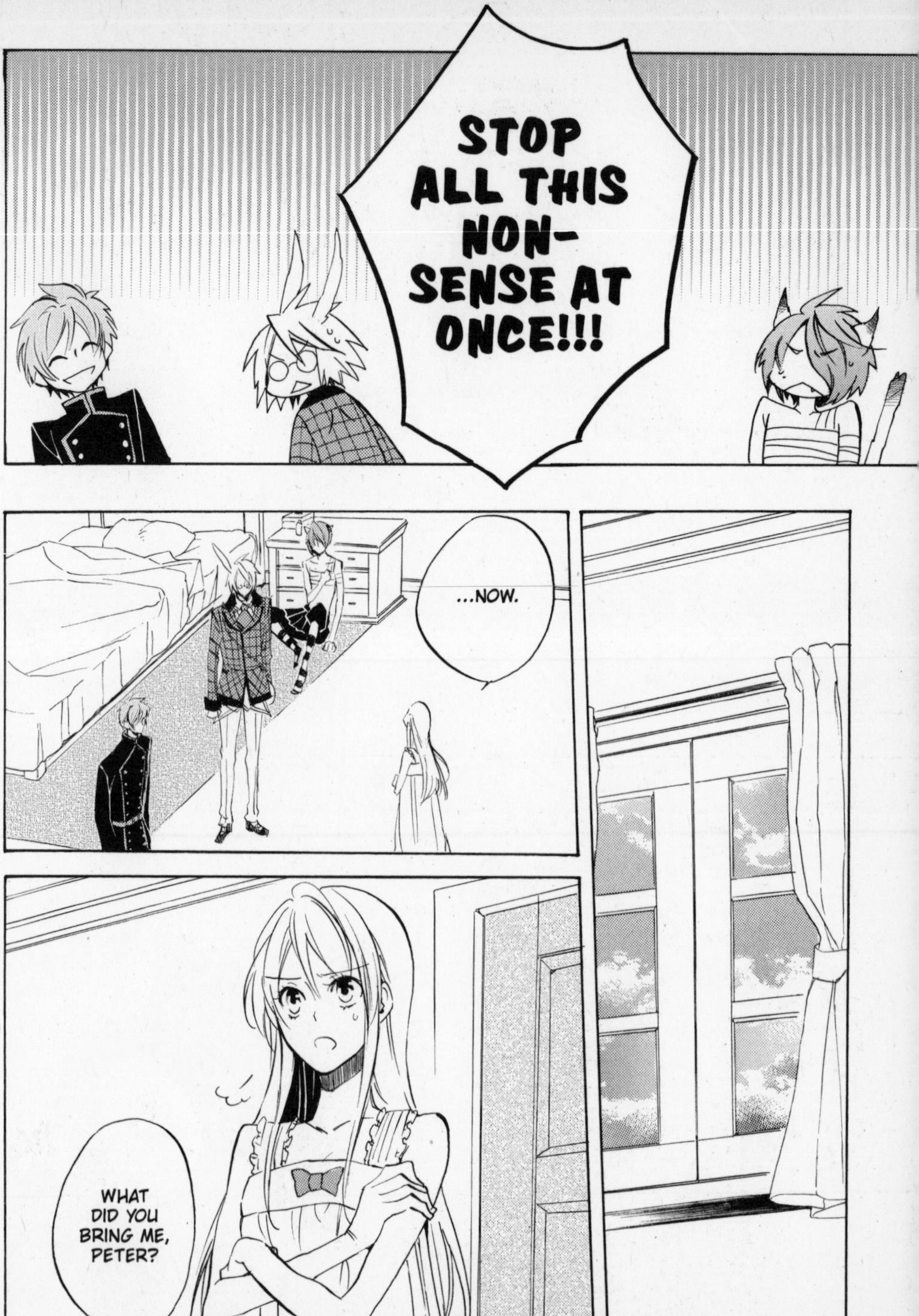
STOP ALL THIS NON-SENSE AT ONCE!!!
...NOW.
WHAT DID YOU BRING ME, PETER?

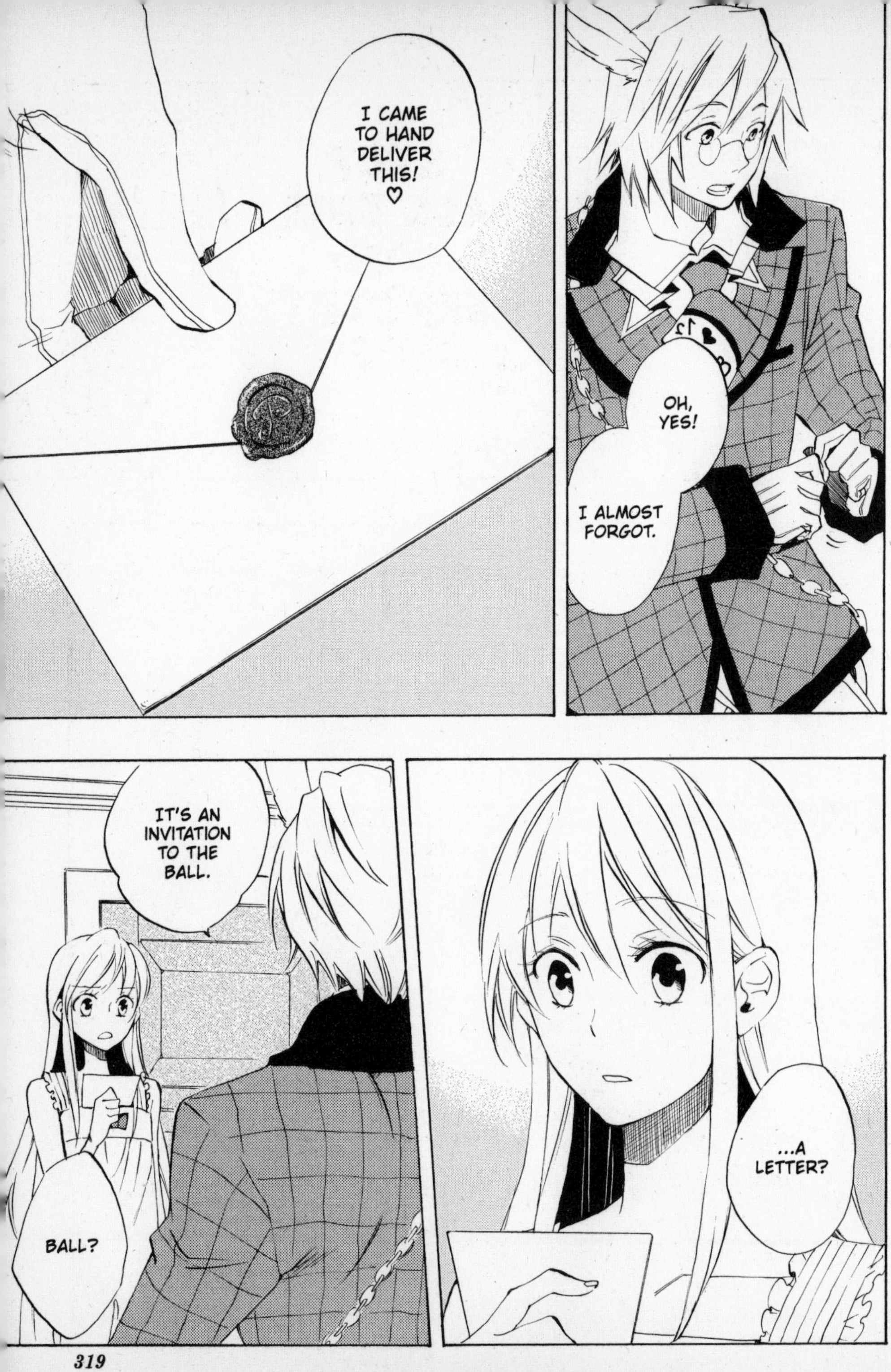
OH, YES!
I ALMOST FORGOT.
I CAME TO HAND DELIVER THIS! ♡
...A LETTER?
IT'S AN INVITATION TO THE BALL.
BALL?

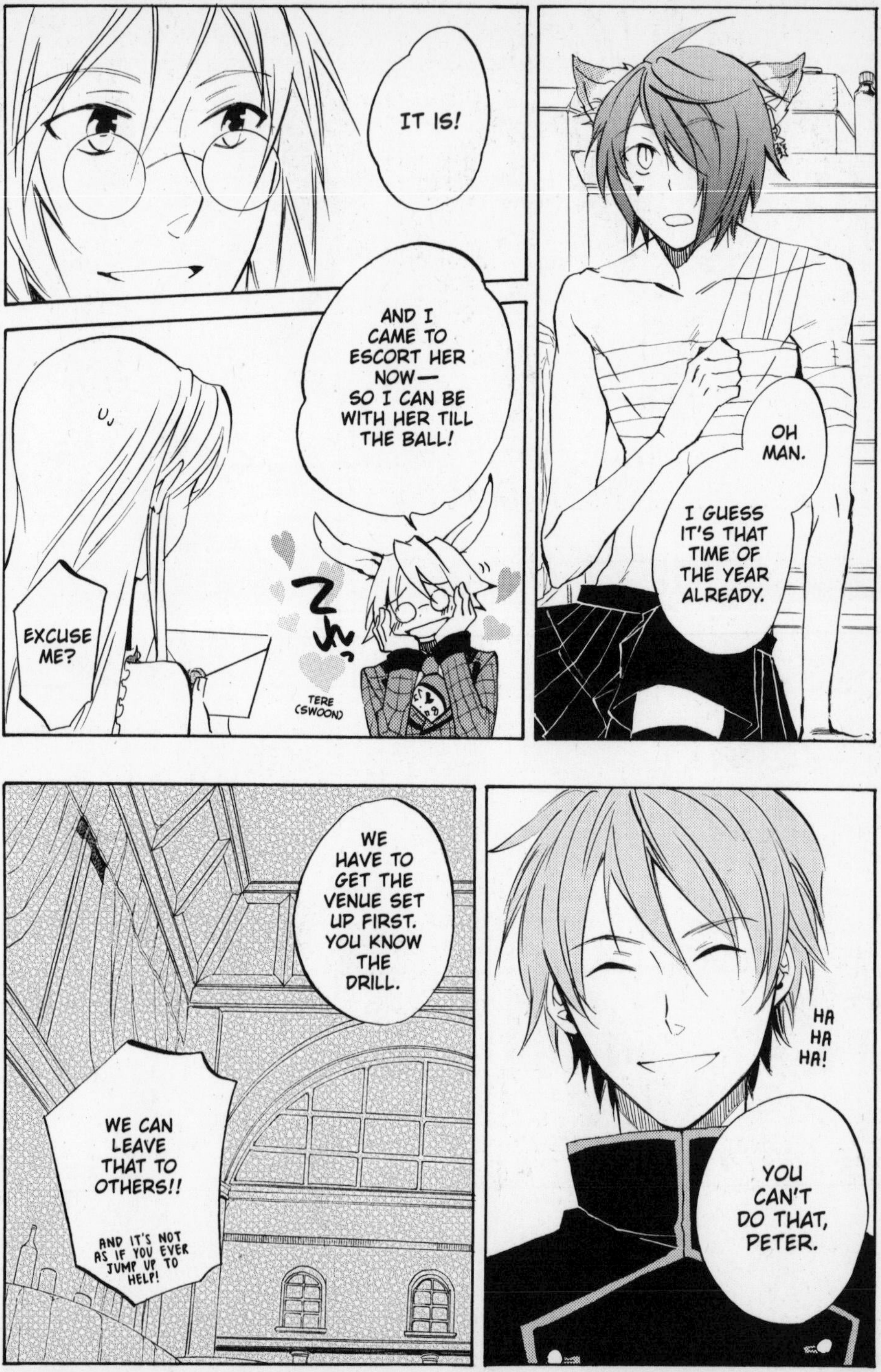
OH MAN.
I GUESS IT'S THAT TIME OF THE YEAR ALREADY.
IT IS!
AND I CAME TO ESCORT HER NOW— SO I CAN BE WITH HER TILL THE BALL!
TERE (SWOON)
EXCUSE ME?
HA HA HA!
YOU CAN'T DO THAT, PETER.
WE HAVE TO GET THE VENUE SET UP FIRST. YOU KNOW THE DRILL.
WE CAN LEAVE THAT TO OTHERS!!
AND IT'S NOT AS IF YOU EVER JUMP UP TO HELP!

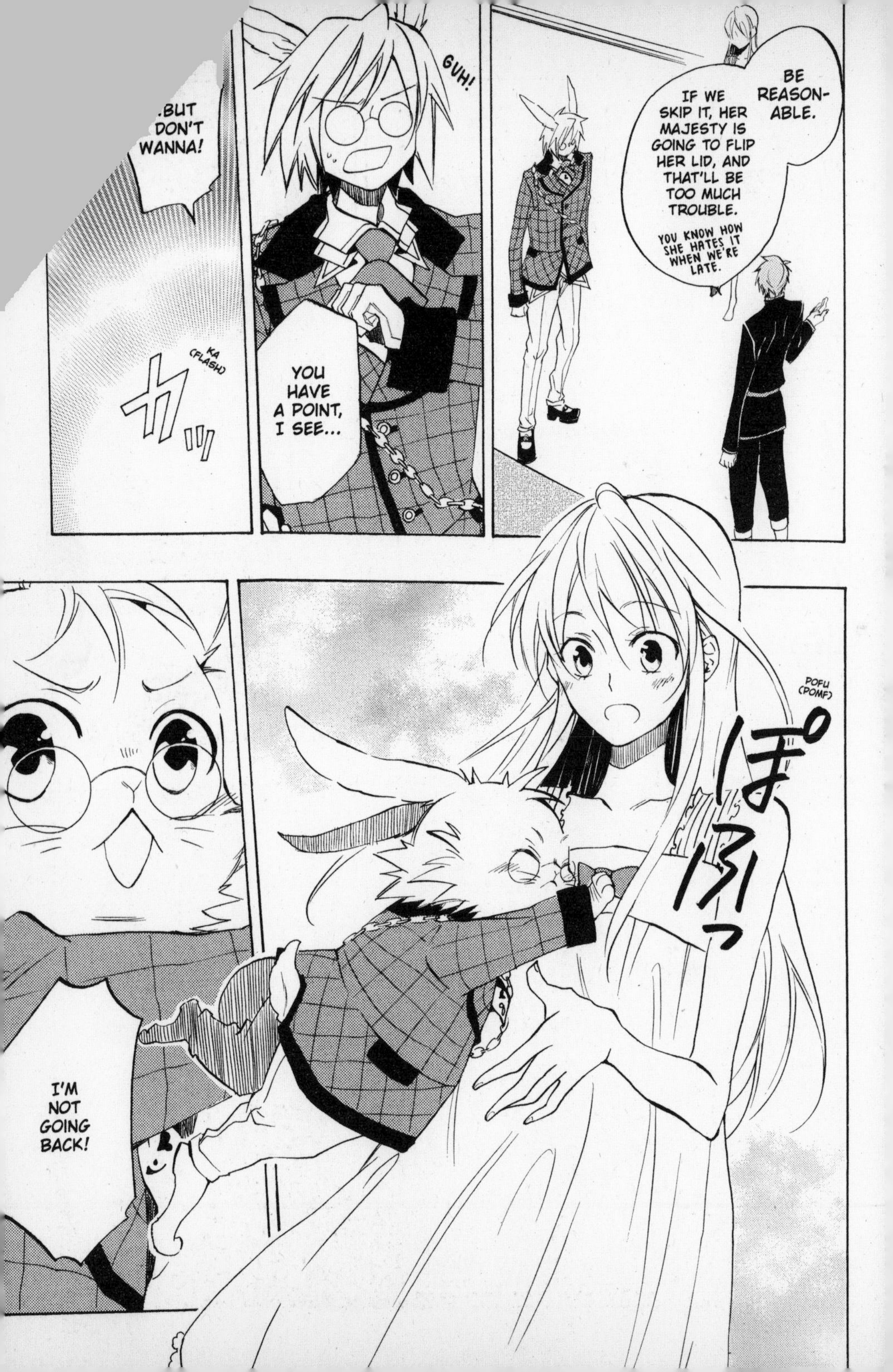
BE REASONABLE.
IF WE SKIP IT, HER MAJESTY IS GOING TO FLIP HER LID, AND THAT'LL BE TOO MUCH TROUBLE.
YOU KNOW HOW SHE HATES IT WHEN WE'RE LATE.
GUH!
YOU HAVE A POINT, I SEE...
.BUT DON'T WANNA!
KA (FLASH)
カッ
POFU (POMF)
ぽふっ
I'M NOT GOING BACK!

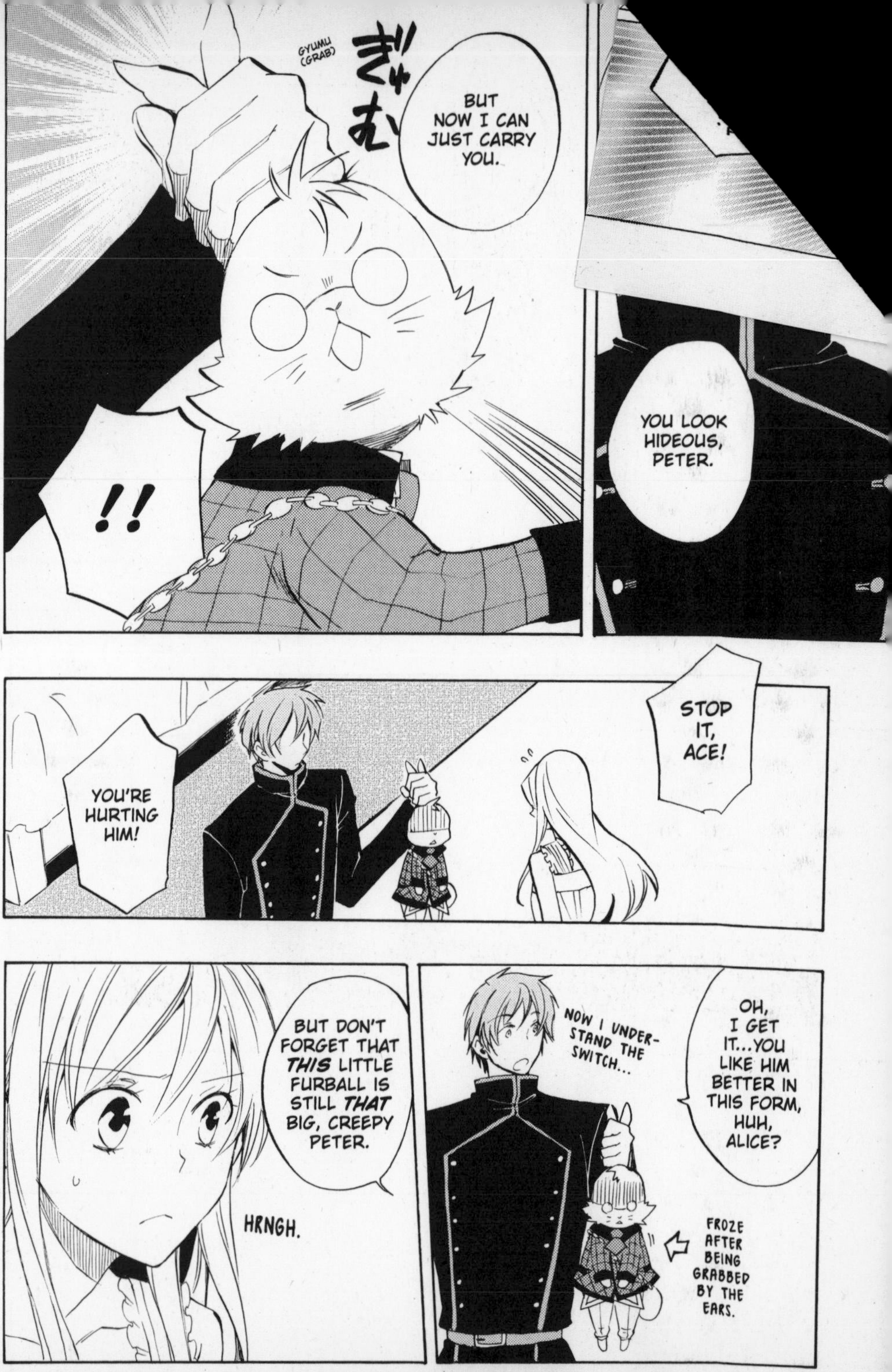
YOU LOOK HIDEOUS, PETER.
ぎゅむ
GYUMU (GRAB)
BUT NOW I CAN JUST CARRY YOU.
!!
STOP IT, ACE!
YOU'RE HURTING HIM!
OH, I GET IT...YOU LIKE HIM BETTER IN THIS FORM, HUH, ALICE?
NOW I UNDERSTAND THE SWITCH...
FROZE AFTER BEING GRABBED BY THE EARS.
BUT DON'T FORGET THAT *THIS* LITTLE FURBALL IS STILL *THAT* BIG, CREEPY PETER.
HRNGH.

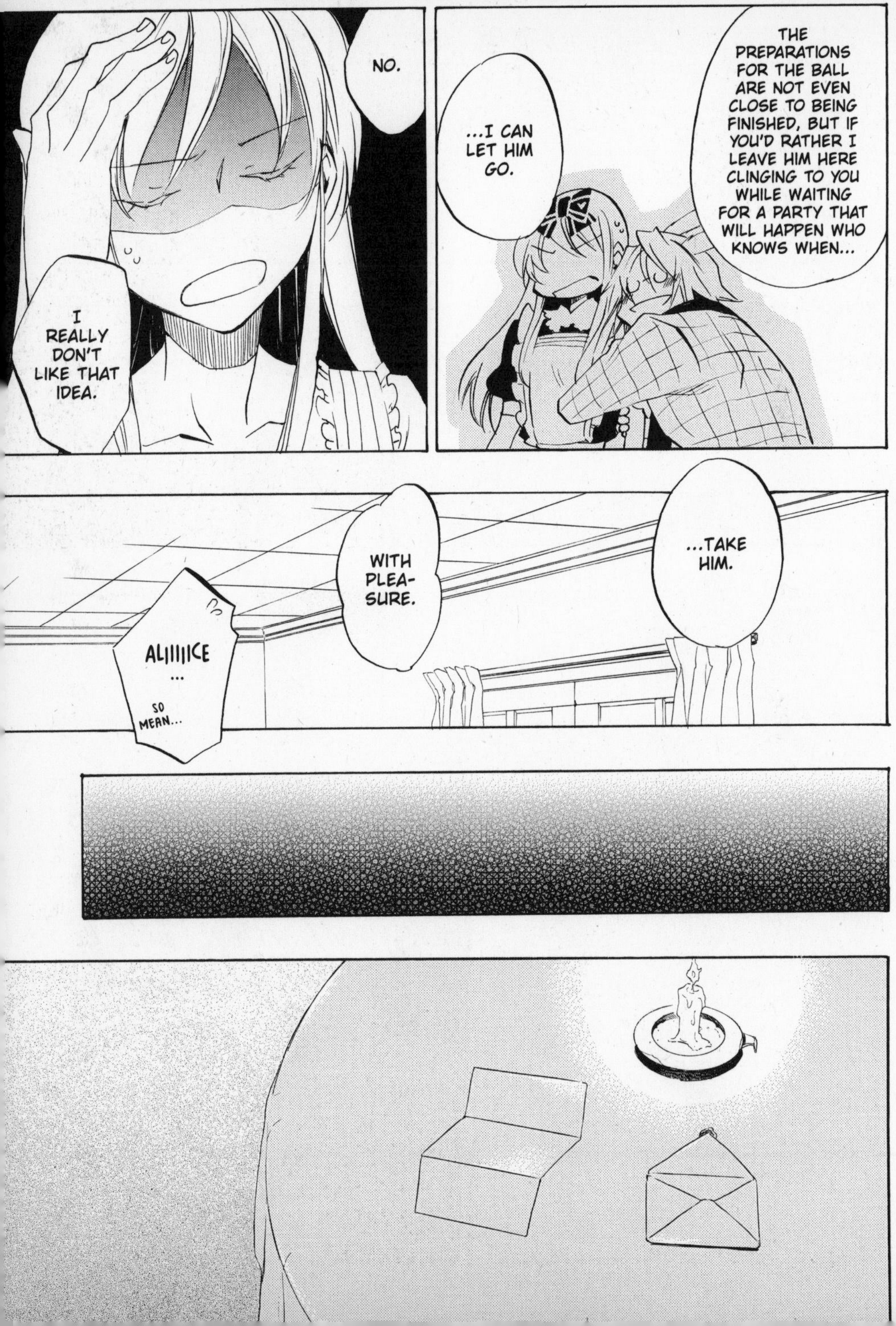
THE PREPARATIONS FOR THE BALL ARE NOT EVEN CLOSE TO BEING FINISHED, BUT IF YOU'D RATHER I LEAVE HIM HERE CLINGING TO YOU WHILE WAITING FOR A PARTY THAT WILL HAPPEN WHO KNOWS WHEN...
...I CAN LET HIM GO.
NO.
I REALLY DON'T LIKE THAT IDEA.
...TAKE HIM.
WITH PLEA-SURE.
ALIIIIICE...
SO MEAN...

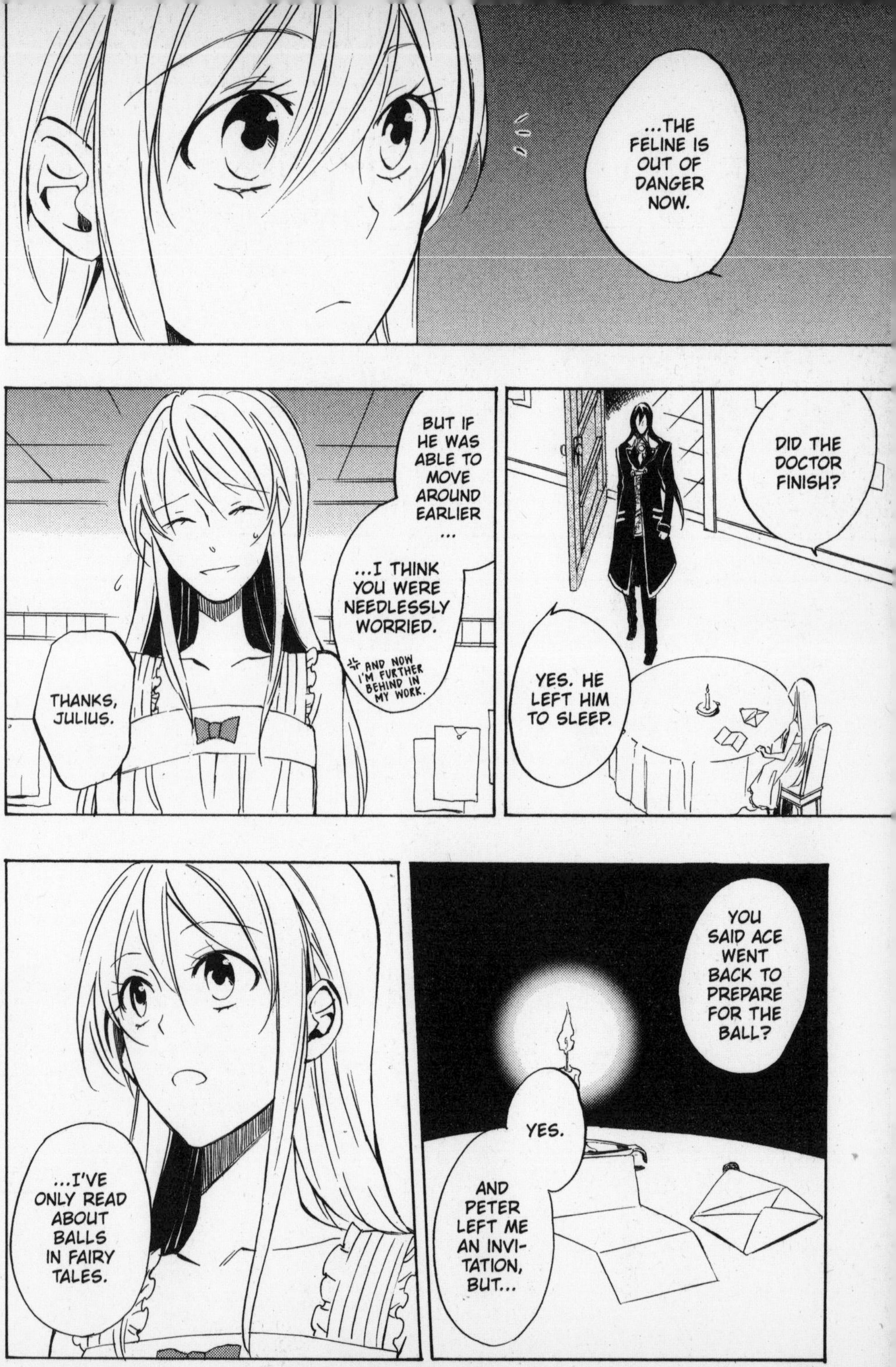
...THE FELINE IS OUT OF DANGER NOW.
DID THE DOCTOR FINISH?
YES. HE LEFT HIM TO SLEEP.
BUT IF HE WAS ABLE TO MOVE AROUND EARLIER...
...I THINK YOU WERE NEEDLESSLY WORRIED.
AND NOW I'M FURTHER BEHIND IN MY WORK.
THANKS, JULIUS.
YOU SAID ACE WENT BACK TO PREPARE FOR THE BALL?
YES.
AND PETER LEFT ME AN INVITATION, BUT...
...I'VE ONLY READ ABOUT BALLS IN FAIRY TALES.

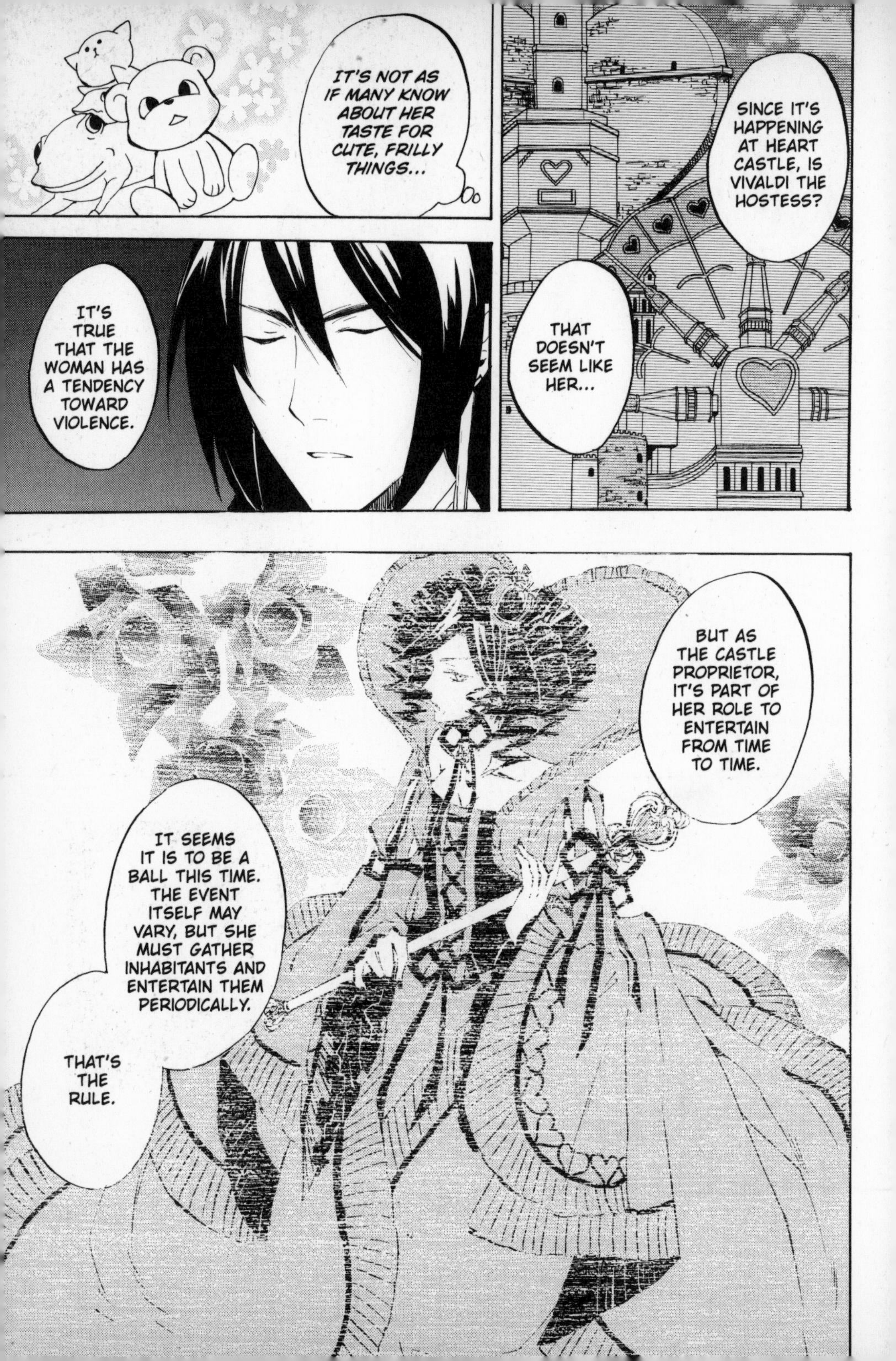
SINCE IT'S HAPPENING AT HEART CASTLE, IS VIVALDI THE HOSTESS?
THAT DOESN'T SEEM LIKE HER...
IT'S NOT AS IF MANY KNOW ABOUT HER TASTE FOR CUTE, FRILLY THINGS...
IT'S TRUE THAT THE WOMAN HAS A TENDENCY TOWARD VIOLENCE.
BUT AS THE CASTLE PROPRIETOR, IT'S PART OF HER ROLE TO ENTERTAIN FROM TIME TO TIME.
IT SEEMS IT IS TO BE A BALL THIS TIME. THE EVENT ITSELF MAY VARY, BUT SHE MUST GATHER INHABITANTS AND ENTERTAIN THEM PERIODICALLY.
THAT'S THE RULE.

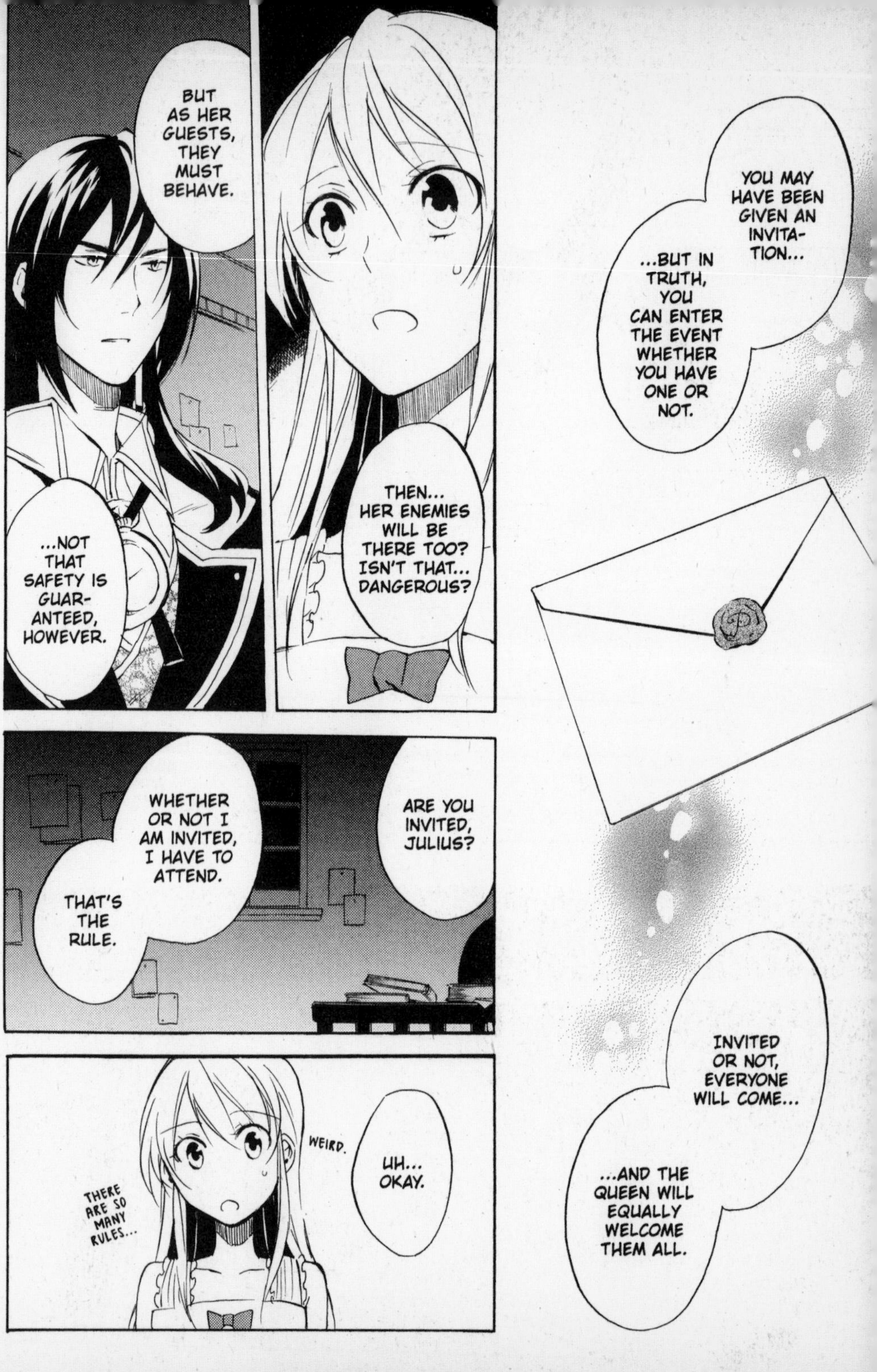
YOU MAY HAVE BEEN GIVEN AN INVITA-TION...
...BUT IN TRUTH, YOU CAN ENTER THE EVENT WHETHER YOU HAVE ONE OR NOT.
INVITED OR NOT, EVERYONE WILL COME...
...AND THE QUEEN WILL EQUALLY WELCOME THEM ALL.
THEN... HER ENEMIES WILL BE THERE TOO? ISN'T THAT... DANGEROUS?
BUT AS HER GUESTS, THEY MUST BEHAVE.
...NOT THAT SAFETY IS GUAR-ANTEED, HOWEVER.
ARE YOU INVITED, JULIUS?
WHETHER OR NOT I AM INVITED, I HAVE TO ATTEND.
THAT'S THE RULE.
UH... OKAY.
WEIRD.
THERE ARE SO MANY RULES...

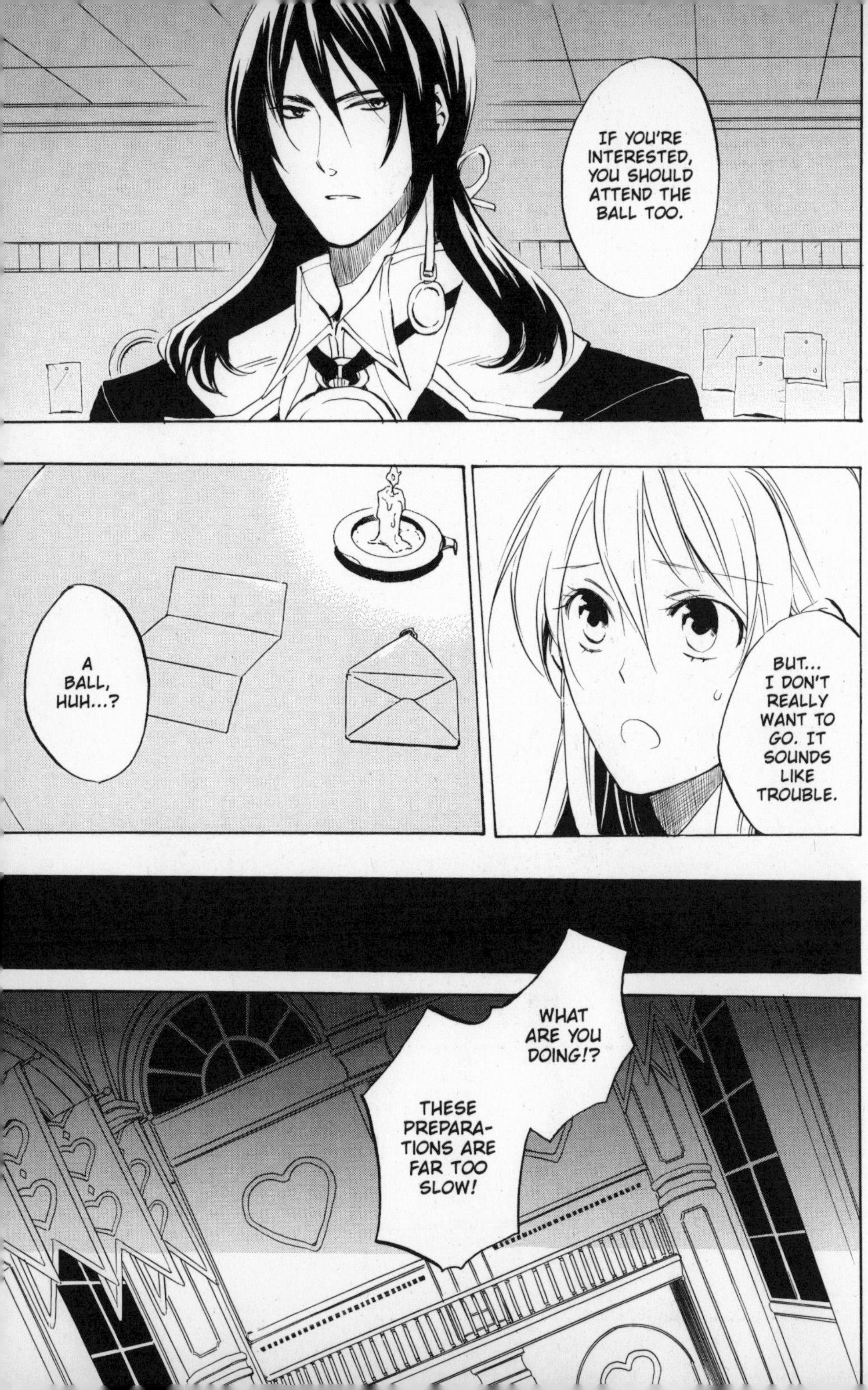
IF YOU'RE INTERESTED, YOU SHOULD ATTEND THE BALL TOO.
BUT... I DON'T REALLY WANT TO GO. IT SOUNDS LIKE TROUBLE.
A BALL, HUH...?
WHAT ARE YOU DOING!?
THESE PREPARATIONS ARE FAR TOO SLOW!

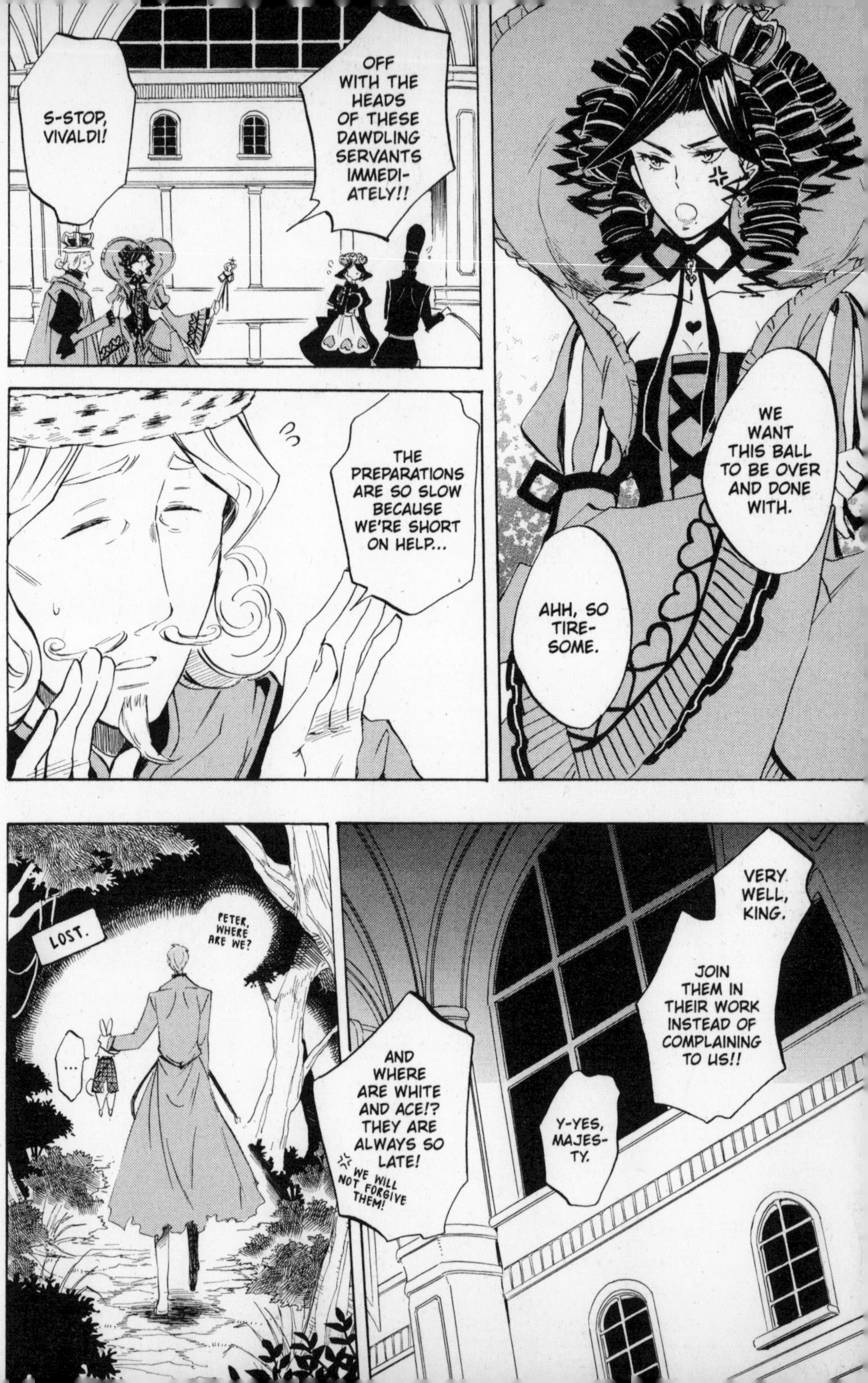

WE WANT THIS BALL TO BE OVER AND DONE WITH.
AHH, SO TIRE-SOME.
OFF WITH THE HEADS OF THESE DAWDLING SERVANTS IMMEDI-ATELY!!
S-STOP, VIVALDI!
THE PREPARATIONS ARE SO SLOW BECAUSE WE'RE SHORT ON HELP...
VERY WELL, KING.
JOIN THEM IN THEIR WORK INSTEAD OF COMPLAINING TO US!!
AND WHERE ARE WHITE AND ACE!? THEY ARE ALWAYS SO LATE!
WE WILL NOT FORGIVE THEM!
Y-YES, MAJES-TY.
PETER, WHERE ARE WE?
LOST.
...

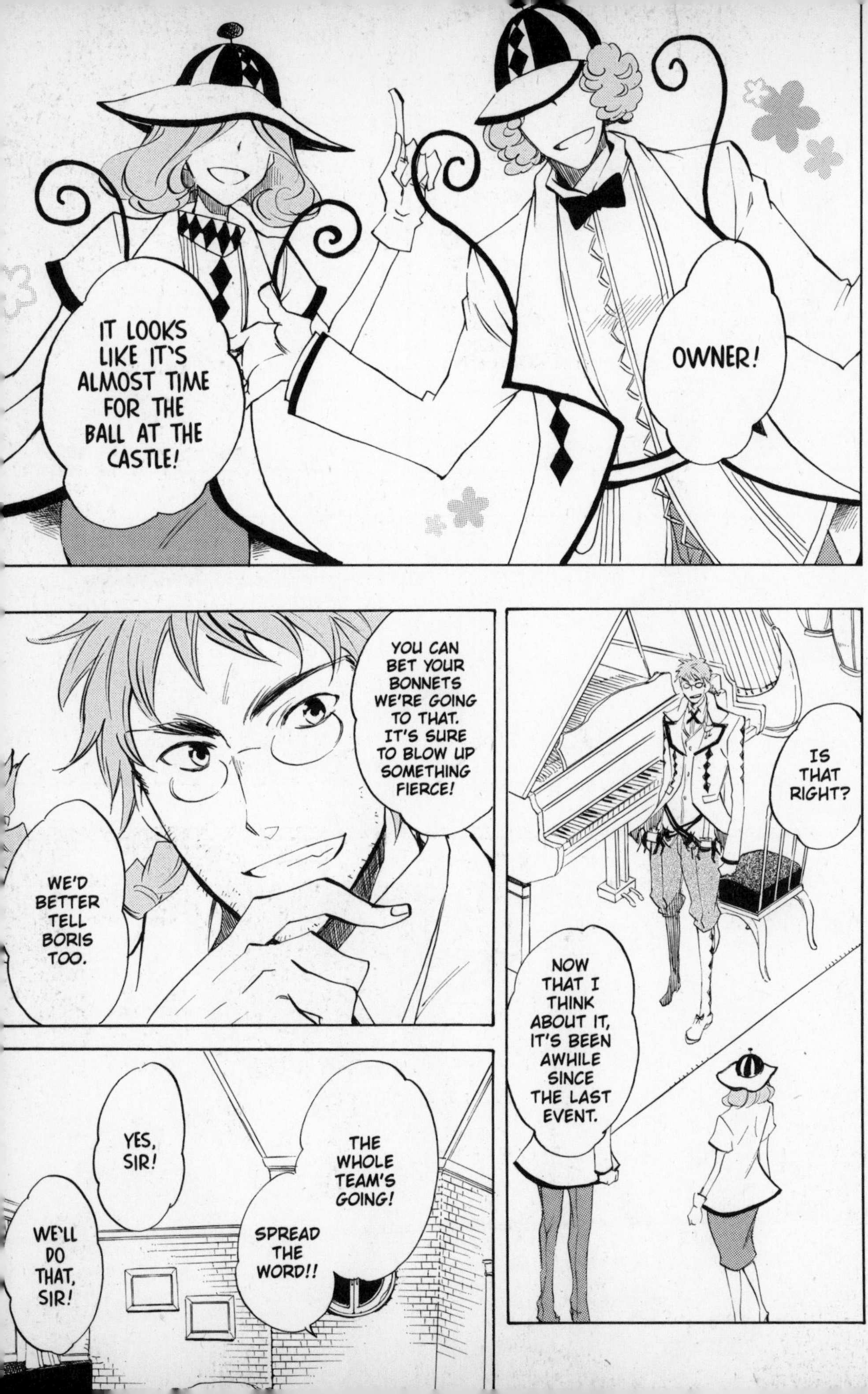
OWNER!
IT LOOKS LIKE IT'S ALMOST TIME FOR THE BALL AT THE CASTLE!
IS THAT RIGHT?
NOW THAT I THINK ABOUT IT, IT'S BEEN AWHILE SINCE THE LAST EVENT.
YOU CAN BET YOUR BONNETS WE'RE GOING TO THAT. IT'S SURE TO BLOW UP SOMETHING FIERCE!
WE'D BETTER TELL BORIS TOO.
THE WHOLE TEAM'S GOING!
YES, SIR!
SPREAD THE WORD!!
WE'LL DO THAT, SIR!

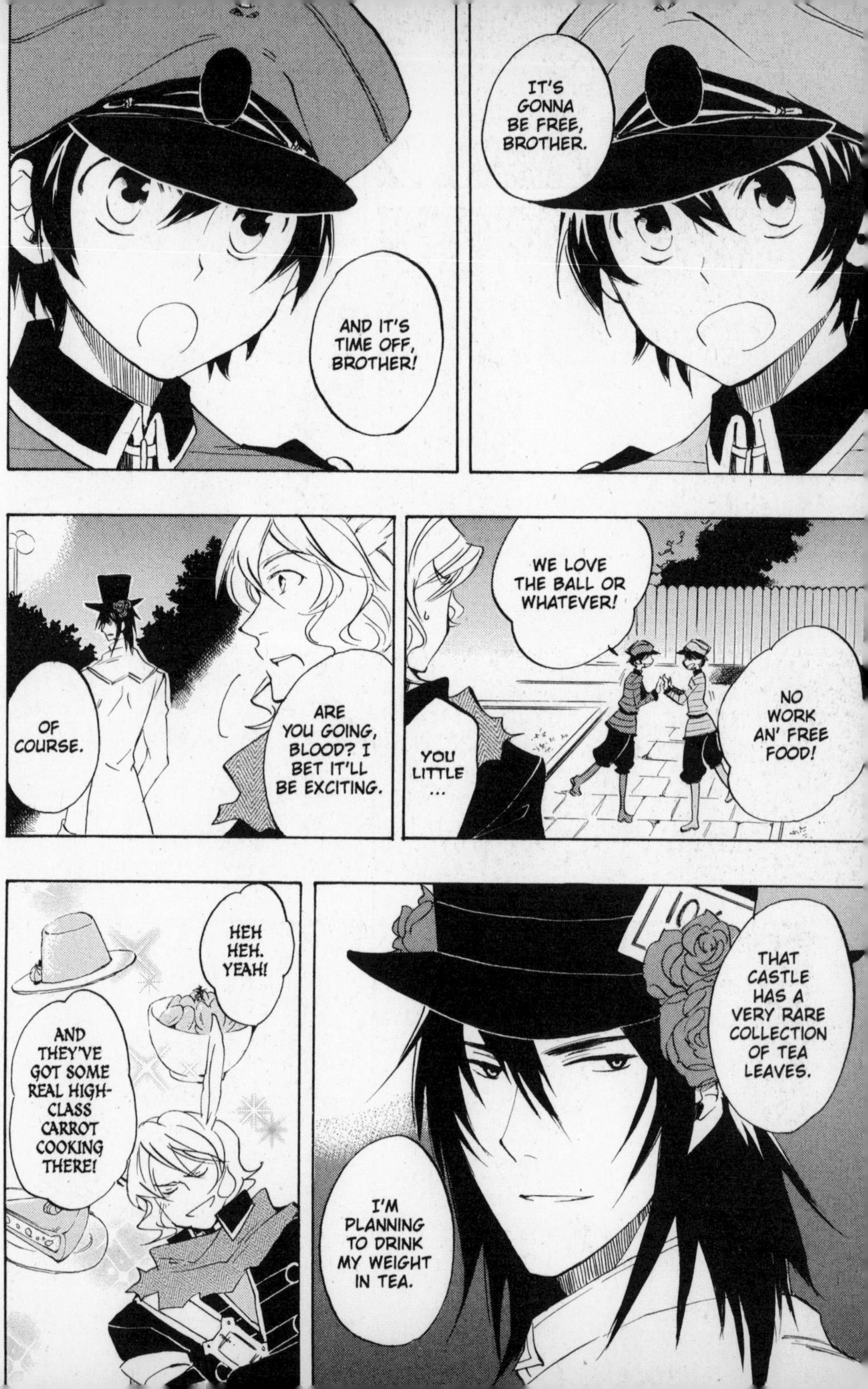
IT'S GONNA BE FREE, BROTHER.
AND IT'S TIME OFF, BROTHER!
WE LOVE THE BALL OR WHATEVER!
NO WORK AN' FREE FOOD!
YOU LITTLE ...
ARE YOU GOING, BLOOD? I BET IT'LL BE EXCITING.
OF COURSE.
THAT CASTLE HAS A VERY RARE COLLECTION OF TEA LEAVES.
I'M PLANNING TO DRINK MY WEIGHT IN TEA.
HEH HEH. YEAH!
AND THEY'VE GOT SOME REAL HIGH-CLASS CARROT COOKING THERE!

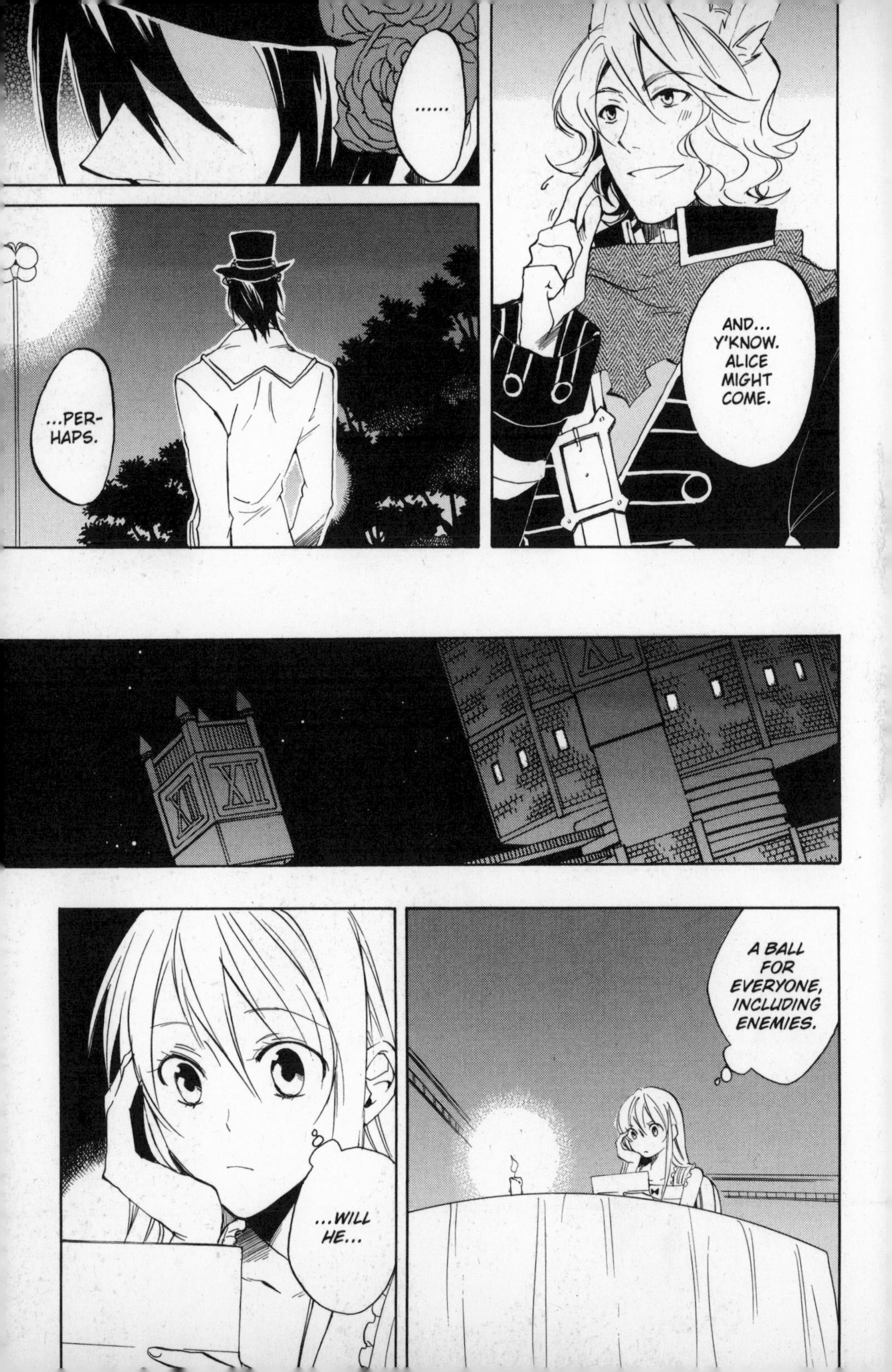
AND... Y'KNOW. ALICE MIGHT COME.
......
...PER-HAPS.
A BALL FOR EVERYONE, INCLUDING ENEMIES.
...WILL HE...

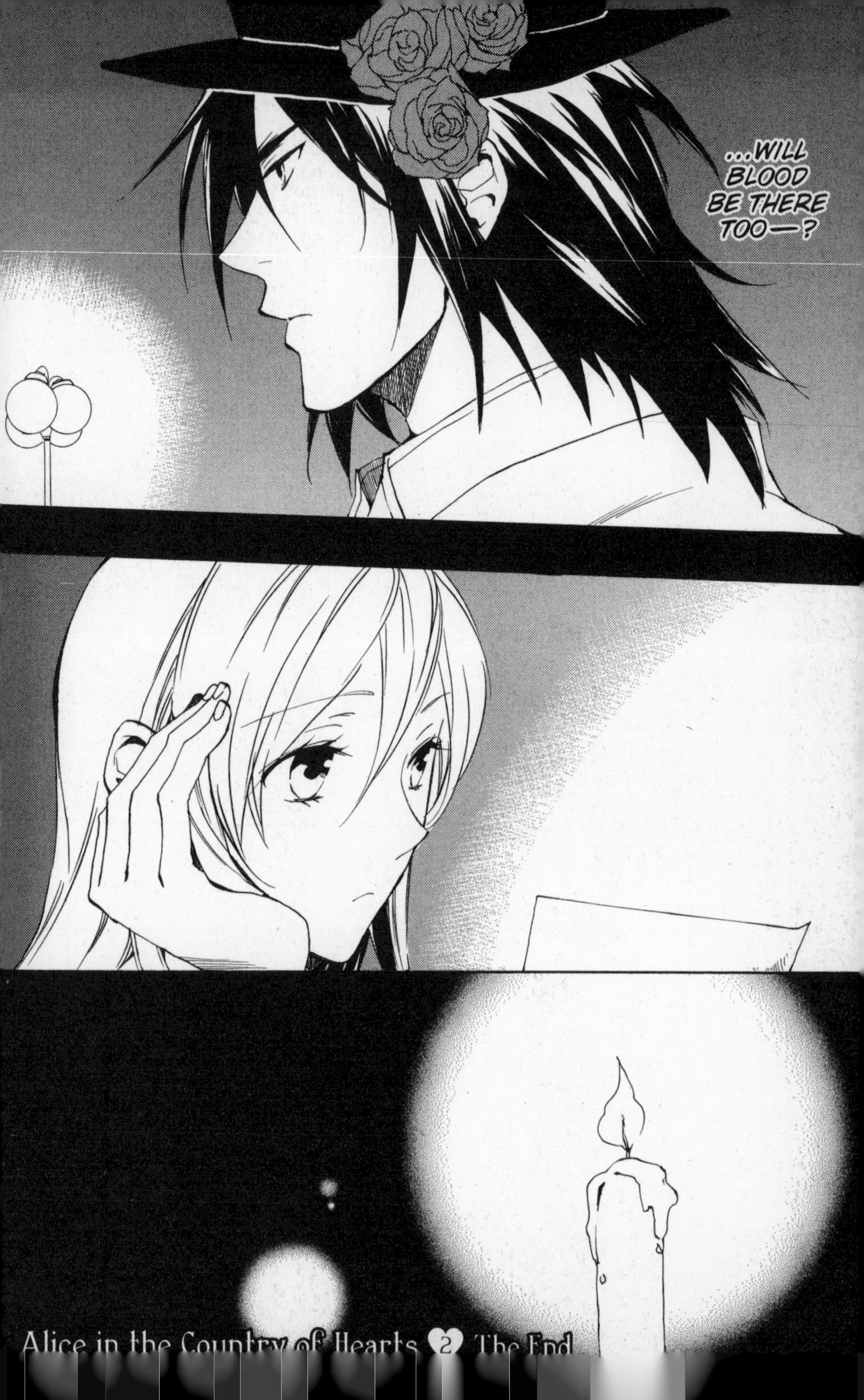
...WILL BLOOD BE THERE TOO—?
Alice in the Country of Hearts 2 The End

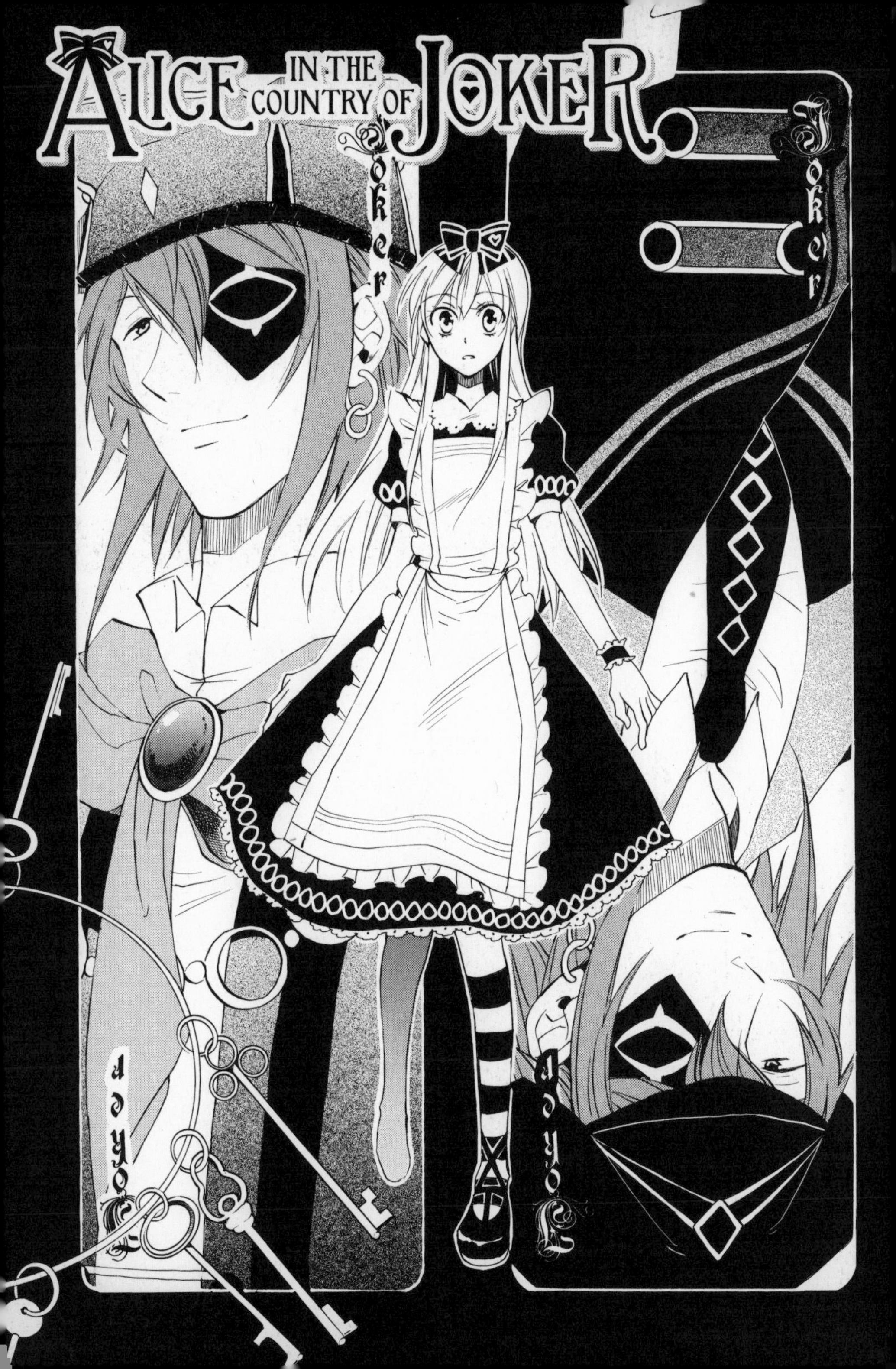
ALICE IN THE COUNTRY OF JOKER
Joker
Joker
Joker
Joker

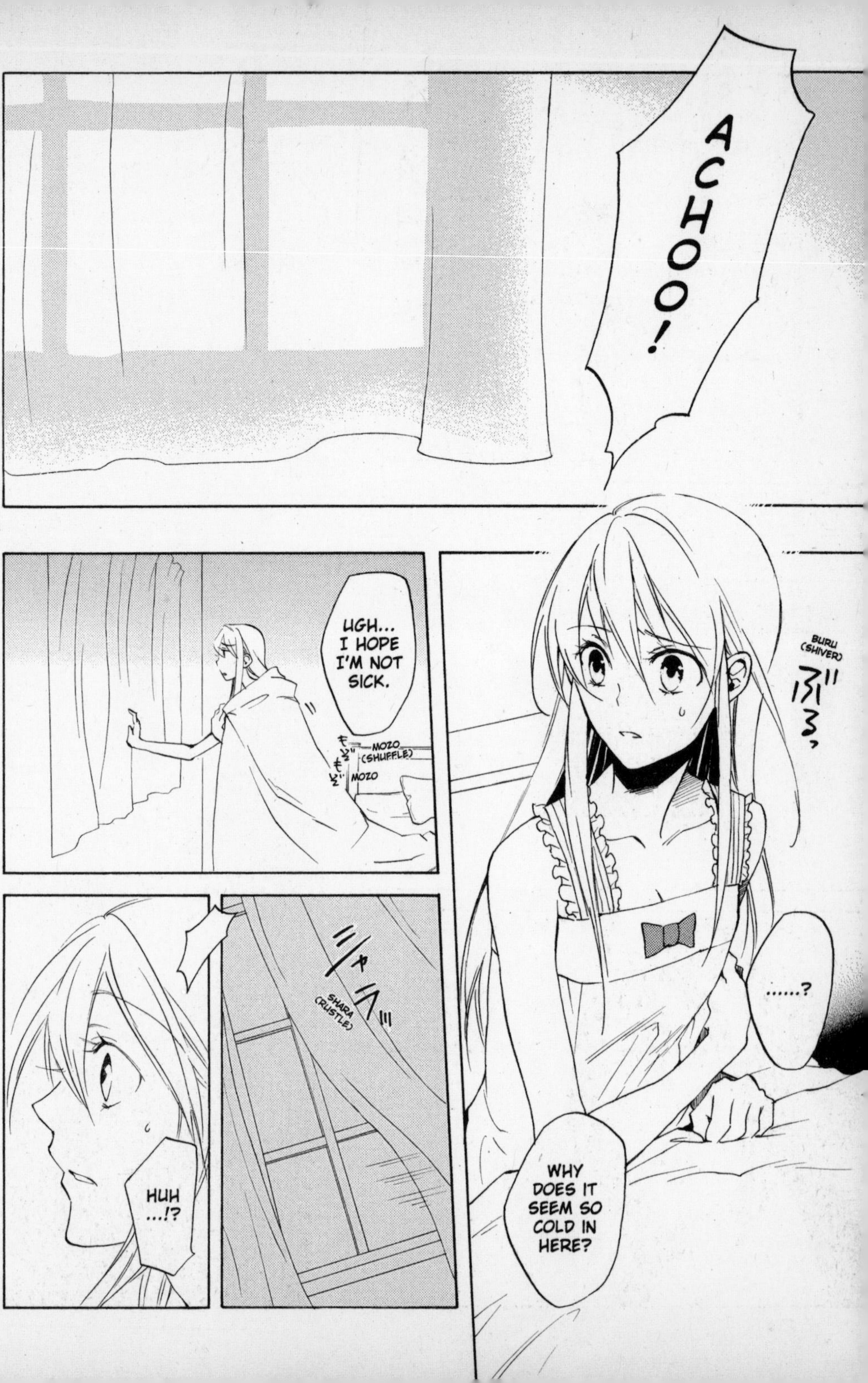
ACHOO!
BURU (SHIVER)
ぶるっ
......?
WHY DOES IT SEEM SO COLD IN HERE?
UGH... I HOPE I'M NOT SICK.
MOZO (SHUFFLE) MOZO
SHARA (RUSTLE)
シャラ
HUH ...!?

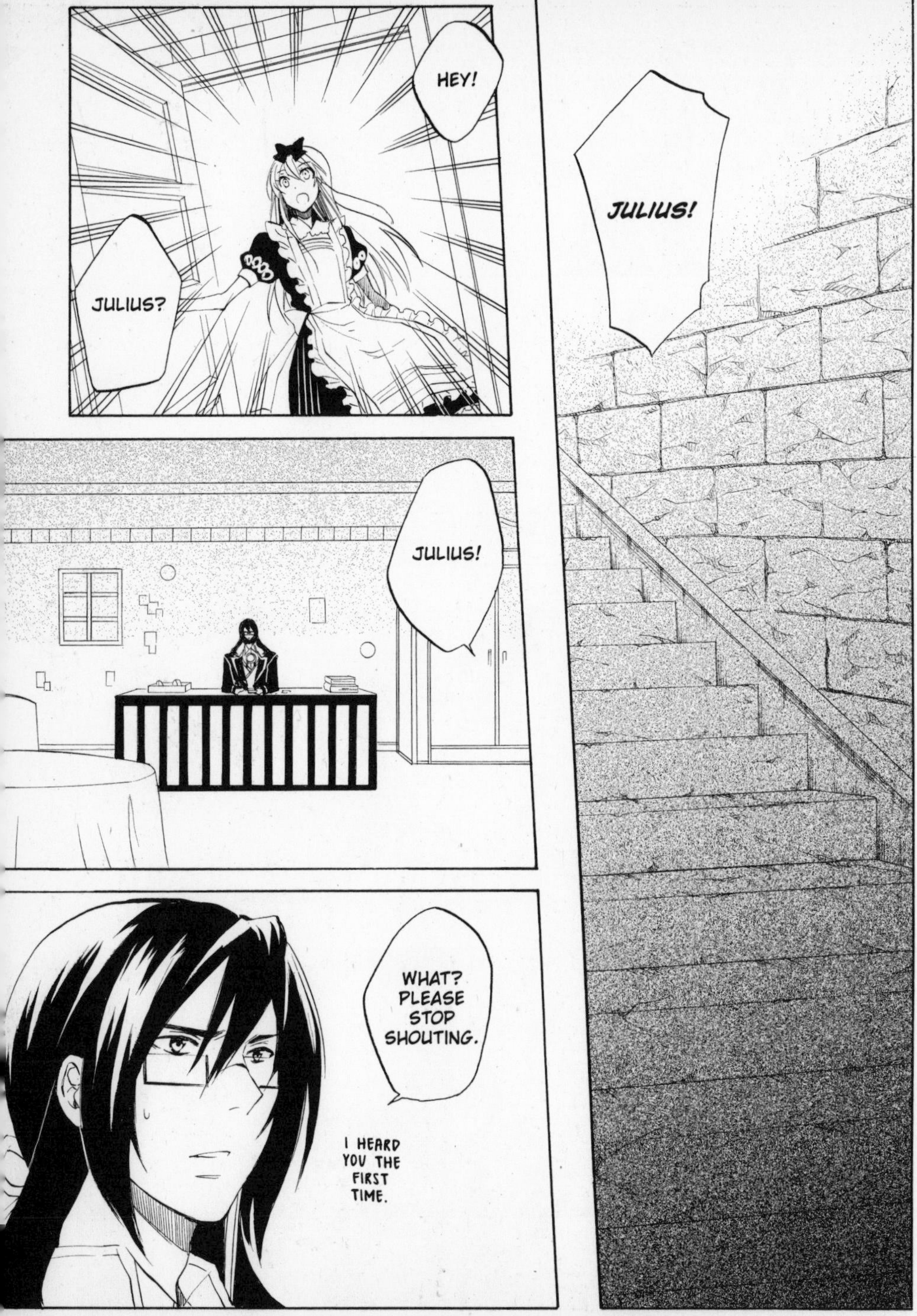
JULIUS!
HEY!
JULIUS?
JULIUS!
WHAT? PLEASE STOP SHOUTING.
I HEARD YOU THE FIRST TIME.

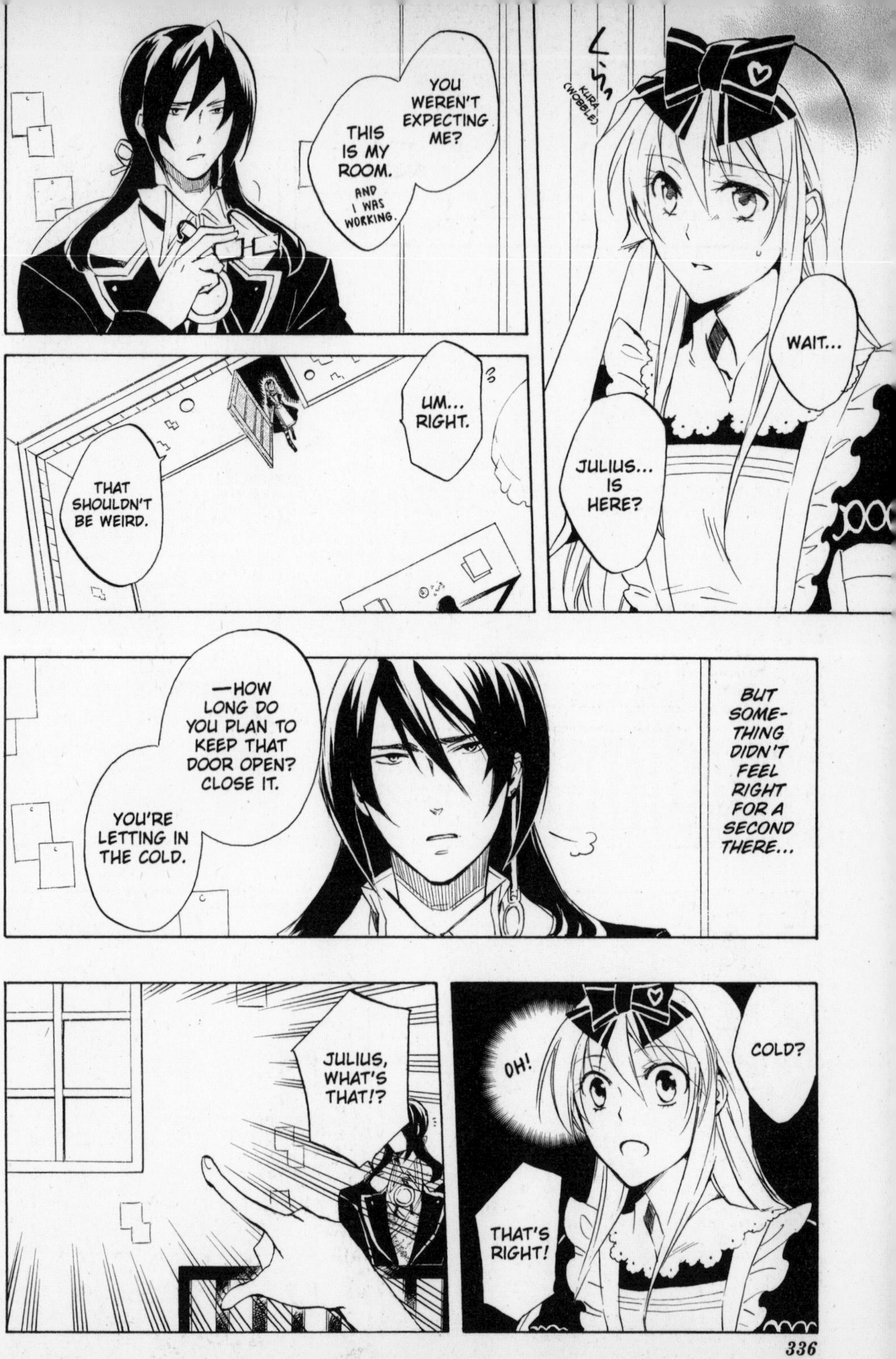
KURA (WOBBLE)
WAIT...
JULIUS... IS HERE?
YOU WEREN'T EXPECTING ME?
THIS IS MY ROOM.
AND I WAS WORKING.
UM... RIGHT.
THAT SHOULDN'T BE WEIRD.
BUT SOMETHING DIDN'T FEEL RIGHT FOR A SECOND THERE...
—HOW LONG DO YOU PLAN TO KEEP THAT DOOR OPEN? CLOSE IT.
YOU'RE LETTING IN THE COLD.
COLD?
OH!
THAT'S RIGHT!
JULIUS, WHAT'S THAT!?

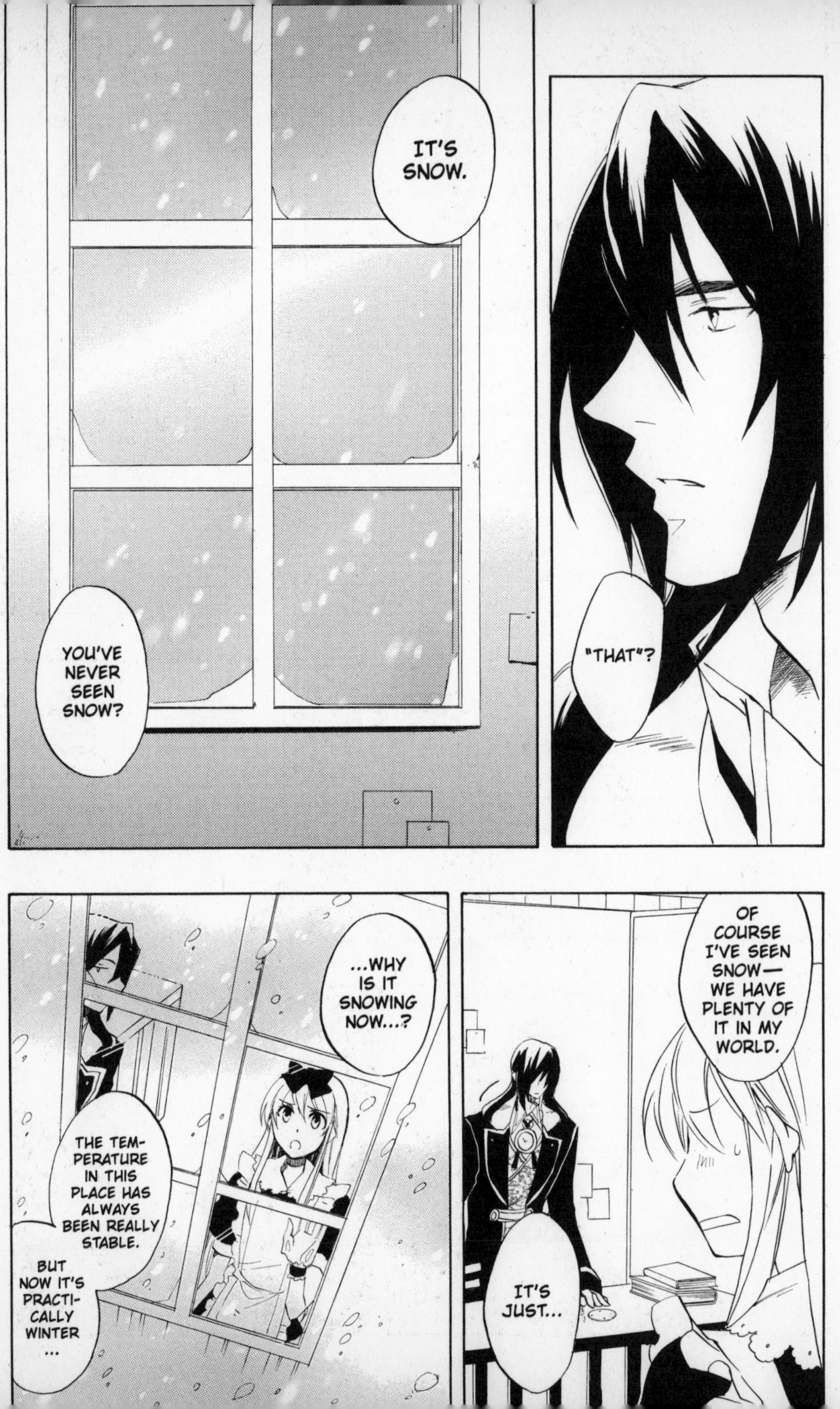
"THAT"?
IT'S SNOW.
YOU'VE NEVER SEEN SNOW?
OF COURSE I'VE SEEN SNOW— WE HAVE PLENTY OF IT IN MY WORLD.
IT'S JUST...
...WHY IS IT SNOWING NOW...?
THE TEMPERATURE IN THIS PLACE HAS ALWAYS BEEN REALLY STABLE.
BUT NOW IT'S PRACTICALLY WINTER...

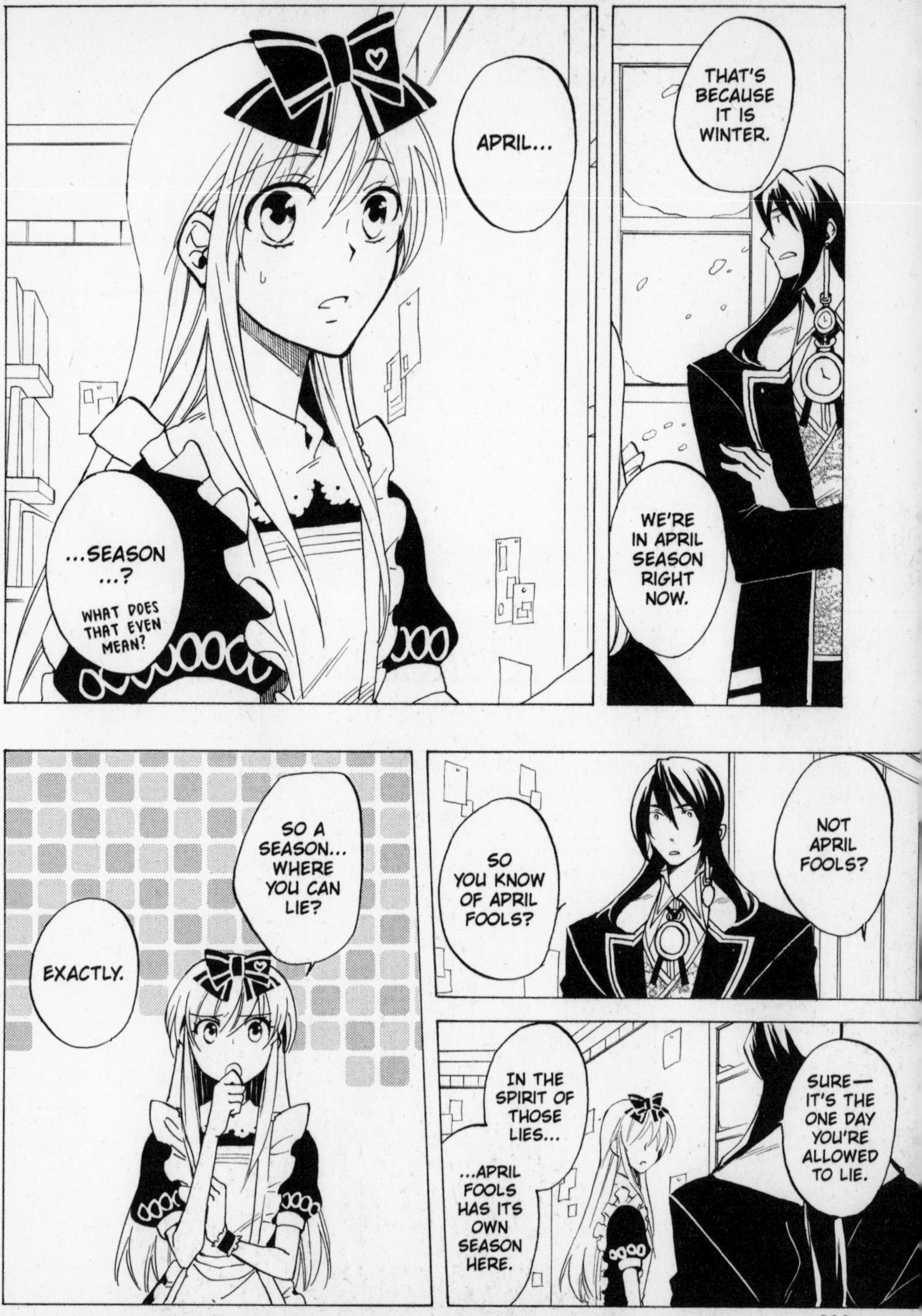
THAT'S BECAUSE IT IS WINTER.
WE'RE IN APRIL SEASON RIGHT NOW.
APRIL...
...SEASON ...?
WHAT DOES THAT EVEN MEAN?
NOT APRIL FOOLS?
SO YOU KNOW OF APRIL FOOLS?
SURE— IT'S THE ONE DAY YOU'RE ALLOWED TO LIE.
IN THE SPIRIT OF THOSE LIES...
...APRIL FOOLS HAS ITS OWN SEASON HERE.
SO A SEASON... WHERE YOU CAN LIE?
EXACTLY.

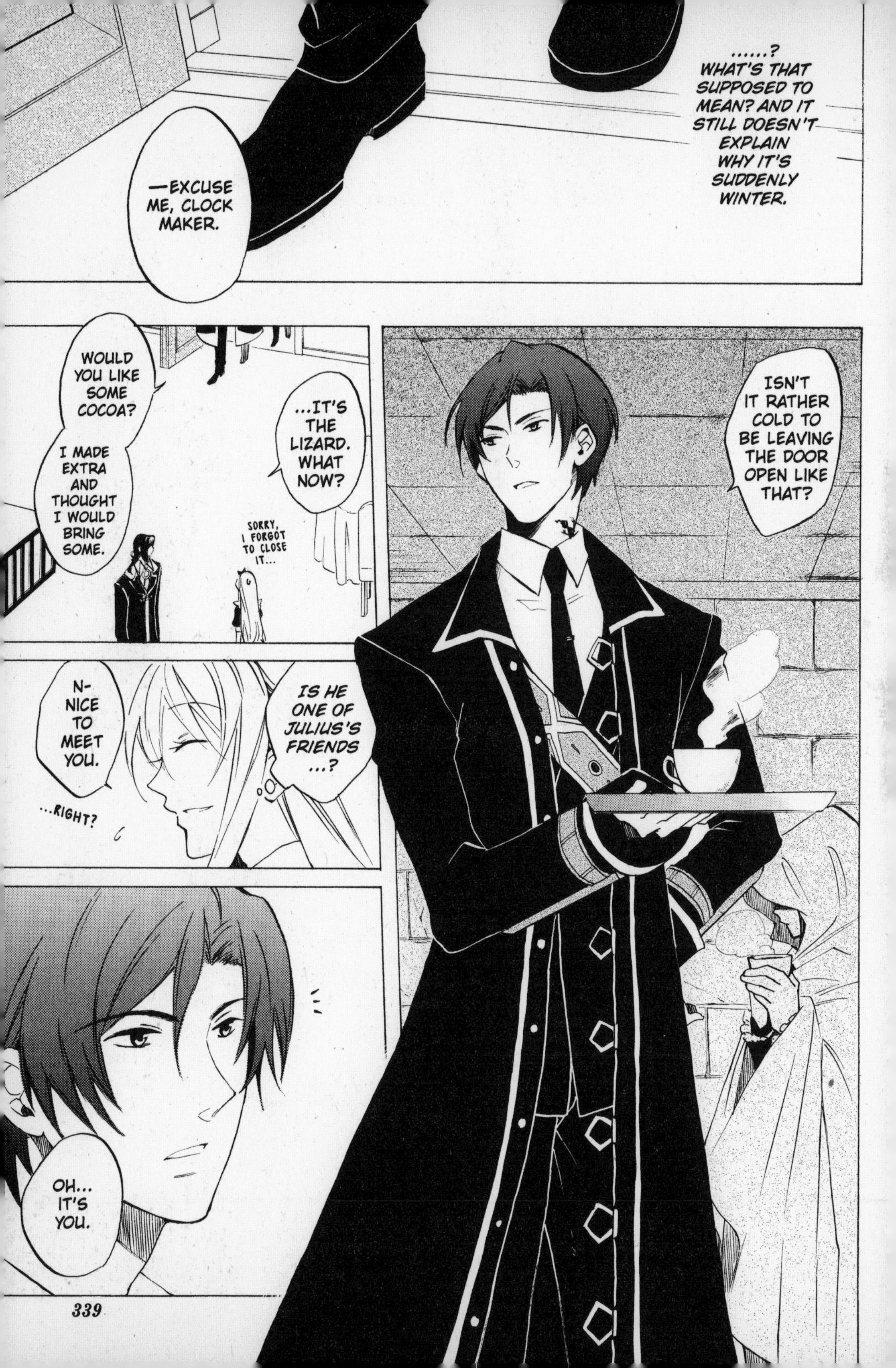
......? WHAT'S THAT SUPPOSED TO MEAN? AND IT STILL DOESN'T EXPLAIN WHY IT'S SUDDENLY WINTER.
—EXCUSE ME, CLOCK MAKER.
ISN'T IT RATHER COLD TO BE LEAVING THE DOOR OPEN LIKE THAT?
...IT'S THE LIZARD. WHAT NOW?
WOULD YOU LIKE SOME COCOA?
I MADE EXTRA AND THOUGHT I WOULD BRING SOME.
SORRY, I FORGOT TO CLOSE IT...
IS HE ONE OF JULIUS'S FRIENDS ...?
N-NICE TO MEET YOU.
...RIGHT?
OH... IT'S YOU.

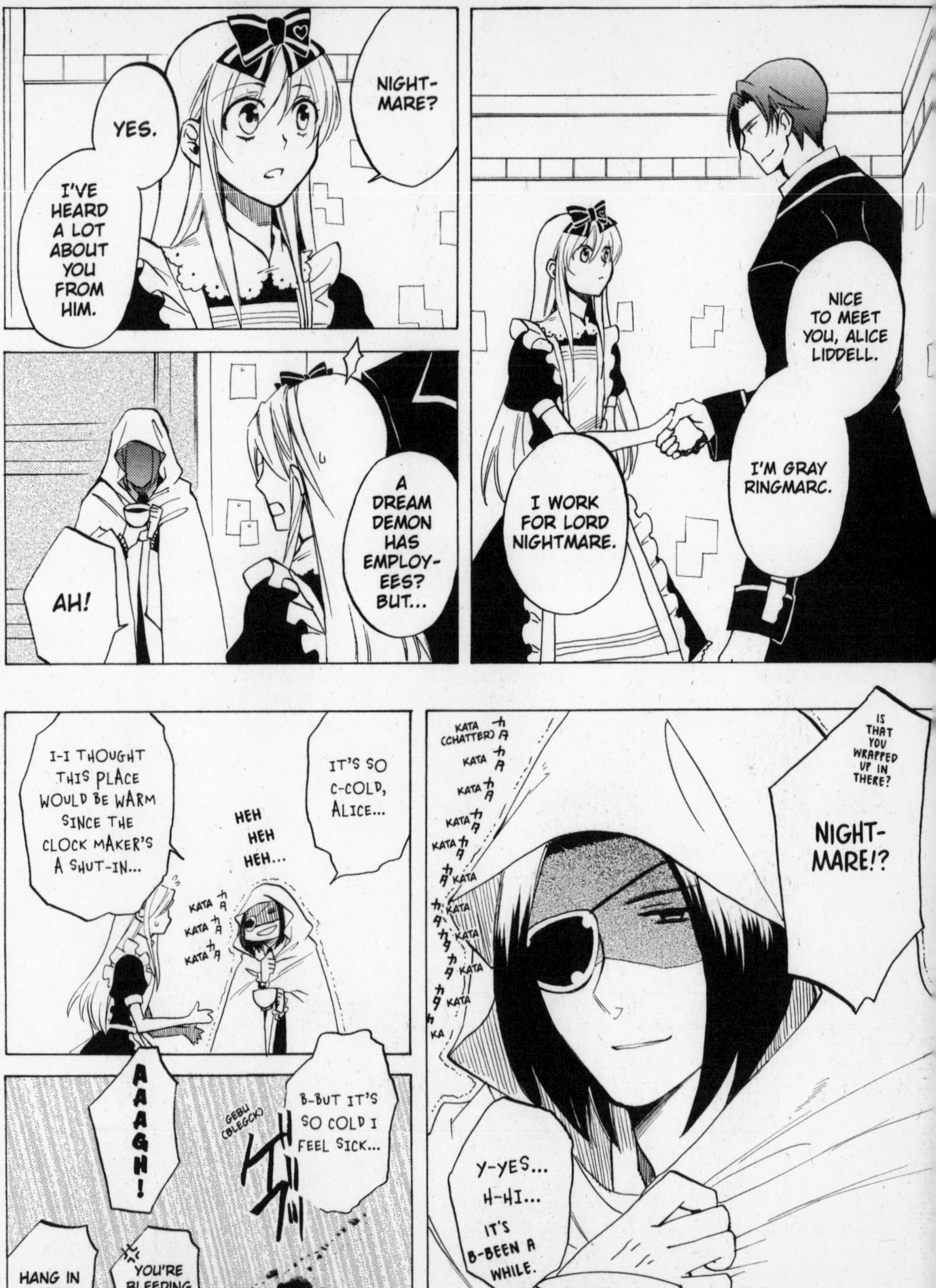
NICE TO MEET YOU, ALICE LIDDELL.
I'M GRAY RINGMARC.
I WORK FOR LORD NIGHTMARE.
NIGHT-MARE?
YES.
I'VE HEARD A LOT ABOUT YOU FROM HIM.
A DREAM DEMON HAS EMPLOY-EES? BUT...
AH!
IS THAT YOU WRAPPED UP IN THERE?
NIGHT-MARE!?
KATA (CHATTER) カタ
KATA カタ
KATA カタ
KATA カタ
KATA カタ
カタ KATA
カタ KATA
カタ KATA
カタ KATA
カタ KATA
カ KA
Y-YES... H-HI... IT'S B-BEEN A WHILE.
IT'S SO C-COLD, ALICE...
HEH HEH HEH...
I-I THOUGHT THIS PLACE WOULD BE WARM SINCE THE CLOCK MAKER'S A SHUT-IN...
KATA カタ
KATA カタ
KATA カタ
B-BUT IT'S SO COLD I FEEL SICK...
GEBU (BLEGGK)
AAAGN!
YOU'RE BLEEDING ON MY FLOOR ...!
HANG IN THERE, MY LORD!

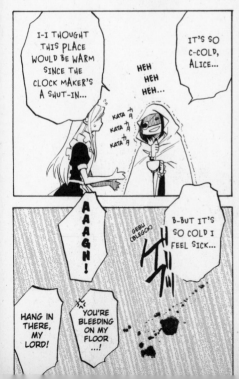

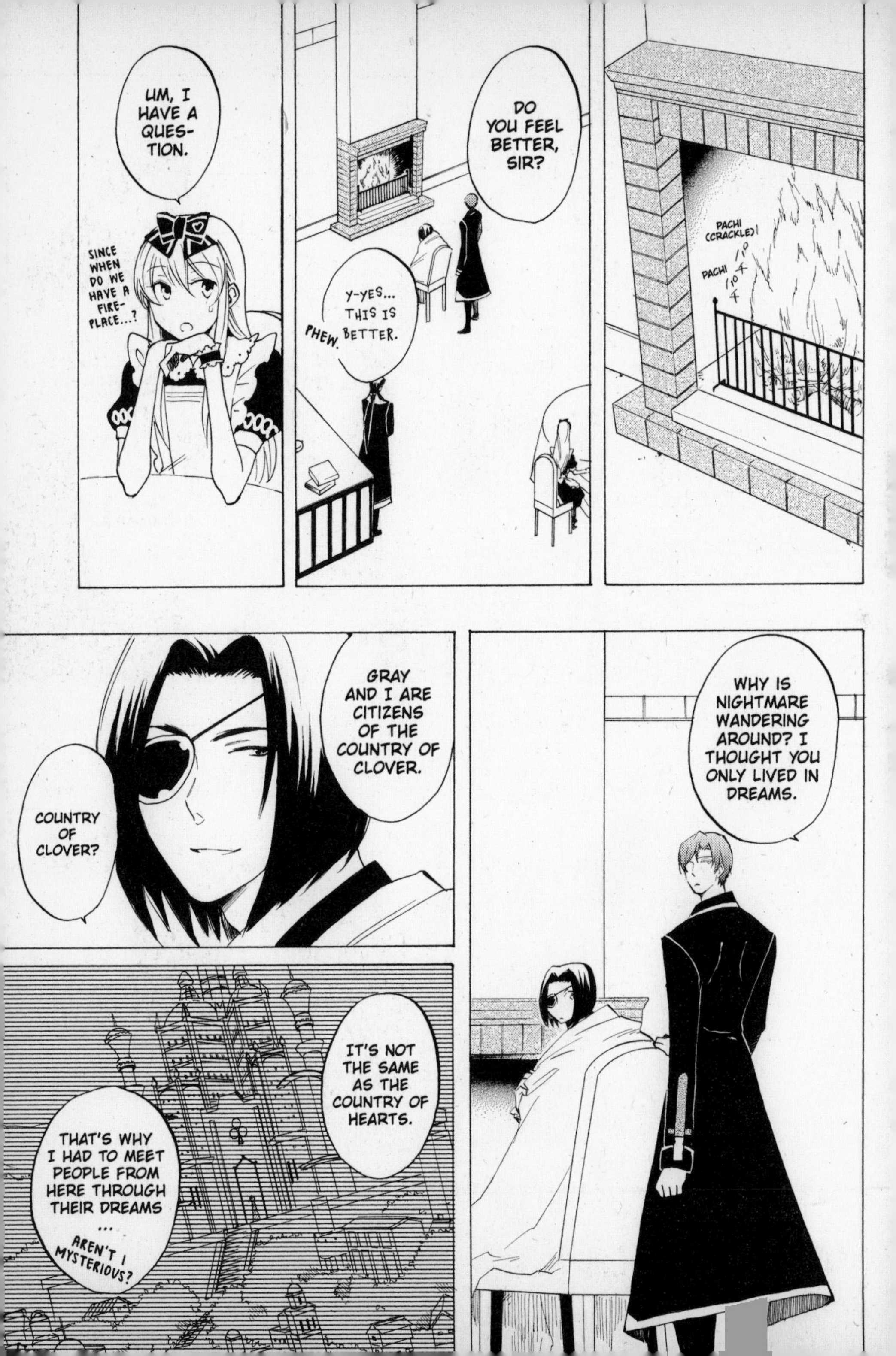
PACHI (CRACKLE)
PACHI
DO YOU FEEL BETTER, SIR?
Y-YES... THIS IS BETTER.
PHEW.
UM, I HAVE A QUES-TION.
SINCE WHEN DO WE HAVE A FIRE-PLACE...?
WHY IS NIGHTMARE WANDERING AROUND? I THOUGHT YOU ONLY LIVED IN DREAMS.
GRAY AND I ARE CITIZENS OF THE COUNTRY OF CLOVER.
COUNTRY OF CLOVER?
IT'S NOT THE SAME AS THE COUNTRY OF HEARTS.
THAT'S WHY I HAD TO MEET PEOPLE FROM HERE THROUGH THEIR DREAMS ...
AREN'T I MYSTERIOUS?

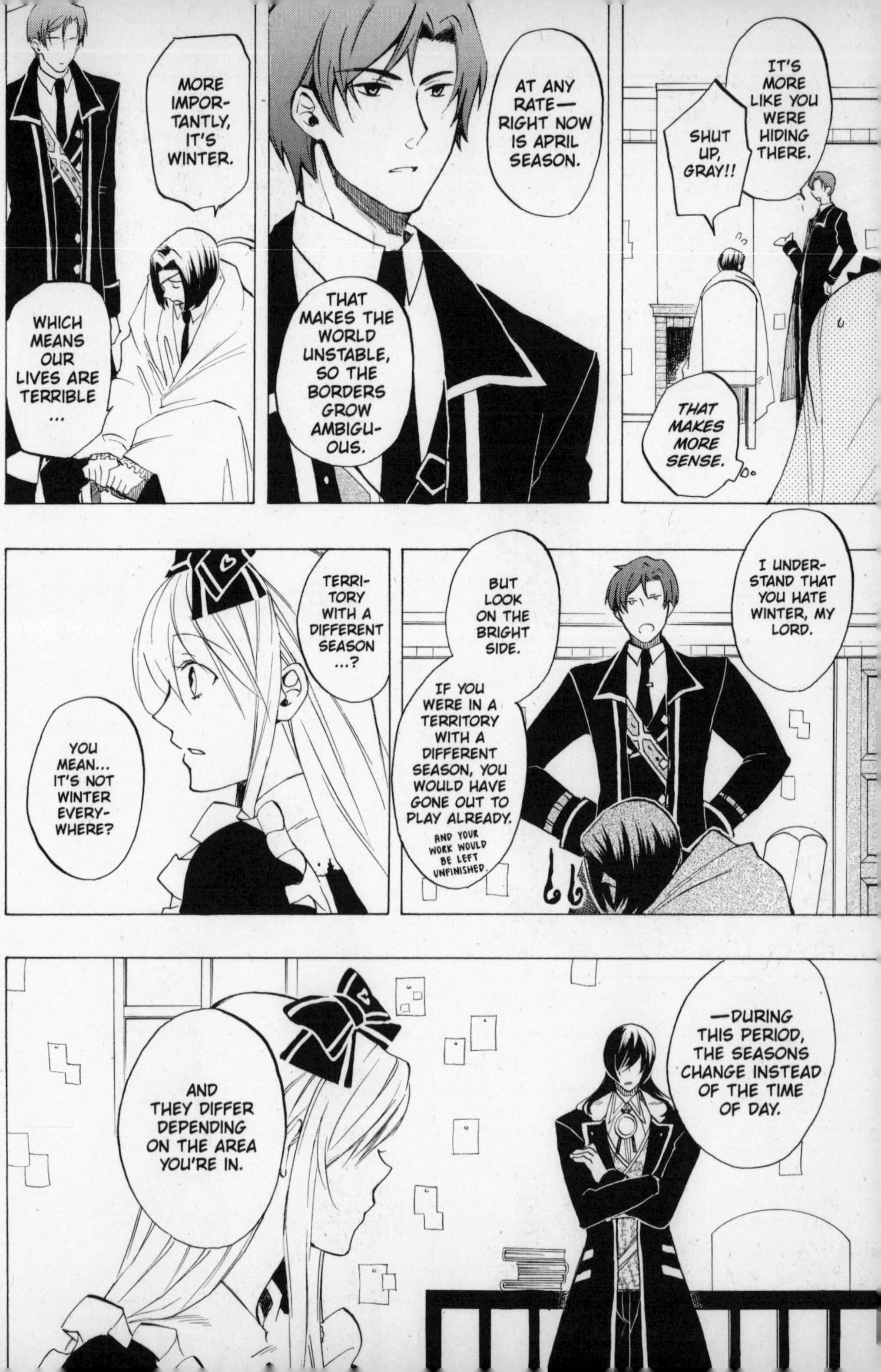
IT'S MORE LIKE YOU WERE HIDING THERE.
SHUT UP, GRAY!!
THAT MAKES MORE SENSE.
AT ANY RATE— RIGHT NOW IS APRIL SEASON.
THAT MAKES THE WORLD UNSTABLE, SO THE BORDERS GROW AMBIGUOUS.
MORE IMPORTANTLY, IT'S WINTER.
WHICH MEANS OUR LIVES ARE TERRIBLE...
I UNDERSTAND THAT YOU HATE WINTER, MY LORD.
BUT LOOK ON THE BRIGHT SIDE.
IF YOU WERE IN A TERRITORY WITH A DIFFERENT SEASON, YOU WOULD HAVE GONE OUT TO PLAY ALREADY.
AND YOUR WORK WOULD BE LEFT UNFINISHED.
TERRITORY WITH A DIFFERENT SEASON...?
YOU MEAN... IT'S NOT WINTER EVERYWHERE?
—DURING THIS PERIOD, THE SEASONS CHANGE INSTEAD OF THE TIME OF DAY.
AND THEY DIFFER DEPENDING ON THE AREA YOU'RE IN.

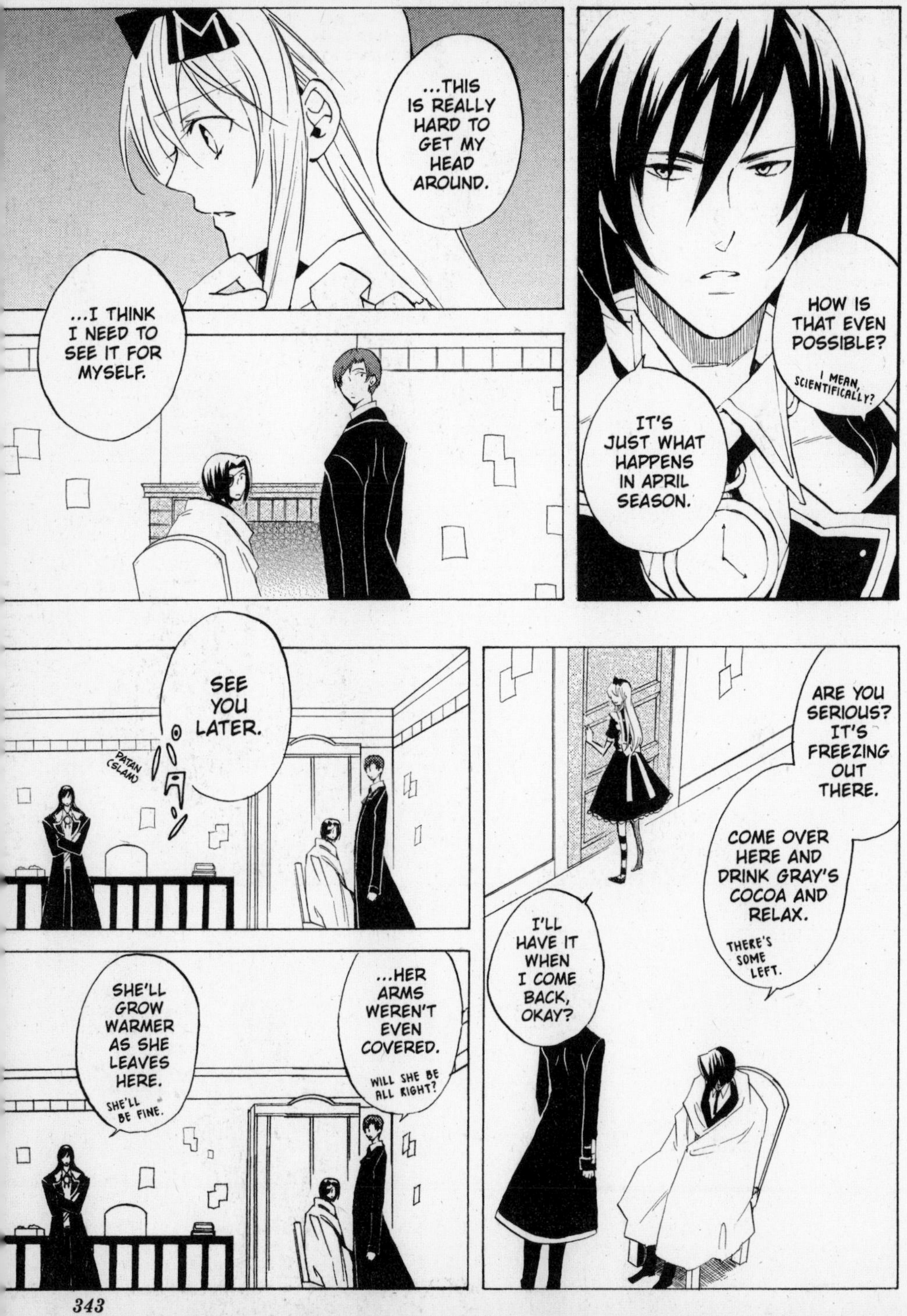
HOW IS THAT EVEN POSSIBLE?
I MEAN, SCIENTIFICALLY?
IT'S JUST WHAT HAPPENS IN APRIL SEASON.
...THIS IS REALLY HARD TO GET MY HEAD AROUND.
...I THINK I NEED TO SEE IT FOR MYSELF.
ARE YOU SERIOUS? IT'S FREEZING OUT THERE.
COME OVER HERE AND DRINK GRAY'S COCOA AND RELAX.
THERE'S SOME LEFT.
I'LL HAVE IT WHEN I COME BACK, OKAY?
SEE YOU LATER.
PATAN (SLAM)
...HER ARMS WEREN'T EVEN COVERED.
WILL SHE BE ALL RIGHT?
SHE'LL GROW WARMER AS SHE LEAVES HERE.
SHE'LL BE FINE.

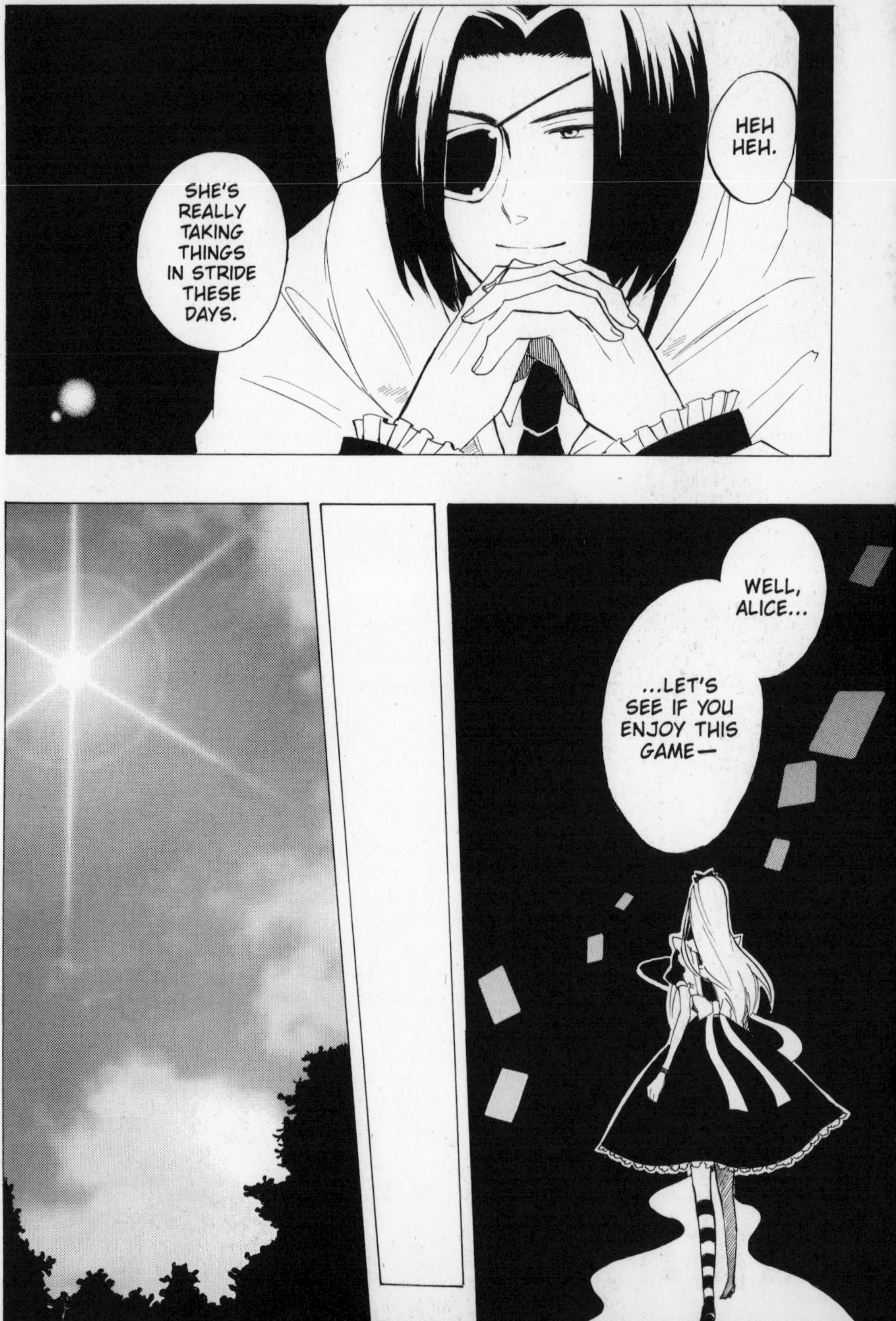
HEH HEH.
SHE'S REALLY TAKING THINGS IN STRIDE THESE DAYS.
WELL, ALICE...
...LET'S SEE IF YOU ENJOY THIS GAME—

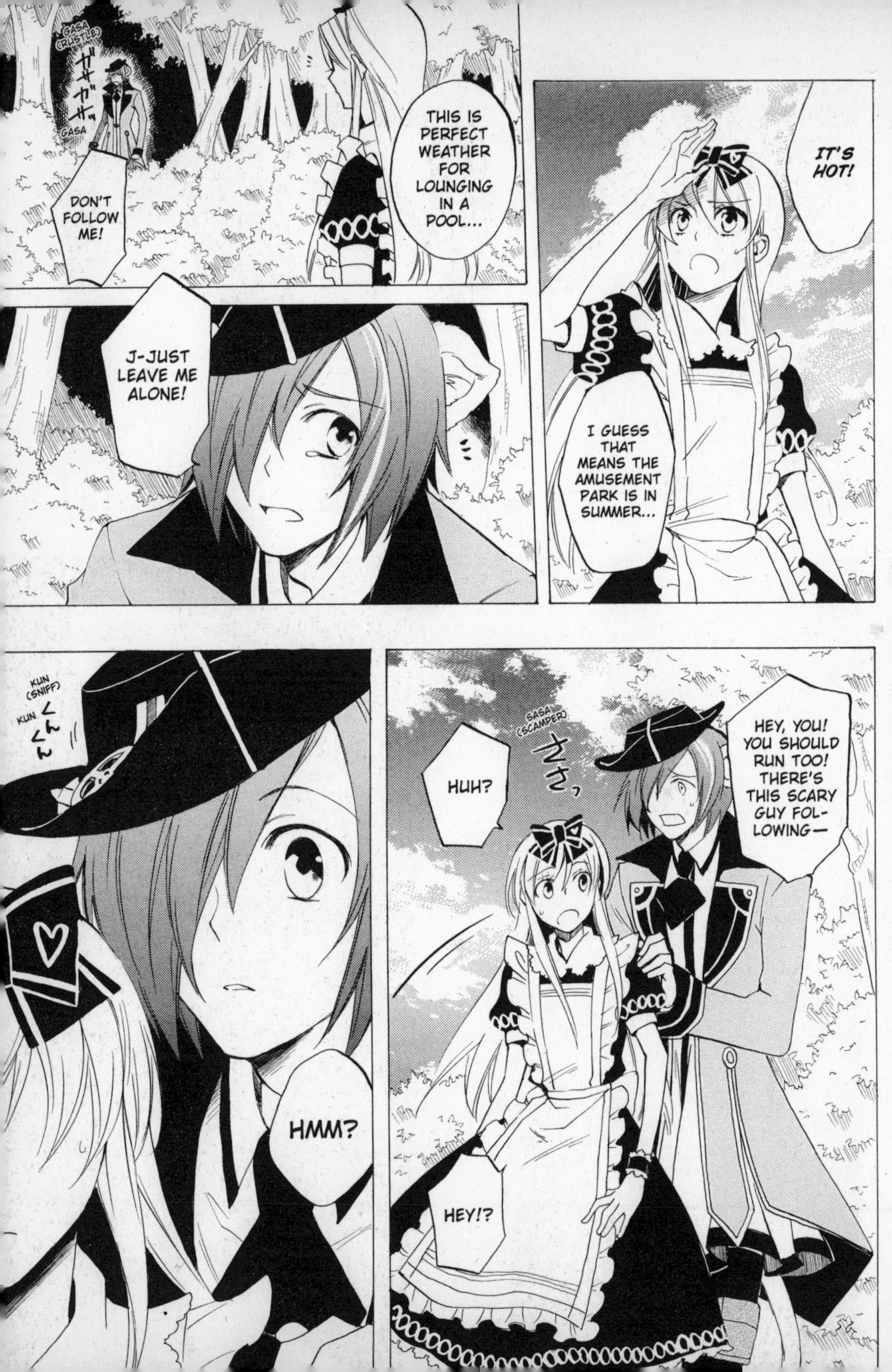
IT'S HOT!
I GUESS THAT MEANS THE AMUSEMENT PARK IS IN SUMMER...
THIS IS PERFECT WEATHER FOR LOUNGING IN A POOL...
GASA (RUSTLE) GASA
ガサガサッ
DON'T FOLLOW ME!
J-JUST LEAVE ME ALONE!
HEY, YOU! YOU SHOULD RUN TOO! THERE'S THIS SCARY GUY FOL-LOWING—
SASA (SCAMPER)
ささっ
HUH?
HEY!?
KUN (SNIFF) KUN
くんくん
HMM?

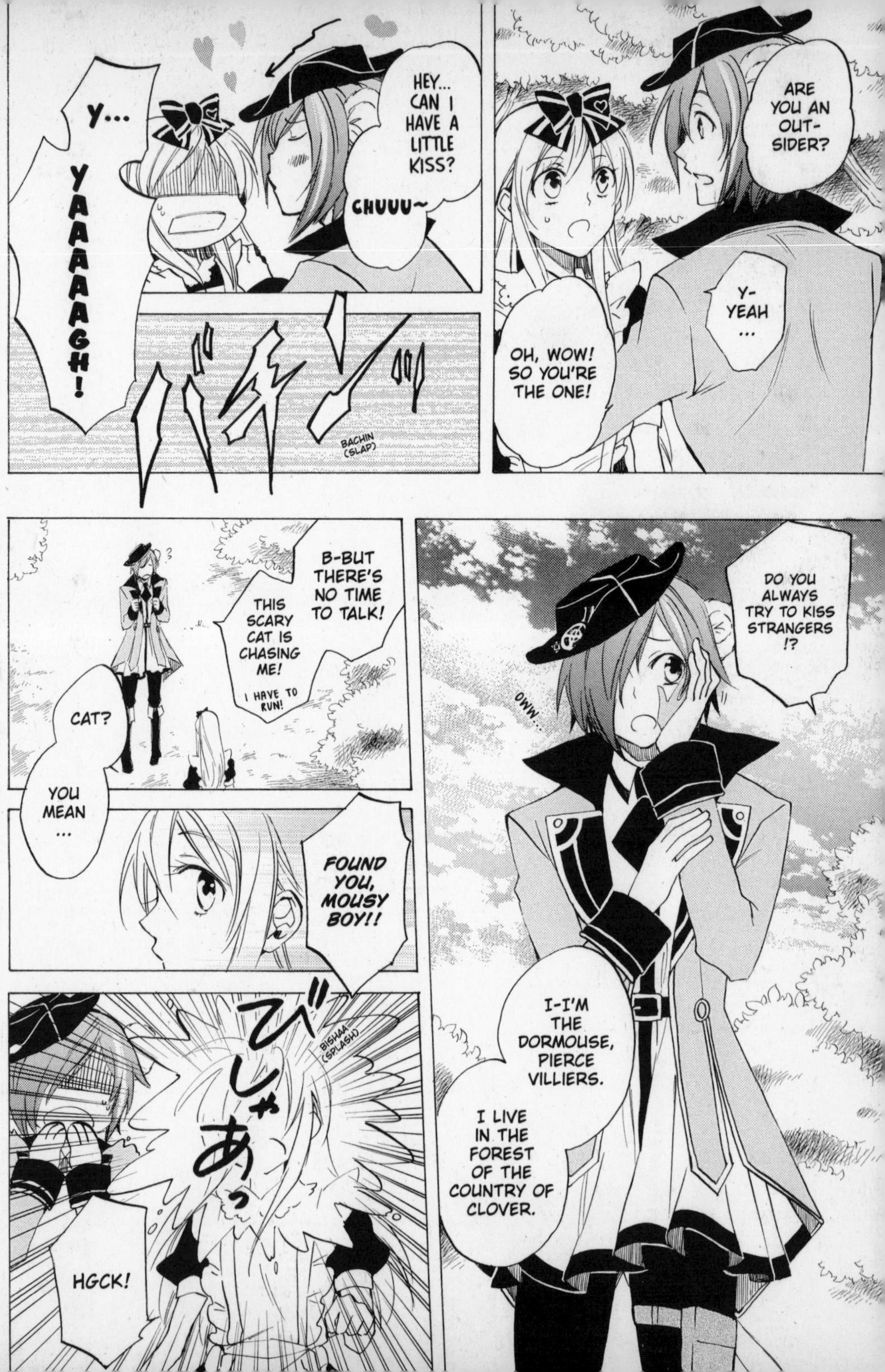
ARE YOU AN OUT-SIDER?
Y-YEAH ...
OH, WOW! SO YOU'RE THE ONE!
HEY... CAN I HAVE A LITTLE KISS?
CHUUU~
Y...
YAAAAAGH!
バチン
BACHIN (SLAP)
DO YOU ALWAYS TRY TO KISS STRANGERS !?
OWW...
I-I'M THE DORMOUSE, PIERCE VILLIERS.
I LIVE IN THE FOREST OF THE COUNTRY OF CLOVER.
B-BUT THERE'S NO TIME TO TALK!
THIS SCARY CAT IS CHASING ME!
I HAVE TO RUN!
CAT?
YOU MEAN ...
FOUND YOU, MOUSY BOY!!
びしゃあっ
BISHAA (SPLASH)
HGCK!

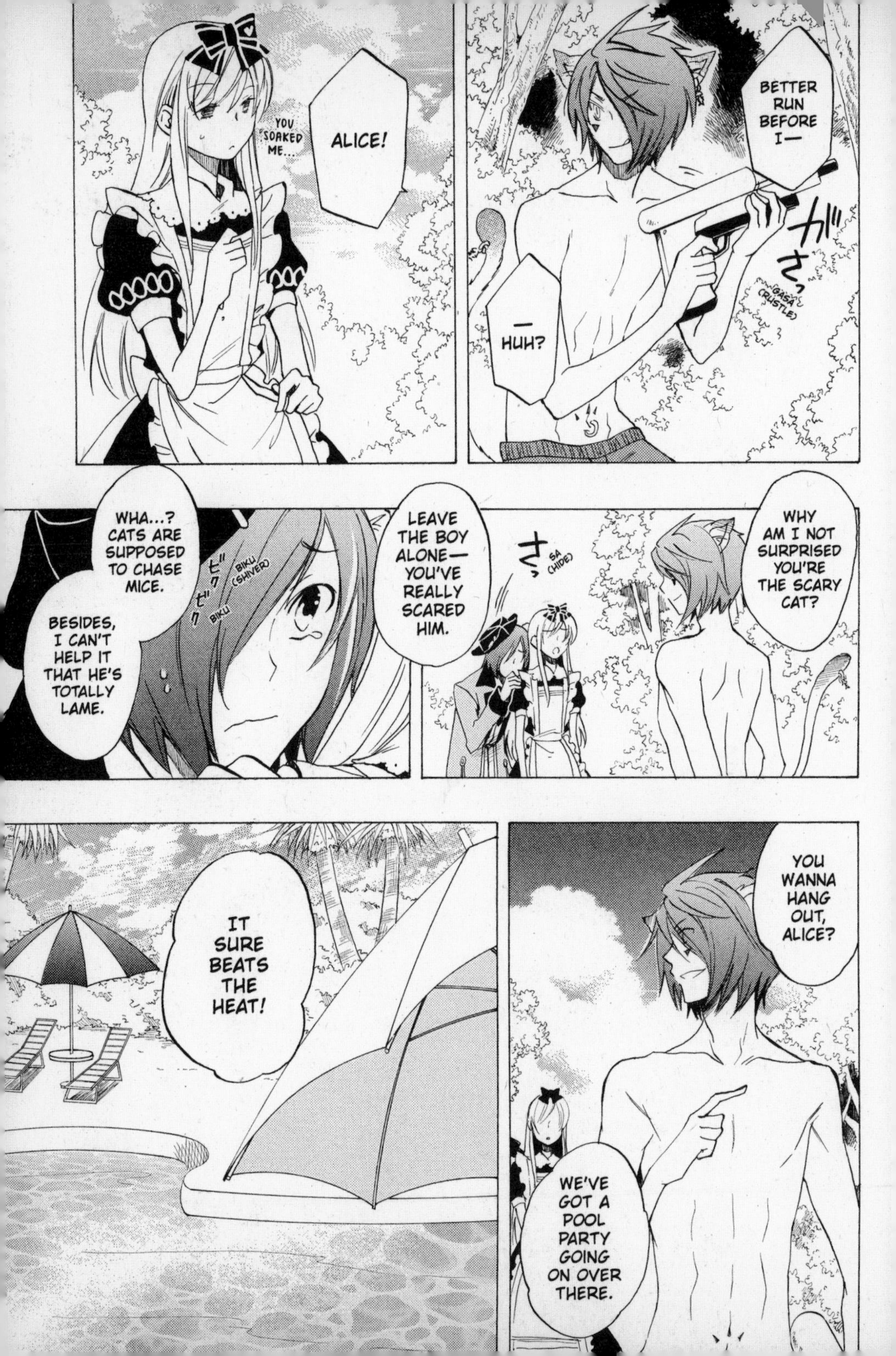
BETTER RUN BEFORE I—
がさっ
GASA (RUSTLE)
—HUH?
ALICE!
YOU SOAKED ME...
WHY AM I NOT SURPRISED YOU'RE THE SCARY CAT?
さっ
SA (HIDE)
LEAVE THE BOY ALONE—YOU'VE REALLY SCARED HIM.
ビクビク
BIKU BIKU (SHIVER)
WHA...? CATS ARE SUPPOSED TO CHASE MICE.
BESIDES, I CAN'T HELP IT THAT HE'S TOTALLY LAME.
YOU WANNA HANG OUT, ALICE?
WE'VE GOT A POOL PARTY GOING ON OVER THERE.
IT SURE BEATS THE HEAT!

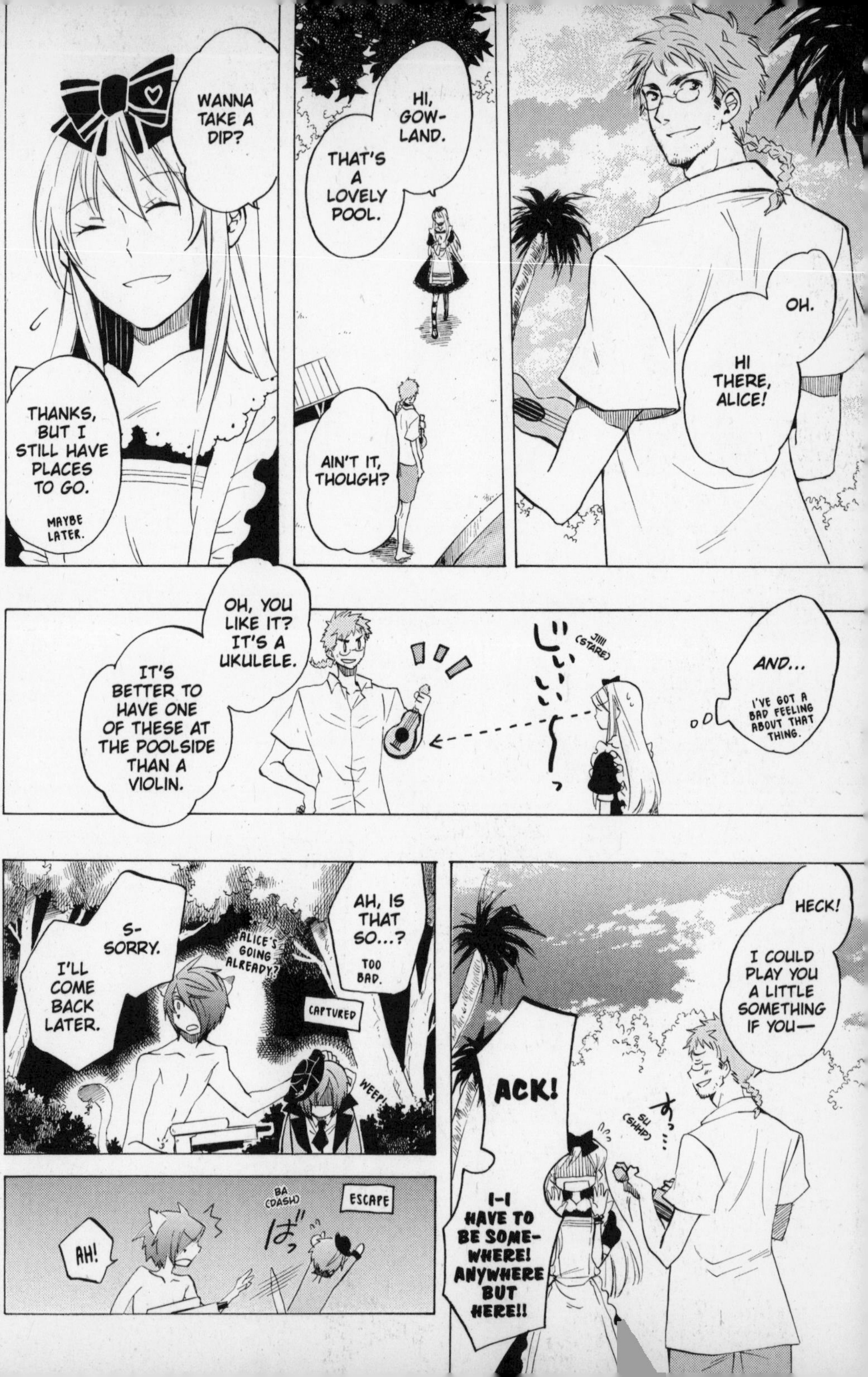
OH.
HI THERE, ALICE!
HI, GOW-LAND.
THAT'S A LOVELY POOL.
AIN'T IT, THOUGH?
WANNA TAKE A DIP?
THANKS, BUT I STILL HAVE PLACES TO GO.
MAYBE LATER.
AND...
I'VE GOT A BAD FEELING ABOUT THAT THING.
JIIII (STARE)
OH, YOU LIKE IT? IT'S A UKULELE.
IT'S BETTER TO HAVE ONE OF THESE AT THE POOLSIDE THAN A VIOLIN.
HECK!
I COULD PLAY YOU A LITTLE SOMETHING IF YOU—
SU (SHHP)
ACK!
I-I HAVE TO BE SOME-WHERE! ANYWHERE BUT HERE!!
AH, IS THAT SO...?
TOO BAD.
ALICE'S GOING ALREADY?
S-SORRY.
I'LL COME BACK LATER.
CAPTURED
WEEP!
ESCAPE
BA (DASH)
AH!

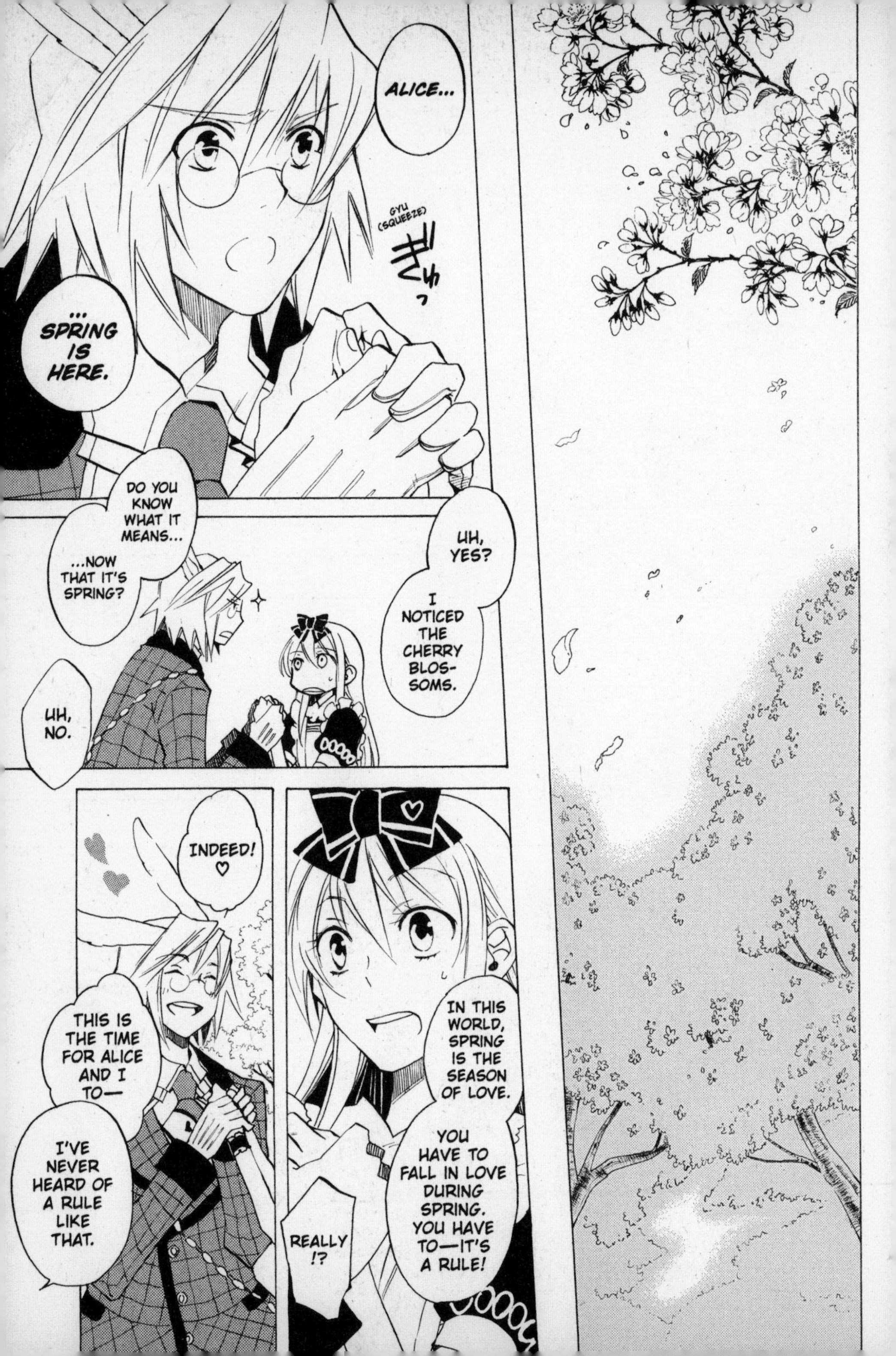
ALICE...
GYU (SQUEEZE)
...SPRING IS HERE.
UH, YES?
I NOTICED THE CHERRY BLOSSOMS.
DO YOU KNOW WHAT IT MEANS...
...NOW THAT IT'S SPRING?
UH, NO.
IN THIS WORLD, SPRING IS THE SEASON OF LOVE.
YOU HAVE TO FALL IN LOVE DURING SPRING. YOU HAVE TO—IT'S A RULE!
REALLY!?
INDEED! ♡
THIS IS THE TIME FOR ALICE AND I TO—
I'VE NEVER HEARD OF A RULE LIKE THAT.

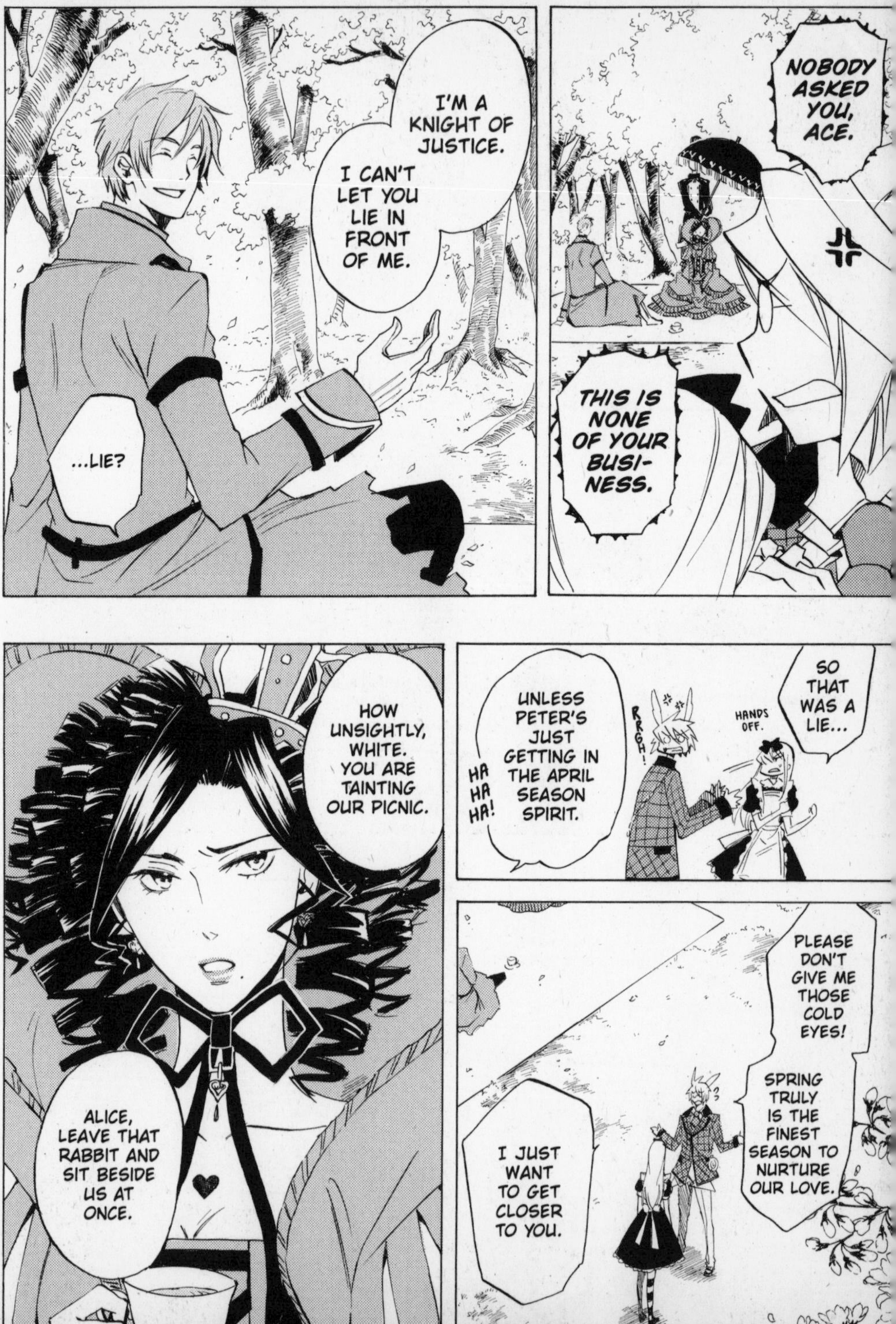
NOBODY ASKED YOU, ACE.
THIS IS NONE OF YOUR BUSI-NESS.
I'M A KNIGHT OF JUSTICE.
I CAN'T LET YOU LIE IN FRONT OF ME.
...LIE?
SO THAT WAS A LIE...
HANDS OFF.
RRGH!
UNLESS PETER'S JUST GETTING IN THE APRIL SEASON SPIRIT.
HA HA HA!
PLEASE DON'T GIVE ME THOSE COLD EYES!
SPRING TRULY IS THE FINEST SEASON TO NURTURE OUR LOVE.
I JUST WANT TO GET CLOSER TO YOU.
HOW UNSIGHTLY, WHITE. YOU ARE TAINTING OUR PICNIC.
ALICE, LEAVE THAT RABBIT AND SIT BESIDE US AT ONCE.

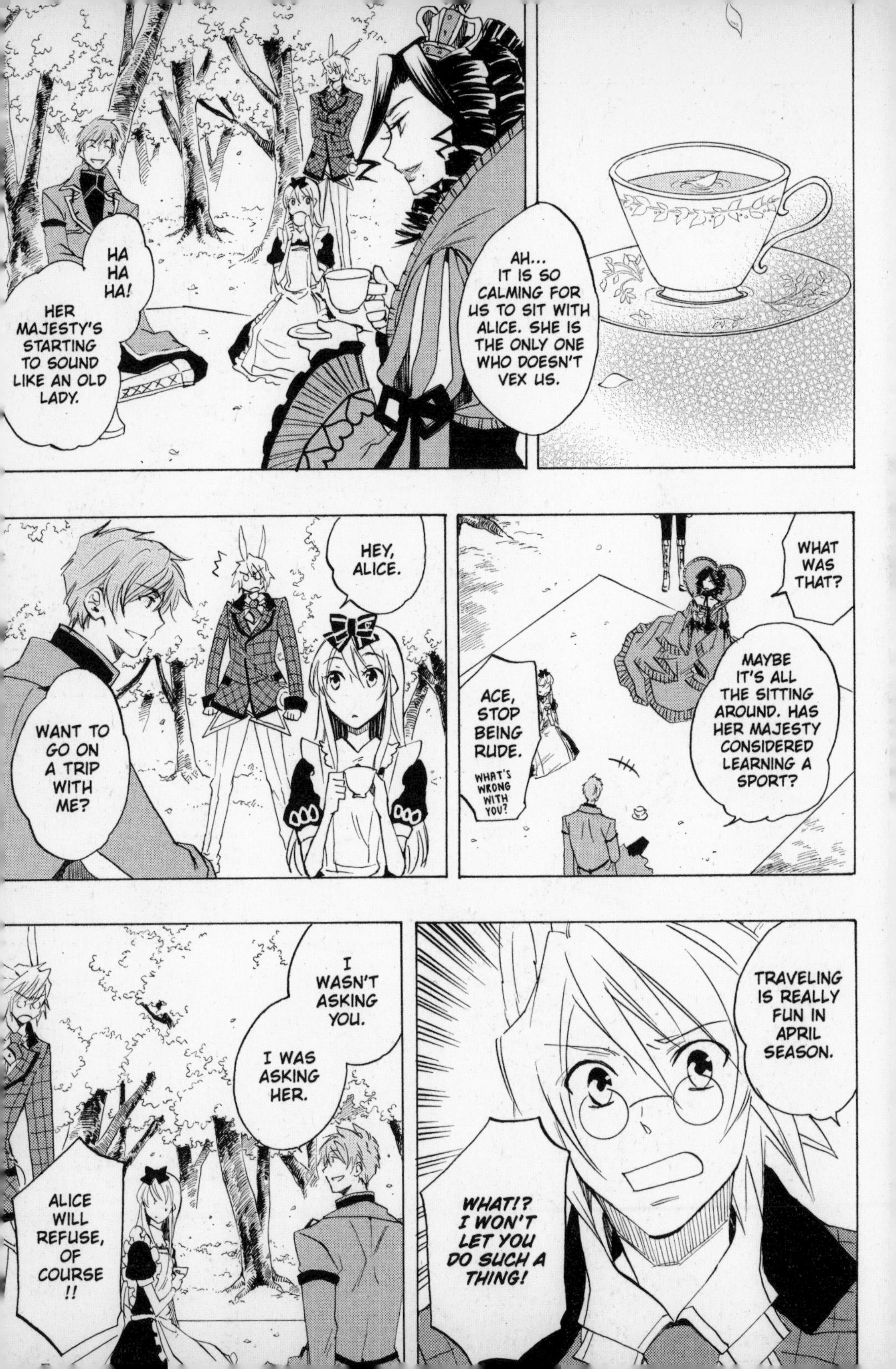
AH... IT IS SO CALMING FOR US TO SIT WITH ALICE. SHE IS THE ONLY ONE WHO DOESN'T VEX US.
HA HA HA! HER MAJESTY'S STARTING TO SOUND LIKE AN OLD LADY.
WHAT WAS THAT?
MAYBE IT'S ALL THE SITTING AROUND. HAS HER MAJESTY CONSIDERED LEARNING A SPORT?
ACE, STOP BEING RUDE.
WHAT'S WRONG WITH YOU?
HEY, ALICE.
WANT TO GO ON A TRIP WITH ME?
TRAVELING IS REALLY FUN IN APRIL SEASON.
WHAT!? I WON'T LET YOU DO SUCH A THING!
I WASN'T ASKING YOU.
I WAS ASKING HER.
ALICE WILL REFUSE, OF COURSE !!

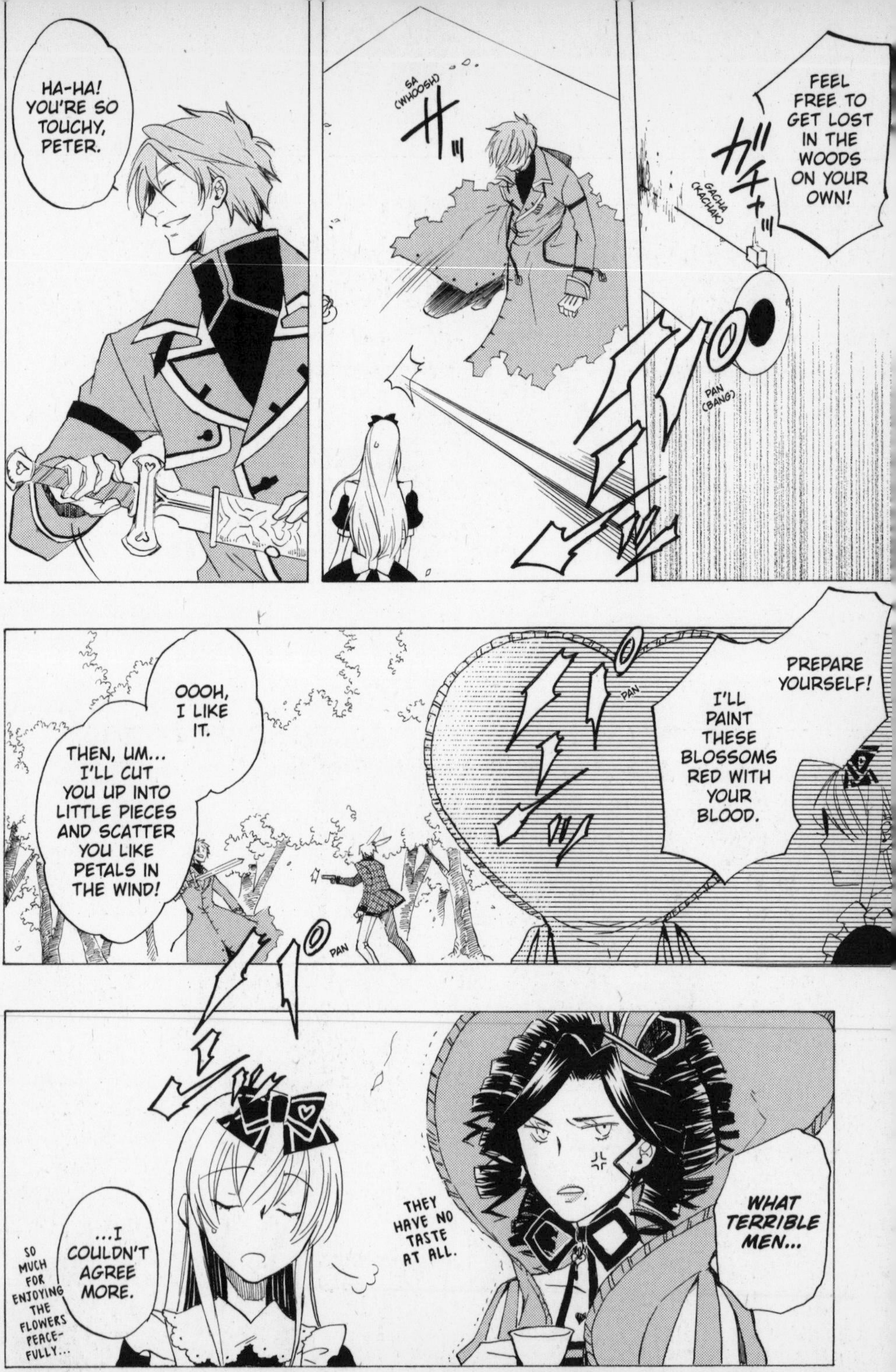
FEEL FREE TO GET LOST IN THE WOODS ON YOUR OWN!
GACHA (KACHAK)
PAN (BANG)
SA (WHOOSH)
HA-HA! YOU'RE SO TOUCHY, PETER.
PREPARE YOURSELF!
I'LL PAINT THESE BLOSSOMS RED WITH YOUR BLOOD.
PAN
OOOH, I LIKE IT.
THEN, UM... I'LL CUT YOU UP INTO LITTLE PIECES AND SCATTER YOU LIKE PETALS IN THE WIND!
PAN
WHAT TERRIBLE MEN...
THEY HAVE NO TASTE AT ALL.
...I COULDN'T AGREE MORE.
SO MUCH FOR ENJOYING THE FLOWERS PEACE-FULLY...

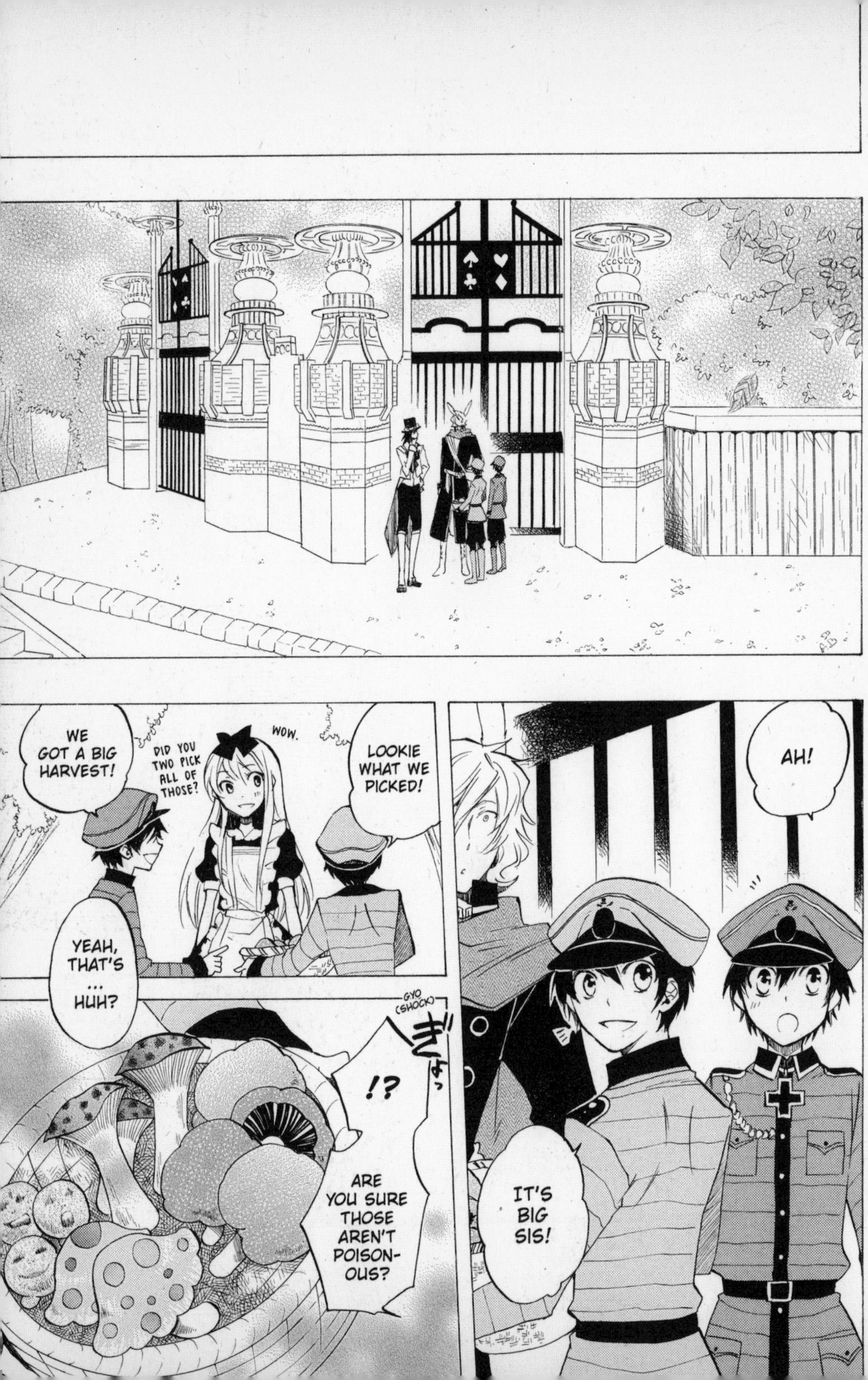
AH!
IT'S BIG SIS!
LOOKIE WHAT WE PICKED!
WOW.
DID YOU TWO PICK ALL OF THOSE?
WE GOT A BIG HARVEST!
YEAH, THAT'S ... HUH?
GYO (SHOCK)
ぎょっ
!?
ARE YOU SURE THOSE AREN'T POISON-OUS?

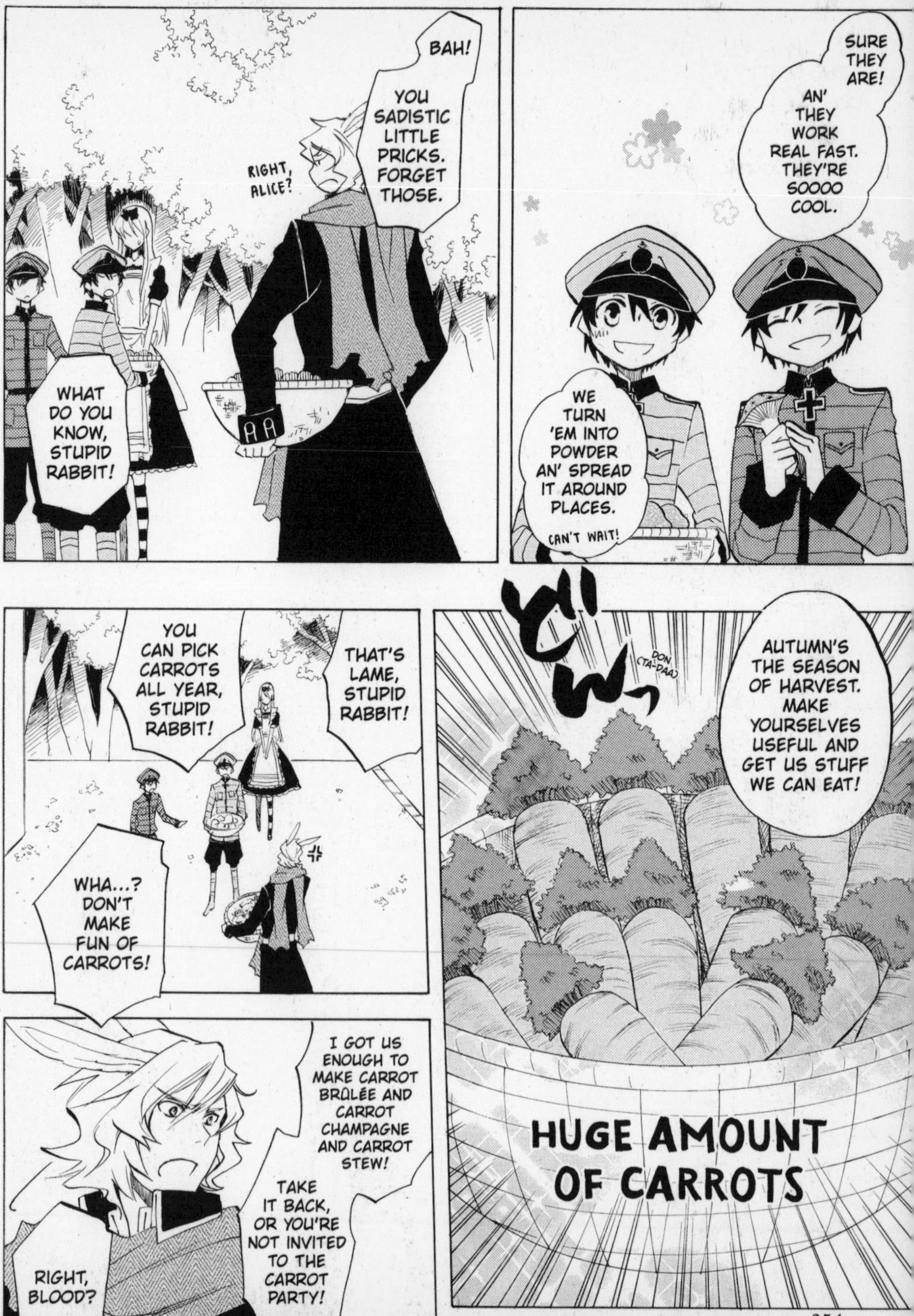

SURE THEY ARE!
AN' THEY WORK REAL FAST. THEY'RE SOOOO COOL.
WE TURN 'EM INTO POWDER AN' SPREAD IT AROUND PLACES.
CAN'T WAIT!
BAH!
YOU SADISTIC LITTLE PRICKS. FORGET THOSE.
RIGHT, ALICE?
WHAT DO YOU KNOW, STUPID RABBIT!
AUTUMN'S THE SEASON OF HARVEST. MAKE YOURSELVES USEFUL AND GET US STUFF WE CAN EAT!
DON (TA-DAA)
HUGE AMOUNT OF CARROTS
THAT'S LAME, STUPID RABBIT!
YOU CAN PICK CARROTS ALL YEAR, STUPID RABBIT!
WHA...? DON'T MAKE FUN OF CARROTS!
I GOT US ENOUGH TO MAKE CARROT BRÛLÉE AND CARROT CHAMPAGNE AND CARROT STEW!
TAKE IT BACK, OR YOU'RE NOT INVITED TO THE CARROT PARTY!
RIGHT, BLOOD?

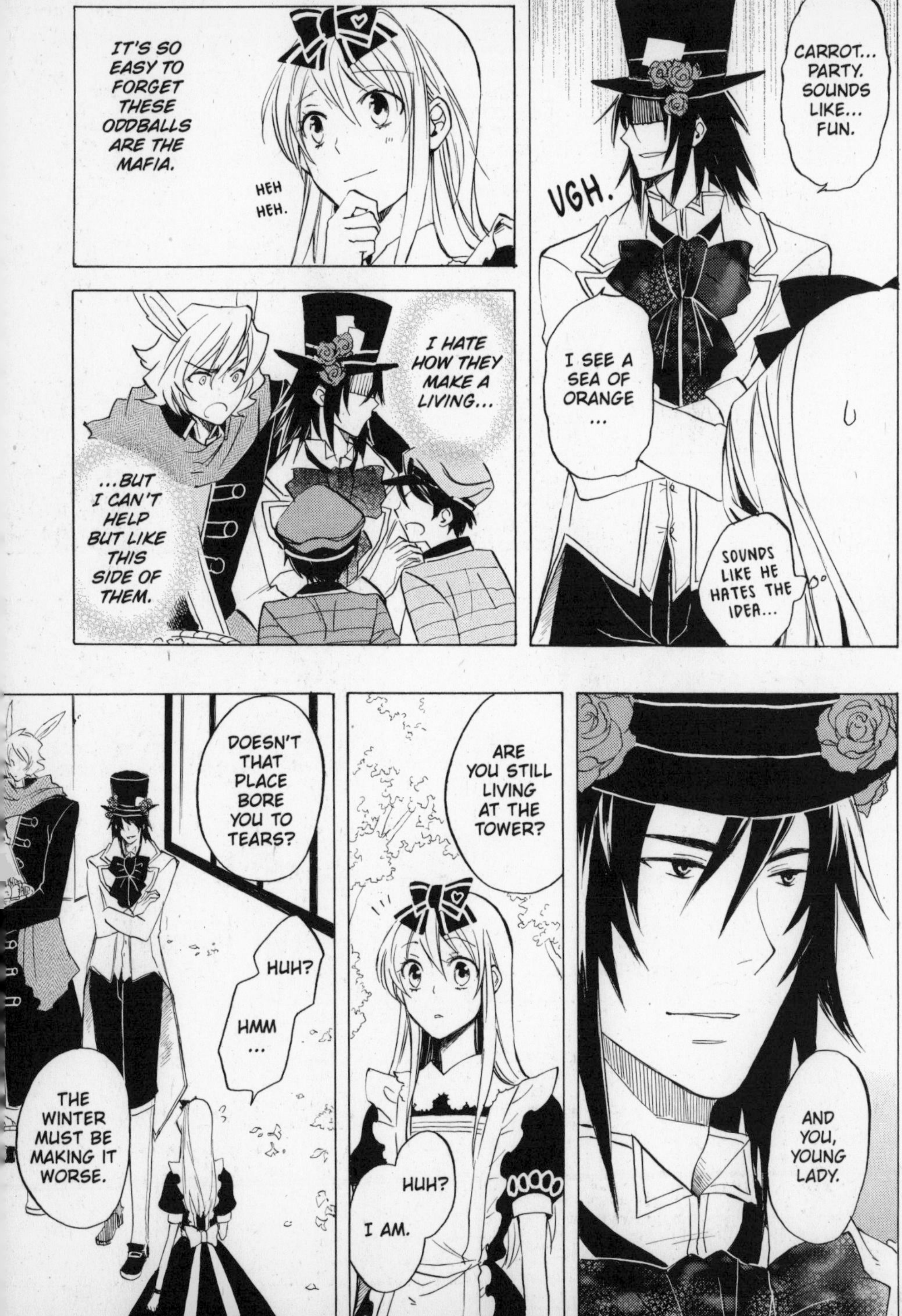
CARROT... PARTY. SOUNDS LIKE... FUN.
UGH.
I SEE A SEA OF ORANGE ...
SOUNDS LIKE HE HATES THE IDEA...
IT'S SO EASY TO FORGET THESE ODDBALLS ARE THE MAFIA.
HEH HEH.
I HATE HOW THEY MAKE A LIVING...
...BUT I CAN'T HELP BUT LIKE THIS SIDE OF THEM.
AND YOU, YOUNG LADY.
ARE YOU STILL LIVING AT THE TOWER?
HUH?
I AM.
DOESN'T THAT PLACE BORE YOU TO TEARS?
HUH?
HMM ...
THE WINTER MUST BE MAKING IT WORSE.

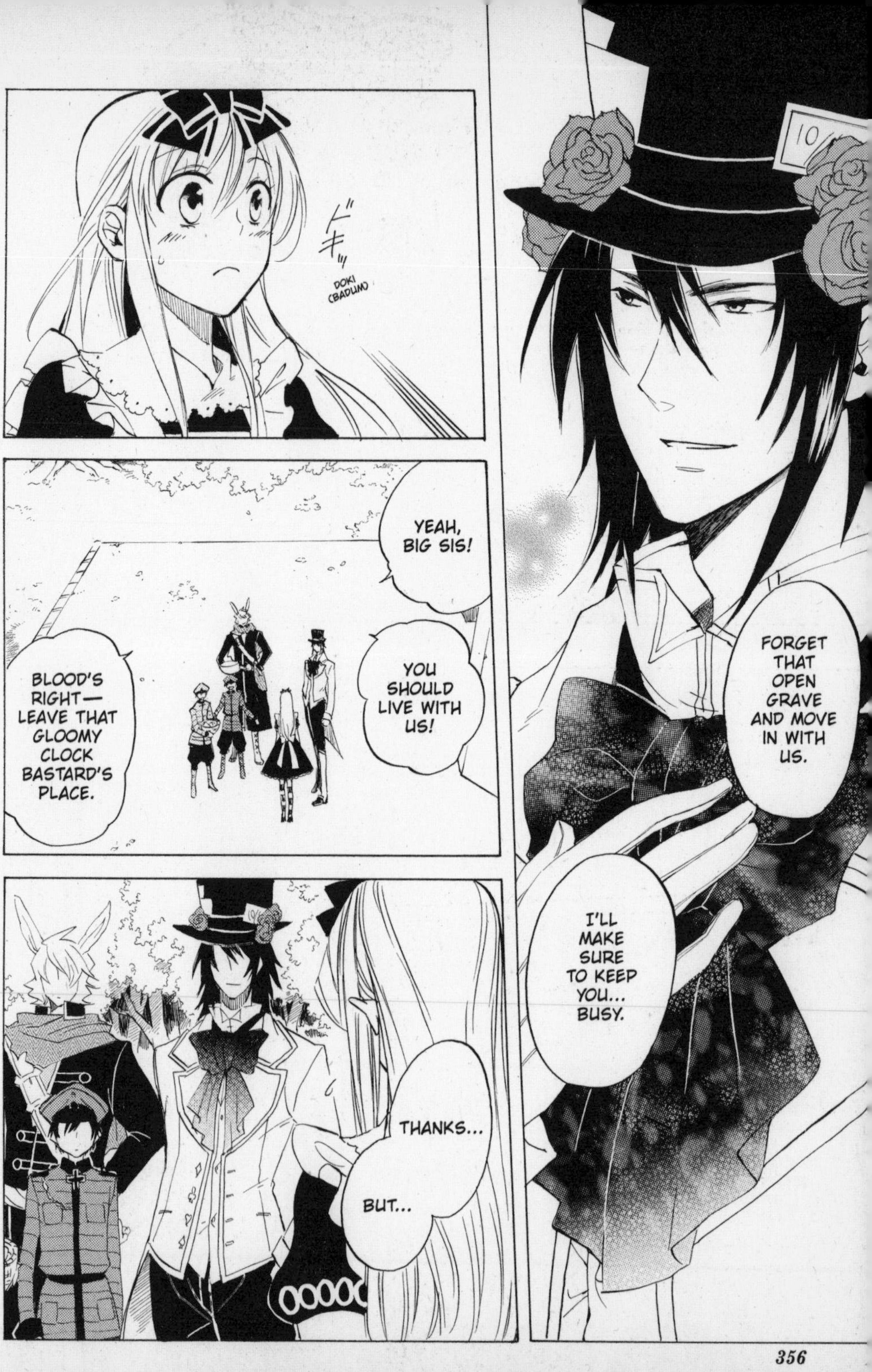
FORGET THAT OPEN GRAVE AND MOVE IN WITH US.
I'LL MAKE SURE TO KEEP YOU... BUSY.
ドキッ
DOKI (BADUM)
YEAH, BIG SIS!
YOU SHOULD LIVE WITH US!
BLOOD'S RIGHT—LEAVE THAT GLOOMY CLOCK BASTARD'S PLACE.
THANKS...
BUT...

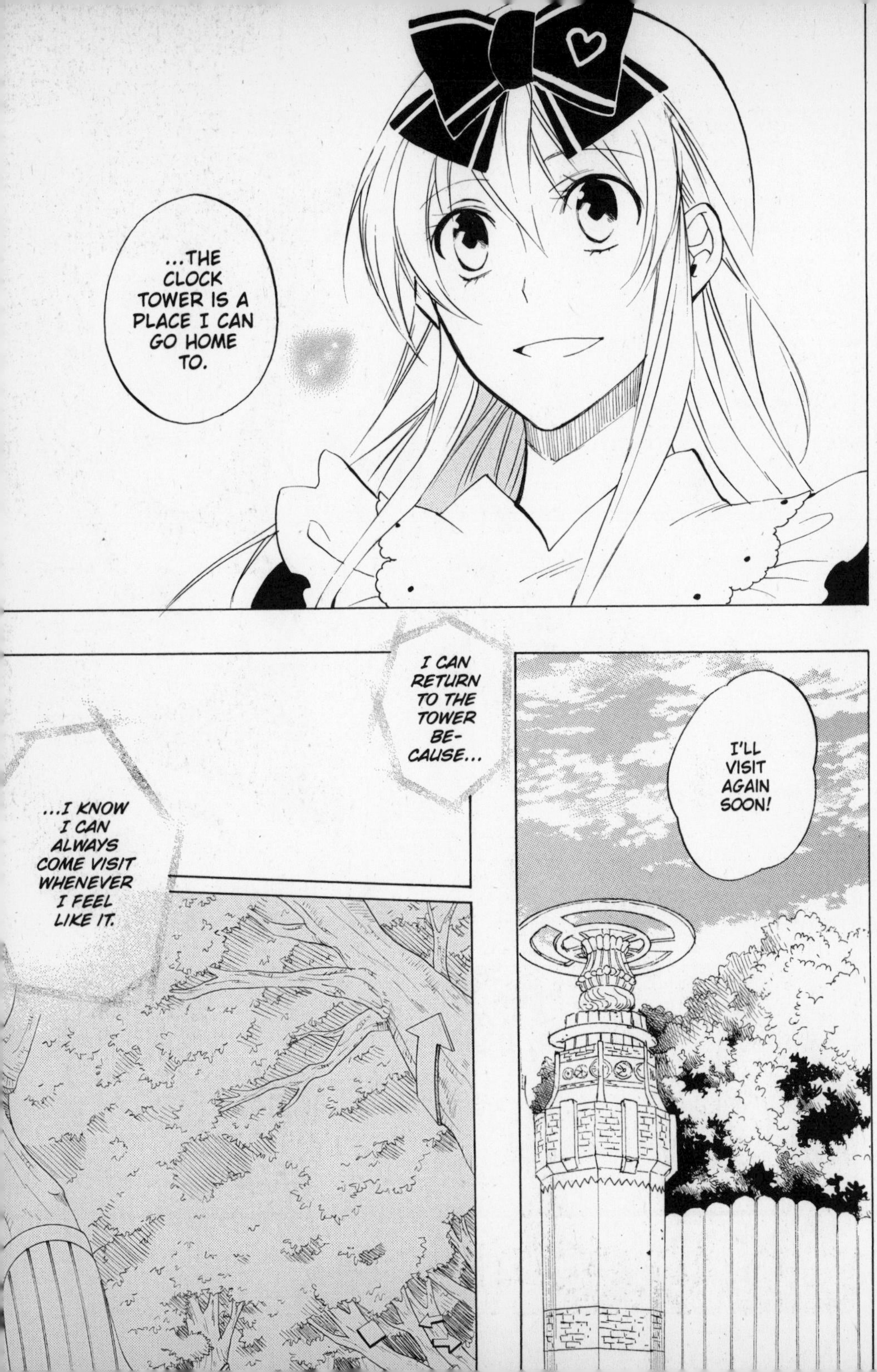
...THE CLOCK TOWER IS A PLACE I CAN GO HOME TO.
I'LL VISIT AGAIN SOON!
I CAN RETURN TO THE TOWER BE-CAUSE...
...I KNOW I CAN ALWAYS COME VISIT WHENEVER I FEEL LIKE IT.

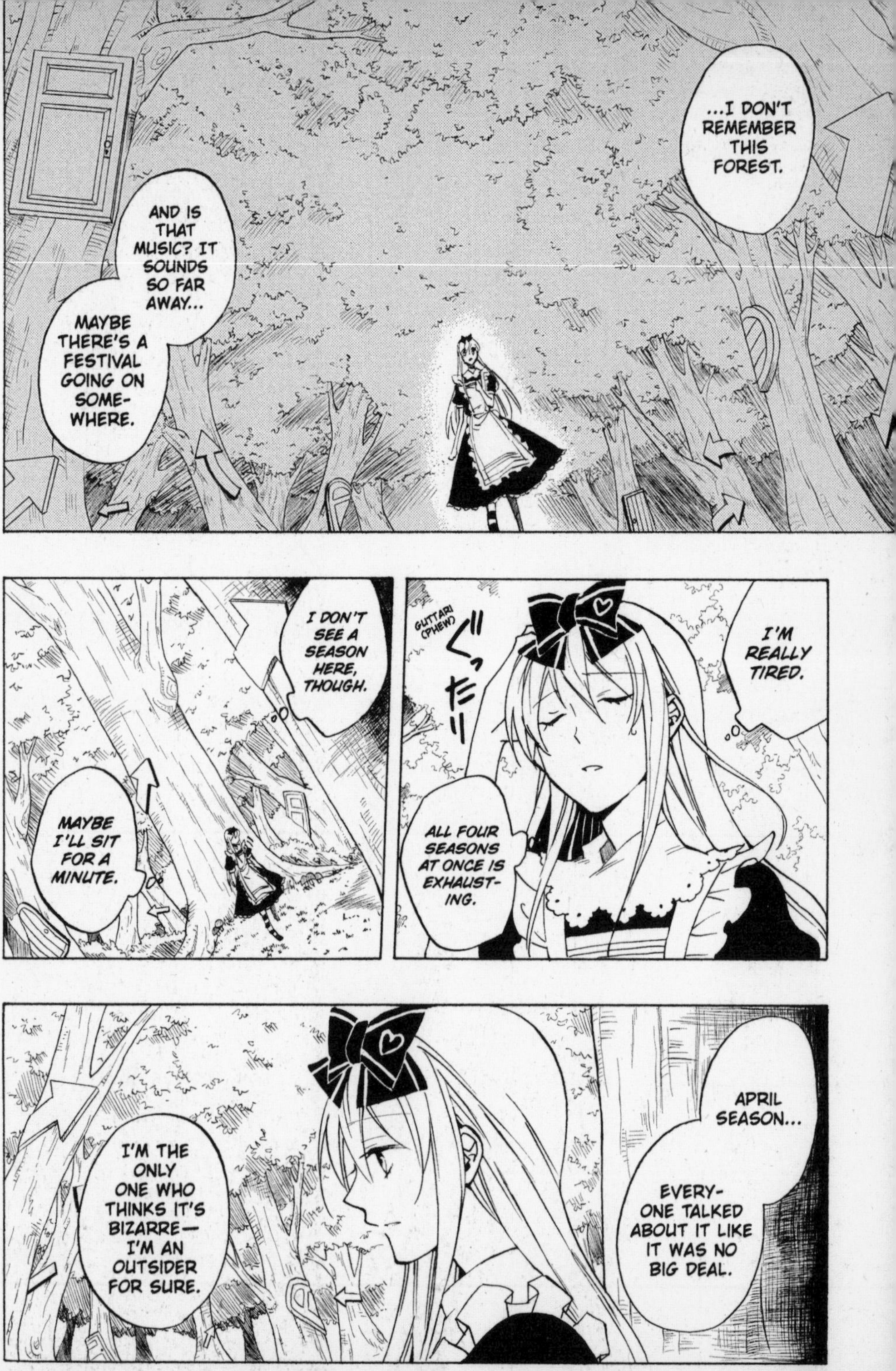
...I DON'T REMEMBER THIS FOREST.
AND IS THAT MUSIC? IT SOUNDS SO FAR AWAY...
MAYBE THERE'S A FESTIVAL GOING ON SOMEWHERE.
I'M REALLY TIRED.
GUTTARI (PHEW)
ぐったり
ALL FOUR SEASONS AT ONCE IS EXHAUSTING.
I DON'T SEE A SEASON HERE, THOUGH.
MAYBE I'LL SIT FOR A MINUTE.
APRIL SEASON...
EVERYONE TALKED ABOUT IT LIKE IT WAS NO BIG DEAL.
I'M THE ONLY ONE WHO THINKS IT'S BIZARRE—I'M AN OUTSIDER FOR SURE.

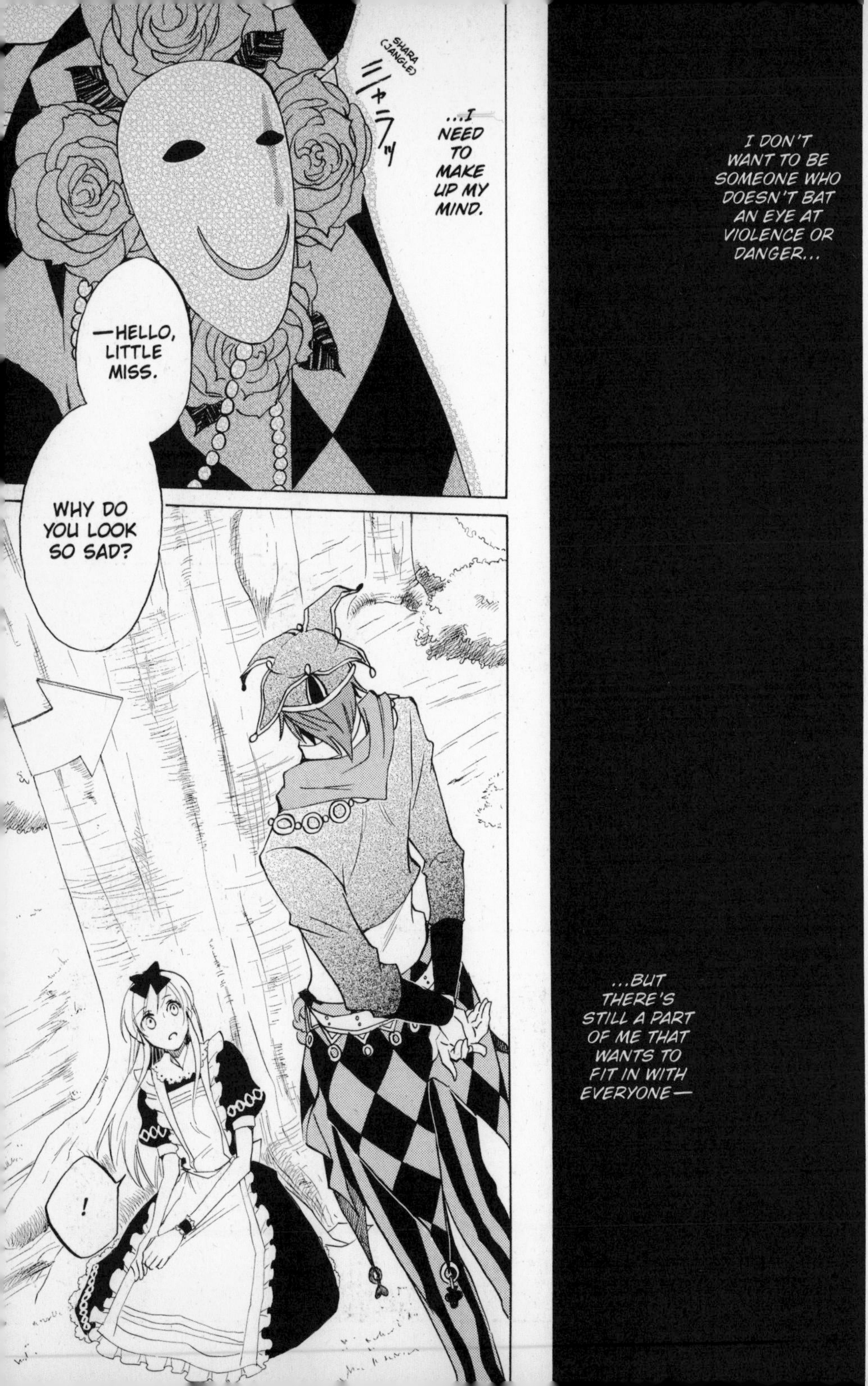
I DON'T WANT TO BE SOMEONE WHO DOESN'T BAT AN EYE AT VIOLENCE OR DANGER...
...BUT THERE'S STILL A PART OF ME THAT WANTS TO FIT IN WITH EVERYONE—
シャラッ
SHARA (JANGLE)
...I NEED TO MAKE UP MY MIND.
—HELLO, LITTLE MISS.
WHY DO YOU LOOK SO SAD?
!

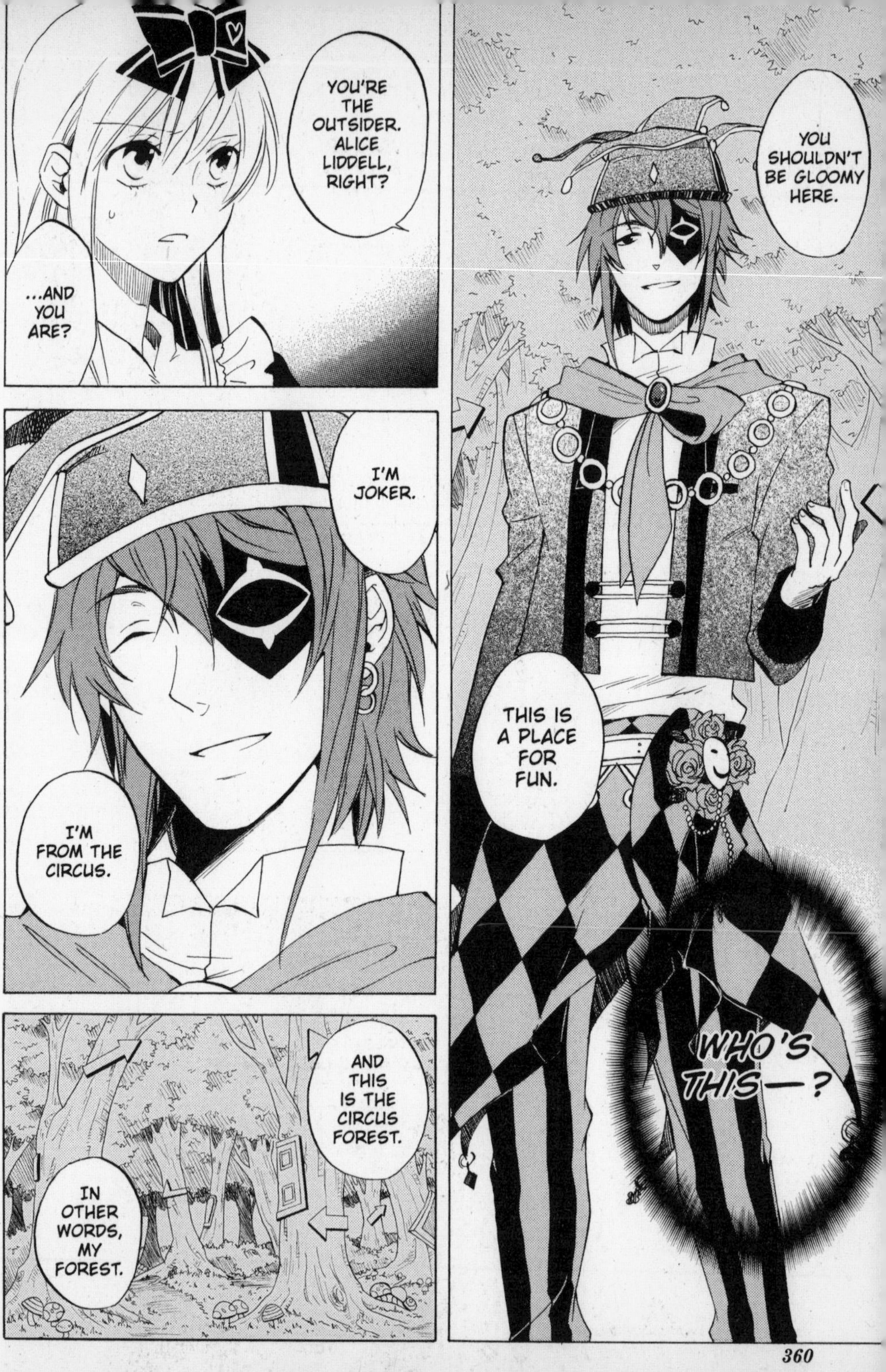
YOU SHOULDN'T BE GLOOMY HERE.
THIS IS A PLACE FOR FUN.
WHO'S THIS—?
YOU'RE THE OUTSIDER. ALICE LIDDELL, RIGHT?
...AND YOU ARE?
I'M JOKER.
I'M FROM THE CIRCUS.
AND THIS IS THE CIRCUS FOREST.
IN OTHER WORDS, MY FOREST.

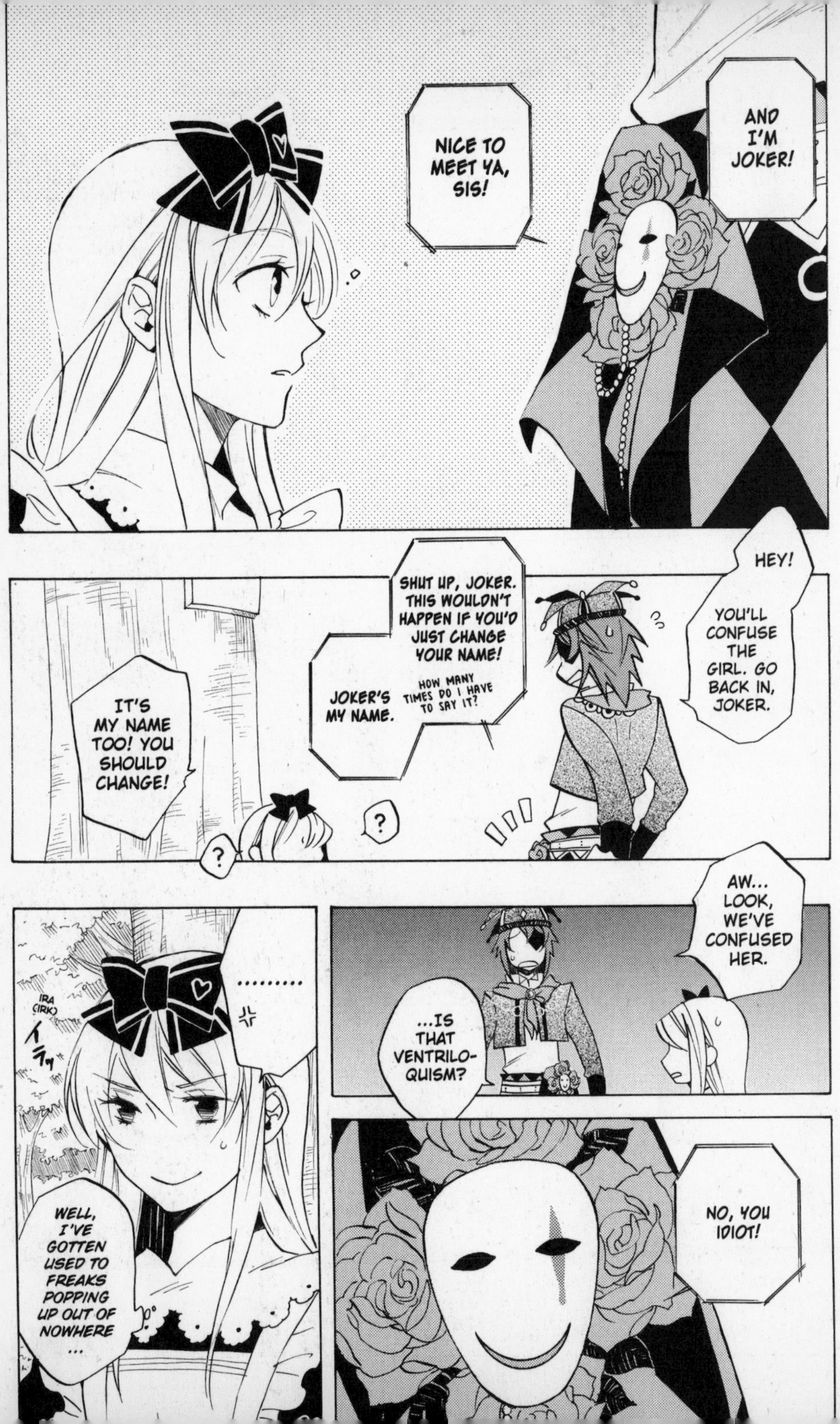
AND I'M JOKER!
NICE TO MEET YA, SIS!
HEY!
YOU'LL CONFUSE THE GIRL. GO BACK IN, JOKER.
SHUT UP, JOKER. THIS WOULDN'T HAPPEN IF YOU'D JUST CHANGE YOUR NAME!
HOW MANY TIMES DO I HAVE TO SAY IT?
JOKER'S MY NAME.
IT'S MY NAME TOO! YOU SHOULD CHANGE!
?
?
AW... LOOK, WE'VE CONFUSED HER.
...IS THAT VENTRILOQUISM?
NO, YOU IDIOT!
....
IRA (IRK)
WELL, I'VE GOTTEN USED TO FREAKS POPPING UP OUT OF NOWHERE ...

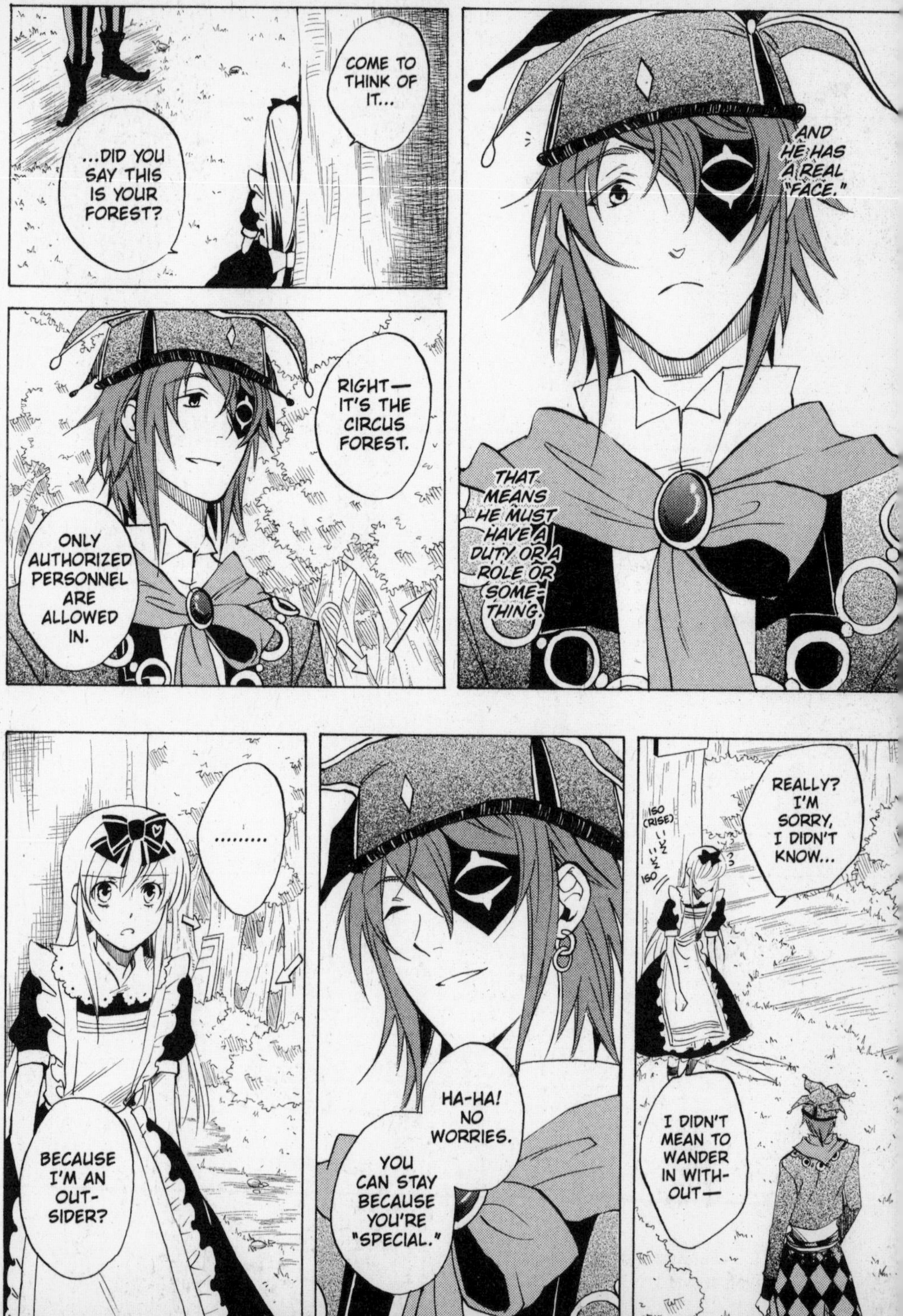
AND HE HAS A REAL "FACE."
THAT MEANS HE MUST HAVE A DUTY OR A ROLE OR SOME-THING.
COME TO THINK OF IT...
...DID YOU SAY THIS IS YOUR FOREST?
RIGHT— IT'S THE CIRCUS FOREST.
ONLY AUTHORIZED PERSONNEL ARE ALLOWED IN.
REALLY? I'M SORRY, I DIDN'T KNOW...
ISO (RISE)
ISO
I DIDN'T MEAN TO WANDER IN WITH-OUT—
HA-HA! NO WORRIES.
YOU CAN STAY BECAUSE YOU'RE "SPECIAL."
....
BECAUSE I'M AN OUT-SIDER?

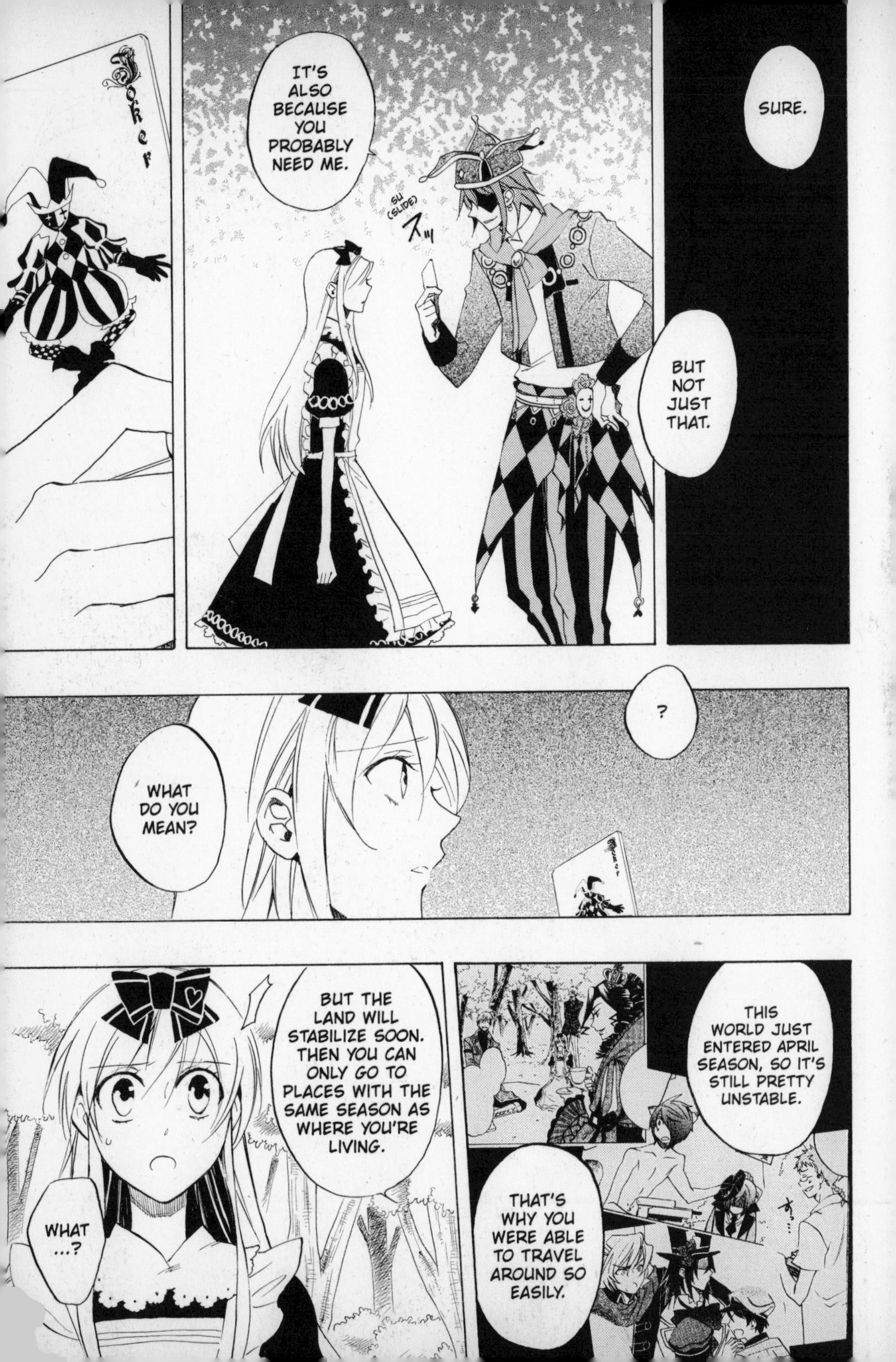
SURE.
BUT NOT JUST THAT.
IT'S ALSO BECAUSE YOU PROBABLY NEED ME.
SU (SLIDE)
ズッ
Joker
?
WHAT DO YOU MEAN?
THIS WORLD JUST ENTERED APRIL SEASON, SO IT'S STILL PRETTY UNSTABLE.
THAT'S WHY YOU WERE ABLE TO TRAVEL AROUND SO EASILY.
す…
BUT THE LAND WILL STABILIZE SOON. THEN YOU CAN ONLY GO TO PLACES WITH THE SAME SEASON AS WHERE YOU'RE LIVING.
WHAT ...?

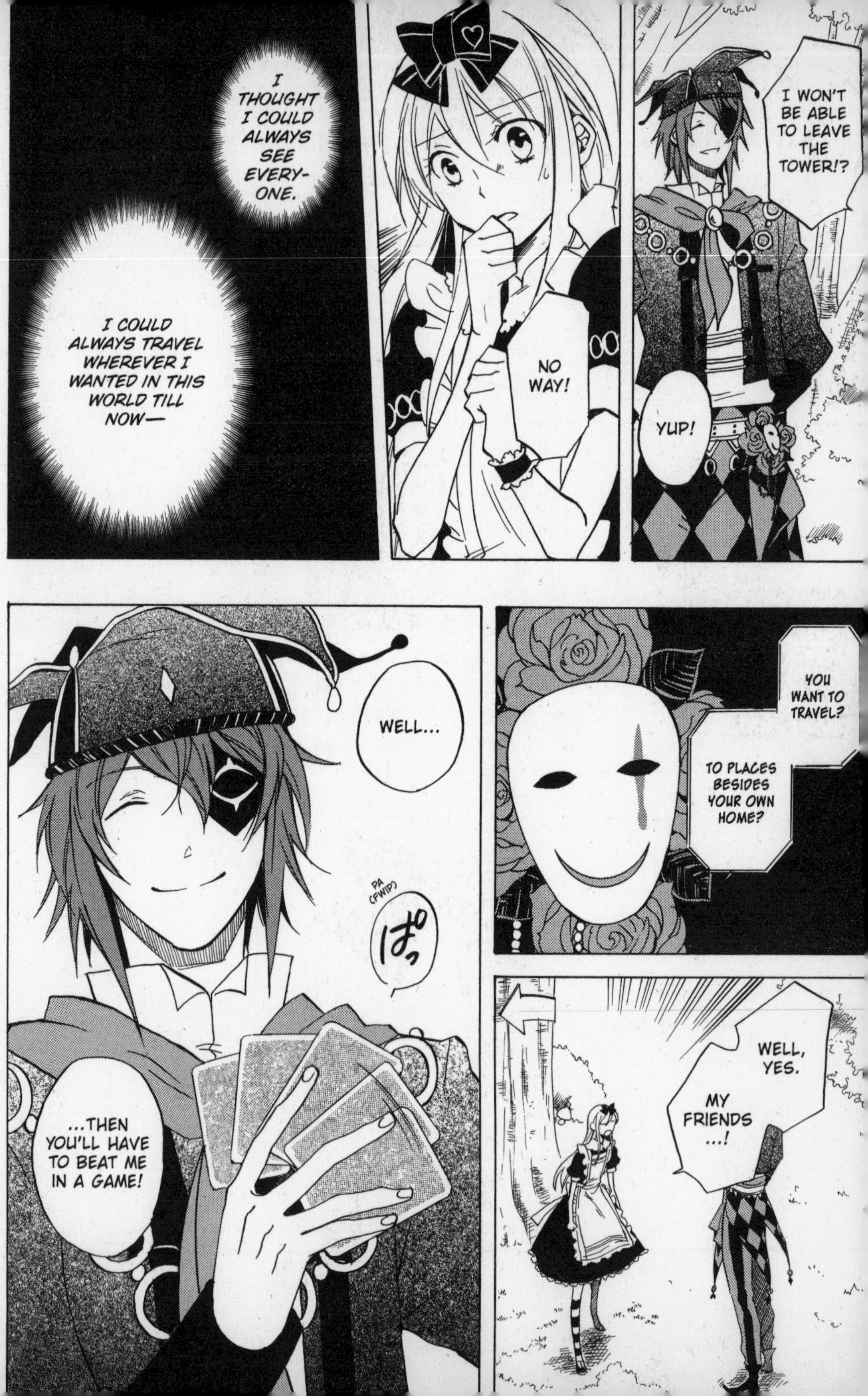
I WON'T BE ABLE TO LEAVE THE TOWER!?
YUP!
NO WAY!
I THOUGHT I COULD ALWAYS SEE EVERY-ONE.
I COULD ALWAYS TRAVEL WHEREVER I WANTED IN THIS WORLD TILL NOW—
YOU WANT TO TRAVEL?
TO PLACES BESIDES YOUR OWN HOME?
WELL, YES.
MY FRIENDS ...!
WELL...
PA (FWIP)
ぱっ
...THEN YOU'LL HAVE TO BEAT ME IN A GAME!

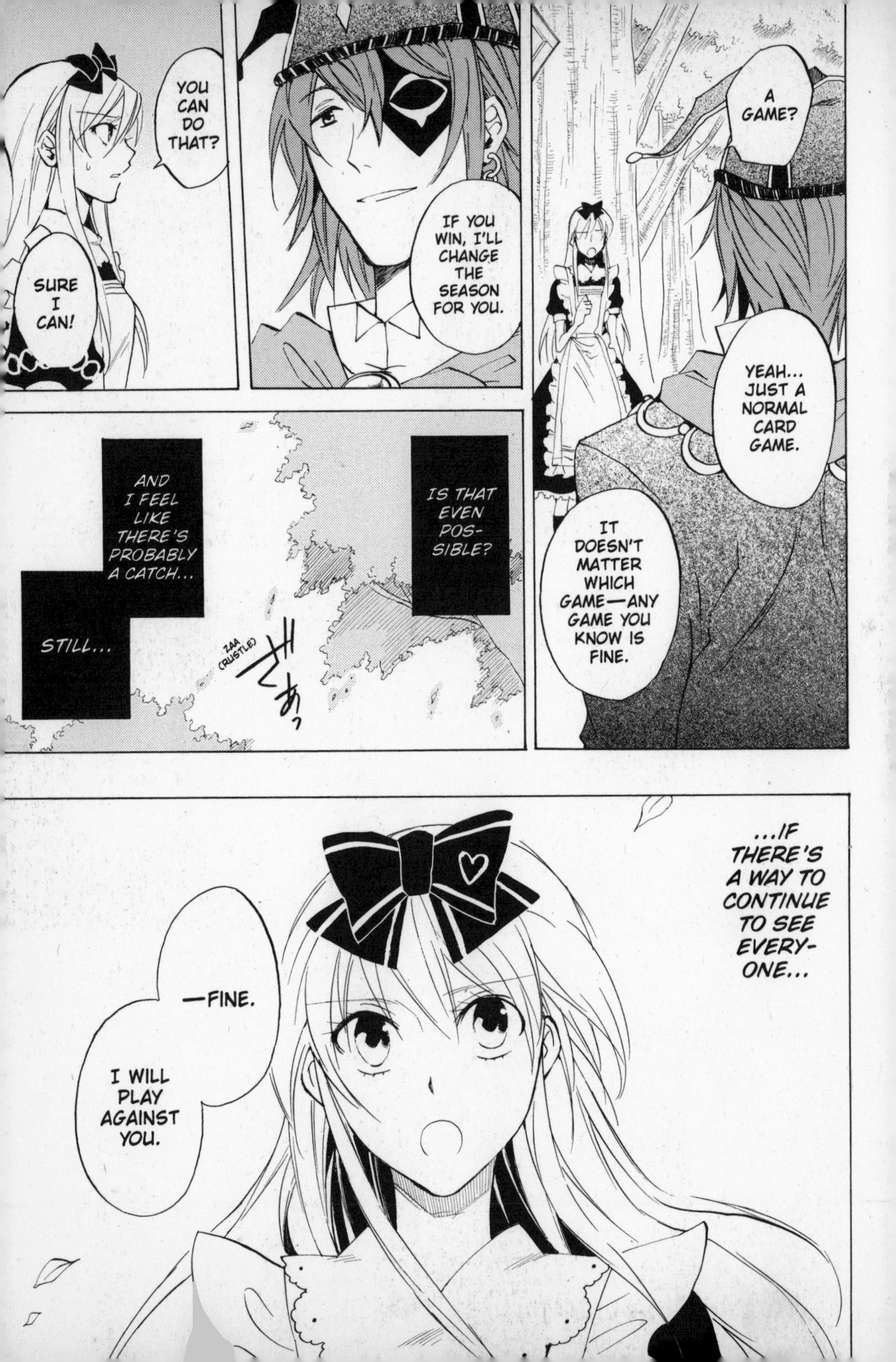
A GAME?
YEAH... JUST A NORMAL CARD GAME.
IT DOESN'T MATTER WHICH GAME—ANY GAME YOU KNOW IS FINE.
IF YOU WIN, I'LL CHANGE THE SEASON FOR YOU.
YOU CAN DO THAT?
SURE I CAN!
IS THAT EVEN POS-SIBLE?
AND I FEEL LIKE THERE'S PROBABLY A CATCH...
STILL...
ざあっ
ZAA (RUSTLE)
...IF THERE'S A WAY TO CONTINUE TO SEE EVERY-ONE...
—FINE.
I WILL PLAY AGAINST YOU.

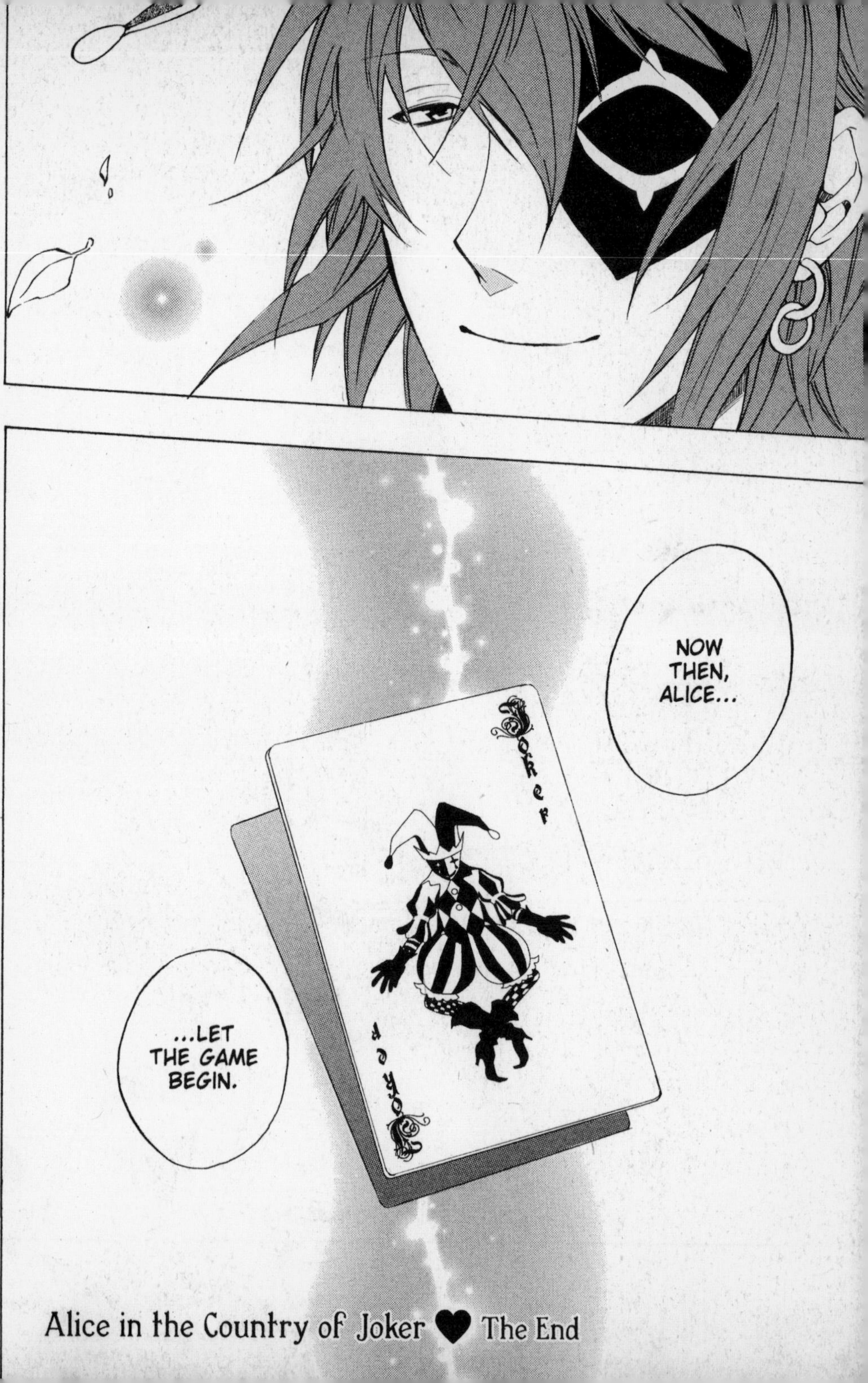
NOW THEN, ALICE...
Joker
...LET THE GAME BEGIN.
Alice in the Country of Joker ♥ The End

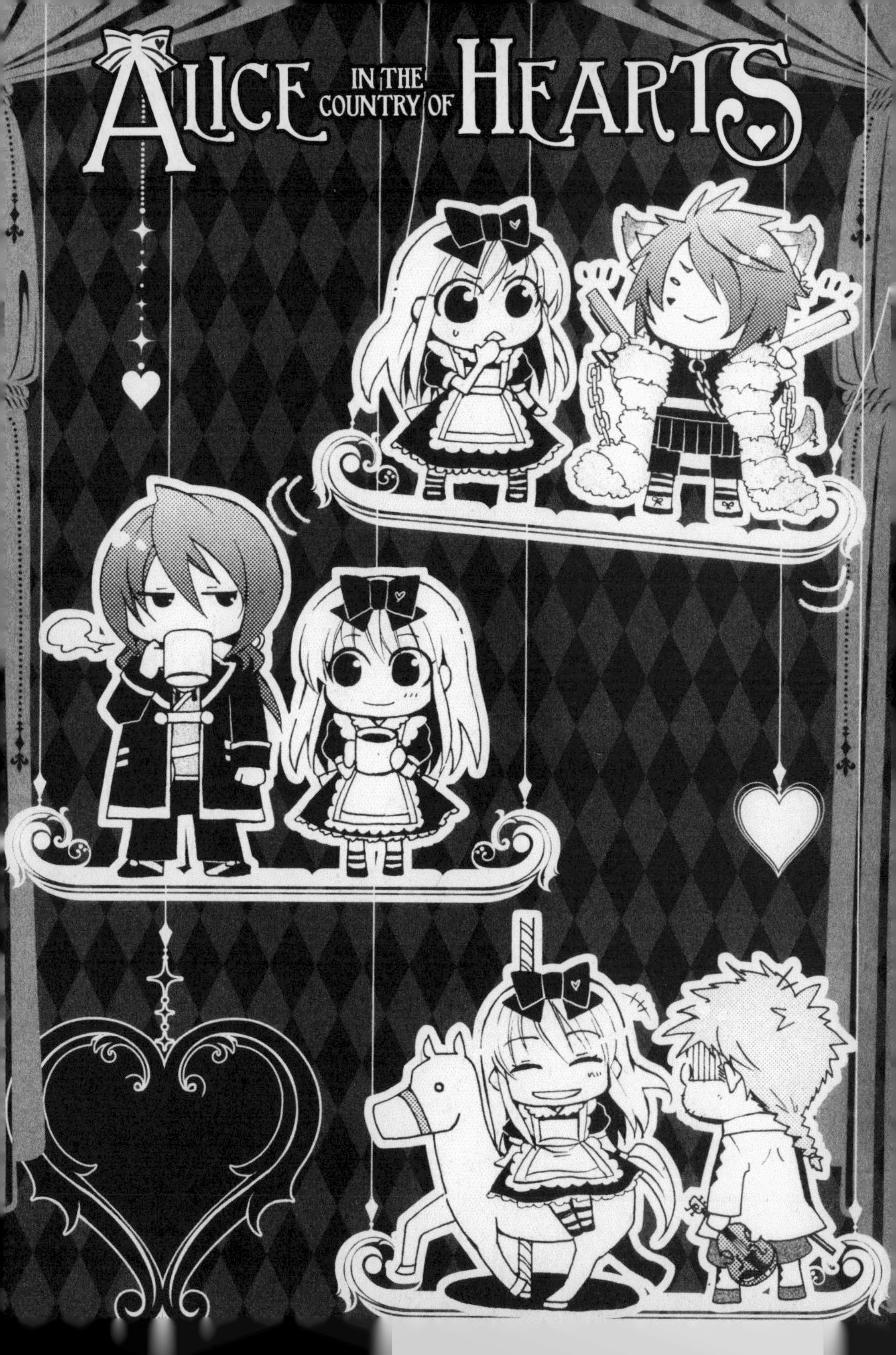

ALICE IN THE COUNTRY OF HEARTS